QuickBooks 2006
THE MISSING MANUAL

Bonnie Biafore

POGUE PRESS™
O'REILLY®

Beijing · Cambridge · Farnham · Köln · Paris · Sebastopol · Taipei · Tokyo

QuickBooks 2006: The Missing Manual

by Bonnie Biafore

Published by O'Reilly Media, Inc., 1005 Gravenstein Highway North, Sebastopol, CA 95472.

O'Reilly books may be purchased for educational, business, or sales promotional use. Online editions are also available for most titles (*safari.oreilly.com*). For more information, contact our corporate/institutional sales department: (800) 998-9938 or *corporate@oreilly.com*.

Printing History:

December 2005:   First Edition.

 This book uses RepKover™, a durable and flexible lay-flat binding.

ISBN: 0-596-10184-8
[M]

Table of Contents

Part Two: Accounting with QuickBooks

Part Three: Managing Your Business

Part Five: Appendixes

The Missing Credits

About the Author

 **Bonnie Biafore** writes about personal finance, investing, and project management, although she dreams of writing a best-selling crime novel and selling the movie rights for oodles of money. As an engineer, she's steadfastly attentive to detail but uses her sense of humor to transform drool-inducing subjects into entertaining reading. Her *NAIC Stock Selection Handbook* won major awards from the Society of Technical Communication and APEX Awards for Publication Excellence.

Bonnie is also the author of O'Reilly's *Online Investing Hacks* and *Quicken for Starters: The Missing Manual*. She writes a monthly column called WebWatch for *Better Investing* magazine and is a regular contributor to The Microsoft Work Essentials Web site (*www.microsoft.com/workessentials*) and Womenswallstreet. com. As a consultant, she wins accolades for her ability to herd cats. When not chained to her computer, she hikes in the mountains with her dog, cooks gourmet meals, and practices saying no to additional work assignments. Web: *www. bonniebiafore.com*. Email: *bonnie.biafore@gmail.com*.

About the Creative Team

Nan Barber (editor, copy editor) is associate editor for the Missing Manual series. She works in O'Reilly's Cambridge office and enjoys at least reading about people who have their finances organized. Email: *nanbarber@mac.com*.

Michele Filshie (editor) is O'Reilly's assistant editor for the Missing Manual series and editor of four Personal Trainers (another O'Reilly series). Before turning to the world of computer-related books, Michele spent many happy years at Black Sparrow Press. Email: *mfilshie@oreilly.com*.

Debra Chamra (technical reviewer) is the chief financial officer for Hesketh.com, the Southeast's first user experience firm specializing in Web technology. She earned her MBA with concentrations in electronic commerce, marketing, and operations and supply chain management at NC State University; and her Masters in Healthcare Administration from the University of NC at Chapel Hill. Email: *debra@hesketh.com*.

Vikki Ellison (technical reviewer) is the owner of Astute Business Solutions, an enterprise management consulting service. She's been in the enterprise management and education fields for 20 years. Vikki says that QuickBooks is a staple of her business process. Email: *vikki.ellison@abizsol.com*.

Tim Oswald (technical reviewer) is a CPA in Colorado and California. After graduating from St. Mary's College, he worked in public and corporate accounting before becoming president of the Accounting and Business School of the Rockies. The school offers hands-on accounting and business classes and a Professional Bookkeeping Certificate Program. Email: *tim@usefultraining.com*

Rose Cassano (cover illustration) has worked as an independent designer and illustrator for 20 years. Assignments have ranged from the nonprofit sector to corporate clientele. She lives in beautiful Southern Oregon, grateful for the miracles of modern technology that make working there a reality. Email: *cassano@highstream. net*. Web: *www.rosecassano.com*.

Acknowledgements

Writing a book is hard work, but the folks at O'Reilly make the hours and sweat tolerable. Thanks to Sarah Milstein for convincing me to write this book, for handling all the details so dependably, and, most importantly, for laughing at my jokes. My eternal gratitude goes to Nan Barber for reining in my rambling words. And thanks to everyone else at O'Reilly for doing their usual amazing job.

I also want to thank the technical reviewers, Tim Oswald, Vikki Ellison, and Debra Chamra, for reviewing the manuscript and providing so many great tips for wrangling QuickBooks into submission.

Of course, no set of my acknowledgements is complete without thanks to my husband, Pete Speer, for putting up with me while I work to meet book deadlines. I am not fun to be around when I'm writing a book, but he always handles it with aplomb. Just ask him. And finally, my special thanks go to our dog, Emma, who graciously negotiated one walk a day for the duration of the manuscript.

—Bonnie Biafore

The Missing Manual Series

Missing Manuals are witty, superbly written guides to computer products that don't come with printed manuals (which is just about all of them). Each book features a handcrafted index; cross-references to specific page numbers (not just "see Chapter 14"); and RepKover, a detached-spine binding that lets the book lie perfectly flat without the assistance of weights or cinder blocks.

Recent and upcoming titles include:

Access 2003 for Starters: The Missing Manual by Kate Chase and Scott Palmer

AppleScript: The Missing Manual by Adam Goldstein

AppleWorks 6: The Missing Manual by Jim Elferdink and David Reynolds

Creating Web Sites: The Missing Manual by Matthew MacDonald

Dreamweaver 8: The Missing Manual by David Sawyer McFarland

eBay: The Missing Manual by Nancy Conner

Excel: The Missing Manual by Matthew MacDonald

Excel for Starters: The Missing Manual by Matthew MacDonald

FileMaker Pro 8: The Missing Manual by Geoff Coffey and Susan Prosser

FrontPage 2003: The Missing Manual by Jessica Mantaro

GarageBand 2: The Missing Manual by David Pogue

Google: The Missing Manual, Second Edition by Sarah Milstein and Rael Dornfest

Home Networking: The Missing Manual by Scott Lowe

iLife '05: The Missing Manual by David Pogue

iMovie HD & iDVD 5: The Missing Manual by David Pogue

iPhoto 5: The Missing Manual by David Pogue

iPod & iTunes: The Missing Manual, Third Edition by Jude Biersdorfer

iWork '05: The Missing Manual by Jim Elferdink

Mac OS X Power Hound, Panther Edition by Rob Griffiths

Mac OS X: The Missing Manual, Tiger Edition by David Pogue

Office 2004 for Macintosh: The Missing Manual by Mark H. Walker and Franklin Tessler

PCs: The Missing Manual by Andy Rathbone

Photoshop Elements 4: The Missing Manual by Barbara Brundage

Quicken 2006 for Starters: The Missing Manual by Bonnie Biafore

Switching to the Mac: The Missing Manual, Tiger Edition by David Pogue and Adam Goldstein

Windows 2000 Pro: The Missing Manual by Sharon Crawford

Windows XP Power Hound by Preston Gralla

Windows XP for Starters: The Missing Manual by David Pogue

Windows XP Home Edition: The Missing Manual, Second Edition by David Pogue

Windows XP Pro: The Missing Manual, Second Edition by David Pogue, Craig Zacker, and Linda Zacker

Introduction

Thousands of small companies and nonprofit organizations turn to QuickBooks to keep company finances on track. And over the years, Intuit has introduced editions of QuickBooks to satisfy the needs of different types of companies. Back when milk was simply milk, you either used QuickBooks or you didn't. Now that milk comes from soy beans as well as cows, and sports five different amounts of fat, it's no surprise that you can choose from QuickBooks Simple Start, Pro, Premier, Online, and Enterprise editions, as well as six industry-specific editions. From the smallest of sole proprietorships to thriving enterprises that aren't small at all, one of the QuickBooks editions is likely to meet your organization's needs *and* budget.

QuickBooks isn't hard to learn. Many of the techniques that you're familiar with from other programs work just as well in QuickBooks—windows, dialog boxes, drop-down lists, and keyboard shortcuts to name a few. With each new version, Intuit adds enhancements and new features to make your work flow more smoothly and finish much faster. The challenge that remains is knowing what to do according to accounting rules, as well as how to do so in QuickBooks.

What's New in QuickBooks 2006

Despite the malleable size of the tax code each year, accounting and bookkeeping practices don't change all that much. Many changes in QuickBooks 2006 are small tweaks and subtle improvements. But a few additions might make you sit up and take notice:

- **The QuickBooks Home page** is a slick new launch pad for your accounting tasks. For easy navigation, this window consolidates the many navigators and centers from previous versions into a single diagram (page 144). Whether you're a beginner or a QuickBooks veteran, you can quickly get an overview of your accounting system and then trace the workflow diagram to find the specific task you want to perform. Along with accounting tasks, the Home page gives you quick access to your Chart of Accounts, online banking, and more.

- **The Customer Center, Vendor Center, Employee Center**, and **Report Center** windows organize your QuickBooks information into compact dashboards. For example, the Customer Center displays your Customer List, as well as the contact information and transactions for the customer whose name you select. The same window lets you add or edit customer records and create any kind of customer transaction. (You can open the Centers by clicking their names on the left side of the Home page or in the navigation bar.)

- **Streamlined QuickBooks menus** remove the duplicate entries for some commands. For example, you now find Make General Journal Entries only on the Company menu, instead of both Company and Banking (as in QuickBooks 2005). Add-on services, which used to pop up on several QuickBooks menus, now congregate neatly in one place. Click Add Services in the Home page to find all the add-ons that Intuit offers.

- The **Payroll Setup wizard** has been totally revamped in QuickBooks 2006. As you step through the screens, selecting payroll items and setting up employees, the wizard creates the payroll items, accounts, and employee records you need.

- **Audit trail tracking** is always on in QuickBooks 2006, so you can always tell who's done what in your books.

- In QuickBooks 2006, the **Report Center** does the same things as QuickBooks 2005's nifty Report Navigator, but like the other Center windows, it's more easily accessible. By clicking Report Center in the navigation bar, you can read what each report does, view an example of one, and click a link to run the report. (See Chapter 19.)

- **Synchronizing contact information with Microsoft Outlook** is now a one-step process with the new—and free—download, QuickBooks Contact Sync for Outlook (page 526).

- Behind the scenes, QuickBooks now uses an industry-standard **SQL database**, which can handle accounting for larger operations and more concurrent users, while dramatically improving performance.

Getting to Know QuickBooks

When you run a business (or a nonprofit), you track company finances for two reasons: to keep your business running smoothly and to generate the reports required by the IRS, the SEC, and any other stakeholders to whom you are responsible. QuickBooks helps you perform your basic financial tasks, track your financial situation, and manage your business to make it even better. Before you read any further, here are a few things you *shouldn't* try to do with QuickBooks:

- **Work with more than 14,500 unique inventory items or 14,500 contact names.** QuickBooks Pro and Premier company files can contain up to 14,500 inventory items and a combined total of up to 14,500 Company:Job, Vendor, Employee, and Other names. The Enterprise Edition increases these limits to 29,000.

- **Track personal finances.** Even if you are a company of one, keeping your personal finances separate from your business finances is a good move, particularly when it comes to tax reporting. In addition to opening a separate checking account for your business, track your personal finances somewhere else. If that somewhere else is QuickBooks, at least create a separate company file for your personal financial information.

- **Track the performance of stocks and bonds.** QuickBooks isn't meant to keep track of the capital gains and dividends you earn from investments such as stocks and bonds. But companies have investments, of course. A machine that costs hundreds of thousands of dollars is an investment that you hope will generate lots of income and you should track it in QuickBooks. However, in QuickBooks, these types of investments show up as *assets* of the company (page 122).

- **Manage customer relationships.** Lots of information goes into keeping customers happy. With QuickBooks, you can stay on top of customer activities with features like To Do items, Reminders, and Memorized Transactions. But for tracking details like membership, items sold on consignment, project progress, and scheduled events, another program would be a better solution.

Tip: Intuit sells an add-on product called Customer Manager (page 542). Also, some third-party customer management products integrate with QuickBooks (page 530).

Choosing the Right QuickBooks Product

QuickBooks comes in a gamut of editions, offering options for organizations at both ends of the small-business spectrum. QuickBooks Simple Start and Online Edition cover the basic needs of very small operations. Enterprise Solutions are the most robust and powerful editions of QuickBooks, boasting enhanced features and speed for the biggest of small businesses.

This book focuses on QuickBooks Pro because its balance of features and price make it the most popular edition. Throughout this book, you'll also find notes about features offered in the Premier edition, which is one step up from Pro. Whether you're willing to pay for these advanced features is up to you. Here's an overview of what each edition does:

- **QuickBooks Simple Start** is the new, low-cost option for small businesses with simple accounting needs. It's easy to set up and easy to use, but it doesn't handle features like payroll, inventory, accounts payable, or even purchase orders. (If you outgrow this edition, you can always move your data to QuickBooks Pro or Premier.)

- **QuickBooks Online Edition** offers most of the features of QuickBooks Pro, but you access it via the Web instead of running it on your PC. Since it lets you use QuickBooks anywhere, on any computer, this edition is ideal for the consultant who's always on the go.

Note: The edition called QuickBooks Basic is no more. But Intuit has revised its pricing, so you can move up to the more powerful QuickBooks Pro for what you used to spend on Basic ($199.95 for a single user).

- **QuickBooks Pro** is the workhorse edition. It lets more than one user work in a company file at a time. (You can purchase licenses in single- or five-user packs.) QuickBooks Pro includes features such as job costing; creating estimates; saving and distributing reports and forms as email attachments; creating budgets automatically; projecting cash flow; tracking mileage; customizing forms; customizing prices with price levels; printing shipping labels for FedEx and UPS; and integrating with Word, Excel, and hundreds of other programs. All QuickBooks Pro lists—customers, vendors, employees, and so on—can include up to a combined total of 14,500 entries.

- **QuickBooks Premier** is another multiuser edition. For business owners, its big claim to fame is handling inventory items assembled from other items and components. In addition, Premier edition can generate purchase orders from sales orders or estimates, and it can apply price levels to individual items. You can also track employee information and access data remotely. This edition includes a few extra features typically of more interest to accountants, like reversing general journal entries. Premier edition comes in different flavors targeted to several specific industries (see the section, "The QuickBooks Premier Choices"). Like the Pro edition, Premier can handle a combined total of up to 14,500 list entries.

- **Enterprise Solutions** is the edition for larger operations. It's faster, bigger, and more robust. Up to 15 people can access a company file at the same time, and this simultaneous access is at least twice as fast as in the Pro or Premier edition. The database can handle twice as many names in its customer, vendor, employee, and other names lists. You can have multiple company files, work in several locations, and produce combined reports for those companies and locations. With more people in your company file, this edition offers features such as an enhanced audit trail, more options for assigning or limiting user permissions, and the ability to delegate administrative functions to other users.

The QuickBooks Premier Choices

If you work in one of the industries covered by QuickBooks' industry editions, you can get additional features unique to your industry—for only a few hundred dollars more than QuickBooks Pro. Some people swear that these customizations are worth every extra penny. Others say the extra features don't warrant the Premier price. On the QuickBooks Web site (*http://quickbooks.intuit.com*), you can tour the Premier editions to decide for yourself.

- **Accountant Edition** is designed to help professional accountants deliver services to their clients. In addition to being compatible with all other editions of QuickBooks, it lets you design financial statements and other documents, process payroll for clients, reconcile client bank accounts, and prepare client tax returns. This edition comes with a one-year subscription to WebEx, an online conferencing service that makes it easy to work with your clients.

- **Contractor Edition** includes special features near and dear to construction contractors' hearts: job cost reports, different billing rates by employee, managing change orders, and other contractor-specific reports.

- **Manufacturing & Wholesale Edition** is targeted to companies that manufacture products. It includes a Chart of Accounts and menus customized for manufacturing and wholesale operations. You can manage inventory assembled from components and track customer return materials authorizations (RMAs) and damaged goods.

- If you run a nonprofit organization, you know that several things work differently in the nonprofit world. **Nonprofit Edition** includes features such as a Chart of Accounts customized for nonprofits, forms and letters targeted to donors and pledges, help about using QuickBooks for a nonprofit, and the ability to generate the Statement of Functional Expenses 990 form.

Note: You may be tempted to save some money by using QuickBooks Pro for your nonprofit organization, but be prepared to live with some limitations. As long as funding comes primarily from unrestricted sources, the Pro edition fits reasonably well. Your biggest annoyance is using the term "customer" when you mean donor or member, or the term "job" for grants you receive. Throughout this book, you'll find notes and tips about tracking nonprofit finances with QuickBooks Pro.

However, if you receive restricted funds or track funds by program, you must manually post them to equity accounts and allocate funds to accounts in your Chart of Accounts: QuickBooks Pro doesn't automatically perform these staples of nonprofit accounting. Likewise, the program doesn't generate all the reports you need to satisfy your grant providers or the government, though you can export reports (page 535) and then modify them as necessary in a spreadsheet program.

- **Professional Services Edition** (not to be confused with QuickBooks Pro) is designed for the company that delivers services to its clients. Features unique to this edition include project costing reports, templates for proposals and invoices, billing rates that you can customize by client, billing rate by employee, and professional service-specific reports and help.

- **Retail Edition** customizes much of QuickBooks to work for retail operations. It includes a specialized Chart of Accounts, menus, reports, forms, and help. Intuit offers companion products that you can integrate with this edition to support all aspects of your retail operation. For example, QuickBooks' Point of Sale tracks sales, customers, and inventory as you ring up sales, and it shoots the information over to your QuickBooks company file. Similarly, Merchant Services (page 508) and Virtual Terminal Plus let you take credit cards as payment, often far more cheaply than the deal you can get at your bank.

Accounting Basics—The Important Stuff

Intuit claims that you don't need to understand most accounting concepts to use QuickBooks. However, the accuracy of your books *and* your productivity will benefit if you understand the following concepts and terms:

- **Double-entry accounting** is the standard method for tracking where your money comes from and where it goes. Following the old saw that money doesn't grow on trees, with double-entry accounting, money always comes from somewhere. For example, as demonstrated in Table I-1, when you sell something to a customer, the money on your invoice comes in as income and goes into your Accounts Receivable account. Then, when you deposit the payment, the money comes out of the Accounts Receivable account and goes into your checking account.

Tip: Each side of a double-entry transaction has a name: debit or credit. As you can see in Table I-1, when you sell products or services, you credit your income account (you increase your income when you sell something), but debit the Accounts Receivable account (selling something also increases how much customers owe you). You'll see examples throughout the book of how transactions equate to account debits and credits.

Table I-1. Following the money through accounts

Transaction	Account	Debit	Credit
Sell products or services	Accounts Receivable	$1,000	
Sell products or services	Service Income		$1,000
Receive payment	Checking Account	$1,000	
Receive payment	Accounts Receivable		$1,000
Pay for expense	Office Supplies	$500	
Pay for expense	Checking Account		$500

- **Chart of Accounts.** In bookkeeping, an account is a place to store money, just like your checking account is a place to store your ready cash. The difference is that you need an account for each kind of income, expense, asset, and liability you have. The Chart of Accounts is simply a list of all the accounts you use to keep track of money in your company. (See Chapter 4 to learn about all the different types of accounts you might use.)

- **Cash vs. Accrual Accounting.** Cash and accrual are the two different approaches companies can take to document how much they make and spend. Cash accounting is the choice of many small companies because it's easy. You don't show income until you've received a payment, regardless of when that might occur. And, you don't show expenses until you've paid your bills.

The accrual method follows something known as the matching principal, which matches revenue with the corresponding expenses. This approach keeps income and expenses linked to the period in which they occurred, no matter when cash comes in or goes out. With accrual accounting, you recognize income as soon as you record an invoice, even if you'll receive payment during the next fiscal year. If you pay employees in January for work they did in December, those wages are part of the previous fiscal year. The advantage of the accrual method is that it provides a better picture of profitability because income and its corresponding expenses appear in the same period.

- **Financial Reports.** You need a triumvirate of reports to evaluate the health of your company (described in detail in Chapter 14). The *income statement*, which QuickBooks calls a *Profit & Loss report*, shows how much income you've brought in and how much you've spent over a period of time. The QuickBooks report gets its name from the difference between the income and expenses, which results in your profit (or loss) for that period.

The *balance sheet* is a snapshot of how much you own and how much you owe. Assets are things you own and that have value such as buildings, equipment, and brand names. Liabilities are the money you owe to others (perhaps money you borrowed to buy one of your assets). The difference between assets and liabilities is the *equity* in the company—like the equity you have in your house when the house is worth more than you owe on the mortgage.

The *Statement of Cash Flows* tells you how much hard cash you have. You might think that the Profit & Loss report would tell you that, but noncash transactions, such as depreciation, prevent it from doing so. The statement of cash flow removes all noncash transactions and shows the money generated or spent operating the company, investing in the company, or financing.

About This Book

Despite the many improvements in QuickBooks over the years, one feature has remained mostly stagnant: Intuit documentation. For a topic as complicated as accounting software, all you get with QuickBooks is a small Fundamentals manual, which is little more than a guide to tasks QuickBooks performs, with a reference to the Help topic for each. Any detail to be found is in the program's online help.

Even if you have no problem reading instructions in one window as you work in another, you'll quickly discover that QuickBooks help is often unworthy of the screen space it consumes. Topics are terse, offer little in the way of technical background or troubleshooting tips, and lack useful examples. In many cases, you get nothing more helpful than "Choose the command you want and follow the onscreen instructions." Well, *duh.* The help system rarely tells you what you *really* need to know, like *when* and *why* to use a certain feature. And marking your place, underlining key points, jotting notes in the margins, or reading about QuickBooks while sitting in the sun are all out of the question.

The purpose of this book, then, is to serve as the manual that should have accompanied QuickBooks 2006. It focuses on the Windows version of QuickBooks, though many features work similarly on a Mac.

Tip: Although each version of QuickBooks introduces new features and enhancements, you can still use this book if you're keeping your company books with earlier versions of QuickBooks. Of course, the older your version of the program, the more discrepancies you'll run across.

In this book's pages, you'll find step-by-step instructions for using every QuickBooks Pro feature, including those you might not have quite understood, let alone mastered: progress invoicing (page 219), making general journal entries (page 374), customizing templates (page 550), writing off losses (page 347), and so on. As mentioned earlier in this introduction, you'll learn about some of the extra bells and whistles in the QuickBooks Premier edition as well. (All of the features in QuickBooks Pro—and in this book—are also in Premier.) To keep you productive, the book includes evaluations of features that help you figure out which ones are useful and when to use them.

QuickBooks 2006: The Missing Manual is designed to accommodate readers at every technical level. The primary discussions are written for advanced-beginner or intermediate QuickBooks users. But if you're a first-time QuickBooks user, special boxes with the title "Up To Speed" provide the introductory information you need to understand the topic at hand. On the other hand, advanced users should watch for similar boxes called "Power Users' Clinic." These sidebars offer more technical tips, tricks, and shortcuts for the experienced QuickBooks fan.

About the Outline

QuickBooks 2006: The Missing Manual is divided into five parts, each containing several chapters:

- **Part 1, Getting Started,** covers everything you must do to set up QuickBooks based on your organization's needs. These chapters explain how to create and manage a company file; create accounts, customers, jobs, invoice items, and other lists; and configure preferences.

- **Part 2, Accounting with QuickBooks,** follows the money from the moment you add charges to a customer's invoice to the tasks you must perform at the end of the year to satisfy the IRS and other interested parties. These chapters describe how to bill customers, manage the money that your customers owe you, pay for expenses, run payroll, manage your bank accounts, and perform other book-keeping tasks.

- **Part 3, Managing Your Business,** delves into the features that help you make your business a success—or even more successful than it was before. These chapters explain how to keep your inventory at just the right level, how to keep track of time and mileage, how to build budgets and plan for the future, and how to use QuickBooks reports to evaluate every aspect of your enterprise.

- **Part 4, QuickBooks Power,** helps you take your copy of QuickBooks to the next level. Save time and prevent errors by downloading transactions electronically. Boost your productivity by integrating QuickBooks with other programs. Customize QuickBooks components to the way you like to work. And, most important, set up QuickBooks so your financial data is secure.

- **Part 5, Appendixes,** provides a guide to installing and upgrading QuickBooks, a reference to help resources for QuickBooks, and a quick review of the most helpful keyboard shortcuts.

The Very Basics

To use this book, and indeed to use QuickBooks, you need to know a few basics. This book assumes that you're familiar with a few terms and concepts:

- **Clicking.** This book gives you three kinds of instructions that require you to use your computer's mouse or track pad. To *click* means to point the arrow pointer at something on the screen and then—without moving the pointer at all—press and release the left button on the mouse (or laptop track pad). To *double-click*, of course, means to click twice in rapid succession, again without moving the pointer at all. And to *drag* means to move the pointer while holding down the button the entire time.

  When you're told to *Shift+click* something, you click while pressing the Shift key. Related procedures, such as *Ctrl+clicking*, work the same way—just click while pressing the corresponding key.

- **Menus.** The *menus* are the words at the top of your screen: File, Edit, and so on. Click one to make a list of commands appear, as though they're written on a window shade you've just pulled down. Some people click to open a menu and then release the mouse button; after reading the menu command choices, they click the command they want. Other people like to press the mouse button continuously as they click the menu title and drag down the list to the desired command; only then do they release the mouse button. Either method works, so choose the one you prefer.

- **Keyboard shortcuts.** Nothing is faster than keeping your fingers on your keyboard to enter data, choose names, and trigger commands. You'll save time by not needing to grab the mouse, carefully position it, and then choose a command or list entry. That's why many experienced QuickBooks fans prefer to trigger commands by pressing combinations of keys on the keyboard. For example, in most word processors, you can press Ctrl+B to produce a **boldface** word. When you read an instruction like "Press Ctrl+A to open the Chart of Accounts window," start by pressing the Ctrl key; while it's down, type the letter A, and then release both keys.

About → These → Arrows

Throughout this book, and throughout the Missing Manual series, you'll find sentences like this one: "Choose Lists → Customer & Vendor Profile Lists → Customer Type List." That's shorthand for a much longer instruction that directs you to navigate three nested menus in sequence, like this: "Choose Lists. On the Lists menu, point to the Customer & Vendor Profile Lists menu entry. On the submenu that appears, choose Customer Type List." Figure I-1 shows the menus this sequence opens.

Similarly, this arrow shorthand also simplifies the instructions for opening nested folders, such as Program Files → QuickBooks → Export Files.

About MissingManuals.com

At *www.missingmanuals.com*, you'll find news, articles, and updates to the books in this series.

But the Web site also offers corrections and updates to this book (to see them, click the book's title, and then click Errata). In fact, you're invited and encouraged to submit such corrections and updates yourself. In an effort to keep the book as up-to-date and accurate as possible, each time we print more copies of this book, we'll make any confirmed corrections you've suggested. We'll also note such changes on the Web site, so that you can mark important corrections into your own copy of the book, if you like.

In the meantime, we'd love to hear your suggestions for new books in the Missing Manual line. There's a place for that on the Web site, too, as well as a place to sign up for free email notification of new titles in the series.

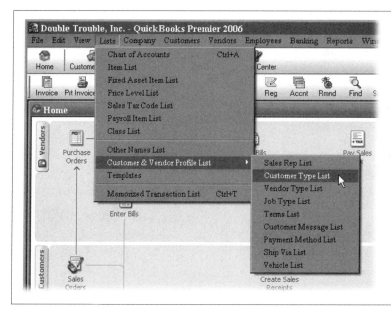

Figure I-1:
Instead of filling pages with long and hard-to-follow instructions for navigating through nested menus and nested folders, the arrow notations are concise, but just as informative. For example, "Choose Lists → Customer & Vendor Profile List → Customer Type List" takes you to the menu shown here.

Safari® Enabled

When you see a Safari® Enabled icon on the cover of your favorite technology book, that means the book is available online through the O'Reilly Network Safari Bookshelf.

Safari offers a solution that's better than e-books. It's a virtual library that lets you easily search thousands of top tech books, cut and paste code samples, download chapters, and find quick answers when you need the most accurate, current information. Try it for free at *http://safari.oreilly.com*.

Part One:
Getting Started

Creating a Company in QuickBooks

A *company file* is where you store your company's records in QuickBooks, and it's the first thing you need to work on in the program. You can create a company file from scratch or convert records previously kept in Quicken, but the most agreeable approach is to use a file that *someone else* created. If you've worked with an accountant to set up your company, she might provide you with a company file configured precisely for your business so that you can hit the ground running.

If you must create your own company file, this chapter tells you how to use the QuickBooks EasyStep Interview to get started, and it points you to the other chapters in this book that tell you how to finish the job. If you already have a company file, you'll learn how to open it and modify basic company information.

Opening QuickBooks

Here are the easiest methods for opening QuickBooks:

- **Desktop icon.** If you requested during installation that QuickBooks create a desktop shortcut, double-click that shortcut to launch QuickBooks.

- **Quick Launch toolbar.** The fastest way to open QuickBooks is to click its icon on the toolbar (Figure 1-1).

QuickBooks icon

Figure 1-1:
The Quick Launch toolbar (no relation to QuickBooks) keeps your desktop tidy.

If you have a QuickBooks desktop shortcut, right-drag (that's dragging while holding down the right mouse button) the desktop shortcut onto the Quick Launch toolbar and then choose Copy Here to create a second shortcut on the toolbar. (If you're trying to clean up your desktop, choose Move Here to move the desktop shortcut to the Quick Launch toolbar.) You can also use the right-drag technique to copy or move a shortcut in Windows Explorer or from the Start menu.

Tip: If you don't see the Quick Launch toolbar, in the Windows taskbar, right-click an empty area and then choose Toolbars → Quick Launch. When a checkmark appears to the left of the Quick Launch menu entry, the appearance of the toolbar in the Windows taskbar should follow.

- **Programs menu.** Without a desktop icon, you can launch QuickBooks from the Windows Start menu. Click Start, and then choose Programs → QuickBooks → QuickBooks Pro 2006 (or QuickBooks Premier 2006).

The first time you launch QuickBooks, you're greeted by the "Welcome to Quick-Books" window. Later, if you close a company file, the No Company Open window appears, as shown in Figure 1-2. These two windows are nearly—but not quite—the same. The rest of this chapter tells you when and how to use each one.

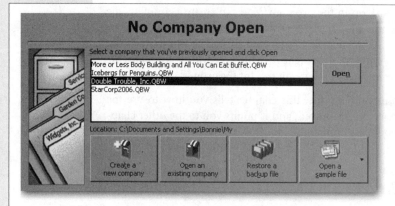

Figure 1-2:
The No Company Open window includes "Restore a backup file," which you'll gladly click should something go terribly wrong with your QuickBooks company file. To reopen a file that you worked on recently, double-click its name on the list. (If you'd like to play around with an unfamiliar feature, click "Open a sample file" as described in the box on page 18.)

You still have to create or open a company file the first time you launch Quick-Books. But after you've opened a company file in one session, QuickBooks kicks off your next session by opening the same company file. If you use only one company file, you might never have to actively open a QuickBooks file again.

Tip: If you're transferring your books from Quicken to QuickBooks, choose File → Utilities → Convert and then choose either From Quicken or From Peachtree. In the dialog box that opens, click View Help for a full explanation of the conversion process.

Creating a New Company

Keeping books requires accuracy, attention to detail, and persistence, hence the customary image of spectacled accountants hunched over ledgers. QuickBooks can help you keep your books without ruining your vision or your posture—as long as you start your QuickBooks company file with good information.

The EasyStep Interview tries to make creating a company file as painless as possible, but the process isn't pain *free*. Indeed, the EasyStep Interview is much like a family reunion, where you're asked a lot of questions that you don't want to answer. Unlike the reunion, however, you can skip parts of the Interview or return to it when you're better prepared for the interrogation.

In QuickBooks 2006, the Interview is short and sweet. All it wants to know is some company information, the industry you're in, and the features you want to use. The Interview sets your preferences and creates a few accounts, but you have to do the bulk of the work yourself later. For example, the company file that EasyStep Interview creates doesn't even know what tax form you use to file your business tax return. You must fill in this information in the Company Information dialog box *and* slog through individually assigning each account to a tax line.

UP TO SPEED

The Fastest Way to a New Company File

The proud owners of brand-new businesses face a dilemma. They have more important things to do than muddle around setting up a company file in QuickBooks, but money is usually as short as free time. If you don't know much about bookkeeping or accounting, paying for a few hours of your accountant's time is a valuable investment. You'll not only save untold hours of tedium and confusion, but you'll also feel confident that your books are set up properly. Accountants well-versed in QuickBooks can create a flawless company file without breaking a sweat.

If you plan to do without an accountant, but you want some help setting up your company file, choose Help → Access Support Resources. Under the Certified QuickBooks Pro-Advisor heading, click the Learn More link. QuickBooks opens your Web browser to the Certified QuickBooks ProAdvisor Search window, where you can seek out someone in your area to help you get started.

Steps to Take Before You Create Your Company File

If you've just started a business and want to inaugurate your books with Quick-Books, your prep work will be a snap. On the other hand, if you have existing books for your business, you have a few small tasks to complete before you jump into QuickBooks' setup. Whether your books are paper ledgers or electronic files in another program, gather your company information *before* you open Quick-Books. Then, you can hunker down in front of your computer and crank out a company file in record time. Here's a guide to what you need to create your company file in QuickBooks.

A Start Date

To keep your entire financial history at your fingertips, you need every transaction and speck of financial information in your QuickBooks company file. But you know that you have better things to do than enter years worth of checks, invoices, and deposits, so the comprehensive approach is practical only if you started your company quite recently.

GEM IN THE ROUGH

Using a Sample File

QuickBooks comes with two sample files: one for a product-based business and the other for a service-based business. To experiment with QuickBooks features before you put them in production, in either the "Welcome to QuickBooks" window or the No Company Open window, click "Open a sample file" and then choose either "Sample product-based business" or "Sample service-based business." If you botch your experiment, you can always reinstall the sample files from the QuickBooks CD.

These files aren't suitable as your company file because they come with accounts, customers, vendors, and transactions such as checks, invoices, and purchase orders. Besides, QuickBooks sets the date to 12/15/2007, which makes transactions later than you or your vendors would like.

The more realistic approach is to enter your financial state as of a specific date (ideally the beginning of a fiscal year) and from then on, add all new transactions in QuickBooks. In QuickBooks, the date you choose is called the *start date* and you shouldn't choose it arbitrarily. Here are your start date options and the ramifications of each:

• **The first day of the fiscal year.** If you're setting up QuickBooks during the first half of the year, bite the bullet and choose the first day of your company's fiscal year as the QuickBooks start date.

Yes, you have to enter checks, credit card charges, invoices, and other transactions that occurred since the beginning of the year, but that won't take as much time as you think. You'll regain those hours when tax time rolls around and you nimbly generate the reports you need to complete your tax returns. During the second half of the year, the best approach is to be patient and postpone your QuickBooks setup until the next fiscal year. Intuit releases its new versions in November for just that reason.

• **The first day of a fiscal period.** The next best start date is the first day of a fiscal quarter (or fiscal month at the very least).

Waiting until next year isn't always an option, particularly if your old accounting system vendor wants a truckload of cash for an upgrade. Starting in the middle of a fiscal year makes the entire year's accounting more difficult. Even if you fill in year-to-date values for all your accounts, since your company file doesn't contain a full year's worth of detail, you'll have to switch between QuickBooks and your old filing cabinets to prepare your tax returns and look up any financial information. Starting at the beginning of a fiscal period mitigates this hassle but doesn't eliminate it.

Account Balances

Unless you begin using QuickBooks when you start your business, you need to know your account balances as of the start date to get things rolling. For example, if your checking account has $342 at the end of the year, that value feeds into QuickBooks during setup. Here are the balances you need to know and where you can find them in your records:

- **Cash balances.** For each bank account you use in your business (checking, savings, money market, petty cash, and so on), find the bank statements with statement dates as close to but earlier than the start date for your QuickBooks file.

  Gather deposit slips and your checkbook register to identify the transactions that haven't yet cleared in your bank accounts. You'll need them to enter transactions, as described in the upcoming chapters. If you have petty cash lying around, count it and use that number to set up your petty cash account.

- **Customer balances.** If customers owe you money, pull the paper copy of every *unpaid* invoice or statement out of your filing cabinet. If you didn't keep copies, you'll have to figure out how much you sold in services and products, the discounts you applied, what you charged for shipping and other charges, and the amount of sales tax. As a last resort, you can ask your customers for copies of the invoices they haven't paid or create invoices in QuickBooks to match the payments you receive. QuickBooks needs this information to calculate your Accounts Receivable balance.

- **Vendor balances.** If your company considers handing out cash more painful than data entry, find the bills you haven't paid and get ready to enter them in QuickBooks. If you'd rather reduce the transactions you have to enter, pay those outstanding bills.

- **Asset values.** When you own assets such as buildings or equipment, the value of those assets depreciates over time. If you've filed a tax return for your company, you can find asset values and accumulated depreciation on your most recent tax return (yet another reason to begin using QuickBooks at the beginning of a year). If you haven't filed a tax return for your company, the asset value is typically the price you paid for the asset, and you won't have any depreciation until you file that first return.

- **Liability balances.** Unpaid vendor bills that you enter in QuickBooks generate the balance for your Accounts Payable liability account. However, you must find the current balances you owe on any loans or mortgages.

- **Inventory.** For each product you stock in inventory, you need to know how many items you had in stock as of the start date, how much you paid for them, and what you expect to sell them for.

> **Note:** QuickBooks isn't very good at working with inventory that you assemble from components or raw materials. The QuickBooks Premier Manufacturing Edition offers inventory assembly, which is a start.

- **Payroll.** Payroll services offer great value for the money, which you'll grow to appreciate as you collect the information you need for payroll (including salary and wages, tax deductions, benefits, pensions, 401(k) deductions, and other stray payroll deductions you might have). You also need to know who receives withholdings, such as tax agencies or the company handling your 401(k) plan. Oh yes, you need payroll details for each employee. Chapter 11 explains the ins and outs of payroll using QuickBooks.

> **Tip:** If you have outstanding payroll withholdings such as employee payroll taxes, send in those payments so you don't have to enter those open transactions in QuickBooks.

Other Important Information

If you're going back to the beginning of the fiscal year for the start date, you need every transaction that has occurred since the beginning of the year: sales you've made, expenses you've incurred, payroll and tax transactions, and so on, to re-establish your asset, liability, equity, income, and expense accounts. So, dig that information out of your existing accounting system (or shoebox). Federal tax returns and payroll tax returns (federal and state) include all sorts of information that QuickBooks setup wants to know, like your federal tax ID number. And the balance sheet that goes with the return is a great starting point for your account balances.

> **Note:** Intuit totally revamped the EasyStep Interview for QuickBooks 2006. That's why, if you've been through the process before, much of what you see here looks unfamiliar.

Starting the EasyStep Interview

You can create a brand-new company file from either the "Welcome to Quick-Books" window or the No Company Open window by clicking "Create a new company." Although the wizard doesn't provide hints about which step comes next, the interview covers the basics for creating and customizing a company file to fit your business. Click Next or Back to move from screen to screen.

The Get Started screen assures you that you'll be ready to start using QuickBooks in about 30 minutes. Start by choosing one of the following three buttons:

- **Convert Data.** If you have existing records in Quicken or Peachtree, you're in luck. Converting your books is easier than starting from scratch.

- **Skip Interview.** If you're something of a QuickBooks expert, this option lets you set up a company file without a safety net. It opens the bare-bones Creating New Company window, followed by a few screens of data entry. If you need help during the process, you can always click the Help button.

- **Start Interview.** If you don't fit into either of the previous categories, this one's for you.

Company Information

The first setup screen asks you for the basic 411 about your company, as you can see in Figure 1-3. If any of the fields are confusing, try clicking "Get answers" in the upper-right corner. Click Next when you're done.

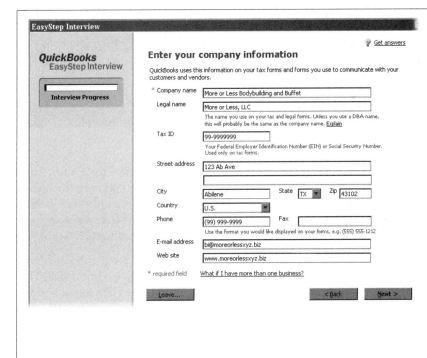

Figure 1-3:
On the Company Information screen, fill in both fields, even if the name your company commonly uses is the same as its legal name. In the "Company name" field, type the name that you want to appear on invoices, reports, and other forms. In the "Legal name" field, type the company name as it should appear on contracts and other legal documents. If you own a corporation, the legal name is what appears on your Certificate of Incorporation. The Tax ID box is for the federal tax ID number you use when you file your taxes—your Social Security number or Federal Employer Identification Number.

The Administrator Password

The second screen in the EasyStep Interview asks you to set a password for the administrator login. The administrator can do absolutely anything in your company file: set up other users, log in as other users, and access any area of the company files. Surprisingly, the administrator password is optional. QuickBooks lets you click Next and skip right over it, but this is no time for shortcuts. Type the password you want to use in both the "Administrator password" and "Retype password" boxes. Keep the login name and password in a safe but memorable place; see the box below for more password advice.

Safe Login Practices

Don't even think about sharing one login among everyone who works with a company file. You wouldn't want everyone to have access to payroll data, and you'd never know whom to fire if you find any less-than-legal transactions in the file. Even if you run a small business from home, an administrator password prevents the chimney sweep from swiping your business credit card number. Chapter 23 has much more about keeping your QuickBooks files secure, but here are some password basics:

• Be focused when you set the administrator password. If you forget the administrator login and password or lose the paper they're written on, you won't be able to open your company file. Passwords are case-sensitive, so make sure that Caps Lock isn't turned on by mistake.

• Type the administrator's password in both the "Administrator password" and "Retype password" boxes. If you copy and paste the password from the "Administrator password" box into the "Retype password" box, you could copy a typographical error and not be able to access the company file you just created.

You can pay Intuit to unlock a company file if you've forgotten your password. A four-day turnaround costs you $65; express service is $110.

Create Your Company File

After you set the administrator password and click Next, the Create Your Company File screen appears. If you're new to QuickBooks, the first screen includes a link "Where should I save my company file?", which opens a QuickBooks Help window that explains the pros and cons of storing files in different places (page 167). QuickBooks veterans can click Next to specify the file name and location.

QuickBooks opens the "Filename for New Company" dialog box, which is really just a Save File dialog box. Initially, it sets the "Save as" type to QuickBooks Files and the location to Program Files → QuickBooks → Company Files. But you're free to change the name or navigate to a different folder for saving. Here are some guidelines:

• QuickBooks fills in the "File name" field with the company name that you entered earlier in the Interview. Keep this name or type one that is shorter or that better identifies the company's records within.

• Instead of the Program Files → QuickBooks folder, consider storing your company file in a folder with the rest of your company data so that it gets backed up along with everything else. (Typically, backup programs skip the Program Files folder.) For example, you could create a Company Files folder in My Documents, if you're the only person who uses QuickBooks.

When you click Save, QuickBooks can take a minute or so to create the new file, and, in the meantime, the "Creating new company file" message box appears. When the company file is ready, the Easy Step Interview displays the Customizing QuickBooks for your business screen. Click Next to dig in.

Tip: At this point, the progress bar in the left margin is depressingly short because the bulk of company file setup still remains. If you need a break before continuing, click Leave. The EasyStep Interview recommences where you left off the next time you open the company file.

Customizing Your Company File

The next several screens in the EasyStep Interview ask you about your business to decide which features to turn on, what to include on your QuickBooks Home page, and so on.

Unlike its counterpart in QuickBooks 2005, this interview sticks to the basics, so you'll have more setup to do later. As you step through the screens in this section, make a list of the features you're turning on (and the corresponding page number in this book) for reference.

Here are some guidelines for answering the questions on the screens that follow:

- Choose carefully on the **"Select your industry"** screen. As shown in Figure 1-4, the list of industries is robust, so chances are good you'll find one that's close to what your organization does. Based on choice, QuickBooks recommends accounts and preferences. If QuickBooks makes assumptions that you don't like, you can change preferences later (page 132).

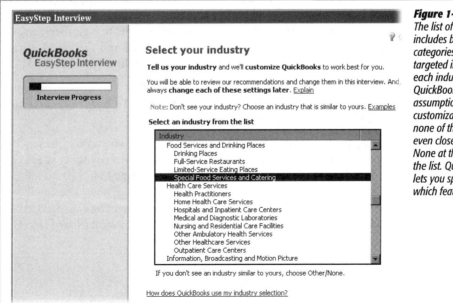

Figure 1-4:
The list of industries includes both high-level categories and more targeted industries. For each industry, QuickBooks makes assumptions about customization for you. If none of the choices are even close, choose Other/None at the bottom of the list. QuickBooks then lets you specify exactly which features you want.

• The **"What do you sell?"** screen is where you tell QuickBooks whether you sell services, products, or both. When you choose one of these options, Quick-Books knows which types of income accounts you need. The interview asks about whether you track inventory later.

• If your business sells things, you see the **"Do you sell products online?"** screen. Whether you want to sell online or not, you can bypass Intuit's marketing pitch for their add-on sales services by selecting the "I don't sell online and I am not interested in doing so" option.

• The **"Do you charge sales tax?"** screen contains only Yes or No options. If you're one of the unfortunate souls who must navigate the rocky shoals of sales tax, select Yes. If you don't charge sales tax, select No and breathe a sigh of relief. For detailed instructions on sales taxes in QuickBooks, see page 87.

• On the **"Do you want to create estimates in QuickBooks?"** screen, select Yes or No to turn the estimate feature on or off. If you prepare quotes, bids, or estimates for your customers and want to do so in QuickBooks (page 216), select Yes.

Tip: If you use QuickBooks Premier, the "Tracking customer orders in QuickBooks" screen asks whether you want to use sales orders to track back orders or other orders that you plan to fill at a later date.

• The **"Using sales receipts in QuickBooks"** screen is targeted to retailers who provide sales receipts when customers purchase or pick up products and pay in full. Simply select Yes if you want to create sales receipts in QuickBooks (see page 192).

• **"Using statements in QuickBooks"** is where you tell the program whether you generate statements to send to your customers (page 193). For example, your wine-of-the-month club might send monthly statements to your members. Or, a consultant could send invoices for work performed and then send a statement that summarizes the fees, payments, and outstanding balance.

• The **"Using progress invoicing"** screen asks whether you invoice customers based on the percentage you've completed on a job. To learn why (and how) you might use this feature, see page 219.

• **"Managing bills you owe"** asks whether you plan to write checks to pay bills immediately (No) or enter bills in QuickBooks and then pay them later (Yes). You can read about bill and payment preferences on page 154.

Tip: It's more work to enter bills in QuickBooks instead of just writing checks, but if you do, QuickBooks can remind you when bills are due or qualify for timely payment discounts, and it can keep track of how much you owe in total.

- **"Tracking inventory in QuickBooks"** is the screen where you tell QuickBooks whether you keep track of the products you have in stock. This screen provides a few examples of when to track or bypass inventory, but page 77 includes more guidelines for whether tracking inventory makes sense for your business.

- The **"Do you accept credit cards?"** screen lets you tell QuickBooks whether you take credit cards for payment (as well as whether you want to get a sales pitch about Intuit's card).

- If you bill by the hour, **"Tracking time in QuickBooks"** is ideal. Select Yes to track the hours that people work and create invoices for their time. You can turn time tracking on in the Interview, but you'll need the instructions on page 424 to set it up properly.

- **"Do you have employees?"** is where you specify whether you need QuickBooks payroll and 1099 features. If you use non-Intuit services to run payroll or generate contractors' 1099s, select No.

When you click Next on the "Do you have employees?" screen, you see the "Using accounts in QuickBooks" screen and the progress bar indicating that you're about three-quarters through the interview. With a few more steps, you'll have your start date and most of the accounts you want to use. Here are the last things to set up:

- The **"Enter your start date"** screen offers a summary of what you learned about starting dates on page 18. If you've already decided which start date to use, simply type or choose that date in the "Start date" box and click Next.

- The **"Add your bank account"** screen asks if you'd like to add an existing bank account. Select Yes if you'd like QuickBooks to walk you through setting up a bank account. If you're comfortable setting up the account on your own, select "No, I'll add a bank account later."

  If you select Yes, the next screen asks for the bank account name, bank account number, and when you opened the account. Click Next again and another screen asks for the statement ending date and ending balance prior to your company file start date. After you create that account, you can add additional bank accounts, or select No to add the rest after you finish the interview.

- The **"Review expense accounts"** screen lists the expense accounts typically used by companies in your selected industry, as shown in Figure 1-5. You can't change these accounts now, but if you need to, make a note to edit your Chart of Accounts once you complete the interview (page 33).

- The **"Review income accounts"** screen mimics the expense accounts screen. You'll see a short list of income accounts typically used by companies in your industry. Select Yes to use the accounts that the program suggests as a start. If you want to create your income accounts from scratch, select "No, I will create my own accounts later."

When you click Next, you'll see a bright yellow Congratulations! Click Finish, and you end up in the QuickBooks Learning Center, which contains several tutorials about the remaining setup options. If you made a list of your interview choices, you can start setting up those features now, or you can wait until you need them.

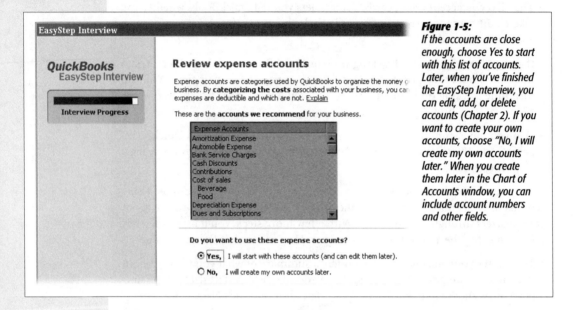

Figure 1-5:
If the accounts are close enough, choose Yes to start with this list of accounts. Later, when you've finished the EasyStep Interview, you can edit, add, or delete accounts (Chapter 2). If you want to create your own accounts, choose "No, I will create my own accounts later." When you create them later in the Chart of Accounts window, you can include account numbers and other fields.

What's Next

The EasyStep Interview in QuickBooks 2006 doesn't tell you what to do next. Because the interview sets up only a bare framework, you may be looking for guidance. Look no further than the book in your hands. Here are the ways you can flesh out your company file:

- Specify the first month of your fiscal year and tax year. See page 29.

- Specify the income tax form you use. See page 29.

- Set up your users and passwords. See page 564.

- Review and/or change the preferences that QuickBooks set. See page 132.

- Set up or edit the accounts in your Chart of Accounts. If you set up accounts in the EasyStep Interview, you must edit them to assign them to the tax lines on your tax form. See page 40.

- Create a journal entry to specify account opening balances. See page 374.

- Create items for the products and services you sell. See page 75.

- Set up sales tax codes. See page 86.

- Set up your 1099 tracking. See page 166.

- **Sign up for Intuit Payroll Service if you want help with payroll.** See page 316.

- **Enter your historical transactions.** For invoices, see page 194; for bills, see page 276; for payroll, see page 326.

- **Create a backup copy.** See page 168.

- **Customize your forms.** See page 550.

Open an Existing Company File

"Open an existing company" appears in both the "Welcome to QuickBooks" window and the No Company Open window. When you click this button, the "Open a Company" dialog box appears, and you can double-click the name of the company file you want to open. However, the fastest route to opening your company file (in the No Company Open window) is by double-clicking one of the file names in the list of recently opened files, as shown in Figure 1-6.

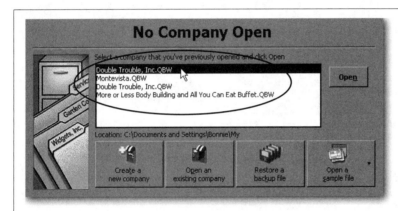

Figure 1-6:
When you select a filename in this list, QuickBooks tries to display its folder path. But unless you store your company files in a top-level folder, you won't likely see the entire pathname. Initially, QuickBooks tries to store company files in the same folder as the software. But backups are much easier if you store your company files in folders dedicated to data.

Convert a Quicken File to QuickBooks

If you're like many small business owners, your accountant probably recommended that you make the leap from tracking your business in Quicken to using QuickBooks. Quicken doesn't report your business performance in the way that most accountants want to see, nor does it store your business transactions the way QuickBooks does. If you want the conversion to proceed as smoothly as possible, do some cleanup in your Quicken file first.

For example, you have to record overdue scheduled transactions and send online payments before you convert your Quicken file. Make sure that customer names are consistent and unique. QuickBooks doesn't support repeating online payments, so you must also send an instruction in Quicken to delete any repeating online payments you've set up. In addition, you need complete reports of your past payroll because Quicken payroll transactions don't convert to QuickBooks.

Intuit has published a detailed guide to help you prepare for a Quicken conversion. The easiest way to locate this document is to point your browser to *http:// quickbooks.com/support*, which displays a section for searching the knowledge base. In the Enter search terms box, type *Quicken convert* to find topics that include links to the Quicken to QuickBooks Conversion Guide.

When your Quicken file is ready for QuickBooks prime time, you have two options in QuickBooks:

- Choose File → New. In the EasyStep Interview window, click Convert Data and choose Quicken.

- Choose File → Utilities → Convert → From Quicken.

FREQUENTLY ASKED QUESTION

Upgrading a QuickBooks File

How do I upgrade a company file to the newest version of QuickBooks?

If you've used a previous version of QuickBooks, your company file is set up to work with that version of the program. When you upgrade to QuickBooks 2006, the program must make some changes to the format of your company file. Fortunately, updating a company file is easy. During installation, the wizard asks if you want to update your data file. Type *Yes*, and the wizard updates the company file you opened last.

From then on, all you have to do to update other company files is open them in the new version of QuickBooks. Click

"Open an existing company file" and then select the company file. When prompted to update the file, type *Yes*, and then click OK. You'll see several message boxes as QuickBooks first backs up your original file and then converts the file to QuickBooks 2006. Each one gives you the opportunity to stop before updating your company file, in case you change your mind.

Once you upgrade the company file, your co-workers won't be able to open it until you upgrade the QuickBooks program on their computers. To prevent work disruption, plan to upgrade all copies of QuickBooks and the company file during downtime.

Restore a Backup File

In the No Company Open window, you'll see "Restore a backup file." Backup files are the answer to the adrenaline rush you get when you do something incredibly stupid with your company file or when your hard drive crashes. To learn how to create backup files in the first place, as well as how to restore them, see page 168.

Modifying Company Information

In the EasyStep Interview, QuickBooks extracts the basic information about your company in small chunks spread over several screens. After your company file exists, you can edit any of this information in one dialog box, as illustrated in

Figure 1-7. Remember, the legal name and address are the ones you use on your federal and state tax forms. To open this dialog box, choose Company → Company Information.

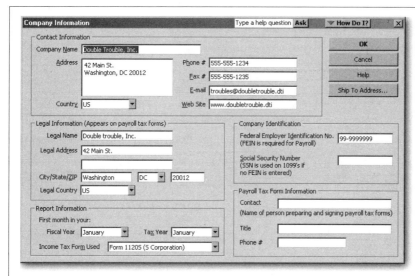

Figure 1-7:
Some company information changes more often than others. For instance, you might relocate your office or change your phone number, email, or Web site. However, information such as your legal name and address, the Federal Employer Identification Number, and your choice of business type (corporation, sole proprietor, and so on) usually remain the same.

Setting Up a Chart of Accounts

If you've just begun to run a business or keep books, all this talk of credits, debits, and accounts could have you flummoxed. Accounting is the cross between mathematics and black arts that records and reports the performance of an organization. The end result of bookkeeping and accounting is a set of financial statements (page 381), but the starting point is the Chart of Accounts.

In accounting, an account is like a bucket of money. When you earn money, you document those earnings in an income account, just as you might toss the day's take at the lemonade stand into the jar on your desk. When you buy supplies for your business, that expense shows up in an expense account. If you buy a building, its value ends up in an asset account. And if you borrow money to buy a building, the mortgage owed shows up in a liability account. Accounts come in a variety of types to reflect whether you've earned or spent money, whether you own something or owe money to someone else, as well as a few other financial situations. The Chart of Accounts isn't actually a chart; it's a list of all the accounts you use to track money in your business.

Neophytes and experienced business folks alike should be relieved to know that no one has to build a Chart of Accounts from scratch in QuickBooks. This chapter explains how to acquire a ready-made Chart of Accounts for your business and what to do with it once you've got it. If you want to add or modify accounts in your Chart of Accounts, you'll learn about that, too.

Obtaining a Chart of Accounts

The easiest—though probably not the cheapest—way to obtain a Chart of Accounts is to get one from your accountant. Accountants understand the accounting guidelines set by the Financial Accounting Standards Board (FASB—pronounced "faz bee"—a private-sector organization that sets standards with the SEC's blessing). When your accountant builds a QuickBooks Chart of Accounts for you, you can be reasonably sure that you have not only the accounts you need to track your business, but that those accounts conform to accounting standards.

Note: Don't worry too much about the cost for your accountant to build a Chart of Accounts in Quick-Books. Your accountant won't start from scratch either. Many financial professionals maintain spreadsheets of accounts and build a Chart of Accounts by importing a customized list of accounts into QuickBooks.

If you've opted to work without an accountant, QuickBooks tries to help you do the right thing accounting-wise. If you use QuickBooks' EasyStep Interview (page 20) to create your QuickBooks file, you can tell the program to create income, expense, and bank accounts for you. As you learned on page 3, if you choose an industry during the interview, QuickBooks lists accounts typical for that industry, which you can use as a starting point for your Chart of Accounts.

Tip: You might find a ready-made Chart of Accounts from other sources. For example, the National Center for Charitable Statistics Web site (*http://nccsdataweb.urban.org/FAQ/index.php?category=77*) includes a downloadable QuickBooks file that contains the Unified Chart of Accounts for nonprofits (known as the UCOA).

For a few hundred dollars more than QuickBooks Pro, QuickBooks Premier offers editions for several different types of business: accounting, construction, manufacturing, nonprofit, professional services, retail, and wholesale. With an industry-specific Premier edition, QuickBooks provides a Chart of Accounts, an item list, payroll items, and preferences already tuned to your industry. The industry-specific editions also offer features unique to an industry, such as enhanced job costing in the Contractor Edition.

If you don't see any accounts in your Chart of Accounts after completing the EasyStep Interview, in the "Chart of Accounts" window, turn on the Show All checkbox. If an X appears to the left of an account that you want to use, click the X to reactivate the account (see page 45 for more about hiding accounts).

With the QuickBooks Chart of Accounts in place, you can add more accounts, hide accounts you don't need, or edit the accounts on the list—all of which is described in the remaining sections of this chapter.

Account Naming and Numbering

Accountants and bookkeepers tend to refer to accounts by both numbers *and* names. This section explains why you should set up naming and numbering conventions—and suggests some rules you can follow—but it won't explain the meaning of all the different names you'll find in your Chart of Accounts. If you accept the accounts that QuickBooks recommends in the EasyStep Interview, your accounts already have assigned account numbers, as shown in Figure 2-1. You might think that lets you off the hook. By taking the time to learn standard account numbers and names, you'll find working with accounts more logical, and you'll understand more of what your accountant and bookkeeper say.

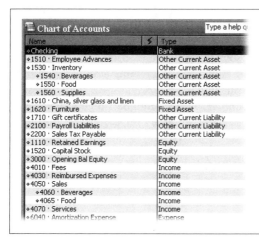

Figure 2-1:
Accounts that QuickBooks adds to your Chart of Accounts during the EasyStep Interview come with account numbers assigned. If you don't see account numbers in the "Chart of Accounts" window, choose Edit → Preferences. In the Preferences window, click Accounting and then click the Company Preferences tab. When you turn on the "Use account numbers" checkbox and click OK, the numbers appear in the "Chart of Accounts" window.

Setting Up Account Numbers

Companies reserve ranges of numbers for different types of accounts; the benefit is that you can identify the type of account by its account number alone. Business models vary, so you'll find account numbers carved up in different ways depending on the business. If you think about your personal finances, you know that you spend money on many different things, but your income derives from a precious few sources. Businesses and nonprofits are no different. You might find expense accounts using numbers anywhere from 5000 through 9999 (see Table 2-1).

Table 2-1. *Account numbers*

Number Range	Account Type
1000–1999	Assets
2000–2999	Liabilities
3000–3999	Equity
4000–4999	Income
5000–5999	Sales, cost of goods sold, or expenses
6000–6999	Expenses or other income

Table 2-1. *Account numbers (continued)*

Number Range	Account Type
7000–7999	Expenses or other income
8000–8999	Expenses or other expenses
9000–9999	Other expenses

Note: The account-numbering scheme is consistent for most types of businesses until you reach the number 4999. Some companies require more income accounts, but in most businesses, expense accounts are the most plentiful.

Account numbering conventions don't end with number ranges for account types. If you read annual reports as a hobby, you know that companies further compart-mentalize their finances. For example, assets and liabilities split into *current* and *long-term* categories. Current means something happens in the next 12 months, such as a loan that is due in 3 months. Long-term is anything beyond 12 months. Typically, companies show assets and liabilities progressing from the shortest to the longest term, and the asset and liabilities account numbers follow suit. Here's one approach to allocating the asset account numbers for current and progressively longer-term assets:

- **1000–1099.** Immediately available cash, such as a checking account, savings account, or petty cash.

- **1100–1499.** Assets you can convert into cash within a few months to a year, including accounts receivable, inventory assets, and other current assets.

- **1500–1799.** Long-term assets, such as land, buildings, furniture, and other fixed assets.

- **1800–1999.** Other assets.

Companies also break down expenses into smaller categories. Many companies track whether the sales team is doing its job by tracking sales expenses separately and monitoring the ratio of sales to sales expense. Sales expenses often appear in the number range from 5000 through 5999. QuickBooks reinforces this standard by automatically creating a "Cost of Goods Sold" account with the account number 5001. Other companies assign overhead expenses to accounts in the range between 7000 and 7999—this way, they can assign a portion of those expenses to each job performed.

Tip: When you add new accounts to your Chart of Accounts, increment the account number by 10 to leave room in the numbering scheme for similar accounts that you might need in the future. For example, if your checking account number is 1000, assign 1010, not 1001, to your new savings account.

In QuickBooks, an account number can contain up to seven digits, but Quick-Books sorts numbers beginning with the leftmost digit, as illustrated in Figure 2-2. If you want to categorize in excruciating detail, slice your number ranges into sets of 10,000. For example, assets range from 10000 to 19999; income accounts span 40000 to 49999.

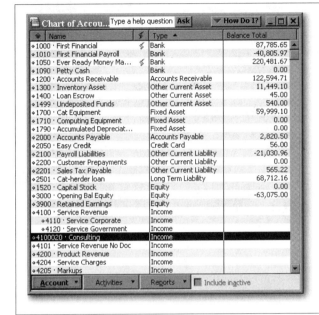

Figure 2-2:
QuickBooks sorts accounts first by account type, then by account number. By looking at the income account numbers, you can see that QuickBooks sorts numbers beginning with the leftmost digit. Account 4100020 appears before account 4101. The "Making Sense of Account Types" box on page 37 lists account types in the order in which they appear in the QuickBooks Chart of Accounts window.

Standardizing Account Names

Accounts should be unique both in name and function because you don't need two accounts for the same type of income, expense, or financial bucket. For instance, if you consider advertising and marketing as two distinctly different activities, create an account for each. But if advertising and marketing blur in your eyes, create one account, with a name such as Marketing & Advertising. Quick-Books does its part to enforce unique account names. Suppose you try to create a new expense account with the name Samovar Rental, but an account by that name already exists. QuickBooks displays the message "This name is already in use. Please use another name."

QuickBooks doesn't help ensure that each account represents a unique category of money. Without a naming standard, you could end up with multiple accounts with unique names, yet each representing the same category, as demonstrated by the following names for the account you use to track postage:

Expense-postage
Mail expense
Post

Postage
Postage and delivery
Shipping

Naming Rules for Accounts

If you haven't used QuickBooks before, you probably don't know all the different ways that account names can cause trouble. Here are some rules you can apply to introduce consistency into your account names:

- **Word order.** Decide whether to include the account type in the name: Postage or Postage Expense. If you include the account type in the name, append it to the end of the name. You'll spot Postage Expense more easily than Expense Postage.

- **Consistent punctuation.** Choose "and" or "&" for accounts that cover more than one item, e.g., "Dues

and Subscriptions." Decide whether to include apostrophes, such as "Owners Draw" or "Owners' Draw."

- **Spaces.** Decide whether to include spaces for readability or to eliminate spaces for brevity (e.g., "Dues and Subscriptions" or "Dues&Subscriptions").

- **Abbreviation.** If you abbreviate words in account names for brevity, choose a standard abbreviation length. If you choose a four-letter abbreviation, for example, Postage would become "Post." With a three-letter abbreviation, you might choose "Pst."

Someone might conclude that an account for postage doesn't exist if the account is named Mail Expense or Expense-postage. If that person creates a postage account, you're on your way to inconsistency and confusion. A naming standard can help you keep expenses in their proper accounts.

Warning: QuickBooks won't enforce your naming standards. After you set the rules for account names, write them down so that you don't forget what they are. A consistent written standard encourages everyone (yourself included) to trust and follow the naming rules. Also, urge everyone to search the Chart of Accounts, using synonyms to see if such an account already exists, before creating a new one. These rules are easier to enforce if you limit the number of people who can create and edit accounts (page 568).

Creating Accounts and Subaccounts

The different types of accounts represent dramatically different financial animals, as described in the "Making Sense of Account Types" box on page 37. The good news is that accounts of every type share most of the same fields, so you have to remember only one procedure for creating accounts.

If you look closely at the Chart of Accounts list in Figure 2-1, you'll notice that accounts fall into two main categories: those with balances and those without. If you're really on your toes, you might also notice that accounts with balances are the ones that appear on the Balance Sheet report. Accounts without balances appear on the Profit & Loss report. To learn more about financial statements and the accounts they reference, see page 381.

Creating an Account

After you've had your business for a while, you won't add new accounts very often. However, you might need a new account if you start up a new line of income and want a new income account, take on a mortgage for your new office building, or want a new expense account for the ostrich infertility insurance you took out for your ostrich farm. The procedure for creating accounts is simple, which is a refreshing change from many accounting tasks.

Making Sense of Account Types

If the account types you see in QuickBooks are unfamiliar, rest assured that they are standard types used in finance. Here's a quick introduction to the account types and what they represent:

- **Bank.** An account that you hold at a financial institution, such as a checking, savings, money market account, or petty cash.

- **Accounts Receivable.** The money that your customers owe you from sources, such as outstanding invoices or goods purchased on credit.

- **Other Current Asset.** Things you own that you'll use or convert to cash within 12 months, such as prepaid expenses.

- **Fixed Asset.** Fixed assets are things that your company owns, which decrease in value over time (depreciate), such as equipment as it wears out or becomes obsolete.

- **Other Asset.** If you won't convert an asset to cash in the next 12 months, and it isn't a depreciable asset–you guessed it–it's an Other Asset. A long term note receivable is one example.

- **Accounts Payable.** This is a special type of current liability account (money you owe in the next 12 months), in which QuickBooks calculates the balance from the amounts you owe each of your vendors.

- **Credit Card.** A credit card account.

- **Current Liability.** Money you owe in the next 12 months, such as sales tax and short-term loans.

- **Long-term Liability.** Money you owe that you'll pay over several years, such as a mortgage.

- **Equity.** The owners' equity in the company, including the original capital invested in the company and retained earnings. Money that owners withdraw from the company shows up in an Equity account, but the values are negative.

- **Income.** The revenue (that is, money) you generate through your main business functions, such as sales.

- **Cost of Goods Sold.** The cost of products and materials that you held originally in inventory but then sold.

- **Expense.** The money you spend to run your company.

- **Other Income.** Money you receive from sources other than business operations, such as interest income.

- **Other Expense.** Money you pay out for things other than business operations–e.g., interest.

- **Non-posting Account.** QuickBooks creates non-posting accounts automatically when you use features such as estimates and purchase orders. When you create an estimate (page 216), you don't want that money to appear on your financial reports, so QuickBooks stores those values in non-posting accounts.

Before you can create an account, you must first open the "Chart of Accounts" window. The easiest way is by pressing Ctrl+A (which you can do from anywhere in the program), but because the Chart of Accounts is central to accounting, QuickBooks provides several additional methods for opening this window:

- On the Home page in the Company section, click Chart of Accounts.

- In the menu bar, choose Lists → Chart of Accounts.

- On the icon bar, click Accnt.

Once you've opened the Chart of Accounts, here's how to create an account:

1. **To open the New Account dialog box, press Ctrl+N.**

    Alternatively, on the menu bar at the bottom of the window, click Account, and then choose New.

    QuickBooks opens the New Account dialog box, shown in Figure 2-3, and highlights the Bank account type in the Type drop-down list. As it turns out, the Bank account type includes all but one of the fields that apply to accounts. If you create another type of account and don't see one of the fields mentioned here, it simply doesn't apply to that account type.

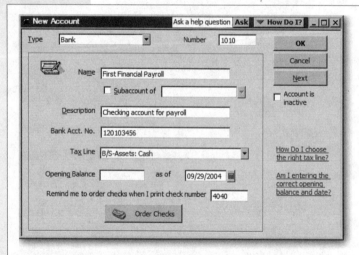

Figure 2-3:
The Bank account type includes every account field except for the Note field. It also includes one field that you won't find on any other account type. If you want QuickBooks to remind you to order checks, in the "Remind me to order checks when I print check number" box, type the check number you want to use as a trigger. Clicking the Order Checks button opens the browser to the Order Supplies Web page, which is useful only if you use checks from Intuit. If you obtain checks from another source, you'll have to follow your regular procedure for reordering checks.

2. **To create a Bank account, just press Tab to accept the account type and move on to naming the account. If you want to create any other type of account, in the Type drop-down list, choose the type of account.**

    If you prefer your fingers glued to the keyboard, you can select the account type by typing. Because Bank and Income are the only account types with unique first letters, this approach doesn't help as often as you'd like.

3. **In the Number box, type the Chart of Accounts account number you want to use.**

If you keep the Chart of Accounts in view while you create new accounts, review the account numbers for similar types of accounts. Then, when you generate your new account number by incrementing one of those account numbers by 5 or 10, the new account snuggles in nicely with its compatriots in the Chart of Accounts.

Note: If the Number box doesn't appear, you haven't turned on account numbers in QuickBooks preferences. To turn on account numbers, choose Edit → Preferences. In the Edit Preferences dialog box, click the Accounting icon, then click the Company Preferences tab. Turn on the "Use account numbers" checkbox.

If you want to turn an account into a subaccount to track your business (see the box below), turn on the "Subaccount of" checkbox. Then, in the drop-down list, choose the account that you want to act as the parent.

UP TO SPEED

Adding Detail with Subaccounts

Your company's travel expenses are sky-high and you want to start tracking what you spend on different types of travel, such as airfare, lodging, and limousine services. You could try creating reports that categorize expenses by vendor, but subaccounts are easier to use, and they produce more dependable results. Subaccounts are nothing more than further partitions within a higher-level account (a parent account).

When you post transactions to subaccounts only, not the parent account, your reports show the subtotals for the subaccounts and a grand total for the parent, with the Travel account (number 6336) and its subaccounts Airfare (6338), Lodging (6340), and Limousine (6342).

Subaccounts help categorize transactions with more precision, but they're indispensable for assigning similar expenses

to different lines on a tax form. For example, the IRS doesn't treat all travel expenses the same. You can deduct only half of your meal and entertainment expenses, while other travel expenses are fully deductible. In the figure, Meals and Entertainment are separate subaccounts from Travel for this very reason.

6330 · Travel & Entertainment		
6332 · Entertainment		125.00
6334 · Meals		289.15
6336 · Travel		
6338 · Airfare	3,642.00	
6340 · Lodging	2,416.25	
6342 · Limousine	1,185.00	
Total 6336 · Travel		7,243.25
Total 6330 · Travel & Entertainment		7,657.40

4. **To add a more meaningful description of the account, in the Description box, type** *text.*

For example, you can define whether a bank account is linked to another account or give examples of the types of expenses that apply to an expense account. Inexplicably, the account Description field can contain no more than 29 characters.

For several types of accounts, you'll see the Bank Acct. No. field. Fill that in next.

5. **In the Bank Acct. No. box, type the account number for the account at your financial institution, such as a checking account, money market account, or mortgage.**

This field appears for Bank, Other Current Asset, Other Asset, Credit Card, Other Current Liability, and Long-term Liability account types. The field label for a credit card account is Card No.

When an account type doesn't include the Bank Acct. No. field, you'll see the Note field. Type any additional information you want to document about the account.

6. **To associate the account with a tax form and a specific line on that tax form, in the Tax Line drop-down list, choose the entry for the appropriate tax form and tax line.**

The Tax Line field is unassigned if you haven't specified the tax form that your company files with the IRS. To see QuickBooks tax line assignments, start by choosing Company → Company Information. In the Company Information dialog box, in the Income Tax Form Used field, choose the tax form appropriate for your business, such as Form 1120S for an S corporation.

If QuickBooks hasn't assigned a tax line for you, you can scan the entries in the drop-down list for a likely match. If you don't find an entry that seems correct, your best bet is to call your accountant or the IRS.

To remove a tax line from an account, in the drop-down list, choose *<Unassigned>*.

Note: For a brand-new account, the value for the Opening Balance field is easy—it's zero. But if you're setting up QuickBooks with accounts that existed prior to your starting date, those accounts *do* have opening balances. Even so, you should leave the Opening Balance field blank. See the box on page 374 to learn how to specify opening balances for all your accounts with only a few steps.

---

7. **Click Next to save the current account and begin the next one.**

If you want to save the account you just created and close the New Account dialog box, click OK, or click Cancel to discard the account in progress and close the New Account dialog box.

Viewing Account Names and Numbers

Perhaps it's the nature of accounting, but financial professionals put great store in account numbers. You can earn the eternal gratitude of your bookkeeper or accountant by assigning and displaying account numbers in QuickBooks.

Turning on the "Use account numbers" preference (page 133) displays account numbers in the "Chart of Accounts" window, account drop-down lists, and account fields. With the "Use account numbers" checkbox turned on, the New Account and Edit Account dialog boxes display the Number box, so you can add or modify an account's number.

Tip: Turning off the "Use account numbers" checkbox doesn't remove any account numbers you've already added. You can see them again by simply turning this preference checkbox back on. However, you won't be able to add account numbers to any accounts that you create while the checkbox is turned off.

When you use subaccounts, QuickBooks displays both the parent account name and the subaccount name in account fields, which often makes it impossible to tell which account a transaction uses, as illustrated in Figure 2-4. If you use account numbers and want to see only the lowest-level subaccount in Account fields, turn on the "Show lowest subaccount only" checkbox (page 134).

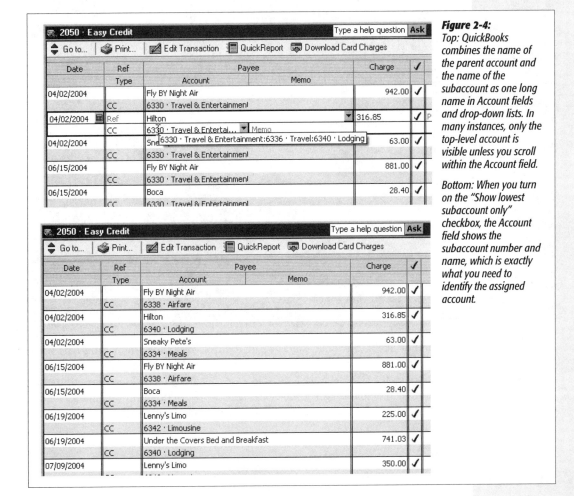

Figure 2-4:
Top: QuickBooks combines the name of the parent account and the name of the subaccount as one long name in Account fields and drop-down lists. In many instances, only the top-level account is visible unless you scroll within the Account field.

Bottom: When you turn on the "Show lowest subaccount only" checkbox, the Account field shows the subaccount number and name, which is exactly what you need to identify the assigned account.

Modifying Accounts

If you stick to your account numbering and naming conventions, you'll have few reasons to edit accounts. In the Edit Account dialog box, you can tweak an account name or description, adjust an account number to make room for new accounts, or change an account's level in the Chart of Accounts hierarchy.

You're not likely to change the Type field unless you chose the wrong type when you created the account. If you do want to change the account type, back up your QuickBooks file first (see page 168), in case the change has disastrous effects that you didn't anticipate. QuickBooks has several restrictions on changing account types. You can't change account types under the following conditions:

- An account has subaccounts.

- You try to change an Accounts Receivable or Accounts Payable account to another account type, and vice versa.

- QuickBooks automatically created the account, such as Undeposited Funds.

To modify an account, in the Chart of Accounts window, select the account that you want to edit and press Ctrl+E. In the Edit Account dialog box, make the changes you want and click OK when you're done.

Note: If your company owns multiple copies of QuickBooks Pro, Premier, or Enterprise, no one else can access the QuickBooks file while you're editing accounts. To switch QuickBooks to single-user mode, ask others to exit QuickBooks. When everyone has logged off, choose File → Switch to Single-user Mode. After you complete your account changes, choose File → Switch to Multi-user Mode. Don't forget to tell your co-workers that they can log into QuickBooks again.

Merging Accounts

Suppose you find multiple accounts for the same purpose—Postage and Mail Expense, for example—lurking in your Chart of Accounts. Rather than punishing your QuickBooks experts, it's more productive to merge the accounts into one and then reiterate the account naming conventions to everyone who creates accounts in QuickBooks. If you haven't gotten around to setting up an account naming convention, see page 35 for some guidelines.

When you merge accounts, QuickBooks sweeps all the transactions from both accounts into the account that you keep. Each type of account has a distinct purpose, so you can merge accounts only if they are the same type. As an experienced manager, you can imagine the havoc that merging income and expense accounts would cause in your financial statements.

Note: If you find two accounts with similar names but different types, those accounts might not represent the same thing. For instance, a Telephone Ex. expense account probably represents what you pay for your monthly telephone service; the Telephone Eq. asset account might represent the big telephone switch that your mega-corporation owns. In this situation, the accounts should be separate, although more meaningful names and descriptions would help differentiate them.

Here's how to eliminate an extraneous account:

1. **Switch to single-user mode.**

   You must be in single-user mode to merge accounts. Show your fellow QuickBooks workers courtesy by making these changes outside of working hours. If you want to merge accounts during the workday, remember to tell your co-workers they can log into the program after you've switched the company file back to multiuser mode.

---

2. **To open the "Chart of Accounts" window, press Ctrl+A. Then, in the Chart of Accounts list, select the name of the account that you want to eliminate and press Ctrl+E.**

   The Edit Account dialog box opens.

   Accounts must be at the same level in the Chart of Accounts hierarchy (page 36) before you can merge them. If the accounts are at different levels, move the account you plan to eliminate to the level of the account you're keeping. (Drag the diamond to the left of the account name to the left or right to change the account's level in the hierarchy.)

3. **In the Edit Account dialog box, change the account number and name to match the values for the account you want to keep.**

   If you don't remember the account number and name for the account you want to keep, drag the "Chart of Accounts" window and the Edit Account dialog box so you can see both at the same time. If QuickBooks won't let you do that, you might have the One Window preference set. To change your window display to show multiple windows, choose Edit → Preferences. In the Edit Preferences dialog box, click the Desktop View icon, and then click the My Preferences tab. Choose the Multiple Windows option.

   As long as you get the words and numbers right, QuickBooks takes care of matching uppercase and lowercase for you.

4. **Click OK.**

   QuickBooks displays a message informing you that the name is in use and asks if you want to merge the accounts.

5. **Click Yes to merge the accounts.**

   In the Chart of Accounts list, the account you renamed disappears and any transactions for that account now belong to the account that remains.

Hiding and Deleting Accounts

If you create an account by mistake, you can delete it. However, because Quick-Books drops your financial transactions into account buckets and you don't want to throw away historical information, you'll usually want to hide accounts that you don't use anymore. You don't delete your Nutrition Service account just because you've discontinued your nutrition consulting service to focus on selling your new book, *The See Food Diet*. The income you earned from that service in the past must remain in your records.

Hiding Accounts

The records of past transactions are important, whether you want to review the amount of business you've received from a customer or the IRS is asking unsettling questions. Hiding accounts doesn't mean you withhold key financial information from prying eyes. When you hide an account, the account continues to hold your historical transactions, but account lists in QuickBooks no longer display it, so you can't choose it by mistake with a misplaced mouse click.

Hiding and reactivating accounts, demonstrated in Figure 2-5, also comes in handy when you use QuickBooks' predefined Charts of Accounts, explained on page 32. If QuickBooks overwhelms you with accounts you don't think you need, hide the accounts for the time being. When you find yourself saying, "Gosh, I wish I had an account for the accumulated depreciation of vehicles," the solution might be as simple as reactivating a hidden account.

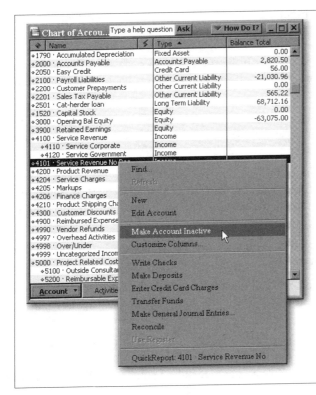

Figure 2-5:
To hide an account, in the "Chart of Accounts" window, right-click the account and choose Make Account Inactive from the shortcut menu. The account and any subaccounts disappear from the Chart of Accounts.

To view all accounts, at the bottom of the "Chart of Accounts" window, turn on the "Include inactive" checkbox. QuickBooks adds a column with an X as its heading and displays an X in that column for every inactive account in the list.

To reactivate an account, first view all accounts, and then click the X next to the account name. If the account has subaccounts, in the Activate Group dialog box, click Yes to reactivate the account and any subaccounts.

Deleting Accounts

You can delete an account only if nothing in QuickBooks references it in any way. An account with references within QuickBooks is a red flag that deleting it might not be the right choice. If that red flag isn't enough to deter you, the sheer tedium of removing references to an account should nudge you toward hiding the account instead. If you insist on deleting an account, here are the conditions that prevent you from doing so and what you must do to remove the constraints:

- **At least one transaction references the account.** If you create a transaction that uses the account, either edit the transaction to use a different account or consider hiding the account if you want to keep the transaction the way it is.

  To delete transactions, in the Chart of Accounts list, double-click the account name. For bank accounts and other accounts with balances, QuickBooks opens a register window, in which you can select a transaction and then press Ctrl+D.

  For accounts without balances, QuickBooks opens an Account QuickReport window. To delete a transaction that appears in the report, double-click the transaction in the report. QuickBooks opens a dialog box (for instance, the Write Checks dialog box appears if the transaction is a check). Choose Edit → Delete Check or the corresponding delete command for the type of transaction you chose.

- **The account has a balance.** An account balance comes from either an opening balance transaction or other transactions that reference the account. You remove an account balance by deleting all the transactions in the account.

- **An item uses the account.** If you create any items that use the account as an income account, an expense account, cost of good sold account, or inventory asset account, you can't delete the account. Edit the items to use other accounts, as described on page 102.

- **The account has subaccounts.** You must first delete all subaccounts before you can delete the parent account.

- **Payroll uses the account.** You can't delete an account if your payroll setup uses it. See Chapter 11 to learn how to modify your payroll and payroll liabilities accounts.

After you have deleted all references to the account, in the "Chart of Accounts" window, select the account you want to delete. Press Ctrl+D or choose Edit → Delete Account. If references to the account are indeed gone, QuickBooks asks you to confirm that you want to delete the account. Click Yes.

Setting Up Customers and Jobs

You might be fond of strutting around your sales department proclaiming, "Nothing happens until somebody *sells* something!" As it turns out, you can increase your self-satisfaction by quoting that tired adage in your accounting department, too. Whether you sell products or services, the first sale to a new customer can initiate a flurry of activity, including creating a new *customer* in QuickBooks, assigning a *job* for the work, and the ultimate goal of all this effort—*invoicing* your customer (sending her an invoice, which shows the services and products that you sold and how much she owes) to collect some income.

The people who buy what you sell have plenty of nicknames: customers, clients, consumers, patrons, patients, purchasers, donors, members, shoppers, and so on. QuickBooks throws out the thesaurus and applies one term, *customer*, to every person or organization that buys from you. To be precise, a customer in QuickBooks is a record of information about your real-life customer. QuickBooks takes the data you enter for customers and fills in invoices and other sales forms with your customers' names, addresses, payment terms, and other information. If you play it safe and define a credit limit, QuickBooks even reminds you when an order puts customers over their limits.

To QuickBooks, a *job* is simply a record of a real-life project that you agreed, perhaps begged, to perform for a customer—remodeling a kitchen, designing an advertising campaign, or tracking down the safety deposit box that matches your customer's key. Some organizations don't track jobs, and if your company is one of those, you don't have to create jobs in QuickBooks. For example, retail stores sell products, not projects. Even consultants who usually work on projects sometimes work on retainer, which provides a steady income that isn't related to one specific project. In these situations, you simply create your customers in Quick-Books and move on to invoicing them for their purchases without assigning the income to a job.

Regardless of how your organization works, customers and jobs are inseparable in QuickBooks. Both the New Customer dialog box and the Edit Customer dialog box, which you'll meet in this chapter, include tabs for customer information *and* job information. When you create a customer, in effect, you get one job built in automatically.

Tip: In QuickBooks 2006, the Customer Center (page 54) is a brand-new dashboard that provides easy access to everything related to your customers and jobs.

So, what if you own a store and don't *do* jobs? For that matter, do you even need QuickBooks customers? Creating customers in QuickBooks is still a good idea, even when you run a primarily cash business. For example, creating customers in QuickBooks for your repeat customers saves time by filling in their information on each of their sales receipts, giving you time to help them become even better customers. Because your business isn't job-oriented, you can pretend the fields for job information aren't there.

On the other hand, when your business revolves around projects, you can create a job in QuickBooks for each project you do for a customer. Suppose you're a plumber and you work regularly for a general contractor. You might create several jobs, one for each place you plumb: Smith house, Jones house, and Gates house. With QuickBooks jobs, you can keep income and expenses by job and gauge each one's profitability. This chapter guides you through customer and job creation and helps you decide how to apply customer and job fields in your business.

What to Do Before You Create Customers and Jobs

QuickBooks doesn't care if you create customers and jobs without any fore-thought, but you *should* take the time to set them up properly. If you want to report and analyze your financial performance to see where your business comes from and which type is most profitable, categorizing your QuickBooks customers and jobs is the way to go. For example, customer and job types help you produce a report of kitchen remodel jobs that are in progress for residential customers. With that report, you can order catered dinners to treat those clients to customer service that they'll brag about to their friends.

With the handy <Add New> menu command in every drop-down list of customer and job types, QuickBooks gives you just-in-time customer and job type creation. Spending a few minutes up front planning your customers and jobs in Quick-Books can save you hours of effort when you want to get information about your business.

Tip: You can add customer and job categories, as well as customers and jobs at any time. If you don't have time to add categories now, come back to this section to learn how to categorize them all.

Categorizing Customers and Jobs

Categorizing your customers and jobs is one way to slice and dice your business reports to show where your business is doing well and what needs closer attention. In a construction company, knowing that your commercial customers cause fewer headaches, *and* that doing work for them is more profitable than residential jobs, is a strong motivator to focus your future marketing efforts on commercial work. Organize your customers and jobs by type, and you'll easily get some insightful analysis.

GEM IN THE ROUGH

Categorizing with Classes

The Class Tracking feature, explained in detail on page 114, is a powerful and often misunderstood way to categorize business. When you turn on Class Tracking, *Classes* appear in one additional field in your transactions so you can classify your business in various ways. They derive their power from their ability to cross income, customer, and job boundaries. Suppose you want to track how much you sell in each state to figure out where to open new stores. If you sell products and services in each state, your income accounts show you sales by products and services—not by state. For a tunnel you built between the states of New York and New Jersey, job types won't help either.

To solve this sales-by-state dilemma, you can create a class for each state. When you enable class tracking, every transaction includes a Class field. Unlike the Customer Type and Job Type fields, which you assign when you create a customer or job, the Class field is initially blank when you begin a transaction. For each invoice, sales receipt, and so on, choose the class for the state in which the sale took place. By doing so, you can produce a report sorted by class that will show sales by state.

As you'll learn on page 113, you can create classes to track information by categories, such as business unit, company division, and location. But don't expect miracles—classes work best when you stick to only one type of class. Mixing business unit and location classes tend to render the classes ineffective.

Creating types of customers

Business owners often like to look at the performance of different segments of their business. Over the years, Home Depot has expanded its business to include sales to professional contractors, so Home Depot probably wants to know how much it sells to homeowners versus construction contractors. Home Depot is too large a company to use QuickBooks, but a small building supply business could designate customers as Homeowner or Contractor to obtain this same comparison, as shown in Figure 3-1. In QuickBooks, you categorize customers with customer types, which appear as entries in the aptly named Customer Type List.

Tip: As you'll see throughout this book, QuickBooks lists make it easy to fill in information in most Quick-Books dialog boxes by choosing from a list instead of typing.

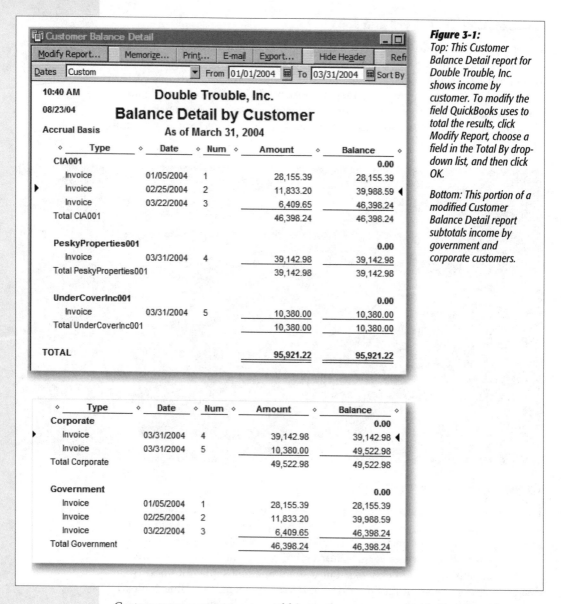

Figure 3-1:
Top: This Customer Balance Detail report for Double Trouble, Inc. shows income by customer. To modify the field QuickBooks uses to total the results, click Modify Report, choose a field in the Total By drop-down list, and then click OK.

Bottom: This portion of a modified Customer Balance Detail report subtotals income by government and corporate customers.

Customer types are yours to mold into whatever categories help you analyze your business. For example, a healthcare provider might classify customers by their insurance, because reimbursement levels depend on whether a patient has Medicare, major medical, or pays privately. A clothing maker might classify customers as custom, retail, or wholesale, because the markup percentages are different for each. A training company could categorize customers by how they learned about the company's services. When you create your company using industry-specific editions of QuickBooks or the EasyStep Interview described on page 20, Quick-Books fills in the Customer Type List with a few typical types of customers for the kind of business you own.

If your business sense tends to the eccentric, you can delete the QuickBooks suggestions and create your own entries in the Customer Type List. As a gardener, you might include customer types such as Lethal, Means Well, and Green Thumb, so you can decide whether Astroturf, cacti, or orchids are more appropriate. As you'll learn in the section "Creating a New Customer" on page 54, categorizing a customer is as easy as choosing an entry from the Customer Type List.

A common beginners' mistake is defining customer types that don't relate to customer characteristics. For example, if you provide consulting services in several areas, such as financial forecasting, investment advice, and reading fortunes, your customers might hire you to perform any or all of those services. If you classify your customers by the services you offer, you'll be wondering which customer type to choose when one of your customers hires you for two different services. Here are some suggestions for applying customer types and other QuickBooks features to analyze your business in different ways.

- **Services.** To track how much business you do for each service you offer, set up separate income accounts in your Chart of Accounts, as outlined on page 36.

- **Products.** To track product sales, create an income account in your Chart of Accounts.

- **Marketing.** To identify the income you earned based on how customers learned about your services, create customer types such as Referral, Web, Newspaper, and Blimp. With these categories, you can create a report that shows the revenue you've earned from different marketing efforts—and whether each marketing strategy is worth the money.

- **Nonprofit "customers."** For nonprofit organizations, customer types such as Member, Individual, Corporation, Foundation, and Government Agency, can help you target fundraising efforts.

- **Customer support.** You may find it handy to categorize customers by their headache factor, such as High Maintenance, Acceptable, and Easy To Please (as long as you're careful to keep the customer type off of the invoices you send out).

You can create the types of customers you want when you set up your Quick-Books company file or at any time after the setup is complete. To create a customer type, follow these steps:

1. **If the company file isn't already open, choose File → Open Company. Then navigate to the company file and double-click it.**

If the QuickBooks Login window appears (which it will if you've assigned a password to the Admin account or set up multiple users), type your user name and password, and then click OK.

2. Choose Lists → **Customer & Vendor Profile Lists** → **Customer Type List.**

The Customer Type List window opens, displaying the customer types that already exist.

3. **To create a new customer type, press Ctrl+N or, at the bottom of the Customer Type List window, click Customer Type, and then choose New.**

The New Customer Type dialog box opens.

4. **Type the name of the customer type in the Customer Type box.**

To define a customer type as a subtype of another, turn on the "Subtype of" checkbox. Then, in the drop-down list, choose the higher-level customer type. For example, if individual members of an industry association can pay annually or month by month, the top-level customer type could be Individual and contain subtypes of Annual and Monthly. Click OK when you're done.

5. **To create additional customer types, click Next and add another type.**

Lather, rinse, repeat.

When you close the New Customer Type dialog box, the new customer type appears in the Customer Type List.

Categorizing jobs

Jobs are optional in QuickBooks, so job types matter only when you track your work by job. If your sole source of income is selling organic chicken fat ripple ice cream to health-obsessed carnivores, jobs and job types don't matter. Your relationship with your customers is one long run of selling and delivering products. On the other hand, for project-based businesses, job types add another level of filtering to the reports you produce. For example, if you're a writer, you can track the type of documents you produce and filter the Job Profitability Report by job type to see which types of writing are the most lucrative. For technical writing, job types might include Article, White Paper, and Marketing Propaganda.

Creating a job type is similar to creating a customer type, described in the previous section. With the company file open, choose Lists → Customer & Vendor Profile Lists → Job Type List. With the Job Type List window open, press Ctrl+N to open the New Job Type window. As you do for customer types, type a name for the job type. For a subtype, turn on the "Subtype of" checkbox and choose the job type to which you want to add this subtype.

Creating Customers in QuickBooks

If bringing in business were as easy as creating customers in QuickBooks, sales of QuickBooks would propel Intuit past Microsoft as the software company with the largest market capitalization. Face facts—you still have to convince customers to work with your company. But once you've cleared *that* hurdle, you create customers in QuickBooks so you can charge for the products you sell and the services you deliver.

WORD TO THE WISE

Making Customers Easy to Identify

In QuickBooks, the Customer Name field uniquely identifies each of your customers. Although you are free to choose from a palette of alphanumeric characters and punctuation, the Customer Name is a code that makes it easy to differentiate the customers on your list, not the name that appears on invoices.

If you own a small company with only a few customers, you're not likely to create multiple records for the same customer. Your customer list is short, so you know which ones you've created and you can see them without scrolling in the Customer Center. Even so, it's a good idea to define a standard for customer names. Perhaps you hide customers you haven't worked with in a while, or you have so many customers that it takes all day to scroll through the list.

Consistent naming can help you avoid multiple records for each customer by preventing you from creating slightly different values in the Customer Name field for the same customer. For example, you could end up with three customers in QuickBooks, such as Cales's Capers, Cales Capers, and CalesCapers, all representing the same events organizer.

QuickBooks doesn't enforce naming conventions. After you define rules that work for your business, you must discipline yourself to apply those rules each time you create a new customer. Here are a few of the more common naming conventions:

- **The first few letters of the customer's company name followed by a unique numeric identifier.** This standard is easy to apply and differentiates customers as long as their names all don't begin with

the same words. For example, if most of your customers are wine stores with unimaginative owners, your customer names could end up as Wine001, Wine002, and Wine003. But if your customers are Zinfandels To Go, Merlot Mania, and Cabernet Cabinet, this system works nicely.

- **For individuals, the last name followed by the first name and a numeric ID to make the name unique.** Although unusual names such as Zaphod Beeblebrox render a numeric ID unnecessary, using this standard ensures that all customer names are unique.

- **The actual company name with any punctuation and spaces omitted.** Removing spaces and punctuation from company names helps eliminate multiple versions of the same name. If you choose to remove punctuation and spaces from names, capital letters at the beginning of each word make the customer name more readable. For instance, Icantbelieveitsyogurt is a headache waiting to happen, but ICantBelieveItsYogurt looks much like its spaced and punctuated counterpart.

- **A unique alphanumeric code.** Customer:Job drop-down lists and reports sort customers by the Customer Name field. Codes such as X123Y4JQ use only a few characters to produce unique identifiers, but cryptic codes make it difficult to pick out the customer you want from drop-down lists, and sorting reports in a meaningful way is challenging. Stick with using part of the customer name whenever possible.

Creating a New Customer

QuickBooks is quite accommodating when it comes to creating customers. If you run a mom-and-pop shop and don't add new customers very often, you can create a customer at the same time that you create the customer's first invoice. For larger outfits that sign up new customers all the time, creating customers in batches is much more efficient. Without closing and reopening the New Customer dialog box, you can create several customers at a time. Then, when it's time to create invoices, you can create several of those at once, choosing the customer you want for each one from the Customer:Job drop-down list.

The Customer Center, new to QuickBooks 2006 and shown in Figure 3-2, is your starting point for creating, modifying, and viewing customers and jobs. QuickBooks provides three easy ways to open the Customer Center window:

- On the left side of the QuickBooks Home page, click Customers.

- On the icon bar, click Customer Center.

- Choose Customers → Customer Center.

Tip: You can add notes to a customer or job record, like a reminder to call the customer about a sale you're having. Simply click Edit Notes and type away. QuickBooks adds the notes to the list in the middle of the Customer Center window.

In the Customer Center icon bar, create a new customer by clicking New Customer & Job → New Customer. If you're a keyboard fan, press Ctrl+N. The New Customer dialog box opens, as shown in Figure 3-3.

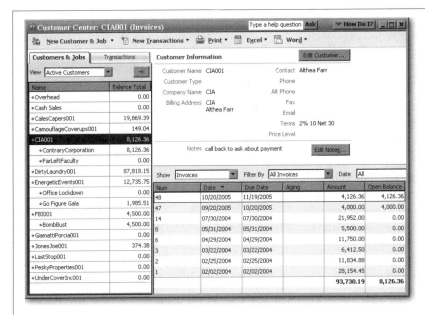

Figure 3-2:
The Customer Center, new in QuickBooks 2006, eliminates the chain of windows you had to open in previous versions. You can filter the customers in the Customers & Jobs tab (left pane) by choosing a category in the View drop-down list. When you choose a customer or job, the right side of the center displays information about your selection and its transactions. The Show, Filter By, and Date drop-down lists let you filter customer or job-related transactions, like all open invoices for the current quarter.

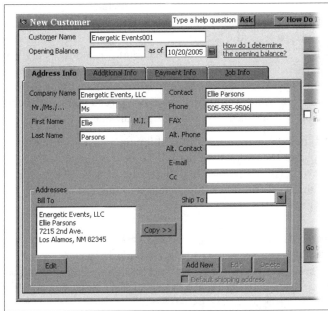

Figure 3-3:
Customer Name is the only field you need to create a customer. Type the name for your new customer, following the customer naming convention you've chosen, as described in the box on page 53.

Entering address information

If you plan to bill your customers, ship them products, or call them to make them feel appreciated, address and contact information is important. In the New Customer dialog box on the Address Info tab, you can specify address and contact information. Here's a guide to the fields you can enter and what they're good for:

- **Company Name.** Unlike Customer Name, which acts as an identifier, the Company Name field is nothing more than the name of the company as you want it to appear on invoices and other forms you create. QuickBooks automatically copies the company name that you type into the Bill To box.

- **Contact.** To address invoices, letters, and other company communications, enter the primary contact's salutation or title, first name, middle initial, and last name in the appropriate fields. As often happens, the first person you contact isn't the person who gets things done day after day. If this turns out to be the case, you can always make this dependable resource the primary contact and assign the figurehead as the alternate contact. QuickBooks automatically copies the salutation and name that you type to the Bill To box.

- **Bill To address.** To complete the address for invoices, type the street address, city, state, country, and postal code, or copy the information from another program.

  To view or enter address information as separate fields, including Address, City, State/Province, Zip/Postal code, and Country, click Edit. In the Edit Address Information dialog box, turn on the "Show this window again when address is incomplete or unclear" checkbox if you want QuickBooks to notify you when you forget a field like the city or when the address is ambiguous. For example, if the address for your biggest customer for toys is Santa Claus, North Pole, QuickBooks opens the Edit Address Information dialog box so that you can fatten the address up a bit with a street, city, and artic postal code.

- **Ship To address.** If the billing address and the shipping address are the same, click Copy>> to replicate the contents of the Bill To field in the Ship To field. (The greater-than symbols on the button indicate the direction that QuickBooks copies the address.) If you don't ship products to the customer, skip the Ship To field altogether.

- **Additional contact information.** QuickBooks gets you started by copying the contents of the First Name and Last Name fields into the Contact field. If you plan to look up contact information such as phone number and email in Quick-Books rather than in your contact program (Outlook or Act! for example), fill in the other fields on the Address Info tab to specify the contact's phone number, a fax number, an alternate phone number such as a mobile phone number, an email address, an email address to carbon copy, and an alternate contact.

Specifying additional customer information

In the New Customer dialog box, the Additional Info tab, shown in Figure 3-4, serves up several fields that categorize your customers and simplify your book-keeping. Although they're optional, some fields speed up entering transactions by storing the values you use most frequently. Other fields appear or disappear depending on the preferences you choose (preferences are the topic of Chapter 6). For example, if you charge sales tax, you must turn on QuickBooks Sales Tax preferences if you want to look on the Additional Info tab to see the Tax Code, Tax Item, and Resale Number fields.

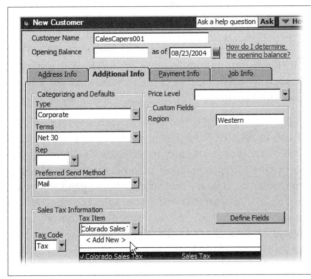

Figure 3-4:
Most of the fields on the Additional Info tab use QuickBooks' lists. To jump directly to the entry you want in lists of epic length, in any text box with a drop-down list, type the first few characters of the entry. QuickBooks selects the first entry that matches the characters you've typed and continues to reselect the best match as you type more characters. You can also scroll to the entry in the list and click to select it. If the entry you want doesn't exist, click <Add New> to create it.

Here's a description of the fields you might see on the Additional Info tab and some ideas for how you can use them:

- **Type.** Choose a type from the Customer Type List to categorize the customer (see page 49). For a healthcare services company, you might categorize customers as government, health insurance, or private pay, so you know how patient you must be while waiting to receive payment. If you want to see if the marketing firm you hired is worth its fee, you can use the Type field to track how customers heard about your company.

• **Terms.** The Terms field represents the payment terms the customer has agreed to. But the entries you see come from the Terms List (page 18), which represents payment terms for your customers *and* the ones you accept from your vendors. QuickBooks provides several of the most common payment terms, such as "Due on Receipt" and Net 30, but you can choose *<Add New>* to define additional payment terms in the Terms List. If you leave the Terms field blank in a customer record, you must choose the payment terms every time you create an invoice for the customer.

• **Rep.** Choosing a name in the Rep field links a customer to a sales representative, which is helpful if you want to track sales representatives' results and calculate their sales commissions. Reps don't have to be *sales* representatives. One of the best ways to provide good customer service is to assign a customer service representative to a customer. When you choose *<Add New>* to create a new Rep entry (page 116), you can select existing names from the Employee List, Vendor List, and the Other Names List.

• **Preferred Send Method.** Choose None, Mail, and E-mail to identify the method that your customer prefers for receiving documents. You can't add a new entry to the Preferred Send Method list, so if you use carrier pigeons to correspond with your incarcerated customers, you'll just have to remember that preference. Choose None if you typically print documents and mail them the old-fashioned way instead of using QuickBooks' add-on mail feature (page 243). If you choose E-mail, QuickBooks automatically turns on the E-mail checkbox when you create forms such as invoices. The Mail method uses an add-on QuickBooks service to mail invoices (page 542).

• **Sales Tax Information.** The Sales Tax Information area with several fields for sales tax appears only if you enable the Sales Tax preference in QuickBooks. If the customer must pay sales tax, choose an entry in the Sales Tax Item list (see page 89), which specifies the tax rate percentage. Customers who buy products for resale usually don't pay sales tax because that would tax the products twice. Who says tax authorities don't have hearts? To bypass the sales tax, choose Non (for nontaxable sales) in the Tax Code List, and then type the customer's resale number in the Resale Number field. If tax auditors pay you a visit, the resale number tells them where the burden of sales tax should fall.

• **Price Level.** More often than not, customers pay different prices for the same product. Consider the labyrinth of pricing options for seats on airplanes. In QuickBooks, price levels represent discounts or markups that you apply to transactions. For example, you might have one price level, called Top20, which applies a 20 percent discount for your best customers, and another price level, called AuntMabel, that extends a 50 percent discount to your Aunt Mabel because she fronted you the money to start your business.

Note: In QuickBooks Pro, your only choice is fixed percentage price levels, which means that you can increase or decrease prices on all items by a fixed percentage. On the other hand, QuickBooks Premier adds the Per Item price level type as an option. Per item price levels open the door to setting the dollar amount of individual items you sell for different customers or jobs.

- **Custom Fields.** QuickBooks provides 15 customer fields, which you can use to store important information that QuickBooks didn't see fit to offer out of the box. Because custom fields don't use drop-down lists, you must type your entries and take care to enter values consistently. Learn more about custom fields on page 128.

Designating payment information

That's right. The New Customer dialog box offers still more fields for storing customer information. The Payment Info tab, shown in Figure 3-5, is the place to say how the customer pays and how much credit you're willing to extend.

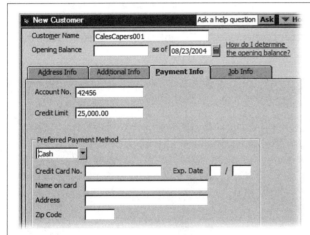

Figure 3-5:
QuickBooks doesn't seem as concerned about your productivity on the Payment Info tab because only one field contains a small set of commonly used values. You must type the values you want to add to all the fields except the Preferred Payment Method field, which displays the Payment Method List in the drop-down list.

You can use the following fields to specify the customer's payment information:

- **Account No.** Account numbers are optional in QuickBooks. Large accounting programs based on database management systems often assign unique account numbers, which greatly reduce the time it takes to locate a customer record. In QuickBooks, the Customer Name field works like an identifier, so the Account No. field is best reserved for an account number generated by another of your business systems. You can use account numbers or the codes in the Customer Name field to both identify and classify your customers. For example, R402 could represent one of your retail customers, whereas W579 represents a wholesale customer.

- **Credit Limit.** You can specify a dollar value of credit that you are willing to extend to the customer. QuickBooks warns you when an order or invoice exceeds the customer's credit limit, but that's as far as it goes. It is up to you to reject the order or ship your products COD. If you don't plan to enforce the credit limits you assign, don't bother entering a value in this field.

- **Preferred Payment Method.** Choose the payment method that the customer uses most frequently. The Payment Method List includes several common payment methods such as Cash, Check, and Visa, but you can add others by choosing *<Add New>*. The payment method you specify for the customer appears automatically in the Receive Payments window when you choose the customer. If a regular customer forgets her checkbook and pays with cash, you can simply replace Check with Cash as you create the Sales Receipt.

- **Credit card information.** For credit card payments, you can specify the customer's credit card number, the name as it appears on the card, the billing address for the credit card, the Zip code, and the expiration date. But before you enter this sensitive and valuable information into your QuickBooks file, check for government and merchant card provider restrictions on storing credit card numbers. Even if the laws allow you to store the numbers, consider whether your security procedures are sufficient to protect your customers' credit card information.

ALTERNATE REALITY

Tracking Donors for Nonprofits

For nonprofit organizations, any individual or organization that sends money is a donor (as well as generous), but you won't see the term *donor* appear anywhere in QuickBooks. Even the Premier Nonprofit Edition of QuickBooks focuses single-mindedly on customers, so get used to mentally saying "donor" whenever you see "customer" in QuickBooks.

Likewise, a job in QuickBooks is the equivalent of a contract or grant. If you must report on a grant or contract, add a separate job for it to the customer (donor, that is) who donated the funds.

Entering members or individual donors as separate customers can max out QuickBooks' customer name limit (10,000) or increase your QuickBooks file to a size that makes QuickBooks' response slower than your great-grandmother's driving. True, the Enterprise Edition of QuickBooks provides a larger number of customers, but most nonprofits would choke at the software's price tag.

To solve this dilemma, create customers in QuickBooks to represent generic pools, such as donors and members, reserving the details of your membership and donor names for a separate database or spreadsheet. For example, create a customer called Unrestricted and post all unrestricted donations to that customer.

Note: The New Customer window includes a Job Info tab, which includes fields for job-related information. If you don't track jobs, you can use the Job Status field to store the overall status of your work for the customer. Document the dates for the work you are currently doing for the customer in the Start Date, Projected End, and End Date fields. If you perform projects or job-based work for a customer, skip the Job Info tab because you're going to create separate jobs, as described on page 67.

Importing and Exporting Customer Information

Chances are you store customer information in other applications besides Quick-Books, such as a customer relationship management program to track customer interactions or a word processing application to produce mailing labels. Entering the same information more than once is not only mind-numbingly tedious, it also wastes time you should spend on more important aspects of your business, such as selling, managing cash flow, or finding out who has the incriminating pictures from the Christmas party. If the other programs you use support *delimited text files*, you can avoid data entry grunt work by transferring data to or from Quick-Books. Delimited text files are nothing more than files that separate each piece of data with a comma, a space, a tab, or another character. The same kind of information appears in the same position in each line, so other programs can pull the information into the right places.

Exporting Customer Information

To extract customer information from QuickBooks, you have three choices:

- **Export your customer information directly to Excel** if you're not sure what information you need, and you'd rather delete and rearrange columns in a spreadsheet program. QuickBooks exports every field for customers and you can edit the spreadsheet all you want and transfer the data to yet another program when you're done. (The one downside to this approach is that the spreadsheet includes blank columns between each field column.)

- **Create a report** when you want control over exactly which fields to export. By creating a customized version of the Customer Contact List report, you can export the same set of records repeatedly, creating delimited files, spreadsheets, and so on.

- If you need a delimited file to load into another program, QuickBooks lets you **export a text file** of your customer data. The delimited file contains each customer in its own row with each field separated by tabs.

Exporting to Excel

In QuickBooks 2006, exporting the Customer List to Excel is a snap, as Figure 3-6 demonstrates.

Customized exports using the Contact List report

By modifying the settings for the Contact List report, you can export exactly the fields you want for specific customers. For example, storing emails in QuickBooks is perfect when you email invoices to customers, but you probably want customer emails in your email program for the steady stream of emails that you exchange with your customers about the work you're doing for them. Exporting the entire

Customer List is overkill when all you want is the contact name and email address; that's where exporting a report shines.

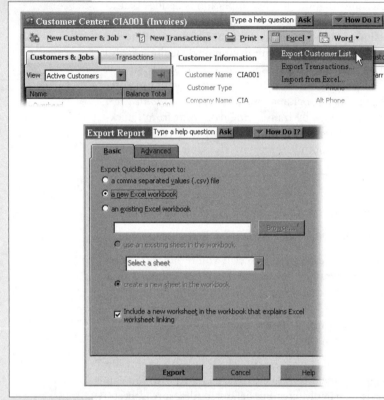

Figure 3-6:

Top: To export all the customer data stored in QuickBooks to an Excel file, in the Customer Center icon bar, click Excel and then click Export Customer List. This menu also contains commands for exporting transactions and for importing spreadsheet data into QuickBooks.

Bottom: The Export Report dialog box that appears is already set up to create a new spreadsheet. Click Export and you'll be looking at the Customer List in Excel in a few seconds. If you'd rather give QuickBooks more guidance on creating the spreadsheet, click the Advanced tab and specify options before clicking Export.

FREQUENTLY ASKED QUESTION

Opening Act

Should I add an opening balance?

With the Opening Balance and As Of fields always visible at the top of the New Customer dialog box, you might conclude that these fields are incredibly important. Actually, you're better off skipping these fields altogether.

Entering an opening balance as of a specific date is a shortcut that eliminates having to create the invoices that generate the customer's current balance. But that shortcut comes at a price. If customers haven't paid, you might have a hard time collecting the money if you can't tell them what services

and products you delivered, how much they cost, the invoice numbers, and when the invoices were due. In addition, when your customers *do* pay, you can't accept those payments against specific invoices to track your accounts receivable.

The best way to build your customer's balance is to create invoices in QuickBooks for the invoices that the customer hasn't paid yet. You'll have complete documentation about those sales and detailed records in your Accounts Receivable account. Also, you can apply the payments that come in to settle those invoices.

Out of the QuickBooks box, the Customer Contact List report includes the Customer Name, Bill To address, Contact, Phone, FAX, and Balance fields. To transform the Contact List report into an export tool, choose Reports → Customers & Receivables → Customer Contact List. To make changes to the fields that appear in the report, in the Customer Contact List window, click Modify Report, which opens the Modify Report:Customer Contact List dialog box. You can use the following techniques to filter the data that you export, or refer to page 489 to learn about other ways to customize the report.

- **Change the report fields.** The Contact, Phone, and FAX fields might be a good start for the fields you want to export. Then again, they might not. You can add or remove a few fields in the report or make wide-scale changes to the list of fields. To modify the fields that appear in the report, in the Modify Report: Customer Contact List dialog box, select the Display tab, choose the fields that you want to export in the report, and then click OK.

  To change the fields that appear in the report, you must click every field you want to add or remove from the list. Clicking a field in the Columns list toggles the field on and off. When a checkmark appears in front of the field name, the field appears in the report. When no checkmark is present, the report doesn't show the field.

- **Filter the customer list.** To produce a report for only the customers you want, in the Modify Report:Customer Contact List dialog box, select the Filters tab. In the Filter list, choose Customer. To specify the customers whose information you want to export, choose a customer name in the Customer drop-down list or choose Selected Names to select more than one.

Tip: Saving the modified report reduces the export steps the next time around. After you've made the changes you want in the Modify Report dialog box and clicked OK to display the customized report, in the Customer Contact List window, click Memorize. In the Memorize Report dialog box, type a name for the report and click OK.

Exporting a text file

To create a delimited file of the entire Customer:Job List (or any other QuickBooks list), choose File → Utilities → Export → Lists to IIF Files. The first Export dialog box that appears includes checkboxes for each QuickBooks list, as described in detail on page 534. If you want to export *only* customer names and addresses to a tab-delimited file, choose File → Utilities → Export → Addresses to Text File.

Importing Customer Information

Salespeople learn a lot about companies long before they become customers. For example, knowing who the decision makers are and what they want is at the heart of most sales strategies. If your sales team stores contact names, phone numbers, email addresses, and other information in a program that exports data to delimited files or Excel spreadsheets, why not import the relevant data into QuickBooks when the company finally decides to buy from you?

Note: You don't have to import every field you have captured so far. Salespeople build relationships with clients by remembering spouses' and kids' names or favorite sports teams, but much of that information doesn't belong in QuickBooks.

The Easy Way to View Data

Data is easier to examine when you view an export or import file with a spreadsheet program, such as Excel, as described in Chapter 21. Most programs can open or import text delimited files, but Excel is a master at reading the records stored in these text files. When you export data to a text delimited file and then open it in Excel, the program pigeonholes the data into cells in a spreadsheet. Because records and fields appear in rows and columns, respectively, you can quickly identify, select, and edit the data you want.

Furthermore, in spreadsheet programs, you can eliminate entire rows or columns with a few deft clicks or keystrokes. A detailed explanation of opening a delimited text file with Excel starts on page 537, but the following steps should be enough if you are at least familiar with Excel:

1. Choose File → Open (as you would to open any worksheet).

2. The delimited text files won't appear in the Open dialog box at first because they're not Excel worksheets. Delimited text files come with a range of file extensions (the three characters that follow the last period in the file name). Because of this, the only way to be sure to see your delimited file—in the "Files of Type" drop-down list—is to choose All Files (*.*).

3. To open the file, navigate to the folder that contains the delimited text file and double-click the file name. The Text Import Wizard dialog box appears.

4. As you tell the wizard which characters act as delimiters and what type of data appears in each column, the wizard shows you what the data will look like after it's imported into Excel. When the interpretation of the data is correct, click Finish.

When you export data from another program to use in QuickBooks, the result is a delimited text file or a spreadsheet. The data is compartmentalized by separating each bit of information with commas or tabs, or by cubbyholing them into columns and rows in an Excel file. Just because another program exports data, the resulting export file isn't necessarily ready to import into QuickBooks. Headings in the delimited file or spreadsheet might identify the field names in the program that held the information, but QuickBooks has no way of knowing the relationship between the other program's fields and its own. As a result, you have some work to do to transform an export file produced by another program into an import file that QuickBooks can read.

Fortunately, Excel and other spreadsheet programs are obliging with this kind of transformation. QuickBooks looks for keywords in the import file to tell it what to do, as illustrated in Figure 3-7.

When you export a file from another program and it looks something like the file in the bottom image of Figure 3-7, save the export file without changing its format. To do this, choose File → Save.

Tip: To see how an import file should look, export your current QuickBooks customer list to an .iif file (page 534) and open it in Excel.

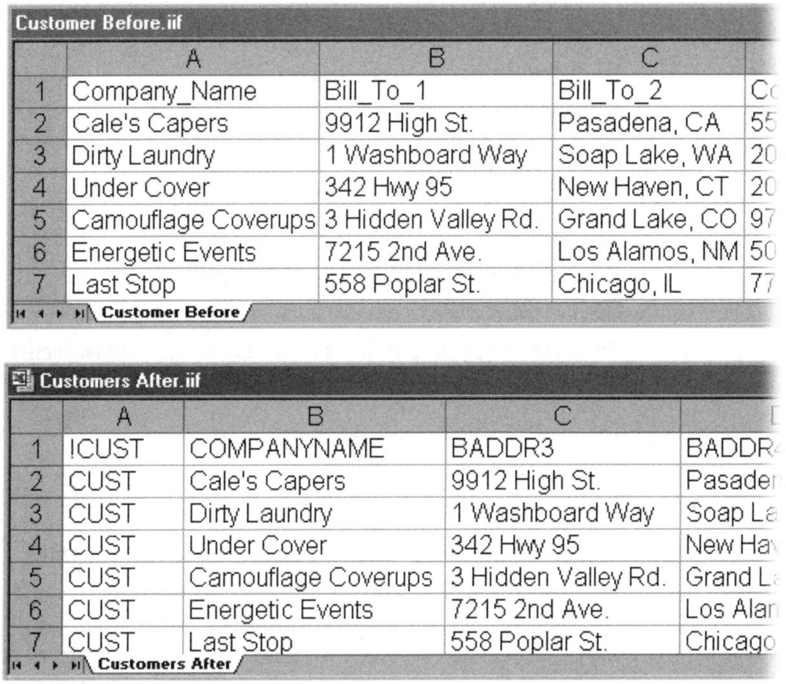

Customer Before.iif			
	A	B	C
1	Company_Name	Bill_To_1	Bill_To_2	C
2	Cale's Capers	9912 High St.	Pasadena, CA	55
3	Dirty Laundry	1 Washboard Way	Soap Lake, WA	20
4	Under Cover	342 Hwy 95	New Haven, CT	20
5	Camouflage Coverups	3 Hidden Valley Rd.	Grand Lake, CO	97
6	Energetic Events	7215 2nd Ave.	Los Alamos, NM	50
7	Last Stop	558 Poplar St.	Chicago, IL	77

Customer Before

Customers After.iif			
	A	B	C
1	!CUST	COMPANYNAME	BADDR3	BADDR
2	CUST	Cale's Capers	9912 High St.	Pasader
3	CUST	Dirty Laundry	1 Washboard Way	Soap La
4	CUST	Under Cover	342 Hwy 95	New Hav
5	CUST	Camouflage Coverups	3 Hidden Valley Rd.	Grand L
6	CUST	Energetic Events	7215 2nd Ave.	Los Alan
7	CUST	Last Stop	558 Poplar St.	Chicago

Customers After

Figure 3-7:
Top: This imported file uses field names that don't match QuickBooks field names. Also, the first column doesn't include the keywords QuickBooks looks for to identify customer records. The first cell in the first row of a customer import file must contain the text, !CUST.

Bottom: To link the columns in the import file to QuickBooks fields, type the keyword for a field in the first cell of the column. For example, replace the Last_Name heading with LASTNAME, which is the keyword for the last name field in QuickBooks. (Table 3-1 provides customer keywords and the fields they represent.)

Table 3-1. *When these keywords appear in the first row of an import file created in another program, such as your contact management program, QuickBooks imports the values in columns to the corresponding fields in your QuickBooks customer records*

Keyword	Field Contents
NAME	(Required) The Customer Name field, which specifies the name or code that you use to identify the customer.
BADDR1	The first line of the customer's billing address.
BADDR2	The second line of the customer's billing address.
BADDR3	The third line of the customer's billing address.
BADDR4	The fourth line of the customer's billing address.
BADDR5	The fifth line of the customer's billing address.
SADDR1	The first line of the customer's shipping address.

Table 3-1. *When these keywords appear in the first row of an import file created in another program, such as your contact management program, QuickBooks imports the values in columns to the corresponding fields in your QuickBooks customer records (continued)*

Keyword	Field Contents
SADDR2	The second line of the customer's shipping address.
SADDR3	The third line of the customer's shipping address.
SADDR4	The fourth line of the customer's shipping address.
SADDR5	The fifth line of the customer's shipping address.
PHONE1	The phone number stored in the Phone Number field.
PHONE2	The customer's alternate phone number.
FAXNUM	The customer's FAX number.
EMAIL	The customer's email address.
NOTE	The name or number of the account, stored in the Account No. field. To set up a customer as an online payee (see page 520), you must assign an account number.
CONT1	The name of the primary contact for the customer.
CONT2	The name of an alternate contact for the customer.
CTYPE	The customer type category. If you import a customer type that doesn't exist in your Customer Type List, QuickBooks adds the new customer type to the list.
TERMS	The payment terms by which the customer abides.
TAXABLE	Y or N indicates whether you can charge sales tax to the customer.
SALESTAXCODE	The code that identifies the sales tax to charge.
LIMIT	The dollar amount of the customer's credit limit with your company.
RESALENUM	The customer's resale number.
REP	The representative who works with the customer. The format for a rep entry is *name:list ID:initials,* such as "Saul Lafite:2:SEL." *Name* represents the name of the representative; the list ID equals 1 if the rep name belongs to the Vendor List, 2 for the Employee List, or 3 for the Other Names List. *Initials* are the rep's initials.
TAXITEM	The name of the type of tax you charge this customer. The name you enter must correspond to one of the sales tax items on your Item list, described on page 89.
NOTEPAD	This field is your chance to wax poetic about your customer's merits or simply document details you want to remember.
SALUTATION	The salutation or title to prefix to the contact's name, such as Mr., Ms., Dr.
COMPANYNAME	The name of the customer's company, as you want it to appear on invoices or other documents.
FIRSTNAME	The primary contact's first name.
MIDINIT	The primary contact's middle initial.
LASTNAME	The primary contact's last name.

Table 3-1. When these keywords appear in the first row of an import file created in another program, such as your contact management program, QuickBooks imports the values in columns to the corresponding fields in your QuickBooks customer records (continued)

Keyword	Field Contents
CUSTFLD1–CUSTFLD15	Custom field entries for the customer, if you have defined any. To learn how to create custom fields, see page 128.
HIDDEN	This field is set to N if the customer is active in your QuickBooks file. Inactive customers are set to Y.
PRICELEVEL	The price level for the customer.

Note: QuickBooks also exports the fields for job information into six columns with the keywords JOBDESC, JOBTYPE, JOBSTATUS, JOBSTART, JOBPROJEND, and JOBEND.

Creating Jobs in QuickBooks

Project-based work means that your current effort for a customer has a beginning and an end, although it sometimes seems like your project will last forever. Whether you build custom software programs or apartment buildings, you can use job tracking in QuickBooks to analyze financial performance by job.

If you sell products to retailers and don't give a hoot about job tracking, you can simply invoice your customers for the products and services you sell without ever creating a job in QuickBooks. On the other hand, suppose you want to know whether you're making more money on the mansion you're building or the bungalow remodel. What's more, you want to know the percentage of profit you made on each project. These financial measures are the reason you create jobs for each project you want to track.

In QuickBooks, jobs connect to customers like baby possums clinging to their mothers. A QuickBooks job *always* belongs to a customer. In fact, if you try to choose the Add Job command before you create a customer, you'll see a message box telling you to create a customer first.

Creating a New Job

Because a job belongs to a customer, you must first create a customer before you can create any of that customer's jobs. Follow these steps to add a job to an existing customer:

1. **Open the Customer Center. Right-click the customer you want, and then choose Add Job from the shortcut menu.**

   The New Job dialog box appears. You can also click New Customer & Job in the Customer Center icon bar and then choose Add Job.

2. **In the Job Name box, type the name for the job.**

The name that you type appears on invoices and other customer documents. You can type up to 41 characters in the Job Name box. The best names are short but easily recognizable by both you *and* the customer.

QuickBooks fills in most of the remaining job fields with the information you entered for the customer who owns the job. Unless the information on the Address Info, Additional Info, and Payment Info tabs is different for the job, you can skip the fields on these tabs. For example, if materials for the job go to a different shipping address than the one stored with the customer, type the job shipping address in the fields on the Address Info tab.

3. **If you want to add information about job type, dates, or status, in the New Job dialog box, click the Job Info tab and enter values in the fields.**

If you add job types, you can analyze jobs with similar characteristics, no matter which customer hired you to do the work. Fill in the Job Status field to see what's going on just by scanning the Customer Center. If you want to see whether you're going to finish the work on schedule, you can document your estimated and actual dates for the job in the Date fields.

Tip: To change the options for Job Status, modify the status text in Preferences (see page 151).

---

4. **After you have filled in the job fields, click Next to create another job for the same customer, or click OK to save the job and close the New Job dialog box.**

Modifying Customer and Job Information

As long as you enter a customer name when you create a new customer, you can leave the remaining customer fields blank. You can change customer information at any time to add more data or to change what's already there. Similarly, you can create a job with only the job name and come back later to modify or add more. To modify a customer or job, open the Customer Center and then double-click the customer or job that you want to edit.

Tip: If double-clicking isn't your favorite action, select the customer or job you want to edit and then press Ctrl+E. If you can't remember keyboard shortcuts, in the Customer Center, click Edit Customer (or Edit Job).

In the Edit Customer dialog box, you can make changes to all customer fields—that is, all except for the customer balance. QuickBooks pulls the customer balance from the opening balance (if you provide one) and shows any unpaid invoices for that customer. Once a customer exists, creating invoices (page 194) is your only option for reproducing the customer's current balance. Similarly, all the fields in the Edit Job dialog box are editable, except for the customer balance.

Remember that the changes you make to fields on the Address Info, Additional Info, Payment Info, and Job Info tabs apply only to the job, not the customer.

Warning: Unless you have revamped your naming standard for customers, don't edit the value in a customer's Customer Name field. Because the Customer Name field uniquely identifies your customers, you might customize QuickBooks based on the Customer Name field. For example, if you created a customized report filtered by a specific customer name, the report isn't smart enough to take on the new customer name. If you do modify the Customer Name, make sure to modify any customization to use the new name.

Specifying Job Information

The fields on the Job Info tab are optional. You can invoice a customer even if every Job Info field is blank. However, Job Status and Job Type both help you analyze your business performance, past and future. You don't even have to use the terms that QuickBooks provides for status. However, defining the text that appears for each phase isn't a matter of creating a QuickBooks list. You need to set the Jobs and Estimates preferences as described on page 151.

Here's a guide to the Job Info fields and how you can put them to use:

• **Job status.** The Job Status can indicate trends in your business. If several jobs are set to Pending status, a resource crunch might be headed your way.

• **Start date.** When you start the job, in the Start Date box, select the actual start date on the calendar.

• **Projected end.** If you have estimated when you will complete the job, in the Projected End box, select that date on the calendar.

• **End date.** By comparing the actual end date with your projections, you can improve future projections or decide to change how you work in order to finish jobs on time. When you complete the job, in the End Date box, select the actual end date on the calendar.

• **Description.** Type a more detailed description of the job to remind you about the work when the job name doesn't ring any bells.

• **Job type.** If you categorize the jobs you deliver, choose the job type (page 52) from the Job Type drop-down list, which QuickBooks fills in with the entries from the Job Type List.

Adding Notes About Customers

Attention to detail. Follow through. These are a few of the things that keep customers coming back for more. Following up on promises or calling if you can't make your meeting is good business. But sending reorder brochures after customers have made purchases can just make them mad. If you use another program for customer relationship management, you can track these types of details there. On the other hand, if you prefer to use the smallest number of software programs, stay in customers' good graces by using QuickBooks notes to keep track of personal information and customer to-do lists.

In the Customer Center, select the customer to which you want to add a note. Click Edit Notes to open the Notepad window shown in Figure 3-8.

To-do items are handy little reminders of what you want to do for a customer and when. In the Notepad window, click New To Do. In the New To Do dialog box, type the text for your to-do item. If you want QuickBooks to remind you when it's time to take action, choose a date in the Remind Me On box. The to-do item shows up on the QuickBooks Reminder List on the date you asked QuickBooks to remind you. Of course, QuickBooks reminders work only if you open QuickBooks on that day and you remember to look at the Reminders List.

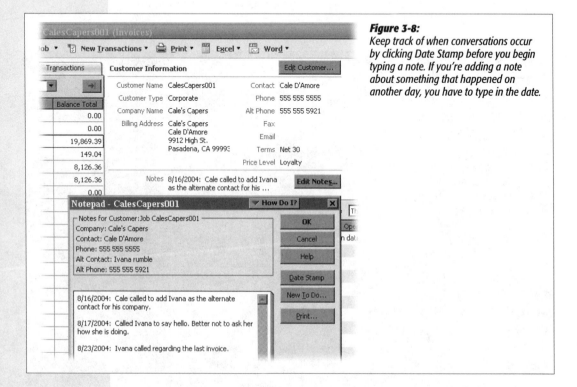

Figure 3-8:
Keep track of when conversations occur by clicking Date Stamp before you begin typing a note. If you're adding a note about something that happened on another day, you have to type in the date.

Merging Customer Records

Suppose you remodeled buildings for two companies run by brothers: Morey's City Diner and Les' Exercise Studio. The brothers conclude that their businesses have a lot of synergy—people are either eating or trying to lose weight, and usually doing both. To smooth out their cash flow, they decide to merge their companies into More or Less Body Building and All You Can Eat Buffet. You have to figure out how to create one customer in QuickBooks from the two businesses, and you also want to retain the jobs, invoices, and other transactions that you created when the companies were separate.

If you don't use a standard naming convention as recommended on page 53, you could end up with multiple customer records representing one real-life customer, such as Les's Exercise Studio and LesEx. You can merge these doppelgangers into one customer just as you can merge two truly separate companies into one.

Merging customers in QuickBooks results in one customer that retains the entire transaction history for the two original customers. You don't so much merge two customers as turn one customer's records into those of another's. If your customers have jobs associated with them, you have to move all the jobs to the customer you intend to keep before you start the merge. Subsume the customer with fewer jobs so you don't have to move as many jobs. If you don't use jobs, subsume whichever customer you want.

Merging customers in QuickBooks won't win any awards for best intuitive process. You merge two customers by renaming one customer to the same name as another. But that's not all. The customer you rename can't have any jobs associated with it. Finally, if you work in multiuser mode (described in Chapter 23), you must switch to single-user mode for the duration of the merging operation. (Warn your fellow QuickBooks users and then choose File → Switch to Single-user Mode. When you're done, switch back to multiuser mode and tell your colleagues they can work in QuickBooks once more.)

To merge customers with a minimum of angry outbursts, follow these steps:

1. **Open the Customer Center.**

   In the icon bar, click Customer Center or, on the QuickBooks Home page, click Customers.

2. **If the customer you're going to merge has jobs associated with it, position the mouse pointer over the diamond to the left of the job you want to reassign.**

   If you have hundreds of jobs, moving them is tedious at best, but move them you must.

3. **Drag the job under the customer you plan to keep after the merge, as shown at left in Figure 3-9.**

   Repeat steps 2 and 3 for each job that belongs to the customer you are going to merge.

4. **In the Customer:Job List, right-click the name of the customer you are going to merge and, on the shortcut menu, choose Edit Customer:Job.**

   You can also edit the customer by selecting the customer name on the Customer & Jobs tab and then, when the customer information appears on the right side of the Customer Center, clicking the Edit Customer button.

   Either way, the Edit Customer dialog box opens.

5. **In the Edit Customer dialog box, change the name in the Customer Name field to match the name of the customer you intend to keep. Click OK.**

   QuickBooks displays a message informing you that the name is in use and asks if you want to merge the customers.

6. **Click Yes to merge the customers.**

In the Customer Center, the customer you renamed disappears and any customer balances now belong to the remaining customer, as illustrated at right in Figure 3-9.

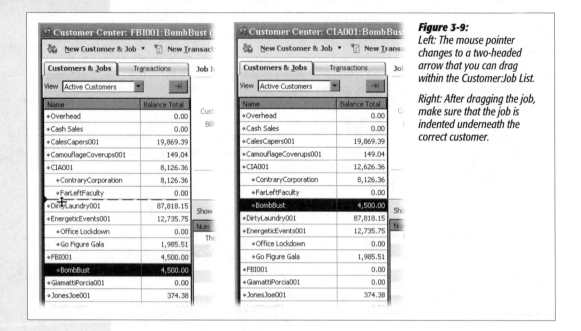

Figure 3-9:
Left: The mouse pointer changes to a two-headed arrow that you can drag within the Customer:Job List.

Right: After dragging the job, make sure that the job is indented underneath the correct customer.

Hiding and Deleting Customers

Hiding customers isn't about secreting them away when the competition shows up to talk to you. Because you can delete customers only in very limited circumstances, hiding customers keeps your list of customers manageable and is a much easier way to prevent selecting inactive customers by mistake.

Deleting Customers

You can delete a customer only if there is no activity for that customer in your QuickBooks file. If you try to delete a customer that has even one transaction, QuickBooks warns you that you can't delete the record.

If you create a customer by mistake, you can remove it, as long as you first remove any associated transactions—which are likely to be mistakes as well. But QuickBooks doesn't go so far as to tell you which transactions are preventing you from deleting this customer. You can see all the transactions for the customer by selecting that customer in the Customer Center and setting the Show box to All Transactions and the Date box to All. Or, you can run the Transaction List by Customer report (described on page 483). In the report, open the transaction you want to delete by double-clicking it. For example, double-click an invoice that you charged the customer. Then choose Edit → Delete Invoice.

After you have deleted all the transactions for this accidental customer, open the Customer:Job List window and select the customer you want to delete. Press Ctrl+D or choose Edit → Delete Customer:Job. If the customer has no transactions, QuickBooks asks you to confirm that you want to delete the customer. Click Yes.

Hiding Customers

Although your work with a customer might be at an end, you still must keep records about your past relationship. But old customers can clutter up your Customer Center, making it difficult to select the customers that are active on your list. Hiding customers is a better solution. It retains the historical transactions for a customer, so you can reactivate them if they decide to work with you again. Hiding removes customer names from all the lists that appear in transaction windows so you can't select them by mistake. Figure 3-10 shows you how to hide and reactivate customers.

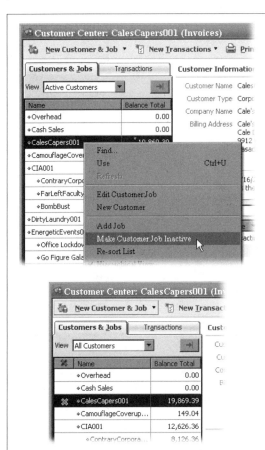

Figure 3-10:
Top: To hide a customer, in the Customer Center, right-click the customer and choose Make Customer:Job Inactive from the shortcut menu. The customer and any associated jobs disappear from the list.

Bottom: To view all customers, in the View drop-down list, choose All Customers. QuickBooks displays an X to the left of every inactive customer in the list. Click that X to restore the customer to active duty.

Setting Up Invoice Items

Whether you build houses, sell gardening tools, or tell fortunes on the Internet, you'll probably use *items* in QuickBooks. In QuickBooks, items are the products and services you sell. But to the program, things like subtotals, discounts, and sales tax are items, too. *Nothing* appears in the body of a QuickBooks sales form (such as an invoice) unless it's an item.

Put another way, when you want to create invoices (Chapter 8) in QuickBooks, you need customers *and* items to do so. So, now that you've got your customers and your Chart of Accounts set up, it's time to dive into items.

This chapter begins by helping you decide whether you need items at all. But if your organization is like most and uses business forms such as invoices, sales receipts, and so on, you'll read the rest of the chapter to learn how to create, name, edit, and manage the items you add to them.

What Items Do

For your day-to-day work with QuickBooks, items save time and increase consistency on your sales forms. Here's the deal. When you create an item, you specify its characteristics. The fields you fill in include what the item is, how much you pay for it, how much you sell it for, and the accounts to which you post the corresponding income and expense. For example, the bookkeeping service you provide might cost $75 an hour, and you want the income to show up in your Financial Services income account. Then, when you add an item to a sales form, QuickBooks fills in the fields on the form with the information you stored in the item.

You can work out which accounts to assign items to on your own or with your accountant (a good idea if you're new to bookkeeping), and then specify the accounts in your items. QuickBooks remembers these assignments from then on, as illustrated in Figure 4-1.

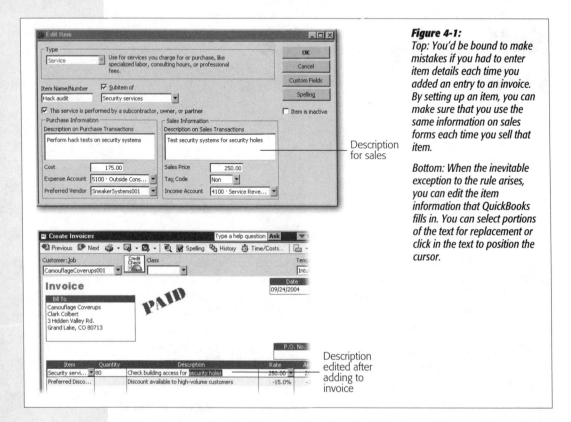

Figure 4-1:

Top: You'd be bound to make mistakes if you had to enter item details each time you added an entry to an invoice. By setting up an item, you can make sure that you use the same information on sales forms each time you sell that item.

Bottom: When the inevitable exception to the rule arises, you can edit the item information that QuickBooks fills in. You can select portions of the text for replacement or click in the text to position the cursor.

When it's time to analyze how your business is doing, items shine. QuickBooks has built-in reports based on items, which show the dollar value of sales or the number of units of inventory you've sold. To learn how to use inventory reports, see page 412. For other item-based reports, read Chapter 19.

When You Don't Need Items

Bottom line: without items, you can't create any type of sales form in QuickBooks, which includes invoices, statements, sales receipts, credit memos, and estimates. Conversely, if you don't use sales forms, you don't need items. Few organizations operate without sales forms, but here are a few examples:

- Old Stuff Antiques sells antiques on consignment. Kate, the owner, doesn't pay for the pieces; she just displays them in her store. When she sells a consignment item, she writes paper sales receipts. When she receives her cut from the seller, she deposits the money in her checking account.

- Tony owns a tattoo parlor specializing in gang insignias. He doesn't care how many tattoos he creates and—for safety's sake—he doesn't want to know his customers' names. All Tony does is deposit the cash he receives upon completing each masterpiece.

- Dominic keeps the books for his charity for icebergless penguins. The charity accepts donations of money and fish, and it doesn't sell any products or perform services to earn additional income. He deposits the monetary donations into the charity's checking account and enters the checking account deposit in QuickBooks. Dominic does keep track of the donors and fish inventory in a spreadsheet.

Should You Track Inventory with Items?

If your business is based solely on selling services, you can skip this section entirely. But if you sell products at all, you can handle them in two ways: by stocking and tracking inventory, or by buying products only when customer work requires them. The system you use affects the types of items you create in QuickBooks. When you use QuickBooks' inventory feature, the program keeps track of how many products you have on hand as you purchase and sell them to customers. When you purchase products specifically for customers, you still need items, but there's no need to track the quantity on hand. In this case, you can create Non-inventory Part items, which you'll learn more about shortly.

For example, general contractors rarely work on the same type of project twice, so they usually purchase the materials they need for a job and charge the customer for those materials. Because general contractors don't keep materials in stock, they don't have to track inventory and can use Non-inventory Part items. On the other hand, specialized contractors such as plumbers install the same kinds of pipes and fittings over and over. These contractors often purchase parts and store them in a warehouse, selling them to their customers as they perform jobs. These warehoused parts should be set up as Inventory Part items in QuickBooks.

Tracking inventory requires more effort than buying just the materials you need. Use the following questions to determine whether your business should track inventory:

- **Do you keep products in stock to resell to customers?** If your company stocks faux pony bar stools to resell to customers, those bar stools are inventory. By tracking inventory, you know how many units you have on hand, how much they're worth, and how much money you made on the bar stools you sold.

  The faux pony mouse pads you keep in the storage closet for your employees are business supplies. Most companies don't want the overhead of tracking inventory for supplies they consume in the course of business.

- **Do you want to know when to reorder products so you don't run out?** If you sell the same items over and over, keeping your shelves stocked means more sales. QuickBooks can remind you when it's time to reorder a product.

• **Do you purchase products specifically for jobs or customers?** If you special order products for customers or purchase products for a specific job, you don't need to track inventory. After you deliver the special order or complete the job, your customer has taken and paid for products, and you must account only for the income and expense you incurred.

Your business model might dictate that you track inventory. However, Quick-Books' inventory-tracking feature has some limitations. For example, it lets you store up to 14,500 items, and then you're stuck. If you answer yes to any of the following questions, QuickBooks isn't the program to use to handle the products you sell:

• **Do you sell products that are unique?** In the business world, tracking inventory is meant for businesses that sell commodity products, such as electronic equipment, and stock numerous units of each product. If you sell unique items, such as fine art or compromising Polaroid photos, you'd eventually use up the 14,500 items that QuickBooks can store. For unique items, consider using a spreadsheet to track the products you have on hand. When you sell your unique handicrafts, you can record your sales in QuickBooks using items that *aren't* unique. For example, use an item called Oil Painting on the sales receipts for the oils you sell.

• **Do you manufacture the products you sell out of raw materials?** QuickBooks inventory can't follow materials as they wend through a manufacturing process or track inventory in various stages of completion.

Note: QuickBooks Premier and Enterprise editions can track inventory for products that require light assembly. For instance, if you create Wines from Around the World gift baskets using the wine bottles in your store, you can build an Inventory Assembly item out of wine and basket Inventory items.

• **Do you sell on consignment or rent equipment to customers?** When you sell on consignment, you don't purchase products before you sell them, so you don't need Inventory items for them. If you want to keep track of consignment items, create a separate spreadsheet or database. Similarly, if you rent or lease equipment, you receive income for the rental or lease of assets you own. In this case, you can show the value of the for-rent products as an asset in QuickBooks, but you don't need Inventory items.

• **Do you value your inventory by a method other than average cost?** Quick-Books calculates inventory value by average cost. If you want to use other methods, like last in, first out (LIFO) or first in, first out (FIFO), you can export inventory data to a spreadsheet and calculate inventory cost outside of Quick-Books (page 535).

• **Do you use a point-of-sale system to track inventory?** Point-of-sale inventory systems often blow QuickBooks inventory tracking out of the water. If you forego QuickBooks' inventory feature, you can periodically update your Quick-Books file with the value of your inventory from the point-of-sale system.

Tip: If you like the point-of-sale idea but don't have a system yet, Intuit offers QuickBooks Point of Sale, an integrated, add-on product for retail operations that tracks store sales, customer information, and inventory.

You don't have to use QuickBooks' inventory feature at all if you don't want to. For example, if you perform light manufacturing, you can track the value of your manufactured inventory in a database or other program. Periodically, you can add journal entries to QuickBooks to show the value of in-progress and completed inventory.

The QuickBooks Item Types

Ten types of items are all it takes to satisfy most of the sales needs of small businesses and nonprofit organizations. Learning what each type of item does seems like an unnecessary delay if you're anxious to start keeping books, but choosing the *wrong* type of item can lead to a dead end that only a major overhaul can fix. This section explains the 10 item types. Avoid a six-Advil headache, and read it before you dive in.

Note: You can change only Non-inventory Part and Other Charge items into different types of items. Moreover, these two types convert only into Service, Non-inventory Part, Inventory Part, or Other Charge items. Because of this limitation, be careful when you change item types. If you make the wrong choice, you might not be able to change the item back.

WORD TO THE WISE

Catch-All Items

When you develop a hierarchy of parent items and sub-items, eventually someone in your company will run across a service or product that doesn't fit any of your existing sub-items. For every parent item, create a catch-all subitem to give these outcasts a home. "Other" is a popular name for these catch basins.

For example, if you use a parent item called Security Services, be sure to add a subitem, such as Security Services-Other.

Catch-all items also act as holding pens while you figure out which item you should use. You can create a transaction using the Security Services-Other item, and then change the item in the transaction later when you've identified (or created) the correct item.

Items for Services

Services are less tangible things that you sell, like time or the output of your brain. For example, you might sell consulting services, Internet connection time, magazine articles, or Tarot card readings. In construction, services represent phases of construction, which makes it easy to bill customers based on progress and to compare actual values to estimates. In some companies, such as law practices, the partners get paid based on the hours they bill, so the partners' compensation is an expense associated directly with the firm's income.

The mighty Service item single-handedly manages all types of services, whether you charge by the hour or by the service, associated expenses or not.

Items for Products

Products you sell to customers fall into three categories: products you keep in inventory, products that you special order, and products you assemble. QuickBooks can handle inventory as long as your company passes the tests on page 77. Likewise, products purchased specifically for customers or jobs are no problem. As explained on page 97, QuickBooks can handle only lightly assembled products like gift baskets or gizmos made from widgets—and you'll need a QuickBooks Premier Edition to do even that.

In QuickBooks, choose one of these three item types for the products you sell:

- **Inventory Part.** Use this type for products you purchase and keep in stock for resale. Retailers and wholesalers are the obvious examples of inventory-based businesses, but other types of businesses track inventory, too. You can create Inventory Part items only if you turn on the inventory feature as described on page 154. With inventory parts, you can track how many you have, how much they're worth, and when you should reorder.

- **Non-inventory Part.** If you purchase products specifically for a job or a customer, and you don't track how many products you have on hand, use Non-inventory Part items. Unlike an Inventory Part item, the Non-inventory Part item has at most two account fields: one for income you receive when you sell the part, and the other for the expense of purchasing the part in the first place.

- **Inventory Assembly.** This item type is perfect when you sell products built from your inventory items. For example, you stock wine bottles and related products like corkscrews and glasses, and you assemble them into gift baskets. With an Inventory Assembly item, you can track the number of gift baskets you have on hand as well as the individual inventory items. You can assign a different price for the gift basket than the total of the individual products, as described in the box on page 97. (Inventory Assembly items are available only in QuickBooks Premier and Enterprise editions.)

Tip: Many companies don't bother with purchase orders—forms that record what you order from a vendor—to buy office supplies. But if you want to track whether you receive the supplies you bought, you can create purchase orders for them (page 283). Then use Non-inventory Part items for supplies you add to purchase orders but don't track as inventory.

Other Items

If a line on a sales form isn't a service or a product, look to one of the following items:

- **Other Charge.** The Other Charge item is aptly named because you use it for any charge that isn't quite a service or a part—for instance, shipping charges, finance charges, or the charges for bounced checks. Other Charge items can be percentages or fixed amounts. For example, you can set up shipping charges as the actual cost for shipping, or you can estimate shipping as a percentage of the product cost.

  If a customer holds back a percentage of your charges until you complete the job satisfactorily, create an Other Charge item for the retainer (that is, the portion of your invoice that the customer doesn't pay initially). In this case, enter a negative percentage so QuickBooks deducts the retainer from the invoice. When your customer approves the job, create an invoice using another Other Charge item, called Retention, to charge the customer for the amount she withheld.

Note: Progress invoices (page 219) are another way to invoice customers for a portion of a job and are ideal if you invoice the customer based on the percentage you've completed.

- **Sales Tax.** If you sell taxable products or services, QuickBooks' sales tax items let you calculate and organize sales taxes charged by state and local authorities. Planning how you're going to handle sales taxes is part of getting set up to use QuickBooks' sales items; see page 86 for details.

ACCOUNTING CONCEPTS

Following the Inventory Money Trail

Inventory Part items are the most complicated items, because, in accounting, the cost of inventory moves from place to place as you purchase, store, and finally sell your products. Here's the path that the inventory money trail takes:

1. You spend money to purchase faux pony bar stools to sell in your store and that money buys something of value. The cost shows up in your checking or credit card account. Because inventory has value, it represents an asset of your company. Hence, the value of your inventory appears in an inventory asset account in your Chart of Accounts.

2. When you sell some bar stools, QuickBooks posts the sale to an income account (such as Product Sales) and you receive some amount of money into Accounts Receivable. The stools leave inventory, so QuickBooks deducts the cost of the stools you sold from the inventory asset account. As accounting aficionados already know, the cost of the sold stools has to go somewhere. QuickBooks posts the cost to a *cost of goods sold account*. In the financial reports that you create, the gross profit of your company represents your income minus the cost of goods sold.

• **Subtotal.** You'll need Subtotal items if you charge sales tax on the products you sell, or if you discount only some of the items on a sales form. The Subtotal item adds up all the preceding entries up to the last subtotal item, which means you can have more than one subtotal on an invoice.

For example, you can use one Subtotal item to add up the services you sell before applying a preferred customer product discount and a second Subtotal for product sales when you have to calculate sales tax.

• **Group.** The Group item is a great timesaver, and it's *indispensable* if you have a tendency to forget things. Create a Group item that contains items that always appear together, such as each service you provide for a landscaping job. As demonstrated in Figure 4-2, you can show or suppress the individual items that a Group item contains.

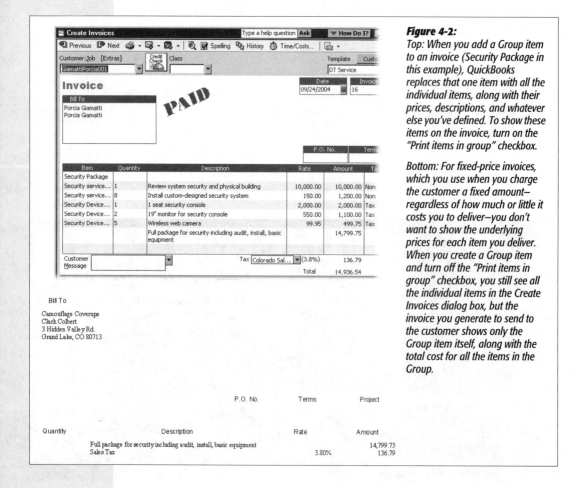

Figure 4-2:

Top: When you add a Group item to an invoice (Security Package in this example), QuickBooks replaces that one item with all the individual items, along with their prices, descriptions, and whatever else you've defined. To show these items on the invoice, turn on the "Print items in group" checkbox.

Bottom: For fixed-price invoices, which you use when you charge the customer a fixed amount—regardless of how much or little it costs you to deliver—you don't want to show the underlying prices for each item you deliver. When you create a Group item and turn off the "Print items in group" checkbox, you still see all the individual items in the Create Invoices dialog box, but the invoice you generate to send to the customer shows only the Group item itself, along with the total cost for all the items in the Group.

- **Discount.** As a bookkeeper, you know that a discount is an amount you deduct from the standard price you charge. Volume discounts, customer loyalty discounts, or sale discounts are examples, and the Discount item in QuickBooks calculates deductions like these. By using both Subtotal and Discount items, you can apply discounts to some or all of the charges on a sales form.

Note: Early payment discounts don't appear on a sales form because you won't know that a customer pays early until long after the sales form is complete. You apply early payment discounts in the Receive Payments dialog box, described on page 257.

- **Payment.** When your customers send you payments, you can log them into your QuickBooks file using the Receive Payments command. If you're in the middle of creating invoices when the checks arrive, it's easier to log those payments by adding a Payment item to the customers' sales forms. A Payment item does more than reduce the amount owed on the invoice; see Figure 4-3.

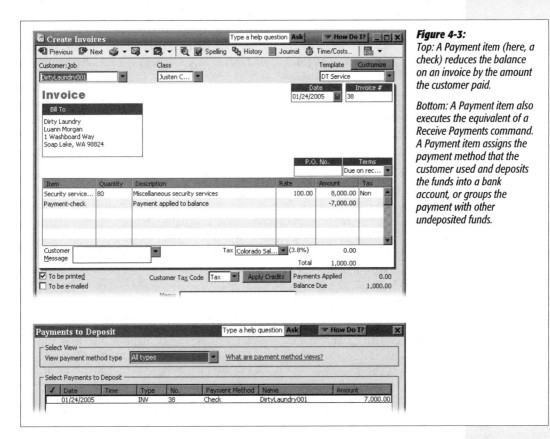

Figure 4-3:
Top: A Payment item (here, a check) reduces the balance on an invoice by the amount the customer paid.

Bottom: A Payment item also executes the equivalent of a Receive Payments command. A Payment item assigns the payment method that the customer used and deposits the funds into a bank account, or groups the payment with other undeposited funds.

Planning Your Items

Setting up items in QuickBooks is a lot like shopping at the grocery store. If you need only a few things, you can shop without a list. Similarly, if you use just a few QuickBooks items, you don't need to write it all out. But if you use dozens or even hundreds of items, planning your item list can save you from experiencing all sorts of unpleasant emotions.

If you jumped feet first into this section, now's the time to read the "Should You Track Inventory with Items?" section on page 77 and "The QuickBooks Item Types" section on page 79. Those sections help you with your first decision: whether to use Service, Inventory Part, or Non-inventory Part items. Read on to learn the other issues you should consider before creating your items in QuickBooks.

Generic or Specific?

Conservation can be as important with QuickBooks items as it is for the environment. QuickBooks Pro and Premier can hold no more than 14,500 items, which is a problem if you sell unique products, such as antiques, or products that change frequently, such as the current clothing style for teenagers. Once you use an item in a transaction, you can't delete that item, so your item list could fill up with items you no longer use (see page 103).

By planning up front how specific your items are, you can keep your QuickBooks list lean with generic items. For instance, a generic item such as Top can represent a girl's black Goth t-shirt one winter and a white poplin button-down shirt the next summer.

Generic items have their limitations, though, so use them only if necessary. First, you can't track inventory properly when you use generic items. QuickBooks might show that you have 100 tops in stock, but that doesn't help when your customers are clamoring for white button-downs and you have 97 black Goth t-shirts. In addition, the information you store with a generic item won't match the specifics of each product you sell. So, when you add generic items to an invoice or sales form, you'll have to edit a few fields, such as description or price.

Item Naming

With item names, brevity and recognizability are equally desirable characteristics. On the one hand, short names are easier to type and manage, but they can be unintelligible. Longer names are harder to type and manage but easier to read. Decide ahead of time which type of naming you prefer and stick with it as you create items.

QuickBooks encourages brevity by allowing no more than 31 characters in an item name. If you sell only a handful of services, you can name your items as you would when you're talking. For a tree services company, names like cut, limb, trim, chip, and haul work just fine. If your item list runs in the hundreds or thousands, some planning is in order. Here are some factors to consider when naming your items:

- **Abbreviation.** If you have to compress a great deal of information into an item name, you'll have to abbreviate. For example, suppose you want to convey all the things you do when you install a carpet, including installing tack strips, padding, and carpet; trimming carpet; vacuuming; and hauling waste. That's more than the 31 characters you have to work with. Poetic won't describe it, but something like "inst tkst,pad,cpt,trim,vac,haul" says it all in very few characters.

- **Aliases.** Create a pseudonym to represent the item. For the carpet job, "Standard install" can represent the installation with vacuuming and hauling waste, while "Deluxe install" includes the standard installation plus moving and replacing furniture. You can include the detail in the item description.

- **Sort order.** QuickBooks lists the items you create in the Item List first by item type and then in alphabetical order. If you want your items to appear in some logical order on drop-down lists (for instance, in an invoice item table), pay attention to the order of characteristics in your item names. Other service items beginning with the intervening letters of the alphabet would separate "Deluxe install" and "Standard install." If you name your installation items "Install, deluxe" and "Install, standard," they'll show up one after the other in your item list.

POWER USERS' CLINIC

Other Ways to Identify Items

If you want to keep item names lean, but still include detailed information, look to these two item features:

- **Descriptions.** Items have fields for both *names* and *descriptions*. When you create an invoice, you choose the item name from a drop-down list. The invoice that the customer sees includes the item description. Keep your item names brief by placing text for the details in the Description field, which is, for all practical purposes, unlimited in length.

- **Group.** Instead of creating one item that represents several phases of a job, you can create separate items for each phase and create a Group item to include those phases on an invoice. For instance, create one item for installing the tack strips, padding, and carpet. Create additional items for vacuuming, hauling, and moving and replacing the furniture. Then, when you add a Group item to the invoice, QuickBooks adds each item to a line in the invoice.

Tip: Construction companies in particular can forego long hours of item data entry with a nifty trick using third-party estimating programs. Construction estimating programs usually include thousands of entries for standard construction services and products. If you build an estimate with a program that integrates with QuickBooks, you can import that estimate into QuickBooks and then sit back and watch as it automatically adds all the items in the estimate to your item list. To find such programs that integrate with QuickBooks, go to *http://marketplace.intuit.com* and then click the Construction link.

Subitems

If you keep all your personal papers in one big stack, you probably have a hard time finding everything from birth certificates to tax forms to bills and receipts. If you've got one big list of items in QuickBooks, you're in no better shape. To locate items more easily, consider designing a hierarchy of higher-level items (*parents*) and one or more levels of subitems, as illustrated in Figure 4-4.

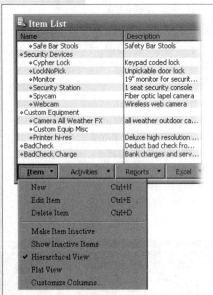

Figure 4-4:
The Hierarchical View indents subitems in the Item List window, making it easy to differentiate the items that you use to structure the list from the items you actually sell. If you work with long lists of subitems, the parent might scroll off the screen. To keep the hierarchy of items visible at all times, in the menu bar at the bottom of the window, click Item and then choose Flat View. QuickBooks uses colons to separate the names for each level of item and subitem.

For example, a landscaping business might create top-level items for trees, shrubbery, cacti, and flower bulbs. Within the tree top-level item, the landscaper might create items for each species: maple, oak, elm, sycamore, and dogwood. Additional levels of subitems can represent categories such as size (seedling, established, and mature, for example).

Taxing Decisions

For most product sales in most areas, you have to keep track of the sales taxes you collect and then send them to the appropriate tax agencies. Labor is usually not taxable, whereas products usually are. Creating separate items for labor and materials makes it easy to apply sales tax to the appropriate items or subtotals on your invoices. Separating the items you've identified into taxable and nontaxable categories can help you decide whether you need one or more items for a particular service or product.

In addition to sales tax codes, QuickBooks lets you create individual sales tax items, which give you more flexibility. If you have to collect sales tax for more than one jurisdiction, for example, sales tax items are the way to go.

Note: If you charge sales taxes, set them up as described in the next section before you go on to "Creating Items" on page 90.

Once you've decided how to name and organize your items, you're ready to get down to business creating items. By planning your item list before you create individual items, you won't waste time editing and reworking existing items to fit your new naming scheme.

ALTERNATE REALITY

Subitems for Nonprofits

Service items are the workhorses of nonprofit organizations. Donations, dues, grants, and money donated in exchange for services all fall into the Service item bucket. The only time you'll need another type of item is if you raise money by selling products from inventory (calendars and note cards, for instance). But subitems come in handy for categorizing the money you receive for different types of services, particularly when donors give money and want to see detailed financial reports in return.

You don't make the big subitem-related decision yourself, the organizations that contribute do. If your organization receives money from the government or a foundation with specific reporting requirements, you can set up subitems and classes (see page 113) to track the details you need for the reports they require. Here's an example of an item list that differentiates type of income and different donors:

Grant
    Government
    Corporate

Donation
    Regular
    Matching

Membership Dues
    Individual
    Corporate
    Contributing
    Platinum Circle

For nonprofits without heavy reporting requirements, you can make do with one item for each type of revenue you receive (grants, donations, dues, fundraising campaigns), with a link to the corresponding income account. For example, a Service subitem called Donation would link to an income account that might be called Donations.

Setting Up Sales Tax

If you don't have to collect and remit sales tax, skip this section and give thanks. Sales taxes aren't much more fun in QuickBooks than they are in real life. Confusingly, QuickBooks gives you two ways of dealing with sales tax: sales tax *codes* and sales tax *items*. Sales tax codes simply specify whether an invoice item is taxable. Sales tax items actually calculate the sales tax for the items on your invoices or other sales forms. This section describes both features and when to use each.

Note: Before you can dive into the details of setting up sales tax, you must turn it on. Choose Edit → Preferences. In the Preferences dialog box, click Sales Tax and then click the Company Preferences tab. In the Do You Charge Sales Tax? section, select the Yes option. Click OK.

Sales Tax Codes

Sales tax codes are QuickBooks' way of letting you specify whether to apply sales tax. Out of the box, the Sales Tax Code List comes with two self-explanatory options: Tax and Non. (If you'd like to further refine taxable status, you can add more options.)

You can apply tax codes in two places: to customers or to individual sales items. For example, nonprofit organizations and government agencies are usually tax-exempt (Non). In many states, food and services are not taxable, although some states tax almost everything.

Assigning tax codes to customers

To tell QuickBooks whether a customer pays sales tax, open the Edit Customer dialog box and click the Additional Info tab. Here's how QuickBooks interprets a customer's tax-exempt status:

- **Nontaxable customer.** When you assign Non or another nontaxable sales tax code to customers, QuickBooks doesn't calculate any sales tax on any items you sell to them.

- **Taxable customer.** When you assign Tax or any taxable sales tax code to a customer, the program calculates sales tax only on the taxable items on their invoices.

Assigning tax codes to items

Sometimes a customer has to pay taxes, but not on all items. As mentioned earlier, most services and non-luxury goods like foods don't get taxed in most states. If you look carefully at the top invoice in Figure 4-2, you'll notice "Non" or "Tax" to the right of some of the amounts, which indicates nontaxable and taxable items, respectively. QuickBooks applies the sales tax only to taxable items to calculate the sales taxes and tax on the invoice.

Items include a Tax Code field, so you can designate each item as taxable or nontaxable. In the Edit Item dialog box, choose the code in the Tax Code drop-down list.

Creating additional sales tax codes

Tax codes aren't QuickBooks' most powerful feature. They let you mark customers and items as either taxable or nontaxable, and that's that. So, the two built-in options, Tax and Non, pretty much cover all possibilities. The only reason you may want to create additional sales tax codes is to classify nontaxable customers by their *reason* for exemption (nonprofit, government, wholesaler, out-of-state, and so on), or perhaps to show which customers are taxable in other states.

Note: If you sell products in more than one state, sales tax items are a much easier and more efficient way of dealing with varying tax regulations. See "Sales Tax Items" (below) to learn the whys and hows.

With that caveat in mind, here are the steps for creating additional sales tax codes in QuickBooks:

1. **Choose Lists → Sales Tax Code List.**

   The Sales Tax Code List window opens.

2. **To create a new code, press Ctrl+N. Or, at the bottom of the list window, click the Sales Tax Code drop-down menu and choose New.**

   The New Sales Tax Code dialog box opens.

3. **In the Sales Tax Code box, type a one- to three-character code.**

   For example, type *Gov* for a nontaxable sales tax code for government agencies, *Whl* for wholesalers who resell your products, or *Oos* for out-of-state customers, and so on.

4. **In the Description box, add some helpful details about the code.**

   For example, type a description that explains the purpose for the code, like *Government* for Gov.

5. **Choose the Taxable or Non-taxable option.**

   Sales tax codes are limited to taxable or nontaxable status.

6. **Click Next to add another code.**

   The code you created appears in the Sales Tax Code List window.

When you've added all the codes you want, click OK to close the New Sales Tax Code dialog box.

As you can see, QuickBooks' sales tax codes sport only a three-code ID, a description, and a taxable or nontaxable setting. They don't let you specify a sales tax percentage or note which tax office to send the collected sales taxes. If your sales tax tango is the least bit complex, use sales tax items, described next.

Sales Tax Items

If you have to worry only about your home state's 5% flat sales tax, then QuickBooks' built-in sales tax codes are fine for turning taxable status on and off at will. Sales tax items and sales tax groups take more time to set up, but they're so much more helpful that you may never add a new sales tax code.

For example, suppose *both* local and state taxes apply to products you sell in your store. And, for customers to whom you ship goods in other states, sales taxes for those *other* states apply as well. You can create separate sales tax items for your local tax and the state sales taxes for each state in which you do business. Or, if one tax authority collects several sales taxes, QuickBooks offers its Sales Tax Group feature to help you collect them all in one shot.

When you create a sales tax item, you specify the sales tax rate for the sales tax and the tax authority that levies the tax. Unlike sales tax codes, which can apply to both customers and products, sales tax items apply only to customers, which, when you think about it, makes perfect sense since sales tax rates usually depend on the customer's location. If the customer is in the boonies, you might assign the state sales tax item because the customer pays only that one tax. Alternatively, a customer smack in the middle of downtown might have to pay state tax, city tax, and a special district tax. If you assign sales tax items to customers (page 58), QuickBooks automatically fills in the sales tax item on your invoices to show the customer the sales taxes they pay.

Creating sales tax items follows the same procedure as other sales items. For the specific details on filling out the dialog box and applying sales tax items to customers, see page 101.

Creating Items

The best time to create items is *after* you've created your accounts but *before* you start billing customers. Each item links to an account in your Chart of Accounts, so creating items goes quicker if you don't have to stop to create an account as well. Similarly, you can create items while you're in the midst of creating an invoice, but you'll find creating items goes much faster when you create one item after the other. The amount of time it takes to create items depends on how many items you need. If you sell only a few services, a few minutes should be sufficient. On the other hand, construction companies that need thousands of items often forego hours of data entry by importing items from third-party programs (page 537).

Each type of item has its own assortment of fields, but the overall procedure for creating items is the same for every type. With the following procedure under your belt, you'll find that you can create many of your items without further instruction. If you *do* need help with fields for a specific type of item, read the sections that follow to learn what each field does.

1. **In the QuickBooks Home window, click Items & Services to open the Item List window.**

   When you first display the Item List, QuickBooks sorts entries by item type. The sort order for the item types isn't alphabetical, but it is in the order that item types appear in the Type drop-down list. You can change the sort order of the list, as shown in Figure 4-5.

2. Open the New Item dialog box by pressing Ctrl+N. Alternatively, on the menu bar at the bottom of the window, click Item, and then choose New.

QuickBooks opens the New Item dialog box and highlights the Service item type in the Type drop-down list.

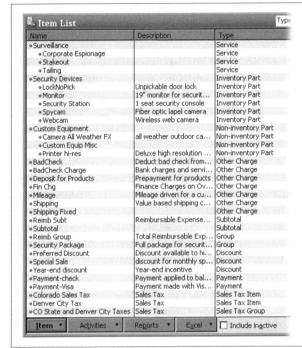

Figure 4-5:
QuickBooks lists items in alphabetical order within each item type. You can change the sort order of the Item List by clicking a column heading. If you click it again, QuickBooks toggles the list order between ascending and descending order. To return the list to sort by item type, click the diamond to the left of the column headings (which appears any time the list is sorted by a column other than Type).

3. If you want to create a Service item, just press Tab to proceed to naming the item. If you want to create any other type of item, choose the type of item in the Type drop-down list.

The Inventory Part type won't appear in the list if you haven't turned on inventory tracking, as described on page 154. The Sales Tax Item and Sales Tax Group items won't appear if you haven't turned on the sales tax feature (see page 162).

4. In the Item Name/Number box, type a unique identifier for the item.

For example, if you opt for long and meaningful names, you might type *Install carpet and vacuum*. For short names, you might type *Inst Carpt*.

5. To make this item a subitem of another item, as shown in Figure 4-5, turn on the "Subitem of" checkbox and choose the item that you want to act as the parent.

You can create the parent item in the midst of creating a subitem, but creating the parent first puts much less strain on your brain. When the parent item already exists, simply choose it from the "Subitem of" drop-down list. To create the parent *while* creating the subitem, choose *<Add New>* on the "Subitem of" drop-down list, and jump to step 3 to begin the parent creation process. Subitems and parents must be the same type. (You can't create subitems for Subtotal, Group, or Payment items.)

You have to assign an account to every item, whether it's a parent or not. However, you need Rate or Price values only if you plan to use items on invoices or other sales forms.

6. **Complete the other fields as described in the following sections ("Service Fields," "Inventory Part Fields," and so on) for the type of item that you're creating.**

   You can enter information that QuickBooks will later use to fill in fields on sales forms. For example, you can type in the sales price, and QuickBooks uses that sales price on an invoice when you sell some units. If the sales price changes each time, simply leave the item's Sales Price field at zero. In this case, QuickBooks doesn't fill in the price, so you can type the price each time you sell the item. Even if you set up a value for an item, you can overwrite it whenever you use the item on a sales form.

7. **When you have many items to create, simply click Next to save the current item and begin another. If you want to save the item you just created and close the New Item dialog box, click OK.**

   If you've made mistakes in almost every field or need more information before you can complete an item, click Cancel to throw away the current item and close the New Item dialog box.

Service Fields

Suppose you offer a telephone answering service. You earn income when your customers pay you for the service. You pay salaries to the people who answer the phones, regardless of whether you have 2 service contracts or 20. For this business, you earn income with your service, but your costs don't link to the income from specific customers or jobs.

Services that you farm out to a subcontractor work differently. For example, if you offer a 900 number for gardening advice, you might have a group of freelancers who field the calls and whom you pay only for their time on the phone. You still earn income for the service you sell, but you also have to pay the subcontractors to do the work. The subcontractors' cost relates to the income for that service. QuickBooks displays different fields depending on whether a service has costs associated with income.

Here's how the Service fields work:

- **"This service is used in assemblies or is performed by a subcontractor or partner" checkbox.** As shown in Figure 4-6, this checkbox is the key to displaying the fields you need when you purchase services from someone else.

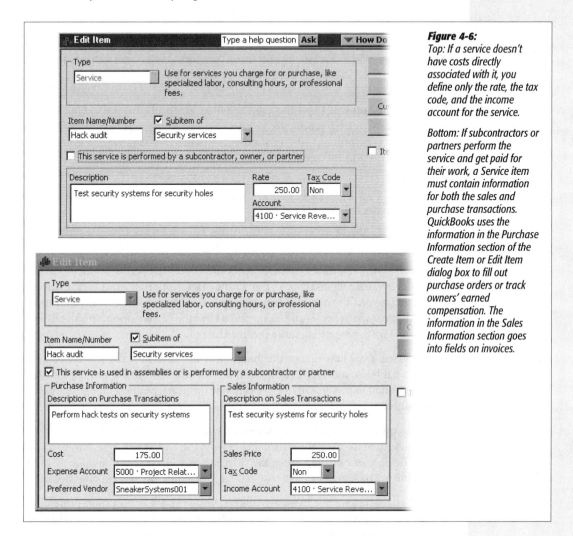

Figure 4-6:
Top: If a service doesn't have costs directly associated with it, you define only the rate, the tax code, and the income account for the service.

Bottom: If subcontractors or partners perform the service and get paid for their work, a Service item must contain information for both the sales and purchase transactions. QuickBooks uses the information in the Purchase Information section of the Create Item or Edit Item dialog box to fill out purchase orders or track owners' earned compensation. The information in the Sales Information section goes into fields on invoices.

- **Description on Purchase Transactions.** Type the description that you want to appear on the purchase orders you issue to subcontractors.

- **Cost.** Enter what you pay for the service, which can be an hourly rate or a flat fee. For example, if a partner performs the service and receives $100 for each hour of work, type *100* in this field. If the cost varies, type *0* in the Cost field. You can then enter the actual cost when you create a purchase order.

- **Expense Account.** Choose the account to which you want to post what you pay for the service. If a subcontractor does the work, choose an expense account for subcontractor or outside consultants' fees. If a partner or owner performs the work, choose an expense account for job-related costs.

Tip: QuickBooks multiplies the cost and sales prices by the quantities you add to sales forms. Be sure to define the cost and sales price in the same units so that QuickBooks calculates your income and expenses correctly.

- **Preferred Vendor.** If you choose a vendor in this drop-down list, QuickBooks selects the preferred vendor for a purchase order when you add this Service item. This is helpful only if you almost always use the same vendor for this service *and* you add the service item to a purchase order before you choose the vendor.

- **Description on Sales Transactions.** If you create a Service item without associated costs, type a detailed description for the service in this box. This description appears on invoices and sales forms, so use terms your customers can understand.

  For items *with* associated costs, QuickBooks copies the text from the "Description on Purchase Transactions" box to the "Description on Sales Transactions" box. However, if your vendors use technical jargon that your customers wouldn't recognize, you can change the text in the "Description on Sales Transactions" box to something more meaningful.

- **Sales Price.** Type how much you charge your customers for the service. You can enter a flat fee or a charge per unit of time. For example, *you* might charge $9.95 for unlimited gardening advice per call, but Intuit telephone support charges by the minute.

  When you add the item to an invoice, QuickBooks multiplies the quantity by the sales price to calculate the total charge. If the cost varies, type *0* in the Sales Price field. You can then enter the price when you create an invoice or other sales form. For services that carry a flat fee, use a quantity of *1* on your invoices.

- **Tax Code.** Most service items are nontaxable, so you'll choose Non more often than not. This field appears only if you've turned on the sales tax feature, as described on page 162.

- **Income Account.** Choose the income account to which you want to post the income for this service. For example, when you create a Service item for snowplowing, choose the corresponding snowplowing income account.

Inventory Part Fields

As described in the "Following the Inventory Money Trail" box on page 81, dollars move between accounts as you buy and sell inventory. Here's how you use the fields for an Inventory Part item (shown in Figure 4-7) to define your company's inventory money trail *and*, at the same time, keep track of how much inventory you have:

- **Manufacturer's Part Number.** If you want your purchase orders to include the manufacturer's part number or unique identifier for the product, add it here.

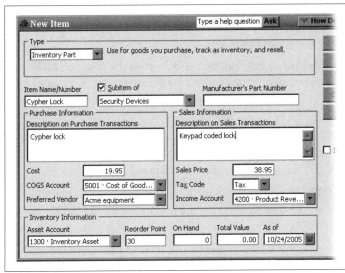

Figure 4-7:
When you create a new Inventory Part item, QuickBooks includes fields for purchasing and selling the item. The fields in the Purchase Information section show up on purchase orders. The Sales Information section sets the values you see on sales forms, such as invoices and sales receipts. The program simplifies building your initial inventory by letting you type the quantity you have on hand and their value.

- **Description on Purchase Transactions.** This is the description that you want to appear on the purchase orders you issue to purchase inventory items. Describe the product in terms that the vendor or manufacturer understands, because you can use a different and more customer-friendly description for the invoices that customers see.

- **Cost.** Enter what you pay for one unit of the product. QuickBooks counts on your selling products in the same units that you buy them. For example, if you purchase four cases of merlot but sell wine by the bottle, enter the price you pay per bottle in this field.

- **COGS Account.** Choose the account to which you want to post the costs *when you sell the product*. (COGS stands for cost of goods sold, which is an account for tracking the underlying costs of the things you sell in order to calculate your gross profit.)

Note: If you don't have a cost of goods sold account in your Chart of Accounts, QuickBooks creates a Cost of Goods Sold account for you as soon as you type the name for your first inventory item in the New Item dialog box.

- **Preferred Vendor.** If you choose a vendor in this drop-down list, QuickBooks selects the preferred vendor when you add this Inventory Part item to a purchase order.

- **Description on Sales Transactions.** When you type a description in the "Description on Purchase Transactions" box, QuickBooks copies that description into the "Description on Sales Transactions" box. If your customers wouldn't recognize the description you use to buy the product, type a more customer-friendly description in this field.

- **Sales Price.** In this field, type how much you charge for the product. Make sure that the Cost field uses the same units. For example, if you sell a bottle of merlot for $15, type *15* in this field and type the cost per bottle in the Cost field.

- **Tax Code.** When you add an item to an invoice, QuickBooks checks this code to see whether the item is taxable. (QuickBooks comes with two tax codes set up: "Non" for nontaxable items and "Tax" for taxable items.) Most products are taxable, although groceries are the most familiar exception.

- **Income Account.** This drop-down list includes the accounts in your Chart of Accounts. Choose the income account for the money you receive when you sell one of these products.

- **Asset Account.** Choose the asset account for the value of the inventory you buy. Suppose you buy 100 bottles of merlot, which are worth the $8-a-bottle you paid. QuickBooks posts $800 into your inventory asset account. When you sell a bottle, QuickBooks deducts $8 from the inventory asset account and adds that $8 to the COGS Account.

- **Reorder Point.** Type the quantity on hand that would prompt you to order more. When your inventory hits that number, QuickBooks notifies you to reorder the product on the Reminders List (page 155).

Tip: If you can receive products quickly, use a lower reorder point to reduce the money tied up in inventory and prevent write-offs due to obsolete inventory. When products take some time to arrive, set the reorder point higher. Start with your best guess and edit this field as business conditions change.

- **On Hand.** If you already have some of the product in inventory, type the quantity in this field. However, if you use QuickBooks' inventory feature (page 411) to record inventory you receive, you can rely on it to accurately post inventory values in your accounts.

- **Total Value.** If you filled in the On Hand field, fill in *this* field with the total value of the number of the products on hand. QuickBooks increases the value of your inventory asset account accordingly.

- **As of.** The program uses this date for the transaction it creates in the inventory asset account.

Note: You can enter values for the last three fields only when you create a new item. From then on, QuickBooks calculates how many you have on hand based on the number you've sold and the number you've received.

POWER USERS' CLINIC

Assembling Products

In the Premier and Enterprise editions of QuickBooks, you can create an Inventory Assembly item (page 80) that gathers Inventory Part items into a new item that you sell as a whole.

As shown here, the New Item dialog box for an assembled item is similar to the one for an Inventory Part. The main difference is that you select other inventory items or Inventory Assembly items as the building blocks of your new item. In the Bill of Materials section, you specify the components and the quantity of each. The program calculates the total cost of the bill of materials. Moreover, you set the price you charge for the entire ball of wax in the Sales Price field, regardless of the cost of the individual pieces.

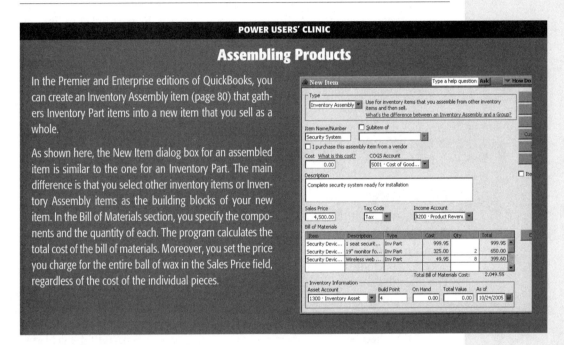

Non-inventory Part Fields

You'll need Non-inventory Part items if you use purchase orders to buy supplies or other products that you don't track as inventory. For example, suppose you're a general contractor and you purchase materials for a job. When you use Non-inventory Part items, QuickBooks posts the cost of the products to an expense account and the income from selling the products to an income account. You don't have to bother with the inventory asset account because you transfer ownership of these products to the customer almost immediately. See page 291 to learn how to charge your customer for these reimbursable expenses.

The good news about Non-inventory Part items is that they use all the same fields as Service items. The bad news is the few subtle differences you need to know. Take the following disparities into account when you create Non-inventory Part items:

- **"This item is used in assemblies or is purchased for a specific Customer:Job" checkbox.** The checkbox goes by a different name than the one in Service items, but its behavior is the same. Turn on this checkbox when you want to use different values on purchase and sales transactions. If the Non-inventory Part item is for office supplies you want to place on a purchase order, turn this checkbox off because you won't have sales values. For items you resell, be sure to turn this checkbox on.

  When you turn this checkbox on, QuickBooks displays an Income Account field and an Expense Account field, like the fields you see in Figure 4-6 (bottom). For Non-inventory Part items, the accounts that you choose are income and expense accounts specifically for products. Read the next bullet to find out what happens when you turn this checkbox off.

- **Account.** If you don't resell this product and you thus turn off the "This item is used in assemblies or is purchased for a specific Customer:Job" checkbox, you see only one Account field. QuickBooks considers the account in this field as an expense account for the purchase.

- **Tax Code.** The Tax Code field works exactly the same way as the Tax Code field for a Service item. Choose Non if the products are nontaxable, such as groceries. Choose Tax if the products are taxable.

Other Charge Fields

For Other Charge items, the checkbox for hiding or showing cost fields comes with the label "This item is used in assemblies or is a reimbursable charge." For example, turn on this checkbox when you want to set the Cost field to the actual sales price and include the shipping and handling fees you charge your customers. You'll see the same sets of fields for purchases and sales as you do for Service and Non-inventory Part items.

Alternatively, you can create charges that don't link directly to expenses by turning off this checkbox. You can create a percentage, which is useful for calculating shipping based on the value of the products being shipped, as shown in Figure 4-8.

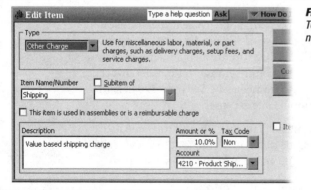

Figure 4-8:
To create a percentage-based charge, type a number followed by % in the "Amount or %" field.

You can also define a dollar value charge, such as for a country club's one-time initiation fee. When you turn off the "This is used in assemblies or is a reimbursable charge" checkbox, the Cost and Sales Price fields disappear, and the "Amount or %" field takes their place. If you want to create a dollar charge, type a whole or decimal number in this field.

Tip: When you add a percentage-based Other Charge item to an invoice, such as shipping, QuickBooks applies the percentage to the previous line in the invoice. If you want to apply the Other Charge percentage to several items, add a Subtotal item to the invoice before the Other Charge item.

Subtotal

You need only one Subtotal item, because a Subtotal item does only one thing—it totals all the amounts for the preceding lines up to the last subtotal. Because you can't change a Subtotal item's behavior in any way, a Subtotal item has just two fields: Item Name/Number and Description. You can type any name and description you wish in these fields, but in practically every case, Subtotal says it all.

Group

A Group item can add several items to an invoice at once. For example, you can create a Group item, such as Landscaping, that contains the individual Service items for every phase of a construction project. When you add this Landscaping Group item to an invoice, QuickBooks adds the Service items for phases, such as Excavation, Grading, Planting, and Cleanup.

You can also use a Group item to *hide* the underlying items, which is useful mainly when you create fixed-price invoices (page 204) and you don't want the customer to know how much profit you're making. Here's how you set up a Group item to do these things:

- **Print items in group.** To show all the underlying items on your invoice, turn on the "Print items in group" checkbox. Figure 4-2 (page 82) shows examples of both showing and hiding the items within a group.

- **Item.** To add an item to a group, click a blank cell in the Item column, as shown in Figure 4-9, and choose the item you want.

- **Description.** Type a description of the group that gives a sense of the individual items within it, such as Landscaping Project.

- **Qty.** When you create a Group item, you can include different quantities of items, just like a box of note cards usually includes a few more envelopes than cards. For each item, type how many you typically sell as a group. If the quantity of each item varies, type *0* in the Qty cells. You can then specify the quantities on your invoices after you've added a Group item.

Discount

The Discount item deducts either a dollar amount or a percentage for discounts you apply at the time of a sale, such as volume discounts, damaged goods discounts, or the discount you apply because your customer has incriminating pictures of you.

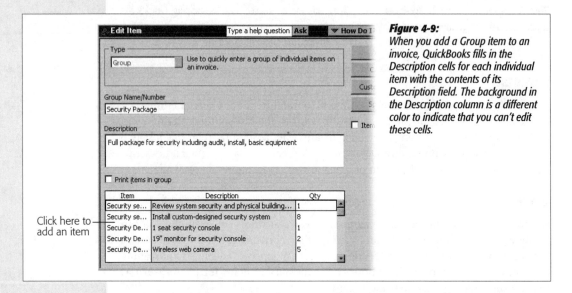

Figure 4-9:
When you add a Group item to an invoice, QuickBooks fills in the Description cells for each individual item with the contents of its Description field. The background in the Description column is a different color to indicate that you can't edit these cells.

Note: QuickBooks applies early payment discounts in the Receive Payments dialog box, so you don't create Discount items for those.

The fields for a Discount item are similar to those of an Other Charge item with a few small differences—described here:

- **Amount or %.** This field is always visible for a Discount item. To deduct a dollar amount, type a positive number (whole or decimal) in this field. To deduct a percentage, type a whole or decimal number followed by %, for instance, *5.5%*.

- **Account.** Choose the account to which you want to post the discounts you apply. You can post discounts to either income accounts or expense accounts.

  When you post discounts to an income account, they appear as negative income, so your gross profit reflects what you actually earned after deducting discounts. Posting discounts to expense accounts, on the other hand, makes your income look better than it actually is. The discounts increase the amounts in your expense accounts, so your net profit is the same no matter which approach you use.

- **Tax Code.** When you choose a taxable code in the Tax Code field, QuickBooks applies the discount before it calculates sales tax. For instance, if customers buy products on sale, they pay sales tax on the sale price, not the original price.

When you choose a nontaxable code in the Tax Code field, QuickBooks applies the discount *after* it calculates sales tax. You'll rarely want to do this because you'll collect less sales tax from your customers than you must send to the tax agencies.

Payment

Beyond the Type, Item Name/Number, and Descriptions fields, the Payment item boasts fields unlike those for other items. These fields, shown in Figure 4-10, should look familiar if you've already set up customers in QuickBooks.

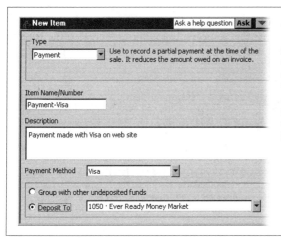

Figure 4-10:
The fields for a Payment item designate the method of payment that a customer uses and whether you deposit the funds to a specific bank account or group them with other undeposited funds. For example, if your customers send checks, you save up the checks you receive each week and make one trip to deposit them in your bank. Banks sometimes transfer credit card payments into a bank account individually and sometimes group all the charges for the same day.

- **Payment Method.** Choose the payment method, such as cash, check, or brand of credit card. In the Make Deposits dialog box, you can filter pending deposits by the type of payment method.

- **Group with other undeposited funds.** Choose this option if you want to add the payment to other payments you received. When you add the Payment item to a sales form, QuickBooks adds the payment to the list of undeposited funds. To actually complete the deposit of all your payments, choose Banking → Make Deposits.

- **Deposit To.** If payments flow into an account without any action on your part, such as credit card or electronic payments, choose this option and then choose the bank account in the drop-down list.

Sales Tax Item

Like the IRS, each tax agency wants to receive the taxes it's due. To track the taxes you owe to each agency, create a sales tax item for *each* agency. As described on page 89, if you sell products through direct mail, you'll need a sales tax item for each state that you ship to.

To create a sales tax item, in the New Item dialog box, in the Type drop-down list, choose Sales Tax Item. Then fill in the fields (see Figure 4-11) as follows:

- **Tax Name.** Fill in this box with a name for the sales tax. You can use the identifiers that the tax authority uses or a more meaningful name like Denver city tax.

- **Description.** If you want QuickBooks to display a description of the sales tax on your invoices or sales forms, type the description that you want to appear.

- **Tax Rate (%).** In this box, type the percentage rate for the sales tax. QuickBooks automatically adds the percent sign (%), so simply type the decimal number—for example, *4.3* for a 4.3% tax rate.

- **Tax Agency.** In this drop-down list, choose the tax authority that collects the sales tax from the list of vendors that appears. If you haven't created the vendor for the tax authority, choose *<Add New>*.

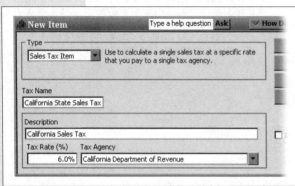

Figure 4-11:
The Tax Name field can include up to 31 characters—more than enough to use the 4- or 5-digit codes that many states use for sales taxes. The Tax Rate (%) field sets the percentage of the sales tax. The Tax Agency drop-down list shows the vendors you've set up, so you can choose the tax agency to which you remit the taxes. If a tax authority collects the sales taxes for several government entities, a Sales Tax Group is the way to go. (See the box on page 103.)

Tip: Unlike most other invoice items, you apply sales tax items to *customers*, not products or services. After all, it's usually your customers' location that determines what sales tax they pay. See the box on page 104 for instructions.

Modifying Items

You can change information about an item even if you've already used the item in transactions. The changes you make don't affect existing transactions. When you create *new* transactions using the item, QuickBooks grabs the updated information to fill in fields.

To modify an item, open the Item List window by clicking Items & Services in the QuickBooks Home page, and then double-click the item that you want to edit. QuickBooks opens the Edit Item window. Make the changes you want and click OK when you're done.

Be particularly attentive if you decide to change the Type field. You can change only Non-inventory Part or Other Charge items to other item types, and they can morph into only certain item types: Service, Non-inventory Part, Other Charge, Inventory Part, or Inventory Assembly (this last type is available only in QuickBooks Premier and Enterprise). If you conclude from this that you can't change a Non-inventory Part item back once you change it to an Inventory part, you're absolutely correct. To prevent type change disasters, back up your QuickBooks file before switching item types (see page 168).

Note: Parts that you keep in inventory have value that shows up as an asset of your company, but non-inventory parts show up simply as expenses. If you change an item from a Non-inventory Part to an Inventory Part, be sure to choose a date in the "As of" field that is *after* the date of the last transaction that uses the item in its Non-inventory Part guise.

GEM IN THE ROUGH

Sales Tax Group

A Sales Tax Group item calculates the total sales tax for multiple Sales Tax Items—perfect when you sell goods in an area rife with state, city, and local sales taxes. The customer sees only the total sales tax, but QuickBooks tracks how much you owe to each agency. This item works in the same way as the Group item, except that you add Sales Tax Items to cells instead of items such as Service, Inventory, and Other Charges.

A Sales Tax Group item applies several Sales Tax items at once. For example, businesses in Denver charge a combined sales tax of 7.6%, which is made up of a Denver sales tax, the Colorado sales tax, an RTD tax, and a few special district taxes. Before you can create a sales tax group, you must first create each of the sales tax items that you plan to include.

As shown here, after you type the name or number of the sales tax group and a description, click the Tax Item drop-down list to choose one of the individual sales tax items to include in the group. QuickBooks fills in the rate, tax agency, and description from the sales tax item. The program also totals the individual tax rates into a total rate for the group, which is what the customer sees on an invoice.

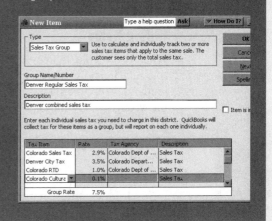

Hiding and Deleting Items

Deleting items and hiding them are two totally different actions, although the visible result is the same—QuickBooks doesn't display the items in the Item List window. The only time you'll delete an item is when you create it by mistake and want to eliminate it permanently from the Item List. As you might discover when you attempt to delete an item, deleting an item is possible only if you have never used it in a transaction.

Hiding items doesn't have the same restrictions and offers a couple of advantages to boot. First, when you hide items, they don't appear in your Item List, which prevents you from selecting the wrong item as you create an invoice or other sales form. Unlike deleting, hiding is reversible. You can switch items to active status if you start selling them again. Suppose you hid the item for bell-bottom hip huggers in 1974. Decades later, when 70s retro becomes cool again, you can reactivate the item and use it on sales forms. Of course, you'll probably want to edit the cost and sales price to reflect today's higher prices.

UP TO SPEED

Assigning Sales Tax Items to Customers

Once you've created sales tax items, you associate then with customers. To do so, in the New Customer or Edit Customer dialog box, click the Additional Info tab. In the Tax Code box, choose a sales tax code (page 86); in the Tax Item box, choose the corresponding Sales Tax Item or Sales Tax Group.

If you prefer to assign sales tax items as you go, in an invoice or other sales form, choose the sales tax item or group you want to assign to the customer. When you save the form, the program asks if you want to change the customer record to use that item. Click Yes. QuickBooks adds the sales tax item or group to the customer record, which means it'll appear in the Tax box automatically the next time you create an invoice or other sales transaction for the customer.

Hiding Items

When you've sold an item in the past, the only way to remove it from the Item List is to hide it. Hiding items means that your Item List shows only the items you currently use. You'll scroll less to find the items you want and you're less likely to pick the wrong item by mistake. If you start to sell an item again, you can reactivate it so that it appears on the Item List once more. If you're wondering how you make an item reappear if it isn't visible, here's a guide to hiding and reactivating items in your Item List:

- **Hide an item.** In the Item List, right-click the item and choose Make Item Inactive from the shortcut menu. The item disappears from the Item List.

- **View all items, active or inactive.** At the bottom of the Item List window, turn on the "Include inactive" checkbox. QuickBooks displays a column with an X as its heading and displays an X in that column for every inactive item in the list. The "Include inactive" checkbox is grayed out when all the items are active.

- **Reactivate an item.** First, turn on the "Include inactive" checkbox to display all items. To reactivate the item, click the X next to its name. When you click the X next to a parent item, QuickBooks opens the Activate Group dialog box. If you want to reactivate all the subitems as well as the parent, click Yes.

If you find that you're constantly hiding items that you no longer sell, your item list might be too specific for your constantly changing product list. For example, if you create 100 items for the clothes that are in with teenagers in May, those items will be obsolete by June. Consider creating more generic items, such as pants, shorts, t-shirts, and bathing suits. You can reuse these items season after season, year after year, without worrying about running out of room on the Item List, which is limited to 14,500 items.

Tip: To see how many items you have, press F2 to open the Product Information window. Then, head to the List Information section in the lower-right corner of the window.

Deleting Items

If you improperly create an item and catch your mistake immediately, deleting the offender is no sweat. Use any one of these methods to delete an item:

- In the Item List window, select the item you want to delete and press Ctrl+D.

- In the Item List, select the item, and then choose Edit → Delete Item (if commands on menus are more to your liking).

- In the menu at the bottom of the window, click Item and then choose Delete.

If you try to delete an item used in even one transaction, QuickBooks warns you that you can't delete the item. For example, you created an item by mistake and then compounded the problem by inadvertently adding the item to an invoice. When you realize your error and try to delete the item, QuickBooks refuses to oblige. If you used the item in one or two recent transactions, you can probably find those transactions and replace the item without thinking too hard. When you've removed the item from all transactions, use one of the methods above to delete it.

If you blasted out a bunch of transactions, it's easier to find the transactions with the Sales by Item Detail report, which includes a heading for each item you sell, and groups transactions underneath each heading. If you sell lots of items, you probably want the report to show the transactions only for the item you want to delete. Here's how you modify the Sales by Item Detail report and then edit the transactions:

1. **To create a Sales by Item Detail report, choose Reports → Sales → Sales by Item Detail.**

   QuickBooks opens the Sales by Item Detail report in its own window.

2. **To modify the report, in the button bar at the top of the "Sales by Item Detail" window, click Modify Report.**

   QuickBooks opens the "Modify Report: Sales by Item Detail" dialog box. To produce a report with transactions for one item, modify the date range and filter the report based on the item name, as demonstrated in Figure 4-12.

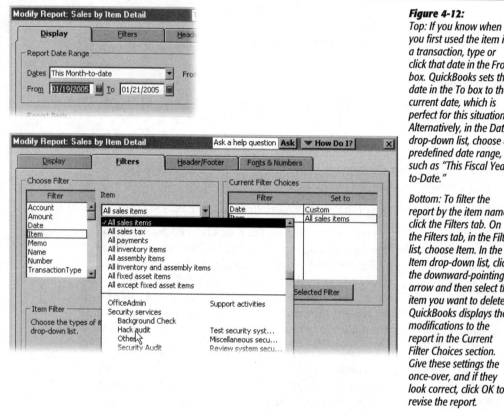

Figure 4-12:
Top: If you know when you first used the item in a transaction, type or click that date in the From box. QuickBooks sets the date in the To box to the current date, which is perfect for this situation. Alternatively, in the Dates drop-down list, choose a predefined date range, such as "This Fiscal Year-to-Date."

Bottom: To filter the report by the item name, click the Filters tab. On the Filters tab, in the Filter list, choose Item. In the Item drop-down list, click the downward-pointing arrow and then select the item you want to delete. QuickBooks displays the modifications to the report in the Current Filter Choices section. Give these settings the once-over, and if they look correct, click OK to revise the report.

3. **To edit a transaction to remove an item, in the "Sales by Item Detail" window, double-click the transaction.**

   Based on the type of transaction you double-click, QuickBooks opens the corresponding dialog box. For example, if you double-click an invoice, QuickBooks opens the Create Invoices dialog box and displays the invoice you chose.

   In the Item Code column, click the cell that contains the item you want to delete, click the downward-pointing arrow in the cell, and then choose the correct item from the Item drop-down list.

4. To save the transaction with the revised item, click Save & Close.

   You'll know that you've successfully eliminated the item from all sales transactions when the report in the "Sales by Item Detail" window shows none.

Tip: To be sure that you have removed all links to the item, in the menu bar at the top of the report window, click Refresh to update the report based on the current data in your QuickBooks file.

---

5. Finally, back in the Item List window, select the item you want to delete and press Ctrl+D. In the Delete Item message box, click Yes to confirm the deletion of the item.

   The item disappears from your Item List for good.

6. To close the report window, click the Close box at the upper right.

   The item is gone and you're ready to get back to work.

Setting Up Other QuickBooks Lists

Open any QuickBooks window, dialog box, or form, and you're bound to bump into at least one QuickBooks list. These drop-down lists make it easy to fill in information for transactions and forms. Creating an invoice? If you pick the customer and job from the Customer:Job List, QuickBooks fills in the customer's address, payment terms, and other fields for you. Selecting the payment terms from the Terms List tells QuickBooks to calculate the due date for the invoice. If you choose an entry in the Tax List, QuickBooks calculates the sales tax due on the goods sold on the invoice. Even the products and services you sell to the customer come from the Item List, but you already learned about that list in Chapter 4.

In this chapter, you'll discover what the different lists actually do for you and whether you should bother setting them up for your business. Because some lists have their own unique fields (such as the "Vendor eligible for 1099" checkbox for a vendor entry), you'll also learn what the fields do and how to fill them in. If you already know which lists and list entries you want, you can skip to "Creating and Editing List Entries" (page 123) to master the techniques that work for every type of list in QuickBooks, such as creating and editing entries, merging entries, hiding, and so on. Learn how to work with one QuickBooks list, and the doors to every other list open as well.

Note: A few of the QuickBooks lists warrant their own chapters. If you don't find a list that you want to use in this chapter, look in these other chapters:

- **Chapter 2.** Covers the Chart of Accounts, which is a list of your bookkeeping accounts.

- **Chapter 3.** Describes the Customer:Job List, which contains entries for both customers and their jobs.

- **Chapter 4.** Explains how to use the Item List to fill in invoices and other sales forms with services and products you sell.

- **Chapter 11.** If you turn on the payroll feature (page 152), the Lists menu contains the Payroll Item List command, which covers the deposits and deductions on your payroll. Payroll Items are quite specialized, and QuickBooks offers tools to help you set them up, which are explained in detail on page 318.

- **Chapter 22.** Describes how to create or modify templates for your QuickBooks business forms.

The Vendor List

There's no way around it: you're going to work with vendors and pay them for their services and products. The telephone company, your accountant, and the subcontractor who installs Venetian plaster in your spec houses are all vendors. You can create vendors one at a time, whenever you get the first bill from a new vendor. However, if you already know who most of your vendors are, it's easier to create those entries all at once so that you can write checks or enter bills with no interruptions.

In QuickBooks 2006, creating, editing, and reviewing your vendors is a breeze with the new Vendor Center. Like the Customer Center (page 54), the Vendor Center lists the details of your vendors and their transactions in one easy-to-use dashboard. To open the Vendor Center window, use any of the following methods:

- In the icon bar, click Vendor Center.

- Choose Vendors → Vendor Center.

- On the left side of the QuickBooks Home page, click Vendors.

With the Vendor Center window open, press Ctrl+N (or in the Vendor Center menu bar, click New Vendor) to open the New Vendor dialog box. You'll notice some of the same fields you see for customers. For example, the Vendor Name field corresponds to the Customer Name field, which you might remember is actually more of a code than a name. Use the same sort of naming convention for vendors that you chose for customers (see the "Making Customers Easy to Identify" box on page 53). As with customer records, you're better off leaving the Opening Balance field empty and building your current vendor balance by entering the invoices or bills they sent.

Entering Address Information

If you print checks and envelopes to pay your bills, you'll need address and contact information for your vendors. In the New Vendor dialog box (which you opened in the previous paragraph) on the Address Info tab, you can specify address and contact information, as shown in Figure 5-1. Because the fields on the Address Info tab are identical to customer address and contact fields; see page 56 if you need help filling in these fields.

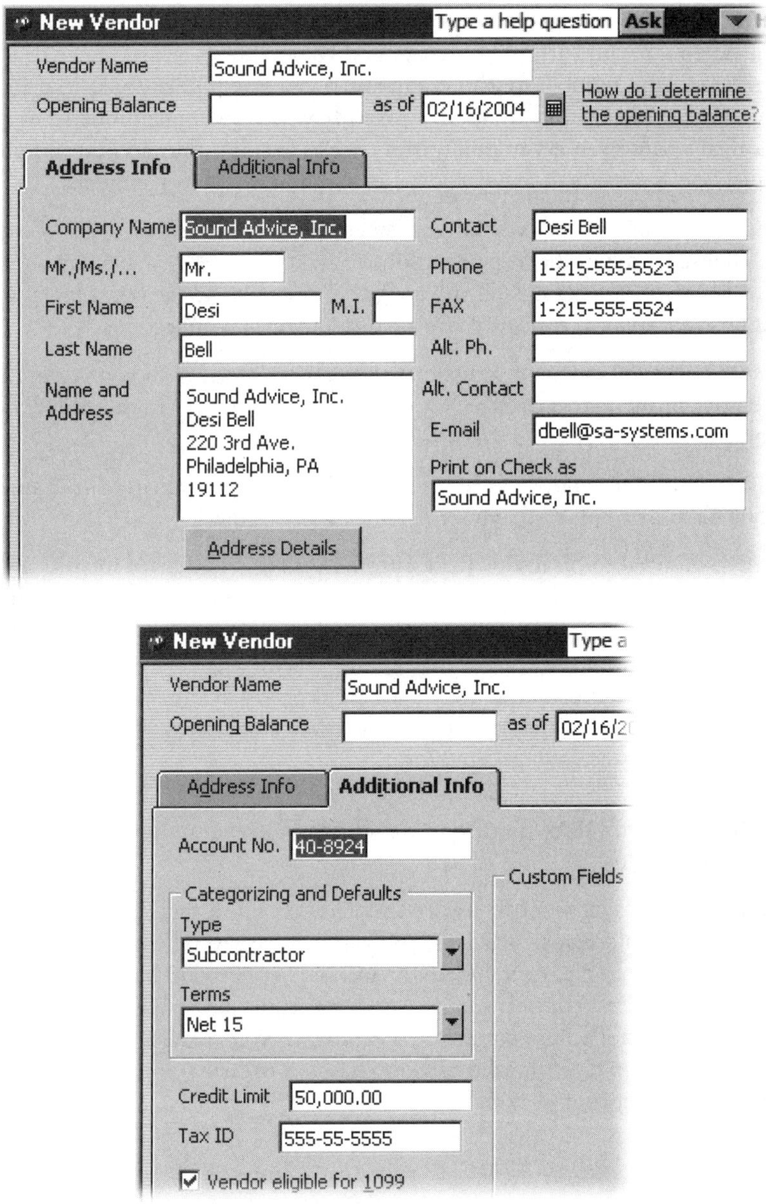

Figure 5-1:
Top: The Address Info tab has one field that doesn't show up for customers. When you print checks, QuickBooks fills in the payee with the name in the "Print on Check as" field. In most cases, you don't have to do a thing because QuickBooks fills in this field with the name you enter in the Company Name field. If you want a different name to appear, simply edit the name in this box.

Bottom: In the New Vendor dialog box, the fields on the Additional Info tab are pretty easy to fill in as long as you remember that they represent information about your account with the vendor. For example, in the Account No. field, type the account number that the vendor assigned to your company. The Credit Limit field represents how much credit the vendor extends to your company.

Additional Info

The Additional Info tab contains fields that are a bit different than the ones you see for customers. The following list describes what they are and what you can do with them:

- **Account No.** When you create customers, you can assign an account number to them. When it's your turn to be a customer, your vendors return the favor and assign an account number to *your* company. If you want QuickBooks to print it in the memo field of the checks you print, type the account number that the vendor gave you. Even if you don't print checks, keeping your account number in QuickBooks is handy if a question arises about one of your payments.

- **Type.** If you want to sort vendors or generate reports based on types of vendors, choose a type in the Type drop-down list or create a new type by choosing *<Add New>*. For example, if you assign a Tax type to all the tax agencies you remit taxes to, you can easily prepare a report of your tax collections.

- **Terms.** Choose the payment terms that the vendor extended to your company. The entries in the Terms drop-down list (page 118) apply to both vendors and customers.

- **Credit Limit.** If the vendor has set a credit limit for your company, for example $45,500 for your credit card, type that value in this box.

- **Tax ID.** You need to fill in this field with the vendor's Employer Identification Number (EIN) or Social Security number *only* if you're going to create a 1099 for the vendor.

Tip: When you hire subcontractors to do work for you, you document on a 1099 tax form how much you pay them. You can forego some of this paperwork if you pay them as suppliers instead of subcontractors, but that's a choice best advised by an accountant.

- **Vendor eligible for 1099.** Turn on this checkbox if you are going to create a 1099 for the vendor.

- **Custom fields.** If you want to track vendor information that isn't handled by the fields that QuickBooks provides, you can include several custom fields (see page 128). For example, your subcontractors are supposed to have current certificates for workers' comp insurance, and you could be in big trouble if you hire a subcontractor whose certificate is expired. If you create a custom field to hold the expiration date for each subcontractor's workers' comp certificate, you can generate a report of workers' comp expiration dates.

Classes

Not everyone needs classes, so don't feel that you *must* use them. However, classes are the only solution if you want to classify income and expenses by business unit, department, location, partner, consultant, or other categories that span multiple accounts in your Chart of Accounts or multiple types of customers, jobs, and vendors.

Tip: Before you decide to turn on classes, use QuickBooks without them for a few weeks or months. If you can generate all the reports you need without classes, don't burden yourself with another field to enter. For example, if you run restaurants in a couple of locations, you don't necessarily need classes to track your business for each restaurant. You could create income accounts for each location instead.

UP TO SPEED

Do You Need Classes?

You can call on several QuickBooks features (such as accounts, customer and job types, and classes) to help you track your business. Each tracking feature has its advantages, so how do you decide which ones to use to evaluate your performance? Here's a brief description of each feature and the best time to use it:

- **Accounts.** You can use accounts to segregate income and expenses in several ways. For instance, keep income from your physical store separate from your Web site sales by creating two separate income accounts. Accounts are the fastest way to see performance because Profit & Loss reports built into QuickBooks (page 382) automatically include results by account.

- **Customer, job, and vendor types.** If you want a report that categorizes income by wholesale, retail, and online customers, use customer types to classify your customers.

  Types are more limited in scope than accounts. Customer types apply only to customers (page 49). When you assign customer types to your customers, you can filter the reports you generate to show results

for a specific type of customer. Likewise, job types (page 52) and vendor types (page 112) help you categorize only by job and vendor, respectively.

- **Classes.** Classes cut across accounts, customers, jobs, and vendors because you assign a class to an individual transaction, such as a check, bill, or invoice. Classes are perfect for categories that span accounts and types. If you use classes to segregate income and expenses by business unit, a Profit & Loss report by class (page 386) tells you how each business unit is performing.

  For instance, suppose the partners in your company help customers implement technology and tighten their security. You've decided to use separate income accounts to track technology sales and security sales, and you use customer types to track work for the government versus the private sector. You also want to track income by partner—but each partner works on any type of service for any type of customer. You can create classes to track partners' sales, regardless of which service the partner delivers or the type of customer.

If you decide to work with classes, be sure to follow these guidelines to get the most out of them:

- **Pick one use for your classes.** QuickBooks has only one list of classes, and every class should represent the same type of classification. Moreover, you can assign only one class to a transaction, so classes add only one additional way to categorize your transactions. For example, once you assign a class for a business unit to a transaction, there's no way to assign another class—for instance to identify the office branch—to the same transaction.

- **Use classes consistently.** Make sure to use classes on *every* transaction. Otherwise, your class-based reports won't be accurate.

Tip: QuickBooks can remind you to enter a class for a transaction should you forget. Choose Edit → Preferences, click the Accounting icon, click the Company Preferences tab, and then turn on the "Use class tracking" and "Prompt to assign classes" checkboxes. If you try to save a transaction without an entry in the Class field, QuickBooks gives you an opportunity to add the class or save the transaction without one.

- **Create a catch-all class.** Set up a class such as Other so that you can still classify transactions even if they don't fit into any of the specific classes that you've defined.

To use classes, you must first turn on the class-tracking feature (page 135); to do *that*, you must be a QuickBooks administrator. If class tracking is off, the Lists menu won't even display the Class List command. If you aren't a QuickBooks administrator, you'll have to convince someone who is to turn on classes because classes affect everyone in your organization who uses QuickBooks.

A Class entry includes a name (in the Class Name field) and fields for making the class a subtype of another. In the Class List window, you can press Ctrl+N to open the New Class dialog box and create all of your classes at once. If you realize you need another class while working on a transaction, you can also create an entry by choosing *<Add New>* in a Class drop-down list, as illustrated in Figure 5-2.

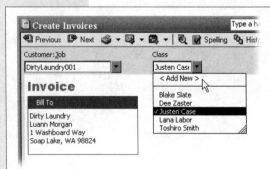

Figure 5-2:
After you turn on class tracking, every transaction that you create includes a Class field. To assign a class to the transaction, choose one of the classes from the drop-down list or choose <Add New>.

Price Levels

If you give your favorite customers price breaks or increase other customers' charges because they keep asking for "just one more thing," you can make those adjustments with discounts or markups on their invoices. Remembering who gets discounts and what percentage you apply is tough when you have a lot of customers, and it's bad form to mark up a favorite customer's prices by mistake. When you assign price levels to customers, QuickBooks takes care of adjusting the prices on every invoice you create.

To use price levels, you must first turn on the Price Level preference. In the Edit Preferences dialog box, click the Sales & Customers icon, and then click the Company Preferences tab. Turn on the "Use price levels" checkbox.

In QuickBooks Pro, a price level can increase or decrease prices by a percentage, as illustrated in Figure 5-3. Think of price levels as standard discounts or markups, and then apply those percentages to specific customers. For example, create a price level called Extras to boost prices by 20 percent. Then, assign that price level in the customer record (page 68) for every nitpicker you work for. Although price level names don't appear on your customer invoices, it's still a good idea to choose names that are meaningful without being rude.

Tip: In QuickBooks Premier, you can create price levels that set the dollar prices for individual items in your Item List. For example, suppose you sell calendars to retail stores for $5 each. You could create a price level so that a nonprofit would pay only $3.50 for a calendar.

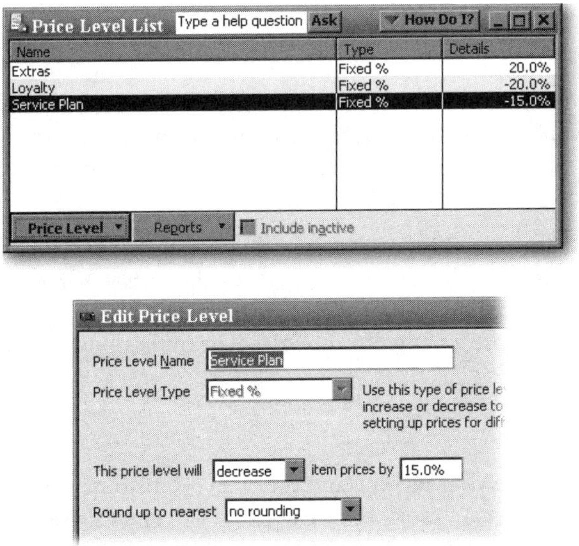

Figure 5-3:
Top: To create a new price level, choose Lists → Price Level List, which opens the Price Level List window, and then press Ctrl+N. If you want to edit an existing price level, double-click the name of the price level or, alternatively, select the price level and then press Ctrl+E.

Bottom: In QuickBooks Pro, the Price Level Type box is automatically set to Fixed % because you can create price levels only with fixed percentage increases or decreases. The "Round up to the nearest" drop-down list lets you set price levels that round the discount or markup to the nearest penny, the nearest dollar, and so on.

Tip: The "Round up to nearest" feature is a welcome addition to QuickBooks 2006, especially if your customers pay cash and you hate making change. In the past, percentage discounts often resulted in prices with fractions of a penny. This setting lets you round discounts to pennies, nickels, dimes, quarters, 50 cents, and even whole dollars (if you *really* hate making change).

Putting a price level to work is actually a two-step process. First, in the Price Level List, you create a price level entry. Then, in the New Customer or Edit Customer dialog box, you apply the price level to a customer record. When you create an invoice for that customer, QuickBooks automatically adjusts the prices by the price level percentage (page 198).

Customer & Vendor Profile Lists

Filling in fields goes much faster when you can choose information from drop-down lists instead of typing. The lists that appear on the Customer & Vendor Profile menu pop up regularly, whether you're creating an invoice, paying a bill, or generating reports. For example, when you create an invoice, QuickBooks fills in the Payment Terms field with the payment terms that you assigned to the customer's record (page 58), but you can also choose different payment terms from the drop-down list if you urge your customer to pay more quickly.

To create an entry on a list choose Lists → Customer & Vendor Profile; when the submenu appears, choose the list you want to tend. For many of these lists, creating entries is no more than typing an entry name and specifying whether the entry is a subentry to another. Here is a breakdown of the information you add to entries in each list and how to put these lists to work for your business.

Sales Rep List

If you pay sales reps on commission or want to assign employees as points of contact for your customers, you can assign people as sales reps to your customers and generate reports by sales rep (page 475). But first you have to add the names of your sales reps and contacts to the Sales Rep List.

To add a name to the Sales Rep List, make sure that name appears on the Employee List (page 323), the Vendor List (page 110), or the Other Names List (page 117). Then, in the New Sales Rep List dialog box, in the Sales Rep Name drop-down list, you simply choose a name. In the Sales Rep Initials box, type the person's initials.

Customer Type List

Customer types help you analyze your income and expenses by customer category (page 49). For example, a health care provider might create Govt and Private customer types to see how much a change in government reimbursement might hurt revenue. You first create customer types in the Customer Type List and then assign one of those types in each customer's record.

A Customer Type entry includes a name (in the Customer Type field) and whether the customer type is a subtype of another. Opening the New Customer Type dialog box and creating all your customer types up front is fast—as long as you already know what your entries are. In the Customer Type List window, press Ctrl+N and create your customer types. After you create one type, click Next to create another. Click OK when you've added all the types you want.

The Right Time to Use the Other Names List

If you have more than a few names in your Other Names List, you're probably not getting the most out of QuickBooks. In fact, unless you're a sole proprietor or several partners share ownership of your company, you can run QuickBooks without *any* names in the Other Names List.

The problem with Other Names is that QuickBooks doesn't track activity for Other Names. You can't find out how much you owe someone—or how much they owe you—if they are in your Other Names List. The entries in the Other Names List show up in the drop-down lists for a few types of transactions, such as checks and credit card charges (page 338), but they're conspicuously absent when you create invoices, purchase orders, sales receipts, or any other type of transaction.

What are Other Names good for? The perfect application for the Other Names List is for *your* name as sole proprietor

or the names of company partners. When you write owners' draw checks to pay partners, you can choose the names from the Other Names List.

To create an entry on the Other Names List, choose Lists → Other Names List. In the Other Names List window, press Ctrl+N. The fields in the New Name and Edit Name dialog boxes are contact information, similar to the fields found in the New Customer and Edit Customer dialog boxes (see page 54).

Should you decide that any of your Other Names entries actually belong on another list, click Activities (below the Other Names List) and then choose Change Other Name Types. In the Change Name Types dialog box, click the cell in the Customer, Vendor, or Employee column to reset Other Name to a new type. Click OK to complete the makeover.

You can also create entries as you work. If you are creating or modifying a customer in the New Customer or Edit Customer dialog boxes, click the Additional Info tab. In the Type drop-down list, choose *<Add New>*, which opens the New Customer Type dialog box. Now, you can create a new customer type, as shown in Figure 5-4.

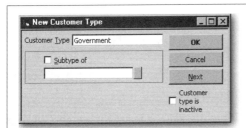

Figure 5-4:
The New Customer Type dialog box is simple. The only thing you must provide is a name in the Customer Type field. If the customer type represents a portion of a larger customer category, turn on the "Subtype of" checkbox and choose the parent customer type. For example, if you have a parent customer type of Utilities, you might create subtypes for Water Utility, Electric Utility, Gas Utility, and so on.

Vendor Type List

Vendor types work similarly to customer types—you can filter reports or subtotal your expenses by different types of vendors. For example, if you create a Communications vendor type, you could generate a report of the expenses you've paid to your telephone, Internet, and satellite communications providers.

You create Vendor Type entries the way you create Customer Type entries. With the Vendor Type List window open, press Ctrl+N to open the New Vendor Type dialog box. To create a new vendor type while you're creating a vendor, in the New Vendor dialog box, click the Additional Info tab, and in the Type drop-down list, choose *<Add New>* to open the New Vendor Type dialog box.

Job Type List

Job types also follow the customer type lead. For instance, you can filter a Profit & Loss report to show how profitable your spec house projects are compared to your remodeling contracts. You create Job Type entries the way you create Customer Type entries (page 49).

Terms List

The Terms List holds both the payment terms you require of your customers and the payment terms your vendors ask of you.

The fields that you fill in to create Terms entries, illustrated in Figure 5-5, are different than many of the other Customer & Vendor Profile Lists.

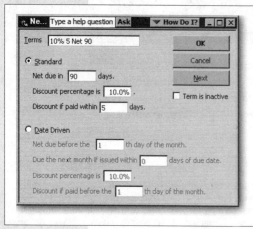

Figure 5-5:
Because payment terms apply to vendors and customers, consider using generic names that say something about the payment terms themselves. For example, the "10% 5 Net 90" entry is an enticement for early payments because it means that the amount is due 90 days from the invoice date, but you can deduct 10 percent from your bill if you pay within 5 days.

Here's an explanation of what the Terms fields do:

- **Standard.** Choose this option when the due date is a specific number of days after the invoice date.

— **Net due in __ days.** Type the maximum number of days after the invoice date that you or a customer can pay without incurring a penalty charge. For example, if you type 30, customers have up to 30 days to pay an invoice and you have up to 30 days to pay a bill.

— **Discount percentage is.** If you offer a discount for early payments, type the percentage discount in this box.

— **Discount if paid within __ days.** Type the number of days after the invoice date within which a customer must pay to receive the early payment discount.

Note: When you use terms that reduce a customer's bill for early payments, QuickBooks deducts these discounts in the Receive Payments dialog box (page 257) when the program can tell if the customer paid early.

• **Date driven.** Choose this option when payments are due on a specific date, regardless of the date on the invoice.

The "Date driven" option is better when you send invoices every month—say, on the last day of the month. For example, your home mortgage might specify that you'll owe a late fee if your payment arrives after the 15th of the month. If you send invoices whenever you complete a sale, choose the Standard option so that payment is due within a number of days of the invoice date.

— **Net due before the __th day of the month.** Type the day of the month that the payment is due. For example, if a mortgage payment is due before the 15th of the month, no matter what date appears on your loan statement, type *15* in the box.

— **Due the next month if issued within __ days of due date.** Your customers might get aggravated if you require payment by the 15th of the month and then send out your invoices on the 14th. Your customers would have no way of paying on time, unless they camped out in your billing department.

You can type a number of days in this box to automatically push the due date to the following month when you issue invoices too close to the due date. For example, if you type *5* in this box, QuickBooks pushes due dates to the next month if you generate invoices within 5 days of the due date. Suppose payments are due on the 15th of each month. For invoices you create between August 10th and August 15th, the program changes the due date to September 15th.

— **Discount percentage is.** If you extend a discount for early payments, type the percentage discount in this box.

— **Discount if paid before the __th day of the month.** Type the day of the month before which a customer receives the early payment discount.

Customer Message

When you create an invoice, you can add a short message to the form, such as "If you like the service we deliver, tell your friends. If you don't like our service, tell us." Save time and prevent embarrassing typographical errors by adding your stock messages to the Customer Message List. The New Customer Message dialog box has only one field, the Customer Message field, which can hold up to 101 characters (including spaces).

Don't use the Customer Message List for messages that change with every invoice, such as a message that specifies the calendar period that an invoice covers. You'll fill your Customer Message List with unique messages and won't be able to add any more. If you want to include unique information, do so in a cover letter (or email) that accompanies your invoice.

Payment Method List

When you select Banking → Make Deposits, you can choose to process all the payments you've received via a specific payment method. For example, you can deposit all the checks and cash you received into your checking account, but you might deposit the payments you receive via credit cards to your money market account. QuickBooks starts the Payment Method List for you with entries for cash, check, and credit cards (such as American Express and Visa). A Payment Method entry has a name and a payment type. For example, if you use two Visa credit cards, you can create two entries with a Visa payment type.

Ship Via List

When you include the shipping method that you use on your invoices, your customers know whether to watch for the mailman or the UPS delivery truck. Quick-Books creates several shipping methods for you, including Airborne, DHL, Federal Express, UPS, and U.S. Mail. If you use another shipping method, for example a bike messenger in New York City or your own delivery truck, simply create additional entries in the Ship Via List. In the Shipping Method field, type the name of the method you want to add.

Tip: If you use one method of shipping most of the time, you can have QuickBooks fill in the Shipping Method with that entry automatically. To do this, choose Edit → Preferences, and then click the Sales & Customers icon. On the Company Preferences tab, in the Usual Shipping Method drop-down list, choose your preferred shipment method. See page 161 to learn about other shipping preferences, such as the "Usual Free on Board" location.

Vehicle List

If you want to track mileage on the vehicles you use for your business, create entries for your cars and trucks in the Vehicle List. Use the Vehicle box to name the vehicle: Ford Prefect 1982 Red, for example. The Description field can hold up to 256 characters, so use it to store the VIN, license plate, and even the insurance policy number. To learn how to track mileage, see page 445. If you want to charge your customer for your mileage, see page 448.

Note: Although the Sales Tax Code List appears on the Lists menu, sales tax codes are inextricably linked to how you handle sales tax. Details for setting up the Sales Tax Code List is described in Chapter 4 on page 68.

Memorized Transactions

When you enter the same transactions over and over, memorizing them for reuse saves time. QuickBooks can fill in most, if not all, of the fields for you. It can also remind you to enter a transaction, such as a recurring client invoice for retainers, or even to add the transaction without any help from you. For example, if your company Internet service costs $259 each month and you use an automatic credit card payment, you can memorize that credit card charge and tell QuickBooks to automatically enter the same credit card charge each month.

The Memorized Transactions List is an anomaly on the List menu because you don't create memorized transactions the way you do entries on other lists. Instead, you memorize existing transactions, as described here:

1. **Enter a transaction, such as a check or credit card charge.**

   For fields that remain the same each time you use a transaction, fill in those transaction fields, as demonstrated in Figure 5-6. For example, enter the payee for a check, the account to post the expense to, and any other fields you want.

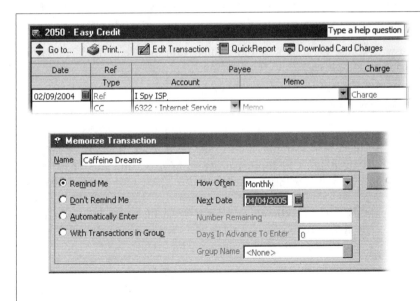

Figure 5-6:
Top: If fields change each time, leave those fields blank. Later, when you use the memorized transaction, QuickBooks fills in all the fields except for the amount. You simply fill in the Amount field with the current balance.

Bottom: In the Register window, select the transaction and press Ctrl+M or choose Edit → Memorize Check (or Edit → Memorize Credit Card Charge) to open the Memorize Transaction window. After memorizing the transaction, you can complete it or press Esc to remove it.

2. **In the Memorize Transaction dialog box, in the Name box, type a name that you'll recognize when you see it in the Memorized Transaction List.**

   For example, you might use names like Monthly Telephone Bill or Health Insurance Premium.

3. **Choose an option to specify whether you want QuickBooks to remind you.**

   Choosing the Remind Me option is the best of both worlds. QuickBooks reminds you when it's time to enter the next transaction, but you can choose to skip the transaction. If you choose this option, specify how often you want to be reminded and pick the next date for a reminder. For example, if you pay your phone bill on the 10th of each month, in the How Often box, choose Monthly and in the Next Date box, pick the 10th of the next month.

   If you don't use a transaction on a regular schedule, choose the Don't Remind Me option. QuickBooks won't add the memorized transaction to the Reminder List. When you want to use the transaction again, press Ctrl+T to open the Memorized Transaction List window. Select the transaction and click Enter Transaction.

   If you want QuickBooks to enter the transaction on its next scheduled date without any intervention on your part, choose the Automatically Enter option. When you select this option, be sure to specify, in the Number Remaining box, the number of times QuickBooks should enter the transaction. Otherwise, your company might continue to make an installment payment long after the last payment was due. You can also specify how many days in advance you want QuickBooks to enter the transaction. Providing a few days of lead time helps you avoid late payments, as well as insufficient funds charges from your bank.

4. **To memorize the transaction, click OK.**

   If you want to use the transaction immediately, in the Memorized Transaction List window, simply click Enter Transaction.

Fixed Asset Items

Assets that you can't convert to cash quickly—such as backhoes, buildings, or the new Deep Thought supercomputers—are called fixed assets. If you track information about your fixed assets in another program or have only a few fixed assets, there's no reason to bother with the Fixed Asset Item List. As shown in Figure 5-7, Fixed Asset Items track information, such as when you bought the asset and how much you paid. But in QuickBooks, *you* have to calculate depreciation (see the "How Depreciation Works" box on page 124) for each asset at the end of the year and create journal entries to adjust the values in your asset accounts.

Tip: QuickBooks Premier Accountant Edition and QuickBooks Enterprise Edition include the Fixed Asset Manager, which not only figures out the depreciation on your assets, but posts depreciation to Quick-Books with a click of the mouse.

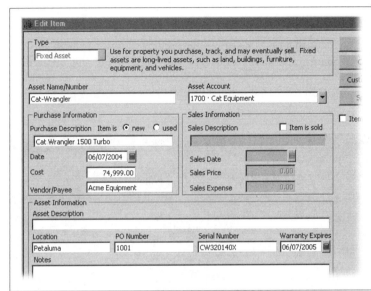

Figure 5-7:
When you buy a fixed asset, you can create a Fixed Asset Item and enter its name and purchase information, where you keep it, the item's serial number, and when the warranty expires. When you create a Fixed Asset Item, QuickBooks doesn't automatically add the purchase price to the Asset Account you choose. As explained on page 298, the account you choose in your purchase transaction (check or credit card charge, for instance) is what adds the purchase price to the Fixed Asset account in your Chart of Accounts.

If you decide to track the details about your fixed assets outside QuickBooks, you still need the *value* of your fixed assets in your financial reports. Simply create Fixed Asset accounts (page 38) to hold the value of your assets. Each year, you'll add a general journal entry to each Fixed Asset account (page 379) to reduce the balance by the amount of depreciation.

When you sell an asset, open the Edit Item dialog box (with the Fixed Asset Item List window open, select the item and press Ctrl+E), and then turn on the "Item is sold" checkbox, which enables the sales fields so that you can specify when you sold the machine, how much you sold it for, and any costs associated with the sale.

Creating and Editing List Entries

Every list in QuickBooks responds to the same set of commands. As your business changes, you can add new entries, edit existing ones, merge two entries into one, or hide entries that you no longer use. If you make a mistake creating an entry, you can delete it. You can also print your QuickBooks lists, for example, to produce a price list of the products you sell. Digest the following techniques and you'll be able to do what you want with any list or entry you might need.

Creating Entries

If you're setting up QuickBooks, creating all the entries for a list at the same time is fast and efficient. Open the New dialog box for the type of list entry you want (New Vendor, for example), and you'll soon find your rhythm creating one entry after another. You can also add new list entries in the middle of bookkeeping tasks without too much of an interruption.

For example, if you launch a new line of business selling moose repellent, you can add a customer type for burly man products in the middle of creating an invoice. But don't rely on this approach to add every entry to every list—you'll spend so much time jumping from New dialog box to New dialog box that you'll never get to your bookkeeping.

UP TO SPEED

How Depreciation Works

When your company depreciates assets, you add dollars here, subtract dollars there, and none of the dollars are real. Sounds like funny money, but depreciation is nothing more than an accounting concept, one which actually presents a better picture of financial performance. To see how it works, here's an example of what happens when a company depreciates a large purchase.

Suppose your company buys a Deep Thought supercomputer for $500,000. You spent $500,000, but you now own an asset worth $500,000. Your company's balance sheet moves that money from your bank account to an asset account, but your total assets remain the same. The problem arises when you sell the computer, perhaps 10 years later when it would make a good boat anchor. The moment you sell, the value of that asset plummets from $500,000 to your selling price—say $1,000. The drop in value shows up as an expense, putting a huge dent in your profits for the 10th year. Shareholders don't like it when profits jump from year to year—up or down. With depreciation, though, you can spread the cost of a big purchase over several years, which matches revenue and expenses. This shows shareholders how well you use assets to generate income.

Depreciation calculations come in several flavors: straight line, sum of the years' digits, and double declining balance. Straight-line depreciation is the easiest and most common.

To calculate annual straight-line depreciation, subtract the *salvage* value (how much the asset is worth when you sell it) from the purchase price, and then divide by the number of years of useful life, like so:

- Purchase price: $500,000

- Salvage value after 10 years: $1,000

- Useful life: the 10 years you expect to run the computer

- Annual depreciation: $499,000/10, which equals $49,900.

Every year, you use the computer to make money for your business, and you show $49,900 as that income's associated equipment expense. On your books, the value of the Deep Thought computer drops by another $49,900 each year, until the balance reaches the $1,000 salvage value at the end of the last year. This decrease in value each year keeps your balance sheet (page 386) more accurate and avoids the sudden drop in asset value in year 10.

The other, more complex methods depreciate your assets faster in the first few years (called *accelerated depreciation*), making for big tax write-offs in a hurry. Your accountant can tell you which is best for your situation.

Each list has its own collection of fields, but the overall procedure for creating entries in lists is the same:

1. **Open the window for the list you want to work on. Simply choose Lists and then select the list you want on the submenu.**

   For example, to open the Price Level List window, choose Lists → Price Level List. Several lists are tucked away one level deeper on the Lists menu. For lists that include characteristics for your customers or vendors, such as Vendor Type or Terms, choose Lists → Customer & Vendor Profile Lists, and then choose the list you want, as demonstrated in Figure 5-8.

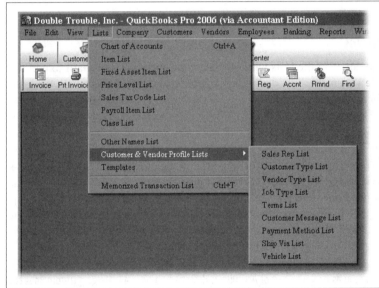

Figure 5-8:
Many of the QuickBooks lists appear directly on the Lists menu, but lists that help you create customers and vendors are one level lower on the Customer & Vendor Profile submenu. To boost your productivity, take note of the keyboard shortcuts for the three lists you're likely to access most often. Ctrl+A opens the Chart of Accounts window. Ctrl+J opens the Customer:Job List window, and Ctrl+T opens the Memorized Transaction List.

2. **To create an entry, you must open the appropriate New dialog box. To do so, press Ctrl+N or, alternatively, at the bottom of the list window, click the list name, and then choose New.**

   For example, to create an entry in the Price Level List, make sure that the Price Level List is the active window and then press Ctrl+N. Or, at the bottom of the Price Level List window, click Price Level and then choose New. QuickBooks opens the New Price Level dialog box.

3. **After you've completed one entry but still have many more to create, simply click Next to save the current entry and begin another. If you want to save the entry you just created and close the dialog box, click OK.**

   If you want to toss an entry that you botched, click Cancel to throw it away and close the dialog box. (Unlike all the other New dialog boxes for lists, the New Price Level dialog box doesn't include a Next button.) A few of the lists on the

Customer & Vendor Profile Lists menu can include subentries, as shown in Figure 5-9.

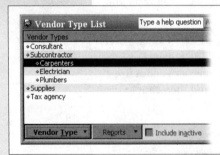

Figure 5-9:
You can create multiple levels of entries in the Customer Type, Job Type, and Vendor Type lists. For example, you might create top-level types for vendors that require 1099 forms and those that don't. Then, you can create subentries for types such as electricians, plumbers, and carpenters.

Editing Entries

To modify an entry, in the Lists window, select the entry that you want to edit and press Ctrl+E. When the Edit dialog box opens, make the changes you want and click OK when you're done.

Merging List Entries

Over time, your lists collect detritus. For example, your Item list (see Chapter 4) has separate inventory items for 1/2" copper pipe cut to 4-, 5-, and 10-foot lengths, but you just need one item for 1/2" copper pipe cut to order. Or, two of your suppliers for copper pipes merge their businesses, and you want to merge their vendor records as well. You can merge entries on only two of the lists discussed in *this* chapter: the Vendor List and the Other Names List.

Note: Merging accounts on your Chart of Accounts is described on page 43. Merging customers is covered on page 70.

When you merge entries, QuickBooks puts all the transactions from both entries into the one that you keep. For example, if you merge Bob's Bazookas into Ari's Armaments, all your purchases at Bob's become purchases for Ari's Armaments.

Here's how you merge two entries, using the Vendor List as an example:

1. **Switch to single-user mode.**

   If you work in multiuser mode, choose File → Switch to Single-user Mode. When you're done, switch back to multiuser mode and tell your colleagues they can work in QuickBooks once more.

2. **Open the Vendor Center.**

   In the icon bar, click Vendor Center or, on the QuickBooks Home page, click Vendors. If you want to merge names on the Other Names list, choose Lists → Other Names List.

3. **In the Vendors tab, right-click the name of the vendor you are going to merge
   and, on the shortcut menu, choose Edit Vendor.**

   The Edit Vendor dialog box opens. You can also edit the vendor by selecting the
   vendor name on the Vendors tab and then, when the vendor information
   appears on the right side of the Vendor Center, clicking the Edit Vendor
   button.

4. **In the Edit Vendor dialog box, change the name in the Vendor Name field to
   match the name of the vendor you intend to keep. Click OK.**

   QuickBooks displays a message informing you that the name is in use and asks
   if you want to merge the vendors.

5. **Click Yes to merge the vendors.**

   In the Vendor Center, the vendor you renamed disappears and any balances
   now belong to the remaining vendor.

Hiding and Deleting List Entries

Deleting entries is only for discarding entries that you create by mistake. If you've
already used list entries in transactions, hide the entries that you don't use anymore so your historical records are complete. For example, you wouldn't delete the
Net 30 payment terms just because you're lucky enough to have only Net 15 clients right now; you may still extend Net 30 terms to some clients in the future.

Hiding Entries

Hiding list entries that you no longer use accomplishes two things:

- Your previous transactions still use the entries you've hidden, so your historical
  records don't change.

- When you create new transactions, the hidden entries don't appear in drop-
  down lists, so a sudden muscle cramp won't choose an entry by mistake.

The methods for hiding and reactivating list entries are exactly the same regardless
of which list you're working on.

- **To hide an entry,** in the list window (or the list in Vendor Center), right-click
  the entry and choose Make *<list name>* Inactive from the shortcut menu, where
  <list name> is the list that you're editing. The entry disappears from the list.

- **To view all the entries in a list,** hidden or active, at the bottom of the window,
  turn on the "Include inactive" checkbox. In the Vendor Center, in the View
  drop-down list, choose All Vendors. QuickBooks adds a column with an X as its
  heading and displays an X in that column for every inactive entry in the list.

• **To reactivate an entry,** first view all the entries, and then click the X next to the entry that you want to reactivate. If the entry has subentries, in the Activate Group dialog box, click Yes to reactivate the entry and all its subentries.

Deleting Entries

You can delete an entry only if nothing in QuickBooks references it in any way. If you create a list entry by mistake, your only hope is to catch it quickly. To delete a list entry, open the appropriate list window and select the entry you want to delete. Press Ctrl+D or choose Edit → Delete *<list name>*. If you haven't used the entry in any records or transactions, QuickBooks asks you to confirm that you want to delete the entry. Click Yes.

GEM IN THE ROUGH

Defining Custom Fields for Lists

QuickBooks provides numerous fields for customer, vendor, employee, and item records, but those fields might not cover all the information you need. For example, you might add a custom field for the branch office that services a customer. For employees, you could set up a custom field to track whether they make charitable contributions that your company matches.

QuickBooks' answer to this issue is custom fields. Unfortunately, these fields are pretty feeble compared to what some of QuickBooks' built-in fields can do. After you create a custom field and apply it to a list, QuickBooks does nothing more than add the custom field label and a text box to the Additional Info tab (see Figure 3-4 on page 57). You have to type your entries each time; there's no drop-down lists or even a comparison to text you entered in other records. It's up to you to make sure that your data entry is correct and consistent.

When you edit a record that can contain custom fields, in the Edit dialog box on the Additional Info tab, you'll see the Define Fields button. Click it, and all you get is the Define

Fields dialog box, shown in the figure. When you create a custom field, you define the field label and the records in which it appears. In one of the 15 label boxes, type the name of the field. If you're associating a custom field to a customer, vendor, or employee record, turn on the checkbox for the appropriate list. For example, the sales region custom field could apply to both the Customer:Job List and the Vendors List.

When you edit an item in the Items List, you click Custom Fields. In the Custom Fields dialog box, click Define Fields to create labels for up to five custom fields for your items.

Define Fields			
		To be used for	
Label	Customers:Jobs	Vendors	Employees
Region	☑	☐	☐
Charity	☐	☐	☑
Branch	☑	☐	☐
Technician	☑	☐	☐
Workmans' Comp	☐	☑	☐

Sorting Lists

QuickBooks usually sorts lists alphabetically by name, which is what you want most of the time. The only reason to sort a list otherwise is if you're having trouble finding the entry you want to edit. For example, if you want to find equipment you bought within the last few years, you could sort the Fixed Asset List by purchase date to find the machines that you're still depreciating. Sorting a list in the list window doesn't even change the order that entries appear in drop-down lists.

Just in case you want to modify the sort order, Figure 5-10 shows you how to do so, and it also shows you how to change it back.

Figure 5-10:
To sort a list by a column, click the column heading, such as Purchase Date. The first time you click a column heading, QuickBooks sorts the list in ascending order. To toggle between ascending and descending order, click the same column heading again. The small black triangle in the column heading points up when the list is sorted in ascending order and points down for descending order.

Tip: If you change the column used to sort a list, QuickBooks displays a gray diamond to the left of the column heading that it uses to sort the list initially. For example, the Fixed Asset Item List shows items listed in alphabetical order by Name. If you sort the list by Purchase Date instead, the gray diamond appears to the left of the Name heading. To return the list to the order that QuickBooks uses, click the diamond.

Printing Lists

After you spend all that time building lists in QuickBooks, you'll be happy to know that it's much easier to get those lists back out of the program. For instance, suppose you want to print a price list of all the items you sell. Or, you want a text file of your customer information to import into your email program. QuickBooks makes short work of printing your lists or turning them into files that you can use in other programs.

Blasting Out a Quick List

Here's the fastest way to produce a list, albeit one that doesn't give you any control over report appearance:

1. **At the bottom of the list window, click the button that contains the list name—Price Level, for example—and then, in the shortcut menu, choose Print List.**

   QuickBooks might display a message box telling you to try list reports if you want to customize or format your reports. That method is covered in the next section. For now, in the message box, click OK. The Print Lists dialog box opens.

Note: Vendors and Employees have their own centers in QuickBooks 2006. To print these lists, in the Vendor Center or Employee Center icon bar, click Print and choose Vendor List or Employee List.

2. **If you want to print the list, choose the Printer option and choose the printer in the drop-down list. If you want to output the list to a file, choose the File option and then select the file format you want.**

You can create ASCII text files, comma-delimited files, or tab-delimited files (page 534). You can also specify printer settings, as you can in many other programs. Twist the report around into landscape or portrait orientation, choose the pages to print, and set the number of copies.

3. **Click Print.**

Customizing a Printed List

If the Print List command described in the previous section scatters fields over the page or produces a comma-delimited file that doesn't play well with your email program, QuickBooks might provide a report closer to what you had in mind. For example, a vendor phone list and employee contact list are only two menu clicks away. To access the reports that come with QuickBooks, choose Reports → List and then choose the report you want. If these reports fall short, you can modify them to change the fields and records they contain, or you can format them in a variety of ways.

Chapter 19 explains how to customize reports, but here are some things you can do if you use a list report to print your list or create a file of your list information:

- **Choose fields.** The Columns box includes every field for a list entry. When you click a field, QuickBooks adds a checkmark before its name and adds the field to the report.

- **Sort records.** Choose the field you want to sort by and whether you want the report sorted in ascending or descending order.

- **Filter the report.** Filters limit the records in a report. For example, you can produce an employee report for active employees, which refers to their employment status—not the level of effort they devote to their jobs. You can also filter by employee name or values in other fields.

- **Set up the report header and footer.** You can choose the information that you want to show in the report title and the footer at the bottom of each page. For example, a report title identifies the information in the report, and the date the report was prepared tells you if the employee list is current.

- **Format text and numbers.** Choose the font that QuickBooks uses for different parts of the report. For instance, labels should be larger than the lines in the report. You can also choose how to display negative numbers; the In Bright Red checkbox controls whether red ink truly applies to your financial reports. You can divide numbers by 1,000 before displaying them in a report so that it's easier to differentiate thousands from millions.

Configuring Preferences to Fit Your Company

An organization's approach to accounting often depends on business objectives, policies, procedures, and the industry in which the organization operates. Maybe you want inventory tracking and payroll or maybe you don't. The way that you and your accountant like to work also influences your organization's accounting practices. For instance, you might prefer the simplicity of cash accounting or the more intimate pairing of income and expenses that accrual accounting (page 159) offers.

Enter QuickBooks, an accounting program with the Herculean task of satisfying every nuance of business operation and personal proclivity. QuickBooks *preferences* are configurable settings that accommodate different business styles and personal tastes. During installation, QuickBooks sets its preferences to settings likely to work for a majority of organizations. And if you set up your QuickBooks file using the EasyStep Interview (page 20), you might already have most preferences set the way you want.

But you can reset preferences to control all sorts of QuickBooks behaviors and features, such as whether you create estimates for jobs you do or assign a password to access your QuickBooks file. Preferences also let you turn on QuickBooks features, such as inventory and payroll. Using QuickBooks a little can make it clear which preferences you need to change. If you find that some of the preferences that QuickBooks chose initially don't work for you, this chapter presents all the preferences that QuickBooks offers and helps you determine which settings are appropriate for you and your organization.

Tip: You can change preferences at any time, so feel free to tweak and tinker with them.

An Introduction to Preferences

You can't quibble over quantity when QuickBooks offers 18 sections of preferences that control QuickBooks' behavior. Each preference section contains several settings, so finding the preferences that do what you want is your biggest challenge. To view and set preferences, open the Preferences dialog box by choosing Edit → Preferences.

On the left side of the Preferences dialog box is a pane that contains icons for each preference section, as illustrated in Figure 6-1. To display the preferences within a section, click the appropriate icon in the pane. QuickBooks highlights the icon you click to indicate that it's active. The preference sections are listed alphabetically, not in order of importance.

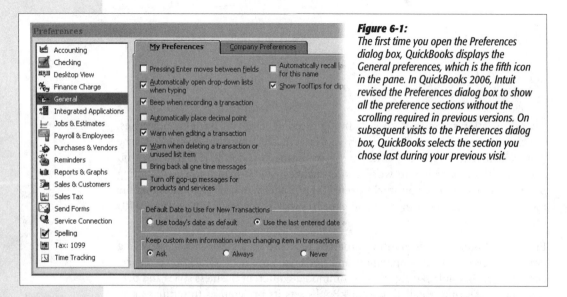

Figure 6-1:
The first time you open the Preferences dialog box, QuickBooks displays the General preferences, which is the fifth icon in the pane. In QuickBooks 2006, Intuit revised the Preferences dialog box to show all the preference sections without the scrolling required in previous versions. On subsequent visits to the Preferences dialog box, QuickBooks selects the section you chose last during your previous visit.

To accommodate both company and personal preferences, QuickBooks includes two tabs for each section: My Preferences and Company Preferences. As you might expect, the My Preferences tab contains options that people who log into QuickBooks can set for their QuickBooks sessions alone. For example, you can choose options in the Desktop View preference section if you want to look at multiple windows using a lurid purple color scheme (called Grappa Granite), without forcing your tastes on everyone else.

Some preferences must remain consistent for everyone within an organization. For example, the IRS won't tolerate some financial reports produced using cash accounting and others using accrual accounting (see page 7 for the pros and cons of each). The preferences that appear on the Company Preferences tab ensure consistency because they are in-force no matter who in your company logs in. To make sure company preferences are set properly, only people who log in as

QuickBooks administrators (see page 564) can change the preferences on the Company Preferences tab.

Note: If you're puzzled by QuickBooks' habit of opening the Preferences dialog box to a My Preferences tab that contains no preferences, rest assured that Intuit has its reasons. Only QuickBooks administrators can change settings on the Company Preferences tab. Rather than taunt the majority of people who log into QuickBooks with preferences that they can't modify, QuickBooks displays the My Preferences tab. Unfortunately, for most preference sections, the Company Preferences tab is usually where the action is.

When you click OK to close the Preferences dialog box, QuickBooks saves the changes you made in the current preference section. What if you are on an energetic mission to reset preferences in several sections? If you make changes to preferences in a section and click the icon for another section, QuickBooks asks you whether you want to save the changes in the section you are about to leave. Make sure you save what you want by clicking one of the following buttons:

- **Yes.** Click Yes to save the changes in the current section before proceeding to the section whose icon you clicked.

- **No.** Click No to discard the changes and move on to the section whose icon you clicked.

- **Cancel.** Click Cancel to discard the changes you made and remain in the current section so that you can make other choices.

The rest of this chapter explains each set of preferences. They're listed in alphabetical order, as they are in the Preferences dialog box.

Accounting Preferences

QuickBooks' accounting preferences control key accounting practices, such as requiring accounts in transactions, assigning transactions to classes, and closing the books at the end of a fiscal year. Accounting practices stay the same throughout a company, so Accounting Preferences reside on the Company Preferences tab. Here's what they do:

- **Use account numbers.** In the accounting world, most people follow a numbering standard, which uses ranges of numbers for different types of accounts. For example, asset account (bank accounts, inventory, and so on) numbers run from 1000 to 1999; liability accounts (credit cards, loans, and so on) appear in the 2000 to 2999 range. If you work with an accountant, she'll probably ask you to turn on this checkbox. By doing so, you can assign a number in addition to a name to each account you create.

Tip: When you assign an account to a transaction, such as applying your rent check to the Rent expense account, you can locate the account in the Account drop-down list by typing either the account number *or* the first few letters of the account name.

• **Show lowest subaccount only.** If you use only top-level accounts in your Chart of Accounts, you have no need for this behavior. But if your company is like most, your Chart of Accounts is a hierarchy of accounts and subaccounts as described on page 33. You must turn on this checkbox if you want to easily identify the subaccount you've selected in an Account field, as demonstrated in Figure 6-2.

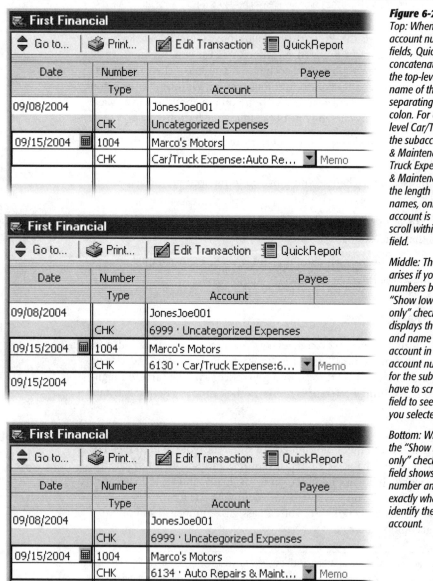

Figure 6-2:

Top: When you don't use account numbers, in Account fields, QuickBooks concatenates the name of the top-level account and the name of the subaccount, separating the two with a colon. For example, the top-level Car/Truck Expense and the subaccount Auto Repairs & Maintenance become Car/Truck Expense:Auto Repairs & Maintenance. Because of the length of these combined names, only the top-level account is visible unless you scroll within the Account field.

Middle: The same problem arises if you use account numbers but turn off the "Show lowest subaccount only" checkbox. QuickBooks displays the account number and name for the top-level account in addition to the account number and name for the subaccount. You still have to scroll in the Account field to see which account you selected.

Bottom: When you turn on the "Show lowest subaccount only" checkbox, the Account field shows the subaccount number and name, which is exactly what you need to identify the assigned account.

- **Require accounts.** Detail helps you manage your business, but it's *essential* to surviving the toughest of IRS audits. If detail isn't your strong suit, turning on this checkbox forces you to assign an account to every item and transaction you create, which, in turn, creates a trail that you and the IRS can follow. For example, when you turn on the "Require accounts" checkbox and then click Record without an assigned account, QuickBooks warns you that you must enter an account. To record the transaction, in the Warning message box, click OK. Then, choose the account in the transaction Account field. Now, when you click Record, QuickBooks completes the transaction without complaint.

  You can turn this checkbox off and record transactions without assigned accounts, but QuickBooks assigns the transaction amounts to either the Uncategorized Income or Uncategorized Expense accounts. For example, if you receive a payment from a customer and don't assign an account to the deposit, that income posts to the Uncategorized Income account.

Warning: If the IRS decides to audit your tax returns, you'll have to go back and move your uncategorized income and expenses into the right accounts to prove that you paid the right amount of taxes. And, if you happened to pay too little, the IRS will charge you penalties and interest.

- **Use class tracking.** When you want to track your business in more ways than accounts, customer types, and job types can offer, you can use classes to add one more level of categorization to your reports, which you'll learn in detail on page 492. For example, you can create classes to track the income that the company partners generate, regardless of which types of customers they support or the type of work they do. To enable the Class feature, turn on the "Use class tracking" checkbox. With classes enabled, a Class field appears in every transaction window, and QuickBooks reminds you to assign a class if you try to save or record a transaction without one.

- **Prompt to assign classes.** If you turn on the Class feature, your reports by class won't accurately reflect your business performance unless you assign classes to *all* of your transactions. To make sure that you assign classes consistently, turn on the "Prompt to assign classes" checkbox so that QuickBooks reminds you when you forget a class assignment for a transaction.

Note: In QuickBooks 2006, audit tracking is *always* turned on, so unlike previous versions, you won't find an option in Preferences to turn it on or off. Refer to page 572 to learn how to review your audit trail.

- **Automatically assign general journal entry number.** Journal entries refer to the traditional approach to accounting, in which accountants used to assign credits and debits to accounts in paper-based journals. If you miscategorized a transaction, your accountant creates a journal entry to move dollars from your incorrectly assigned account to the correct account. For instance, a journal entry might move company-paid health club dues from the Membership & Dues account you used to a more appropriate Employee Benefits account.

Discussing changes that you and your accountant make to your books is much easier when you can refer to journal entries by an identifier or number. Unless you use an unusual numbering scheme for general journal entries, there's no reason to turn this checkbox off. When you turn this checkbox on, QuickBooks makes sure that each general journal entry has a unique number. When you create a new general journal entry (see page 374), QuickBooks increments the previous general journal entry number by one, as demonstrated in Figure 6-3.

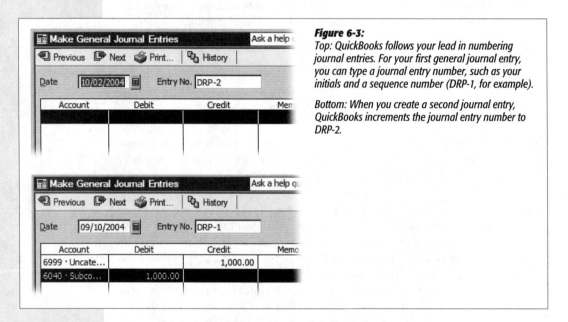

Figure 6-3:
Top: QuickBooks follows your lead in numbering journal entries. For your first general journal entry, you can type a journal entry number, such as your initials and a sequence number (DRP-1, for example).

Bottom: When you create a second journal entry, QuickBooks increments the journal entry number to DRP-2.

Note: If the previous entry number is blank, QuickBooks won't assign a general journal entry number to the next entry. If you notice that QuickBooks has begun to shirk its automatic numbering duties, look for a blank entry number. Add numbers to any existing journal entries without entry numbers. Then, when you add a new journal entry, QuickBooks will number the next entry as it should.

- **Warn when posting to Retained Earnings account.** The program automatically turns on this checkbox, and it's a good idea to leave it that way. QuickBooks creates the Retained Earnings account to track past profits that have been retained in the company's coffers. For example, if your company earned $10,000 in 2005 and didn't distribute that money to the owners or as profit-sharing bonuses to employees, that money becomes Retained Earnings once you begin 2006. QuickBooks updates the balance in the account automatically at the beginning of a new fiscal year by transferring the previous year's earnings into it. This preference warns you before you post a transfer directly to the Retained Earning account and inadvertently create inaccurate records.

- **Closing date.** After producing the financial reports for a fiscal year and paying corporate income taxes, most companies close their books, which means locking the transactions so no one can change anything. By closing the books, you ensure that your past transactions continue to match what you submitted to your accountant, reported to the IRS, and communicated to your shareholders. When you use QuickBooks, your QuickBooks file is synonymous with your "books." Therefore, you close your books by choosing a date in the "Date through which books are closed" box. For example, if you run your company on a calendar year and just reported and paid taxes for 2005, type or choose 12/31/2005.

QuickBooks gives you an out if you absolutely must edit a transaction that occurred before the closing date. In this preference section, you can assign a password so that you can edit, delete, or create transactions that would alter account balances. To set the password, click the Set Password button. In the Change Closing Date Password dialog box, type the password in the New Password and Confirm New Password boxes, and then click OK. If you *must* edit a transaction prior to the closing date, you'll first have to type the password.

Note: For QuickBooks Premier and Enterprise, the My Preferences tab contains only one preference: the "Autofill memo in general journal entry" checkbox. You keep the debit and credit sides of the entry linked by adding memos to the lines of general journal entries. Turn on this checkbox if you want QuickBooks to copy the memo you type for the first line of a journal entry to every subsequent line of the entry.

Checking

Checking preferences let you set company-wide settings to control the appearance of the checks your company prints through QuickBooks. In this section, you can also set preferences for the accounts that QuickBooks selects automatically for several types of financial transactions, as demonstrated in Figure 6-4.

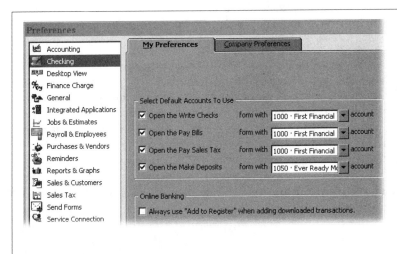

Figure 6-4:
When you choose accounts in Checking preferences, you have one less field to fill in for each banking transaction. For example, if you always deposit money into your money market account, you can set your preferences so the Write Checks dialog box selects your checking account, whereas the Make Deposits dialog box selects your money market account. In addition, if you always use the same accounts, setting these preferences prevents errors from selecting the wrong account in a drop-down list.

If you have only one bank account, you can ignore the preferences for default accounts. QuickBooks automatically chooses your checking account for writing checks, paying bills, and making deposits.

Choosing the Bank Accounts You Use

Using the options on the My Preferences tab, each person who logs into Quick-Books can choose her own default accounts for banking transactions. Suppose a company has stores in several states and each store has its own checking account. The person in Miami wants the Florida checking account to appear in the Write Checks dialog box, but the person in New York would want to see the Manhattan checking account. To save some time when creating transactions, consider setting these default accounts:

- **Open the Write Checks form with _ _ account.** In the account drop-down list, choose the account you typically use to write checks. When you open the Write Checks dialog box (see page 305), QuickBooks automatically fills in the Bank Account field with the account you specified here, as shown in Figure 6-4 (top).

- **Open the Pay Bills form with _ _ account.** In real life, paying bills and writing checks usually mean the same thing. In QuickBooks, you can enter bills you receive and pay them at a later date, as described on page 276. For this preference, choose the account you typically use to pay bills in the account drop-down list. If you choose the same checking account that you chose in the "Open the Write Checks form with" preference, you're in good company with the majority of other small business owners. When you open the Pay Bills dialog box, QuickBooks automatically fills in the Payment Account field with the account you specify in this preference.

- **Open the Pay Sales Tax form with _ _ account.** If you collect sales tax from your customers (see page 87), you must remit the taxes you collect to the appropriate tax authority, such as the state where your business is. When it's time to send the taxes in, you open the Pay Sales Tax dialog box and create a payment. This preference sets the account that QuickBooks uses in the Bank Account field.

- **Open the Make Deposits form with _ _ account.** Unlike the other options on the My Preferences tab, this preference sets up the account you use when you *deposit* money. For many small businesses, the deposit account and the checking account are one and the same. Some businesses, however, deposit money into a savings account that pays interest, and then transfer money into a checking account only when it's time to pay bills. Choose the account you typically use to deposit money. When you open the Make Deposits dialog box (see page 271), QuickBooks automatically fills in the Deposit To field with the account you specify in this preference, as Figure 6-4 illustrates.

Tip: The My Preferences tab includes an Online Banking section with one checkbox: "Always use 'Add to Register' when adding downloaded transactions." If you turn this checkbox on, QuickBooks automatically adds all downloaded transactions to the register. Leave it turned off for greater control so that you can choose to, say, add a deposit to the register yourself and link it to a payment, rather than having it download unlinked behind your back.

Setting the Way Company Checks Work

Although a company might have several checking accounts, QuickBooks assumes that company checks should look the same no matter who prints them. Most preferences on the Company Preferences tab let you set the company standard for printing checks from QuickBooks. If you use preprinted checks and write them out by hand, you can skip these options.

- **Print account names on voucher.** If the paper checks that you print include check stubs, you might as well turn on this checkbox. When you do so, QuickBooks prints on the stub the account name for the account you used to pay the check. If you use only one bank account, printing the account name might not seem all that useful. But QuickBooks also prints the payroll item on the stub for payroll checks, and for checks used to purchase inventory, it prints the name of the inventory item you purchased—both of which can help you keep track of where your money is going.

Note: Regardless of how you set this preference, QuickBooks always prints the payee, date, memo, amount, and total amount on stubs.

- **Change check date when check is printed.** When you turn on this checkbox, QuickBooks inserts the date that you *print* checks as the check date, which is just fine in most situations. You can enter checks into QuickBooks over several days, but date all the checks with the day you print them.

  Turn off this checkbox if you want to control the check dates. For example, if your cash flow situation is grim, you might resort to post-dating checks to defer some payments for a few days.

- **Start with payee field on check.** Turning on this checkbox is a small but satisfying time-saver. If you always write checks from the same account, or you use the "Open the Write Checks form with" preference to specify an account (see page 138), tabbing to skip the Bank Account field for each transaction grows old quickly. When you turn on this checkbox, you can save one pesky keystroke each time you write a check, as illustrated in Figure 6-5.

  This preference also works with credit card charges. When you turn on the "Start with payee field on check" checkbox and then choose Banking → Record Credit Card Charges → Enter Credit Card Charges, QuickBooks opens the Enter Credit Card Charges dialog box, with the cursor in the Purchased From box.

• **Warn about duplicate check numbers.** Not surprisingly, turning on this checkbox means that QuickBooks warns you that you are trying to record a check with the same number as one you already entered.

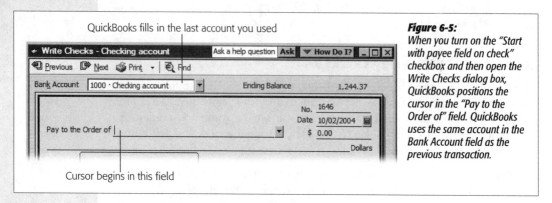

QuickBooks fills in the last account you used

Cursor begins in this field

Figure 6-5:
When you turn on the "Start with payee field on check" checkbox and then open the Write Checks dialog box, QuickBooks positions the cursor in the "Pay to the Order of" field. QuickBooks uses the same account in the Bank Account field as the previous transaction.

• **Autofill payee account number in check memo.** Just as you assign account numbers to your customers, the vendors you do business with assign your company an account number, too. Printing account numbers on the checks you write helps a vendor credit your account, even if the check becomes orphaned from its accompanying payment slip. If you enter your company's account number in each Vendor record in QuickBooks (see page 112), turn this checkbox on to print these account numbers on your checks.

Choosing Company-Wide Payroll Accounts

The two Checking preferences in the Select Default Accounts To Use section of the Company Preferences tab let you set the accounts you use for payroll. QuickBooks might seem to jump the gun by offering company-wide settings for the accounts used for payroll and payroll liabilities, but most companies centralize payroll no matter how regional other operations are. If you don't use QuickBooks payroll features, don't bother with these preferences because you'll never open the Create Paychecks or Pay Payroll Liabilities forms. (To learn how to turn on QuickBooks payroll features, refer to page 152 for the Payroll & Employees preference section.)

Tip: A separate account for payroll simplifies reconciling your regular checking account, particularly for companies with numerous employees and weekly paychecks. Otherwise, you'll have to reconcile dozens or even hundreds of paychecks each month in addition to the other checks you write.

• **Open the Create Paychecks form with _ _ account.** In the account drop-down list, choose the account you use to write payroll checks. When you open the Create Paychecks dialog box (see page 329), QuickBooks automatically fills in the Bank Account field with the account you specify in this preference.

• **Open the Pay Payroll Liabilities form with _ _ account.** From the Account drop-down list, choose the account you use to pay payroll taxes.

• **Payee aliasing.** New in QuickBooks 2006, this helpful online banking option is turned on automatically. If QuickBooks downloads a transaction with a payee it doesn't recognize, you can associate that name to an existing payee in your company file. The next time you download a transaction for that payee name, the program automatically replaces the downloaded name with the one in your company file.

POWER USERS' CLINIC

Integrated Applications

As you'll learn in more detail in Chapter 21, QuickBooks plays well with other programs, such as Microsoft's Excel and Access. For example, by integrating Microsoft Outlook with QuickBooks, you can easily keep your contact information synchronized in both programs. Third-party vendors create all sorts of programs that integrate with QuickBooks for tasks such as document management, project tracking, creating bar codes, and so on. If you're a QuickBooks administrator, the Integrated Applications preferences section is the place to go to control which applications can interact with QuickBooks and the extent of their interaction. For example, you might use another program to produce estimates and want to transfer the completed estimates into QuickBooks to fill out invoices and other forms.

To find programs that integrate with QuickBooks, at the bottom of the Company Preferences tab, click the Quick-Books Solutions Marketplace link. QuickBooks opens a browser window and navigates to the QuickBooks Solutions Marketplace Web site. You can look for programs based on your industry or by the type of software.

Sometimes, third-party programs alter QuickBooks features such as your Chart of Accounts and items. So, before you try to integrate a new program, back up your QuickBooks file. After you integrate a program, check your QuickBooks file for unwanted changes, such as new accounts or classes that you don't want to use. Depending on what you find, you can restore your backup, modify your lists manually, or leave things the way they are.

To access these preferences, choose Edit → Preferences, click the Integrated Applications icon, and then click the Company Preferences tab. Here's a guide to setting preferences to allow or restrict other programs' access to your QuickBooks file:

• **Don't allow any applications to access this company file.** The quickest way to lock down a QuickBooks file against access by other programs is to turn on this checkbox. When you do so, Quick-Books prevents integrated applications from accessing the file and also suppresses the display of screens that allow people to authorize access. If you want QuickBooks to display access screens, turn on this checkbox. Others can authorize access only if a QuickBooks administrator enables their accounts to do so, which is discussed on page 568.

• **Notify the user before running any application whose certificate has expired.** The most security conscious of administrators might turn on this checkbox to see a warning if an application trying to access the QuickBooks file has an expired certificate. But an expired certificate doesn't mean that the program has changed or has morphed into malicious code—it indicates only that the certificate has expired. For most administrators, turning off this checkbox is preferable.

• **Applications that have previously requested access to this company file.** When programs request access to a QuickBooks file, QuickBooks displays an access screen to the QuickBooks administrator who must approve or deny access. Programs that have received approval to access your company file appear in this list. To deny access to one of these programs, click the checkmark in the Allow Access column, or select the application and then click Remove.

Desktop View

Each person can customize the QuickBooks desktop for herself. You can fulfill your every desktop desire with the preferences on the My Preferences tab—your choices affect no one else who logs into QuickBooks. In QuickBooks 2006, the Company Preferences tab now includes preferences that control what appears on the QuickBooks Home page (page 144).

Window Preferences

You can keep your desktop neat with only one window at a time, or you can view multiple windows.

- **One Window.** If you're not good at multitasking or you simply prefer full-size windows, choose the One Window option so that QuickBooks displays only one full-size window at a time, as shown in Figure 6-6.

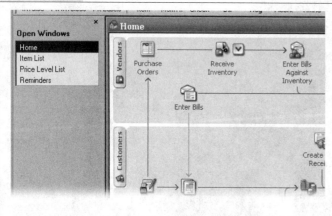

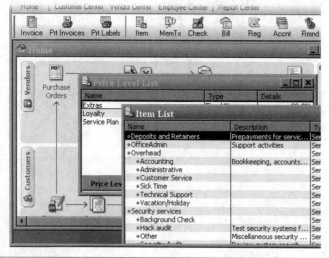

Figure 6-6:

Top: Although you can open multiple windows, they are stacked on top of each other so you see only the top one. When you use the One Window approach, you can switch windows by choosing windows in the Open Window List. If the Open Window List isn't visible, choose View → Open Window List. On the menu bar, you can also choose Window and then choose the name of the window you want to display.

Bottom: The Multiple Windows option displays multiple windows. In this mode, you can also reposition windows by dragging their title bars or resize windows by dragging their edges and corners.

- **Multiple Windows.** If you like to view several windows at a time or want to size windows based on how much information they show, as illustrated in the bottom screen of Figure 6-6, choose the Multiple Windows option. When you choose this option, the Windows menu offers commands such as Cascade and Tile Vertically for arranging windows.

Preferences for Saving the Desktop

On the My Preferences tab, the Desktop section gives you four options that control what QuickBooks does with the windows that are open when you exit the program. For example, if you have your windows arranged just the way you like, you can save your QuickBooks desktop so the windows open in exactly the same arrangement the next time you log in. Here's the lowdown on why you might choose each option:

- **Save when closing company.** If you typically continue your work from one QuickBooks session to the next, this option saves the open windows and their positions when you exit QuickBooks. The next time you log in, QuickBooks opens the same windows and positions them where they were so you can finish entering the remaining 300 checks you have to write.

  Choosing this option adds a small delay to the time it takes QuickBooks to close. If you would rather have QuickBooks live up to its name and close more quickly, choose one of the other desktop options.

- **Save current desktop.** If you have a favorite arrangement of windows that works well for the bulk of your efforts in QuickBooks, you can save that arrangement and display it every time you log in. To do this, first open the windows you want and position them. Then, open the Preferences dialog box, choose this option, and click OK.

  When you choose the "Save current desktop" option, QuickBooks adds the "Keep previously saved desktop" option to the My Preferences tab.

- **Don't save the desktop.** Choosing this option displays a desktop with only the menu bar, the icon bar, and the Shortcuts and Navigator bars. QuickBooks opens faster because it opens no windows, but you're likely to spend the time you save by opening the windows you want.

- **Keep previously saved desktop.** Once you've saved a desktop you like, this option appears on the Desktop View My Preferences tab. Choose this option so that QuickBooks opens with the desktop as it was when you selected "Save current desktop."

- **Show Home page when opening a company file.** The Home page (page 144) in QuickBooks 2006 shows the entire workflow of your accounting tasks, as well as links to oft-opened windows like the Chart of Accounts. Keep this checkbox turned on to see the Home page each time you log in.

Choosing a Color Scheme

The last preference of note on the My Preferences tab is Color Scheme. The standard color scheme that QuickBooks applies is neutral and easy on the eyes. If you're color blind or simply like some color to brighten an otherwise dull financial day, choose one of the other built-in color schemes that QuickBooks offers.

Note: The Desktop View My Preferences tab includes a Windows Settings section at the bottom of the tab. The Display button and the Sounds button take you to the appropriate section of your Windows Control Panel to change the display options or sounds that you use for Windows. If you make display and sound changes by following this path, you might not realize that your changes affect every program on your computer. To avoid confusion, change your Windows options only in the Windows Control Panel.

Setting Up the QuickBooks Home Page

Since QuickBooks automatically displays its new Home page when launched, you probably know that this window lets you access almost any accounting task. As you can see in Figure 6-7, the Home page has three horizontal panels for tasks related to vendors, customers, and employees. The Desktop View Company Preferences tab is where you can customize what you see here.

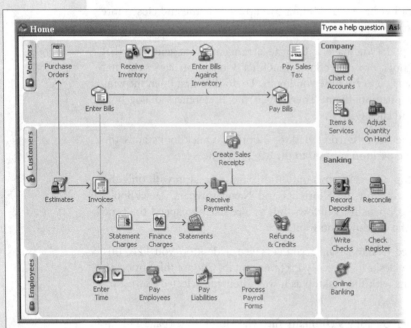

Figure 6-7:
If you click one of the buttons on the left side of the Home page (Vendors, Customers, or Employees), the program opens the corresponding center (page 2). To open a dialog box for an accounting task, click the icon in the workflow. To the right of these panels, you can launch banking activities (like reconciling or depositing money) and open the Chart of Accounts and Items windows.

In the Home page, clicking "Customize Home page and set preferences" takes you exactly where you need to go—the Desktop View Company Preferences tab, as shown in Figure 6-8. Simply turn on the checkboxes on this tab to display the Home page icons for various tasks. To work with the preferences for other features, like Inventory, click their links in the Related Preferences section.

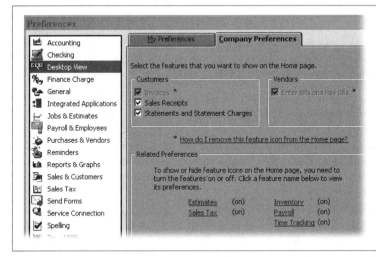

Figure 6-8:
If the checkboxes for invoices or bill payment tasks are dimmed and you want to remove those tasks from the Home page, you must first turn off other preferences. For example, for invoices, you must turn off the Estimate and Sales Orders preferences (in other Preference sections). Click the "How do I remove this feature icon from the Home page?" link to read a Help topic that lists the settings you must change.

Finance Charge

If you're lucky enough to have customers who always pay on time or you run a nonprofit organization that graciously accepts donations, you can bypass this section of preferences. But if you want to add an incentive for customers to pay on time, finance charge preferences determine your level of leniency.

Because you probably don't want each of your employees deciding how to charge customers for late payments, all the preferences in the Finance Charge section appear on the Company Preferences tab. Only someone logged into QuickBooks as an administrator can change these settings. To learn how to add the finance charges configured here to the invoices you create, see page 264.

Tip: If you plan to charge late fees, include the finance charge terms in your contracts. If your customers know about them ahead of time, they are less likely to complain if the added charges aren't a surprise.

Here are the finance charge preferences you can set and what they mean to your customers:

- **Annual Interest Rate** (%). Type the interest rate that you charge per year for overdue payments. For example, if you charge 18 percent per year, type *18* in the Annual Interest Rate box. QuickBooks calculates the finance charge due by prorating the annual interest date to the number of days that the payment is late.

- **Minimum Finance Charge.** If you charge a minimum finance charge no matter how inconsequential the overdue amount, type that minimum value in this box. For example, to charge at least 20 dollars, type *20*.

- **Grace Period (days).** Just like the grace period that you probably enjoy on your mortgage, the grace period in QuickBooks is the number of days that a payment can be late before finance charges kick in. In the "Grace Period (days)" box, type the number of days of grace you are willing to extend to your customers.

- **Finance Charge Account.** Choose the account that you use to track finance charges you collect. Most companies create an income account to track finance charges, which are interest income. For example, create an account following the instructions on page 36. For the account type, choose Other Income.

- **Assess finance charges on overdue finance charges.** If a customer goes AWOL and doesn't pay the bill *or* the finance charges, you can get tough and levy finance charges on the finance charges that the customer already owes. If your customer owes $100 in finance charges, turning on this checkbox would result in an additional $18 a year on the outstanding finance charges alone.

Tip: Most companies find it excessive to tack finance charges on overdue finance charges. Moreover, you should check the lending laws that apply to your location and business. Some laws restrict your ability to charge interest on outstanding interest payments.

- **Calculate charges from.** You can calculate finance charges from two different dates, depending on how painful you want the finance charge penalty to be. Choosing the "due date" option is the more lenient approach. For this option, QuickBooks assesses finance charges only on the days that an invoice is paid past its due date. For example, if the customer pays 10 days after the due date, QuickBooks calculates the finance charges for 10 days. If you want to assess finance charges from the date on an invoice, choose the "invoice/billed date" option. If the customer pays 10 days late on a *Net 30 invoice* (meaning payment is due no more than 30 days after the invoice date), QuickBooks calculates finance charges based on 40 days—the 30 days until the invoice was due and the 10 days that the payment was late.

- **Mark finance charge invoices "To be printed."** If you want QuickBooks to remind you to print invoices with finance charges, turn on this checkbox. Invoices that you haven't printed yet appear as alerts in the Reminders window.

General

You might find it odd that the most common preferences appear in the middle of the preferences list. And it's even stranger that QuickBooks selects the General preferences section the very first time you open the Preferences dialog box. What gives? The answer is simply that preference sections appear in alphabetical order.

Don't bypass the General settings; they can affect whether your QuickBooks sessions breeze by or cause you unending annoyance. Most of the General preferences appear on the My Preferences tab, but a few apply to everyone who logs into QuickBooks.

Tuning QuickBooks to Your Liking

The following settings on the My Preferences tab can help you fine-tune QuickBooks' behavior.

- **Pressing Enter moves between fields.** In the Windows world, pressing the Enter key usually activates the default button in a dialog box, while the Tab key advances the pointer to the next field. If you press Enter in QuickBooks and find that your dialog box closes unexpectedly, this QuickBooks checkbox can provide some relief. When you turn on this checkbox, pressing Enter moves the pointer between fields in a dialog box rather than closing it. However, because Enter no longer closes a dialog box, you must click a button to do so, such as OK, Record, Save & Close, or Save & New (depending on the dialog box). You can also press Ctrl+Enter to close a dialog box.

- **Automatically open drop-down lists when typing.** This preference is new in QuickBooks 2006, and to show it off, the program starts out with it turned on. It makes drop-down menus spring open as soon as you type a letter in a field, as illustrated in Figure 6-9. You can then click the entry you want.

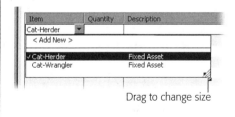

Drag to change size

Figure 6-9:
QuickBooks 2006 has added several enhancements to drop-down lists. First, the drop-down list appears as soon as you begin typing an entry in a field so that you can keep typing or simply click if you prefer. Second, the list narrows down to the choices that match the letters you've typed so far (like showing Cat-Herder and Cat-Wrangler for the letters "cat"). The third improvement is the ability to expand or contract the width of the drop-down list to show as much or as little information as you want.

- **Beep when recording a transaction.** If you like auditory assurance that your software is working along with you, turn on this checkbox to have QuickBooks beep when it records a transaction. If you grow tired of your QuickBooks sessions sounding like an arcade game, simply return to the Preferences dialog box and turn off this checkbox. (Remember, you'll hear beeps only if you haven't muted the audio on your computer.)

- **Automatically place decimal point.** When you turn on this checkbox, QuickBooks automatically places a decimal so that the last two numbers you type represent cents. For example, typing *19995* becomes 199.95 without any action on your part. If you want to enter a whole dollar, type the decimal point at the end of the number. In fact, having QuickBooks place decimal points in numbers for you can be quite addictive once you get used to it, particularly if you haven't graduated to rapid-fire numeric entry on the numeric keypad of your computer—or, if you work on a laptop and haven't realized that your keyboard *has* a numeric keypad.

- **Warn when editing a transaction.** QuickBooks turns on this checkbox by default, which means that the program displays a warning if you edit a transaction and attempt to leave it (for instance, by clicking another transaction) without explicitly recording the change. If you inadvertently modify a check or invoice, this warning gives you a chance to exit without saving the changes.

  If you decide to turn off this feature, QuickBooks automatically records transactions that aren't linked to other transactions. However, if a transaction has links, such as a payment that links to a customer invoice, you must record transactions after you change them regardless of how you've set this preference.

- **Warn when deleting a transaction or unused list item.** QuickBooks turns this checkbox on by default, so you must confirm that you want to delete a transaction, such as a deposit or check, or a list item that has never been used in a transaction.

  Caution is a watchword in the financial world. Although QuickBooks lets you delete transactions, it's a good idea to include this extra step to make sure you're deleting what you *want*. If you turn off this checkbox, you can delete a transaction without confirmation.

Note: Regardless of how this preference is set, QuickBooks won't let you delete a list item if it has been used even once in a transaction. As explained in Chapter 5, QuickBooks includes numerous lists, such as the Vendor List and Customer Type List, which make it easy to fill in fields in transactions by choosing from a list rather than typing in an entry; list items are the entries in these lists. Learn what you must do to delete list items on page 103.

- **Bring back all one-time messages.** One-time messages instruct beginners in the ways of QuickBooks, but for experienced users, these messages are merely annoyances. The only time you might want to turn on this checkbox is if you were overly enthusiastic about hiding one-time messages and find yourself in need of QuickBooks mentoring once more.

- **Turn off pop-up messages for products and services.** Out of the box, QuickBooks displays its own pop-up messages about other products and services it would love to sell to you. Turn this checkbox off to stop the marketing.

- **Automatically recall last transaction for this name.** Do you write similar checks or incur similar credit charges each month? For instance, you might write checks each month from the same account for your Internet access or mobile phone. Those transactions include the same vendor, the same amount, and post to the same account. QuickBooks turns on the "Automatically recall last transaction for this name" checkbox specifically to make these recurring transactions easy. When you type a name in a transaction, QuickBooks fills in the rest of the fields in the transaction with the values you used in the last transaction for that name.

AutoRecall has a couple of limitations you should keep in mind. You can't recall a transaction in one account if the previous transaction was in another account. In addition, you can recall transactions for bills, checks, and credit card charges only. For other transactions, such as purchase orders, invoices, sales receipts, and credit memos, you must fill in all the fields.

Tip: If most of your transactions differ from month to month, you might find this automated data entry more of a hindrance than help. If that is the case, turn off the "Automatically recall last transaction for this name" checkbox. You can still reuse transactions by memorizing them and choosing them from the Memorized Transaction List, described on page 121.

- **Show ToolTips for clipped text.** You'll find that text in many QuickBooks fields is longer than what you can see on the screen. For example, if you see the text "Make sure you always" in a text box, you'll wish there was an easy way to see the rest of the message. This checkbox, which QuickBooks turns on by default, tells QuickBooks to display the entire contents of a field when you position the mouse over it.

- **Default date to use for new transactions.** In this section of the My Preferences tab, choose the "Use today's date as default" option if you want QuickBooks to fill in the date field with the current date for every new transaction you create.

  If you create invoices over the course of several days but you want each invoice to reflect the first day of the month, choose the "Use the last entered date as default" option. In the first invoice you create, type the date you want for all your invoices. For subsequent invoices, QuickBooks fills in the Date field with the date you entered on the previous invoice. When you want to use a new date (after all the invoices are complete), simply type the new date in your next transaction.

- **Keep custom item information when changing item in transactions.** This setting determines how QuickBooks responds when you change an item in a transaction after customizing its description. Say you add an item to an invoice, edit the description in the invoice, and *then* realize that you added the wrong item. When you choose a new item to replace it, if you've selected the Ask option in Preferences, QuickBooks asks you if you want to use the edited description for the new item. The Always option automatically applies the edited description to the new item. With the Never option, QuickBooks creates the new item immediately, using the existing description in the Item record.

Company-Wide General Preferences

The Company Preferences tab includes three preferences, shown in Figure 6-10. Only a QuickBooks administrator can change these settings. Here's what these preferences do:

- **Show portions of an hour as.** You can enter hours in one of two ways—as decimal numbers that represent hours and fractions of an hour, or as hours and minutes separated by a colon, as you can see in Figure 6-10.

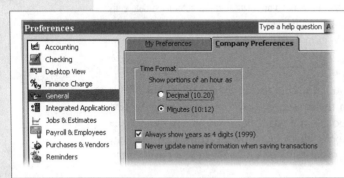

Figure 6-10:
To display hours and minutes as a decimal number, choose the Decimal option. For example, if you type 15:45 in a time field, QuickBooks converts the value to 15.75. To display hours and minutes, choose the Minutes option. For this option, QuickBooks displays an entry of 5.4 as 5:24.

- **Always show years as 4 digits.** Turning on this feature tells QuickBooks to display all four digits of the year whether you type two digits or four. For example, if you type 99, then QuickBooks displays 1999. Turning off this checkbox shows years with two digits.

When you type a two-digit number for a year, QuickBooks translates numbers from 00 through 27 as years 2000 through 2027. Numbers 28 through 99 become 1928 through 1999.

Tip: When you turn off the "Always show years as 4 digits" checkbox, QuickBooks does as it's told and displays only two digits for the year. If a date field shows 28 and you want to see whether that stands for 1928 or 2028, in the date field, click the Calendar icon. The Calendar shows both the month and the full four-digit year.

- **Never update name information when saving transactions.** QuickBooks comes set so that when you change information for a name, such as a customer or vendor, the program asks if you want to replicate that change back in the original record—on the Customer:Job List or Vendor List. Possibly the only time you might want to change this behavior (which you can do by turning on this checkbox) is if you use generic names, such as donor or member. If you receive donations and your donors want receipts with their name and address filled in, you don't want the names and addresses you enter on sales receipts to alter your generic donor record.

Jobs & Estimates

If you create estimates or document job progress in QuickBooks, head to the Jobs & Estimates preferences section to set up your progress terminology and estimating features. QuickBooks forces nonprofits to think in terms of customers, but it does allow you to choose the terminology you prefer for progress on a job. For example, if you're a professional gigolo, your terminology for a woman you didn't win over might be "TooSmart," and you can instruct QuickBooks to display that term in the Job Status field.

QuickBooks includes five fields for job status: Pending, Awarded, In progress, Closed, and Not awarded. You might wonder why Intuit bothered to name these fields as they did because the status terms do nothing more than appear in Job Status fields and columns (see the box on page 69 to learn more). Despite QuickBooks' field names, you can type any term you want for status in any of the five boxes. Type *Waiting* in the Pending box, *Whoopie!* in the Awarded box, and *Finally* in the Closed box. When you edit a job and display the Job Status drop-down list, you can choose from these terms.

The rest of the preferences on the Company Preferences tab relate to estimates and progress invoicing. Choose any or all of the following preferences:

- **Do You Create Estimates?** This question is simple but, unfortunately, misleading. If you create estimates in a program other than QuickBooks, you still choose the No option. Only choose the Yes option if you want to create estimates in QuickBooks, which is described on page 216. Selecting Yes adds an Estimates icon to the Home page.

- **Do You Do Progress Invoicing?** Also known as partial billing, progress invoicing means that you invoice your customer for work as you go instead of billing for the entire job at the end. For example, if you're building a shopping mall, you don't want to carry the costs of construction until shoppers are walking in the front door. You want to charge your customer as you meet milestones. To simplify creating invoices for portions of your estimates, choose the Yes option. Then, you can invoice for part of an estimate and show how much you billed previously, described in more detail on page 219.

  If you choose the No option, you can create progress invoices based on your entire estimate. After you bring the entire estimate into your invoice, remove entries until the invoice includes only what you want to bill. The flaw in this approach is that you can't show previous totals billed or compare the amount billed and remaining to your estimate.

- **Warn about duplicate estimate numbers.** Turn on this checkbox if you want QuickBooks to warn you that you are creating an estimate with the same number as one you already entered. You can change preferences any time you want, so turn this checkbox on to start. If you notice an unreasonable delay when you record your estimates while QuickBooks searches for duplicates, you can open the Preferences dialog box and turn this checkbox off.

• **Don't print items that have zero amount.** When you produce progress invoices, you might not charge for every estimated item on every progress invoice. To keep your progress invoices tidy, suppress the items that you're not charging for by turning on this checkbox.

Payroll & Employees

Perhaps the most infuriating characteristic of employees is their insistence on being paid. Sad to say, using QuickBooks for payroll doesn't eliminate the need to transfer money from your company into your employees' pockets, but it can simplify the task. For almost every company, you'll choose one of the payroll service options. The Payroll & Employees preference section is command central for configuring your payroll service and how it operates. Payroll and employee preferences appear on the Company Preferences tab, so only QuickBooks administrators can set these preferences.

On the Company Preferences tab, the QuickBooks Payroll Features area contains three options for choosing a payroll service: Full Payroll, No Payroll, and Complete Payroll Customers. Because the option labels don't tell the entire story, this list helps you determine which one you should choose:

• **Full Payroll.** If you want to produce payroll documents such as paychecks; payroll reports; and payroll forms, including 940 (employer federal unemployment tax), 941 (employer quarterly federal taxes), W-2 (employee wage and tax statement), and W-3 (transmittal of W-2s), choose this option. Full Payroll is the option you want if you plan to calculate payroll yourself and use QuickBooks features to produce the documents—or, if you use QuickBooks Standard Payroll (previously known as Do-It-Yourself Payroll), Enhanced Payroll, or QuickBooks Assisted Payroll to figure out payroll amounts.

If you want to allocate wages and payroll taxes to jobs, choose the Full Payroll option, even if you use an outside payroll service (see page 316 for details).

Tip: If you would rather have someone else handle the brain damage of government payroll requirements, choose Employees → Add Payroll Service → Learn About Payroll Options. The Payroll Services window opens with links to learn more or sign up for services.

• **No Payroll.** Only two situations warrant choosing the No Payroll option: you do not run payroll in any way, or you use a third-party payroll service and don't want to assign payroll amounts to job costs. For example, if you are a sole proprietor and pay yourself by taking owner's draws, this is the right option. Likewise, if you use an outside payroll service, such as Paychex or ADP, and have no need to print payroll documents or assign payroll costs to jobs, choose this option. With this option selected, QuickBooks suppresses the appearance of payroll-related commands on the Employees menu and in the Employee Center.

Tip: Even if your third-party payroll service performs your payroll calculations; produces payroll checks, reports, and government filings; and transfers money for payroll and payroll liabilities; you need Quick-Books payroll features to assign payroll and payroll taxes to jobs.

If you have transactions from prior payrolls and switch to using an outside payroll service, the past payroll data remains in your QuickBooks file.

- **Complete Payroll Customers.** If you use Intuit Complete Payroll, a full-blown outsourced payroll service, described on page 317, choose this option. When you use Intuit Complete Payroll, you transmit your payroll data from Quick-Books to the payroll service and then import the processed payroll transactions from the service into QuickBooks.

The Payroll & Employees preference section offers plenty of additional preferences, which are intimately linked to payroll and described in detail in Chapter 11. For example, you can specify the deductions and payroll items that affect every employee, or you can control the fields that appear on paychecks and paycheck stubs. Whether you run payroll or not, here's the lowdown on the remaining employee preferences that don't relate to payroll:

- **Display Employee List by.** When your company employs only a few people, you can choose the First Name option so that QuickBooks sorts the Employee List by first names. However, if you employ hundreds of employees or you want practice remembering your employees' last names, choose the Last Name option. Regardless of which option you choose, QuickBooks prints paychecks with employee names with the first name first and last name last.

- **Mark new employees as sales reps.** If only a few of your employees act as customer contacts and receive commissions, you can reserve the Sales Rep List for them by turning off this checkbox and adding names to the Sales Rep List manually (page 116). On the other hand, if you consider every employee a potential sales rep, you can turn on this checkbox so that QuickBooks automatically adds every employee you create to the Sales Rep list, saving you a five-step process each time.

- **Display employee Social Security numbers in headers on reports.** QuickBooks automatically turns off this checkbox, which is preferable if you want to protect your employees' financial privacy.

- **Print Employee List one per page.** QuickBooks starts out with this checkbox turned on, so it prints each employee's payroll information on a separate page. This setup is ideal when you want to keep each employee's payroll information with the rest of your paper records for that person. Turn it off to print the Employee List as compactly as possible.

Purchases & Vendors

To turn inventory on and off or to control QuickBooks' billing behavior, click the Purchases & Vendors icon. The Purchases & Vendors preferences all appear on the Company Preferences tab and are changeable only by QuickBooks administrators. Although the preferences are relatively straightforward, here's a guide to why you might want to use each one:

- **Inventory and purchase orders are active.** If you want to track inventory using QuickBooks, turn on this checkbox. After doing so, you can perform inventory related tasks, such as creating inventory part items, producing purchase orders, and generating inventory reports. Turning this checkbox on adds icons, such as Purchase Orders and Receive Inventory to the Home page.

- **Warn about duplicate purchase order numbers.** Turn on this checkbox if you want QuickBooks to warn you when you are creating a purchase order with the same number as one you already entered.

- **Warn if not enough inventory quantity on hand (QOH) to sell.** If you prepare an invoice to sell more doodads than you have in stock, QuickBooks warns you—if this checkbox is turned on. Suppose you sell 500 quarts of sesame soy swirl frozen yogurt, but you have only 400 quarts in stock. When you attempt to save the invoice for the 500-quart order, QuickBooks displays a warning message box informing you of your shortage. QuickBooks doesn't go any further than that. You can save the invoice but it's up to you to order more inventory.

- **Bills are due _ _ days after receipt.** The first time you access Purchases & Vendors preferences, you'll find that QuickBooks has set this preference so that bills you enter show a due date 10 days after the date of the bill. For instance, if you receive a bill dated June 15, and in the Enter Bills dialog box you fill in the Date field as such, QuickBooks automatically changes the Bill Due field to June 25. This value is fine in most cases. If a few of your bills are due in a different number of days, you can change the date in the Bill Due field on only those bills.

- **Warn about duplicate bill numbers from same vendor.** Surely, you don't want to pay the same bill twice, so be sure to turn on this checkbox so QuickBooks warns you that you are entering a bill with the same number as one you already entered from the same vendor.

- **Paying Bills.** If you want QuickBooks to automatically apply to your bills any credits and discounts to which you're entitled, turn on the "Automatically use discounts and credits" checkbox. For example, if you typically receive a 15 percent discount on all purchases and also have a $100 credit, QuickBooks applies these adjustments to your bill before calculating the total. When you turn on this checkbox, choose the account to which you want to post the discounts you take. For example, if you use an expense account specifically for vendor discounts, choose that account.

Tip: Set up the discounts that vendors extend to you in vendor records, as described on page 110.

Reminders

QuickBooks reminds you when to perform many of your accounting and business tasks, so you can save your brain cells for remembering more important things—like your employees' names. Even with a brain the size of a planet, you're likely to rely on QuickBooks reminders to nudge you when it's time to print checks or reorder inventory. And when you turn on reminders for To Do Notes, the program can give you hints about any task that you don't want to forget for a customer, vendor, or employee.

POWER USERS' CLINIC

Service Connection Preferences

If your company uses QuickBooks Business Services, such as online banking, QuickBooks administrators can control how people log into those services. The easiest way to learn about or sign up for these services is to choose Help → Add QuickBooks Services and then click the link for the service you want. Each person who uses QuickBooks Business Services can control the behavior of online sessions. Security is a company-wide issue, so the options for whether to prompt for a password appear on the Company Preferences tab. Here are the service connection preferences that administrators can set and when you might want to use them:

- **Automatically connect without asking for a password.** Choosing this option automatically logs people into the QuickBooks Business Services network without a login name or password. This option is appropriate if you are the only person who accesses the network or you aren't concerned about security.

- **Always ask for a password before connecting.** Choose this option if you want everyone to provide a login name and password each time they access QuickBooks Business Services. Choose this option if several people access QuickBooks Business Services or different people have different privileges with the services you use.

- **Allow background downloading of service messages.** If you want QuickBooks to check for messages and updates when your Internet connection isn't tied up with other work, turn on this checkbox.

QuickBooks checks the Intuit web site periodically and downloads QuickBooks updates or messages. If you turn off this checkbox, you can check for updates at a convenient time by choosing Help → Update QuickBooks.

If you aren't a QuickBooks administrator, you can still make some choices about your connection to QuickBooks Business Services:

- **Give me the option of saving a file whenever I download Web Connect data.** Suppose you download transactions from your bank or another financial institution (page 513), but it's the end of the day and you want to process them later. If you want QuickBooks to ask you whether you want to process downloaded transactions immediately or save them to a file, turn on this checkbox. If you turn this checkbox off, QuickBooks automatically and immediately processes downloaded transactions.

- **If QuickBooks is run by my browser, don't close it after Web Connect is done.** You can launch QuickBooks by downloading Web Connect data or by double-clicking a QuickBooks file that contains Web Connect data that you downloaded previously. When you open QuickBooks in this manner, you often want to continue working in QuickBooks after you process the downloaded transactions. To keep QuickBooks open after processing transactions, turn on this checkbox.

Reminders on the My Preferences Tab

In the Reminders preference section of the My Preferences tab, you'll find only one preference, but it can render all the settings on the Company Preferences tab useless. If your short-term memory is mere nanoseconds, turn on the "Show Reminders List when opening a Company file" checkbox. That way, QuickBooks opens the Reminders List window whenever you open your company file, and it stays open unless you close it.

Reminders for Everyone

The Company Preferences tab contains 13 different types of reminders, which are available only if you have enabled the corresponding QuickBooks feature. For example, if you don't use QuickBooks' inventory, the "Inventory to Reorder" reminder is dimmed. As shown in Figure 6-11, you can specify the level of detail for each type of reminder and when you want QuickBooks to remind you.

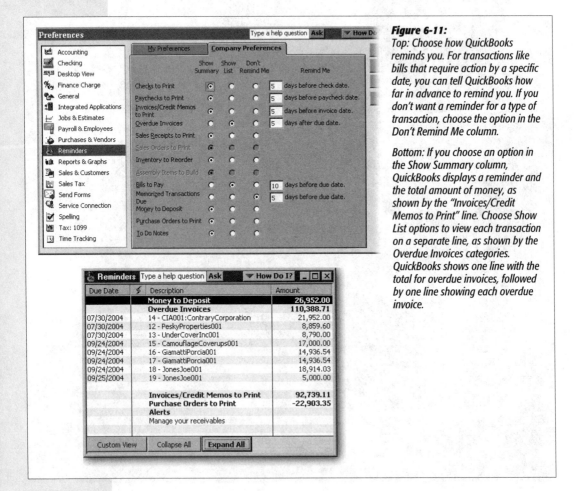

Figure 6-11:
Top: Choose how QuickBooks reminds you. For transactions like bills that require action by a specific date, you can tell QuickBooks how far in advance to remind you. If you don't want a reminder for a type of transaction, choose the option in the Don't Remind Me column.

Bottom: If you choose an option in the Show Summary column, QuickBooks displays a reminder and the total amount of money, as shown by the "Invoices/Credit Memos to Print" line. Choose Show List options to view each transaction on a separate line, as shown by the Overdue Invoices categories. QuickBooks shows one line with the total for overdue invoices, followed by one line showing each overdue invoice.

QuickBooks can generate reminders for the following transactions:

- **Checks to Print.** As described on page 305, you can queue up checks to print in the Write Checks dialog box by turning on the To Be Printed checkbox for each check you create. This reminder tells you that you have checks queued up to print. You can also specify how many days notice you want before the date you entered to print the checks.

- **Paychecks to Print.** This reminder tells you that paychecks generated when you ran payroll are waiting to print. You can specify how many days notice you want before the payroll date you entered.

- **Invoices/Credit Memos to Print.** If you want to print invoices or credit memos in batches, as described on page 194, in the Create Invoices dialog box, turn on the To Be Printed checkbox. Then, to receive a reminder of unprinted invoices or credit memos, select the Show Summary or Show List option in the "Invoices/Credit Memos to Print" row. You can specify how many days notice you want before the invoice or credit memo date you entered.

- **Overdue Invoices.** This reminder warns you about invoices that have passed their due date with no payment from the customer. You can specify how many days an invoice is late before QuickBooks reminds you.

- **Sales Receipts to Print.** If you queued up sales receipts to print as a batch (page 238), this is the reminder about printing them. QuickBooks reminds you as soon as you have any sales receipts to print.

- **Sales Orders to Print.** This preference is available only if you use QuickBooks Premier or Enterprise, and it reminds you to print sales orders you queued up.

- **Inventory to Reorder.** When you create inventory part items in QuickBooks, you can set a reminder for when you need to reorder inventory. This reminder warns you when a sales form you create reduces the number of items on hand below your reorder point. The program generates a reminder immediately.

- **Assembly Items to Build.** This preference is available only if you use Quick-Books Premier or Enterprise. It warns you when the quantity of assembled items drops below your build point (page 97).

- **Bills to Pay.** This reminder nudges you about the bills you have to pay. Creating bills is described on page 276. You can specify how many days notice you want before the date the bills are due.

- **Memorized Transactions Due.** When you memorize transactions, you can specify a date for the next occurrence, as described on page 121. This reminder tells you about recurring memorized transactions. You can specify how many days notice you want before the date for the next occurrence.

- **Money to Deposit.** When you receive payments, you can group them with other undeposited funds (page 261), so you aren't running to the bank every five minutes as checks pour in. If you want to put your money to work as soon as possible, turn on this checkbox to receive a reminder as soon as you have any funds to deposit.

- **Purchase Orders to Print.** This reminder gives you a prod about purchase orders you haven't yet printed.

- **To Do Notes.** To-do items that you associate with customers can include dates, as described on page 69. This reminder shows you when to-do items are due.

Reports and Graphs

QuickBooks administrators can modify settings for reports and graphs that apply to every report and graph the company produces. Each person who logs into QuickBooks can specify a few preferences for the reports and graphs she generates.

Preferences for the Reports You Generate

Here's a guide to the personal preferences shown in Figure 6-12 and the effect they have on performance:

- **Prompt me to modify report options before opening a report.** The reports you want usually require small tweaks—a different date range perhaps—so turning on this checkbox works for most people. QuickBooks automatically opens the Modify Report window when you generate a report. You can make any change you want to the report and click Refresh to view the results. If you turn off this checkbox and want to modify a report, on the report's button bar, click Modify Report.

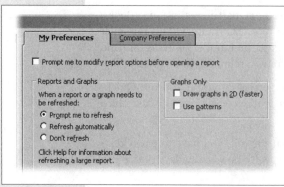

Figure 6-12:
Keeping reports up-to-date with the information in your company's QuickBooks file can be time-consuming. To accommodate the inclinations of each person who logs into QuickBooks, the preferences on the My Preferences tab control how QuickBooks updates reports and graphs.

- **Prompt me to refresh.** If your QuickBooks file changes frequently and you don't want to wait while QuickBooks incessantly refreshes every report you have open, choose this option. If you want a reminder when you have changed data that affects the reports you have generated, this is the best option to choose. QuickBooks prompts you to refresh whenever the data in your QuickBooks file has changed and rendered a report or graph inaccurate. For example, suppose you generated a Profit & Loss report and then created a new invoice for a customer. QuickBooks would prompt you to refresh your report. Refreshing your report requires a small amount of time, so you can choose whether you want to refresh or not. When you're ready to refresh your report or graph, in the Report window, simply click the Refresh button.

- **Refresh automatically.** This option can be slow and disruptive to your work, particularly if numerous people are frantically changing data in the company file, as is often true as year-end approaches. However, if it's critical that your reports and graphs are always accurate, choose this option so QuickBooks automatically refreshes reports and graphs whenever the underlying data changes.

- **Don't refresh.** If you find yourself distracted by refreshes or even prompts about refreshing, choose this option. QuickBooks won't refresh your reports and graphs or remind you—no matter how significant the changes to the underlying data. When you have finished your report and graph customizations, click the Refresh button to generate the report with the current data.

- **Draw graphs in 2D.** If you care about time more than fancy graphics, turn on this checkbox. QuickBooks displays graphs in two dimensions, which is faster than drawing the 3D graphs that appear if you turn off the checkbox.

- **Use patterns.** When you turn on this checkbox, QuickBooks uses black and white patterns instead of colors to differentiate areas on graphs. If you turn off this checkbox, QuickBooks displays colors on color monitors or shades of gray on black-and-white monitors.

Preferences That Apply to Every Company Report

The Company Preferences tab contains several preferences for the reports and graphs you generate for your company. If you are a QuickBooks administrator, use the following preferences to format reports and graphs:

- **Summary Reports Basis.** Nothing starts adrenaline flowing like financial reports that aren't what you expect, particularly when the IRS auditors are on their way over. If you use cash or accrual accounting, be sure to choose the corresponding Cash or Accrual option so that the reports you generate reflect your financial performance accurately. If you choose Cash, your reports show income when you receive payments for income and show expenses when you pay for them. If you choose Accrual, your reports show income as soon as you record an invoice or enter a sale regardless of whether you received payment. Expenses appear as soon as you enter a bill.

Note: In most cases, when your accountant recommends cash or accrual, you choose the appropriate option, and you can forget about it. If you upgrade or reinstall QuickBooks, make sure that QuickBooks didn't reset the Summary Reports Basis choice.

- **Aging Reports.** You can control how QuickBooks calculates age for invoices, statements, and bills. If you choose the "Age from due date" option, Quick-Books shows the number of days between the due date and the current date. If you choose "Age from transaction date," QuickBooks shows the number of overdue days from the date of the transaction to the current date. For example, consider an invoice dated September 1 with a due date of October 1. On October 10, the "Age from due date" option shows the invoice age as 10 days. The "Age from transaction date" option shows the invoice age as 40 days.

- **Reports – Show Accounts by.** Reports typically show accounts by name. If you use especially short account names, you can use the account description in reports. You can also show both names and descriptions.

- **Statement of Cash Flows.** Although QuickBooks does a great job of associating your accounts with the Operating, Investing, and Financing sections of the Statement of Cash Flows report, some companies are bound to require a customized cash flow report. If you're lucky enough to need a customized cash flow statement, click Classify Cash button to open the Classify Cash dialog box. See page 389 to learn how to generate and customize a cash flow statement for your company.

- **Format.** Click Format to set up standards for all of your reports. For example, you can choose the information that you want to appear in headers and footers, and whether they are aligned to the left, right, or center of the page.

Sales & Customers

With the Sales & Customers preferences section, shown in Figure 6-13, you can control how QuickBooks handles the sales you make to your customers, whether it be the shipping method you choose, tracking reimbursed expenses as income, or simply finding out that you've created a duplicate invoice number.

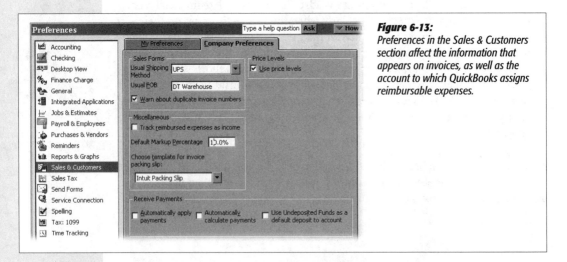

Figure 6-13:
Preferences in the Sales & Customers section affect the information that appears on invoices, as well as the account to which QuickBooks assigns reimbursable expenses.

Here's a guide to the Sales & Customers preferences, all of which only QuickBooks administrators can change:

- **Usual Shipping Method.** If you negotiate a sweet deal with a shipping company and use it whenever possible, choose that company in the Usual Shipping Method drop-down list. When you do so, QuickBooks fills in sales form Ship Via fields with this shipping method. If the method you want to use isn't on the list, choose *<Add New>* to open the New Shipping Method dialog box.

- **Usual FOB.** FOB stands for Free on Board and represents the location at which the customer becomes responsible for the products you ship. For example, suppose you ship products from your warehouse in Severance, CO and you use Severance as your FOB location. As soon as your shipments leave Severance, the customer becomes the official owner of the products and is responsible for them should they be lost, damaged, or stolen in transit. Type a brief description of your FOB location in this box. QuickBooks fills in the FOB field on invoices and other sales forms with this information.

Tip: To keep you on your toes, the Intuit developers used a standard size for the Usual FOB text box, but you can type no more than 13 characters in the box.

- **Warn about duplicate invoice numbers.** Turn on this checkbox if you want QuickBooks to warn you when you create an invoice with the same number as one you already entered.

- **Track reimbursed expenses as income.** Companies differ in their approach to reimbursed expenses, as explained on page 291. Some companies assign reimbursed expenses as income and then deduct the expenses as costs. The method chosen doesn't affect the profit you earn—the reason for tracking reimbursable expenses as income is to charge sales tax on those expenses. If you want to post reimbursed expenses to an income account, turn on this checkbox.

- **Default Markup Percentage.** Suppose you are an interior decorator and you mark up the furniture and bric-a-brac you sell by a standard percentage. When you specify your markup percentage in this text box and create new items, QuickBooks calculates the item sales price based on the item's cost (see page 90 for detailed instructions on creating items). For example, if you create an inventory part for a black leather sofa and enter its cost as $10,000, a 20 percent markup percentage results in a sales price of $12,000.

When you charge a different markup on a few of the things you sell, simply modify the sales price that QuickBooks calculates.

- **Choose template for invoice packing slip.** If you ship products to customers, you can print a packing slip with QuickBooks to include in your shipments. When you create an invoice, on the Print menu, choose Print Packing Slip. To specify the packing slip you want to use, in the drop-down list, choose the form you want to use as a packing slip. QuickBooks selects its predefined packing slip, Intuit Packing Slip, when you first access these preferences. If you insist on your own style of packing slip, you can create your own template by following the instructions on page 550.

- **Use price levels.** You can set up multiple discount levels on the items you create by setting price levels. Refer to pages 58 and 115 to learn how to define and apply price levels. To turn on the price level feature, turn on this checkbox.

- **Round all sales prices up to the next whole dollar for fixed % price levels.** In QuickBooks Premier and Enterprise, you can ensure that your sales prices calculated with price levels are whole dollars by turning on this checkbox. When you do so, QuickBooks rounds any sales prices—even one penny more than a whole dollar—to the next whole dollar.

- **Automatically apply payments.** You're better off keeping this checkbox turned off, which means you have to manually match payments you receive to the corresponding customer invoices. When you turn this checkbox on, QuickBooks applies customer payments to invoices for you. If a payment doesn't match any of the invoice amounts, QuickBooks applies the payment to the oldest invoices first, which could mask the fact that a payment wasn't received or that a customer's check was for the wrong amount.

- **Automatically calculate payments.** The "Automatically calculate payments" checkbox is another preference that's better kept turned off. When you receive a payment from a customer, in the Receive Payments window, in the Amount box, you typically type the amount that the customer sent. Then, as you choose the invoices to apply the payment to, you can see if the payment balances the amount the customer owes. If the customer underpaid, QuickBooks asks you if you want to keep the underpayment or write off the amount that the customer did not pay. If you turn on this checkbox, QuickBooks calculates the payment for you as you choose invoices, so discrepancies aren't easily apparent.

- **Use Undeposited Funds as a default deposit to account.** If you typically collect a few payments before heading to the bank to deposit them, turn on this checkbox so that QuickBooks automatically adds payments you receive to the Undeposited Funds account. When you turn on this checkbox, QuickBooks doesn't show the "Deposit to" box in the Receive Payments window, so you have no choice but to deposit payments to Undeposited Funds. If you want a choice about whether to deposit payments right away, keep this checkbox turned off. Then, in the Receive Payments window, in the Deposit To field, you can choose a bank account to deposit funds immediately, or you can choose Undeposited Funds to collect several payments before you make a deposit.

Sales Tax

Charging sales tax can be a complicated business, as the number of preferences on the Sales Tax Company Preferences tab indicates. If you don't charge sales tax, in the Do You Charge Sales Tax? area, simply choose the No option and move on to more important endeavors. If you do charge sales tax, you'll learn how to use the rest of the preferences as you set up sales tax items (page 84), charge sales tax on your sales (page 202), and pay sales tax to the appropriate authorities (page 309).

Send Forms

As you'll learn throughout this book, you can include a cover note when you send invoices, purchase orders, and other business forms via email, as illustrated in Figure 6-14. For example, if you email a purchase order, you can include details about the delivery in the note. Or, you can include a cover note along with an invoice to add some personal interaction with your customer.

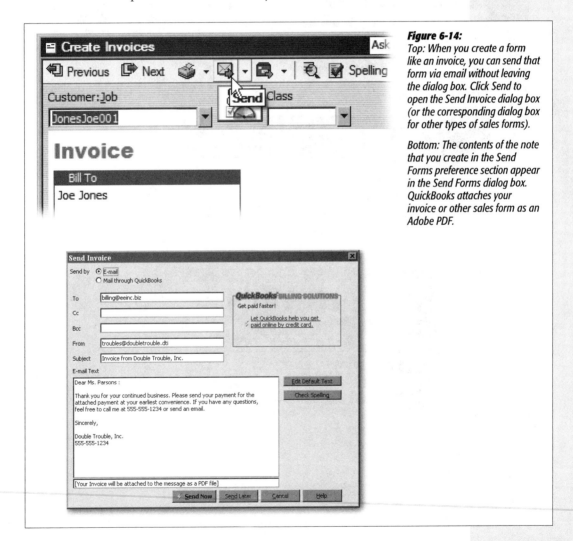

Figure 6-14:
Top: When you create a form like an invoice, you can send that form via email without leaving the dialog box. Click Send to open the Send Invoice dialog box (or the corresponding dialog box for other types of sales forms).

Bottom: The contents of the note that you create in the Send Forms preference section appear in the Send Forms dialog box. QuickBooks attaches your invoice or other sales form as an Adobe PDF.

QuickBooks includes standard messages for each type of form you send via email. These messages, illustrated in Figure 6-15, won't win any awards for creativity, but QuickBooks administrators can change the standard messages. With Send Forms preferences, shown in the bottom screen of Figure 6-15, you can create standard notes for invoices, estimates, statements, sales orders, sales receipts, credit memos, purchase orders, and reports.

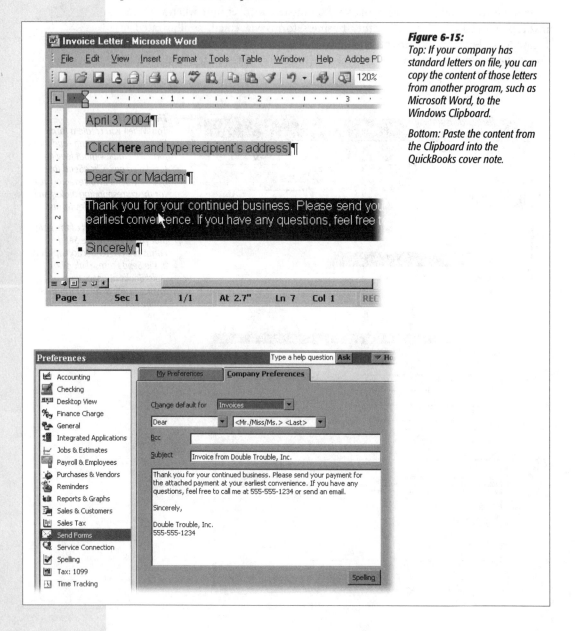

Figure 6-15:
Top: If your company has standard letters on file, you can copy the content of those letters from another program, such as Microsoft Word, to the Windows Clipboard.

Bottom: Paste the content from the Clipboard into the QuickBooks cover note.

To configure a standard note for a particular type of business form, follow these steps:

1. **To modify the note that accompanies a particular type of form, in the "Change default for" drop-down list, choose the form that you want to customize.**

   For example, if you want to set up a cover letter to go with your invoices, choose Invoice in the list.

2. **To specify the salutation you want, choose one from the drop-down list.**

   Your choices include "Dear" and the impersonal "To."

3. **To specify the format for the recipient's name, choose it from the format drop-down list.**

   Depending on how formal or chummy you like to be, you can choose to display the person's first name only, the first and last name, or a title and last name. For example, if you choose *<First>*, your note begins with something like To Dana or Dear Dana. For more formal notes, choose *<Mr./Miss/Ms.> <Last>* to begin with Dear Ms. Dvorak.

4. **Edit the content of the note using typical editing techniques.**

   For instance, double-click a word to select the entire word. Click in the text to position the pointer where you want to add text. Drag the pointer to select text you want to replace.

5. **To save the changes to your notes and close the Preferences dialog box, click OK.**

   If you make changes to notes and click another preference icon, QuickBooks displays a Save Changes dialog box. To save the changes you made, click Yes. When you email an invoice or other form, QuickBooks opens the Send Invoice dialog box (or the dialog box corresponding to the business form you're sending) with your note filled in, as described on page 243.

Spelling

The Spell Checker in QuickBooks isn't the all-knowing, willing-to-learn assistant that you might encounter in other programs, but it helps you find common misspellings in most text fields, as described on page 195. Spell checking is a personal preference. Each person who logs into QuickBooks can choose whether to use spell checking by turning on or off the "Always check spelling before printing, saving, or sending supported forms" checkbox.

If you turn on spell checking, you can also choose words that you want the Spell Checker to ignore. For example, you can ignore Internet addresses, words that contain numbers, words beginning with a capital letter, all uppercase words, and words with a mixture of upper- and lowercase letters.

Tax: 1099

The Company Preferences tab in the Tax: 1099 preference section begins with the most important 1099 question: "Do you file 1099-MISC forms?" If you don't use 1099 vendors, such as self-employed subcontractors, or you delegate 1099 generation to your accountant, simply choose the No option and ignore the rest of the preferences in this section. If you do file 1099-MISC forms, you can specify the accounts you use to track 1099 vendor payments and the minimum amount you must report to the IRS. To learn how to generate 1099s and set the preferences that control them, refer to page 403.

Time Tracking

The time tracking preferences are refreshingly few in number. Available only on the Company Preferences tab, preferences include the options to turn time tracking on and off and a drop-down list to set the first day of the work week that appears if you use weekly timesheets in QuickBooks (see page 427).

Managing QuickBooks Files

When company books were paper ledgers, you had to be careful not to tear the pages, and a spilled drink spelled misfortune. Today, electronic books require their own sort of care and feeding. Protecting your QuickBooks files is essential, not only because your books tell the financial story of your company, but because the computer environment is notorious for chewing up data in all sorts of ways.

QuickBooks files have a few advantages over their paper-based relatives. Most importantly, you can make copies of your company files for safekeeping. (Quick-Books can also create a *special* copy of your company file so you and your accountant can both work on your company file at the end of the year; see page 399.) QuickBooks files have a few other features that you *might* consider advantages, but you'll use them so infrequently that they hardly count. This chapter focuses on backing up your QuickBooks files, but it also explains why and how to verify, condense, and delete your files.

Tip: If you aren't totally at ease working with files in your computer operating system, *Windows XP Pro: The Missing Manual* will make you an expert in no time.

Where to Store Your Company Files

Left to its own devices, QuickBooks saves your company files in the same folder as the program's software files (on a PC, usually *C:\Program Files\Intuit\QuickBooks <edition>* depending on your edition—Pro, Premier, or Enterprise). But intermingling your data files with software files is asking for trouble. First, when you store data files in the software folder, you could delete or rename a software file by accident and have to reinstall QuickBooks. Second, scattering data files around your folders makes it hard to herd them all together for backups. QuickBooks doesn't care where you store your company files, so you might as well keep them with the rest of your data.

If you use Windows XP, you're probably familiar with the My Documents folder, which happens to be an ideal place to store your company files. When you store your data within the My Documents folder structure, your backup procedure has to process only one target: the My Documents folder (and all its subfolders).

For many companies, creating a folder for QuickBooks files makes a lot of sense. In addition to company files, you'll probably create backup files, message templates, files that you export from QuickBooks, and files for importing data into your company file. With a QuickBooks folder as a container, you can create subfolders for each type of file, as demonstrated in Figure 7-1.

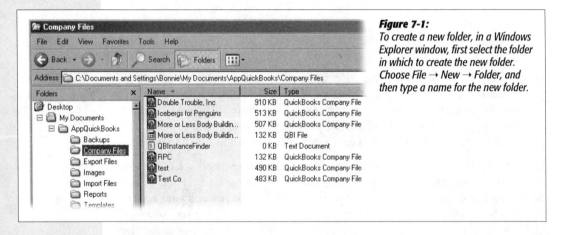

Figure 7-1:
To create a new folder, in a Windows Explorer window, first select the folder in which to create the new folder. Choose File → New → Folder, and then type a name for the new folder.

Backing Up Files

If you already have a backup procedure for *all* your company data, the QuickBooks Backup command might seem as useful as your appendix. Your company-wide backups regularly squirrel your data files away in a safe place, ready to rescue you should disaster strike.

Note: What you back up and how often are up to you (or your company's system administrators). But the decision hinges on the information you can't afford to lose and how much data you're willing to recreate in case of a disaster.

Still, the QuickBooks Backup command is worth learning. For example, before you experiment with a new QuickBooks feature, you don't want to back up *all* your data—just the company file. If the experiment goes terribly wrong, you can restore your backup and try a different approach. You can also call on the QuickBooks

Backup command when you've worked hard on your company file, for instance entering hundreds of inventory items in one sweaty session, and the thought of losing that work makes you queasy. In both of these situations, running a Quick-Books *manual backup* creates a backup file immediately.

Tip: QuickBooks backup files aren't merely copies of your company files. They are compressed files that take up less space, which is helpful whether you back up to floppy disks, CDs, another hard drive, or an online location.

If you have trouble remembering to back up your work, QuickBooks' automatic backups are just what you need. You can set it up to automatically back up your company file after you've opened it a certain number of times. If you mangle that data or it becomes corrupt in some way, you can use one of these backups to recover. If QuickBooks is the only program on your computer—so your company file is the only data that you want to back up—the program can run company file backups automatically according to the schedule you specify. For example, Quick-Books can automatically back up your company file Tuesdays through Saturdays at 2:00 AM.

Tip: If you have other data on your computer, such as customer correspondence or your email file, QuickBooks scheduled backups won't protect those files. You'll have to back up those files using your operating system or third-party backup program.

Whether you want to set up a schedule for backups or run a backup immediately, open the QuickBooks Backup dialog box using any of the following methods:

- On the icon bar, click Backup.

- Choose File → Backup.

Note: You must run QuickBooks in single-user mode to open the Backup dialog box, whether you want to create a manual backup or set up a schedule of backups. Furthermore, once you've scheduled a backup, no users must be working in the company file when the backup takes place.

Manual Backups

If you just spent four hours of tedious typing to create a dozen new customers in QuickBooks, you definitely want to save that work. To run a backup right away, here's what you have to do:

1. **If the QuickBooks Backup dialog box isn't open, on the icon bar, click Backup.**

   The QuickBooks Backup dialog box opens with the Backup Company File tab displayed, as shown in Figure 7-2. So you know which file QuickBooks will back up, the Current Company section displays the name of the company file that's open and shows the full path to the folder that contains the file.

2. **If you want to back up your company file to a hard drive or removable media, select the Disk option.**

QuickBooks automatically fills in the Filename box with the same file name prefix as your company file, but with the extension .qbb (for QuickBooks backup). To make the file name more meaningful, include "backup" in the file name prefix or append the date you made the backup. The file name in Figure 7-2 ends with "051026" to indicate that the backup date was October 26, 2005.

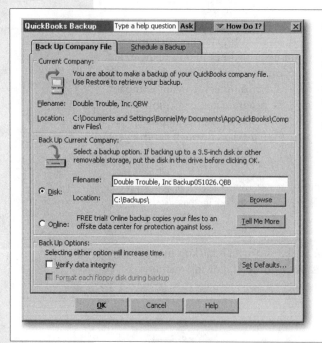

Figure 7-2:
The first time you back up a company file, QuickBooks automatically sets the backup location to the folder that contains the QuickBooks software. As described on page 167, it's wise to choose a different location, such as removable media or a folder dedicated to data. Once you choose a location, QuickBooks uses it for every subsequent backup of that file.

To change the location for the backup for *this* company file, click Browse. In the "Back Up Company to" dialog box, navigate to the hard drive, folder, or removable media you want to use, and then click Save.

Tip: Saving a backup file to the same hard drive that contains your company file won't help if your hard disk crashes. To protect your data from human error *and* hardware failure, back up your file to a *different hard drive* or to removable media, such as a CD. When a company-wide backup transfers data to removable media every night, backing up your company file to a hard drive is fine for protection during the day.

---

3. **To make sure your company file isn't corrupt (for example, to confirm that it conforms to the structure that QuickBooks requires), turn on the "Verify data integrity" checkbox.**

Verifying data integrity increases the time it takes to back up your file. To keep your backup procedures short and sweet, turn off this checkbox. Then, verify your company file at a more convenient time, as described on page 180.

4. **To begin the manual backup, click OK.**

If you've already created a backup file with the same name, QuickBooks asks if you want to replace that file. When you click Yes, QuickBooks overwrites the previous backup. To retain your previous backups, click No and, in the Filename box, edit the file name to make it unique.

When QuickBooks displays the message that your data bas been backed up successfully, click OK. If you back up your company file to a CD, you might have to burn the backup to the CD (see the box below).

GEM IN THE ROUGH

Back Up Directly to CD

In the Set Defaults dialog box, you'll find that QuickBooks turns on the Use Windows CD Writing Wizard checkbox automatically if your computer runs on the Windows XP operating system. When this checkbox is turned on, the program turns over responsibility for backing up to CD to the Windows XP CD burning feature—which can be confusing. Here's what you have to do to make sure your backups reach the CD:

1. Choose a CD drive as your backup location. To do this, in the QuickBooks Backup dialog box, on the Back Up Company file tab, click Browse and select the CD drive you want to use. When you click OK, QuickBooks displays a message telling you that your data has been backed up successfully. But the backup file isn't on the CD yet!

2. You might not notice the balloon just above your Windows System Tray (in the lower-right corner of your screen) that tells you that you have files waiting to be burned to a CD. When you use the Windows CD Writing Wizard, QuickBooks creates the backup file in the folder for your CD or DVD drive. To see these files, open Windows Explorer and navigate to your CD or DVD drive. To burn any files waiting to be written to a CD, click "Write these files to CD," as illustrated in the figure.

3. After the CD contains the backup, you can remove the CD from the drive. If you haven't labeled the CD yet, be sure to add a label with the name of the backup and the date.

Using the Windows CD Writing Wizard is fine if you want to stockpile files to burn to a CD all at once. However, if you run scheduled backups at 3 AM, you don't want to stick around to tell the wizard to burn the CD. To write your QuickBooks backups directly to a CD without any action on your part, turn off the Use Windows CD Writing Wizard checkbox. When you turn off this feature, you'll need to install other CD burning software, such as Roxio's DirectCD, and be sure to insert a CD or DVD into the drive before you leave the office.

DirectCD runs in the background on your computer and treats the CD or DVD as if it were another hard disk. When QuickBooks runs the backup, the CD-burning software kicks in and writes the file to the CD or DVD. When you eject the CD or DVD, you'll have to decide how you plan to access the disk in the future. If you leave the disk as is, it continues to act as another drive, but other CD drives won't be able to read the CD. If you want to read the CD on other computers, you must close the CD.

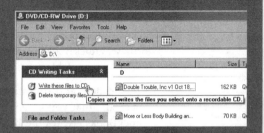

Choosing Standard Settings for Your Backups

For each company file that you back up, you can choose settings for QuickBooks to use during the backup. These standard settings are great timesavers and make for more consistent backups. For example, you can tell QuickBooks to remind you to back up your data after you've opened the company file a specific number of times. Or, you can automatically append the date and time that you run the backup to the name of the backup file. You choose these settings once for each company file and QuickBooks uses them for every backup of that company until you change the settings once more.

In the QuickBooks Backup dialog box, on the Back Up Company File tab, click Set Defaults. QuickBooks opens the Set Defaults dialog box, as shown in Figure 7-3. The settings in this dialog box apply only to the current company file.

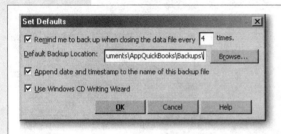

Figure 7-3:
In the "Remind me to back up when closing the data file every __ times" box, type a number based on how often you open your company file. For example, if you work on it daily, type 1, so QuickBooks reminds you to back up every time you close the file. If you open the file occasionally and add only a few transactions, your regular company backup should be enough protection, so you might type 4.

Here are the settings you can choose and what they're good for:

- **Remind me to back up when closing the data file every __ times.** If you want QuickBooks to remind you to back up your file every so often, turn on this checkbox. When you've closed the company file the number of times you specified, QuickBooks displays the Automatic Backup message box. If you decide to bypass this automatic backup, click No. To create a backup of your company file, click Yes, which opens the QuickBooks Backup dialog box so you can run a manual backup.

- **Default Backup Location.** If you'd rather not search for backups saved by mistake to unconventional locations, choose a default location for your backups. To tell QuickBooks to store the backup file in the same folder each time, click Browse. QuickBooks opens the "Browse for Folder" dialog box. Navigate to the folder or removable media device on your computer or network; click OK.

- **Append date and timestamp to the name of this backup file.** If you want to make sure that you *never* overwrite a backup file, turn on this checkbox. When QuickBooks creates the backup file, it adds the date and time to the file name. Unless you make multiple backups within a minute of each other, you can be sure that your file names are unique. For example, the file name for a backup that QuickBooks created on October 17, 2004 at 2:30 PM would be something like: Double Trouble, Inc Oct 17, 2004 02 30 PM.qbb.

Automated QuickBooks Backups

QuickBooks can back up your data automatically in two different ways—automatically or unattended—both of which are available in the QuickBooks Backup dialog box on the Schedule Backup tab, as shown in Figure 7-4.

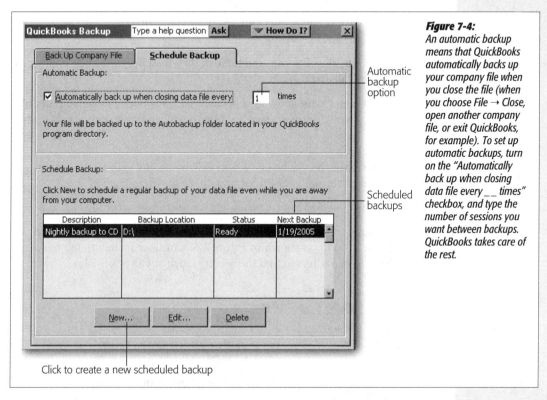

Figure 7-4:
An automatic backup means that QuickBooks automatically backs up your company file when you close the file (when you choose File → Close, open another company file, or exit QuickBooks, for example). To set up automatic backups, turn on the "Automatically back up when closing data file every __ times" checkbox, and type the number of sessions you want between backups. QuickBooks takes care of the rest.

QuickBooks creates automatic backup files in the Autobackup folder within the QuickBooks program folder, typically *C:\Program Files\Intuit\QuickBooks <edition>\Autobackup*, where *<edition>* is Pro, Premier, or Enterprise. The file naming convention that QuickBooks uses for the backup files is:

ABU_0_<company name> <date stamp> <time stamp>

ABU stands for Automatic Backup. For example, the first automatic backup file might be ABU_0_Double Trouble, Inc Mar 22, 2005 05 17 PM. However, when QuickBooks creates the next automatic backup, QuickBooks renames the file that begins with ABU_0 to start with ABU_1 (and renames the ABU_1 file to start with ABU_2), so that the ABU_0 file is always the most recent.

Unattended Backups

You can also schedule QuickBooks backups to run when you aren't around. The only time you'd use this feature is when your QuickBooks data is the *only* data on your computer. Otherwise, you're better off using the Backup utility within your operating system to schedule a backup that captures *all* your data.

If you want to back up only your QuickBooks data during off hours, here are the steps to create a scheduled backup:

1. **On the icon bar, click Backup, and then, in the QuickBooks Backup dialog box, click the Schedule Backup tab.**

   This tab includes a table showing scheduled backups you've already set up, plus each backup's description, storage location, status, and next occurrence.

2. **Click New.**

   QuickBooks opens the "Schedule a Backup" dialog box with all the options you need to set up a regularly scheduled backup, as shown in Figure 7-5.

3. **In the Description box, type a meaningful name for the scheduled backup.**

   The description that you type appears on the Schedule Backup tab in the Description column, as shown in Figure 7-5. Consider including the frequency of the backup and where to find the backup (such as CD or off-site).

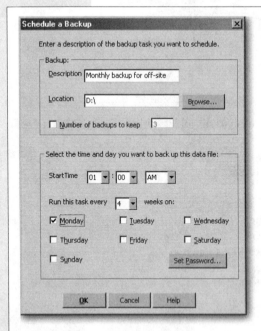

Figure 7-5:
You won't need more than a few scheduled backups. For instance, you can create one scheduled backup to save your data every weeknight from Monday through Thursday. A second scheduled backup might save a weekly backup every Friday night. Finally, you could set up a third scheduled backup to run every Saturday night to create a backup that you can store off-site.

4. **The easiest way to specify the backup location is to click Browse.**

   QuickBooks opens the "Browse for Folder" dialog box. To choose a folder, hard drive, or CD drive on your computer, expand the My Computer entry and choose the backup location you want. If you want to store the backup on another computer on your network, expand the My Network Places entry and then choose the backup location.

Tip: With scheduled backups, you can't turn off your computer when you go home or your backup won't work. If you back up to a hard drive on another computer, that computer must be running as well. If you back up to any kind of removable media, be sure to place a blank disk in the drive before you leave the office. (Yet another reason to stop using floppy disks: your company file almost always requires more than one floppy disk, and you won't be there to insert the second disk.)

---

5. **If you back up your company file to a hard drive and don't want to overwrite your last backup each time the scheduled backup runs, turn on the "Number of backups to keep" checkbox and, in the box to the right of the label, type the number of previous backups you want to keep.**

   When you turn on this checkbox, QuickBooks uses a file name SBU_0_<*company name*> <*date stamp*> <*time stamp*>. For example, a scheduled backup file might be SBU_0_Double Trouble, Inc Mar 228, 2004 01 00 AM. (SBU stands for Scheduled Backup.) Each time QuickBooks creates a new scheduled backup file, it renames the previous backups to the next number in the list, and then replaces the SBU_0 file with the new backup. For example, if you keep four backups, the SBU_2 backup becomes the SBU_3 file; the SBU_1 file becomes the SBU_2 file; the SBU_0 backup file becomes the SBU_1 file; and the new backup becomes the new SBU_0 file.

6. **In the Start Time boxes, choose the time you want the backup to run.**

   The Start Time boxes work on a 12-hour clock, so you specify the hour, minutes, and AM or PM.

   It's easy to confuse midnight and noon on a 12-hour clock. Midnight is 12 AM. Noon is 12 PM. Avoid this gotcha by running your scheduled backups at 11 PM, 1 AM, or later.

7. **To set up the frequency for the backup, in the "Run this task every __ weeks on" box, type the number of weeks that you want between backups, and then turn on the checkboxes for each day of the week on which you want the backup to occur.**

   For example, for your daily backups, in the "Run this task every __ weeks on" box, type *1*, and then turn on the checkbox for each weekday.

When you're done, click OK. QuickBooks adds the scheduled backup to your list of scheduled backups.

Tip: You can ignore the Set Password button unless your computer runs Windows NT, Windows 2000, Windows XP, or Windows 2003 Server, *and* uses the NTFS (a secure filesystem that controls access to files). To see if your hard drive uses NTFS, in Windows Explorer, right-click the hard drive and choose Properties. In the Local Disk Properties dialog box, you'll see NTFS to the left of the file System label. To run a backup on a secure filesystem, you must click Set Password and type your Windows user name and password.

Restoring Backups

Having backup files can reduce your adrenaline level in a number of situations:

- You merge two customers into one by mistake or make another type of major faux pas that you want to undo.

- Your company file won't open, which can happen if the file's been damaged by a power outage or power surge.

- Your hard disk crashes and takes all your data with it.

- You recently assigned a password to your administrator login and can't remember what it is.

Warning: Hard disk crashes used to be dramatic events accompanied by impressive grinding noises. With the closer tolerances of today's smaller hard disks, crashes can be deceptively quiet. If you hear odd sounds emanating from your computer—little chirps or squeaks, for instance—stop what you're doing and try to back up your key files. You might be able to save them to a CD or a USB thumb drive if you act quickly. If you shut down your computer and it won't reboot because of a disk crash, a data recovery company can sometimes recover some of your data, but the price is usually in the thousands of dollars.

GEM IN THE ROUGH

The Intuit Online Backup Service

In the QuickBooks Backup dialog box on the Back Up Company File tab, Intuit entices you with a free trial offer for their Online Backup Service. Yes, this service costs money, but as long as your Internet connection has respectable speed, Intuit's Online Backup Service is worth evaluating.

The service can automatically select all your company files or you can choose the files you want to back up. Plus, Online Backup Service isn't just for QuickBooks company files. You can back up databases, documents, email, and more. The price depends on the number of megabytes of storage you use. Up to 200 megabytes costs $99.95 a year, but your back-

ups reside in a data center managed by IT experts who live, eat, and breathe effective backup procedures.

The service first compresses and encrypts the backup files and then transfers them via the Internet to the data center. Any time you're connected to the Internet, you can schedule backups or download your backups to your computer.

If you want to learn more about this service, in the Quick-Books Backup dialog box, on the Back Up Company File tab, click Tell Me More, which opens a browser to the Intuit web page for the service.

Here are the steps to restoring a QuickBooks backup:

1. **If you backed up your data to removable media, put the disk containing your backup in the appropriate drive.**

   If you backed up your data to another hard drive on your computer or on a network, you must be able to access that drive. For example, if the shared network drive that you used is offline, you'll have to reconnect to it before restoring your backup. If you need some guidance on how to reconnect an offline drive, consult your operating system's online help or refer to your copy of *Windows XP Pro: The Missing Manual.*

2. **If the No Company Open window is visible, click "Restore a backup file."**

   If a company file is already open, choose File → Restore. Either method opens the Restore Company Backup dialog box, shown in Figure 7-6.

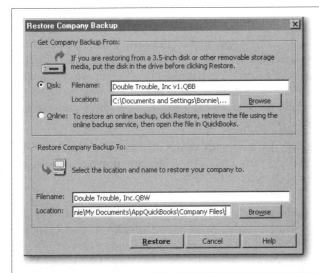

Figure 7-6:
To restore a backup file, you have to specify the file name and location for the backup file you want to restore, as well as the company file that you want to restore the backup file to. QuickBooks makes a guess to fill in the file names and locations for both the backup file and the restored company file, which are almost always wrong. Be sure to check the file names, but also take extra care to scroll through the entire path in the Location boxes to make sure the locations are correct.

3. **In the Restore Company Backup dialog box, find the Get Company Backup From section, and in the Filename box and Location box, specify the backup file that you want to restore and where it is located.**

   File names and path names are usually quite long and your chance of typing them correctly is small. The easiest way to choose your backup file is to click Browse, which opens the Restore From dialog box. You can navigate to the folder or removable media that contains your backup file and double-click the file name to automatically fill in both the Filename and Location boxes.

4. **In the Restore Company Backup dialog box, move to the Restore Company Backup To section, which also contains a Filename box and Location box. In the Filename box, specify the company file you want to restore. In the Location box, click Browse to open the Restore To dialog box and specify the folder to which you want to restore the backup.**

If you want to replace a company file that's corrupt or contains evidence of your big gaffe, in the Restore To dialog box, navigate to the folder that contains your company file and double-click the file name. QuickBooks fills in the Filename and Location boxes.

If you want to restore the backup to a computer that doesn't contain the original company file, you can *still* click Browse. In this case, in the Restore To dialog box, navigate to the folder in which you want to restore the company file and, in the Filename box, type the company file name. Make sure that the "Save as Type" box displays QuickBooks Files (*.QBW, *.QBA). Then, click Save.

5. **In the Restore Company Backup dialog box, click Restore.**

If you are restoring a backup of a company file that already exists, QuickBooks warns you that you are about to overwrite an existing file. If the file is corrupt or won't open for some reason, click Yes because that's exactly what you want to do. You'll have to type Yes once more to confirm that you want to delete the file. It's better to take these precautions than to overwrite the wrong file and have to dig out yet another backup.

When you see the message that says your data has been restored successfully, you're ready to open the company file and re-enter any transactions that the backup doesn't contain.

Tip: If your backup copy won't restore, try copying the contents of the backup media (CD, DVD, Zip disk, or floppy) to your hard drive and restoring the backup file from there. If the restore still doesn't work, your backup file is probably damaged. Try the next most recent backup to restore your company file.

If none of your backups work, Intuit offers data recovery services to extract data from your backup files. The service isn't free, but it might be cheaper than rebuilding your entire company file. To arrange for this service, choose Help → Access Support Resources, and click one of the links for support. In addition, you should spend some time sorting out the problem so you can fix your backup procedure.

Sending Company Files to Others

In previous versions of QuickBooks, company files were unwieldy to transport. To give a copy to your accountant, you needed a lightning-fast Internet connection, a CD or DVD, or a forklift truck. QuickBooks 2006 includes portable company files, a slim new file format that flies through the email ether and slips effortlessly into limited-capacity removable media like USB thumb drives and Zip disks. You can now email a portable company file to your accountant so she can take a quick look or transfer the file to a colleague in another office before you head out on vacation. But, before you transmit your file electronically, be sure you've added a password to it, so that someone can't intercept and access your financial data.

For example, a company file that runs 10 megabytes in size turns into a portable company file of less than 1 megabyte. Portable company files come with a .qbm file extension, but QuickBooks converts them to a regular company file with a .qbw file extension when opened.

Note: If the person you send the file to is going to make any changes and send the file back, she needs the administrator password to do so. Remember that this password lets her use any and every QuickBooks feature on your file, so don't give it out lightly.

Creating a Portable Company File

Creating a portable company file is just a wee bit more complicated than saving a file. Here are the steps:

1. **Choose File → Portable Company File → Create File.**

   When a message box warns you that QuickBooks must close and reopen your file, click OK.

2. **In the Create Portable Company File dialog box, fill in the Filename and Location boxes with the name and location for the file you want to create.**

   The program automatically assigns a .qbm file extension.

3. **Click Save.**

   When you see a message that the company file was created successfully, click OK.

Feel free to view the portable company file's icon in Windows Explorer and admire its sleek size.

Opening a Portable Company File

Opening a portable company file is almost as easy as creating one. However, since QuickBooks essentially converts the portable-format file into a full-size, bona fide company file, there's an extra wrinkle. Here's the full procedure:

1. **Choose File → Portable Company File → Open File.**

   Similar to the Restore Backup dialog box (page 176), the Open Portable Company File dialog box includes a Get Portable Company File From section and a "Name and Location of New Company File" section.

2. **In the Get Portable Company File section, select the portable company file you want to open.**

   The program automatically looks in your QuickBooks software folder, so you'll usually click Browse to navigate to the folder that holds your portable company file.

3. **In the Name and Location of New Company File section, specify the name to use for the *regular* company file and the folder where to put it.**

   When you click Open, the program converts the portable company file into a regular company file, which might take several minutes.

Note: The regular company file that QuickBooks creates from a portable company file is often a little smaller than your original company file. Don't worry; the file contains exactly the same data as your original file.

Verifying Your QuickBooks Data

QuickBooks files hiccup now and then. Perhaps you worked through a spectacular thunder storm and a power spike zapped a bit of your company file. The Quick-Books Verify Data utility scans your company files and tells you whether your file has suffered any damage. It's a good idea to run the Verify Data utility every so often, just to make sure that your company file is OK. How often you run this utility depends on how hard you work your company file, but monthly verifications are in order for most companies. However, the utility is indispensable if you notice any of the following symptoms:

- **Invalid Protection Faults or Fatal Errors.** If these types of errors appear when you run QuickBooks, you almost certainly have a damaged data file.

- **Discrepancies on reports.** Your Balance Sheet might not show all of your accounts, or transactions show negative values instead of positive ones.

Tip: If the totals in your reports don't seem right, first check that the report dates are correct and that you are using the correct cash or accrual accounting setting (see page 159).

- **Missing transactions and names.** Transactions or names that you're sure you entered don't appear in reports or lists.

Running the Verify Data Utility

Whether you're just giving your company file a checkup or you see signs of problems, the Verify Data utility is easy to use. To run the utility, choose File → Utilities → Verify Data. When the utility completes its task, you'll see one of two possible outcomes:

- If QuickBooks displays a message that it detected no problems with your data, your file is healthy.

- If you see the message "Your data has lost integrity," your company file has some problems. QuickBooks displays instructions for running the Rebuild Data utility, which tries to repair the damage. Continue reading to learn what to do.

Reviewing Problems

If your company file has "lost integrity," the Verify Data utility writes any errors it finds to a file named QBWIN.log. Before you run the Rebuild Data utility, take a look at this log file to review your file's problems. The method that QuickBooks provides for viewing the log file is obscure and requires several steps. Here's an easier and more direct way to view the most recent entries in the log file:

1. **In Windows Explorer, navigate to the folder that contains your QuickBooks software.**

   This folder is typically *C:\Program Files\Intuit\QuickBooks <edition>* where edition is Pro, Premier, or Enterprise.

2. **To open the log file, locate and then double-click QBWIN.log.**

   The file opens in Windows Notepad, and you can use Notepad commands to move around the file, as illustrated in Figure 7-7. If the file doesn't open, launch Notepad, choose File → Open, and double-click the QBWIN.log file name.

Figure 7-7:
When you verify data, QuickBooks automatically renames the previous QBWIN.log file to QBWin.log.old1 so that the QBWin.log file contains information for only the most recent verification. It renames other old files, for example, changing QBWin.log.old1 to QBWin.log.old2, and so on.

Running the Rebuild Data Utility

If your file is damaged in some way, the Rebuild Data utility tries to fix it. Unfortunately, it can also make matters worse. Intuit recommends that you run the Rebuild Data utility only if an Intuit technical support person tells you to. *Always* make a backup of your company file before trying to rebuild your company file. Take extra care to prevent overwriting your previous backups—those files might be your only salvation if the rebuild doesn't work.

To run the Rebuild Data utility, choose File → Utilities → Rebuild Data. When the utility finishes, close your company file and reopen it, which refreshes the lists in your data file so that you can see if the problems are gone.

Run the Verify Data utility once more after you run the Rebuild Data utility to see if any damage remains. If this second Verify Data run still shows errors, restore a recent backup of your company file.

Cleaning Up Data

As you add transactions and build lists in QuickBooks, your company file gets larger. Now that QuickBooks 2006 uses an industry-standard SQL database, larger company files don't cause as much hassle as they used to. Still, you might grow alarmed when your company file reaches hundreds of megabytes or more. And, if you still use floppy disks to back up your file, you know that your backups take up too much of your valuable time.

The Archive & Condense Data wizard in QuickBooks 2005 and earlier is now called Clean Up Company Data. As the name implied, Archive & Condense Data created an archive file *and* shrank the size of your company file. The new version doesn't change the size of your company file. However, like its predecessor, Clean Up Company Data still creates an archive file and deletes obsolete list items and transactions prior to a date of your choosing.

When QuickBooks cleans up data, it replaces the detailed transactions prior to your specified date with general journal entries that summarize the deleted transactions by month. As a result, some of your financial detail is no longer available for running reports, filing taxes, and other accounting activities. Still, there are a couple of compelling reasons to do a data cleanup:

- **You no longer refer to old transactions.** If you've used QuickBooks for years, you probably *don't* need the finer details from eight or more years ago. If you ever do need details from the past, you can open an archive file to run reports.

- **You have obsolete list items.** Cleaning up a company file can remove list items that you don't use, like inventory items you no longer sell. (QuickBooks lets you remove inventory items only if you remove all the transactions that use them.) This comes in handy if you're nearing the 14,500 limit on inventory items and want to make room for new products.

An archive file created by the Clean Up wizard is a regular company file that contains all of your transactions, but it's read-only, so you can't inadvertently enter new transactions. If QuickBooks runs into trouble cleaning up your file, it automatically pulls transaction details from the archive file.

Note: It's counterintuitive, but an archive copy is not a backup file, so it won't let you use the QuickBooks Restore command to replace a corrupt company file. Even with an archive copy, you still need to back up your data.

If you want to keep your company file intact and responsive to any reporting needs you have, consider these simple and relatively inexpensive alternatives:

- **Slow backups.** If you're backing up to floppies, consider installing a CD drive on your computer. Backing up to CD is not only faster, but CDs aren't as prone to failing as floppy disks, which means your backups are also more dependable.

- **Disk space.** If disk space is the issue, first clean out the temporary files on your computer. Back up old files to CDs or other removable media and then delete the files on your hard disk. If you've been limping along with a minuscule disk drive, consider buying a large hard disk. You can get disks that hold gigabytes of data for a few hundred dollars.

If you decide to clean up your company file, here's what you can expect to find afterward:

- **General journal entries summarize deleted transactions.** QuickBooks replaces all the deleted transactions that occur during one month with one general journal entry. For example, instead of 20 separate invoices for the month of June, you'll see 1 journal entry transaction with the total income for June for each income account.

Note: If you see other transactions for the same month, QuickBooks couldn't delete those transactions for some reason. For example, QuickBooks won't delete unpaid invoices or other transactions with an open balance, nor will it delete any transactions marked "To be printed" (page 240) or transactions that you haven't yet reconciled (page 352).

- **Inventory adjustments reflect the average cost of items.** QuickBooks removes inventory transactions that are complete, such as invoices that have been paid in full. When QuickBooks finds an inventory transaction that it can't condense, perhaps because the payment is outstanding, it keeps all the inventory transactions from that date forward. Because inventory transactions use the average cost of inventory items, QuickBooks also adds an inventory adjustment to set the average cost of the inventory items as of that date.

- **Reports might not include the details you want.** You can still generate summary reports using condensed data because QuickBooks can incorporate the information in the monthly general journal entries. Likewise, sales tax reports still include the information about your sales tax liabilities. However, detailed reports won't include transaction detail before the cutoff date you choose for condensing the file (see below). Cash accounting reports (see page 484) aren't accurate because they need the dates for detailed transactions.

- **Payroll for the current year remains.** QuickBooks removes payroll transactions only if they occur before the current year and before the cutoff date you choose for condensing the file.

- **QuickBooks deletes estimates for closed jobs.** If a job has any status other than Closed, QuickBooks keeps the estimates for that job.

- **QuickBooks keeps time data that you haven't billed.** QuickBooks keeps any time you've tracked that's billable but that you haven't yet billed to your customers. Also, if you pay employees by the time they work, QuickBooks keeps data for time for which you *haven't* compensated your employees.

Running the Clean Up Company File Tool

If you're ready to clean up your company file, first consider *when* to do it. The cleaning process can take several hours for a large company file, and a slow computer or a small amount of memory exacerbates the problem. You might want to clean your company file at the end of a workday so it can run overnight.

Here's how you condense a company file:

1. **Choose File → Utilities → Clean Up Company Data.**

   If you've created budgets in QuickBooks, you'll see a message that the clean up might remove budget data. If the loss of some budget data doesn't scare you, click Yes. The Clean Up Company Data dialog box opens.

Tip: You can export your budget before you clean up your data and then import the budget back into your company file after cleanup (page 460).

---

2. **Select the "Remove transactions as of a specific date" option.**

   The first screen of the wizard provides two options for condensing your data, explained in Figure 7-8.

3. **In the "Remove closed transactions on or before" box, type or select the ending date for the period you want to condense.**

   If you use a QuickBooks Payroll Service for your payroll (page 316), you can't clean up data for the current year. Besides, QuickBooks won't let you clean up transactions that are later than the closing date on your company file (page

407). Choosing a date at least two years in the past ensures that you can compare detailed transactions for the current year and the previous year. For example, if it's August 1, 2005, consider using December 31, 2003 or earlier as your cutoff date.

4. **Click Next to advance to the "Select Additional Criteria for Removing Transactions" screen.**

   If you want QuickBooks to remove transactions that the condensation process would normally leave alone, turn on the appropriate checkboxes. Figure 7-8 shows your choices.

   Before you turn on these checkboxes, carefully review your company file to make sure that you won't delete transactions that you want to keep. Click Next to proceed to the next screen.

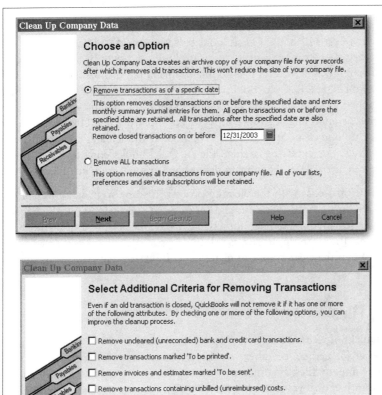

Figure 7-8:
Top: The "Remove transactions as of a specific date" option removes old transactions and other things like unused accounts and items. The "Remove ALL transactions" option removes transactions but keeps your preferences, lists, and service subscriptions—such as payroll—intact. You won't want to use this option often, but it comes in handy if, for example, you wanted to offer your clients a template company file that contains typical list entries, but without any transactions.

Bottom: The tool includes settings to remove transactions that it would normally leave alone—for example, transactions marked "To be printed" that you don't need to print. If you have very old, unreconciled transactions, invoices or estimates marked "To be sent," or transactions with unreimbursed costs, turn on these checkboxes to remove them during the cleanup.

5. **If you want to remove list items no longer referenced in the cleaned up file, turn on the appropriate checkboxes. Then click Next.**

   When you delete old transactions, accounts, customers, vendors, other names, and invoices items might become orphans without any links to the transactions that still remain. Removing these list items neatens your file and lists. Keep in mind that you might still use a vendor or work with a customer even though the cleaning process deleted all of their previous transactions.

   If seeing all the To Do notes that you've completed gives you a sense of accomplishment, leave the "'Done' To Do notes" checkbox turned off. But to show only To Do notes that you haven't completed, turn this checkbox on.

6. **On the "Proceed with cleanup?" screen, click Begin Cleanup.**

   If you're not sure of the options you chose, or if you have any doubts about cleaning up your file, click Prev to return to a previous screen in the tool, or click Cancel to exit without taking any action.

When you click Begin Cleanup, QuickBooks tells you that it will back up your file before condensing the transactions. If you want QuickBooks to back up the file to a CD or other removable media, insert a blank formatted disk in the appropriate drive. When you click OK, QuickBooks opens the QuickBooks Backup dialog box. You can change the name of the backup file or its location (for instance, to select a network drive or another hard drive on your computer). Click OK when you're ready to back up *and* clean up your data. QuickBooks first creates a backup file of your data. Then, it creates the archive file (a QuickBooks company file, not a backup file; see page 182) in the same folder as your original company file.

As QuickBooks proceeds with the cleanup process, it scans your data *three* times. You might see dialog boxes wink on and off in rapid succession and, then again, you might not see anything happen for a while if your file is large. But if your hard disk is working, the clean up process is still in progress. Be patient and resist clicking Cancel. When the cleanup is complete, QuickBooks displays a message telling you so.

Deleting Files

Although QuickBooks lets you delete transactions (which is risky because doing so makes it easier for people to embezzle), the program *doesn't* provide a command for deleting company files. If someone else has taken responsibility for your non-profit's accounting, or if you want to get rid of a practice file you no longer use, it's easy enough to delete QuickBooks files using operating system commands. But you have some housekeeping to do to remove all references to that file from QuickBooks. A company that you delete still appears in the list of previously opened files, as demonstrated in Figure 7-9, but QuickBooks won't be able to find the file if you choose that entry. Here's how you eliminate those stale entries:

1. Navigate to the folder that contains your QuickBooks company files.

2. Use Windows Explorer, for example, or a My Computer window. Right-click the company file that you want to delete.

   What you look for depends on how you've set up your folder view. If your folder shows the full names of your files, look for a file with a .qbw file extension, such as DoubleTrouble,Inc.qbw. If the folder includes a Name column and a Type column, the type you want is "QuickBooks Company File."

   .qbx file extensions represent accountant's copies. Files with .qbb file extensions are backup copies of your company files. If you delete the company file, go ahead and delete the backup and accountant's copies as well.

3. On the shortcut menu, choose Delete.

   Windows displays the Confirm File Delete message box. Click Yes to move the file to the Recycle Bin. If you have second thoughts, click No to keep the file.

Tip: If you find that you always seem to need a file the day after you delete it, consider copying files to a CD before you delete them.

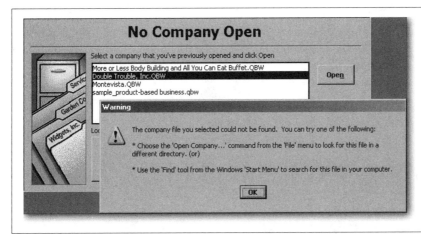

Figure 7-9:
If you double-click the name of a file that QuickBooks can't find, the program suggests that you choose File → Open Company and then look for the file in another directory, or, alternatively, that you use the Windows Find command. If you know that the file doesn't exist, simply click OK and select another file.

4. In QuickBooks, to eliminate the deleted company file from the list that you see when you choose File → Open Previous Company, you must first open another company file.

   If QuickBooks displays the No Company Open window, open the company file that you typically work with by double-clicking it.

5. To clear out old companies in the previously opened file list, you must reset the number of companies displayed in the No Company Open window. To do this, choose File → Open Previous Company → Set number of previous companies.

In the "How many companies do you want to list (1 to 20)?" box, type *1*, and then click OK. When you choose File → Open Previous Company, you'll notice that only one company appears—the company file you opened last. In the No Company Open window, the "Select a company that you've previously opened and click Open" list also contains only the last file you opened.

6. **Now that you've removed the deleted company from these lists, you can reset the number of previously opened companies. With a company file open, choose File → Open Previous Company → Set number of previous companies.**

   In the "How many companies do you want to list (1 to 20)?" box, type *4* (or the number of companies you'd like to see in the list), and then click OK.

As you open different company files, QuickBooks displays these files in the No Company Open window and on the Open Previous Company menu.

2

Part Two: Accounting with QuickBooks

Invoicing

Telling your customers how much they owe you (called *accounts receivable*) and how soon they must pay is an important first step in accounting. Because if money isn't flowing into your organization from outside sources, eventually you'll close up shop, closing your QuickBooks company file with it.

Although businesses use several different sales forms to bill customers, the *invoice* is the most popular, and, unsurprisingly, customer billing is often called *invoicing*. This chapter begins by explaining the difference between invoices, statements, and sales receipts—each of which is a way of billing customers in QuickBooks—and when each is most appropriate. Then, you'll learn how to fill in the QuickBooks versions of these sales forms, and how to get those forms into your customers' hands.

Choosing the Right Type of Form

In QuickBooks, you can choose from three different sales forms to document what you sell, and each form has its own strengths and limitations. Invoices can handle any billing task you can think of, so an invoice is the best choice if you have any doubts about which one to use. Table 8-1 summarizes what each of the three sales forms can do. The sections that follow explain each form's capabilities in detail and when to choose each one.

Table 8-1. *Sales receipts and statements have limitations, but an invoice always works*

Action	Sales Receipt	Statement	Invoice
Track customer payments and balances		Yes	Yes
Accept payments in advance		Yes	Yes
Accumulate charges before sending sales form		Yes	Yes
Collect payment in full at time of sale	Yes	Yes	Yes
Create summary sales transaction	Yes	Yes	Yes
Apply sales tax	Yes		Yes
Apply percentage discounts	Yes		Yes
Use group items to add charges to form	Yes		Yes
Add long descriptions for services or products	Yes		Yes
Subtotal items	Yes		Yes
Include customer message	Yes		Yes
Include custom fields on form	Yes		Yes

Sales Receipts

The sales receipt is the simplest sales form that QuickBooks offers, but it's only appropriate if your customers pay the full amount at the time of the sale—for example, in a retail store, restaurant, or beauty salon. Because sales receipts don't include a field for customer payments, you can't use them to keep track of how much your customers owe.

When your customers pay in full, sales receipts are the shortest path from making a sale to having money in the bank (at least in QuickBooks). When you create and save a sales receipt in QuickBooks, the program posts the money to the Undeposited Funds account or the back account you choose. As you'll learn in this chapter and the next, invoices and statements take several steps to move from billing to bank deposits.

Despite their shortcomings in the customer payment department, sales receipts *can* handle sales tax, discounts, and subtotals—in fact, any item in your Item List. But when you operate a cash business, creating a sales receipt in QuickBooks for each newspaper and pack of gum your newsstand sells is *not* good use of your time. Instead, consider creating a sales receipt that reflects a day's or week's sales, using a customer named Cash Sales created specifically for that purpose (see page 54).

Statements

Suppose you're a lawyer and you spend 15 minutes here and 15 minutes there working on a client's legal problem over the course of a month. Each time you spend some time, that's another charge to the client's account. In QuickBooks, each of those charges is called a *statement charge*, and you enter them individually (page 223). Businesses often turn to statements when they charge the same amount each month, such as a fixed monthly fee for full-time work as a contract programmer. But memorized invoices (page 213) are just as easy.

Note: Although statements can track customer payments and balances, they don't handle the following billing tasks:

- Tracking sales tax.
- Using Group items to add several items.
- Typing multiparagraph descriptions of services or products.
- Subtotaling items.
- Applying percentage discounts to items sold.
- Including a customer message.
- Including custom fields.
- Summarizing the services and products sold. (On statements, each separate service or product you sell must appear as a separate statement charge.)

Behind the scenes, a statement adds up all the accounts receivable transactions for the customer over a period of time, which includes statement charges, payments, and invoices. When you invoice customers, you can create statements to notify your customers that they have overdue invoices. If you want a more thorough paper trail to face any disputes about invoices, you can send statements to your customers to show how much money is outstanding, whether or not it's overdue.

Invoices

The bottom line: if statements or sales receipts don't work, don't be afraid to use invoices. They accept any item you've created in your Item List (see Chapter 4) without complaint, *and* they track what your customers owe you.

Besides the features in Table 8-1, an invoice is the only type of sales form that you can generate from an estimate (page 216). If you're a general contractor and prepare a detailed estimate of the services and products for a job, you'll save a huge chunk of time by turning that estimate into an invoice for billing.

Note: QuickBooks Premier and Enterprise editions include one more type of sales form: the sales order. In those editions of the program, when you create a sales order for the products that a customer wants to buy, you can keep track of out-of-stock items that you'll need to ship to your customer when a new shipment arrives.

Creating Invoices

Invoices tell your customers everything they need to know about what they purchased and the payment they are about to make. If you created your customers and jobs with settings such as payment terms and sales rep (page 58), filling in your typical invoice is almost effortless. As soon as you choose a customer and job in the Customer:Job field, QuickBooks fills in most of the fields for you.

Some fields on an invoice are more influential than others, but they all come in handy at some point. To digest the purpose of the fields on an invoice more easily, you can break an invoice up into three basic sections, as illustrated in Figure 8-1. Because the invoices you create for product sales include a few more fields than the invoices for services only, the following sections use a product invoice to explain how to fill in each field you might run into on the invoices you create. If the information that QuickBooks fills in for you is incorrect, these sections also tell you where to go to correct the problem.

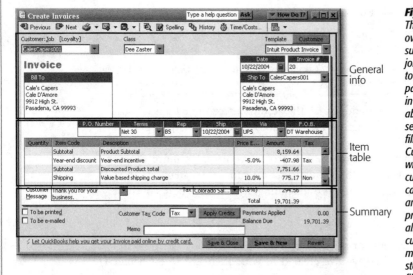

Figure 8-1:
The top of the invoice has overall sale information, such as the customer and job, the invoice date, who to bill and ship to, and the payment terms. The table in the middle has info about each product and service sold. QuickBooks fills in the Tax field and the Customer Tax Code field with values in the customer's record, but you can change these values and any others that the program fills in. You can also add a message to the customer, choose your send method, or type a memo to store in your QuickBooks file.

Note: If you charge your customers based on the progress you've made, invoices are a *little* more complicated, but you'll learn how to handle this situation on page 219.

In the sections that follow, you'll find details about filling in all the fields on an invoice. For now, here's the basic procedure for creating and saving one or more invoices:

1. To create invoices, first open the Create Invoices dialog box. On the Quick-Books Home page, for example, click Invoices.

   You can also open the Create Invoices dialog box from the icon bar by clicking Invoice, or by pressing Ctrl+I.

2. In the Customer:Job box, choose the customer or job associated with the invoice.

   When you choose a customer or job, QuickBooks fills in many of the invoice fields with values from the customer record (see page 54), job record (page 67), and the preferences you set (page 151). For example, QuickBooks pulls the data for the Bill To address, Terms, and Rep fields from the customer or job record. The values for the Ship Via and FOB (which stands for Free on Board, or the physical point at which the customer becomes responsible for damage or loss to the shipment) fields come from your Sales & Customers preferences.

3. For each product or service sold, in the line item table, enter the information for the item, including the quantity and price (or rate).

   If you want, fill in the boxes below the line-item table, such as Customer Message and Memo.

   You can also turn on the checkboxes below the line-item table to specify how to send the invoice. Rarely will you find the need to change the sales tax rate associated with the customer, but you can.

4. If you have additional invoices to create, simply click Save & New to save the current invoice and begin another.

   To save the invoice you just created and close the Create Invoices dialog box, click Save & Close.

   If you're unhappy with most of the choices you made in the current invoice, click Clear to start over with a fresh, blank invoice.

Tip: Maintain your professional image by checking for spelling errors before you send your invoice. To run the QuickBooks spell checker, in the Create Invoices dialog box icon bar, click Spelling. If you checked spelling when you created your customers and invoice items, the main source for spelling errors is edits you've made to item descriptions. If the QuickBooks spell checker doesn't work the way you want, change your Spelling preferences (see page 165).

Filling in Invoice Header Fields

If you fill in all the fields in your customer and job records (see Chapter 3), your work in the invoice header section is limited to filling in a few fields. Here's what the header fields do and where QuickBooks gets the values it fills in automatically.

Choosing an Invoice Template

As you scan from the top left of the Create Invoices dialog box (Figure 8-1), the first box you encounter is the Customer:Job field—but it shouldn't be the first field you fill in. The template you choose in the Template field determines the fields that appear on your invoices and how they're laid out. For example, you might have two templates: one for printing on your company letterhead and another one for invoices you send electronically. Choosing a template is the best way to prevent printing the wrong invoice to your expensive letterhead. But you can switch templates any time you want. If you've already filled in an invoice, changing the template doesn't throw out the data; QuickBooks simply displays the data in the new template.

When you choose a template, in the Create Invoices dialog box, you'll see the fields and layout for the new template. However, QuickBooks won't display settings like your company logo, fonts, and other formatting until you print or preview your invoice (page 238).

Note: QuickBooks remembers the template you chose when you created your last invoice. If you use only one invoice template, choose it on your first invoice and the program chooses it for you from then on.

Templates aren't linked to customers. If you pick a different template when you create an invoice for one customer, QuickBooks chooses that same template for your next invoice, regardless of which customer it's for.

Many small companies are perfectly happy with the invoice templates that Quick-Books provides. When you create your first invoice, you might not even think about the layout of the fields on the invoice. But if you run across a billing task that the current template can't handle, don't panic: you can choose from more than one built-in invoice template. And if you want your invoices to reflect your company's style and image, you can create your own templates (see page 550).

Before you accept the template that QuickBooks chooses, in the Template drop-down list, quickly select and review each of the following templates to see whether you like them better:

- **The Intuit Product Invoice.** If you sell products with or without services, the Intuit Product Invoice is set up to show information like the quantity, item code, price for each item, the total charge for each item, sales tax, and shipping information—including the ship date, shipping method, and FOB.

- **The Intuit Service Invoice.** This invoice doesn't bother with shipping fields because services are performed, not shipped. The template includes fields for item, description, quantity, rate, amount, tax, and purchase order number.

- **The Intuit Professional Invoice.** The only difference between this template and the Intuit Service Invoice is that this template doesn't include a purchase order number field, and the Quantity column follows the Description column.

- **The Progress Invoice.** If you bill your customers based on the progress you've made on their jobs, the Progress Invoice has columns for your estimates, prior charges, and new totals. It appears in the Template drop-down list only if you turn on the preference for progress invoicing (see page 151).

Tip: The Packing Slip template also appears in the Template drop-down list, but it isn't an invoice template. When you ship products to customers, you can print an invoice *and* packing slip from within the Create Invoices dialog box (see page 242).

- **The Fixed Fee Invoice.** This invoice drops the quantity and rate fields, since the invoice shows only the total charge. The template includes the date, item, description, tax, and purchase order number.

- **The Time & Expense Invoice.** If you bill your customers by the hour, this template includes a column for hours and hourly rate, and it calculates the resulting total amount.

Tip: The second entry in the Template drop-down list is Download Templates. When you choose this entry, QuickBooks opens a Web browser to an online template gallery. If you're looking for something special, you can choose your industry in one drop-down list or, in the Enter Search Term box, type keywords such as *progress* or *invoice*.

WORKAROUND WORKSHOP

Saving and Printing Invoices

If you prefer to save an invoice before you print it, the two Save options in the Create Invoices dialog box are inadequate. You can't save an invoice *and* keep it in view in the Create Invoices dialog box.

If you want to save the invoice and then print it, click Save & New, which saves the current invoice and displays a blank invoice. Then, click Previous to return to the invoice you just saved. Now, you can print it or perform any other tasks you want.

But the QuickBooks save options have another hole—and this one is big enough to drive a truck through. You can print an invoice and then *not* save it either by clicking Clear, which erases the current invoice; or the Close button, which closes the Create Invoices dialog box without saving the current invoice.

The problem with this behavior is that it makes embezzling much too easy. For example, an employee can create and print an invoice for a sale with the payment going to the employee instead of the company. This is particularly problematic because you have no record of the sale. You might think an Audit Trail (page 572) would catch this—because an audit trail keeps track of deleted transactions—but in this case, the audit trail doesn't help because the employee never saved or deleted the invoice.

The only solution is to be careful when hiring your financial folks and limit QuickBooks access to only those employees who require it.

Choosing the Customer or Job

The selection you make in the Customer:Job field is your most important choice for any invoice. In addition to billing the correct customer for your work, QuickBooks uses the settings from your customer and job records to fill in many of the invoice fields.

To choose a customer or job, in the Customer:Job drop-down list, choose the customer or job you want, as demonstrated in Figure 8-2.

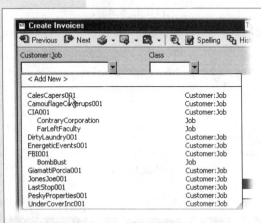

Figure 8-2:
If you work on different jobs for a customer, click the name of the job, which is indented underneath the customer's name. If your work for a customer doesn't relate to jobs, click the customer's name. The column to the right of the customer and job names provides another way to differentiate customers and jobs. You'll see Customer:Job for a customer entry, whereas the second column displays Job for a job entry.

After you choose a customer, QuickBooks displays the "Price level" box immediately to the right of the Customer:Job box if the customer has an assigned price level (page 58). When you add an invoice item and the price isn't what you expect, the price level may be the culprit. You can change a customer's price level by editing the customer record (page 68), or you can choose existing price levels to change the price you charge as you add items to your invoice (page 200).

The Rest of the Header Fields

As you can see in Figure 8-3, QuickBooks can fill in most of the remaining header fields for you. Here's what you do to fill in any empty fields or change the ones that QuickBooks didn't complete the way you want:

- **Class.** If you turned on the class tracking feature (page 135) to categorize your income and expenses in different ways, choose a class for the invoice. If you skip this box, QuickBooks politely reminds you that the box is empty when you try to save the invoice. Although you *can* save the invoice without a class, it's important to assign classes to every transaction if you want your class-based reports to be accurate. For example, if you use classes to track income by partner and save an invoice without a class, the partner who delivered the services on the invoice might complain about the paucity of her paycheck.

- **Date.** QuickBooks fills in the current date, which is fine if you create invoices when you make a sale. But service businesses often send invoices on a schedule—the last day of the month is a popular choice. If you want to get a head start on your invoices, type or choose the invoice data you want. QuickBooks uses the same date for every subsequent invoice, making your end-of-month invoicing a tiny bit easier.

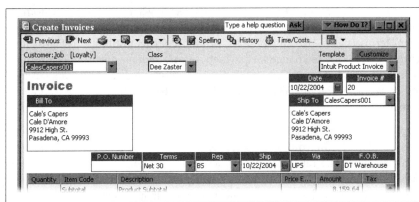

Figure 8-3:
The only field that QuickBooks can't fill in under any circumstances is the P.O. Number field, and that's because you get that number from your customer.

- **Invoice #.** When you create your first invoice, type the number that you want to start with. For example, if you'd rather not reveal that this is your first invoice, type a number such as 245. Each time you create a new invoice, QuickBooks increases the number in the "Invoice #" box by one: 246, 247, and so on.

Tip: Press the plus (+) key or the minus (–) key to increase or decrease the invoice number by one, respectively. When you save the current invoice, QuickBooks considers its invoice number the starting point for subsequent numbers.

If your last invoice was a mistake and you delete it (page 231), you'll end up with a gap in your invoice numbers. For example, when you delete invoice number 203, QuickBooks already has set the next invoice number to 204. Your invoice numbers don't *have* to be sequential, but it's easier to spot missing payments and other issues when your invoice numbers are in numeric order. If you notice the gap, in the Invoice # box, type the invoice number you want to use to get QuickBooks back on track.

- **Bill To.** The Bill To field is essential when you mail your invoices. When the customer record includes a billing address (page 56), QuickBooks uses that address to fill in this field. If you email invoices, a billing address isn't necessary—the customer name in the Bill To field identifies the customer on the emailed form.

Tip: If QuickBooks fills in fields with incorrect values, make the corrections on the invoice. You can't lose. When you save the invoice, QuickBooks asks if you would like the new values to appear the next time. If you click Yes, QuickBooks changes the corresponding fields in the customer and job records. If you click No, QuickBooks changes the values only on the invoice.

- **Ship To.** If you sell services, you don't need an address for the Ship To box. But when you sell products, you need a Ship To address to send the products to your customer. When the customer record includes a shipping address (page 56), QuickBooks uses that address to fill in the field.

- **P.O. Number.** If your customer issued a purchase order for the goods and services on your invoice, type that purchase order number.

- **Terms.** Typically, you set up the payment terms when you create customers, which you then use for every invoice. When the customer record includes payment terms (page 118), QuickBooks uses those terms to fill in this field. However, if you decide to change the payment terms, perhaps due to the customer's failing financial strength, choose a different term, such as "Due on receipt." When you save the invoice, QuickBooks offers to save that change to the customer record.

- **Rep.** If you assigned a sales rep in the customer record (page 116), QuickBooks fills in this field for you. If the sales rep changes from invoice to invoice (for instance, when the rep is the person who takes a phone order), leave the Rep field in the customer record blank. When you create an invoice, QuickBooks leaves the Rep box blank and you can choose the right person.

- **Ship Date.** QuickBooks fills in the current date. If you plan to ship on a different date (when the products arrive from your warehouse, for example), type or choose the ship date.

- **Ship Via.** If you set the Usual Shipping Method preference (page 161), QuickBooks uses that value to fill in the Ship Via box. To choose a different shipping method for this purchase—for instance when your customer needs the order right away—in the invoice Ship Via box, choose the shipping method you want.

- **FOB.** FOB stands for Free on Board and signifies the physical point at which the customer becomes responsible for the shipment. That means that if the shipment becomes lost or damaged beyond the FOB point, it's the customer's problem. If you set the Usual FOB preference, QuickBooks uses that preference to fill in the FOB box. To choose a different shipping method for this order, you must type the FOB location you want.

***

Note: Unlike many of the other fields in the invoice header, the FOB box doesn't include a drop-down list. QuickBooks doesn't keep a list of FOB locations because most companies pick one FOB location and stick with it.

***

Entering Invoice Line Items

If you dutifully studied the material in Chapter 4, you already know about the different types of items that you can add to an invoice. This section describes how to fill in a line in the line-item table to charge your customers for the things they buy.

The order in which you add items to an invoice is important. For example, when you add a Subtotal item, QuickBooks subtotals all the preceding items up to the previous Subtotal item (if one is present). QuickBooks does nothing to check that you add items in the correct order. You can add a Subtotal item as the first line item, even though that does nothing for your invoice. See page 208 for info on adding Subtotal, Discount, and Sales Tax items in the right order.

The columns in the line-item table vary from template to template, but this section and Figure 8-4 show the columns in the order they appear on the Intuit Product Invoice template:

- **Quantity.** For products, type the quantity. For services you sell by the hour (or other unit of time), type the number of hours. If you sell services with a flat rate, you can leave the Quantity cell blank.

  When you use the Intuit Product Invoice, the Quantity column is the first column. After you choose an item, make sure to check the value in the Amount field. If the number looks too large or too small, the quantity that you entered might not match the units for the item. For example, if you charge for developing training materials by the hour, but charge for teaching a training class by the day, your quantity for developing training materials must be in hours and your quantity for teaching must be in days.

  You can't edit the Quantity field when the item is a discount, subtotal, or sales tax. If you choose one of these items after entering a quantity, QuickBooks removes the value in the Quantity field.

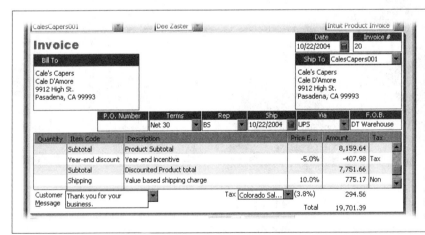

Figure 8-4:
It seems odd to set the quantity before you choose an item, but that's how the Intuit Product Invoice works. If you realize that you entered the wrong quantity after you pick an item, simply edit the Quantity field. After you've added your first line item, start another line item by clicking any field in the first empty line of the table.

- **Item Code.** From the Item drop-down list, choose an item (see Chapter 4).

  Depending on the information you entered when you created the item in the Item List (page 91), QuickBooks can fill in the Description field and Price Each (or Rate) field for you.

- **Description.** You can keep the description that comes with the item you added or you can edit it. For example, when you set up your inventory items with standard descriptions, you don't have to change the description in the invoice. On the other hand, you can add detail to a vague description—for instance, editing the description "Lawn service" to "Mow lawn, June 2005."

- **Price Each (or Rate).** Depending on the type of item you're adding to the invoice, QuickBooks uses the value in the Sales Price field or Rate field in the item record (see Chapter 4). For example, service items use the Rate field, unless a partner or subcontractor performs the work, and then it uses the Sales Price field. An inventory part always uses the Sales Price field.

Tip: Don't forget that different items can use different units for their price. If you charge for a service by the hour, the value in the Rate or Price Each field is the price per hour and the value you type in the Quantity field should be the number of hours. Conversely, if you use a fixed fee for your "How to Get Along with Your Mother-in-law" seminar, type *1* in the Quantity field (or simply leave the field blank). Alternatively, if you use the Time & Expense or Fixed Fee templates (page 197), you don't have to remember these rules.

ALTERNATIVE REALITY

Invoicing for Nonprofits

When you sell products and services for a living, you create invoices when someone buys something. For nonprofits, invoices record the pledges, donations, grants, or other contributions you've been promised.

Invoicing for nonprofits differs from the profit world's approach. First of all, many nonprofits don't bother sending invoices to donors. Nonprofits might send reminders to donors who haven't sent in the pledged donations, but they don't add finance charges to late payments.

Moreover, because some donors have specific reporting, nonprofits often use several Accounts Receivable accounts to track money coming from grants, dues, pledges, and other sources. When you use multiple Accounts Receivable accounts, the Create Invoices dialog box includes an Account field where you can choose the Accounts Receivable account. For example, if you create an invoice for pledges, you'll choose the Pledges Receivable account.

To compensate for this additional field, QuickBooks provides a handy feature when you use multiple Accounts Receivable accounts. The program remembers the last invoice number used for each account, so you can create unique invoice numbering schemes for each account.

- **Amount.** QuickBooks calculates the total in this field by multiplying the quantity by the value in the Price Each (or Rate) field.

- **Tax.** If you set up the taxable status of your customers (page 58) and the items you sell (page 86), QuickBooks automatically handles sales tax on your invoices. For example, when an item is taxable *and* the customer is liable for paying sales tax, the program calculates the total sales tax that appears below the table (see Figure 8-1 on page 194) by totaling all the taxable items on your invoice and multiplying by the tax rate set in the Tax box. (QuickBooks fills this box in with the sales tax item you set in the customer's record.)

Tip: If you notice that the taxable status isn't correct, don't change the value in the Tax field. You're better off correcting the customer's or the item's tax status so you don't affect other customers' invoices.

Inserting and Deleting Line Items

Sometimes, you forget to add line items that you need. For example, you've added several services and inventory items to your invoice, and you realize that you need Subtotal items following the last service and last inventory items so you can apply a shipping charge only to the inventory items.

Here's how you insert and delete lines in the line-item table:

- **Insert a line.** Right-click the line above which you want to insert a line and then choose Insert Line from the shortcut menu. If you prefer keyboard shortcuts, press Ctrl+Insert to insert a line.

- **Delete a line.** Right-click the line you want to delete and choose Delete Line from the shortcut menu. Or, you can press Ctrl+Delete to delete a line.

As shown in Figure 8-5, QuickBooks adjusts the invoice's lines accordingly.

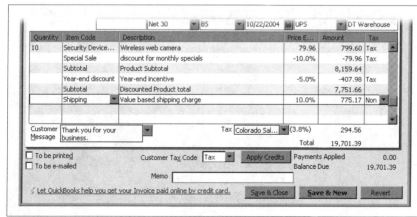

Figure 8-5:
As you add items to the table, QuickBooks adds blank lines (and new pages to your invoice). Tab into or click a blank line to add as many lines as you need. The number of items visible depends on the size of the Create Invoices dialog box. To view more items, resize the window by dragging a corner or move the scroll bar up or down.

Invoicing for Billable Time and Costs

When you work on a time and materials contract, you charge the customer for the job expenses plus labor costs. Cost-plus contracts are similar except that you charge a fee on top of the job costs. Contracts like these are both low-risk and low-reward—in effect, you're earning an hourly wage for the time you work. For these types of contracts, it's critical that you capture all the expenses associated with the job or you'll lose the profit that the contract offers.

Assigning time and expenses to customers or jobs

QuickBooks has features for tracking your time and expenses. The features don't guarantee that you'll remember to enter every hour you worked and every expense you incurred for a job. But once you enter those things into QuickBooks, it's easy to build an invoice that captures them.

Before you can pop your billable time and expenses into your invoices, you must first record them as billable items and assign them to the correct customer or job. Here are the billable items you can add to your invoices and the chapters where you'll learn how to track them:

- **Billable time.** Chapter 17 (page 424) describes how to track your billable time and assign your hours to a customer or job.

- **Mileage.** Chapter 17 (page 445) describes how to track mileage and assign mileage to a customer or job.

- **Purchases and expenses related to a customer or job.** Reimbursable expenses include products you purchase specifically for a job, services you obtain from a subcontractor, and other expenses such as shipping and postage. Chapter 10 describes how to assign items you purchase and expenses you incur (page 291) to a customer or job as you enter bills, checks, or credit card charges in Quick-Books.

GEM IN THE ROUGH

Invoicing Fixed-Price Contracts

Fixed-price contracts are risky for contractors because the contractor must swallow any cost overruns on the job. However, if you've sharpened your skills on similar projects in the past and can estimate the costs with reasonable accuracy, a fixed-price contract provides opportunity for better-than-average profit.

Once you and your customer agree on the fixed price, that price is all that matters to the customer. Even if *you* track the costs of performing a job, your customer never sees those numbers. In QuickBooks, you can invoice fixed-price contracts two different ways:

- If you use the same sets of services and products for multiple jobs, create a Group item that contains each service and product you deliver and set up the

Group item to hide the details of the underlying services and products (page 99). After you add the Group item to your invoice, change the price of the Group item to your fixed price.

- If every fixed price job is different, create a Service item (page 92) called something like Fixed Fee. When you create the item, fill in the Rate field with the full amount of the fixed-price contract. Then, when you reach a milestone that warrants a payment, create a progress invoice (page 219). In the Qty column, type the decimal that equates to the percentage complete (.25 for 25 percent). QuickBooks calculates the payment by multiplying the quantity by the fixed price amount.

Adding billable time and expenses to invoices

Here's how to include billable time and expenses on an invoice:

1. To create a new invoice, in the QuickBooks icon bar, click Invoice.

   QuickBooks opens the Create Invoices dialog box and displays a blank invoice. You can also open this dialog box by clicking Invoices in the QuickBooks Home page.

2. In the Customer:Job box, choose a customer or job.

   As soon as you choose a customer or job, QuickBooks checks to see whether it has billable time or costs that you haven't billed. If the program finds any, you'll see a message box telling you to click Time/Costs to include those costs on the invoice, as shown in Figure 8-6.

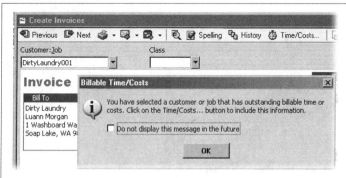

Figure 8-6:
Although you can turn on the checkbox to prevent the reminder from appearing in the future, it's better to leave it turned off. Having to click OK to dismiss the reminder is a small inconvenience compared to forgetting to invoice your customer for time and expenses.

3. To add billable time and costs, in the Create Invoices dialog box icon bar, click Time/Costs.

   QuickBooks opens the "Choose Billable Time and Costs" dialog box, which includes tabs for different types of reimbursable items, as shown in Figure 8-7.

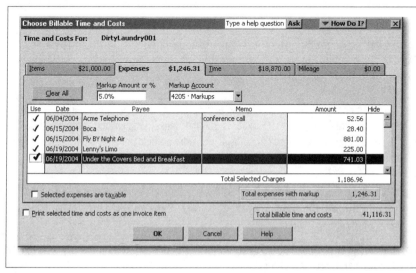

Figure 8-7:
If you mark up expenses, such as phone calls and postage, the Expenses tab lets you track them. In the "Markup Amount or %" box, type the markup's dollar value or percentage. Choose the income account for the markup. If applicable, turn on the "Selected expenses are taxable" checkbox to have QuickBooks calculate the sales tax. If the customer is tax exempt, QuickBooks doesn't add sales tax no matter what.

4. **To include items that you purchased specifically for this customer or job, click the Items tab.**

   To the left of every item you want to include, click the cell in the Use column.

Tip: To add all the entries on a tab, click Select All.

Adding Different Markups to Billable Expenses

The Expenses tab contains only one "Markup Amount or %" box, which is frightfully inconvenient if you add markup to some, but not all, of the billable expenses. But there's nothing stopping you from adding these expenses to your invoice in two batches. And you can assign a different markup amount or percentage to each batch. Here's how it works:

1. In the Create Invoices dialog box icon bar, click Time/Costs, and, in the "Choose Billable Time and Costs" dialog box, click the Expenses tab.

2. In the "Markup Amount or %" box, type the markup for the first batch of expenses.

3. Click the Use field for each expense that you want to mark up.

4. Click OK to add the selected expenses to the invoice.

5. In the Create Invoices dialog box icon bar, click Time/Costs again, and, in the "Choose Billable Time and Costs" dialog box, click the Expenses tab.

6. Change the value in the "Markup Amount or %" to the next markup.

7. Repeat steps 3 and 4.

This technique works just as well when some of the expenses are taxable while others aren't. Choose the taxable items, turn on the "Selected expenses are taxable" checkbox, and add the taxable expenses to the invoice. Reopen the "Choose Billable Time and Costs" dialog box, choose the nontaxable items, turn off the "Selected expenses are taxable" checkbox, and add the nontaxable expenses to the invoice.

---

5. **To include reimbursable expenses such as postage and telephone calls, click the Expenses tab.**

   To the left of every expense you want to include, click the cell in the Use column. As shown in Figure 8-7, the pointer changes to a checkmark when you position it in the Use column.

Tip: On the Expenses tab, the Memo column displays what you typed in the Memo field for the original vendor bill, check, or credit card charge. QuickBooks uses the entries in this column as the description on the invoice, so you don't want to leave these fields blank. If you didn't enter a Memo in the original expense transaction, you'll have to type the description for each expense once they're added to the invoice.

---

6. **To include the billable hours worked, on the Time tab, click the Use field for each time entry.**

   To change how your billable hours appear on the invoice, click Options. You can display each activity as a separate line or combine all activities for the same

---

Service item on one line. If each activity is on its own line, you can transfer activity descriptions, notes, or both to the invoice.

Note: In the "Choose Billable Time and Costs" dialog box, the tabs display the total amount for the billable expenses that you've selected on that tab.

7. **To include mileage, on the Mileage tab, click the Use column for each entry.**

   You can control how mileage charges transfer in the same way you can control billable hours.

8. **If you want to summarize the costs on the Expenses tab and the time on the Time tab on one line of the invoice, turn on the "Print selected time and costs as one invoice item" checkbox.**

   When you turn on this checkbox, you'll still see all the individual entries in the Create Invoices dialog box. QuickBooks displays the detail in the Create Invoices dialog box, so you can review the invoice for accuracy. The printed invoice shows only one line labeled Total Reimbursable Expenses.

Tip: Once you've created the invoice with one line for time and costs, it takes several steps to recreate it showing individual costs. To change an invoice back to a line-by-line listing, in the Create Invoices dialog box, delete the Total Reimbursable Expenses line item. Click Time/Costs to open the "Choose Billable Time and Costs" dialog box and reselect all the entries you want. Turn off the "Print selected time and costs as one invoice item" checkbox and then click OK.

9. **When you've selected all the billable items you want to add from every tab, in the "Choose Billable Time and Costs" dialog box, click OK.**

   QuickBooks adds all the billable items you selected to the invoice, as demonstrated in Figure 8-8.

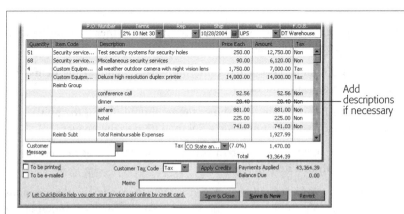

Add descriptions if necessary

Figure 8-8:
This invoice shows the time spent on each Service item on a separate line. If you didn't type memos in the original expense transactions, you have to type the descriptions for billable expenses directly on the invoice. After that, you can edit the quantities, descriptions, and prices on the invoice, but doing so could lead to confusion later when you try to correlate income to your expenses.

Applying Subtotals, Discounts, and Percentage Charges

Services, Inventory Parts, and Non-inventory Parts (see Chapter 4) are standalone items. When you add them to the line-item table, they don't affect their neighbors in any way. However, with percentage discounts on what you sell or Other Charge items that calculate shipping as a percentage of price, the order that you add items becomes crucial. And, if you want to apply a percentage to several items, you'll also need one or more Subtotal items to make the calculations work.

You first learned about Subtotal, Discount, and Other Charge items in Chapter 4, but Figure 8-9 shows how to combine them to calculate percentage discounts and add markups to the items on your invoice.

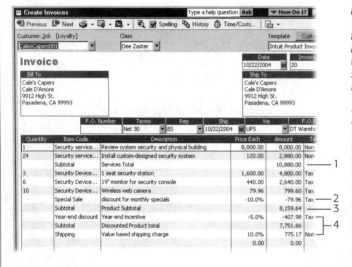

Figure 8-9:
1: A Subtotal item adds the values of all the items up to the previous Subtotal item. For example, if you want to keep the Service items out of the product subtotal, add a Subtotal item after the last Service item.

2: For Discount items and Other Charge items created as percentages, QuickBooks multiplies the percentage by the total on the preceding line. If the discount applies only to one item, add the Discount item immediately below the item you want to discount.

3: If you want to apply a percentage discount to several items, use a Subtotal item to total their cost.

4: Add a percentage Discount or Other Charge item on the line following a Subtotal.

Here are the steps for arranging Subtotal, Discount, and Other Charge items to calculate percentages on invoice items:

1. **If you want to discount several items on your invoice, add all the items you want to discount one after the other.**

   Even though the Balance Due field shows the total of all items, to apply a discount to all of them, you must first add a Subtotal item to the invoice.

2. **Add a Subtotal item after the last item you want to discount, as demonstrated by the Product Subtotal item in Figure 8-9.**

   The Subtotal item adds up all the preceding line items up to the previous Subtotal. For example, in Figure 8-9, the Services Total item is a subtotal of the Service items on the invoice. The Product Subtotal item adds up all items between the Services Total and the Product Subtotal items.

3. To apply a percentage discount or charge to the subtotal, simply add the Discount or Other Charge Item to the line immediately below the Subtotal item.

   If you've already added other items to your invoice, right-click the line immediately below the Subtotal item and choose Insert Line from the shortcut menu.

4. **If you have additional items that you don't want to include in the discount or charge, add those below the Discount or Other Charge item.**

Tip: These steps also work for Other Charge items that you set up as percentages.

FREQUENTLY ASKED QUESTION

Adjusting Price Levels

I run a doggie spa, and one of my Service items is Deluxe Spa Day, with the price set to $300. But when I was doing a customer invoice, the Price Each came up as $250! What's going on?

Before you rush to correct that Service item's price, look near the top of the Create Invoices dialog box, immediately to the right of the Customer:Job label. If you see text in square brackets, such as "[Preferred]", you'll know that you set up your customer with a price level (page 58). Instead of a mistake, this price adjustment on your invoice is actually a clever and convenient feature.

Price levels are percentages (either increases or decreases) that you can apply to the prices you charge. For example, you can set up price levels to give discounts to your high-volume customers or mark up prices for customers well-known for their thorough exercising of your customer service line. If you apply a price level to a customer, Quick-Books automatically applies the price level percentage to every item you add to invoices for that customer. The only indication you'll see is the price level name next to the Customer:Job label. To use price levels, you must first turn on the price level preference (page 162).

You can also apply price levels to individual items in an invoice. For example, suppose you offer a 20 percent discount on a different item each month. When an item is the monthly special, you can apply the Monthly Special price level to just that item. To do so, click the Price Each (or Rate) field for the item that's on special. When QuickBooks displays a downward-pointing triangle to indicate that a drop-down list is available, click the triangle and then choose the price level you want to apply, as demonstrated in the figure.

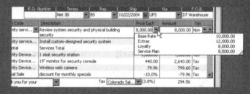

When you use price levels, your customers don't see that the price increases or decreases, which could mean that they could take your discounts for granted. If you want to emphasize the discounts you apply, use a Discount item instead to visibly reduce prices on your invoice (see page 208).

Adding a Message to the Customer

You can include a message to your customers on your invoices—for instance, reminding them that you'll send your cousin Guido over if they don't pay. In the Customer Message drop-down list, choose the message you want to include. The messages that appear in the drop-down list are the ones you've added to the Customer Message List.

Tip: If the message you want to use doesn't exist, in the drop-down list, click <*Add New*> to open the New Customer Message dialog box.

Choosing How to Send the Invoice

Below the line-item table, you'll find two checkboxes that simplify sending your invoices to your customers: "To be printed" and "To be mailed." But these checkboxes don't tell the whole story because you actually have five options for sending your invoices:

- **Print immediately.** If you create only the occasional invoice and send it as soon as it's complete, turn off both checkboxes. In the Create Invoices dialog box icon bar, click the Print icon and follow the instructions on page 235.

- **Email immediately.** In the Create Invoices dialog box icon bar, click the Send icon and follow the detailed instructions on emailing invoices on page 243.

- **Print later.** If you want to add the invoice to a queue to print later, turn on the "To be printed" checkbox. Then, you can print all the invoices in the queue, as described on page 240.

- **Email later.** If you want to add the invoice to a queue to email later, turn on the "To be e-mailed" checkbox. You can send all the invoices in the queue via email, as described on page 244.

- **Print and email later.** You can turn on both checkboxes if you want to email invoices to get the ball rolling and follow up with paper copies.

Adding a Memo to Yourself

The Create Invoices dialog box includes a Memo box, which works identically to Memo boxes throughout QuickBooks. You can use the Memo box to remind yourself about something special on the invoice or to summarize the transaction. For example, if the invoice is the first one for a new customer, you can note that in the Memo box. The memo appears in your sales reports, although it won't print on the invoices you send to your customers.

Invoicing for Backordered Products

Placing a product order to fulfill your customers' orders is known as a *backorder*. If backorders are a big part of your business, you should consider finding suppliers who deliver more quickly, but you might also consider upgrading to QuickBooks Premier, which has a built-in sales order form for tracking backordered items. By combining a few of QuickBooks Pro's features, you can handle backorders with no trouble.

When you tell your customers that a product is out of stock, they might ask you to handle the backorders in different ways. Here are the most common requests for backorders:

- **Remove the backordered items from the order.** Customers in a hurry ask you to fill the order with only the products you have in stock. If they can't find the backordered products anywhere else, they can call in a new order.

- **Ship all items at once.** If convenience is more important than delivery date, you can hold the customer order until the backordered products arrive and ship the entire order at once.

- **Ship backordered items when they arrive.** Many customers request that you process their orders for the products you *do* have in stock and send the back-ordered products when you receive them.

If you remove backordered items from an order, you can ship the entire order and invoice the customer immediately. But when customers ask you to hold all or part of their orders until backordered products arrive, they usually expect you to invoice for backordered products only when you ship them. In the meantime, you don't want the income appearing in your account balances until the order ships.

Tip: If you need help remembering *how* customers prefer that you handle their backorders, store back-order preferences in a custom field in the customer record (page 128) or in the Customer Center (select the customer and click Edit Notes). Any information you add to the customer Notepad appears front and center whenever you select the customer on the Customers & Jobs tab.

Using Pending Invoices for Backorders

In QuickBooks, setting an invoice status to Pending places it in a holding pattern with no income or expenses posting to your accounts. But they're easy to spot in the Create Invoices dialog box—QuickBooks adds a Pending stamp to the form.

To set an invoice to Pending status, display the invoice in the Create Invoices dialog box (Ctrl+I) and choose Edit → Mark Invoice as Pending. After QuickBooks adds the "Pending (non-posting)" stamp to the invoice, click Save & Close.

When the backordered products arrive, open the invoice in the Create Invoices dialog box, choose Edit → Mark Invoice as Final. When you save the invoice, QuickBooks posts its values to the appropriate accounts.

Pending invoices are also great for entering transactions ahead of time, but holding them until you receive approval for a sale or reach the milestone that the invoice represents.

Tip: You can set sales receipts and credit memos to Pending status as well. To see all your pending sales, choose Reports → Sales → Pending Sales.

Using Sales Orders for Backorders

QuickBooks Premier and Enterprise have a Sales Order form, which also comes in handy for backorders. The Create Sales Orders dialog box looks like the Create Invoices dialog box, except that the item table includes an Ordered column, which holds the number of items the customer ordered but that you haven't yet invoiced. In effect, it's a record of how much stock you need to have on hand to fill the order.

Tip: To see all your sales orders at once, choose Reports → Sales and then choose either "Open Sales Order by Customer" or "Open Sales Orders by Item."

If you create an invoice for items that you don't have in stock, you'll see an error message warning of the shortfall. This message tells you how many you have on hand, how many are on other sales orders, and the remaining quantity available. Because the products aren't in stock, the Quantity is a negative number. You can then cancel the invoice and create a sales order instead.

If you already know that your inventory is woefully low, simply create a sales order for the customer's order. Then, if a review of your inventory shows that some items aren't in stock, you can create a partial invoice for the items in stock and use the sales order to track the backordered items. Since the sales orders keep a running balance of backordered items, you can easily create a purchase order to restock the products you need. Here are the steps:

1. **To open the Create Sales Orders dialog box, click Sales Orders on the Home page (or choose Customers → Create Sales Orders).**

   Fill in the fields for the sales order as you would the fields in an invoice (page 194). The only difference is that you record the quantity of items ordered in the Ordered column, instead of an invoice's Quantity column.

2. **In the icon bar, click Create Invoice.**

   The aptly named "Create Invoice Based on Sales Order(s)" dialog box opens.

3. **To create a partial invoice for the items you have in stock, select the "Create invoice for selected items" option and click OK.**

   The "Specify Invoice Quantities for Items on Sales Order(s)" dialog box appears, showing you how many items you have in stock. QuickBooks automatically fills in the To Invoice column with the number of items on hand because you usually invoice for only the products you can ship, but you can edit the quantity if you wish.

4. **Click OK to create an invoice for the in-stock items.**

   When you click OK, the program creates the invoice. If you return to the Create Sales Orders dialog box and look at the sales order on which you based the invoice, you'll see the backordered items in the Ordered column. You can place an order for the backordered items while it's still fresh in your mind.

5. In the icon bar, click the down arrow to the right of Create Invoice, and choose Purchase Order.

The "Create Purchase Order Based on the Sales Transaction" dialog box appears, already filled in with the items you need to fulfill the backorder. You can adjust this number if you wish.

6. Select the "Create purchase order for selected items" option, and click OK to create a purchase order for only the items on backorder.

You have to choose the vendor who supplies the items you want to order. And if you purchase the items from multiple vendors, you have to create separate purchase orders for each vendor.

After you replenish your inventory, you can create a final invoice from the sales order, as described previously.

POWER USERS' CLINIC

Adding Group Items to Invoices

If you find the same items frequently appearing together on your invoices, you can add those items in one step by first creating a Group item (page 99).

For example, your customers seem to buy your deluxe vinyl sofa covers with the dirt-magnet front hall runner and the deluxe garage floor liner. A Group item, perhaps called the Neat Freak Package, can include the items for the sofa covers, runner, and garage floor liner. You can create a Group item with the quantity you typically sell of each item. Any type of item is fair game for a Group item, so you can include discounts, subtotals, and other charges as well.

To add a Group item to an invoice, in the Create Invoices dialog box, in the Item Code drop-down list, choose the Neat Freak Package Group item. QuickBooks fills in the first line by adding the name of the Group item in the Item Code field. Then, the program adds additional lines (including quantity, description, and price) for the sofa cover, runner, and garage floor liner.

Memorizing Recurring Invoices

If you charge a fixed monthly fee for your services or work on retainer, the invoices you create are basically the same each month except for the invoice date. If you would rather sleep than do paperwork, it's easy to get QuickBooks to create your invoices for you. With a memorized invoice, QuickBooks handles the entire process or reminds you when it's time to create your invoice.

Here's how to automate a recurring invoice:

1. In the Create Invoices dialog box, create the invoice that you want to reuse.

Fill in the fields that remain the same on each invoice, such as the Service item and rate. If your hours change from invoice to invoice, leave the Quantity field blank.

2. When the invoice is set up the way you want, press Ctrl+M.

The Memorize Transaction dialog box opens.

---

3. **Give the reusable invoice a name in the Name box.**

For example, you might include the customer's name or the type of retainer, such as Full-time Programming Contract.

4. **Choose an option to specify whether you want QuickBooks to remind you.**

If you select Remind Me, QuickBooks adds the memorized transaction to the Reminders list.

When you memorize a transaction and choose the Automatically Enter option, you don't have to do anything to add the next invoice. QuickBooks enters it for you based on the schedule you specified.

The Don't Remind Me option is asking for trouble because you don't want to forget to send recurring invoices. However, it's perfect when you want to cancel a recurring invoice.

Note: To make sure you actually *see* these reminders, choose Edit → Preferences. In the icon bar, click Reminders, and, on the My Preferences tab, turn on the "Show Reminders List when opening a Company file" checkbox. That way, when you open the company file, the program displays a Start Up box that asks if you want to enter memorized transactions. Click Now to add them.

---

5. **To memorize the invoice, click OK.**

QuickBooks closes the Memorize Transaction dialog box and adds the invoice to the Memorized Transaction List.

6. **In the Create Invoices dialog box, click Save & Close to save the invoice.**

The program creates the invoice and also adds a memorized invoice for later use. If you created the invoice simply to set up a memorized transaction, click Clear and then click the Close button to close the dialog box without saving the invoice.

Editing a Memorized Invoice

Editing a memorized invoice is technically editing and rememorizing it. To do so, choose Lists → Memorized Transaction List (or press Ctrl+T) to open the Memorized Transaction List. Select the invoice and click Enter Transaction, which opens the invoice in the Create Invoices dialog box. Do your editing, and then press Ctrl+M to rememorize it with the changes you've made. When you click Replace, the edited invoice takes the place of the previous one in the Memorized Transaction List.

If the invoice *information* is correct but you want to change the recurrence schedule, select the invoice in the Memorized Transaction List and press Ctrl+E to edit the memorized transaction. The Schedule Memorized Transaction dialog box appears with settings for reminders and the recurrence (page 280).

Estimating Jobs

Many customers ask for an estimate before hiring you to perform a job. If you're good with numbers, you might tot up the costs in your head and scribble the estimate on a napkin. But creating estimates in QuickBooks not only generates a more professional-looking estimate for your customer, it also makes it easier to invoice your customer as you perform the work. QuickBooks estimates make short work of pricing small-time and material jobs. When you create an estimate in Quick-Books, you add the items you'll sell or deliver and set the markup on those items.

UP TO SPEED

The Link Between Sales Forms and Accounts

An invoice or other sales form is the first step in the flow of money through your company, so it's a good time to look at how QuickBooks posts income and expenses on your invoices to the accounts in your Chart of Accounts. If you're still getting used to double-entry accounting, balancing the debit and credit amounts for an invoice is a brainteaser. Suppose your invoice has the entries shown here:

Here's how the amounts on the invoice post to accounts in your Chart of Accounts:

Account	Debit	Credit
Accounts Receivable	5812.62	
Services Revenue		5000
Product Revenue		990
Sales Discounts	250	
Sales Tax Payable		37.62
Shipping		35
Cost of Good Sold	420.50	
Inventory		420.50

And, here's why the amounts post the way they do. You sold $5,000 of services and $990 of products, which is income. The values appear as credits to your Services Income and Product Revenue accounts to show that you sold something. In this example, the discount is in an income account, so the discount *reduces* your income. The sales tax you collect is a credit to the Sales Tax Payable account. Your shipping charge reduces your shipping expense account.

All those credits must balance against a debit. Because your customer owes you money, the amount owed belongs in the Accounts Receivable account, indicated by the debit.

You also sold some products from inventory. You credit the Inventory account with the cost of the products, which decreases the Inventory account balance. You offset that credit with a debit to the Cost of Good Sold account, which is an income statement account.

Truth be told, QuickBooks estimating is not for every business. Particularly in construction, when you might require hundreds or even thousands of items for a major project, you definitely don't want to enter all the data you'd need to build the Item List for your project. That's why most construction firms turn to third-party estimating packages, which come with databases of the services and products you need. Many of these estimating packages integrate with QuickBooks, which means you can import an estimate you created in another program and use it to produce your invoices (see Chapter 21).

Note: The totals on estimates don't post to accounts in your Chart of Accounts. After all, an estimate doesn't mean that your customer has committed to going ahead with the job. But the estimates show the potential value of a job without showing up in your financial reports, like the Project & Loss report. When you turn on the preference for estimates (page 151), QuickBooks creates a *non-posting* account, called Estimates, which is where it stores estimate values. (If you use account numbers, its account number is 4.)

Creating an Estimate

If you've mastered QuickBooks invoices, you'll feel right at home with the fields that appear in a QuickBooks estimate, as the Create Estimates window shown in Figure 8-10 confirms.

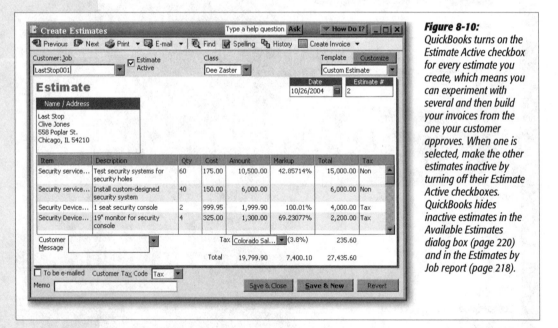

Figure 8-10:
QuickBooks turns on the Estimate Active checkbox for every estimate you create, which means you can experiment with several and then build your invoices from the one your customer approves. When one is selected, make the other estimates inactive by turning off their Estimate Active checkboxes. QuickBooks hides inactive estimates in the Available Estimates dialog box (page 220) and in the Estimates by Job report (page 218).

Here's how you create an estimate and handle the small differences between invoices and estimates:

1. **To begin an estimate, on the Home page, click Estimates (or choose Customers → Create Estimates).**

   QuickBooks opens the Create Estimates window. QuickBooks automatically chooses the Custom Estimate template in the Template box. If you've created your own estimate template (page 550), in the Template drop-down list, choose your customized template.

2. **As you do for an invoice, build your estimate by adding items to the line-item table.**

   In a blank line in the line-item table, in the Item drop-down list, choose the item that you want to add to the estimate. When you fill in the quantity, Quick-Books uses the cost and sales price from the item record to fill in the Cost, Amount, Markup, and Total fields. QuickBooks calculates the markup percentage by dividing the sales price for the item by the cost of the item.

Note: The calculated value in the Total field isn't set in stone. If you change the Total value, QuickBooks recalculates the markup percentage for you. Likewise, if you change the percentage in the Markup field, QuickBooks recalculates the value in the Total field.

---

3. **To email the estimate to your customer, turn on the "To be e-mailed" checkbox.**

   QuickBooks queues up the estimate to be emailed later (page 244). For reasons unknown, you can't queue up an estimate to print later. If you want to print an estimate, in the Create Estimates window icon bar, click the Print icon.

4. **When the estimate is complete, click Save & Close to save the estimate and close the Create Estimates window.**

After you've created an estimate and printed it or emailed it to your customer, you don't do much with it until the customer gives you the nod for the job. At that point, you can base progress invoices on the estimate (page 219) as you reach milestones on the job.

Creating Multiple Estimates

Whether you're creating a second estimate because the customer thought the first price was too high, or you're creating separate estimates for each phase of a multi-year job, it's easy to build and manage several estimates for the same job. You've got the following methods at your disposal:

- **Creating an estimate.** You can create additional estimates for a job simply by creating a new estimate (as described in the previous section). When you create additional estimates, QuickBooks makes them active so that they appear in the Available Estimates dialog box and in the Estimates by Job report.

- **Duplicating an estimate.** If you want to play what-if games with an existing estimate, duplicate it and then make your adjustments. To duplicate an estimate, in the Create Estimates window, display the estimate you want to copy and then choose Edit → Duplicate Estimate. QuickBooks pulls everything from the existing estimate onto a new one, and it uses the next estimate number in sequence. After you make the changes you want, click Save & Close or Save & New.

- **Making an estimate inactive.** When you create several estimates for the same work, eventually you and your customer will pick one to run with. When you reach that point, you *can* delete the other estimates. If you want a record of your other attempts, make them inactive instead. To make an estimate inactive, in the Create Estimates window, display the estimate and then turn off the Estimate Active checkbox. Click Save & New to save the estimate while keeping the Create Estimates window open. If you want to make another estimate inactive, click Previous or Next until the estimate appears, and then repeat the steps.

POWER USERS' CLINIC

Building Boilerplate Estimates

Suppose you've put a lot of thought into the typical tasks you perform and the materials you need for different types of jobs. You can capture this information in QuickBooks estimates so that you can quickly produce an estimate for a new customer that takes into account your performance on similar jobs in the past. To create a boilerplate estimate, build an estimate with all the information you reuse and then memorize that estimate. Here's how:

1. In the Create Estimates window, fill in all the fields and line items you want in the boilerplate estimate. If you want to capture the items you use but not the quantities, in the line-item table, leave the Qty cells blank.

2. To memorize the transaction, press Ctrl+M.

3. QuickBooks tells you that it removes the Customer: Job so you can use the memorized estimate for any customer. Click OK to dismiss the message.

4. In the Memorize Transaction dialog box, type a name for the memorized transaction. For example, if you're creating a boilerplate estimate for fire mitigation, use a name like Standard Fire Mitigation Estimate.

5. Because you'll recall this estimate only when you get a similar job, choose the Don't Remind Me option.

6. Click OK to add the estimate to your Memorized Transaction List.

7. When you bid on a similar job, press Ctrl+T to open the Memorized Transaction List window.

8. Double-click the memorized estimate to open the Create Estimates window with the memorized estimate information.

9. In the Customer:Job box, choose the new customer.

10. Click Save & Close.

Tip: If you have too many estimates to click Previous and Next, the Estimates by Job report is a convenient place to look. To display it, choose Reports → Jobs, Time & Mileage → Estimates by Job. This report includes an Estimate Active column, which displays a checkmark if the estimate is active. Double-click anywhere in the line to open that estimate in the Create Estimates window.

- **Deleting an estimate.** Deleting an estimate isn't the no-no that deleting an invoice is. Your only risk is that you'll realize that you wanted to keep the estimate as soon as you delete it. In the Create Estimates window, display the estimate and then choose Edit → Delete Estimate. In the Delete Transaction dialog box, click OK to complete the deletion.

Tip: To protect profit margins from being nibbled away by small changes, many businesses keep track of every change that a customer requests (called change orders). The Contractor and Accountant Editions of QuickBooks let you track change orders on estimates.

Creating Progress Invoices

When you work on jobs and projects that take more than a few days, you probably don't want to wait until the job is completely finished to charge for some of your work. Progress invoices include charges based on both your estimate *and* the progress you've made on the job. These invoices are common for jobs that are broken into phases or when payments occur when you reach milestones. Since most large jobs start with an estimate, you won't have to start from scratch when it's time to invoice your customer. QuickBooks can convert your estimates into progress invoices with only a few additional pieces of information.

Note: To produce progress invoices, you must first turn on the preferences for both creating estimates and progress invoicing (page 151).

Progress Invoicing Options

Progress invoices are still invoices; they just happen to link to estimates you've created for a job. In the Create Invoices dialog box, when you choose a customer or job, QuickBooks checks to see if an estimate exists. If at least one estimate for the customer or job *does* exist, QuickBooks opens the Available Estimates dialog box so that you can choose an estimate to invoice against, as illustrated in Figure 8-11.

When you create your first progress invoice, you can choose to invoice the entire estimate or only a portion. Here are the options that appear in the Create Progress Invoice Based On Estimate dialog box and when you might use them:

- **Create invoice for the entire estimate (100%).** This option is perfect if you prepared an estimate to obtain approval before starting a job, but you completed the job in a short period of time. QuickBooks takes care of the grunt work of transferring all the services, products, and other items from the estimate to the invoice.

Tip: You can edit the invoice amounts, which is handy if, for instance, your actual costs were higher than your estimates. However, the contract you signed determines whether your customer will actually pay the revised amounts!

• **Create invoice for a percentage of the entire estimate.** Choose this option if you negotiated a contract that pays a percentage when you reach a milestone, such as 15 percent when the house foundation is complete. (Of course, you and the customer must agree that a milestone is complete; QuickBooks can't help you with that.) This option is also handy if your contract specifies a number of installment payments. In the "% of estimate" box, type the percentage of completion that you've achieved.

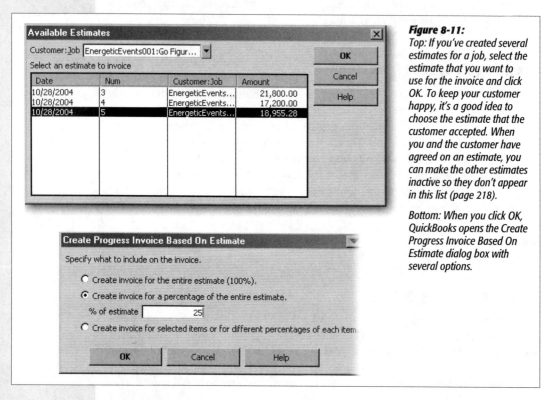

Figure 8-11:
Top: If you've created several estimates for a job, select the estimate that you want to use for the invoice and click OK. To keep your customer happy, it's a good idea to choose the estimate that the customer accepted. When you and the customer have agreed on an estimate, you can make the other estimates inactive so they don't appear in this list (page 218).

Bottom: When you click OK, QuickBooks opens the Create Progress Invoice Based On Estimate dialog box with several options.

Suppose your contract includes a clause that covers cost overruns, and the job ended up costing 20 percent more than the estimate. You might wonder how you can charge for that extra 20 percent. The trick is noticing that the "% of estimate" box doesn't limit the percentage to 100 percent. In this example, type 120 percent for the last invoice to reflect the costs that exceeded the estimate.

• **Create invoice for selected items or for different percentages of each item.** This option is the most flexible and a must if you bill your customers for only the work that is actually complete. For example, if you're building an office complex, one building might be complete while another is still back at the framing phase. When you select this option, you can choose the services and products to include on the invoice and specify different percentages for each one.

Tip: For every progress invoice after the first one for a job, you'll see one additional option for invoicing the remaining amounts in the estimate. Use this option only on your last estimate. Its sole purpose is to save you the brain damage of calculating the percentages that haven't yet billed.

Fine-Tuning a Progress Invoice

In the Create Progress Invoice Based On Estimate dialog box, when you click OK, QuickBooks calculates and automatically fills in the invoice with the estimate items, percentages, and amounts, as demonstrated in Figure 8-12. You don't have to stick with the numbers that QuickBooks comes up with—you can reconfigure the charges on the invoice in any way you want. (However, it's always a good idea to review the customer's contract and get her approval before you make any increases or additions not covered by the contract.)

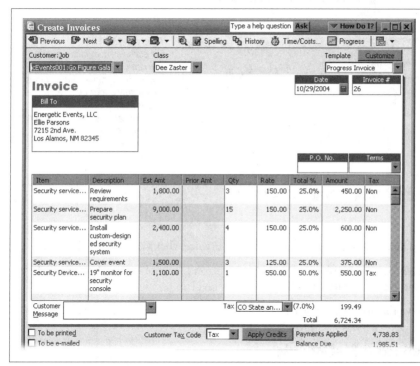

Figure 8-12:
When you provide materials for a job, they're either on site or not. Assigning 50 percent to materials doesn't make any sense unless half the boxes made it. If you want to invoice 25 percent of the services but 100 percent for materials, change the values in the fields in the Total % column. Changing the Total % field also solves the problem of one task that's far behind or far ahead.

You can modify line items directly in a QuickBooks invoice, but that approach doesn't create a history of your changes. If you want to keep a record of the changes you make between estimate and progress invoice, follow these steps instead:

1. **With the progress invoice visible in the Create Invoices dialog box (Ctrl+I) icon bar, click Progress.**

   QuickBooks opens the "Specify Invoice Amounts for Items on Estimate" dialog box.

2. Before you begin changing values, make sure that the correct columns are visible. Turn on the "Show Quantity and Rate" or the Show Percentage checkbox.

   On large projects, you'll probably work with percentages because it's too much effort to track minutiae. But on small jobs, you might prefer knowing the number of items you used and their prices, rather than the resulting percentage. It's rare to use all three, but in QuickBooks, you can turn on both checkboxes to show the Qty, Rate, and Curr % (that's current percentage) columns.

3. To change a value for the progress invoice, click the cell that you want to change, as demonstrated in Figure 8-13.

   Changing a rate is a rare occurrence. However, it might happen, if, for example, you have a contract that bumps your consulting rate by 10 percent for the next calendar year. If the job runs into the next calendar year, you can increase the rate for the hours worked in January.

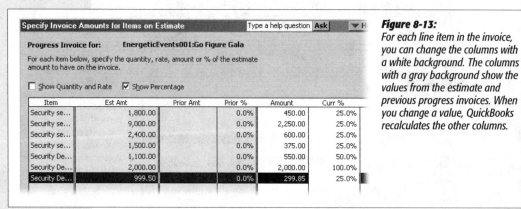

Figure 8-13:
For each line item in the invoice, you can change the columns with a white background. The columns with a gray background show the values from the estimate and previous progress invoices. When you change a value, QuickBooks recalculates the other columns.

4. To apply the changes you made to the invoice, click OK.

   The "Specify Invoice Amounts for Items on Estimate" dialog box closes, taking you back to the now modified progress invoice.

5. Save the progress invoice by clicking Save & New or Save & Close.

Producing Statements

Statements are the least flexible sales forms you can produce (see page 193), but they are perfect for some types of businesses, such as law offices, cable television companies, or pet-walking services. In QuickBooks, creating statements is a two-step process:

1. Enter the statement charges, which are the services or other items you delivered to your customers.

2. **After all the statement charges are complete, generate statements for your customers.**

You don't fill in a statement in QuickBooks the way you do sales receipts and invoices. Think of statements as a view of all the statement charges during the statement period. A statement's previous balance, charges, and customer payments all depend on the dates you choose for the statement. Businesses typically send statements out once a month, but you can generate statements for any time period you want.

Creating Statement Charges

Statement charges look like the line items you see in an invoice, except for a few small but important differences—omissions, to be exact. When you select an item for a statement charge, you won't see any sales tax items, percentage discounts, subtotals, groups, or payment items in your item list.

You can use items in your Item List to create statement charges as long as they're limited to these types:

- Service items
- Inventory Part items
- Non-inventory Part items
- Other Charge items

Unlike invoice line items, you create statement charges directly in the Accounts Receivable register for the customer or job that has racked up charges, as shown in Figure 8-14.

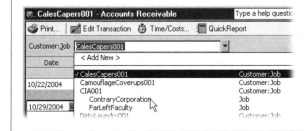

Figure 8-14:
On the Home page, click Statement Charges (or choose Customers → Enter Statement Charges) to open the Accounts Receivable window. In the Customer:Job drop-down list, choose the customer or job for whom you want to create charges.

Tip: If you track time, costs, or mileage, you can create statement charges from those entries. In the Accounts Receivable register in the icon bar, click Time/Costs, and add the items you want (page 224).

CHAPTER 8: INVOICING

A statement charge contains fields much like those for a line item in an invoice. The big difference is that these fields are scrunched into two lines in the Accounts Receivable register, as illustrated in Figure 8-15.

Figure 8-15:
When you choose an item, QuickBooks fills in the Rate, Amt Chrg, and Description fields. QuickBooks set the Type to STMTCHG to denote a charge that appears on a statement rather than an invoice. But invoices and other transactions appear in the register, too, such as invoice number 14.

Here's how to create a statement charge:

1. **In a blank line in the Accounts Receivable window, in the Item field, choose the item you want to charge for. Press Tab to move to the Qty field; type the quantity for the item.**

   Just as you do for invoice line items, enter the quantity based on the units for the item, whether they're hours, days, or physical units. Because QuickBooks fills in the Rate field as soon as you choose an item, it's easier to determine the item units.

   After you enter the quantity and move to another field (by pressing Tab or clicking the field), QuickBooks updates the total amount charged (in the Amt Chrg field) based on the rate and quantity.

Tip: If the item you add has a fixed price, you can skip the Qty field. QuickBooks fills in the Rate field and copies that value to the Amt Chrg field.

---

2. **If the item you add doesn't have a set rate or you want to change the rate, press Tab to move to the Rate field, and type the value you want.**

   When you change the value in the Rate field, QuickBooks recalculates the amount in the Amt Chrg field.

   If you don't use a quantity and rate, you can type the amount charged directly in the Amt Chrg field.

3. **If you want to revise the description for the charge, edit the text in the Description field.**

   QuickBooks automatically fills in the Description field with the first paragraph of the Sales description from the item record, but you can see only a smidgeon of it. To see it all, click the Description field and then keep the pointer over the field. QuickBooks displays the full contents of the field. If this truncated description isn't acceptable, edit the description.

Tip: If you use classes (page 113), in the Class field, choose the one you want.

---

4. **To control which statement the charge appears on, in the Billed Date field, choose the date for the charge.**

   If you don't choose a Billed Date, QuickBooks uses the date in the Date field to corral the charge onto the correct statement.

   When you add a statement charge that you want to save for a future statement, be sure to choose a Billed Date within the correct time period. For example, if a membership fee comes due in April, choose a Billed date during the month of April. The statement charge won't show up until you generate the customer's April statement. On the other hand, if you forgot a charge from the previous month, set its Billed date to a day in the current month so the charge appears on this month's statement.

5. **If you plan to assess finance charges for late payments, in the Due Date field, choose the date when payment is due.**

   QuickBooks uses the date in the Due Date field along with your preferences for finance charges (page 119) to calculate any late charges due. But late charge calculations don't occur until you generate statements.

6. **To save the statement charge, click Record.**

Tip: If you charge the same amount every month, memorize the first statement charge and set its recurrence schedule to the same time each month (page 280). QuickBooks then takes care of entering your statement charges for you, so all you have to do is generate the customer statements once a month.

Generating Customer Statements

QuickBooks is a smart program, but it can't read your mind. The statements that you generate include only the statement charges and other transactions that you've entered. Before you produce your monthly statements, double-check that you've entered all customer payments, credits, or refunds that your customers are due, and all new statement charges for the period.

As Figure 8-16 shows, everything about the statements you generate appears in the Create Statements dialog box, including the date range for the statements, the customers you want to send statements to, the template you use, printing options, and finance charges. To begin creating statements, on the Home page, click Statements (or choose Customers → Create Statements). The sections that follow explain the choices you can make and the best way to apply them.

Choosing the date range

Statements typically cover a set period of time, such as a month. But the date of the statement doesn't have to be during that period. For example, you might wait until the day after the period ends so you're sure to capture every transaction. In the Enter Statement Date and Type section, you can choose the statement date and the date range for the statement charges.

- **Statement Date.** Type the date that you want to appear on the statement. In Figure 8-16, the statement date is the first day after the end of the statement period.

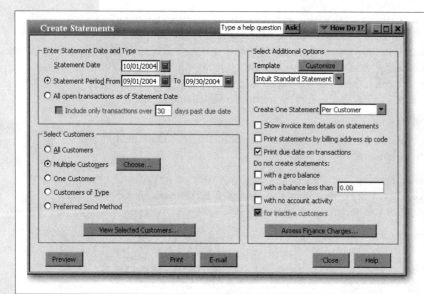

Figure 8-16:
Usually, you'll create statements for all your customers. But you can also generate statements for a subset. For example, if you send statements to some customers by email and to some by U.S. mail, you can generate statements based on the send method. You'll create two sets: one for email and the other for paper. You might also create a statement for a single customer if you made a mistake and want a corrected version.

- **Statement Period From __ To __.** This is the option you choose to create statements for a period of time. For example, if you produce monthly statements, in the From box, choose the first day of the month, and in the To box, choose the last day of the month.

- **All open transactions as of Statement Date.** Choosing this option adds every unpaid statement charge to the statement, regardless of when the original charges occurred. This option is helpful particularly when you want to generate a list of all overdue charges so that you can send a gentle reminder to a woefully tardy customer. To filter the list of open transactions, turn on the "Include only transactions over __ days past due date" checkbox, and type the number of days late.

Selecting customers

QuickBooks automatically selects the All Customers option because most companies send statements to every customer. However, you can choose other options to limit the list of recipients. Here are your customer options and reasons you might choose each one:

- **Multiple Customers.** To specify the exact set of customers to whom you want to send statements, choose the Multiple Customers option. For example, if most of your customers pay in cash, you can choose this option to select the handful of customers that have charge accounts with you.

  When you choose this option, a Choose button appears to the right of the Multiple Customers option. Click the Choose button and, in the Print Statements dialog box that opens, select each customer or job that you want to send a statement to. You can choose individual customers or jobs, or you can specify a search string to select all the customers whose customer name matches the string.

- **One Customer.** To create a corrected statement for only one customer, choose this option. In the drop-down list that appears, click the downward-pointing triangle and then choose the customer or job.

- **Customers of Type.** If you categorize your customers by type and process their statements differently, choose this option. For example, you might spread your billing work out by sending statements to your corporate customers at the end of the month and to individuals on the 15th. In the drop-down list that appears, choose the customer type.

- **Preferred Send Method.** If you print some statements and email others, you'll have to create your statements in two runs. Choose this option and, in the drop-down list that appears, choose one of the send methods. For example, if you choose email, click the E-mail button to send statements to the customers who prefer to receive bills via email. See page 243 for the steps on how to email documents.

Tip: Before you click Print or E-mail to produce statements, click View Selected Customers to make sure that you've chosen the customers you want.

Setting printing options

QuickBooks automatically chooses the Intuit Standard Statement template, but you can choose your own customized template instead. In addition, you can control what QuickBooks adds to statements and which statements to skip:

- **Create One Statement.** In the Create One Statement drop-down list, choosing Per Customer can save some trees. QuickBooks generates one statement for each customer, no matter how many jobs you do for them. Charges are grouped by job. If you want to create separate statements for each job, choose Per Job.

- **Show invoice item details on statements.** Turning this checkbox on is usually unnecessary because your customers already have copies of the invoices you've sent, and extra details merely clutters your statement. Besides, if customers lose invoices or have questions, they're usually not shy about calling you.

- **Print statements by billing address zip code.** You'll want to turn on this checkbox if you have a bulk mail permit, which requires that you mail by Zip code.

- **Print due date on transactions.** QuickBooks turns on this checkbox because you'll typically want to show the due date for each entry on the statement.

- **Do not create statements.** Printing statements that you don't need is a waste of time and paper. QuickBooks includes several settings that you can choose to skip statements. For example, if customers don't owe you anything, you can turn on the "with a zero balance" checkbox. However, if you want to send a statement to show that the last payment arrived and cleared the balance due, turn off this checkbox.

  You might decide to skip customers unless their balance exceeds your typical cost of processing a statement. With a first-class stamp costing 37 cents and the added expense of letterhead, envelopes, and label, you can skip statements unless the balance is at least $5 or so. Turn on the "with a balance less than" checkbox and, in the box to the right of the label, type the dollar value.

  You can also skip customers with no activity during the period, which means *nothing* happened—no charges, no payments, no transactions whatsoever. QuickBooks automatically turns on the "for inactive customers" checkbox because there's no reason to send statements to customers who aren't actively doing business with you.

- **Assess Finance Charges.** If you haven't assessed finance charges already, click Assess Finance Charges to add finance charges due. In the Assess Finance Charges dialog box, you still have an opportunity to turn off the checkmark for individual customers. For example, if a squirrel ate your customer's last statement, you can turn off the checkmark in that customer's entry to prevent QuickBooks from assessing their finance charge.

Previewing Statements

Before you print statements on expensive letterhead or send the statements to your customers, it's a good idea to preview them to make sure that you've chosen the right customers and that the statements appear correct. In the Create Statements dialog box, click Preview. QuickBooks opens the Print Preview window, which works like its counterparts in other programs, as illustrated in Figure 8-17.

Here's how to preview statements before printing:

1. Click "Prev page" or "Next page" to view statements.

   If you left your reading glasses at home, click Zoom In to get a closer look.

2. **When you're ready to print the statements, click Print.**

   See page 235 for more advice on printing.

3. **If you want to return to the Create Statements window to print or email your statements, click Close.**

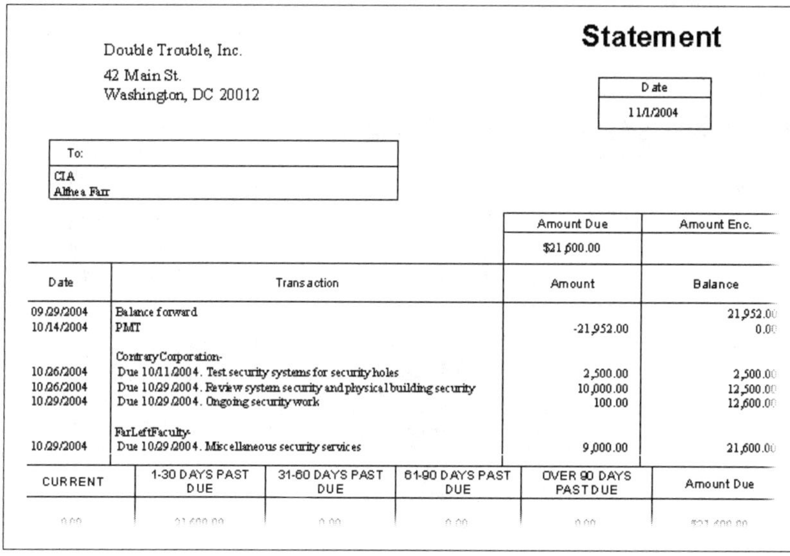

Double Trouble, Inc.
42 Main St.
Washington, DC 20012

Statement

Date
11/1/2004

To:
CIA Althea Farr

Amount Due	Amount Enc.
$21,600.00	

Date	Transaction	Amount	Balance
09/29/2004	Balance forward		21,952.00
10/14/2004	PMT	-21,952.00	0.00
	ContraryCorporation-		
10/26/2004	Due 10/11/2004. Test security systems for security holes	2,500.00	2,500.00
10/26/2004	Due 10/29/2004. Review system security and physical building security	10,000.00	12,500.00
10/29/2004	Due 10/29/2004. Ongoing security work	100.00	12,600.00
	FarLeftFaculty-		
10/29/2004	Due 10/29/2004. Miscellaneous security services	9,000.00	21,600.00

CURRENT	1-30 DAYS PAST DUE	31-60 DAYS PAST DUE	61-90 DAYS PAST DUE	OVER 90 DAYS PAST DUE	Amount Due
0.00	21,600.00	0.00	0.00	0.00	$21,600.00

***Figure 8-17:** The first line in the body of a statement is Balance forward, which is the amount due prior to the first transaction for the current statement. The value in the Amount Due field is the result of the Balance forward–all the transactions for that customer and job that occurred during the statement date range, including payments.*

Warning: In the Print Preview window, clicking Print begins printing your statements immediately. You don't get a chance to set your printer options, such as choosing a printer or the number of copies. If you want to make sure you print properly, click Close and initiate printing from the Create Statements dialog box.

Generating Statements

When you're absolutely sure the statements are correct, in the Create Statements dialog box, click Print or E-mail.

When you click Print, QuickBooks opens the Print Statement(s) dialog box, in which you can choose the printer, forms, letterhead, or blank paper, and the number of copies you want (see page 235 for printing instructions). For example, if you want one copy for the customer and a second one for your files, in the "Number of copies" box, type *2*. When the print options are in place, click Print.

When you click E-mail, QuickBooks opens the Edit E-mail Information dialog box. The program fills in the customer's email address if you added it to the customer record and your company email address. It uses the standard message you've set up for statements (see page 163).

Finding Invoices (and Other Sales Forms)

If you want to resolve a customer's question about what they owe, it's easier when you have the invoice in front of you. The Create Invoices dialog box shows only one invoice at a time, which can mean some furious clicking if you're trying to find one specific invoice out of the hundreds you've sent. In QuickBooks 2006, the Customer Center makes it easy to find the transactions you want, as Figure 8-18 illustrates.

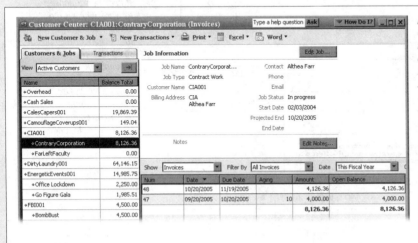

Figure 8-18:
On the Home page, open the Customer Center by clicking Customers. To find a transaction for a specific customer, click the Customer & Jobs tab, and then click the name of the customer or job. To filter the transactions on the right side of the center, in the Show drop-down list, choose the type of transaction you're trying to find, such as Invoices. You can filter the list further by choosing a date range or a category of transactions, such as Open Invoices.

Note: When you locate the invoice or sales form you want, double-click it to open it in its corresponding dialog box. The Find command (page 377) can't help you search the Description field of an invoice. To make invoices easier to locate, consider adding keywords in their Memo fields.

Editing Invoices and Sales Receipts

Editing invoices and sales receipts is easy, even if you've already saved them. If you're still in the process of creating an invoice or sales receipt, you can jump to any field and change its value, delete lines, or insert new ones. In fact, any time you have an invoice visible in the Create Invoices dialog box (or a sales receipt in the Enter Sales Receipts dialog box), you can click any field and make any change you want. If you've already printed the invoice or sales receipt, turn on the "To be printed" checkbox so that you don't forget to reprint the form with the changes you made.

Tip: If you've received a payment against an invoice, editing that invoice is not the way to go. Editing an invoice with a linked payment can disrupt the connections between payment, invoice, and accounts to the point that you'll never straighten it out. If you undercharged the customer, simply create a new invoice with the missing charges on it. If you charged the customer for something she didn't buy, issue a credit memo or refund (see "Handling Refunds and Credits," below).

Voiding and Deleting Invoices and Sales Receipts

Sometimes, you simply want to eliminate an invoice or sales receipt—for instance, when you create an invoice by mistake and want to remove its values from your accounts. QuickBooks provides two options, but for your sanity's sake, you should always void invoices and sales receipts that you don't want.

When you void an invoice or sales receipt, QuickBooks resets the dollar values to zero so that your account balances show no sign of the transaction. However, it also marks the transaction as void, so you know what happened to it when you stumble upon it in the future.

If you delete an invoice or sales receipt, QuickBooks truly deletes the transaction, removing the dollar values from your accounts, but also deleting any sign of the transaction. All that remains is a hole in your numbering sequence of invoice or sales receipt numbers. If your accountant or the IRS looks at your books a few years down the road, your chances of remembering what happened to the transaction are slim. If an invoice has a payment attached to it, deleting the invoice is even more problematic.

To void an invoice or sales receipt, first find and double-click the transaction in the Customer Center. In the Create Invoices dialog box or Enter Sales Receipt dialog box, right-click anywhere and then choose Void Invoice (or Void Sales Receipt) on the shortcut menu. Click Save & Close.

Tip: If you open the Accounts Receivable register window, you might get nervous when you see the word Paid in the Amt Paid column of a voided transaction. Before you get excited about a voided invoice being paid, notice that the amount paid is zero. You'll also see the word Void in the Description field. The word Paid in the Amt Paid column is QuickBooks somewhat skewed way of telling you the invoice isn't open in some way.

Handling Refunds and Credits

If a customer returns a product or finds an overcharge on the last invoice, you have two choices: issue a credit against the customer's balance, or issue a refund by writing a check. In the bookkeeping world, the documents that explain the details of a credit are called credit memos. On the other hand, when a customer doesn't want to wait to get the money she's due, or she isn't planning to purchase anything else from you, a refund check is the logical solution. In either case, refunds and credits both begin with a credit memo, as shown in Figure 8-19.

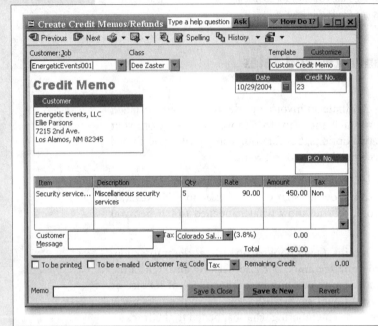

Figure 8-19:
A credit memo is like an invoice but the items you add represent money flowing from you to the customer instead of the other way. Don't enter negative numbers. QuickBooks takes care of calculating the money due based on the value of the items.

Creating Credit Memos

Here's how you create a credit memo:

1. **On the Home page, click Refunds & Credits, or choose Customers → Create Credit Memos/Refunds.**

   QuickBooks opens the Create Credit Memos/Refunds dialog box. If you stay on top of your invoice numbers, you'll notice that the program automatically uses the next invoice number as the credit memo number.

2. **As you would for an invoice, choose the Customer:Job.**

   Choose a class if you use classes; if necessary, choose the credit memo template you want to use.

3. **In the line-item table, add a line for each item you want to credit.**

   Be sure to include all the charges you want to refund, including shipping charges and taxes.

Note: If you want to include a customer message, in the Customer Message box, choose the message from the list.

---

4. **If you want to print or email the credit memo, turn on the "To be printed" or "To be e-mailed" checkbox.**

Click Save & Close when you're done. When you save a credit memo with an available credit balance, you have three options for handling the credit, as demonstrated in Figure 8-20.

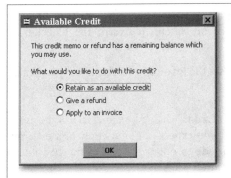

Figure 8-20:
When you save a credit memo with available credit, QuickBooks displays the Available Credit dialog box. If you choose "Give a refund," QuickBooks opens the Write Checks dialog box so you can write the refund check. Choosing "Apply to an invoice" works only if you have an open invoice for the customer. You can also retain the credit and apply it to the next invoice you create for the customer.

Creating Refund Checks

If your customer is dreadfully disgruntled, you'll probably want to write a refund check. To do this, open the Create Credit Memos/Refunds dialog box and find the credit memo for that customer. In the dialog box icon bar, the very last icon on the right is a dollar bill with a hand above it. This picture is Intuit's way of saying you're going to give money back to your customer. To create a refund check, click the downward-pointing triangle to the right of this icon and choose Give refund.

In the "Issue a Refund" dialog box, QuickBooks fills in all the information you need to create the refund. In the "Issue this refund via" box, the program chooses Check. It also chooses the checking account you set in your checking preferences (page 137). If the red face staring at you from across the counter is your customer, in the "Issue this refund via" box, choose Cash.

Note: To refund money via credit card in QuickBooks, you must sign up for the QuickBooks Merchant Service (page 508).

Applying Credits to Invoices

If a customer has an unpaid invoice or statement, you can apply a credit to that invoice or statement and reduce the amount that the customer owes. In the Receive Payments dialog box when you choose a customer or job, QuickBooks displays a message if the customer has available credits and discounts. Here's how to apply that credit to an invoice:

1. **On the Home page, click Receive Payments.**

   QuickBooks opens the Receive Payments dialog box.

---

2. **In the Received From drop-down list, choose the customer whose credit you want to apply.**

In the Receive Payments dialog box, QuickBooks displays a message that the customer has available credit and shows the amount of the credit. If you don't specify a job, the Available Credits value represents the total credits available for all jobs for that customer.

3. **To select the invoice or statement to which you want to apply the credit, click anywhere in the line for the invoice or statement except the Checkmark column.**

Clicking the Checkmark column chooses the invoice to receive a real payment.

4. **Click Discount & Credits.**

QuickBooks opens the "Discount and Credits" dialog box and selects the available credits. If you don't see the credit you expect, it might apply to a different job or to the customer only. If you decide to not apply one of the customer's credits, click the checkmark for that credit to turn it off.

5. **Click Done.**

After all this, the Receive Payments dialog box doesn't look very different, but there's one important change, which you can see in Figure 8-21.

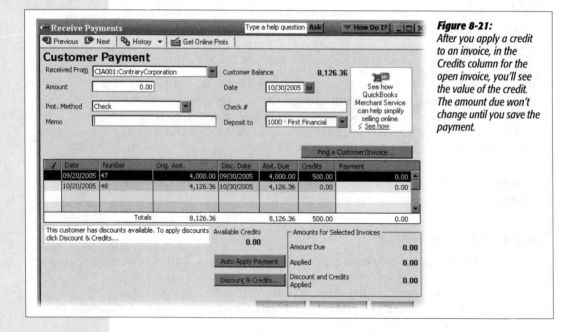

Figure 8-21:
After you apply a credit to an invoice, in the Credits column for the open invoice, you'll see the value of the credit. The amount due won't change until you save the payment.

6. **Click Save & Close to apply the credit to the invoice.**

When you open that invoice in the Create Invoices dialog box, you'll see the credit amount in the Payments Applied field and the Balance Due reduced by the amount of the credit.

Sending Sales Forms

QuickBooks handles the two basic ways you distribute your invoices and other sales forms: on paper and electronically. But within those two distribution camps, you can choose to send your forms as soon as you've completed them or place them in a queue to send in batches. For the sporadic sales forms, it's easier to print or email as you go. But when you generate dozens or even hundreds of invoices or statements, printing and emailing batches is a much better use of your time.

Tip: If you want to make sure that you don't forget to send your sales forms, create reminders (see page 155) for invoices, credit memos, and sales receipts that are queued up to print.

Setting Print Options

Many of the printer options in the "Printer setup" dialog box are the same as options you can set within your operating system, as you'll see in Figure 8-22. To assign and set up printers for forms in QuickBooks, choose File → Printer Setup.

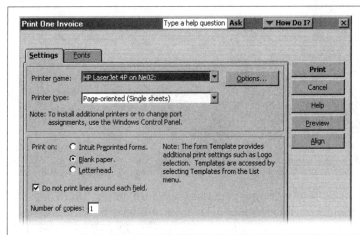

Figure 8-22:
The printers that you set up in your operating system are the ones that appear in the "Printer name" list in QuickBooks. The program starts with the printing preferences you set up outside QuickBooks, but you can adjust those options by choosing a printer and then clicking Options.

- **Printer name.** QuickBooks automatically chooses the printer you set up as the standard for the form you're printing (see the "Setting a Default Printer for Forms" box on page 236). If you want to choose a different printer—for instance, when you switch between printing paper documents and creating Adobe .pdf files—in the "Printer name" drop-down list, choose the printer you want.

- **Options.** If you want to adjust the properties for the printer you chose, click Options. Depending on the type of printer, in the printer Document Properties dialog box, you can change the document orientation, page order, pages per sheet, print quality, paper tray, color, and so on.

- **Printer type.** If the printer feeds individual pages through, such as letterhead or blank paper, choose "Page-oriented (Single sheets)." If a printer feeds continuous sheets of paper with perforations on the edges, such as the green-striped paper so popular in the past, choose Continuous (Perforated Edge).

UP TO SPEED

Setting a Default Printer for Forms

Before you print *any* documents in QuickBooks (not only invoices and other sales forms, but timesheets, pay stubs, reports, and so on), take a few minutes to set up the printers you use with the program. In QuickBooks, you can assign different printers for each type of document you generate. This feature saves a lot of time, wasted paper, and brain damage, especially if you print invoices to multipart forms, paychecks to preprinted check forms, statements to your letterhead, and reports to plain paper. Keep each printer stocked with the right type of paper and you can print your documents with barely a glance at the print options.

Although you can assign a different printer to each of the 21 different QuickBooks forms, you probably have only one or two printers stocked with special paper. In addition, you can bypass printer setup for the forms you print using basic settings, such as printing to your workhorse printer on blank paper and using portrait orientation.

By first setting up printers in QuickBooks, the program fills in the print settings for you automatically when you print.

But Print dialog boxes still appear, and you can change any print options before committing your documents to paper.

QuickBooks keeps the options you choose within the program separate from the settings for the printer within the operating system. For example, if you use Windows printer options to set your most popular printer to portrait orientation, you can set that same printer to landscape in Quick-Books.

Here's how you assign printers and print options to Quick-Books forms:

1. Choose File → Printer Setup.

2. In the "Printer setup" dialog box, in the Form Name box, choose the form for which you want to assign a printer.

3. In the "Printer name" box, choose the printer you want to use.

4. Choose other print options, such as the type of paper.

- **Intuit Preprinted forms.** If you purchase preprinted forms, which typically include your company information, field labels, and lines that separate fields, choose this option. When you print your documents, QuickBooks sends only the data to fill in the form.

Tip: When you use preprinted forms, a small misalignment can make your documents look sloppy and unprofessional. See the next page to learn how to align your documents to the paper in your printer.

- **Blank paper.** When you choose this option, QuickBooks prints everything on your document template: company information, logo, labels, and data. This is also the easiest way to print because you don't have to worry about aligning the paper and the form. If you set up a template with your company logo and attractive fonts (page 550), you can produce a professional-looking form on blank paper.

- **Letterhead.** When you print to letterhead that already contains your company address and other information, you don't need to print that information on your documents. Choose this option to suppress the printing of your company information.

- **Do not print lines around each field.** Turning on this checkbox is a matter of personal preference. Lines around each field make it clear which information belongs to which label, but you might consider those lines unnecessary clutter. If your template separates fields to your satisfaction, turn off this checkbox to print only the labels and data, not borders around each field. Because pre-printed forms include borders, QuickBooks automatically turns on this check-box if you choose the "Intuit Preprinted forms" option.

- **Number of copies.** If you want to print one copy for your customer and one for your files, type *2*. If you need additional copies, type the number you want.

Aligning Forms and Paper

When you use preprinted forms or continuous feed paper with perforations for page breaks, the alignment of the paper is crucial. Otherwise, your data won't appear next to the correct labels or an invoice might print over the page break. It's a good idea to check the alignment of your forms and paper every time you print, but it's particularly important if you're printing a batch of documents. There's no faster way to waste time and paper than printing a big stack of invoices that don't line up with your expensive letterhead or preprinted forms. Here's how to save time, trees, and your sanity:

Note: You can align your form to printer paper in "Printer setup." As long as you don't move the paper in the printer, you won't have to align the paper each time you print. However, if someone else monkeys with the printer, you can align the form from the Print dialog box.

---

1. **To align your form to the paper, in the Print dialog box, click Align.**

   If you have more than one template to choose from, QuickBooks opens the Align Printer dialog box.

2. **Choose the template you want to use to align your paper and click OK.**

   If you're printing to a page-oriented printer, QuickBooks displays the Fine Alignment dialog box. If you're using a continuous feed printer, your first step is a coarse alignment, shown in Figure 8-23.

3. **In the Fine Alignment dialog box, in the Vertical and Horizontal boxes, type numbers to represent the hundredths of an inch to move the form to line it up with the paper.**

After you tweak the alignment, click Print Sample to check the printed form's appearance. When the form is aligned the way you want, click OK, and keep your mitts off the paper in the printer.

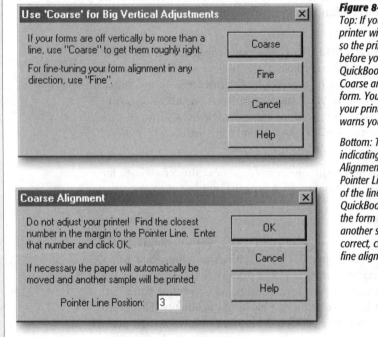

Figure 8-23:
Top: If you're trying to align a dot-matrix printer with perforations, position the paper so the print head is just below a page break before you begin any alignment in QuickBooks. To align perforated paper, click Coarse and then click OK to print a sample form. You don't have to adjust the paper in your printer, which is why QuickBooks warns you several times not to do that.

Bottom: The form that prints includes text indicating a pointer line. When the Coarse Alignment dialog box appears, in the Pointer Line Position box, type the number of the line preprinted in the paper margin. QuickBooks uses that line number to align the form and the paper. Click OK to print another sample. When the alignment is correct, click Close. You can then perform a fine alignment if necessary.

Choosing a Send Method

If you've ever gotten lost at your office supply store, you understand why printing includes so many options. You can print on different types of paper and different types of printer, and making the two line up properly can be a delicate negotiation. Besides the invoices and other sales forms themselves, you might print ancillary documents, such as mailing labels and packing slips.

Each type of sales form in QuickBooks offers the same basic methods and options for sending documents to customers, illustrated in the Create Invoices dialog box in Figure 8-24. In the form windows, the icon bar includes Print and E-mail buttons. You'll find "To be e-mailed" and "To be printed" checkboxes in the dialog boxes for invoices, sales receipts, and credit memos. Estimates work the same way, except that the Create Estimates dialog box doesn't include a "To be printed" checkbox.

Here's a guide to your choices for printing and emailing documents:

- **Print icon.** If you want to print the current form, in the dialog box icon bar, click the Print icon. If you click the downward-pointing triangle to the right of the Print icon, you can choose any of the print commands from the drop-down list. For instance, you can preview the form you're about to print, print the current form, print all the forms in your queue, or print special forms such as packing slips.

- **Send icon.** If you want to email the current form, in the dialog box icon bar, click the Send icon. If you click the downward-pointing triangle to the right of the Send icon, you can choose any of the send commands from the drop-down list. For instance, you can email the form you're about to print, send all the forms in your queue to be emailed, or use QuickBooks' invoice mailing service (a subscription service described in the box on page 245).

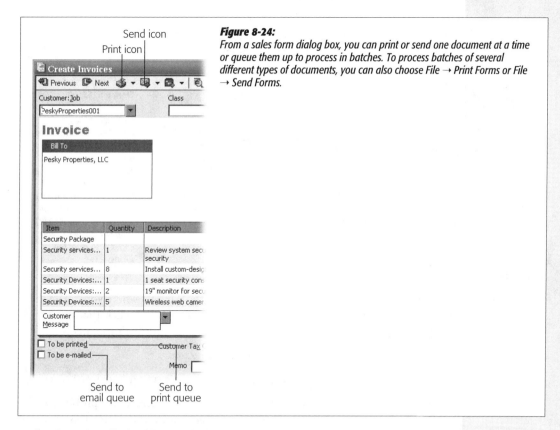

Figure 8-24:
From a sales form dialog box, you can print or send one document at a time or queue them up to process in batches. To process batches of several different types of documents, you can also choose File → Print Forms or File → Send Forms.

- **"To be printed" checkbox.** When you turn on this checkbox, QuickBooks adds the current form to a queue of forms that you'll print as a batch.

- **"To be e-mailed" checkbox.** When you turn on this checkbox, QuickBooks adds the current form to the queue of forms that you'll email all at once.

Print One Form

When you display a form in its corresponding dialog box, you can preview and print it. For example, in the Create Invoices dialog box, to print the displayed invoice, click the Print icon or next to the Print icon, click the downward-pointing triangle and then choose Preview or Print. You'll see the Print One Invoice dialog box, in which you can choose the printer and paper as described on page 235.

Printing in Batches

When you turn on the "To be printed" checkbox before you save a form, Quick-Books adds that form to a print queue. After you've checked that your printer contains the correct paper and the paper is aligned properly, you can print all the forms in the queue with just a few steps:

1. Choose File → Print Forms and then choose the type of forms you want to print.

   QuickBooks opens the "Select *<type of form>* to Print" dialog box with all unprinted forms selected, as shown in Figure 8-25.

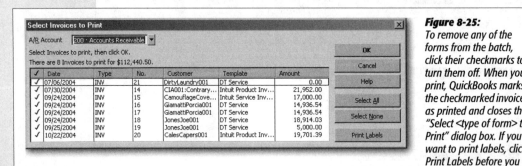

Figure 8-25:
To remove any of the forms from the batch, click their checkmarks to turn them off. When you print, QuickBooks marks the checkmarked invoices as printed and closes the "Select <type of form> to Print" dialog box. If you want to print labels, click Print Labels before you click OK to print the forms.

You can also print the pending forms from the window where you create those forms. For example, in the Create Invoices dialog box, click the downward-pointing triangle to the right of the Print icon, and choose Print Batch.

2. Click OK to print the selected forms in the queue.

   After you've printed the forms, check them to make sure they printed correctly.

If you checked the paper and the alignment before you printed, the problem you're most likely to encounter is a paper jam. QuickBooks anticipates this inconvenience and opens the "Did form(s) print OK?" dialog box. If a problem occurred, you can type the number of the first form that didn't print properly and click OK to reprint that and all following forms.

Printing Mailing and Shipping Labels

QuickBooks can print mailing labels to go with the forms you print. Because the program prints labels for the customers selected in the "Select *<type of form>* to Print" dialog box, you must print the labels *before* you print the forms. Here's how:

1. In the "Select Invoices to Print" dialog box, click Print Labels.

   QuickBooks opens the "Select Labels to Print" dialog box and automatically chooses the Name option, which prints labels for the customers associated with each form waiting to print.

2. If you've created forms for a specific customer type or vendor type, choose the Customer Type or Vendor Type option and, in the drop-down list, choose the type you want to print labels for.

   These options are better suited for printing labels not associated with your queued forms—for example, when you want to send a letter to your retail customers informing them of product rebates. However, you might use them if you process forms for retail and wholesale customers at different times of the month.

Tip: If you want to print labels for a mailing that has nothing to do with money (like an announcement about your new office location) choose File → Print Forms → Labels.

---

3. To filter the labels you print by location, turn on the "with Zip Codes that start with" checkbox, and type the beginning of the Zip code area you want.

   For example, if you're offering a seminar for people in the Chicago area, you can type *606* in the box.

4. In the "Sort labels by" box, choose Name or Zip Code.

   If you use bulk mail, choose Zip Code so you can bundle your mail by Zip code as your bulk mail permit requires.

5. If you want to print shipping labels rather than labels that use billing addresses, turn on the "Print Ship To addresses where available" checkbox.

   The "Print labels for inactive names" checkbox might develop some cobwebs, but it can come in handy from time to time—for instance, if you need to send a letter to past and present customers to tell them about a product recall.

   When you send communication to different addresses for each job, even though the jobs are for the same customer, turn on the "Print labels for jobs" checkbox.

6. After making sure that you've selected the labels you want, click OK.

   QuickBooks opens the Print Labels dialog box.

7. **If you set up the printer you use for labels in Printer Setup, click Print and you're done.**

However, if you want to print to different labels, in the Label Format drop-down list, choose the type of label you use. Check the box of labels you have for the vendor and label number. The drop-down list includes four popular Avery label formats along with several other options.

After you print your labels, QuickBooks closes the Print Labels dialog box, and returns to the "Print *<type of>*" dialog box. Click OK to continue printing your queued forms.

Tip: For invoices and sales receipts, printing a shipping label for the current form is easy. In the Create Invoices or Enter Sales Receipt dialog boxes, click the downward-pointing triangle next to the Print icon and then choose Print Shipping Label. The drop-down menu also includes the Print Envelope command. For envelopes, you'll have to specify the envelope size and whether you want to include the return address. (Turn off this checkbox if your envelopes have your return address on them.) You can even print a delivery barcode for addresses in the United States.

Printing Packing Slips

When you ship products to a customer, it's common to include a packing slip that tells the customer what they should have in their shipment. In QuickBooks, printing packing slips is a labor-intensive task because you must print each packing slip individually from the Create Invoices dialog box. The template that Intuit provides for packing slips is no more than an invoice without prices, no doubt assuming that warehouse workers don't care about the cost of the items they ship.

If you don't perform the steps for printing a packing slip in the right order, you'll end up printing the wrong documents or assigning the wrong templates to your invoices and sales receipts. Here are the steps that keep the correct templates associated with packing slips, invoices, and sales receipts:

1. **In the Create Invoices dialog box, in the Template box, choose the packing slip template you want.**

   The packing slip template is tucked into the Template drop-down list with QuickBooks' invoice templates. (Any templates you've customized are listed here, too.)

2. **Click the downward-pointing triangle next to the Print icon and then choose Print Packing Slip.**

   QuickBooks opens the Print Packing Slip dialog box where you can choose print options if necessary.

3. **To print the packing slip, click Print.**

   QuickBooks closes the Print Packing Slip dialog box and prints the packing slip.

4. Back in the Create Invoices or Enter Sales Receipts dialog boxes, in the Template box, choose the original template for your invoice or sales receipt.

If you skip this step and move on to another invoice, you could end up printing a packing slip by mistake.

Tip: If you want to change the packing slip that QuickBooks chooses automatically, change the packing slip template preference. Choose Edit → Preferences. Click the Sales & Customers icon, and click the Company Preferences tab. In the "Choose Template for Packing Slip" box, choose the packing slip template you want to use in most cases. Click OK.

Emailing Sales Forms

If you've lost interest in paperwork, sending invoices and other sales forms electronically is much more satisfying. But to make your electronic sending as efficient as possible, make sure that all your customer records include the email addresses you want to use. Otherwise, you'll waste time typing email addresses one after another. The chance of typographical errors increase with each address you type. See page 526 to learn how to synchronize QuickBooks and your Outlook addresses.

Emailing One Form

Here's how you email a form when you're looking at it in its corresponding dialog box. These steps use the Create Invoices dialog box as an example, but the steps work equally well for other sales forms.

1. In the Create Invoices dialog box, click the Send icon.

QuickBooks displays the Send Invoice dialog box, shown in Figure 8-26, in which you can change the email addresses and subject, and email text that QuickBooks sends with your form.

2. To copy someone else on this message, in the Cc box, type other email addresses.

Separate each email address you enter with a comma.

3. If you don't like the QuickBooks message, in the E-mail Text box, edit it.

If you edit the message, click Check Spelling to make sure you haven't made any embarrassing typographical errors. If you decide you like your version of the message and want to use it for every email you send for this type of sales form, click Edit Default Text. QuickBooks opens the Preferences dialog box to the Send Forms section, so you can edit the default message (see page 163).

4. To send the form immediately, click Send Now. To add this message to a queue, click Send Later.

When you click Send Now, QuickBooks opens a browser window to the Quick-Books E-mailing site. If you haven't done so already, you must register your email before you can send emails through QuickBooks. The service is free. After the service sends your email, you'll see a message telling you that it was sent successfully.

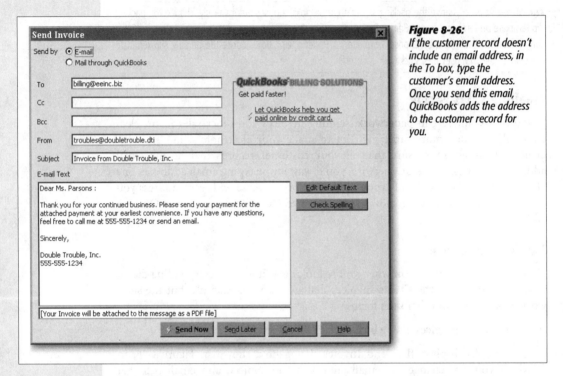

Figure 8-26:
If the customer record doesn't include an email address, in the To box, type the customer's email address. Once you send this email, QuickBooks adds the address to the customer record for you.

Emailing in Batches

When you turn on the "To be e-mailed" checkbox for forms you create, or choose Send Later for several forms, QuickBooks adds them to an email queue. You can send all the forms that you've queued up with a couple of steps:

1. **Choose File → Send Forms.**

   QuickBooks opens the "Select Forms to Send" dialog box, which contains all of your unsent forms of every type. The program selects all pending forms automatically.

2. **If you want to skip some of the forms, click the checkmark in the line to turn it off.**

   When you're ready, click Send Now.

Tip: You can also email pending forms from the dialog box where you create those forms. For example, in the Create Invoices dialog box, click the downward-pointing triangle to the right of the Send icon, and choose Send Batch.

ALTERNATE REALITY

QuickBooks Mail Invoice Service

When you click the downward-pointing triangle next to the Send icon, you'll see the Mail Invoice command. If you're perplexed by Intuit's decision to add a postal mailing option to the Send menu, the answer is in poor command naming. When you choose the Mail Invoice command, QuickBooks opens the Send Invoice dialog box, in which you can choose to email the invoice or send it to QuickBooks mailing service. The "Mail through QuickBooks" option is part of QuickBooks' Billing Solutions services. This service costs money but it prints, folds, and mails your invoices to customers. The cost is $14.95 a month plus $.79 per invoice. But if you're short of both time and office staff, this could be worth the money.

Invoices go to a centralized mail center that prints customized black-and-white invoices using your logo and invoice template, stuffs envelopes, and mails invoices with remittance tear-offs and return envelopes.

When you add the Merchant Services feature (another subscription service), your customers can pay via credit card. Subscribing to the invoice mailing service and Merchant services, your customers can pay you online with a credit card for any invoice—no matter how you sent it. This approach also means you can download payments into QuickBooks reducing your transaction entry *and* the Merchant service gets your payments into your bank account faster.

Note: When you email an invoice, QuickBooks attaches the form as an Adobe .pdf file. Customers that don't have Acrobat Reader installed on their computers can click the Acrobat Reader link to download the reader for free. Otherwise, the customer simply clicks the link to open the attachment.

Managing Accounts Receivable

In between performing work and collecting payments, you have to keep track of who owes you how much (known as *accounts receivable*) and when the money is due. Sure, you can tack on finance charges to light a fire under your customer's accounting departments, but finance charges are rarely enough to make up for the time and effort you spend collecting overdue payments. Far more preferable are customers who pay on time without reminders, gentle or otherwise.

Because companies need money to keep things running, you'll have to spend *some* time keeping track of your accounts receivable and the payments that come in. In this chapter, you'll learn the ins and outs of tracking what customers owe, receiving the payments from them, and dinging them if they don't pay on time.

The Aging of Receivables

You don't have to do anything special to *create* accounts receivable. They're the by-product of billing and invoicing your customers. But receivables that are growing long in the tooth are the first signs of future collection problems. Some companies like to check the state of their accounts receivable every day, and with the Customer Center and built-in QuickBooks reports, you have two ways to do that in record time.

The Customer Center gives you a quick snapshot of the balance each customer owes, as Figure 9-1 demonstrates. (If you don't see it, click Customer Center in the icon bar.)

Accounts Receivable Aging Reports

Aging reports are reports that tell you how many days have passed since you sent each open invoice, and they're the first step to keeping your accounts receivable from growing overly ripe. It's a fact of business life that the longer a customer hasn't paid, the more likely it is that you'll never see that money. Taking action before an account lags too far behind limits bad debts and protects your profits.

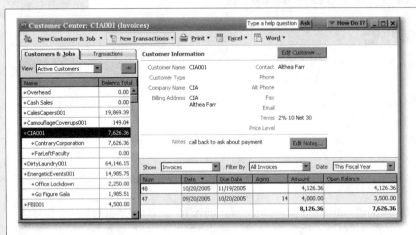

Figure 9-1:
When you open the Customer Center, QuickBooks automatically displays the Customers & Jobs tab, listing your customers and jobs and the balance you have coming from each one. If you select a customer or job name in the list, you can see the invoices or other sales transactions that generated the open balance.

QuickBooks includes two built-in aging reports: the Aging Summary report and the Aging Detail report. Aging reports show how much your customers owe for the current billing period (the past 30 days), as well as unpaid bills and invoices from previous periods (from 31 to 60 days, 61 to 90 days, and more than 90 days).

- **A/R Aging Summary.** For a fast look at how much money your customers owe you and how old your receivables are, choose Reports → Customers & Receivables → A/R Aging Summary, illustrated in Figure 9-2.

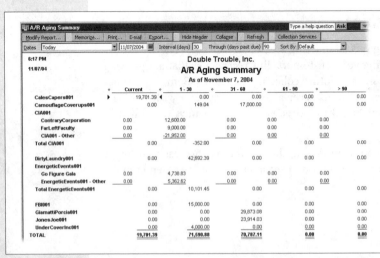

Figure 9-2:
In the A/R Aging Summary report, Quick Books lists customers and jobs and shows the money they owe in each aging period. Ideally, you should see more zero balances as you look at older periods. When you begin a mission to collect overdue accounts, start with the oldest aging period on the right side of the report.

- **A/R Aging Detail.** To see each customer transaction categorized by age, as shown in Figure 9-3, choose Reports → Customers & Receivables → A/R Aging Detail.

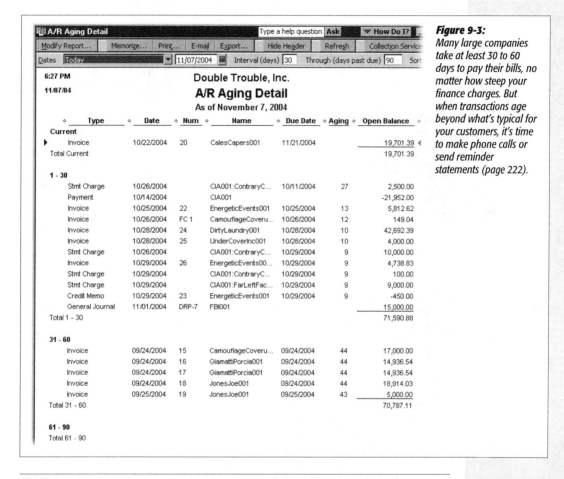

Figure 9-3:
Many large companies take at least 30 to 60 days to pay their bills, no matter how steep your finance charges. But when transactions age beyond what's typical for your customers, it's time to make phone calls or send reminder statements (page 222).

Tip: If the built-in aging reports are too busy for your taste, feel free to remove columns that you don't use (such as P.O. # or Terms), which is explained in Chapter 19.

- **Accounts Receivable Graph.** The Accounts Receivable Graph doesn't show as much detail as either of the A/R Aging reports, but its visual nature makes aging problems stand out, as you can see in Figure 9-4.

Customer & Job Reports

Aging reports aren't the only goodies you can generate in QuickBooks. To see all the reports associated with customers and what they owe, choose Reports → Customers & Receivables. Here's an overview of when it makes sense to use these other reports:

• **Customer Balance Summary.** This report shows the same balance information you see automatically in the Customer Center, but here the job totals appear in one column and the customer totals are offset in a second column to the right. And unlike the Customers & Jobs tab, you can easily print this report.

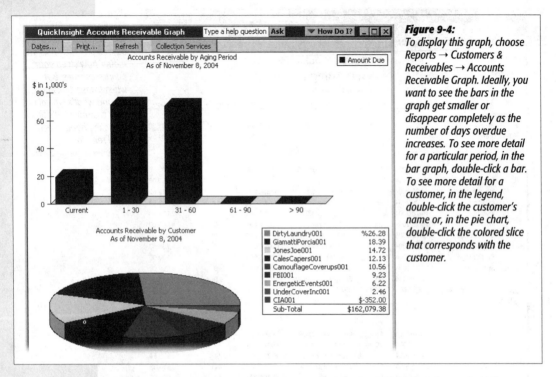

Figure 9-4:
To display this graph, choose Reports → Customers & Receivables → Accounts Receivable Graph. Ideally, you want to see the bars in the graph get smaller or disappear completely as the number of days overdue increases. To see more detail for a particular period, in the bar graph, double-click a bar. To see more detail for a customer, in the legend, double-click the customer's name or, in the pie chart, double-click the colored slice that corresponds with the customer.

• **Customer Balance Detail.** This report is neither short nor focused. It lists every transaction (such as invoices, payments, statement charges, and credit memos) for every customer and job, whether the customer is late or not—which is helpful if you're trying to track down a specific transaction. To inspect transaction details, double-click the transaction value in the Open Balance column.

• **Open Invoices.** This report name isn't entirely accurate because the report includes unpaid invoices and statement charges, as well as payments and unapplied credits, sorted and subtotaled for each customer and job. If you want to find an unpaid invoice without clicking Previous in the Create Invoices dialog box for hours, run this report. When you find the invoice you want, double-click anywhere in the row for the invoice.

• **Collections.** When you're on a mission to collect some of the money that's owed you, the Collections report provides all the information you need. The report shows the past due invoices and statement charges by customer and job with the due date and number of days that the transaction is past due. To make it easy to contact your customers, the report includes the customer contact name and phone number. Give the report to your most persistent employees and get ready to receive payments. If a customer has questions about a transaction, double-click the transaction row to view the transaction in detail.

Tip: When customers have pushed their credit limits—and your patience—too far, you can easily create collection letters by merging information for overdue customers with mail merge collection letters in Word (see page 522).

• **Unbilled Costs by Job.** Another place you might leave money on the table is with job costs that you forget to bill. Run this report to see if there are expenses you haven't billed, the type of expense, when you incurred the cost, and other information. If you spot older expenses that you haven't yet billed, add them to the next invoice (page 200).

POWER USERS' CLINIC

Watching Receivables Trends

In the investment world, financial analysts study trends in accounts receivable. For example, if accounts receivable are increasing faster than sales, that means that customers are not paying as quickly as they used to. Perhaps the billing department is fond of long lunches, but it's more likely that customers aren't paying because they don't like the products or services they've received.

One way to measure how good a job your company does collecting receivables is with *days sales outstanding,* which is the number of days worth of sales it takes to match your accounts receivable. If accounts receivable grow faster than

sales, you'll see this measure get larger. This is the formula for days sales outstanding:

$$\text{Days sales outstanding} = \text{Accounts receivable} / (\text{Sales} / 365)$$

Days sales outstanding below 60 (collecting accounts receivable with two months worth of sales) is good. But if your company is in the retail business, you should aspire to the performance of high-volume giants such as Wal-Mart and Home Depot, who collect their receivables in less than a week.

Receiving Payments for Invoiced Income

How you record an invoice payment depends on the *type* of payment. Most of the time, you'll click Receive Payments on the Home page, but you can also choose Customers → Receive Payments to open the Receive Payments dialog box, which handles full and partial payments for one job or several, early payment discounts, credits, and downloaded online payments. You record some types of payments in other places.

Here are the dialog boxes that can record payments and when you use them:

• **Receive Payments dialog box.** This is the dialog box for full or partial payments that you receive after you've made a sale. Here you can apply early payment discounts, credits for returns, as well as downloaded online payments.

- **Create Invoices dialog box.** See page 262 to learn how to record a partial payment that you receive at the time of sale. These payments appear on the invoice you prepare and reduce its balance.

- **Create Credit Memos/Refunds dialog box.** If your customer makes a down payment or prepays an invoice, create credit memos to record these payments (page 232).

- **Enter Sales Receipts dialog box.** When your customers pay in full at the time of sale, record payments in this dialog box (page 268), whether the customers pays with cash, check, or credit card.

UP TO SPEED

Different Ways to Apply Payments

Most of the time, customers send payments that bear some clear relationship to their unpaid invoices. For those payments, QuickBooks' preference to automatically select invoices (page 162) is a fabulous timesaver. You type in the payment amount, and the program selects the most likely invoice for payment. When a payment matches an invoice amount exactly, this scheme works perfectly almost every time.

But every once in a while, you receive a payment that doesn't match up, and you have to tell QuickBooks how to apply the payment. For example, if the payment and the customer's available credit, taken together, match an open invoice, see page 255 to learn how to apply them to the invoice. If you have no idea what the customer had in mind, don't guess—contact the customer and ask how to apply the payment.

Regardless of the situation, in the Receive Payments dialog box, you can adjust the values in the Payment column to match your customer's wishes. Here's how to handle some common scenarios:

- **Customer includes the invoice number on the payment.** If QuickBooks selects an invoice other than the one the customer specifies, click in the checkmark column to turn off the invoice that the program chose. Turn on the checkmark for the desired invoice to make QuickBooks apply the payment to it.

- **Payment is less than any outstanding invoices.** In this case, QuickBooks applies the payment to the oldest invoice. Click Save & Close to apply the payment as is. Your customers will thank you for helping them avoid your finance charges.

- **Payment is greater than any one invoice.** If the payment is larger than all of the customer's unpaid invoices, also save the payment as is. You can then create a credit or write a refund check for the amount of the overpayment (page 233).

For full or partial payments with or without discounts or credits, follow these steps to record payments you receive from your customers:

1. **On the Home page, click Receive Payments.**

   QuickBooks opens the Receive Payments dialog box.

2. In the Received From box, choose the customer or the job for which you received a payment, as shown in Figure 9-5.

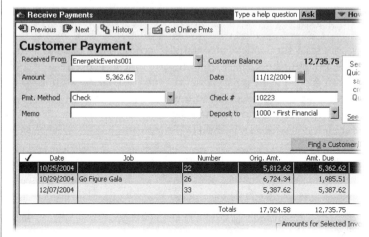

Figure 9-5:
When you choose a customer or job in the Received From box, the Customer Balance to its right shows the corresponding balance (including any credits available). The program also fills in the table here with every unpaid invoice for that customer or job. If an invoice is for a job, the job name appears in the table. When the cell in the Job column is blank, the invoice applies directly to the customer, not a job. If you choose a job and don't see the invoice you expect, in the Received From box, choose the customer to see all invoices for that customer and its jobs.

Tip: If the customer sent a payment that covers more than one job, in the Received From box, choose the customer name—not any of the individual job names. QuickBooks fills in the Receive Payments table with all the outstanding invoices for all of the customer's jobs.

3. **In the Amount box, type the amount of the payment.**

After you type the payment amount and either press Tab or click another box, QuickBooks automatically selects an invoice for you. If the payment amount exactly matches the amount of an unpaid invoice, QuickBooks is smart enough to select that invoice. If the customer sends some other amount of money, however, QuickBooks automatically selects the oldest unpaid invoices.

4. **In the Pmt. Method box, choose the method that the customer used to make the payment.**

If you choose Cash, QuickBooks displays the Reference # box where you can type a receipt number or other identifier. When you choose the Check payment method, QuickBooks displays the Check # box instead. Type the number from the customer's check. For any type of credit card, in the Card No. box and Exp. Date boxes, you can type the card number and the month and year that the card expires. The Reference # box that appears is perfect for storing the credit card transaction number.

Tip: If you subscribe to QuickBooks Merchant Services (page 508), turn on the "Process credit card payment when saving" checkbox. You can download transactions for the payments you received online or via credit card. In the Receive Payments menu bar, simply click Get Online Pmts.

5. **In the Deposit To box, choose the account for the deposit, such as your checking or savings account.**

If you have only one account, you won't see this box at all. However, if you have several accounts, such as checking, savings, and petty cash, you can choose the account for the deposit.

QuickBooks chooses your Undeposited Funds account automatically, which means that the program holds payments in the Undeposited Funds account until you tell it to deposit those payments into a specific bank account. If you're the impatient type, or if your checking account balance is desperately low, you can deposit a payment directly to the bank account—as long as you follow that QuickBooks transaction with a real-world bank deposit.

Tip: To make reconciling your bank statement a bit easier (page 349), choose the Deposit To account based on the way your bank statement shows the deposits you make. If your bank statement shows a deposit total, regardless of how many checks were in the deposit, deposit payments in the Undeposited Funds account. But when your bank shows every check you deposit, deposit each payment separately to your bank account in QuickBooks.

You can set a QuickBooks preference so that the program always chooses Undeposited Funds for payments. Choose Edit → Preferences, and then in the icon bar, click the Sales & Customer icon, and then choose the Company Preferences tab. To always use the Undeposited Funds account for payments, turn on the "Use Undeposited Funds as a default deposit to account" checkbox.

---

6. **If QuickBooks selects the wrong invoices, or if you turned off the Automatically Apply Payments preference, in the first column in the unpaid invoice table, click the cells for the invoices to which you want to apply the payment.**

When the payment doesn't match any unpaid invoices, QuickBooks selects the oldest invoices and adjusts the values in the Payment column to equal the payment total, as demonstrated in Figure 9-6.

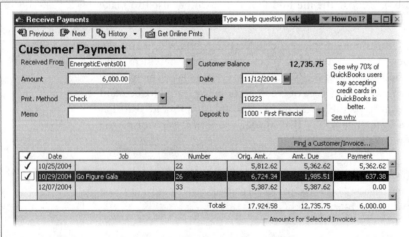

Figure 9-6:
If you select the invoices, you have to edit the values in the Payment column to match the payment amount. Select a cell in the Payment column and type the new amount. When you press Tab or click elsewhere in the dialog box, you'll see the updated amount below the Payment column. When that value equals the value in the Amount box, you're done.

7. **If you have no credits or discounts to apply, click Save & Close to assign the payment to the selected invoices and close the dialog box.**

   If you want to apply another payment, click Save & New.

Tip: If you realize that you've applied a payment to the wrong invoice, you can edit the payment. The easiest way to access a recent payment is to choose Customers → Receive Payments, and then click Previous until the payment transaction appears. Select the correct invoice and click Save & Close.

Applying Credits to Invoices

When something goes awry with the services or products you sell, customers won't be bashful about asking for a refund or credit (page 232). And customers who buy from you regularly might *prefer* a credit against their next order rather than a refund, so that checks aren't flying back and forth in the mail. In a business sense, a credit is a lot like a customer payment that you can apply to invoices. In Quick-Books, you apply credits differently than actual customer payments, although both take place in the Receive Payments dialog box.

Tip: For small credits, it's easier to wait until the customer sends a payment to apply the credit. Quick-Books keeps track of customer credit memos, so you don't have to remember that the credit is available. When the customer sends a payment and you choose that customer in the Receive Payments dialog box, QuickBooks reminds you about the available credits. You can apply the payment and the credit in the same transaction.

If a customer credit is sizable and the customer has unpaid invoices, you can apply the credit to those invoices whether the customer has sent an actual payment or not.

When you're ready to apply a credit to an invoice, here's what you do:

1. **On the Home page, click Receive Payments (or choose Customers → Receive Payments).**

   QuickBooks opens the Receive Payments dialog box.

2. **In the Received From drop-down list, choose the customer or job you want.**

   When you choose a customer or job with an available credit, QuickBooks displays a message to that effect and shows the amount of the credit, as illustrated in Figure 9-7. If you choose a customer, the Available Credits value represents all the credits available for all jobs for that customer.

3. **If your customer gave you instructions about which invoice should get the credit, click anywhere in the line for that invoice or statement except the checkmark column.**

   When you click a cell in the checkmark column, QuickBooks selects that invoice to receive a *real* payment.

4. **To apply the credit to the invoice or statement you selected, click Discount & Credits.**

   QuickBooks opens the "Discount and Credits" dialog box and selects the available credits. If you want to apply only some of the credits, click the check-marked cell for each credit you want to deselect.

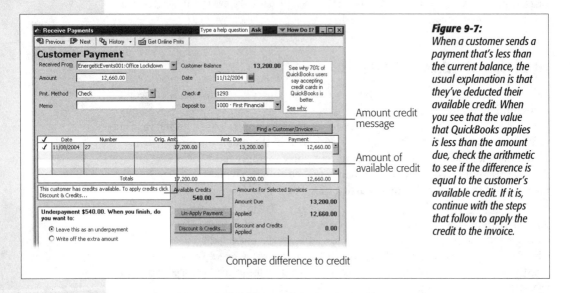

Figure 9-7:
When a customer sends a payment that's less than the current balance, the usual explanation is that they've deducted their available credit. When you see that the value that QuickBooks applies is less than the amount due, check the arithmetic to see if the difference is equal to the customer's available credit. If it is, continue with the steps that follow to apply the credit to the invoice.

Amount credit message

Amount of available credit

Compare difference to credit

Tip: If the credit doesn't appear in the dialog box, it probably relates to a different job or to the customer only. If you want to apply a credit to a different job or to the customer account, see the "Applying a Credit for One Job to a Different Job" box on page 260.

---

5. **Click Done.**

   When QuickBooks closes the "Discount and Credits" dialog box and returns to the Receive Payments dialog box, you'll see the applied credit in two places, as illustrated in Figure 9-8.

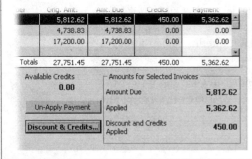

Figure 9-8:
When you apply a credit to an invoice, its amount appears in the Credits cell in the Receive Payments dialog box. The credit also contributes to the "Discount and Credits Applied" value in the "Amounts for Selected Invoices" section. When you've applied all of a customer's credits, the Available Credits box shows 0.00.

6. Click Save & Close to apply the credit to the invoice.

If the customer's available credit is larger than the total for an invoice, you can still apply the credit to that invoice. QuickBooks reduces the invoice's balance to zero but keeps the remainder of the credit available to apply to another invoice. Simply repeat steps 1 through 6 to apply the leftover credit to another invoice.

Discounting for Early Payment

You don't know if customers are eligible for an early payment discount until they actually *pay early*, so it makes sense that you apply early payment discounts in the Receive Payments dialog box. The procedure to apply an early payment discount is almost identical to that of applying a credit. In fact, if an invoice qualifies for both a credit and an early payment discount, you can apply them both while the "Discount and Credits" dialog box is open.

Note: If the discount is for something other than early payment, such as a product that's on sale, add a Discount item to the invoice instead (page 83).

These steps show how to take an early payment discount from the beginning:

1. **On the Home page, click Receive Payments.**

   QuickBooks opens the Receive Payments dialog box.

2. **In the Received From drop-down list, choose the customer or job for the payment you received.**

   In the table of open invoices, the program shows all the invoices or statements that aren't yet paid.

3. **Click anywhere in the line except the checkmark column for the invoice or statement that the customer paid early.**

   Clicking the checkmark column tells QuickBooks to apply a payment to the invoice.

4. **To add an early payment discount to the invoice or statement you selected, click Discount & Credits.**

   QuickBooks opens the "Discount and Credits" dialog box. If the Credits tab is visible, click the Discount tab to display the Discount fields shown in Figure 9-9. If the date for the payment is earlier than the date shown as the Discount Date, QuickBooks uses the early payment percentage from the customer's payment terms to calculate the Suggested Discount. For example, if the customer gets a one percent discount for paying early, the suggested discount is one percent of the invoice total.

Note: Customers often deduct their early payment discounts despite sending their payments after the early payment cutoff date. The typical reaction for most business owners is a resigned sigh. Although QuickBooks shows the suggested discount as zero when a customer doesn't actually pay early, you can show your customer good will and accept their payment. In the "Amount of Discount" box, simply type the discount that the customer took.

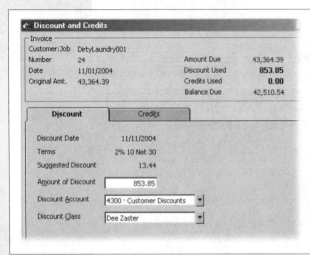

Figure 9-9:
In the "Amount of Discount" box, QuickBooks automatically fills in the suggested discount. You can type a different discount—for instance, when the customer paid only part of the invoice early. The Invoice section at the top of the dialog box shows the amount due on the invoice and the balance due after applying the early payment discount you chose. If the customer has already paid the invoice in full, the early payment discount becomes a credit for the next invoice.

5. **In the Discount Account box, choose the income account you've set up to track customer discounts.**

   At first, you might plan to post customer discounts to one of your income accounts for products or services you sell. But customer discounts tend to fall off the radar screen when they're buried in your regular income. Keep track of the discounts you give by creating an income account specifically for discounts, called something imaginative like Customer Discounts.

   If you spot an *expense* account called Discounts, don't use that as your customer discount account either. An expense account for discounts is meant to track the discounts *you* receive from your vendors.

6. **If you use classes, in the Discount Class box, choose the class you want.**

   This class is typically the same one you used for the invoice in the first place.

7. **Click Done.**

   When QuickBooks closes the "Discount and Credits" dialog box and returns to the Receive Payments dialog box, you'll see the discount in two or three places, as illustrated in Figure 9-10.

   The early payment discount appears both in the Discount column in the table of invoices and in the value shown for "Discount and Credits Applied." If the customer paid the invoice in full, the early payment discount becomes an over-payment.

Tip: If a customer overpays, at the bottom left of the Receive Payments dialog box, QuickBooks displays two options: creating a credit for future use, or refunding the amount to the customer. Unless your customer wants a refund, keep "Leave the credit to be used later" selected.

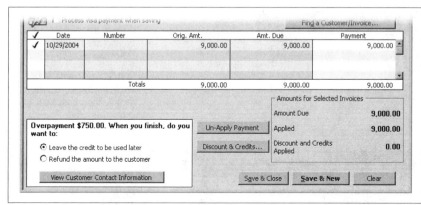

Figure 9-10:
When you apply an early payment discount to an invoice, it appears in the Discount cell. The discount also contributes to the "Discount and Credits Applied" value in the "Amounts for Selected Invoices" section.

Click Save & Close when you're done. You've just processed the payment with the discount applied.

Deposits, Down Payments, and Retainers

Deposits, down payments, and retainers are all *prepayments*: money that a customer gives you that you haven't actually earned. For example, a customer might give you a down payment to reserve a spot in your busy schedule. Until you perform services or deliver products to earn that money, the down payment is more like a loan from the customer than it is income.

Receiving money for something you didn't do feels good, but don't make the mistake of considering that money as yours. Prepayments belong to your customers until you earn them, and they require a bit more care than payments you receive for completed work and delivered products. This section explains how to manage all the intricacies of customer prepayments.

Setting Up QuickBooks for Prepayments

If you accept prepayments of any kind, you'll need an account in your Chart of Accounts to keep that money separate from your income. You'll also need an item that you can add to your invoices to deduct prepayments from what your customers owe.

- **Prepayment account.** If your customer gives you money and you never do anything to earn it, chances are excellent that your customer is going to ask for the money back. Because unearned money from a customer is like a loan, create an Other Current Liability account in your Chart of Accounts (see Chapter 2) to hold prepayments. Call it something like Customer Prepayments.

• **Prepayment item.** If you accept prepayments for services, create prepayment items in your Item List, as illustrated in Figure 9-11.

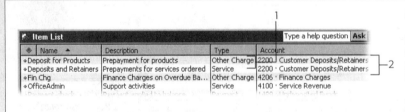

Figure 9-11:

1: If you accept deposits or retainers for services, create a Service item for them. For product deposits, create an Other Charge item.

2: When you create items for prepayments, assign them to the prepayment account.

WORKAROUND WORKSHOP

Applying a Credit for One Job to a Different Job

If you work on several jobs for the same customer, your customer might ask you to apply a credit from one job to another. For example, perhaps the job with the credit is already complete and your customer wants to use that credit toward another job still in progress. QuickBooks doesn't offer a ready-made feature to transfer credits between jobs.

The easy solution is to delete the credit memo for the first job and create a new one applying the credit to the job your customer specified. Your accountant probably won't approve, but the credit amount ends up applied to the job you want.

If you want to transfer the credit and satisfy your accountant, a couple of journal entries do the trick. But first you must create an account to hold these credit transfers. In your Chart of Accounts, create an account (page 36) using

the Other Expense type and call it something like Credit Memo Transfers or Credit Memo Swap Account.

Because you're moving money in and out of Accounts Receivable, and QuickBooks allows only one Accounts Receivable account per journal entry, you need *two* journal entries to complete the credit transfer. The first journal entry moves the credit from the first job into the transfer account, while the second journal entry completes the transfer from the transfer account to the new job. The first journal entry transfers the amount of the job credit memo from the first job into the transfer account; you must choose the customer and job in the Name cell. (Adding a memo helps you follow the money later.) The second journal entry transfers the amount of the job credit memo from the transfer account to the second job. Here you can see what the two journal entries look like.

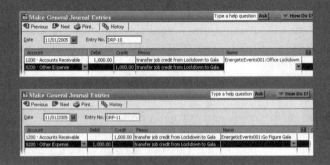

Recording Prepayments

When a customer hands you a check for a deposit or down payment, the first thing you should do is wait until you're out of earshot to yell "Yippee!" The second thing is to record the prepayment in QuickBooks. You haven't done any work yet, so there's no invoice to apply the payment to. A sales receipt not only records a prepayment in QuickBooks, but when printed, it acts as a receipt for your customer at the same time. Here's how to create one:

1. **On the Home page, click Create Sales Receipts.**

   QuickBooks opens the Enter Sales Receipts dialog box to a blank sales receipt. In the Customer:Job box, choose the customer or job for which you received a deposit or down payment.

2. **Fill in the other header boxes as you would for a regular sales receipt or an invoice (page 195).**

   If you use classes, in the Class box, choose a class to track the prepayment. If you have a customized template just for prepayments (page 500), in the Template drop-down list, choose that template. In the Date box, choose the date that you receive the prepayment. In the Payment Method box, choose the method the customer used to pay you. If the customer paid by check, in the Check No. box, type the check number for reference.

3. **Here's the key to recording a prepayment to the correct account: in the Item table, click the first Item cell, and in the Item drop-down list, choose the prepayment item you want to use.**

   Depending on whether the deposit covers services or products, choose the Service item or Other Charge item you created for prepayments (page 81). Because your prepayment items are tied to an Other Current Liability account, QuickBooks doesn't post the payment as income, but rather as money owed to your customer.

4. **In the Amount cell, type the amount of the deposit or down payment.**

   You don't need to bother with entering values in the Qty or Rate cells. The sales receipt simply records the total that the customer gave you. You add the detail for services and products when you create invoices later.

5. **Complete the sales receipt as you would for any other payment.**

   For example, add a message to the customer. If you want to provide the customer with a receipt, turn on either the "To be printed" or "To be e-mailed" checkbox. In the Deposit To box, choose Undeposited Funds if you plan to hold the payment to deposit with other payments. If you're going to race to the bank as soon as your computer shuts down, choose your bank account.

6. **Click Save & Close.**

   QuickBooks posts the payment to your prepayment account and closes the Enter Sales Receipts dialog box.

Applying a Deposit, Down Payment, or Retainer to an Invoice

When you finally start to deliver stuff to customers who've paid up front, you invoice them as usual. But the invoice you create has one additional line item that deducts the customer's prepayment from the invoice balance.

Create the invoice as you normally would with items for the services, products, charges, and discounts (Chapter 8). After you've added all those items, add the item to deduct the prepayment, as illustrated in Figure 9-12.

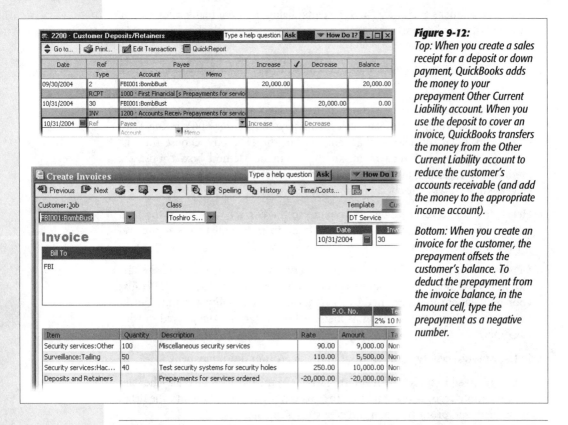

Figure 9-12:

Top: When you create a sales receipt for a deposit or down payment, QuickBooks adds the money to your prepayment Other Current Liability account. When you use the deposit to cover an invoice, QuickBooks transfers the money from the Other Current Liability account to reduce the customer's accounts receivable (and add the money to the appropriate income account).

Bottom: When you create an invoice for the customer, the prepayment offsets the customer's balance. To deduct the prepayment from the invoice balance, in the Amount cell, type the prepayment as a negative number.

Tip: If the charges on the invoice are less than the amount of the customer's deposit, deduct only as much of the deposit as you need. You can use the rest of the deposit on the next invoice.

Refunding Prepayments

Deposits and down payments don't guarantee that your customers follow through with their projects or orders. For example, a customer might make a deposit on décor for his bachelor pad. But when he meets his future wife at the monster truck rally, the plan for the bachelor pad is crushed as flat as the cars under the wheels of a truck. Of course, your customer wants his money back, which means you share some of his disappointment.

Your first step is to determine how much money your customer gets back. For example, if your customer cancels an order before you've purchased the products, you might refund the entire deposit. However, if the leopard print wallpaper has already arrived, you might keep part of the deposit as a restocking fee.

After you decide how much of the deposit you're going to keep, you have to do two things. First, you must move the portion of the deposit that you're keeping from the prepayment account to an income account. Second, you must refund the rest of the deposit. Here's how you accomplish both of these tasks:

1. **To turn the deposit you're keeping into income, create an invoice for the customer or job. Open the Create Invoices dialog box (Ctrl+I), and in the Customer:Job box, choose the customer. Then, in the first Item cell, choose an item related to the cancelled job or order.**

   For example, if you're keeping a deposit for products you ordered, choose the "Non-inventory Part" item for those products. If the deposit was for services worked, choose the appropriate Service item.

2. **In the Amount cell, type the amount of the deposit that you're keeping.**

   Because items are connected to income accounts (see Chapter 4), this first line in the invoice posts the amount of the deposit that you're keeping to the correct income account for the products or services you sold.

3. **In the second line, add the prepayment item, as shown in Figure 9-13.**

   This item removes the prepayment from your liability account so you no longer owe the customer that money.

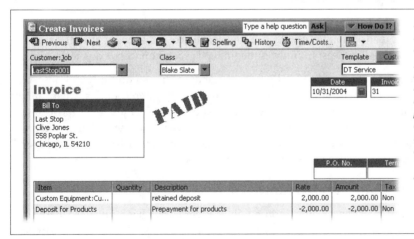

Figure 9-13:
In the Amount cell, type the amount of the deposit you're keeping as a negative number. The negative value makes the invoice balance zero. The prepayment item also deducts the deposit from the prepayment liability account, so you no longer "owe" your customer that money.

4. **Click Save & Close.**

   In saving the invoice, QuickBooks removes the deposit you're keeping from the prepayment liability account and posts that money to one of your income accounts. But if you aren't keeping the entire deposit, you have to refund the rest to the customer.

5. **To refund the rest of the deposit, create a credit memo for the remainder (page 232).**

   In the Create Credit Memos/Refunds dialog box, in the Item cell, choose the same prepayment item you used in the invoice (a Service item for a deposit for services, an Other Charge item for deposits on products). In the Amount cell, type the amount that you are refunding.

6. **Click Save & Close.**

   QuickBooks removes the remaining deposit amount from your prepayment liability account. Because the credit memo has a credit balance, QuickBooks opens the Available Credit dialog box.

7. **In the Available Credit dialog box, choose the "Give a refund" option and click OK.**

   QuickBooks opens the "Issue a Refund" dialog box and fills in the customer or job, the account from which the refund is issued, and the refund amount. If you want to refund the deposit from a different account, choose a different refund payment method or account.

8. **Click OK to create the refund to your customer.**

   As soon as you mail the refund check, you're done.

Applying Finance Charges

If you've tried everything but some customers won't pay, you can resort to finance charges. Finance charges usually don't cover the cost of keeping after the slackers, but QuickBooks at least minimizes the time you spend on this vexing task.

Customers tend to get cranky if you spring finance charges on them without warning. Up front, spend some time determining your payment policies: what interest rate you'll charge, what constitutes "late," and so on. Include these terms in the contracts your customers sign and on the sales forms you send. Then, after you configure QuickBooks with your finance charge settings, a few clicks is all you'll need to add those penalties to customer accounts.

Finance Charge Preferences

The Preferences dialog box (choose Edit → Preferences) has a Finance Charge section. Because your finance charge policies should apply to *all* your customers, these preferences appear on the Company Preferences tab, which means only a QuickBooks administrator can change them. The ins and outs of setting finance charge preferences begin on page 119. Here's a quick review of the finance charge preferences you can set before you move on to assessing them:

- **Annual Interest Rate (%).** Enter the interest rate for an entire year. For example, to charge 15 percent a year, type *15* in the box. (The program adds the % for you.) When you assess finance charges, QuickBooks calculates the finance charge by prorating the annual interest rate to the number of days that a payment is overdue.

Note: Because most companies would rather receive payments on time and forego finance charges, they set the annual interest rate quite high, like the double-digit interest rates so common on credit cards.

- **Minimum Finance Charge.** Because finance charges require time and effort on your part, you might want to charge a minimum amount to recoup some of your processing costs. Type the minimum dollar value in this box.

- **Grace Period (days).** Most companies extend a grace period to their customers: a number of days beyond the due date before finance charges kick in. The grace period gives mailed payments some extra time to wend through the postal system. In the "Grace Period (days)" box, type the number of days after the due date that you're willing to wait before assessing finance charges.

- **Finance Charge Account.** Most companies create a separate income account to track finance charges. If QuickBooks didn't create an account for you during the setup of your company file, create an Other Income account (page 37).

- **Assess finance charges on overdue finance charges.** Most companies stop short at tacking finance charges on top of overdue finance charges. This tactic is even illegal in some states. Unless you really want to get nasty (and your state says you can), keep the "Assess finance charges on overdue finance charges" checkbox turned off.

- **Calculate charges from.** If you're a stickler for punctuality, you might prefer to calculate finance charges from the date of an invoice or bill. QuickBooks doesn't assess finance charges until the customer rockets past the due date. But at that point, the program calculates finance charges from the invoice or bill date until the current date. To be less heavy-handed, you can calculate finance charges only from the due date. For example, if the customer pays 5 days late on a *Net 30 invoice* (meaning payment is due no more than 30 days after the invoice date), QuickBooks calculates finance charges for only 5 days—compared to the 35 days it would use with the "invoice/bill date" option.

Assessing Finance Charges on Overdue Balances

Make sure you apply payments and credits to invoices before you assess finance charges. Otherwise, you'll spend most of your time reversing finance charges and working to get back into your customers' good graces.

QuickBooks creates finance-charge invoices for the customers tardy enough to warrant late fees, but you don't have to print or send these invoices. Instead, assess finance charges just before you print customer statements (page 222) to have

QuickBooks include the finance-charge invoices on statements, along with any outstanding invoices and unpaid charges for the customer.

Here's how you assess finance charges for slow-paying customers:

1. **On the Home page, click Finance Charges (or choose Customers → Assess Finance Charges).**

   In the Assess Finance Charges dialog box, QuickBooks precedes a customer's name with an asterisk if the customer has payments or credits that you haven't yet applied, as shown in Figure 9-14.

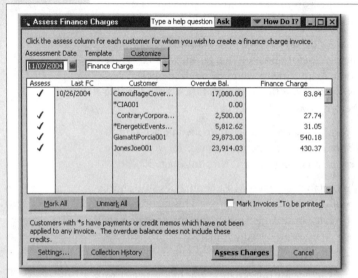

Figure 9-14:
In the Assess Finance Charges dialog box, you'll see an asterisk in front of the name of each customer with unapplied payments or credits. If you see any asterisks, click Cancel. After you've processed those payments (page 251) and credits (page 255), you're ready to start back at step 1. QuickBooks automatically chooses the current date as the date on which you want to assess finance charges, and selects all the customers with overdue balances.

2. **If you begin the process of preparing statements a few days before the end of the month, in the Assessment Date box, change the date to the last day of the month.**

   The last day of the month is a popular cutoff day for customer statements. When you change the date in the Assessment Date box, and move to another field, QuickBooks recalculates the finance charges to reflect the charges through the new assessment date.

3. **Although QuickBooks selects all customers with overdue balances automatically, you can let some of your customers slide without penalty. In the Assess column, click the checkmarked cell for a customer to skip her finance charges.**

   QuickBooks always displays every customer with an overdue balance, and there's no way to flag a customer as always exempt from finance charges. If you reserve finance charges for your most intractable customers, click Unmark All to turn off all the finance charges. Then, in the Assess column, click only the cells for the customers that you want to penalize.

To view the invoices, payments, and credits for a customer, click the row for the customer and then click Collection History. QuickBooks displays a Collections Report with every transaction for that customer.

4. **If you want to change the finance charge amount, in the Finance Charge column, click the cell for the customer and type the new finance charge.**

The only time you might want to do this is when you've created a credit memo (page 232) for a customer, but you don't want to apply it to an invoice. As long as the credit memo is out there, it's simpler to forego the finance charges until you've applied the credit.

5. **If you want to print and send the finance-charge invoices, turn on the "Mark Invoices 'To be printed'" checkbox. Then, to finalize the finance-charge invoices for the selected customers, click Assess Charges.**

QuickBooks adds the finance-charge invoices to the queue of invoices to be printed. When you print all the queued invoices (page 240), the program prints the finance-charge invoices as well. If you plan to send customer statements, turn off the "Mark Invoices 'To be printed'" checkbox. Sending customers a statement to remind them of overdue balances is one thing, but sending a statement *and* a finance-charge invoice borders on nagging.

Cash Sales

Receiving payment at the same time that you deliver the service or products is known as a *cash sale*, even though your customer might pay you with cash, check, or credit card. For example, if you run a thriving massage therapy business, your customers probably pay for their stress relief before they leave your office—and no matter how they pay, QuickBooks considers the transaction a cash sale.

If your customers want records of their payments, you give them sales receipts. In QuickBooks, a Sales Receipt can do double-duty; it records your cash sale in the program *and* you can print it as a paper sales receipt for your customer. Although cash sales are a simultaneous exchange of money and goods (or services), you don't actually have to create a QuickBooks sales receipt at the time of the sale. Here are the two most common approaches for handling cash sales:

- **Recording individual sales.** If you want to keep track of which customers purchase which products, create a separate sales receipt for each cash sale. Individual sales receipts track both customers' purchases and the state of inventory.

Tip: If you keep QuickBooks open in your store, you can print individual sales receipts for your customers. But keeping QuickBooks running on the store computer could be risky if the wrong people started snooping into your records. And, unless you're completely proficient with sales receipts in the program, you might find paper sales receipts faster when your store is swamped. When there's a lull in your store traffic, you can enter individual receipts into your QuickBooks company file.

- **Recording batch sales.** If your shop gets lots of one-time customers, you don't care about tracking who purchases your products. But you still need to know how much inventory you have and how much money you've made. In this situation, you don't have to create a separate sales receipt for each sale. Instead, create a sales receipt for each business day, which shows how much money you brought in for the day and what you sold.

Creating Sales Receipts

Creating sales receipts in QuickBooks is identical to creating invoices (page 194), except for a few small differences that are shown in Figure 9-15. To create a sales receipt, on the Home page, click Create Sales Receipts (or choose Customers → Enter Sales Receipts). If you want to print the sales receipt for your customer after you've filled in all the fields, in the Enter Sales Receipts dialog box icon bar, click Print to have QuickBooks open the Print One Sales Receipt dialog box. To learn more about your printing options, see page 235.

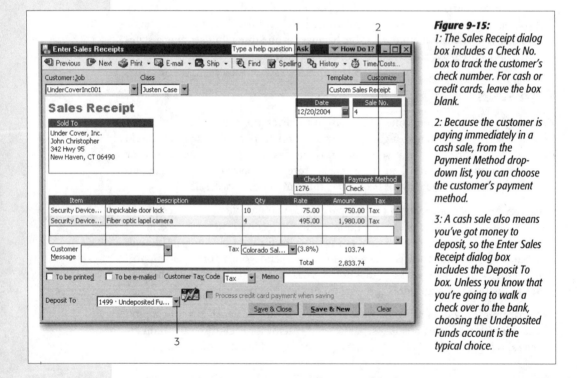

Figure 9-15:
1: The Sales Receipt dialog box includes a Check No. box to track the customer's check number. For cash or credit cards, leave the box blank.

2: Because the customer is paying immediately in a cash sale, from the Payment Method drop-down list, you can choose the customer's payment method.

3: A cash sale also means you've got money to deposit, so the Enter Sales Receipt dialog box includes the Deposit To box. Unless you know that you're going to walk a check over to the bank, choosing the Undeposited Funds account is the typical choice.

Warning: Keeping track of customers who make one-time cash sales can clog your Customer:Job List with unneeded information. Because you can store only 14,500 entries for your Customer:Job, Vendor, Employee, and Other Names lists combined, save the slots in your name lists by creating one customer called Cash Sales (page 54).

Creating a Batch Sales Template

If you want to reduce your paperwork by recording one batch sales receipt for each business day's sales, why not go one step further and *memorize* a batch sales receipt that you can reuse every day? Here's how:

1. **On the Home page, click Create Sales Receipts (or choose Customers → Enter Sales Receipts).**

   QuickBooks opens the Enter Sales Receipts dialog box.

2. **In the Customer:Job box, choose the generic customer you created for cash sales.**

   Don't bother with a payment method because you're likely to receive a combination of cash, checks, and credit cards.

3. **In the Deposit To box, choose the Undeposited Funds account.**

   You'll deposit your money at the same time whether it comes as checks or hard currency.

4. **If you typically sell the same types of items every day, in Item cells, choose the items you sell regularly.**

   Leave the Qty cells blank because those values are almost guaranteed to change every day.

5. **When the sales receipts is set up the way you want, press Ctrl+M to open the Memorize Transaction dialog box.**

   In the Name box, type a name for the reusable sales receipt, such as Day's Cash Sales.

6. **If you want to use this memorized sales receipt only on the days you have cash sales, choose the Don't Remind Me option.**

   If you receive cash sales every day, choose the Remind Me option and then, in the How Often box, choose Daily.

7. **To memorize the sales receipt, click OK.**

   QuickBooks closes the Memorize Transaction dialog box and adds the batch sales receipt to the Memorized Transaction List.

8. **In the Enter Sales Receipts dialog box, click Clear to delete the information you used to set up the memorized sales receipt.**

   To create a new sales receipt for a day, press Ctrl+T to open the Memorized Transaction List window. In the Memorized Transaction List, click the memorized transaction for your batch sales receipt and then click Enter Transaction. QuickBooks open the Enter Sales Receipts dialog box with a sales receipt based on the one you memorized. You can edit the items in the sales receipt, their quantities, and the prices to reflect your day's sales. When the sales receipt is complete, click Save & Close.

Reconciling Excess and Short Cash

When you take in paper money and make change, you're bound to make small mistakes. Unless you're lucky enough to have one of those automatic change machines, the cash in the cash register at the end of the day often disagrees with the sales you recorded. Over time, the amounts you're short or over tend to balance out, but that's no help when you have to record sales in QuickBooks that don't match your bank deposits.

The solution to this reality of cash sales is one final sales receipt at the end of the day that reconciles your cash register total with your bank deposit slip. But before you can create this reconciliation sales receipt, you need an account and a couple of items:

- **Over/Under account.** To keep track of your running total for excess and short cash, create an Income account, such as Over/Under. If you use account numbers, give the account a number so that it appears near the end of your Income accounts. For example, if Uncategorized Income is account number 4999, make the Over/Under account 4998.

- **Over item.** Create an Other Charge item to track the excess cash you collect, and assign it to the Over/Under account. Make sure that you set up this item as nontaxable.

- **Under item.** Create a second Other Charge item to track the amounts that you are short and assign it to the Over/Under account. This item should also be nontaxable.

At the end of each day, compare the income you recorded to the amount of money in your cash register. Create a sales receipt to make up the difference.

If you have less cash than you should, create a Sales Receipt and, in the first line, add the Under item. In the Amount cell, type the amount that you're short as a negative number. When you save the sales receipt, QuickBooks adjusts your income record to match the money in the cash register.

Note: If you notice that your cash count at the end of the day is always short, a fluke of probability could be at work. But the more likely answer is that someone is helping themselves to the cash in your till.

If you have too much cash, create a Sales Receipt and, in the first line, add the Over item. In the Amount cell, type the excess amount as a positive number. This sales receipt increases your recorded income to match the money you have on hand.

Making Deposits

Whether customers mail you checks or hand over a wad of cash, taking those deposits to the bank isn't enough—you also must record those deposits in Quick-Books. If you initially store payments in the Undeposited Funds account, you have to work your way through two dialog boxes to record deposits; otherwise, you have just one step. Both processes are described in this section.

Note: In the Receive Payments dialog box, when you choose a bank account as the Deposit To account (page 253), there's nothing more to do after you save the payment–QuickBooks records the payment as a deposit to the bank account.

Choosing Payments to Deposit

When you store payments in the Undeposited Funds account, you end up with a collection of payments ready for deposit. And when you have payments queued up for deposit and choose Banking → Make Deposits (or on the Home page, click Record Deposits), QuickBooks opens the "Payments to Deposit" dialog box. You can choose the payments you want to deposit in several ways, as shown in Figure 9-16.

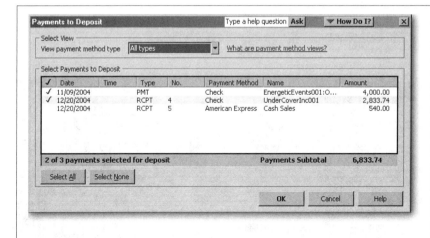

Figure 9-16:
The first method for separating payments to deposit is by payment method. If you have gazillions of payments, in the "View payment method type" box, choose a payment method to display only those types of payments. To choose specific payments to deposit, in the checkmark column, click each payment you want to deposit. To select every payment listed, click Select All.

Tip: If you have other checks that you want to deposit, such as an insurance claim check or a vendor's refund, you'll have a chance to add those to your deposit in the Make Deposit dialog box.

When you've selected the payments you want, click OK. QuickBooks closes the "Payments to Deposit" dialog box and opens the Make Deposits dialog box, described next.

Recording Deposits

The Make Deposits dialog box is like an electronic deposit slip, as you can see in Figure 9-17. If you have other checks to deposit besides customer payments, they won't show up automatically in the Make Deposits dialog box.

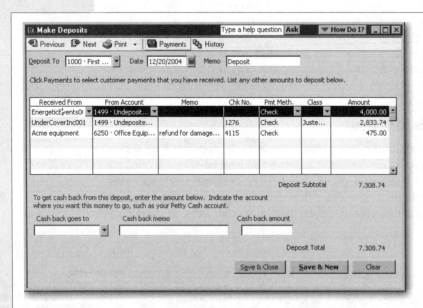

Figure 9-17:
In the Make Deposits dialog box, you can specify the account into which you're depositing funds, the date, and each payment in the deposit. If you're in the habit of withdrawing some petty cash from your deposits, you can record that as well. To prevent yourself from bouncing checks, in the Date box, be sure to choose the date that you actually make the deposit.

UP TO SPEED

Ways to Put Payments to Deposit to Work

Choosing different types of payments *before* you get to the Make Deposits dialog box takes extra work, but it's a good idea for several reasons. Here are a few reasons you might make multiple passes through the deposit process:

- **Different Deposit Types.** Many banks group different types of deposits, such as checks versus electronic transfers. To group your payments in Quick-Books the way your bank groups them on the monthly bank statement, in the "View payment method type" box, choose a payment method, and then click Select All to process those payments as a group.

- **Different Deposit Accounts.** If you deposit some payments in your checking account and other pay-

ments to a savings account, select all the payments you want to deposit in the checking account. Then you can run through the deposit process a second time to deposit other checks to your savings account.

- **Reconciling Cash Deposits.** As you learned on page 270, counting cash is prone to error, so you're probably used to your bank coming up with a different cash deposit total than you did. Although Quick-Books groups cash and checks as one payment type, process your cash and check payments as two separate deposits. Then, if the bank changes the deposit amount, it's easy to edit your cash deposit.

Here's how you add these additional deposits:

1. **Click the first blank Received From cell and choose the vendor or name of the source of your deposit. Then, in the From Account, choose the account to which you're posting the money.**

   For example, if you're depositing a refund check for some supplies, choose the expense account for office supplies.

2. **Fill in the rest of the cells (optional).**

   For customer payments, you can probably skip the Memo cell, but for refunds or checks from other sources, memos can help you remember why people sent you money. In case a question arises, typing the number of the check gives your customer or vendor a reference point.

Tip: If you want to withdraw some money for petty cash from your deposit, in the "Cash back goes to" box, choose your petty cash account. In the "Cash back amount" box, type the amount of cash you're deducting from the deposit.

If your company is a corporation, you can't just withdraw money for your personal use. By accounting for the cash in a petty cash account, you can record your cash expenditures in QuickBooks. If you own a sole proprietorship, you *can* withdraw cash for yourself. In this case, in the "Cash back goes to" box, choose your owner's draw account.

---

3. **When you've filled in all the fields, click Save & Close.**

   QuickBooks posts the deposits to your accounts.

Tip: If you want to turn the Make Deposits virtual deposit slip into a real deposit slip that your bank accepts, you can order printable deposit slips from Intuit. In your browser, navigate to *http://quickbooks.intuit.com*. Under the Additional Solutions heading, click the "Checks, Forms, and Supplies" link.

Depositing Money from Merchant Card Accounts

When you accept payment via credit card, the merchant bank you work with collects your customers' credit card payments and deposits them in your bank account as a lump sum. Regardless of how credit card payments you receive appear on the merchant bank's statement, you record your deposits in QuickBooks the way they appear on your bank statement. For example, your merchant bank might show payments and merchant bank fees separately, whereas the amount deposited in your checking account is the net after the fees are deducted.

Here's how you deposit merchant credit card payments and fees into your bank account:

1. **On the Home page, click Record Deposits (or choose Banking → Make Deposits).**

   In the "Payments to Deposit" window in the "View payment method type" drop-down list, choose the merchant card whose payments you want to deposit.

2. **Select the credit card payments you want to deposit and click OK.**

   QuickBooks opens the Make Deposits window, which lists the credit card payments in the deposit table.

   If the Deposit Subtotal doesn't match the deposit that appears on your bank statement, the merchant bank probably deducted its fees. You'll record those fees in the next step.

3. **In the first blank row in the Account cell, choose the account to which you post merchant card fees (such as Bank Service Charges). Then, in the Amount cell, type the merchant card fees as a negative number.**

   In the Make Deposits dialog box, the Deposit Subtotal should equal the deposit that appears on your bank statement.

4. **Click Save & Close when you're done.**

Note: How soon you can enter your merchant card deposits in QuickBooks depends on how wired your company is. For example, the QuickBooks online banking service (page 514) downloads your merchant card deposits into your company file automatically. If you have online account access to your merchant card account, make the deposit in QuickBooks when you go online and see it in your transaction listing. But if you don't use any online services, you enter the deposit in QuickBooks when the merchant card statement arrives in the mail.

UP TO SPEED

Following the Money Trail

If you use the dialog boxes in QuickBooks to create transactions, the program posts debits and credits to accounts without any action or brain damage on your part. But if you're interested in how money weaves its way from account to account, here's what happens from the time you create an invoice to the time you deposit the customer payment into your bank account.

- **Create Invoices.** When you create an invoice, QuickBooks credits your income accounts because you've earned income. It debits the Accounts Receivable account because your customers owe you money.

- **Receive Payments.** When you receive payments into the Undeposited Funds account, QuickBooks credits the Accounts Receivable account because the customer balance is now paid off. The program debits the Undeposited Funds account because the money is now in that account waiting to be deposited.

- **Make Deposits.** When you deposit the payments queued in the Undeposited Funds account, QuickBooks credits the Undeposited Funds account to remove the money from that account. It debits your bank account to transfer the money into your bank account balance.

Paying for Expenses

Most small business owners sift through the daily mail looking for the envelopes that contain checks. After that, it's time to read all your industry rags and Web sites. And after that, there's nothing to do but open the bills.

When you use QuickBooks, paying bills is a multistep process. If you want your financial records to be right, you have to tell the program about the expenses you've incurred. And, if you want your vendors to leave you alone, you have to pay the bills they send.

Handling expenses can take several forms, just as charging customers for products and services can. QuickBooks accepts this challenge and, aside from a few idiosyncrasies that drive accountants wild, succeeds. This chapter explains the choices you have for paying bills (now or later) and describes how to record your bills and payments either way. If you pay bills right away, you'll find out how to write checks, use a credit card, or pay with cash in QuickBooks. If you enter bills in QuickBooks for payment later, you'll learn how to handle the easy ones, such as rent, as well as reimbursable expenses and inventory.

QuickBooks is happy to help you through every step of the process: recording bills you receive, setting up bill payments, and even printing the checks you mail to your vendors. But for modest enterprises with few expenses, writing checks by hand and recording them in the program works just as well.

When to Pay Expenses

When it comes to paying for expenses, you have three choices. You can choose to *not* pay bills, but QuickBooks can't help you with vendor lawsuits or represent your company in bankruptcy court. The only *viable* choices are paying now or paying later—QuickBooks *can* help with both of these.

If bills arrive about as often as shooting stars, paying each bill immediately doesn't interrupt your work day that much, and you know the bills are paid on time. In QuickBooks, paying immediately means writing a check, entering a credit card charge, making an online payment, or using some money from petty cash—all of which are described in this chapter.

But paying bills later has a lot to offer. When bills arrive as fast as coffee orders at the local Starbucks, you'll probably want to pay bills when it won't interfere with delivering services or selling products. What's more, most companies don't pay bills until just before they're due—unless there's a good reason. Setting up vendor bills for later payment is known as "using accounts payable" because you store your unpaid expenses in an Accounts Payable account.

In QuickBooks, entering bills for later payment goes beyond the obvious advantages of convenience and cash management. You can tell the program when you want to pay bills—for instance, to take advantage of an early payment discount or the grace period that a vendor allows. Then, you can go about your business without distraction until you're ready to pay bills, knowing that QuickBooks knows which bills are on deck for payment.

Tip: For the virulently forgetful, QuickBooks can add bills to your Reminders List (page 55). Choose Edit → Preferences and, in the Edit Preferences dialog box icon bar, click the Reminders icon. Click the Company Preferences tab. For the "Bills to Pay" option, choose Show Summary or Show List and then specify the number of days lead time you want before bills are due.

Once you decide whether you're going to pay bills now or later, you're better off using that method consistently. Otherwise, you could pay for something twice by entering a bill in QuickBooks *and* then, a few days later, writing a paper check for the same expense. If you take the Accounts Payable path, you can still write checks by hand and charge expenses to your credit card, and enter those transactions in QuickBooks without a corresponding bill. To prevent duplicate payments, always enter bills you receive as bills in QuickBooks and pay them using the Pay Bills command (page 292).

Entering Bills in QuickBooks

At first glance, entering bills and then paying them might *seem* like more work than just writing a check. But as you'll learn in this chapter, after you enter bills in QuickBooks, the program makes it incredibly easy to pay them.

To enter bills in QuickBooks, choose any of the following methods to open the Enter Bills dialog box:

- On the Home page, click Enter Bills.

- In the Vendor Center icon bar, click New Transactions → Enter Bills.

- In the QuickBooks icon bar, click Bill.

- Choose Vendors → Enter Bills.

If you've already invoiced your customers for products and services, the fields on a vendor's bill are old friends. In fact, if your vendors use QuickBooks, the bills you receive are just another company's QuickBooks invoices or statements (see Chapter 8).

With the Enter Bills dialog box open, here's what you do to enter a bill in Quick-Books:

1. **In the Vendor box, choose the vendor who billed you.**

   As you can see in Figure 10-1, as soon as you chose a vendor, QuickBooks fills in some information for you.

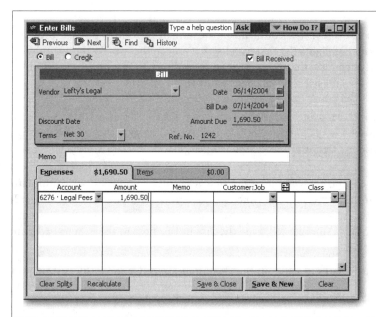

Figure 10-1:
QuickBooks automatically chooses the Bill option so that you can record a vendor bill. It turns on the Bill Received checkbox because you rarely enter a bill you haven't received. Turn off this checkbox only if you receive a shipment of inventory without a bill, which you'll learn about on page 288. The program displays the Expenses tab, which is where you enter information about expenses such as utility bills, office supply bills, and your accountant's fees. See page 289 to learn how to enter bills for inventory purchases using the Items tab.

2. **In the Date box, type or select the date that you received the bill.**

   If you set up payment terms in the vendor's record (page 118), QuickBooks fills in the Bill Due box. For example, as shown in Figure 10-1, the Date is 6/14/2004. Because the vendor's payment terms are Net 30, the bill is due 30 days (one month) after the bill date, which is 7/14/2004. If QuickBooks fills in a date that doesn't match the bill you received, in the Bill Due field, enter the date printed on the vendor's bill—it's more likely to be correct.

Tip: The Terms field shows the payment terms from the vendor record. If you haven't assigned payment terms to a vendor, you can do so right in the Enter Bills dialog box. In the Terms drop-down list, choose the vendor's terms. When you save the bill, QuickBooks asks if you want the new terms to appear the next time. The program is trying to ask if you want to save the terms to the vendor's record; click Yes.

---

3. **In the Amount Due box, type the total from the bill. In the Ref. No. box, type the vendor's invoice number, statement date, or other identifying feature of the bill you're paying.**

   The Ref. No. box accepts any alphanumeric characters, so you can type reference numbers such as "1242," "invoice 1242," or "statement 2/15/2005."

   If you want to include additional notes about the bill, in the Memo box, type a description.

4. **In the first cell in the Account column, choose the expense account from your Chart of Accounts that corresponds to the first expense on the bill.**

   In a cell in the Account column, clicking the downward triangle displays a drop-down list of every account in your Chart of Accounts, but the program automatically highlights the first expense account in the list. To choose a different expense account—the account for your legal fees, for example—scroll in the drop-down list and select the account you want.

Tip: In QuickBooks 2006, you can increase or decrease the width of drop-down lists (to see the full name for the accounts in your Chart of Accounts, for example). Position your cursor over the lower-right corner of the list. When it changes to a two-headed arrow, drag to adjust the width and height.

   When you choose an account in the first Account cell, QuickBooks automatically fills in the first cell in the *Amount* column with the Amount Due value. If the bill covers several types of expenses (such as airfare and your travel agent's fees), in the first Amount cell, type the amount to post to the expense account in the first row.

5. **If an expense relates to a job, in the Customer:Job cell, choose the customer or job.**

   Once you've made your choice, you'll see an icon (which is supposed to look like an invoice) in the Reimbursable column. If you don't want to charge the customer for the expense, click the Reimbursable icon. QuickBooks places a red X over the icon, indicating that the expense is *not* reimbursable.

Tip: If you're recording reimbursable expenses (page 291), which eventually appear on a customer invoice, in the Enter Bills dialog box, be sure to type a meaningful description in each Memo cell. Quick-Books uses the text in the Memo cell as the description of the expense on your invoice. Without text in these Memo cells, your invoice includes charges without descriptions, which is bound to generate a call from your customer.

6. **If you're tracking classes, choose the appropriate class for the expense.**

   The Class column appears only if you're using QuickBooks' classes (page 113).

7. **If the bill you're entering includes different types of expenses, repeat steps 3 through 6 to add a row for each type of expense, as illustrated in Figure 10-2.**

   If the multiple accounts and amounts are hopelessly mangled, click Clear Splits to clear the table so that you can start over.

   If you change the value in the Amount Due box, QuickBooks doesn't automatically adjust the values on the Expenses tab to match. Click Recalculate to automatically modify the last entry amount so that the Amount Due and the total in the table are the same. If you change a value in one or more amount cells, click Recalculate to update the Amount Due.

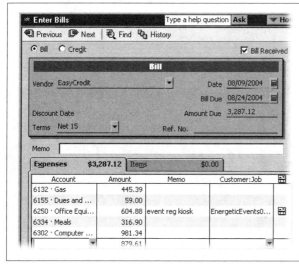

Figure 10-2:
As soon as you choose an account in the next blank line, QuickBooks fills in the Amount cell with the amount that is still unallocated. For the first through the next to last line, you must edit the amount that the program fills in to match your expense. The amount that QuickBooks enters for the last line should be correct if you haven't made any typographical errors.

8. **Click Save & Close to save the bill and close the dialog box.**

   Or, if you haven't had enough, click Save & New to save the bill and then display a blank bill.

Automating Recurring Bills

A lot of your bills are due the same time every month, and some are even the same *amount* every month. For example, your $1,000 rent check is due the first of every month. Your electric bill is due the 19th of the month, but the amount varies each time. When you reorder office supplies or inventory, the items you buy tend to be the same each time. All of these bills are perfect for QuickBooks' memorized transactions.

In QuickBooks, you can memorize bills and reuse them. You can even create a group of bills so that you can process all the bills due on the same day of the month. Even when some fields change, recalling a transaction with *most* of the fields filled in pares time from your bill paying.

TROUBLESHOOTING MOMENT

Turning on Group Features

You're probably spoiled by the QuickBooks feature that lets you create new list entries whenever you need them by choosing *<Add New>* in a drop-down list. Then, when you're hooked on that feature, QuickBooks leaves it out.

You open the Memorize Transaction dialog box and create your first memorized transaction. Tantalizingly visible are the "With Transactions in Group" option and Group Name box, but they are grayed out no matter what you click in the dialog box.

To add a memorized transaction to a group, you must first create the *memorized group*. The steps are easy, once you know the right order:

1. Press Ctrl+T to open the Memorized Transaction List.

2. In the Memorized Transaction List menu bar, click Memorized Transaction and then, on the shortcut menu, choose New Group. QuickBooks opens the New Memorized Transaction Group dialog box—a sibling to the Memorize Transaction dialog box without the With Transactions in Group option and Group Name box.

3. Fill in the fields as you would for a memorized transaction. Name the group. Choose how and when you want to be reminded.

4. Click OK to save the group. Now that the group exists, you can add individual transactions to it.

5. To add an existing memorized transaction to the group, in the Memorized Transaction List, right-click the transaction and, on the shortcut menu, choose Edit Memorized Transaction. In the Schedule Memorized Transaction dialog box, choose the "With Transactions in Group" option. In the Group Name box, choose the group you created. Click OK.

6. To add a new memorized transaction to the group, in the Memorize Transaction dialog box, choose the "With Transactions in Group" option.

When you add a memorized transaction to a group, in the Memorized Transaction List, you'll see that QuickBooks tucks the transactions underneath the memorized group, as shown in the figure. The individual memorized transactions take on the schedule and reminder characteristics of the memorized group.

Memorizing a Bill

Here's how to memorize a bill:

1. **On the Home page, click Enter Bills (or choose Vendors → Enter Bills).**

   QuickBooks opens the Enter Bills dialog box.

2. **Fill in all the fields that will be the same on each bill, as shown in Figure 10-3.**

   If a field changes for each bill, such as the Amount Due, simply leave that field blank. When you use the memorized bill, fill in the empty fields with the values on the bill that your vendor sent.

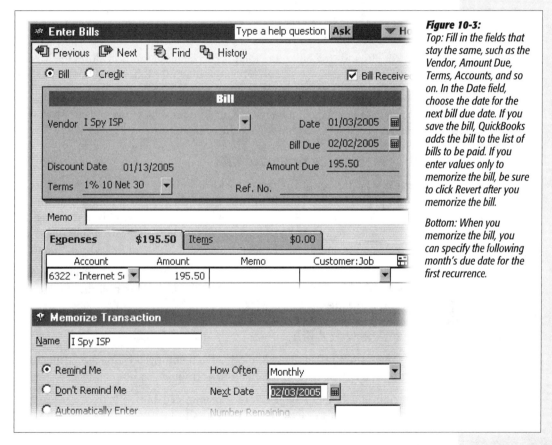

Figure 10-3:
Top: Fill in the fields that stay the same, such as the Vendor, Amount Due, Terms, Accounts, and so on. In the Date field, choose the date for the next bill due date. If you save the bill, QuickBooks adds the bill to the list of bills to be paid. If you enter values only to memorize the bill, be sure to click Revert after you memorize the bill.

Bottom: When you memorize the bill, you can specify the following month's due date for the first recurrence.

3. **When the bill is set up the way you want, press Ctrl+M to open the Memorize Transaction dialog box. In the Name box, type a name for the memorized bill.**

   QuickBooks automatically fills in the Name box with the vendor name, but you can type a more meaningful name. For example, naming a memorized bill Rent is better than using the landlord's name.

4. **If you want QuickBooks to remind you when it's time to pay the bill, choose the Remind Me option and specify when the program should remind you.**

In the How Often box, choose the frequency, such as Monthly. In the Next Date, choose the next due date. For example, if the bill you memorized is set for 1/3/2005, choose 2/3/2005.

Tip: For bills that are identical from month to month, such as rent, choose the Automatically Enter option. You can tell QuickBooks how many days before the due date to enter the bill. When that date arrives, the program tacks the bill onto the list of bills waiting to be paid (see page 292). When you choose Automatically Enter, the Number Remaining box becomes active, so you can type how many payments remain, which is ideal for recurring bills like loan payments, which thankfully don't go on forever.

---

5. **To memorize the bill, click OK.**

QuickBooks adds the bill to the Memorized Transaction List, closes the Memorize Transaction dialog box, and returns to the Enter Bills dialog box.

If you want to add the bill to the queue of bills to be paid, click Save & Close. If you created the bill *only* to memorize it, close the dialog box and click No when QuickBooks asks if you want to save the transaction.

Creating Memorized Groups of Bills

The first day of the month is the nemesis of bill payers everywhere because so many bills are due then. QuickBooks can't ease the pain of watching your money leave, but at least it can ease the burden of entering all those bills in the program. Memorized bills are a start, but why enter individual memorized bills when you can enter several at once?

You can set up memorized transaction groups that act like their individual memorized counterparts—to remind you on a specific day or enter all the transactions automatically. See the box on page 280.

Using a Memorized Bill

How you generate a bill in QuickBooks from a memorized transaction depends on whether you've opted for total automation, a reminder, or no reminder:

- **Automatically Enter.** If you create a memorized bill with the Automatically Enter option, that's exactly what the program does. When the next scheduled date for the bill arrives, QuickBooks creates a new bill and adds it to the list of bills waiting to be paid.

- **Remind Me.** When you ask QuickBooks to remind you, and the scheduled date arrives, the program adds the bill to the Reminders List. In the Reminders List, double-click a bill to open the Enter Bills dialog box. The bill that you see contains only the memorized information. Make any changes you want, fill in the empty fields, and click Save & Close.

Tip: For the most persistent of reminders, tell QuickBooks to display the Reminders List each time you open a company file. As soon as you log into QuickBooks, you'll see the tasks awaiting you. To set this behavior, choose Edit → Preferences and, in the icon bar, click Reminders. Click the My Preferences tab and turn on the only checkbox there: "Show Reminders List when opening a Company file."

- **Don't Remind Me.** When you memorize a bill that you use only occasionally, choosing Don't Remind Me stores the bill in the Memorized Transaction List in case you need it. You must tell QuickBooks to use the memorized bill. In the Memorized Transaction List, right-click the memorized transaction you want and, on the shortcut menu, choose Enter Transaction.

Purchasing Inventory

Purchasing and paying for inventory items is *mostly* the same as paying for other expenses. But as you learned in Chapter 4, inventory always seems more complicated than the other things you sell.

Part of the problem with inventory is that you have to keep track of how much you have. As inventory wends its way from your warehouse to your customers, and it also hops between accounts in your Chart of Accounts (see Chapter 3). An income account tracks the money you make from selling inventory; a second account tracks the costs of the inventory you've sold; and a third asset account tracks the value of the inventory you still own.

Purchasing inventory also involves three transactions in QuickBooks:

- Adding the inventory you purchase to a QuickBooks inventory account.

- Entering the bill you receive for the inventory you bought.

- Paying the bill for the inventory.

What's maddening is that you don't know whether the bill or the inventory will arrive first. In many cases, the bill arrives with the shipment. But you might receive your inventory before the bill, or Samurai Sam could email you a bill while you wait weeks for your swords to arrive.

Furthermore, you don't have to pay bills for products you don't receive. Quick-Books includes several commands for these situations. In the following sections, you'll learn how to handle any order of bill and inventory arrival.

Creating Purchase Orders

Before you get to receiving inventory and paying the corresponding bills, it's a good idea to make sure that you actually *receive* the inventory you ordered. If you ordered corsages for Mother's Day, but the box that shows up contains corsets, the mistake is obvious. Remembering what you ordered is tougher when products and quantities vary. Most businesses address this problem by creating purchase orders for the inventory they buy. When the order arrives, a comparison of the shipment to the purchase order can confirm that the items and quantities are correct.

Note: You can create all the purchase orders you want. Those orders don't alter the balances in your income, expense, and asset accounts; and they won't appear in your Profit & Loss or Balance Sheet reports.

Purchase orders are known as nonposting transactions. No money changes hands (or accounts), so there's nothing to post in your Chart of Accounts. In QuickBooks, the first posting for purchased inventory occurs when you either receive the inventory or the bill.

In QuickBooks, inventory and purchase orders are inseparable. If you want to track inventory, you must first turn on the preference for inventory and purchase orders. (In the Preferences dialog box, in the icon bar, click Purchases & Vendors. Click the Company Preferences tab. Turn on the "Inventory and purchase orders are active" checkbox.) As soon as you turn on this preference, QuickBooks adds icons for purchase orders and inventory to the Home page; the Vendors menu gains commands, such as Create Purchase Orders and Receive Items; and the Chart of Accounts sports a nonposting account called Purchase Orders.

The Create Purchase Orders dialog box is like the Create Invoices dialog box from some mirror-image universe. Instead of choosing a customer, you choose a vendor; the Ship To address is not a customer address, but *your company's* address, as illustrated in Figure 10-4.

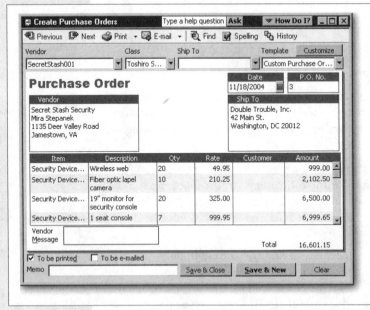

Figure 10-4:
QuickBooks contains one predefined template for purchase orders, which looks a lot like the Intuit Professional Invoice template. If you want to customize your purchase order form (page 550), above the Template box, click Customize.

Otherwise, the fields in a purchase order are practically identical to the ones in an invoice (see Chapter 8). To create a purchase order, on the Home page, click Purchase Orders (or choose Vendors → Create Purchase Orders). Because the forms are so similar, here's a run-through of the fields that work *differently* than their invoicing cousins:

- **Vendor.** Instead of choosing a customer or job to invoice, in the Vendor box, choose the vendor from whom you're ordering your inventory. QuickBooks fills in the Vendor box in the header area with the vendor name and address.

- **Ship To.** QuickBooks fills in the Ship To box with your company address. If you're ordering inventory that you want shipped directly to one of your customers, choose that customer (or job) in the Ship To drop-down list.

- **Date.** QuickBooks fills in the current date, and there's no reason to change that.

- **P.O. No.** When you create your first purchase order, type the number that you want to start with. As you create new purchase orders, QuickBooks increments the number in the P.O. No. box by one. If you order your products over the phone or through an online system and the vendor asks for your purchase order number, give them this number.

- **Item.** The Item drop-down list contains all the entries in your Item List, despite companies' usually creating purchase orders for inventory items only. (As you type the first few letters of an item name, QuickBooks 2006 filters the list to matching entries. You can keep typing or click the item you want as soon as you see it.)

  When you choose an item, QuickBooks fills in fields with information from the item record (see Chapter 4). The Description cell receives the item record Description. The Rate cell grabs the value from the Cost field of the item record (that's the price you pay for the item).

Tip: You can insert and delete lines in a purchase order as you can on invoices and sales receipts. To insert a line, right-click a line and choose Insert Line from the shortcut menu. To delete the line, choose Delete Line from the shortcut menu.

- **Customer.** If you're purchasing inventory specifically for a customer or job, choose the customer or job in the drop-down list.

Note: As you'll learn shortly, when you receive your inventory, you can use the purchase order to record the receipt of inventory into your QuickBooks inventory account and enter the vendor's bill.

Receiving Inventory and Bills Simultaneously

For many orders, you'll find your bill tucked into one of the boxes of your shipment like a bonus gift. Although a bill isn't the most welcome of gifts, receiving a bill and inventory simultaneously is a bonus because you can record your inventory and the accompanying bill at the same time in QuickBooks. To process a shipment and bill at the same time:

1. **On the Home page, click Receive Inventory and then choose "Receive Inventory with Bill" (or choose Vendors → Receive Items and Enter Bill).**

    QuickBooks opens the Enter Bills dialog box that you first met on page 277 and helps you fill in fields, as described in Figure 10-5.

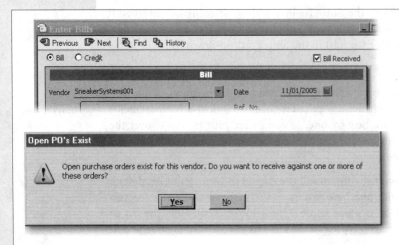

Figure 10-5:
Top: QuickBooks automatically turns on Bill Received. In The Vendor box, choose the vendor who shipped the items you've received.

Bottom: If any open purchase orders exist for the vendor, QuickBooks displays a reminder. If you click Yes, the program displays the Open Purchase Orders dialog box. If you click No, it returns to the Enter bills dialog box where you can click Select PO to display the Open Purchase Orders dialog box.

Regardless of how you access the Open Purchase Orders dialog box, you'll see only purchase order dates, purchase order numbers, and memos. If the vendor bill includes the purchase order number, picking the correct purchase order is easy.

But if you don't memorize purchase order numbers and don't know which one to pick, click Cancel to close the Open Purchase Orders dialog box. To view a report of open purchase orders, choose Reports → Purchases → Open Purchase Orders. Double-click a purchase order to view its details.

2. **In the Date box, fill in the date when you received the bill.**

    If you've already defined the payment terms in the vendor record (page 276), QuickBooks fills in the Terms box and calculates the date in the Bill Due box automatically. If the bill you received shows different terms or a different due date, in the Bill Due and Terms boxes, update the values with those from the vendor's bill. When you save the bill, the program offers to save the new terms in the vendor's record (page 112).

3. If you didn't create a purchase order for the shipment you received, in the Amount Due field, type the amount due from the vendor bill.

When you choose an open purchase order, QuickBooks automatically fills in the Amount Due field in the header and, on the Items tab, the items you received, as shown in Figure 10-6.

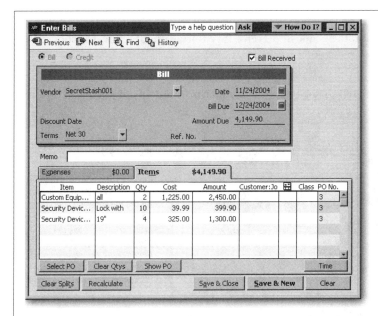

Figure 10-6:
The program uses the information from the purchase order to fill in most of the information about the items you ordered. When you work from a purchase order, QuickBooks displays the purchase order number in the PO No. column. If you don't create purchase orders, you must fill in the item information manually. For each item you receive, in a blank line on the Items tab, specify the item, quantity, customer or job, and class. QuickBooks fills in the Description and Cost cells using the values in the item record (see Chapter 4). The program also calculates the Amount by multiplying the quantity by the item cost.

Tip: Compare the quantities you received in the shipment to the quantities on your purchase order. If you received fewer items than you ordered, in the Qty cell for the item, enter the number you actually received.

4. Click Save & New or Save & Close.

When you save a combination inventory/bill transaction, QuickBooks goes to work. For the inventory you received, QuickBooks first debits your inventory account for the amount you paid for the inventory items. The program also updates the quantity on hand for the item (see Chapter 4). The amount of the bill shows up in your Chart of Accounts as a credit to your Accounts Payable account.

Tip: If you want to see how many of a particular product you have on hand, on the Home page, click Items & Services. In the Item List window, look at the On Hand column for the item you're interested in.

Receiving Inventory Before the Bill

When you receive inventory, you want to record it in QuickBooks, so you know that it's available to sell. In this situation, you use one command to receive inventory in QuickBooks and a second command to enter the bill when it arrives. The fields that you specify and the options at your disposal are the same, but they appear in different dialog boxes:

1. **To receive inventory in your company file, on the Home page, click Receive Inventory and then choose "Receive Inventory without a Bill" (or choose Vendors → Receive Items).**

   QuickBooks opens the Create Item Receipts dialog box, which is a close relative to the Enter Bills dialog box. In fact, other than the title of the dialog box, only three things are different, all shown in Figure 10-7.

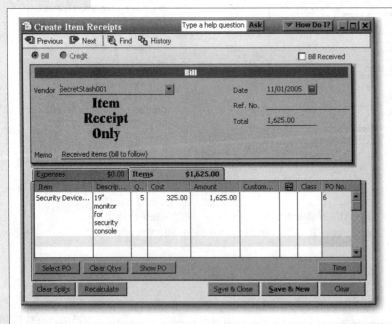

Figure 10-7:
Because you're only adding inventory to your company file, QuickBooks automatically turns off the Bill Received checkbox. To make it crystal clear that you aren't creating a bill, the program displays the words Item Receipt Only and, in the Memo box, adds the message "Received items (bill to follow)."

Tip: If you choose "Receive Inventory without a Bill" (or Vendors → Receive Items) and then realize that you *do* have the bill, there's no need to close the dialog box and choose a different command. Instead, in the Create Item Receipts dialog box, simply turn on the Bill Received checkbox. The program changes the dialog box to the Enter Bills dialog box, so you can receive the items and create the bill at the same time (page 287).

Similar to receiving inventory and a bill at the same time, the Create Item Receipts dialog box reminds you about open purchase orders that you can select to fill in the items received automatically. The rest of the fields behave like the ones in the Enter Bills dialog box.

When you've added all the items you received and updated any quantities that differ from those on your purchase order, click Save & Close.

2. **When the bill arrives, choose Vendors → Enter Bill for Items Received (or on the Home page, click Enter Bills Against Inventory). In the Select Item Receipt dialog box (Figure 10-8), choose the shipment that corresponds to the bill you just received and click OK.**

The Ref. No. and Memo cells identify the shipment that corresponds to the bill in hand. QuickBooks opens the Enter Bills dialog box and fills in the fields with the information from your Receive Items transaction.

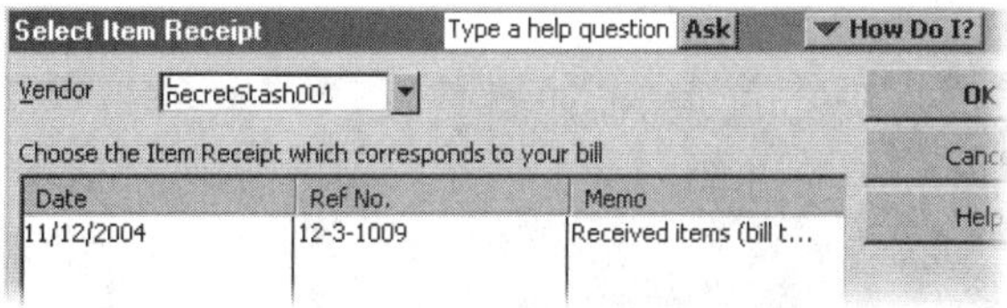

Figure 10-8:
If you don't see any values, click Cancel. Then choose Vendors and, in the Create Item Receipts dialog box, update your records. Use the purchase order number for the shipment or the carrier's tracking number.

TROUBLESHOOTING MOMENT

Posting Inventory Received

When you receive inventory before the bill arrives, your accountant might squawk about how QuickBooks posts inventory to your accounts. In standard accounting practice, only bills show up as credits to the Accounts Payable account. But QuickBooks credits the Accounts Payable account when you receive inventory items.

When you use Receive Items, in the Accounts Payable register, QuickBooks adds an entry for the items you received. (To view the register, in the "Chart of Accounts" window, right-click the account and choose Use Register on the shortcut menu.) The program fills in the Type cell with ITEM RCPT to indicate that the entry isn't a bill. Later, when you enter the bill, QuickBooks overwrites the same transaction, replacing the ITEM RCPT type with BILL.

Although the result in your company file is correct after you both receive inventory and enter bills, accountants typically harp about incomplete audit trails when they see a transaction change without some kind of record. Unfortunately, there's no workaround for keeping track of items received without bills or bills received without shipments. If you want to track inventory, bills, and price differences between your purchase orders and the final bills, you'll have to do so outside of QuickBooks.

---

3. **If the prices and quantities on the vendor bill are different than those Quick-Books used, on the Items tab, you can update the prices and quantities.**

When prices and quantities differ, don't take the vendor bill as the final word. Check your record to see where the discrepancy occurred.

4. **If the bill includes sales tax and shipping that you didn't include on your purchase order, click the Expenses tab, and fill in additional lines for those charges.**

If you changed anything on the Items or Expenses tab, click Recalculate to update the Amount Due field with the new total.

5. **Click Save & Close.**

You'll see a message box that asks if you want to save the changes that you made, even if you didn't make any. QuickBooks asks this question because it has modified the item receipt transaction in your Accounts Payable account. Click Yes to save the changes.

WORKAROUND WORKSHOP

Paying for Inventory Before It Arrives

QuickBooks doesn't provide a command for paying for inventory before you receive it. In the business world, you don't *have to* pay bills for inventory you haven't received. But anything is possible in business, including prepaying for inventory that you order.

Your accountant might not approve of QuickBooks' approach (that incomplete audit trail complaint again), but you can prepay for inventory as long as you first create an account to track what you've prepaid. Here's what you have to do:

1. Create a new Other Current Assets account (page 36) called something like Prepaid Inventory. This account tracks the money you've sunk into inventory that isn't in your warehouse yet.

2. Write a check (page 305) or enter a credit card charge (page 308) to pay for the items. If you have an open purchase order for the inventory, Quick-Books displays a message box about it. Click No because it's too early to use the purchase order.

3. In the Write Checks or Enter Credit Card Charges dialog box, click the Expenses tab.

4. In the first Account cell, choose the Other Current Assets account that you created for your prepaid inventory.

5. Save the transaction.

6. When you receive the inventory items, edit the check or credit card charge. You can edit checks and credit card charges in the Write Checks and Enter Credit Card Charges dialog boxes, or directly in the account register.

7. On the Expenses tab, right-click the line for your Other Current Assets account and choose Delete Line, which removes the posting to your prepaid inventory account.

8. Click the Items tab.

9. Click Select PO and choose the purchase order for the prepaid items. Click OK.

10. Save the check or credit card charge.

If the vendor sent a new bill with additional charges, such as shipping, enter a separate bill for those charges.

Tip: When you want to enter a bill for items you've received, be particularly careful to choose Vendors →
Enter Bills for Received Items (or Enter Bills Against Inventory on the Home page). If you choose Vendors
→ Enter Bills instead, you'll end up with two postings for the same items in your Accounts Payable
account. The first posting appears when you receive the items in QuickBooks (the one identified with the
type ITEM RCPT). The second posting is for the bill.

If this double entry occurs, delete the bill. In the "Chart of Accounts" window, double-click the Accounts
Payable account. In the Accounts Payable register, select the bill and then choose Edit → Delete Bill. Then,
recreate the bill using the "Enter Bills for Received Items" command. Another option is to create a journal
entry to reverse the Accounts Payable entry (page 374).

Handling Reimbursable Expenses

Reimbursable expenses are costs you incur that a customer subsequently pays. For
example, you've probably seen telephone call and photocopy charges on your
attorney's statements. Travel costs are another common type of reimbursable
expense. Products you purchase specifically for a customer or a subcontractor you
hire for a customer's job are all costs you pass on to your customers.

In accounting, as in QuickBooks, there are two approaches to tracking reimbursable expenses:

- **As income.** When you pay a bill, QuickBooks posts the expenses on the bill to
  the expense account you specify. But when you invoice your customer, Quick-
  Books posts the reimbursement as income in a separate income account. Your
  income is higher, but it's offset by higher expenses. This approach is popular
  because it lets you compare reimbursable income and expenses to make sure
  that they match.

- **As expense.** Tracking reimbursements as expenses doesn't change the way
  QuickBooks handles bills—expenses still post to the accounts you specify. But,
  when your customer pays you for the reimbursable expenses, QuickBooks posts
  those reimbursements right back to the expense account. The expense account
  balance looks as if you never incurred the expense in the first place.

Setting Up Reimbursements as Income

If you want to track your reimbursable expenses as income, you have to turn on
the Track Reimbursed Expenses As Income preference. Choose Edit → Preferences
and, in the Edit Preferences icon bar, click Sales & Customers. On the Company
Preferences tab, turn on the Track Reimbursed Expenses As Income checkbox.

When you've turned on this preference, QuickBooks adds an Income Account box
to the Create Account and Edit Account dialog boxes. In this new box, you specify
the income account you want to use to track your reimbursable income. Since
you've already created your expense accounts, you'll have to edit each one that's
reimbursable (travel, telephone, equipment rental, and so on) and add the income
account to the record.

Here's what happens as you progress from paying your bills to invoicing your customers:

- When you assign an expense on a bill as reimbursable to a customer, Quick-Books posts the money to the expense account you specified.

- When you create an invoice for the customer, the program reminds you that you have reimbursable expenses.

- When you add the reimbursable expenses to the customer's invoice, they post to the income account you specified for that type of expense.

Note: If you track reimbursable expenses as expenses, you don't have to set up anything in QuickBooks. When you pay a bill, the expenses post to the expense account. When you invoice a customer, Quick-Books posts the reimbursements back to the same account.

Recording Reimbursable Expenses

As you enter bills (page 276) or make direct payments with checks or credit cards, you add designated expenses as reimbursable, as shown in Figure 10-9.

Tip: Sometimes you want to track expenses associated with a customer or job, but you don't want the customer to reimburse you—such as for fixed-price contracts. In this situation, click the reimbursable icon for that expense. QuickBooks then draws a red X through the icon and the expense won't show up on the customer's invoice.

WORKAROUND WORKSHOP

Accounts for Reimbursable Expenses

QuickBooks won't accept the same income account for multiple reimbursable expense accounts. You have to create a separate income account (see Chapter 2) for each type of reimbursable expense.

To keep your Charts of Accounts neat, create a top-level income account called something like Reimbursed Expenses. Then create an income subaccount for each type of reimbursable expense. When you're done, your income accounts will look like this:

4100 Service Revenue
4200 Product Revenue
4900 Reimbursed Expenses—Income

Subaccounts for account 4900:
4910 Reimbursed Telephone
4920 Reimbursed Postage
4930 Reimbursed Photocopies
4940 Reimbursed Travel

Paying Your Bills

Entering bills in QuickBooks is not *paying* bills. The bills you enter are a record of what you owe and when, but they do nothing to send money to your vendors. In QuickBooks, Pay Bills is the command that pushes your money out the door. With this one command you can select the bills you want to pay, how much to pay for each one, your payment method, the payment account, and the date for the payment. If you have credits or early payment discounts, you can include those, too.

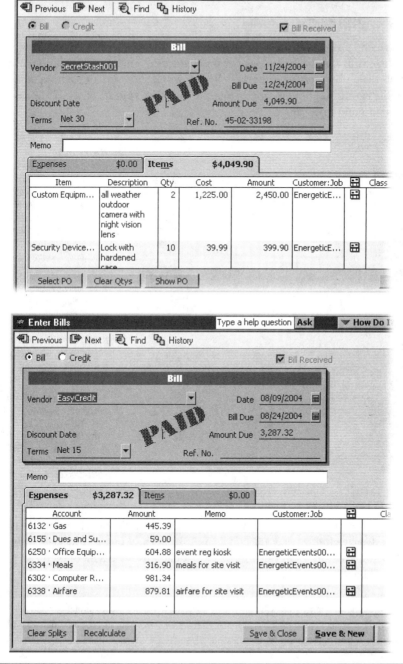

Figure 10-9:
Top: The Enter Bills, Write Checks, and Enter Credit Card Charges dialog boxes all include columns to designate reimbursable expenses and the customers or jobs to which they apply. Even in an account register you can click Splits to access these columns. When you choose a customer or job in the Customer:Job column, in the next column, QuickBooks automatically displays the reimbursable icon (a valiant but uninspired effort to portray an invoice form).

Bottom: When you enter reimbursable expenses, be sure to type a memo to identify the expense to you and your customer. QuickBooks uses the text in the Memo as the description of the reimbursable expense on your invoice.

Tip: If you want to evaluate all your unpaid bills before you begin paying them, choose Reports → Vendors & Payables → Unpaid Bills Detail. QuickBooks displays the bills due up to the current date, grouped by vendor. To include bills due in the future, in the Dates box, choose All. If you want to inspect a bill more closely, double-click anywhere in the line for that bill.

Selecting Bills to Pay

The payment process begins with choosing the bills you want to pay. When you choose Pay Bills (on the Home page or the Vendors menu), QuickBooks opens the Pay Bills dialog box and displays the bills due within the next 10 days. As demonstrated in Figure 10-10, you can change the bills that appear, view bill details, or apply credits and discounts.

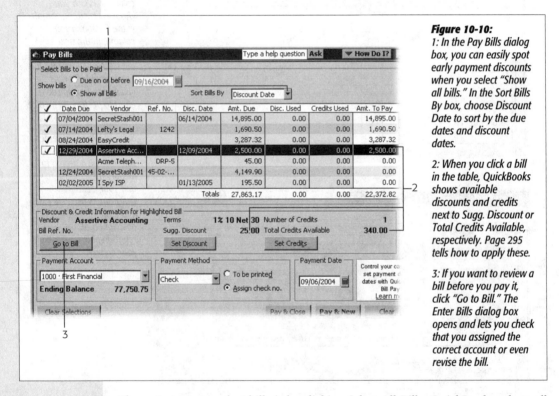

Figure 10-10:
1: In the Pay Bills dialog box, you can easily spot early payment discounts when you select "Show all bills." In the Sort Bills By box, choose Discount Date to sort by the due dates and discount dates.

2: When you click a bill in the table, QuickBooks shows available discounts and credits next to Sugg. Discount or Total Credits Available, respectively. Page 295 tells how to apply these.

3: If you want to review a bill before you pay it, click "Go to Bill." The Enter Bills dialog box opens and lets you check that you assigned the correct account or even revise the bill.

The easiest way to select bills is by clicking Select All Bills. QuickBooks selects all the bills displayed in the Pay Bills table and fills in the Amt. To Pay cells with the total due on each bill. You can choose individual bills for payment by turning on their checkboxes.

Tip: If you pay some bills by check and others by credit card, make two passes through the Pay Bills dialog box. In the first pass, choose all the bills that you pay by check and, in the Payment Method box, choose Check. During the second pass, in the Payment Method box, choose Credit Card.

Modifying Payment Amounts

Whether you select individual bills or QuickBooks selects them for you, the program automatically fills in the Amt. To Pay cells with the total amounts that are due. Paying bills in full means that you don't have to worry about the next due date or paying late fees. But making partial payments can stretch limited resources to appease more of your unpaid vendors. To pay only part of a bill, in a bill's Amt. To Pay cell, type the amount you want to pay.

Tip: If you keep your cash in a money market account until you need it, you'll want to know how much money you must transfer to your checking account to pay the bills. In the Pay Bills dialog box, Quick-Books shows two totals: one for all the bills displayed, and the other for what you've entered in the Amt. To Pay column. Initially, the two totals are the same. If you change a value in an Amt. To Pay cell, click another cell to update the total Amt. To Pay.

UP TO SPEED

When Cash Is Tight

If your cash accounts are dwindling, you may face some tough decisions about whom you pay and when. To keep your business afloat until the hard times pass, here are a few rules to follow:

• Pay government obligations (taxes and payroll with-holdings) first. In the Sort Bills By box, choose Vendor to easily spot all your government bills.

• Pay the vendors whose products or services are essential to your business.

• Make partial payments to all your vendors rather than full payments to some and no payments to others. If you want to pay small bills in full, in the Sort Bills By box, choose Amount Due to see your outstanding bills sorted by dollar value.

Applying Discounts and Credits

Most companies like to use their discounts and credits as soon as possible. By far, the easiest way to deal with discounts and credits from vendors is to let Quick-Books take care of them for you automatically. Here's how you delegate application of early payment discounts and available credits to QuickBooks:

1. Choose Edit → Preferences to open the Preferences dialog box and, in the icon bar, click Purchases & Vendors. Then click the Company Preferences tab.

   The setting you choose for this preference applies to every person who logs into your company file. Because the preference appears on the Company Preferences tab, you must be a QuickBooks administrator to change this setting.

2. Turn on the "Automatically use discounts and credits" checkbox.

   QuickBooks enables the Default Discount Account box.

3. In the Default Discount Account box, choose the account you use to track your vendor discounts.

If you don't have an account for vendor discounts yet, create a new account, called something like Vendor Discounts (page 36).

Note: Whether you create an income account or expense account for vendor discounts is neither an accounting rule nor QuickBooks requirement, but a matter of how you view vendor discounts. If you think of vendor discounts as expenses you've saved by paying early, create an expense account. Conversely, if you view vendor discounts as money you've made, create an income account.

Either way, vendor discounts are different from discounts you extend to your customers. So, in the Default Discount Account box, choose an account specifically for vendor discounts, not your customer discount account.

As you would expect, turning on the "Automatically use discounts and credits" checkbox tells QuickBooks to apply early payment discounts and available credits to bills without further instructions from you. The program uses your payment terms to figure out the discount you've earned, and it adds all available credits to their corresponding bills.

Whether the "Automatically use discounts and credits" preference is on or off, you can control the discounts and credits QuickBooks applies to your bills, as you'll learn on the following pages. For example, you might want to delay a large credit until the following year, which decreases this year's income and the taxes you must pay on that income.

Applying discounts manually

If you want to apply discounts manually or change the discount that QuickBooks added, here's what you do:

1. **In the Pay Bills dialog box (on the Home page, click Pay Bills, or choose Vendors → Pay Bills), in the table, select a bill that isn't already selected for payment by turning on its checkbox.**

   In the "Discount & Credit Information for Highlighted Bill" section, Quick-Books shows the discount and credits that are available for the bill. More importantly, the program enables the Set Discount and Set Credits buttons. If you click cells other than the checkmarked cell in the row, QuickBooks shows the suggested discount and available credits, but the Set Discount and Set Credits buttons are dimmed.

Tip: When you apply discounts manually, you can use the Disc. Date column to identify bills that qualify for early payment. If the date in a cell in that column is in the future, the bill qualifies for an early payment discount.

---

2. **To apply or modify a discount, click Set Discount.**

   QuickBooks opens the "Discount and Credits" dialog box (Figure 10-11).

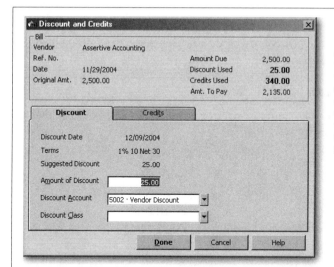

Figure 10-11:
In the "Discount and Credits" dialog box, the program automatically selects the Discount tab and displays your payment terms, the discount date, and the amount of discount you deserve. If the suggested discount is worth an early separation from your money, click Done to continue to the next step. Otherwise, click Cancel. If you also want to work on credits, when you're done modifying the discount, click the Credits tab.

3. **In the "Amount of Discount" box, QuickBooks fills in the suggested discount. If you want to apply a different discount, type the new value.**

   Many companies try to save money by taking early payment discounts when they haven't paid early. Some companies apply discounts regardless of what their payment terms are, and most vendors honor these undeserved discounts in the name of good will.

4. **In the Discount Account box, choose the account you use to track your vendor discounts.**

   If your vendor discount account is an income account, discounts appear as positive numbers and increase the balance of the income account. In vendor discount expense accounts, discounts appear as negative numbers because they reduce the account balance.

Tip: If you want to track discounts on inventory separately, create a Cost of Goods Sold account specifically for inventory discounts. For example, if QuickBooks created account 5000 for Cost of Goods Sold, you can create two subaccounts: 5005 for Cost of Inventory Sold and 5010 for Inventory Discounts.

In your financial reports, the two subaccounts show your original cost and the discounts you receive. But account 5000 adds the two subaccounts together to show your net cost of goods sold.

---

5. **If you track classes, choose the class for the discount.**

Typically, you'll choose the same class for the discount that you used for the original expense.

6. **Click Done.**

QuickBooks closes the "Discount and Credits" dialog box and, in the Pay Bills dialog box, adds the discount you entered in the bill's Disc. Used cell.

Applying credits manually

To apply available credits to a bill or remove credits that QuickBooks applied for you, follow these steps:

1. **In the Pay Bills dialog box (on the Home page, click Pay Bills, or choose Vendors → Pay Bills), select a bill by turning on its checkbox in the table.**

The Pay Bills dialog box doesn't offer an easy way to find all the credits you're due. If you suspect that you have some vendor credits you haven't used, modify the Vendor Balance Detail report to display only the credits you have from vendors.

Choose Reports → Vendors & Payables → Vendor Balance Detail. To see only bill credits, click Modify Report. Click the Filters tab. In the Choose Filter list, choose Transaction Type, and in the Transaction Type drop-down list, select Bill Credit. Click OK.

2. **To apply a credit to the selected bill, click Set Credits.**

QuickBooks opens the "Discount and Credits" dialog box, but displays the Credits tab. Credits that are already applied to the bill are checkmarked.

Tip: If the Discount and Credits dialog box is already open because you've applied a discount, just click the Credits tab and then continue with the steps that follow.

---

3. **As shown in Figure 10-12, click a credit's checkmark cell to toggle between applying the credit and removing it from the bill.**

4. **Click Done.**

QuickBooks closes the dialog box.

Setting the Payment Method and Account

After you've selected the bills to pay and applied any discounts and credits, you still have to tell QuickBooks how and when you want to pay your bills. At the very bottom of the Pay Bills dialog box, these settings are the last choices you have to make before paying your vendors:

- **Payment Account.** Choose the account you use to pay the bills, such as a checking or credit card account.

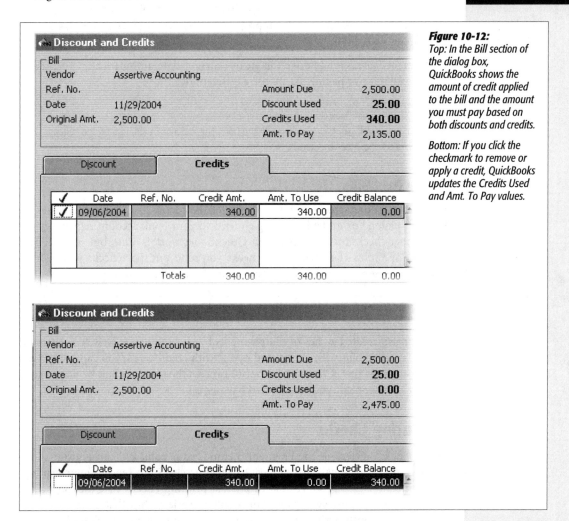

Figure 10-12:
Top: In the Bill section of the dialog box, QuickBooks shows the amount of credit applied to the bill and the amount you must pay based on both discounts and credits.

Bottom: If you click the checkmark to remove or apply a credit, QuickBooks updates the Credits Used and Amt. To Pay values.

- **Payment Method.** In the drop-down list, choose how you want to pay the bills. QuickBooks offers Check, Credit Card, and Online Bank Pmt (if you subscribe to QuickBooks online bill payment).

If you pay bills by check and print your checks within QuickBooks, choose the "To be printed" option. The program automatically adds the bills you selected to the queue of checks to be printed. You'll learn about printing these checks on page 301.

If you write checks by hand, choose the "Assign check no." option. When you click Pay & Close, the program opens the Assign Check Numbers dialog box.

To assign check numbers starting with the next unused check number, choose the "Automatically assigned based on next check number for this bank account" option. If you want to specify the check numbers for each check you write, choose the "Assign the appropriate check number next to each bill payment check" option.

• **Payment Date.** QuickBooks fills in the current date automatically. To predate or postdate your payments, choose a different date.

Tip: If you want QuickBooks to date checks using the day you print your checks, choose Edit → Preferences and, in the icon bar, click Checking. On the Company Preferences tab, turn on the "Change check date when check is printed" checkbox.

Saving Paid Bills

When you're done setting up bills to pay, click Pay & Close. QuickBooks closes the Pay Bills dialog box and adds your payments to your bank account register. If you write paper checks for your bills, your QuickBooks work is done, but you still have to sign your John Hancock to the checks you send out. For checks you print in QuickBooks, see page 301 to learn how to finish the bill paying job.

Note: In the Enter Bills dialog box, QuickBooks adds a PAID stamp to bills you've paid.

You can also create batches of bill payments by clicking Pay & New. For example, if you pay some bills with checks and others with credit cards, you can set up your check payments first. Click Pay & New to process those checks and begin a second batch of payments for your credit card payments.

Producing Checks

When you use Check as the payment method, your bank account register shows check transactions, but you still have to generate checks to send to your vendors. For companies that produce lots of checks, printing checks in QuickBooks can prevent carpal tunnel syndrome. For a sole proprietorship that generates a few checks each month, writing checks by hand is easy enough. QuickBooks accepts either approach with equal aplomb.

Writing Checks by Hand

Writing checks by hand doesn't require any work *in* QuickBooks. But you still have to keep your company file in sync with your paper checks. Whether you're writing checks for bills you've paid in QuickBooks or scratching out a spur-of-the-moment check to the fortune-teller for this week's corporate horoscope, you want to make sure that the check numbers match between your bank account register and your paper checks.

If check transactions already exist in QuickBooks, synchronizing check numbers is as simple as writing the paper checks in the same order as you entered them in QuickBooks. Open the checking account register window and use the check transactions to guide your check writing, as illustrated in Figure 10-13. To open the checking account register, first press Ctrl+A to open the "Chart of Accounts" window. Then, right-click the checking account and choose Use Register.

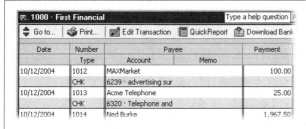

Figure 10-13:
In a register window, the code CHK in the Type cell indicates a check transaction

Tip: If you notice that the next check number in QuickBooks isn't the one on your next paper check, you should figure out why they don't match. The answer might be as simple as a voided check that you forgot to enter in QuickBooks. But if someone is walking off with blank checks, you need to take action.

Until you find the reason for the mismatched check number, editing the check numbers in the checking account register is the easiest way to get checks into the mail. In the register window, double-click an incorrect check number and type the number that's on your paper check.

Setting Up QuickBooks for Printing Checks

If you have scads of checks to generate, printing on preprinted computer checks is well worth the bit of setup you must do. If you dedicate a printer to check printing and keep it stocked with checks, setup is truly a one-time event.

Tip: Lock up your preprinted checks and any printer stocked with them. Otherwise, you might discover checks missing, which often leads to money missing from your bank account.

The first step is telling QuickBooks which printer you use to print checks and the type of checks you use. The program remembers these settings, so you need to go through this process just once. After you've specified your check printing settings, QuickBooks fills them in automatically in the Print dialog box. You can always change those options before you print.

Here's how you set up QuickBooks to print checks:

1. **Open the "Printer setup" dialog box by choosing File → Printer Setup.**

   In the Form Name box, choose Check/Paycheck.

2. **In the "Printer name" box, choose the printer you want to use to print checks.**

If you choose a printer brand that QuickBooks recognizes (and there are few it doesn't), the program automatically fills in the "Printer type" box. If you use a very old or very odd printer, you'll have to choose the type of printer. Page-oriented refers to printers that feed one sheet at a time. Choose Continuous when the printer feeds a roll of paper.

Note: If you print to checks on continuous feed paper, the alignment of the paper in the printer is critical. You can save time and a lot of wasted checks by aligning the paper *before* you print batches of checks, as described on page 238.

---

3. **Choose the option that represents the style of checks you purchased.**

The "Printer setup" dialog box displays examples of each check style it can deal with, making it easy to choose the right one, as illustrated in Figure 10-14.

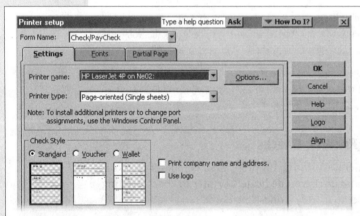

Figure 10-14:
The Standard option sets up QuickBooks to print to checks that fit in a #10 business envelope. These checks typically come three to a page. The Voucher option represents one-page forms that include both a check and a detachable stub for payroll or check information. Wallet checks are smaller than business checks. Because they're narrower than standard business checks, these forms have a perforation on the left for tearing the check off.

Tip: To the right of the Check Style section, you'll see two checkboxes for printing your company name, address, and logo. If you purchase checks with these elements preprinted, leave these checkboxes turned off.

If the company from which you purchase checks wants too much money to print your logo on the checks, turn on the Use logo checkbox. The program opens the Logo dialog box. Click File. In the Open Logo File, locate and double-click the bitmap image (.bmp extension) of your logo.

4. **If you want to change the fonts on the checks you print, click the Fonts tab.**

   You can change the font for the entire check form or designate a special font for the company name and address.

5. **Click OK to save the settings for check printing.**

   The next section tells you how to print your checks.

Printing Checks

In the Pay Bills dialog box, if you choose the "To be printed" option, QuickBooks adds the checks you've selected for payment to a print queue. After you confirm that your printer contains your preprinted checks and the checks are aligned properly, you can print your checks with just two steps:

1. **Choose File → Print Forms → Checks.**

   QuickBooks opens the "Select Checks to Print" dialog box and selects all the unprinted checks, as shown in Figure 10-15.

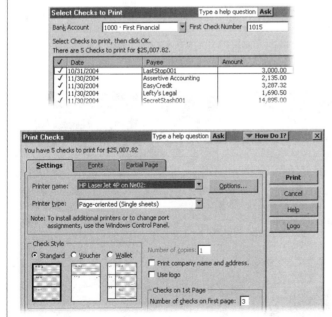

Figure 10-15:
Top: The first time you print checks, QuickBooks sets the first check number to 1. If necessary, in the First Check Number box, type the number of the first check number loaded in your printer. If you want to prevent a check from printing, turn off its checkbox.

Bottom: When you click OK, QuickBooks opens the Print Checks dialog box, which looks much like the Printer setup dialog box for checks. The "Number of checks on first page" box lets you use leftover checks from previous print runs. Type the number of leftover checks and insert that page in the envelope feed of your printer. After the program prints checks to that page, it begins feeding sheets of checks from the paper tray.

2. **Click Print.**

QuickBooks anticipates the problems that can occur during printing (paper jams, low toner, or an ill-timed margarita spill). After the program prints checks, it opens the "Did check(s) print OK?" dialog box. If a problem did occur, in the "First incorrectly printed" checkbox, type the number of the first check that didn't print properly. Click OK to reprint that check and all the checks that followed.

In addition to printing the checks, QuickBooks also removes the words To Print for those checks in your checking account register, replacing them with the check numbers it used.

Writing Checks Without Entering Bills

You might enter bills for the majority of your vendor transactions, but you're still likely to write a quick check from time to time. For example, when the person who plows your parking lot knocks on the door and asks for payment, he won't want to wait while you step through entering and paying bills in QuickBooks—he just wants his $50. And if you write only a couple of checks a month, there's nothing wrong with writing checks to pay your vendors without entering a bill in Quick-Books.

When you first use QuickBooks and want some guidance, use the Write Checks dialog box to make sure you enter everything you need. In no time, you'll grow tired of all the clicking and handholding. At that point, you can switch to recording your checks in the QuickBooks checking account register.

Tip: Entering checks in the register is best reserved for paper checks you write. But you can print a check you enter in the register. First, record the check. Then, right-click it and choose Edit Check to open the Write Checks dialog box. Then, in the dialog box menu bar, click Print.

GEM IN THE ROUGH

Using Leftover Checks

When you print to single sheets of paper, you might print only one or two of the checks on the last sheet. QuickBooks includes a printer setting so that you can print to the orphaned checks.

Open the Printer Setup dialog box and choose Check/Paycheck. Click the Partial Page tab. Choose the option (Left, Center, or Portrait) that corresponds to how your printer feeds envelopes, and then click OK to save the setting. When you start printing, first feed the pages with orphaned checks into the envelope feed on your printer.

If you have an old dot-matrix printer taking up space in a junk closet, consider putting it to work printing your checks. The continuous feed mechanism on a dot-matrix printer means you can stop printing in the middle of a page and resume right where you left off. You won't need the Partial Page printing feature. An added bonus is that you don't have to worry about printing reports on preprinted checks or printing checks to blank paper by mistake.

Using the Write Checks Dialog Box

The Write Checks dialog box is like a trimmed down Enter Bills dialog box. There's no need for fields such as Bill Due or Terms because you're paying immediately. But bills in QuickBooks take care of allocating costs to expense and inventory accounts. So, for a payment without a bill, you have to provide that information, which is why the Write Checks dialog box has tabs for Expenses and Items. QuickBooks fills in a few fields for you, and the rest of the fields are like the ones you've met already in the Enter Bills dialog box (page 276).

Note: The Enter Bills dialog box is no place to write checks for sales tax, payroll, payroll taxes and liabilities, or bills you've paid immediately. To pay sales tax, choose Vendors → Sales Tax → Pay Sales Tax (page 309). See Chapter 11 for paying employees, payroll taxes, and other payroll liabilities.

On the QuickBooks icon bar, click Check for fast access to the Write Checks dialog box. You can also click Write Checks on the Home page. As you can see in Figure 10-16, QuickBooks tries to shorten the learning curve by making the first part of the Write Checks dialog box look like a paper check.

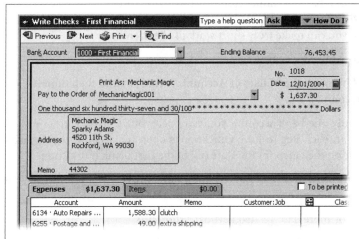

Figure 10-16:
Choosing a vendor fills in not only the "Pay to the Order of" field, but also the Address box, which is perfect for printing checks that you mail in window envelopes. Even though the vendor name appears in the "Pay to the Order of" field, the program displays the company name to show you what it prints on checks. If you include account number in your vendor records, QuickBooks adds the account number to the Memo field.

Note: If you set up default account preferences, such as the bank account to use when you open the Write Checks dialog box (page 305), the program automatically chooses your bank account for you.

The Write Checks dialog box saves time, particularly when you print the checks you enter. The program automatically fills in the No. box with the next check number for the selected bank account. If the check number that the program fills in doesn't match the check you're writing by hand, type the number from your paper check. And, if you type a check number that's already used, QuickBooks warns you about the duplicate when you try to save the check. In the message box, click Cancel, and then, in the Write Checks dialog box, edit the value in the No. field.

The words To Print to the right of the No. label indicate that the "To be printed" checkbox is turned on. This setting adds the checks you create to a print queue. When you print those checks (page 303), QuickBooks replaces To Print with check numbers. To write checks by hand, be sure to turn off the "To be printed" checkbox.

QuickBooks calculates the check amount as you add entries on the Expenses and Items tabs. However, if you fill in the check amount and then start adding expenses and items, you'll know that the check total and the posted amounts match when no unallocated dollars remain.

Adding Checks to an Account Register

Entering checks in a bank account register is fast, easy, and, for the keyboard aficionado, addictive. By combining typing and keyboard shortcuts, such as tabbing from cell to cell, you can make truly short work of check entry.

Here's how you create checks in a register window:

1. **Press Ctrl+A to open the "Chart of Accounts" window, and then double-click your bank account.**

   If you have only one bank account, you can open your register with one click: on the icon bar, click Reg to have QuickBooks open the account register window and position the cursor in the Date cell of the first blank transaction.

2. **If you want to adjust the check date by a few days, press + or − until the date is what you want.**

   See page 591 for more date-related keyboard shortcuts.

3. **Press Tab to move to the Number cell.**

   QuickBooks automatically fills in the next check number for the bank account. If the number doesn't match the paper check you want to write, press + or − until the number is correct. Because the program selects the entire check number, you can also replace the check number by typing the new number. Press Tab to move to the Payee cell.

4. **Start typing the name of the payee.**

   QuickBooks scans the lists of names in your company file and selects the first name that matches all the letters you've typed so far. As soon as QuickBooks selects the one you want, press Tab to move to the Payment cell.

5. **In the Payment cell, type the amount for the check.**

   Press Tab to jump past the Deposit cell to the Account cell.

6. **If the check applies to only one expense account, in the Account drop-down list, click the account you want.**

   You can also choose accounts by typing the account number or the first few letters of the account name. As you type, QuickBooks selects the first account that matches what you've typed so far. When the account is correct, press Tab to move to the Memo cell.

   If your check covers more than one type of expense, you can allocate the payment among several accounts, as demonstrated in Figure 10-17.

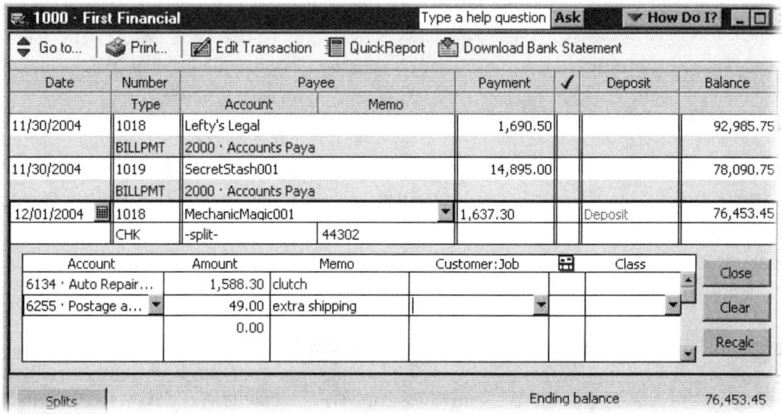

Figure 10-17:
To allocate a check to multiple accounts or to specify a customer, job, or class, click Splits, which opens a window where you can assign them. For each allocation, specify the account, amount, memo, customer, and class. Then, click Close. If you modify the value in the Payment cell or any values in the allocation Amount cells, click Recalc to synchronize payment and any unallocated dollars.

7. **To add a reminder about the check, in the Memo cell, type your notes. When you've filled in all the fields you need, click Record to save the check.**

   Lather, rinse, repeat.

Paying with Cash

If you carry company cash around in your wallet (called petty cash, described in detail on page 368), or if you receive a cash advance toward travel expenses, you must eventually record the details of your cash transactions in QuickBooks. For example, on a business trip, you might pay cash for meals, parking, tips, and tolls.

When you return with your receipts, your bookkeeper can enter a transaction documenting those expenses in the petty cash account.

Entering cash transactions in the petty cash account register is even easier than entering checks in the checking account register (page 369). For cash transactions, the key fields are the amount and the account.

You can skip the Payee field altogether to keep your Vendor List concise. If you want a record of where you spent the cash, type the business name in the Memo cell. QuickBooks assigns a check number to a cash transaction, which you might as well keep. Because you don't reconcile a petty cash account, the number is so irrelevant that it isn't worth deleting.

Paying with Credit Cards

When you make credit card purchases, the easiest way to record those charges in your company file is by signing up for online banking (page 509) and downloading your transactions (page 513). But you can also enter credit charges manually.

Tip: Whether you download charges or not, entering charges manually is a great way to catch erroneous or fraudulent charges that appear on your statement. For example, after entering your charges manually, you can download the charges from your credit card company. If you see additional charges that don't match the ones you entered, either you forgot a charge or there's an error in your account.

Entering credit card charges is similar to writing checks except that you work in the Enter Credit Card Charges dialog box, shown in Figure 10-18. To open it, choose Banking → Enter Credit Card Charges. You can also enter charges directly in the credit card account register, just as you do checks.

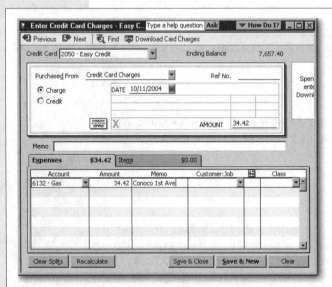

Figure 10-18:
Unless you want your Vendor List awash with every pizza parlor, gas station, and toll booth you patronize, consider creating a vendor called Credit Card Charges (or create several generic vendors such as Gas, Restaurant, and Parking). If you want to track the specific vendors, type their names in the Memo field. In the Ref. No. field, you can type your receipt number. Allocating a charge to multiple accounts or to a customer works the same as for checks.

Recording Vendor Credits

You ordered 30 dozen lightweight polypropylene t-shirts for your summer Death Valley marathon, but your vendor mistakenly silk-screened the logo on long-sleeved cotton t-shirts heavy enough to survive a nuclear blast. Despite your high-temperature ranting, the vendor insists on issuing a credit instead of a refund check. The only good thing about this situation is how easy it is to record a credit in QuickBooks:

1. **On the Home page, click Enter Bills (or choose Vendors → Enter Bills).**

   QuickBooks opens the Enter Bills dialog box as if you are going to enter a bill.

2. **Just below the dialog box menu bar, choose the Credit option.**

   QuickBooks changes the heading in the dialog box to Credit, and the Amount Due label switches to Credit Amount. Otherwise, the fields stay the same.

3. **On the Expenses and Items tabs, fill in the cells with the items for which you are receiving credit.**

   You can enter positive numbers just as you did when you entered the original bill. QuickBooks takes care of the postings. Your inventory account decreases due to the inventory items you return. Expense accounts decrease due to expense credits. And the total credit amount reduces the balance in your Accounts Payable account as well.

4. **Click Save & Close.**

Tip: To enter a refund for a credit card charge, in the Enter Credit Card Charges dialog box, choose the Credit option and fill in the rest of the fields based on the refund you received.

Paying Sales Tax

Sales tax can be a complicated business, particularly in states where the number of tax authorities has metastasized. You might have to pay sales taxes to several agencies, each with its own rules about when and how much. QuickBooks sales tax features can't remove this drudgery, but they can help you pay the right tax authorities the right amounts at the right time—something to be thankful for.

After governmental paperwork, the chief aggravation with sales tax is that setup spans several areas of QuickBooks. If you're new to collecting sales tax for your products, make sure you've completed the following tasks so you're collecting and tracking sales taxes properly. Only then can you pay the sales taxes you owe to government agencies:

• **Sales tax preferences.** If you are liable for sales tax, be sure to turn on the sales tax feature in QuickBooks. Choose Edit → Preferences, and, in the Edit Preferences dialog box icon bar, click Sales Tax. On the Company Preferences tab, in the Do You Charge Sales Tax? section, choose Yes.

Note: When you turn on the sales tax preference, QuickBooks automatically creates a liability account in your Chart of Accounts called Sales Tax Payable. If the sales tax preference is turned off, QuickBooks creates this account for you the first time you add sales tax to an invoice.

To help QuickBooks fill in tax-related fields for you, you can set preferences for the tax codes that you use most often for taxable and nontaxable sales. If you sell predominantly in your own state, set the "Most common sales tax" preference to the Sales Tax Item or Sales Tax Group for your state's sales taxes.

UP TO SPEED

Sales Tax and the Out-of-State Customer

When you sell to out-of-state customers, some states let you place the onus of remitting sales tax on the customer. In theory, the customer informs the state of their purchase and sends in the sales tax that's due. In practice, that may not happen.

What's important is that your company isn't responsible for filling out sales tax forms or mailing remittance payments.

You can track these sales by setting up a nontaxable code for out-of-state sales (page 86), such as OOS. When you create an invoice or other sales forms, in the Customer Tax Code drop-down list, choose the nontaxable code. QuickBooks keeps track of your nontaxable out-of-state sales in case you must prepare a report for a tax agency.

• **Customer records.** When you create a customer in the Customer:Job List, you can assign Tax Codes and Tax Items to the customer record (page87). If you do so, QuickBooks automatically applies the correct sales tax items to taxable sales on the customer's invoices.

• **Items.** When you create items in your Item List, you can specify whether they're taxable or not (page 94). When you add these items to invoices or other sales forms, QuickBooks automatically applies the correct tax status.

Tip: See page 101 to learn how to set up sales tax items and sales tax groups. When you add these to invoices, QuickBooks calculates the sales taxes you must remit.

• **Invoices and other sales forms.** QuickBooks calculates sales tax on invoices and other sales forms based on whether items are taxable and customers are tax-exempt.

Sales Tax Payment Preferences

The preference settings you choose for paying sales taxes aren't up to you. Tax agencies decide when your sales taxes are due, usually based on how much sales tax you collect. When you receive a notice about your required payment interval from the state or other tax authorities, be sure to update your QuickBooks preferences to match.

To set your sales tax preferences, choose Edit → Preferences, and, in the Edit Preferences dialog box icon bar, click Sales Tax. On the Company Preferences tab, QuickBooks provides two sets of payment options to satisfy the tax agencies you're beholden to:

- **Owe Sales Tax.** If your tax agency deems sales taxes due when you add them to customer invoices (known as *accrual basis payment*), choose the "As of invoice date" option. If your tax agency says sales taxes are due when your customers pay them (known as *cash basis payment*), choose the "Upon receipt of payment" option. When you generate sales tax reports (page 478), QuickBooks uses these options to calculate the sales taxes that you must remit.

- **Pay Sales Tax.** Tax agencies determine how frequently you have to remit sales taxes based on how much sales tax you collect. If your sales taxes are only a few dollars, you might pay only once a year. But if you collect thousands of dollars of sales tax, you can be sure that the tax agency wants its money more quickly, such as quarterly or monthly. When your tax agency informs you of your remittance frequency, choose Monthly, Quarterly, or Annually, as appropriate.

Producing Reports of the Sales Tax You Owe

Tax agencies are renowned for their forms. You have to fill out these forms to tell the agencies how much sales tax you've collected and how much you're required to remit to them. Fortunately, QuickBooks can take *some* sting out of your tax paperwork with reports that collate the sales tax information you need. Here are the reports you can generate:

- **Sales Tax Liability report.** This report summarizes the sales taxes you've collected for each tax agency. Choose Reports → Vendors & Payables → Sales Tax Liability. QuickBooks automatically sets the dates for the report to match the payment interval preference you chose, as you can see in Figure 10-19.

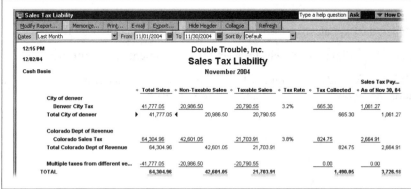

Figure 10-19:
If you remit sales taxes to several tax agencies, each with its own payment interval, you can rerun the report with a different interval to calculate the sales tax you owe to other agencies. In the Dates drop-down list, choose another interval, such as Last Calendar Quarter.

- **Sales Tax Revenue Summary.** This report shows how much of your sales are taxable. Choose Reports → Vendors & Payables → Sales Tax Revenue Summary.

Remitting Sales Taxes

You don't have to enter a bill to pay sales taxes. QuickBooks not only keeps records of the sales taxes you owe, but provides a dialog box especially for sales tax payments. Here's how you keep the tax agency off your back:

1. **On the Home page, click Pay Sales Tax (or choose Vendors → Sales Tax → Pay Sales Tax).**

   QuickBooks opens the Pay Sales Tax window and fills in the sales taxes you owe for the last collection period (as defined in your Sales Tax preferences), as illustrated in Figure 10-20.

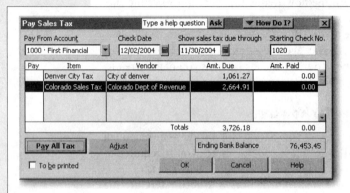

Figure 10-20:
If you remit sales taxes to only one tax agency, or all your sales tax payments are on the same schedule, you can click Pay All Tax to select all the payments in the table. Chances are that you make payments on different schedules to different agencies—in which case, select all the agencies on the same schedule. You'll have to repeat these steps for agencies on a different timetable.

Tip: Make sure that the date in the "Show sales tax due through" box is the last day of the current sales tax reporting period. For example, if you pay sales taxes quarterly, choose a date such as 6/30/2005.

2. **If you use more than one checking account, in the "Pay from Account" drop-down list, choose the account you want to use for payment.**

   QuickBooks fills in the "Pay from Account" box automatically if you set the "Open the Pay Sales Tax form with _ _ account" preference (page 162).

3. **In the Pay column, click cells to select the tax payments you want to make.**

   QuickBooks adds a checkmark to indicate that the payment is selected, and it adds the amount of the remittance in the Amt. Paid cell.

Note: Rare as the situation might be, you may need to adjust the payment you make to a tax agency. Click Adjust to open the Sales Tax Adjustment dialog box. You can increase or decrease the sales by a dollar value, and you must specify the account to which you want to post the adjustment (for instance, the Sales Tax Payable account). If the Entry No. box seems vaguely familiar, it's because this dialog box actually creates a journal entry for the adjustment.

4. **If you want to print the sales tax remittance checks from QuickBooks, turn on the "To be printed" checkbox. When you're done, click OK.**

   If you set up the checks to print in QuickBooks, you'll see them the next time you choose File → Print Forms → Checks. If you didn't turn on the "To be printed" checkbox, whip out your checkbook and write those remittance checks.

Payroll

If you decide to outsource the headaches of payroll to a payroll service company—as many businesses do—you can skip this chapter. The only thing you have to do in QuickBooks payroll-wise is add a couple of transactions for each payroll, allocating salaries and wages, payroll taxes, and any other payroll expenses to the accounts in your Chart of Accounts.

But if you want to process payroll within QuickBooks, you must first sign up for one of the payroll services that Intuit offers. To keep expenses low, you can choose a bare-bones service that provides only updated tax tables. At the other end of the spectrum, you can opt for the full-service payroll that QuickBooks offers. Or you can compromise somewhere in the middle.

After you choose a level of QuickBooks payroll service, your next task is to set up everything QuickBooks needs to calculate payroll amounts. You can walk through each step on your own or use a wizard within the program. Either way, the Payroll Setup wizard keeps track of what you've done and what you still have to do. This chapter takes you through every payroll step from the initial setup to running a payroll, printing checks, and remitting payroll taxes and reports to the appropriate government agencies.

Note: Payroll regulations are complex and vary depending on the size of your payroll and the states to which you remit payroll taxes. This chapter focuses on how to process payroll in QuickBooks. For more information on your company's payroll requirements, check with your accountant or the IRS and state tax agencies you work with.

Choosing a Payroll Service

Without one of QuickBooks' payroll services, trying to process payroll in the program would make a tough job nearly impossible. You'd have to calculate all the deductions by hand, enter your results into the program, and then print the paychecks, remit your payroll taxes, and generate the appropriate payroll tax reports. When you take the value of your time into account, even the most expensive payroll service might look like a good deal.

Intuit offers four payroll services, so you can choose between low-cost basic services, moderately priced and moderately featured services, and a more costly but comprehensive service. Choose Employees → Add Payroll Service → Learn About Payroll Options. QuickBooks opens a Web page that describes Intuit's offerings. Here's a quick overview to get you started:

- **QuickBooks Standard Payroll** used to be called QuickBooks Do-It-Yourself Payroll because you do *everything but* keep the tax tables up-to-date. You set everything up at the start, as you do for all the services. But then, for each payroll, you enter hours or payroll amounts, and QuickBooks uses the data in the tax tables to calculate the deductions and payroll taxes for you. You print the payroll checks (or use direct deposit for an additional fee), print the federal payroll tax forms, and remit your payroll taxes. This service costs as little as $199 per year, so it's perfect for the cost-conscious company.

Note: If employees live in states with income taxes, you must withhold state tax from employee paychecks, too. And that means you have to use QuickBooks Enhanced Payroll because Standard Payroll handles only federal payroll taxes.

- **QuickBooks Enhanced Payroll** is a more robust version of the Standard Payroll service. For starters, if you have to withhold state taxes, you must move up to Enhanced Payroll, which handles both federal and state payroll taxes. This service also handles Workers' Compensation. Its price is higher than Standard Payroll ($299 per year). If you climb one more rung to QuickBooks Enhanced Payroll Plus ($399 per year), you receive automatic upgrades to the latest version of QuickBooks Pro at no additional cost. After subtracting the price of the new version of QuickBooks (normally $199.95), Enhanced Payroll Plus is a better deal than QuickBooks Standard Payroll.

- With **Assisted Payroll**, you no longer have to make federal and state payroll tax deposits, file required tax reports during the year, or prepare W-2 and W-3 forms at the end of the year. The service handles all these tasks for you. In addition, Intuit guarantees that your payroll and payroll tax deposits and filings are accurate and on time. Of course, you have to send Intuit the correct data on time in the first place. But if Assisted Payroll then makes a mistake or misses a deadline, it pays the resulting payroll tax penalties. The price of the service varies depending on your payroll schedule and number of employees, but it's $59 per month for up to 15 employees. (Additional employees are an extra $2 per employee per pay period.)

- **Complete Payroll** is Intuit's outsourced payroll service. You send your payroll data to Intuit and download into your company file the payroll transactions that the service generates. In fact, you can use Compete Payroll even if you don't use QuickBooks. Complete Payroll calculates payroll taxes and deductions; makes federal, state, and local payroll tax payments; makes payroll deposits; and submits federal, state, and local filings (for most states and local agencies). Complete Payroll also guarantees the accuracy and timeliness of its work. The HR Assistant feature helps you handle typical employment procedures, such as hiring and firing. For five employees paid every two weeks, the average price is $100 per month.

Tip: If you want to offer direct deposit for employee paychecks, you can add direct deposit to any Quick-Books payroll service for $0.99 per paycheck and a $3.00 fee per payroll.

Applying for a Payroll Service

Before you begin the mechanics of setting up your payroll, you must select and sign up for one of the QuickBooks Payroll Services. To apply for one of Intuit's services, choose Employees → Add Payroll Service → Order Payroll Service. Quick-Books opens a browser window to the QuickBooks Payroll Services Web site.

Tip: When you install QuickBooks, the preference for payroll is turned on automatically (page 152). If you turned it off initially because you had no employees, but now want to use payroll features, choose Edit → Preferences and click Payroll & Employees. Click the Company Preferences tab. If you've opted to use Complete Payroll, select the Complete Payroll Customers option. Otherwise, select the Full Payroll option.

Before you click Buy Now to launch the online subscription process, gather the following necessary information:

- Your **Federal Employer Identification Number (EIN)**. It's a nine-digit number issued by the IRS.

- The legal names of each **company principal,** and the company's legal name and address.

Tip: If you aren't sure who the company principals are or what the company's legal name and address are, you can find them on your recent tax forms, incorporation documents, and so on.

- A **mailing address** (other than a post office box).

- If you are activating direct deposit, you also need the **bank routing number** and **account number** for the account from which you'll distribute payroll. You must create this account in your company file before you activate direct deposit.

- A **credit card number** for the subscription fee.

After you submit the application, QuickBooks checks the company information and credit card number you provide. If it runs into any problems, a message tells you to contact Intuit (and conveniently lists the telephone number to call).

Setting Up Payroll

The easiest way to begin setting up payroll is by choosing Employees → Payroll Setup, which launches the Payroll Setup wizard. Figure 11-1 shows how the wizard helps you see where you are in the payroll setup process.

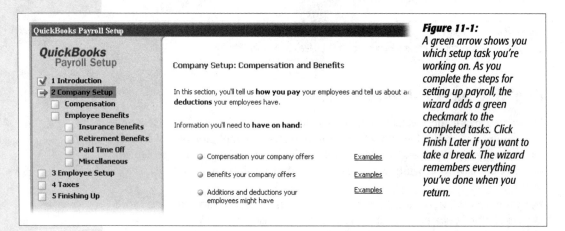

Figure 11-1:
A green arrow shows you which setup task you're working on. As you complete the steps for setting up payroll, the wizard adds a green checkmark to the completed tasks. Click Finish Later if you want to take a break. The wizard remembers everything you've done when you return.

Although you don't have to go through the entire payroll setup process in one shot, you must complete every bit of it before you can run a payroll. Furthermore, don't try to set up payroll the same day that you want to run it for the first time. Intuit needs a few days to turn on your payroll service after you've completed your part of the setup process.

The following sections cover the steps to payroll setup in detail.

Setting Up Compensation and Benefits

The first payroll task is telling QuickBooks how you compensate your employees—whether you pay them a salary, hourly wages, or additional income such as bonuses or commissions. You also specify employee benefits like retirement contributions and insurance premiums—no matter whether the company or the employees pay for them. Thankfully, the new QuickBooks 2006 Payroll Setup wizard takes the guesswork out of choosing items for payroll. All you have to do is turn on checkboxes for the items you use and answer a few simple questions, as described in Figure 11-2.

When you click one of the headings in the navigation bar, the wizard displays the payroll items you've selected. You can then add, edit, or delete items to reflect your payroll needs.

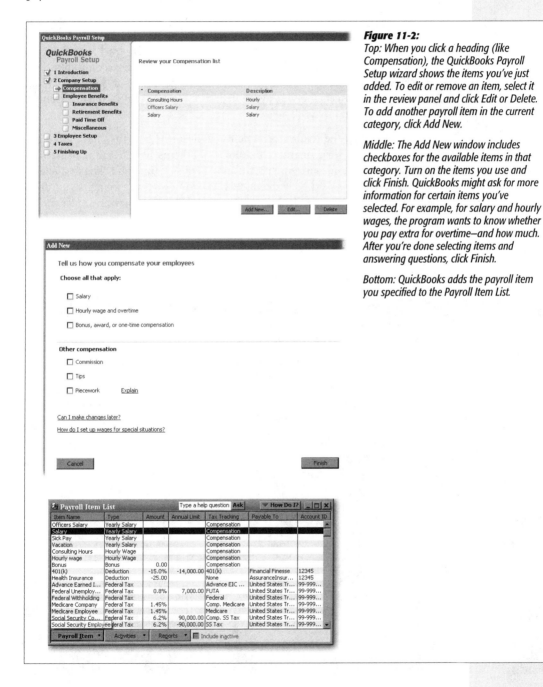

Figure 11-2:
Top: When you click a heading (like Compensation), the QuickBooks Payroll Setup wizard shows the items you've just added. To edit or remove an item, select it in the review panel and click Edit or Delete. To add another payroll item in the current category, click Add New.

Middle: The Add New window includes checkboxes for the available items in that category. Turn on the items you use and click Finish. QuickBooks might ask for more information for certain items you've selected. For example, for salary and hourly wages, the program wants to know whether you pay extra for overtime—and how much. After you're done selecting items and answering questions, click Finish.

Bottom: QuickBooks adds the payroll item you specified to the Payroll Item List.

Tip: You don't have to calculate each employee's pay per payroll cycle in the Payroll Setup wizard. In fact, you can't. Instead, you set up hourly or annual pay rates for each employee (even if they all get the same rate). QuickBooks uses the employee pay rate to calculate the values for the paycheck.

The wizard adds your selected items to the Payroll Item List. It also links those items to accounts in your Chart of Accounts, so you can track your payroll expenses. For example, a salary payroll item links to an Expense account, like Salaries & Wages. Likewise, if you deduct money from paychecks to pay taxes (page 325), the wizard connects the tax payroll item to a vendor (that is, the tax agency), so you're ready to remit payroll taxes.

As you step through the Insurance Benefits, Retirement Benefits, and Paid Time Off sections, simply turn on the checkboxes for items like "Health insurance," Health Savings Accounts, 401(k), 403(b), and "Paid sick time off." The first checkbox in each category's Add New dialog box lets you deactivate benefits you don't provide. For example, under Insurance Benefits, click Add New and turn on the "My company does not provide insurance benefits" checkbox.

The last category for Employee Benefits is Miscellaneous. This is the category to use if you add or remove dollars from paychecks for any other reason, like mileage reimbursement, health club dues, or wage garnishment.

WORKAROUND WORKSHOP

Adding Payroll Transactions Without a QuickBooks Payroll Service

Lots of companies use outsourced payroll services, such as ADP or Paychex, to avoid the brain strain of figuring out tax deductions and complying with payroll regulations. When you use one of these services, you send them your payroll data and receive reports about the payroll transactions that they processed. The payroll service takes care of remitting payroll taxes and other deductions to the appropriate agencies.

The problem is that none of these payroll transactions appear in your QuickBooks company file.

Fortunately, you don't have to enter the details into Quick-Books. In fact, you can create one transaction that distributes the money from your checking account into the appropriate expense accounts, as shown here.

Add a name to the Vendor List or the Other Names List for your payroll transactions. To remember which accounts you allocate payroll to, memorize (page 121) one payroll transaction without any values and use it for each payroll.

Setting Up Employees

Before you dive into setting up employees with the Payroll Setup wizard, completing two prerequisites *first* can speed up your work. Besides, after defining all your payroll items, you probably could use a break. In the Payroll Setup wizard, click Finish Later and perform the following two steps:

- **Gather employee information and records.** You need personal information, such as Social Security numbers and hire dates. For employees already on the payroll, you need their pay rates, the total pay they've received, and deductions taken, along with sick time and vacation balances.

- **Set up employee payroll defaults.** If you have more than a few employees, you can save time by setting up the payroll items that apply to *every* employee, like common deductions. That way, QuickBooks automatically fills in these payroll items for you when you create a new employee record. You need to make only any necessary modifications for that individual. QuickBooks has a feature designed especially for this timesaving scheme, as described in the next section.

The following section explains how to set up the standard payroll items you use for most employees and where to find this command in its new QuickBooks 2006 location.

Setting employee defaults

Typically, you use a common set of payroll items for all your employees, such as salary, tax deductions, health insurance, and 401(k) contributions. Instead of assigning the same payroll items to each employee, you can save these standard items so that QuickBooks fills in most of the payroll fields for you. You can also specify the pay period you use (and the class to apply if you track performance by class).

UP TO SPEED

Choosing the Right Payroll Start Date

QuickBooks doesn't tell you this, but there's a right and wrong time to start using QuickBooks for payroll. You must file 941 reports, Employer's Quarterly Federal Tax Returns, quarterly as their name implies. Therefore, QuickBooks won't let you summarize payroll data for the current quarter; you must enter individual pay period totals from the beginning of the current quarter up to the date you start using QuickBooks payroll.

You can save yourself a lot of data entry by beginning to use QuickBooks for payroll at the beginning of a quarter. You still have to enter summary values for each completed quarter in the current year, but you don't have to enter any individual payrolls.

To set up your default payroll characteristics, on the QuickBooks icon bar, click Employee Center. In the Employee Center window menu bar, choose Related Activities → Employee Defaults. In the Employee Defaults dialog box, you can set up standard items for every type of payroll item you use, as shown in Figure 11-3.

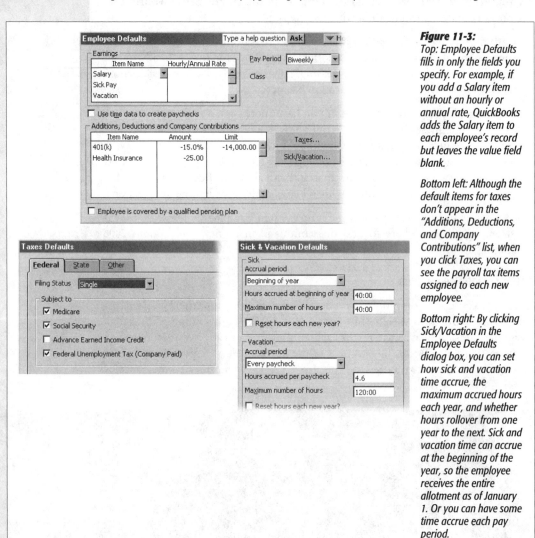

Figure 11-3:
Top: Employee Defaults fills in only the fields you specify. For example, if you add a Salary item without an hourly or annual rate, QuickBooks adds the Salary item to each employee's record but leaves the value field blank.

Bottom left: Although the default items for taxes don't appear in the "Additions, Deductions, and Company Contributions" list, when you click Taxes, you can see the payroll tax items assigned to each new employee.

Bottom right: By clicking Sick/Vacation in the Employee Defaults dialog box, you can set how sick and vacation time accrue, the maximum accrued hours each year, and whether hours rollover from one year to the next. Sick and vacation time can accrue at the beginning of the year, so the employee receives the entire allotment as of January 1. Or you can have some time accrue each pay period.

The Employee Defaults dialog box includes the same set of fields and checkboxes that you'll find in Payroll Setup wizard and the New Employee dialog box (in the Employee Center menu bar, click New Employee) on the Payroll and Compensation Info tab. When you edit an employee record, you can change any default payroll settings that don't apply to that employee.

Tip: If you track employee work hours in QuickBooks (page 427) and pay your employees by the hour, QuickBooks happily calculates their paycheck amounts. Simply turn on the "Use time data to create paychecks" checkbox. To determine the gross amount of paychecks, the program multiplies the hours on employee timesheets for the pay period by the employees' hourly rates.

Creating employee records

With employee records in hand and payroll defaults in place, you can add employees in no time with the Payroll Setup wizard. Choose Employees → Payroll Setup to open the wizard once again. In the wizard's navigation bar, click Employee List. The wizard prompts you to provide all the information it needs to process payroll, as Figure 11-4 illustrates.

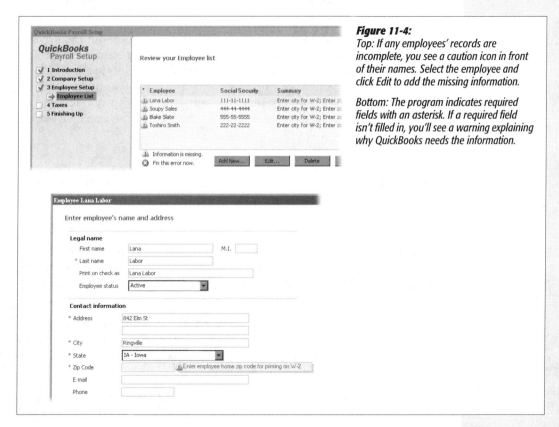

Figure 11-4:

Top: If any employees' records are incomplete, you see a caution icon in front of their names. Select the employee and click Edit to add the missing information.

Bottom: The program indicates required fields with an asterisk. If a required field isn't filled in, you'll see a warning explaining why QuickBooks needs the information.

Whether you create employee records in the Payroll Setup wizard (choose Employees → Payroll Setup) or the New Employee dialog box (in the Employee Center, choose New Employee), the information you provide is equally straightforward. The Payroll Setup wizard happens to be easier to navigate.

Here's how to fill out employee information in the Payroll Setup wizard:

- **Contact information.** For W-2 forms, you need the basic 411 about an employee (employee name and address). In the Payroll Setup wizard, if you add or edit an employee, the name and address screen collects the employee contact information, including phone number and email. This screen also includes the "Employee status" drop-down list, in which you choose Active or Inactive depending on whether the employee is working for you at the moment. If you want to add further contact information, do so in the Edit Employee dialog box (in the Employee Center, right-click an employee name and choose Edit on the shortcut menu).

- **Hiring information.** On this screen, you fill in the basics about the person's employment: whether the employee is an officer, owner, or regular Joe; the state in which the employee lives, which determines the state income tax paid; the state in which the employee works, which determines the unemployment tax you must pay; Social Security number; and hire date. You can also enter a release date, which is a diplomatic name for the last date the employee worked for you.

- **Wages and compensation.** This screen is where you specify the compensation the employee receives, and payroll frequency. The fields are the same as the ones in the Employee Defaults dialog box (page 322). If any of the standard settings don't apply to the employee, edit the record as needed.

- **Benefits.** On this screen, you specify the benefit deductions for the employee, like 401(k) and health insurance. Besides turning benefits on or off, you specify the deduction as a dollar amount or percentage, plus the annual limit (for example, $14,000 for 401(k) contributions).

- **Sick time.** The sick time screen includes fields for specifying your sick time policies: how much the employee earns and when, maximum amounts, and current balances.

- **Vacation time.** The vacation time screen is almost identical to the sick time screen, except that it specifies the employee's vacation earnings.

- **Direct deposit.** If you offer direct deposit, you can turn on direct deposit for an employee and specify whether the deposit goes to only one bank account or to two (checking and savings, for example).

Setting Up Direct Deposit

Direct deposit makes everyone's life a little easier. You don't have to worry about guarding cashable checks until you deliver them to your employees. And your employees don't have to make a trip to the bank to deposit their earnings—the money transfers from your payroll account to the accounts that employees specify, such as checking and savings accounts.

Direct deposit is an add-on service (that means you have to pay extra for it) that you can sign up for no matter which QuickBooks payroll service you choose. Once you've acti-

vated the service (choose Help → Add QuickBooks Services), you have to tell QuickBooks which bank and account gets the directly deposited money for each employee.

To make direct deposit work, you need the nine-digit routing number for the employee's bank and the employee's account number or numbers at that bank. Voided checks from employees are a great way to verify the routing and account numbers. When you split direct deposits between two accounts, the money that goes to each must add up to the total amount of the paycheck.

- **Federal tax.** On this screen, you tell the wizard about the employee's filing status, the number of allowances, extra withholding, and whether the employee is subject to deductions like Social Security and Medicare.

- **State tax.** The state tax screen shows items based on the state in which the employee lives. But this screen sneaks in one additional checkbox—turn on "I need to create custom tax settings for <employee>" if you have other taxes that don't appear in the wizard.

At long last, you'll see the Finish button in the bottom right corner of the Employee dialog box. Click it to complete the setup. You can then add more employees or click Taxes in the Payroll Setup navigation bar, as described in the next section.

Setting Up Payroll Taxes

The next major step in setting up payroll is to tell QuickBooks your company's tax information: your tax identification numbers, the tax agencies you pay, and any local payroll taxes. In the navigation bar, click Taxes to see an overview of what you can expect. Click Continue or, in the navigation bar, click Federal taxes to get down to work.

The Federal tax screen simply lists the federal taxes for which you're responsible. Select a tax and click Edit to change how the tax's name appears on paychecks or to change it to inactive, for instance if you no longer employ people in a particular state.

Note: You specify your federal tax ID number in the Company Information dialog box (choose Company → Company Information).

If you haven't set up state taxes yet (or if some state tax information is missing), the wizard automatically opens the "Set up state payroll taxes" dialog box. For state taxes, in the Payee box, you choose the tax agency from the drop-down list of vendors. You must also specify your account number and the rates.

Entering Historical Payroll

If you start using QuickBooks in the middle of a year, the best approach for record-keeping is to enter all your financial transactions from the beginning of the year. At the end of the year, you and your accountant will be glad you did. But with payroll, it's *essential* to enter all the payrolls you've processed since the beginning of the year. That's the only way to produce W-2s at the end of the year that show the correct totals for the entire year. In addition, by entering previous payroll data into your company file, the payroll calculations take into account deduction limits. For example, for 2005, Social Security taxes apply to only the first $87,000 of income. Income that an employee earns beyond that is free of Social Security tax.

TROUBLESHOOTING MOMENT

Verifying Payroll Summaries

After you've typed in your historical payroll data, it's a good idea to generate payroll summary reports in QuickBooks to compare to the reports you received from your payroll service.

Choose Reports → Employees & Payroll → Payroll Summary. In the report window, in the From and To boxes, type the first and last day of the quarter, respectively.

Compare the values in the QuickBooks report to the payroll service report for the same quarter. If the numbers are wildly disparate, you probably left out an employee or a payroll run when you entered payroll summaries. Check the summary report to make sure that each employee you paid appears and double-check the values.

Small discrepancies are probably data entry errors. Compare each amount in the summary report to the amounts on your payroll service reports. When you find the source of the problem, you can edit the payroll transactions to make the corrections.

Note: Employees pay their taxes based on the calendar year, no matter what fiscal year your company uses. Even in QuickBooks, the payroll year is the calendar year.

Entering previous payrolls by running each one through QuickBooks offers an added bonus: you can take practice runs through the payroll process and verify the values against existing payroll reports from your other system. (If you take the dummy payroll approach, be sure to turn off the "To be printed" checkbox. Instead, fill in the check numbers from those past payrolls.)

You can also add historical payroll manually: follow the instructions described in "Running Payroll" (below) for each past pay period in the current year. Toward the end of the year, the easiest solution is to wait until January 1 to switch to QuickBooks payroll.

If you're switching to payroll services in the middle of the year, you can use the Payroll Setup wizard to add payroll amounts for the payrolls you ran without QuickBooks payroll services. The wizard requires you to complete the steps described in the section "Setting Up Payroll" (page 318). In the Payroll Setup wizard, when you see checkmarks in front of steps 1 through 4, you're ready to enter the year-to-date amounts. Gather your manual payroll records for the year so far and read on.

Running Payroll

Once your payroll setup is complete, generating payroll checks each pay period takes only a few minutes.

Tip: When you use direct deposit services, you must run payroll at least two banking days before the actual pay date so the service can process the payroll and transfer money into your employees' accounts. The transmission date may change due to bank holidays, so be sure to check payroll messages from the bank to see if you must transmit payroll data earlier than usual.

WORD TO THE WISE

Updating Tax Tables

Make a habit of updating your tax tables every time before you run payroll. It's the best way to make sure you withhold the correct amounts. QuickBooks needs the most current tax tables to calculate your payroll taxes correctly and generate the correct payroll tax forms. No matter which Quick-Books payroll service you sign up for, updated tax tables are one of the benefits you receive with your subscription.

Before you run a payroll, download a tax update by choosing Employees → Get Payroll Updates. Click Update to initiate the download. After the progress bar disappears, you'll see a confirmation message. Click OK to view the contents of the update.

If you sign up for the Assisted Payroll service, QuickBooks checks whether your tax information is the most current whenever you send payroll data, and downloads the update for you automatically if your tax tables are out-of-date.

Selecting Employees

The first step in running a payroll is choosing the employees to pay for the period. Usually, you'll select all your employees. But if you pay employees by the hour, you might want to select only the employees who worked during the pay period. Either way, you must choose Employees → Pay Employees to open the "Select Employees to Pay" dialog box (Figure 11-5) and get a payroll run rolling. Data for the last pay period is blank when you run payroll for the first time. However, when you have previous payroll runs, you can use the previous values to generate the next payroll.

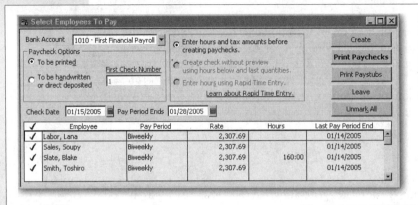

Figure 11-5:
In the Bank Account drop-down list, choose your payroll account. After the first payroll run, QuickBooks fills in this box automatically.

In the Select Employees To Pay dialog box, head to the Paycheck Options section and then choose "To be printed" to add checks to a queue. If all the employees you select use direct deposit, choose "To be handwritten or direct deposited" and, if necessary, in the First Check Number box, type the next check number for the account. Click Mark All to select all the employees listed. Or, to select some, turn on the checkbox in the row for each employee.

Note: Employees that are set to inactive in the Employee List don't appear in the Select Employees To Pay dialog box; neither do employees whose release dates (page 323) are prior to the date in the Pay Period End box.

TROUBLESHOOTING MOMENT

Correcting Paycheck Errors

If you notice that you made a mistake on an employee's pay detail but you've already created paychecks, you still have a chance to make corrections before you send the payroll data to your payroll service. Here's what you do:

1. Open the register window for the payroll bank account (in the Chart of Accounts, double-click the account name).

2. In the payroll account register, double-click the paycheck transaction for the employee, which opens the Paycheck dialog box.

3. Click Paycheck Detail to open the Review Paycheck dialog box.

4. Make the changes you want.

5. Click OK to return to the Paycheck dialog box.

6. Click Save & Close.

The first time you run payroll, QuickBooks automatically selects the "Enter hours and tax amounts before creating paychecks" option. You can enter or change the number of hours employees work, their sick time and vacation time, and other items. For subsequent payrolls, you can select "Create check without preview using hours below and last quantities" option if all the paycheck values are identical to the previous payroll run. In this case, QuickBooks automatically generates the paychecks for the employees you select.

Fill in Paycheck Data

In the Select Employees To Pay dialog box, click Create to begin specifying the information for each paycheck. If you chose the "Enter hours and tax amounts before creating paychecks" option, the Preview Paycheck dialog box is a monster, shown in Figure 11-6, which includes all paycheck values, accrued sick time, and vacation time for the employee. After you review the data, you can change any values if necessary. When the values are correct, click Create to move to the next employee paycheck.

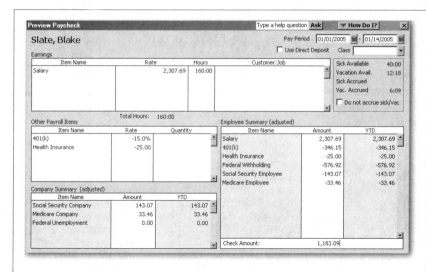

Figure 11-6:
The Earnings section shows the gross amount of the employee's paycheck. For salaried employees, QuickBooks prorates the salary to the length of the pay period. In the Other Payroll Items section and Company Summary section, the program uses the tax tables and your payroll items to calculate paycheck deductions or additions. Below the Class box is available sick and vacation time. The Employee Summary section shows the entries you typically see on a pay stub.

After you step through every employee's paycheck, you'll find yourself back in the Select Employees To Pay dialog box. Now you're ready to print the paychecks or pay stubs.

Printing Paychecks and Pay Stubs

When your employees want paper paychecks that they can deposit at the bank, you print the paychecks you just created. But when employees use direct deposit so the money goes directly to their bank accounts, you don't have to print paychecks. In this situation, your employees still want a record of their pay for the period, so you print pay *stubs* instead. Printing paychecks and pay stubs is almost identical to printing expense checks. This section describes the process, including the minor differences.

Note: If you use direct deposit, you must still *create* paychecks, but you don't *print* them. After you create the direct deposit paychecks, you process them by choosing Employees → Send Payroll Data. (If you haven't signed up for direct deposit, you won't see this menu entry.) To send the paychecks, click Go Online, and then when you're done, click Close.

Before you print paychecks, load the printer with checks for the account you use for payroll, whether it's your regular checking account or a separate one. Then, if the Select Employees To Pay dialog box is still open, click Print Paychecks. Otherwise, you can print paychecks by choosing File → Print Forms → Paychecks.

If you click "Print Pay stubs," the procedure for printing is exactly the same. What's different is the format of the information you print. Instead of printing a check for an employee, QuickBooks prints a report of the employees' payroll data that you can distribute.

QuickBooks opens the "Select Paychecks to Print" dialog box (Figure 11-7) and selects all the unprinted checks. The first time you print paychecks, make sure that you're using the correct bank account and check number. If the account in the Bank Account box is wrong, in the drop-down list, choose the account you use for payroll. In the First Check Number box, type the number on the first check in the printer.

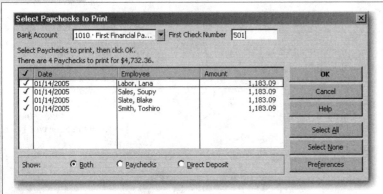

Figure 11-7:
Just above the table of paychecks is a status sentence that tells you how many paychecks you're printing and the total amount. Bounced paychecks are truly bad form, so make sure you have enough money in the account (or transfer enough) to cover the paychecks.

The "Select Paychecks to Print" dialog box automatically displays all paychecks, both direct deposit and paper. If you process paychecks and direct deposit paychecks in different ways, choose one of the Show options (Paychecks or Direct Deposit) to list only one type at a time.

If you want to customize the data that appears on paychecks, click Preferences. In the Payroll Printing Preferences dialog box, you can specify whether to include used and available vacation and sick time, or, if you're security conscious, whether to omit the employees' Social Security numbers and all but the last four digits of bank account numbers.

When you're ready to print the paychecks, in the "Select Paychecks to Print" dialog box, click OK. The Print Checks dialog box opens with the same options you see when you print expense checks (page 303). You can choose the style of check to use and how many checks are on the first sheet in the printer. Click Print to begin printing paychecks.

After the program prints the paychecks, it opens the "Did check(s) print OK?" dialog box. If a problem did occur, in the "First incorrectly printed" checkbox, type the number of the first check that didn't print properly. Click OK to reprint that check and all the checks that followed.

TROUBLESHOOTING MOMENT

Deleting Duplicate Paychecks

If you get called away to handle a crisis before you print paychecks, you might forget where you were and create a second batch of paychecks for the same pay period. When you return to printing paychecks, you'll see the duplicates in the "Select Paychecks to Print" dialog box. What you *won't* see is a way to delete those paychecks. Getting rid of duplicate paychecks is one of the more obscure procedures in QuickBooks.

Choose Reports → Employees & Payroll → "Payroll Transactions by Payee" to run a report of paychecks for every employee. In the report window, double-click a duplicate paycheck transaction to open the Paycheck dialog box. Press Ctrl+D to delete the paycheck. In the confirmation box that appears, click OK.

To get back to printing paychecks, close the report window. If the "Select Employees to Pay" dialog box is still open, click Print Paychecks. The duplicates are no longer in the list.

Paying Payroll Taxes

In addition to paying your employees, you must also remit payroll taxes and withholdings to a number of government agencies. There's no set answer for which payroll taxes you must pay and when you must pay them. The federal government has its requirements; each state has its own rules and schedules; and, in some areas, local governments tack payroll taxes on as well.

Note: QuickBooks Standard Payroll provides tax tables only for federal payroll taxes. Enhanced Payroll Plus, Assisted Payroll, and Complete Payroll provide tables for federal and state payroll taxes. You'll have to calculate local taxes yourself.

Government agencies send you letters telling you what your tax rates are and what payment schedule you must follow. When you set up payroll in QuickBooks (page 318), you can enter these details. The tax tables that the QuickBooks payroll services download update tax rates as well. Because the specifics of remitting payroll taxes vary from company to company, you must follow the instructions you receive from the tax agencies, your bank, and your accountant. Meanwhile, when it's time to remit payroll taxes, here's how you generate the payment checks:

1. **Choose Employees → Process Payroll Liabilities → Pay Payroll Liabilities.**

   QuickBooks opens the "Select Date Range for Liabilities" dialog box, in which you specify the starting and ending dates for the payment period for a payroll tax. For example, the federal government determines payment frequency by the amount that you withhold from your employees' paychecks, and the most common frequency is monthly.

   Note: If your deposit frequency changes, perhaps because you've hired a gaggle of new employees, you'll receive a letter from the IRS with your new deposit frequency.

2. **In the Dates drop-down list, choose the period for which you're paying payroll liabilities, such as Last Calendar Quarter or Last Month.**

   The Dates drop-down list includes the most typical date ranges you'll need. However, if you have a special date range to cover, in the From and To boxes, choose the starting and ending dates, respectively.

3. **Click OK.**

   The Pay Liabilities dialog box opens, listing all the payroll liabilities that you must remit and the agencies or organizations to whom you send the payments. QuickBooks automatically turns on the "To be printed" checkbox, which adds checks to the queue of checks to be printed. If you write the checks by hand, turn off the checkbox.

   Tip: The program also automatically selects the "Review liability check to enter expenses/penalties" option. If you aren't changing the values on the checks, select the "Create liability check without reviewing" option instead.

4. **In the Bank Account box, choose the bank account that you use for payroll.**

   Once you choose the payroll bank account, QuickBooks selects the same account every time you open the Pay Liabilities dialog box.

5. **In the Check Date box, choose the date you want on the checks.**

   Make sure that the check date meets the payment schedule requirements for the tax agency you're paying.

6. **Choose the payroll liabilities that you want to pay by clicking the cell in the checkmark column for each payroll item.**

Figure 11-8 illustrates the procedure.

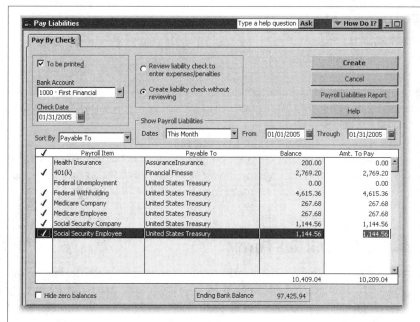

Figure 11-8:
To keep the list as concise as possible, first turn on the "Hide zero balances" checkbox. QuickBooks displays only the liabilities that have a balance. But a payroll liability with a balance doesn't mean a payment is due. Select only the payroll items whose payment frequency requires a payment now. When you click one of the Medicare or Social Security payroll items, QuickBooks automatically selects the other, because both are due at the same time.

7. **When you've chosen the items you want to pay, click Create.**

QuickBooks creates checks for the payroll liabilities, but not as you might expect. Instead of creating one check for each payroll liability, the program creates a single check for each vendor (tax agency, insurance company, or other organization).

Tip: The government isn't known for picking up on small details, such as two different payroll liabilities on the same check—unless the IRS is on an audit kick. So it's a good idea to create separate checks for each payroll liability to the same agency. To separate payments to the same vendor, select one payroll liability for a vendor during the first pass. After you've created the first batch of payroll liability checks, open the Pay Liabilities dialog box once more and select another payment for the same vendor.

If you turned on the "To be printed" checkbox, the program adds the checks to the queue of checks to be printed. If this checkbox is turned off, the program records the transactions in your company file, but you must write the checks by hand.

8. **To print the checks, choose File → Print Forms → Checks.**

The "Select Checks to Print" dialog box opens.

9. **In the Bank Account drop-down list, choose the account you use for payroll.**

   If necessary, in the First Check Number box, type the first check number in your printer. QuickBooks automatically selects all the checks in the queue. If you want to prevent a check from printing in this run, uncheck it.

10. **Click OK to open the Print Checks dialog box.**

    The options for payroll liability checks are the same as paychecks (page 329) and expense checks (page 303).

Note: If you use Assisted Payroll, the payroll service automatically makes your federal and state payroll tax liability payments. But you must send the payroll run data to the service so it can remit withholdings to the appropriate tax agencies.

After you have checks in hand, fill in the coupons or forms that the tax agency sent you and remit the payment and the payment coupon per the agency's instructions. For example, you make federal payments at the bank where you keep your payroll account.

Preparing Payroll Tax Forms

Tax agencies require that you regularly submit forms documenting the payroll taxes and withholdings you're supposed to remit and how much you've already sent in. Depending on the QuickBooks payroll service you use, the program can print payroll tax forms for you. Standard Payroll provides federal tax forms. If you subscribe to Enhanced Payroll Plus, you can generate federal and state tax forms. Although the forms that QuickBooks produces aren't exact replicas of the pre-printed forms you might receive from the government, they are close enough that you can send them in without fear of rejection.

Tip: Many tax agencies are moving to phone and electronic filing. If you use one of these filing options, choose Reports → Employees & Payroll and then choose a report, such as Employee State Taxes Detail, to obtain the values you need for your filing.

Regardless of which tax form you want to generate, the steps are basically the same:

1. **Choose Employees → Process Payroll Forms.**

   QuickBooks opens the Select Form Type dialog box, which includes option buttons for federal and state forms. The "State form" option is dimmed if you've subscribed to QuickBooks Standard Payroll, which doesn't provide state tax tables.

2. Choose the "Federal form" option or the "State form" option, and click OK.

The next dialog box that appears is the Select Payroll Form dialog box, which lists the federal and state forms that QuickBooks can generate. Depending on the form you choose, you specify the filing period, as illustrated in Figure 11-9.

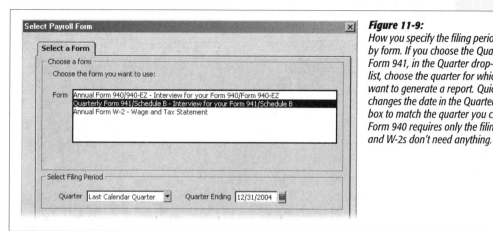

Figure 11-9:
How you specify the filing period varies by form. If you choose the Quarterly Form 941, in the Quarter drop-down list, choose the quarter for which you want to generate a report. QuickBooks changes the date in the Quarter Ending box to match the quarter you choose. Form 940 requires only the filing year, and W-2s don't need anything.

3. To export your payroll data to the form and display the filled in form, click OK.

The form appears in the Payroll Tax Form window. Although QuickBooks formats the form so it's easy for you to read and review, when you print the form, it looks like the preprinted forms you receive from the tax agency. To print the form, in the Payroll Tax Form window, click Print. Now you're ready to mail the report in.

Bank Accounts, Credit Cards, and Petty Cash

You've opened your mail, plucked out your customers' payments, and deposited them in your bank account (see Chapter 9). Your bills and customer refund checks are paid (see Chapter 10). Now you can sit back and relax knowing that *most* of the transactions in your bank and credit card accounts are accounted for. What's left?

Some stray transactions might pop up—an insurance claim check to deposit, restocking your petty cash drawer, or a fee from your bank for a customer's bounced check, to name a few. Plus, running a business typically means that money moves between accounts—from interest-bearing accounts to checking accounts or from merchant credit card accounts to your savings. If you come across a financial transaction in business, you can enter it in QuickBooks, whether you prefer the guidance of dialog boxes or the speed of an account register window.

Reconciling your accounts to your bank statements is another key process you don't want to miss. You and your bank both can make mistakes, and reconciling your accounts is the best way to catch these discrepancies. Once the bane of book-keepers, reconciling is practically automatic now that you can download transactions electronically and let QuickBooks handle the math.

In this chapter, the section on reconciling is the only must-read. If you want to learn the fastest way to enter any type of bank account transaction, don't skip the next section, "Entering Transactions in an Account Register." You can read about transferring funds, loans, bounced checks, and other financial arcana as the need arises.

Entering Transactions in an Account Register

QuickBooks includes dialog boxes for making deposits, writing checks, and transferring funds, but you can also construct these transactions right in a bank account register window. Working in a register window has two advantages over the dialog boxes:

- **Speed.** Entering a transaction in a register window is fast, particularly when keyboard shortcuts, such as pressing Tab to move between fields, are second nature.

- **Visibility.** Dialog boxes, such as Write Checks, keep you focused on the transaction at hand. You can't see other transactions unless you align the dialog box and the register window side by side. In a register window, you can look at previous transactions for reference and to prevent yourself from entering duplicate transactions.

Opening a Register Window

You have to open a register window before you can enter transactions in it. Opening a register window couldn't be easier:

1. **If the "Chart of Accounts" window isn't open, press Ctrl+A (or on the Home page, click Chart of Accounts).**

   The window pops open, listing all accounts you've set up in QuickBooks.

2. **In the "Chart of Accounts" window, double-click the bank account whose register window you want to open.**

   As you can see in Figure 12-1, this method opens register windows for more than bank accounts.

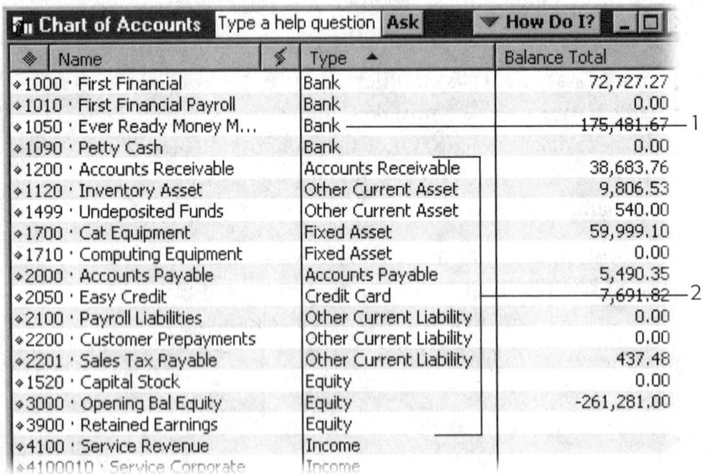

Figure 12-1:
1: You can open a register window by double-clicking any type of bank account, including checking, savings, money market, and petty cash accounts.

2: Every account that appears on your balance sheet (Accounts Receivable, Accounts Payable, Credit Card, Asset, Liability, and Equity accounts) opens the same way.

Note: Income and expense accounts don't have registers in QuickBooks. When you double-click an income or expense account, QuickBooks generate a QuickReport of the transactions for that account. From the report window, you can take a closer look at a transaction by double-clicking it.

Creating a Transaction in an Account Register

The steps to create a check in your checking account register (page 306) work for deposits and transfers with only a few minor adjustments. Here's how to fill in the cells in the register window to create any kind of bank transaction:

- **Date.** When you first open a bank account register window, QuickBooks automatically fills in the Date cell of the first blank transaction with the current date. Tweaking the date by a few days is as easy as pressing + or – until the date is the one you want.

- **Number.** When you jump to the Number cell, QuickBooks automatically fills in the next check number for the bank account. If the number doesn't match the paper check you want to write, press + or – until the number is correct.

Note: QuickBooks keeps track of both handwritten checks and printed checks. When you use the register window to create a check, QuickBooks fills in the Number cell by incrementing the last handwritten check number. When you choose File → Print Forms → Checks, the program fills in the First Check Number box by incrementing the last printed check number.

POWER USERS' CLINIC

Keyboard Shortcuts for Dates

If pressing + or – to increment dates seems rudimentary to you, add some of the following keyboard shortcuts to your date-selection arsenal. When the cursor is in the Date field, jump directly to favorite dates:

- **t (for today).** Press *t* to change the date to today's date.

- **m (for month).** Press *m* to select the first day of the current month. Pressing *m* additional times jumps to the first day of previous months.

- **h (for month).** Press *h* to select the last day of the current month. Pressing *h* additional times jumps to the last day of months in the future.

- **w (for week).** Press *w* to choose the first day of the current week. Pressing *w* additional times jumps to the first day of previous weeks.

- **k (for week).** Press *k* to choose the last day of the current week. Pressing *k* additional times jumps to the last day of future weeks.

- **y (for year).** Press *y* to choose the first day of the current year. Pressing *y* additional times jumps to the first day of previous years.

- **r (for year).** Press *r* to choose the last day of the current year. Pressing *r* additional times jumps to the last day of future years.

You can press these letters multiple times to pick dates further into the past or the future and combine them with pressing + and – to reach any date you want. But face it: After half a dozen different key presses, it might be easier to type a numeric date, such as 12/14/05, or to click the Calendar icon and choose the date.

To make an online payment (see Chapter 20), in the Number cell, type *S*. QuickBooks then fills in the cell with *Send*.

To enter a deposit, you can bypass the Number and Payment cells regardless of what values they contain, as you can see in Figure 12-2.

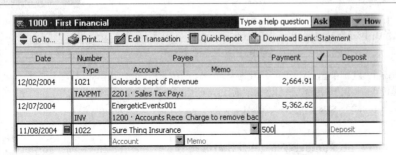

Figure 12-2:
Top: When you start a transaction in the register window, QuickBooks automatically fills in the Number cell with the next check number. You aren't alone if you frequently type a deposit amount in the Payment cell.

Bottom: Simply fill in a value in the Deposit cell and move to another cell, and QuickBooks springs into action. It automatically clears the check number in the Number cell and the value in the Payment cell. And it replaces the code CHK in the Type cell with DEP for deposit.

- **Payee.** QuickBooks doesn't require a value in the Payee cell. In fact, for deposits, transfers, or petty cash transactions, leaving the Payee cell blank and typing a description of the transaction in the Memo cell is preferable to filling up your Vendors list with the occasional payee.

Tip: Many bookkeepers can't stomach leaving the Payee cell blank. But the Vendors list is best reserved for companies and individuals who send you bills. To resolve this dilemma, in the Other Names list (page 117), create more general names, like Deposit, Transfer, Petty Cash, and Gasoline. Then you can fill in the Payee cell for every fuel purchase with *Gasoline* and type the name of the service station in the Memo cell.

If you're entering a *check*, start typing the name of the payee. As you type, QuickBooks scans the names in the various lists in your company file (Vendors, Customers, Other Names, and so on) and selects the first name it finds that matches all the letters you've typed so far. As soon as QuickBooks selects the one you want, press Tab to move to the Payment cell.

- **Payment.** In the Payment cell, type the amount of checks you write, fees that the bank deducts from your account, or petty cash withdrawals.

- **Deposit.** In the Deposit cell, type the amount of deposits you make, interest you earned, or deposits to petty cash.

Note: In QuickBooks transactions, money either goes out or comes in. There's no in-between. When you enter a value in the Payment cell, QuickBooks clears the Deposit cell value, and vice versa.

- **Account.** The Account cell can play many roles. For instance, when you're creating a check, choose the account for the expense it represents. If you're making a deposit, choose the income or expense account to which you want to post the deposit. (Depositing an insurance claim check that pays for equipment repair reduces the balance of the expense account for equipment maintenance and repair.) If you're transferring money from another bank account, choose that bank account.

Tip: If you want to assign a transaction to several accounts, click Splits. Figure 10-9 (page 293) shows how to distribute dollars to different accounts.

FREQUENTLY ASKED QUESTION

Contributing Money to Your Company

How do I record the money I contribute to my company?

If you're incorporating a company, most attorneys suggest that you contribute some cash to get the company off the ground. This money is called *owners' equity.*

The QuickBooks EasyStep Interview (page 20) usually creates an equity account called Owners' Contribution or something similar. If you don't have an owners' equity account, in the "Chart of Accounts" window, create one (page 20). In the New Account dialog box, be sure to choose the Equity account type.

The transaction for your deposit adds the money to your bank account, but you want the money to appear in your owner's equity account on the balance sheet. To accomplish this feat, open the register window for the company checking account. In the Deposit cell, enter the amount of your check and then in the Account cell, choose the Owner's equity account you've created.

- **Memo.** Filling in the Memo cell can jog your memory no matter which type of transaction you create. Enter the bank branch for a deposit (in case your deposit ends up in someone else's account), the location of the gas station for a credit card charge, or the store where you purchased items with petty cash. The transaction reminders just keep coming—the contents of the Memo cell appear in the reports you create.

Tip: Remember your accountant's insistence on an audit trail? If you create a transaction by mistake, don't delete it. Although QuickBooks's audit trail keeps track of transactions that you delete, the omission can be confusing to others or to you after some time passes.

If you void a transaction instead, the amount (payment or deposit) changes to zero. The voided transaction still appears in your company file, so you know that it occurred, but it doesn't affect any account balances or financial reports. Before you void a transaction, add a note in the Memo field that explains why you're voiding it. In a register window, right-click a transaction and choose the Void command (Void Check, Void Deposit, and so on) on the shortcut menu.

Handling Bounced Checks

Bouncing a check is annoying and embarrassing. And banks charge for each check you bounce (and, often, they craftily pay your larger checks before the smaller ones to rack up as many bounced check charges as possible). Besides depositing more money to cover the shortfall and paying those bank fees, you must tell people to re-deposit the ones that bounced or write new checks.

When someone pays your company with a rubber check, it's just as annoying. Besides the charges *your* bank might charge for re-depositing a bounced check, you have to do a few things to straighten out your records in QuickBooks when a customer's check bounces, such as:

- Remove the amount of the bounced check from your checking account, because the money never made it that far.

- Record any charges that your bank levies on your account for your customer's bounced check.

- Invoice the customer to recover the original payment, your bounced check charges, and any additional charges you add for your trouble.

Setting Up QuickBooks to Handle Bounced Checks

Before you can re-invoice your customers, you must first create items for bounced checks and their associated charges.

Bounced check item

When a check bounces, your bank removes the amount of the check from your bank balance. You want to do the same thing in your company file, so you don't overestimate your bank balance and write bad checks of your own. Because the customer hasn't really paid you, the amount of the check should go back into your Accounts Receivable account.

To remove the amount of the bounced check from your bank account, create an Other Charge item, such as BadCheck. In the Create Item dialog box (choose Lists → Item to open the Item List window and then press Ctrl+N), find the Account drop-down list, and then choose your bank account. When you add the Bounced Check item to an invoice, QuickBooks deducts the value of the bad check from your bank account, as you'll see on page 344. In the Tax Code drop-down list, choose a nontaxable code so that QuickBooks doesn't charge tax when you re-invoice the customer.

Service charges for bounced checks

Companies typically request reimbursement for bounced check charges, but many companies tack on *additional* service charges for the inconvenience of processing a bounced check. Depending on how you account for these charges, you'll use one or two Other Charge type items:

- **Bounced check reimbursement.** To request reimbursement for your bank's bounced check charges, you need an item that you can add to an invoice, a "Create an Other Charge" type item, called something like BadCheck Charge.Be sure to choose a nontaxable code for the item so that QuickBooks doesn't calculate sales tax.

  QuickBooks doesn't care whether you post this item to an income account or an expense account. For example, you can post reimbursed bounced check charges to the same income account you use for other types of service charges. Although the customer's reimbursement appears as income, the bank charge you paid is an expense. The effect on your net profit (income minus expenses) is zero.

  You can also post bounced check reimbursements directly to the same expense account you use for bank service charges. Then when you pay your bank's bounced check charge, QuickBooks debits the bank service charge account. When the customer pays you back, QuickBooks credits the bank service charge account. The effect on net profit is still zero.

- **Bounced check service charge.** If you post your bank's bounced check charges to an income account (such as a Service Charge income account), you can use the same item for any extra service charge you apply for bounced checks. However, if you post customers' bounced check reimbursements to your bank service charge *expense* account, you need a separate item for your service charge. Create an Other Charge type item for the service charge. In the Create Item dialog box (choose Lists → Item to open the Item List window and then press Ctrl+N), find the Account drop-down list, and then choose your service charge income account. Like the bounced check reimbursement item, make this charge nontaxable.

Recording Bank Charges

The easiest place to record a bounced check charge is in the bank account register window. This technique works just as effectively for any bank charge your bank drops on your account:

1. **Press Ctrl+A to open the Chart of Accounts.**

   In the "Chart of Accounts" window, double-click your bank account to open its register window.

2. **In the Date cell in the first blank transaction, choose the date on which the bank assessed the charge.**

Note: QuickBooks automatically fills in the Number cell with the next check number. Be sure to delete that number before saving the transaction to keep your QuickBooks check numbers synchronized with your paper checks.

---

3. **Leave the Payee cell blank.**

   Type the details of the bank charge in the Memo cell, as shown in Figure 12-3.

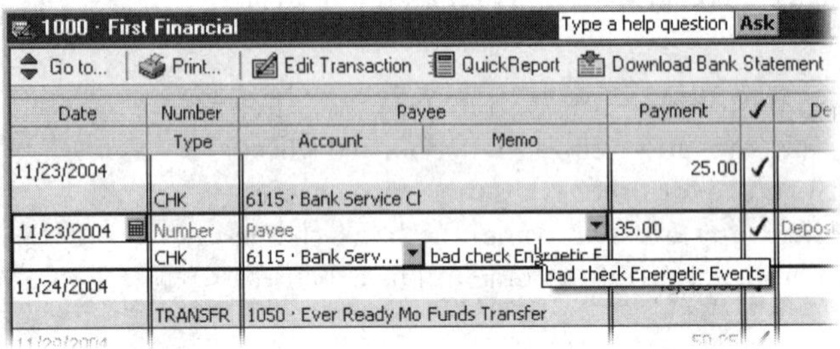

Figure 12-3:
In the Memo cell, type a description of the bank charge, such as "bounced check charge," "minimum balance charge," and so on. For a bounced check charge, add the name of the customer whose check bounced.

4. **In the Payment cell, type the amount of the bank charge. In the Account cell, choose the expense account you use to track bank charges.**

   If you used QuickBooks' sample Chart of Accounts, you probably have an account called Bank Service Charges.

5. **Click Record.**

   QuickBooks saves the bank charge in your account.

Tip: When you re-invoice your customer, don't forget to include a bounced check charge item on the new invoice in order to recoup this cost, as described next.

Bounced Checks

With the bounced check items created on page 342, you can update all the necessary account balances just by re-invoicing the customer for the bounced check. Here's the short and sweet approach:

1. **In the QuickBooks icon bar, click Invoice (or on the Home page, click Invoices).**

   The program opens the Create Invoices dialog box.

2. In the Customer:Job box, choose the customer who wrote you a bad check. Then, in the item table, add an item for the bounced check itself and others for your service fees, as shown in Figure 12-4.

   If you really want to deter customers from writing back checks, in addition to making them pay your bank fee, you can add on a fee for your own trouble. In this example, BadCheck Charge covers the bank's charge plus an additional fee the company collects for itself.

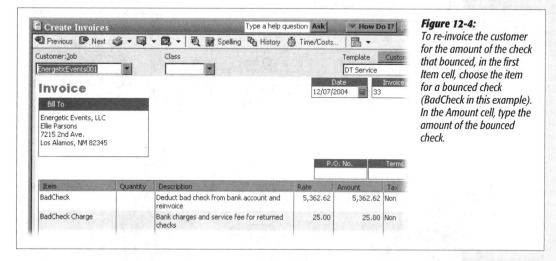

Figure 12-4:
To re-invoice the customer for the amount of the check that bounced, in the first Item cell, choose the item for a bounced check (BadCheck in this example). In the Amount cell, type the amount of the bounced check.

3. In the Amount cell for the bounced check, type the amount of the retuned check itself. In the Amount cell for the bad check charge, type the additional amount you're charging, whether it's just your bank's charge or also includes your service charge.

   QuickBooks added any sales tax owed to the original invoice, so these items include any sales tax.

4. When you save the invoice, QuickBooks updates your bank account and Accounts Receivable account balances, as shown in Figure 12-5.

   When you first invoice a customer, the invoice amount gets added on to your Accounts Receivable balance. The customer's original payment initially reduces the Accounts Receivable balance, but the bounced check requires that you remove the original payment from your records. By re-invoicing the customer, you re-establish the balance as outstanding and add the invoice amount back into Accounts Receivable.

5. When the customer sends you a check for this new invoice, simply choose Receive Payments to apply that check as a payment for the invoice.

QuickBooks reduces the Accounts Receivable balance by the amount of the payment.

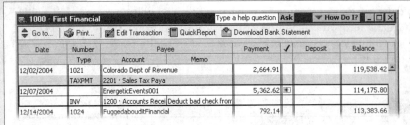

Figure 12-5:
Top: The item for a bounced check is linked to your bank account, so adding it to an invoice deducts the value of the bad check from your bank account balance.

Bottom: The new invoice adds the amount of the bounced check and service charges back into Accounts Receivable.

Managing Credit Card Accounts

Are credit cards accounts or vendors?

In QuickBooks, credit cards can be accounts or vendors, depending on how you prefer to record your credit card transactions. Here's the deal:

- **Credit card vendor.** Setting up a credit card as a vendor has several advantages. You don't have to reconcile a credit card account when you receive your credit card statement. The name of every emporium and establishment you bless with credit card purchases won't fill up your Vendor List. And instead of entering credit card charges as they occur, you can wait until you receive your credit card statement. But you still have to allocate the money you spent to the appropriate accounts. With statement in hand, in the Enter Bills dialog box, enter a bill (page 276) for the total amount on your credit card statement. Then, on the Expenses and Items tabs, add entries to allocate charges to the appropriate expense accounts.

- **Credit card account.** If you prefer to keep your expenditures up-to-date in your company file, create an account for your credit card and enter the charges as they occur (which takes no time at all if you download credit card transactions; page 513 explains how). You have to reconcile a credit card account as you would a checking account (page 349), but QuickBooks makes that easy. To prevent charge payee names from overflowing your Vendor List with names you don't need, add store names in the Memo cell or create more general vendors, such as Gas, Restaurant, and Office Supplies.

Transferring Funds

With the advent of electronic banking services, transferring funds between accounts has become a staple of account maintenance. Companies stash cash in savings and money market accounts to earn interest and then transfer money into checking right before they pay bills.

TROUBLESHOOTING MOMENT

Writing Off Bad Debt

If you try contacting your customer for payment only to find that the telephone is disconnected, the forwarding address has expired, and an eviction notice is stapled to the office door, you'll probably conclude that you aren't going to get your money. In accounting, admitting that the money is gone for good is called *writing off bad debt*.

The invoice you create for a customer represents income *only if* the customer pays it. So, to write off bad debt, you have to remove the income for the unpaid invoice from your financial records. You do that by offsetting the income with an equal amount of expense—you guessed it—the bad debt.

Suppose you invoiced your customer for $5,000, but you realize that you'll never see the money. The $5,000 is sitting in your Accounts Receivable account as an asset. Here's how to remove that money from the Accounts Receivable account by means of a bad debt expense:

1. On the Home page, click Receive Payments.

2. In the Receive Payments dialog box, in the Customer:Job box, choose the customer.

3. Keep the Amount box set to zero (because you haven't received any money from the customer).

4. In the table of invoices, turn on the checkbox for the invoice or statement that you're writing off.

5. QuickBooks opens a warning box, "You cannot apply an amount greater than the total payment plus any existing credits." But if you're writing off bad debt, that's exactly what you want to do, so click OK to close the warning box and boldly continue with the following steps. (The checkmark in the table of invoices now disappears.)

6. Back in the Receive Payments dialog box, click Discounts & Credits.

7. In the "Discount and Credits" dialog box, in the "Amount of Discount" box, type the amount that you've decided to write off ($5,000 in this example).

8. In the Discount Account box, choose the expense account you use to track bad debt. (If you don't have an account for bad debt, create an Other Expense type account and name it Bad Debt.)

9. Click Done.

10. In the Receive Payments dialog box, click Save & Close.

When you apply the write-off as a discount in the Receive Payments dialog box, QuickBooks removes the money from the Accounts Receivable account, so the program no longer thinks your customer still owes the money. And it adds $5,000 to the appropriate income account and to the Bad Debt expense account, so your net profit shows no sign of the income.

Fund transfers have nothing to do with income or expenses—they merely move money from one balance sheet account to another. For example, if you keep money in savings until you pay bills, the money moves from your savings bank account (an asset account in your Chart of Accounts) to your checking bank account (another asset account). Your income, expenses, and, for that matter, your total assets, remain the same before and after the transaction.

Transferring funds in QuickBooks is easy, whether you use the Transfer Funds dialog box or enter the transaction directly in an account register. The steps for creating a transaction in an account register appear on page 338; here's how you use the Transfer Funds dialog box:

1. **Choose Banking → Transfer Funds.**

   QuickBooks opens the transfer Funds dialog box, shown in Figure 12-6.

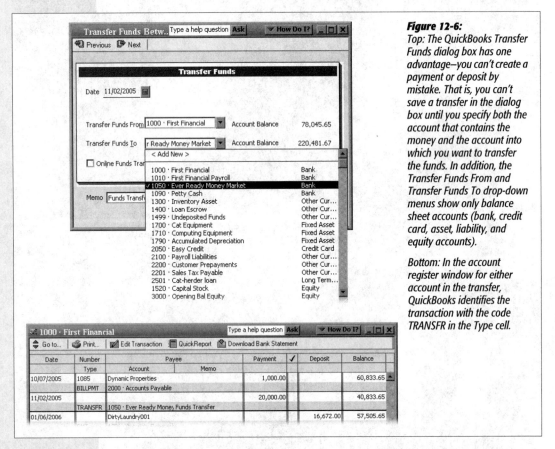

Figure 12-6:

Top: The QuickBooks Transfer Funds dialog box has one advantage—you can't create a payment or deposit by mistake. That is, you can't save a transfer in the dialog box until you specify both the account that contains the money and the account into which you want to transfer the funds. In addition, the Transfer Funds From and Transfer Funds To drop-down menus show only balance sheet accounts (bank, credit card, asset, liability, and equity accounts).

Bottom: In the account register window for either account in the transfer, QuickBooks identifies the transaction with the code TRANSFR in the Type cell.

2. **After you choose the accounts for the transfer, in the Date box, choose the date of the transfer and, on the Transfer Amount $ line, type the amount you're transferring from one account to the other.**

   Typically, you transfer money because you don't have enough money in one of your accounts to pay bills. But if you want to record the reason for the transfer, in the Memo box, type your reason.

3. Click Save & Close.

That's it. Or, if you've got more transfers to make, click Save & New.

Reconciling Accounts

Reconciling a bank statement with a paper check register is tedious and error-prone. Besides checking off items on two different paper documents, the check register and the bank statement never seem to agree—primarily due to arithmetic mistakes you make. With QuickBooks, you can leave your pencils unsharpened and stow your calculator in a drawer.

When all goes well, you can reconcile your account with a few mouse clicks. Discrepancies crop up less often because QuickBooks does math without mistakes. But problems occasionally occur—transactions might be missing or numbers won't match. When your bank statement and QuickBooks account don't agree, QuickBooks helps you find the problems.

Preparing for the First Reconciliation

The first reconciliation for a bank account is often the hardest, because the beginning balance for an account in QuickBooks rarely equals the beginning balance on your bank statement. Short of some extraordinary luck, these two beginning balances typically match only when you start a business and start using QuickBooks at the same time. Your bank statements adhere to their own schedule, so your last statement might have a closing date of December 20. The transactions that occur between the 20th and the 1st generate the difference.

QuickBooks can align your statement and account the first time you reconcile your account, as described in the box, "Adjusting an Account That Won't Reconcile," on page 353. The program generates a transaction that adjusts your account's opening balance to match the balance on your bank statement. A more precise approach, which allocates deposits and checks to the correct accounts, is to enter the transactions that occurred between your last statement end date and the day you started using QuickBooks.

Warning: Account opening balances post to your Opening Bal Equity account, so these adjustments affect your Balance Sheet. If you enter an adjustment as described in the box on page 353, let your accountant know that you changed the opening balance so she can address that change while closing your books at the end of the year.

Preparing for Every Reconciliation

QuickBooks is amenable to your creating and editing transactions right in the middle of reconciliation. But that doesn't mean it's the right way to work. Reconciling your account flows more smoothly when your transactions are up-to-date.

Take a moment *before* you reconcile to make sure that you've entered all the transactions in your account:

- **Bills.** If you paid a bill by writing a paper check and forgot to pay the bill in QuickBooks, on the Home page, click Pay Bills and enter those payments (page 276).

- **Checks.** Checks missing from your checkbook but not in QuickBooks are a big hint that you wrote a paper check and didn't record that check in QuickBooks. Create any missing check transactions in the account register (page 306) or choose Banking → Write Checks.

- **Transfers.** Create missing transfers in the account register (page 347) or choose Banking → Transfer Funds.

- **Deposits.** If you forgot to deposit customer payments in QuickBooks, on the Home page, click Record Deposits to add those deposits to your bank account. If a deposit appears on your bank statement and doesn't show up in the "Payments to Deposit" dialog box, you might have forgotten to receive the payment in QuickBooks. For deposits unrelated to customer payments, create the deposit directly in the account register.

Tip: The easiest way to spot payments that you haven't deposited in QuickBooks is to open the register window for the Undeposited Funds account (double-click it in the "Chart of Accounts" window). If the balance is greater than zero, you haven't deposited all the payment you received.

- **Online transactions.** If you use Online Payment or Online Account Access, download online transactions before you start to reconcile your account.

Starting a Reconciliation

Reconciling an account is a two-part process, and QuickBooks contains separate dialog boxes for each part. The first part of the process includes choosing the account you want to reconcile, entering the ending balance from your bank statement, and entering service charges and interest earned during the statement period. Here's how to kick off account reconciliation:

Tip: If your workload gets ahead of you, several months could go by before you have time to reconcile your account. Don't try to reconcile multiple months at once. Discrepancies are harder to spot, and locating the source of problems will tax your already overworked brain. Put your bank statements in chronological order and then walk through the reconciliation process for each statement.

---

1. **Press Ctrl+A to open the "Chart of Accounts" window. Then right-click the account you want to reconcile and, on the shortcut menu, choose Reconcile.**

   QuickBooks opens the Begin Reconciliation dialog box, which includes information about the previous reconciliation, as shown in Figure 12-7.

Tip: If you're working in the bank account register window, it's easier to start reconciling by choosing Banking → Reconcile. QuickBooks opens the Begin Reconciliation dialog box and automatically selects the active bank account.

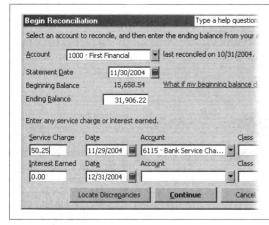

Figure 12-7:
The program uses the ending balance from the previous reconciliation to fill in the Beginning Balance for this reconciliation. If the Beginning Balance in the Begin Reconciliation dialog box doesn't match the beginning balance on your bank statement, click Cancel, and go to page 355 to learn how to correct the problem.

The date of the previous reconciliation appears to the right of the Account box. No date appears if you're reconciling the account for the first time. Quick-Books fills in the Statement Date box with a date one month after the previous reconciliation date, but you can choose the date that matches your bank statement if necessary.

2. **In the Ending Balance box, type the ending balance from your bank statement. And in the Service Charge box, type the monthly service charge for this statement.**

In the Date box, choose the date on which the service charge was levied. In the Account box, choose the account to which you want to post the charge (usually Bank Service Charges or something similar). QuickBooks creates a transaction for you.

Tip: If you use online banking, chances are you've already downloaded your service charge and interest transactions. If this is the case, don't enter them in the Begin Reconciliation dialog box or you'll end up with duplicate transactions.

3. **If you are reconciling an account that pays interest, in the Interest Earned box, type the interest you earned from the bank statement.**

As you did for service fees, specify the date and the account that you use to track interest you earn.

Tip: If you track service fees and interest by class, in the Class boxes, choose the appropriate class. For example, classes might apply if you use them to track performance by region. However, if you use classes to track sales by partner, you don't have to specify a class for interest earned.

4. Click **Continue** to start reconciling individual transactions.

QuickBooks opens the Reconcile dialog box where you reconcile the individual transactions, covered in the next section.

Reconciling Transactions

The Reconcile dialog box groups payments and charges (items that reduce your balance) on the left side with deposits and other credits on the right side. Marking transactions as cleared is a matter of toggling transaction checkmarks on and off, as you can see in Figure 12-8.

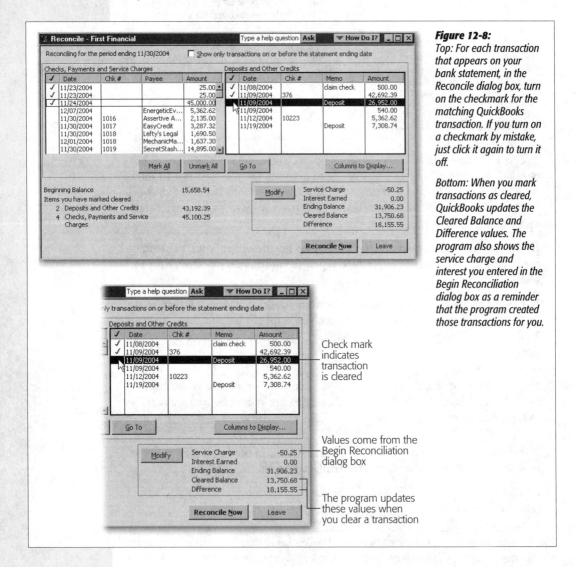

Figure 12-8:
Top: For each transaction that appears on your bank statement, in the Reconcile dialog box, turn on the checkmark for the matching QuickBooks transaction. If you turn on a checkmark by mistake, just click it again to turn it off.

Bottom: When you mark transactions as cleared, QuickBooks updates the Cleared Balance and Difference values. The program also shows the service charge and interest you entered in the Begin Reconciliation dialog box as a reminder that the program created those transactions for you.

Check mark indicates transaction is cleared

Values come from the Begin Reconciliation dialog box

The program updates these values when you clear a transaction

Tip: Initially, the Reconcile dialog box lists all uncleared transactions in the account regardless of when they occur. With transactions after the statement ending date mixed in, you could select transactions by mistake. To filter the list to likely candidates for clearing, turn on the "Show only transactions on or before the statement ending date" checkbox. If you don't see transactions that appear on your bank statement, turn the checkbox off. You might have created a transaction with the wrong date.

QuickBooks includes several shortcuts for marking a transaction as cleared. See whether any of these techniques simplify your work:

• **Mark All.** If you usually end up clearing most of the transactions in the list, click Mark All to select all the transactions. Then uncheck the transactions that don't appear on your bank statement. If you were distracted and selected several transactions by mistake, click Unmark All to start over.

• **Selecting contiguous transactions.** Dragging down the checkmark column selects every transaction you pass. This approach isn't that helpful if you compare one transaction at a time or if your transactions don't appear in the same order as those on your bank statement.

Tip: If you use online account access, click Matched to automatically clear the transactions that you've already matched from your QuickStatement (see Chapter 20). Enter the ending date from the printed statement and click OK.

When the Difference value changes to 0.00, your reconciliation is a success. To officially complete the reconciliation, click Reconcile Now.

WORKAROUND WORKSHOP

Adjusting an Account That Won't Reconcile

When the Difference value in the Reconcile dialog box obstinately refuses to change to 0.00, reconciling without finding the problem *is* an option. For example, if you're one penny off and you can't solve the problem with a quick review, that one cent is not worth more of your time. As you complete the reconciliation, QuickBooks can add an adjustment transaction to make up the difference.

In the Reconcile dialog box, if you click Reconcile Now without zeroing the Difference value, QuickBooks automatically opens the Reconcile Adjustment dialog box. The program

tells you what you already know: there is an unresolved difference between the Ending Balance from your bank statement and the Cleared Balance in QuickBooks. If you decide to try to fix the problem, click Return to Reconcile.

To create an adjustment transaction, click Enter Adjustment. QuickBooks creates a general journal entry to adjust the balance. If you stumble across the source of the discrepancy later, you can delete the adjustment journal entry or create a reversing entry (page 379).

Note: When you reconcile a credit card account and click Reconcile Now, QuickBooks opens the Make Payment dialog box. You can choose to write a check or enter a bill to make a payment for your credit card account.

Reconciliation Reports

After you click Reconcile Now in the Reconcile dialog box, you might notice a short delay while QuickBooks generates your reconciliation reports. These reports come in handy as a benchmark when you try to locate discrepancies in a future reconciliation. Figure 12-9 shows you how to choose your reconciliation reports and what they look like.

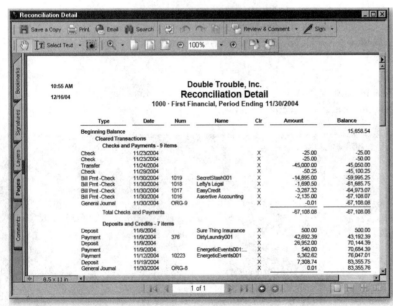

Figure 12-9:
Top: When the Select Reconciliation Report dialog box opens, you can display or print reconciliation reports. To save the reports for future reference, click Print. Choose the Summary option for a report that provides the totals for the checks and payments you made and also for the deposits and credits you received.

Bottom: Choose the Detail option for a report that shows your beginning and ending balances and every transaction you cleared. QuickBooks uses Adobe Acrobat to display the report.

Tip: View a reconciliation report at any time by choosing Reports → Banking → Previous Reconciliation.

Modifying Transactions During Reconciliation

QuickBooks immediately updates the Reconcile dialog box with changes you make in the account register window, so it's easy to complete a reconciliation. Missing transactions? Incorrect amounts? Other discrepancies? No problem. You can jump to the register window and make your changes. When you click the Reconcile dialog box, the changes are there.

Tip: If you can see the register window and the dialog box at the same time, click the one you want to work on. If the Open Windows list appears in the navigation bar on the left side of the QuickBooks window (choose View → Open Window List), you can click names there to change the active window or dialog box.

Here's how you make changes while reconciling:

- **Adding transactions.** If a transaction appears on your bank statement but isn't in QuickBooks, switch to the account register window and add the transaction (page 338).

- **Deleting transactions.** If you find duplicate transactions, in the account register window, select the transaction and press Ctrl+D. You have to confirm your decision before the program deletes the transaction. The Reconcile window removes the transaction if you delete it.

- **Editing transactions.** If you notice an error in a transaction, in the Reconcile dialog box, double-click the transaction to open the corresponding dialog box (Write Checks for checks, Make Deposits for deposits, Transfer Funds for transfers, and so on). Correct the mistake and save the transaction (click Record or Save depending on the dialog box).

Stopping and Restarting a Reconciliation

If your head hurts and you want to take a break, don't worry about losing the reconciliation work you've already done. In the Reconcile dialog box, click Leave. Although QuickBooks closes the dialog box, it remembers what you've cleared. You'll see asterisks in the checkmark column for transactions that you've marked, which indicates that your clearing of a transaction is pending.

When you're refreshed, choose Banking → Reconcile (or on the Home page, click Reconcile). The Begin Reconciliation dialog box opens. Re-enter the ending balance and service charge or interest amounts and click Continue. The transactions you marked are, happily, still marked. Pick up by marking the rest of the transactions that cleared on your bank statement.

Correcting Discrepancies

If you modify a transaction that you've already reconciled, QuickBooks *should* freak out and wave a clutch of red flags at you. After all, if you cleared a transaction because it appeared on your bank statement, the transaction is complete, and changing it in QuickBooks doesn't change it in your bank account. Yet QuickBooks lets you change or delete cleared transactions.

But make no mistake: making changes to previously cleared transactions is the quickest way to create mayhem when reconciling your accounts. For example, in

---

the account register window, clicking a checkmark cell clears that transaction, which then removes that transaction's amount from the Beginning Balance when you try to reconcile the account. And *that* means that the Beginning Balance won't match the beginning balance on your paper bank statement, which is one reason you might be reading this section.

The Discrepancy Report

QuickBooks' only redemption in this matter is the Discrepancy Report, which shows you changes that were made to cleared transactions, illustrated in Figure 12-10. To create the Discrepancy Report, in the Reconcile dialog box, click Locate Discrepancies, and then click Discrepancy Report. You can also choose Reports → Banking → Reconciliation Discrepancy.

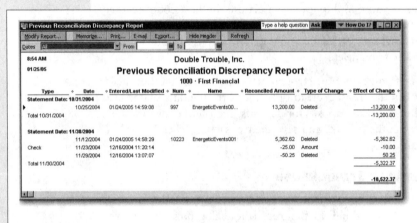

Figure 12-10:
To correct discrepancies created by transaction editing, you must restore each modified transaction to its original state, and the Discrepancy Report provides the information you need to know to do that. To edit a transaction, in the Discrepancy Report, double-click the transaction to open its corresponding dialog box.

Seeing transactions on the Discrepancy Report is a big step toward correcting reconciliation problems. Here's how you interpret the crucial columns in the report:

- **Entered/Last Modified.** This is the date that the transaction was created or modified, which doesn't help you restore the transaction, but might help you find the person who's changing reconciled transactions.

- **Reconciled Amount.** This is the amount for the transaction when you cleared it during reconciliation. If the transaction amount changed, use this value to restore the transaction amount to its original value. For example, in Figure 12-10, -25.00 represents a check written for $25.

- **Type of Change.** This indicates the transaction change. For example, Amount means that the transaction amount changed. Deleted indicates that the transaction was deleted. The only way to restore a deleted transaction is to recreate it from scratch. Uncleared indicates that someone removed the checkmark in the account register.

- **Effect of Change.** This value indicates how the change affected the beginning balance for your reconciliation. For example, the $25 check was changed in a way that subtracted another $10 from your bank account (the new check amount is $35.00). When the Beginning Balance is off and the amount in the "Effect of Change" column matches that discrepancy, you can be sure that restoring these transactions to their original state will fix your problems.

Other ways to find discrepancies

Sometimes, your reconciliation doesn't match because of subtle errors in transactions or because you've missed something in the current reconciliation. Try the following techniques to help spot problems:

- **Search for a transaction equal to amount of the discrepancy.** Press Ctrl+F to open the Find dialog box. In the Choose Filter list, choose Amount. Choose the = option and type the amount in the box. Click Find to run the search.

Note: Using Find in this way works only if the discrepancy is caused by *one* transaction that you cleared or uncleared by mistake. If more than one transaction is to blame for the discrepancy, the amount you're trying to find is the total of all the erroneously cleared transactions, so Find won't see a matching value.

- **Look for transactions cleared or uncleared by mistake.** Compare your bank statement to the transactions in the Reconcile dialog box. Make sure that every transaction on the bank statement is cleared in the Reconcile dialog box. Also, check that no additional transactions are cleared in the Reconcile dialog box.

- **Look for duplicate transactions.** If you both create transactions in QuickBooks and download transactions, it's easy to duplicate them. And when you clear both of the duplicates, the mistake is hard to spot. If that's the case, you have to scroll through the register window looking for multiple transactions with the same date, payee, and amount.

Tip: Count the number of transactions on your bank statement. Compare that number to the number of cleared transactions displayed on the left side of the Reconcile dialog box, illustrated in Figure 12-8. Of course, this transaction count won't help if you enter transactions in QuickBooks differently than they appear on your bank statement. For example, if you deposit every payment individually, but your bank shows one deposit for every business day, your transaction counts won't match.

- **Look for a deposit entered as a payment or vice versa.** To find an error like this, look for transactions whose amounts are half the discrepancy. For example, if a $500 check becomes a $500 deposit by mistake, your reconciliation will be off by $1000 ($500 because a check is missing and another $500 because you have an extra deposit).

- **Look at each cleared transaction for transposed numbers or other differences between your statement and QuickBooks.** It's easy to type $95.40 when you meant $59.40.

Note: If these techniques don't uncover the problem, your bank might have made a mistake (page 359).

Undoing the Last Reconciliation

If you're having problems with this month's reconciliation, but suspect that the guilty party is hiding in *last* month's reconciliation, you can undo the last reconciliation and start over. When you undo a reconciliation, QuickBooks returns the transactions to an uncleared state.

In the Begin Reconciliation dialog box (choose Banking → Reconcile), click Locate Discrepancies. QuickBooks opens the Locate Discrepancies dialog box, where you can undo the last reconciliation or take other measures to correct problems, as shown in Figure 12-11.

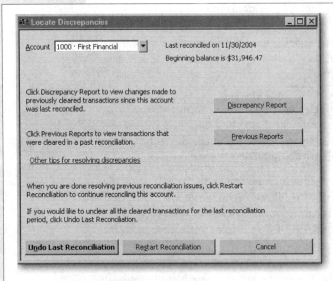

Figure 12-11:
Top: Click Undo Last Reconciliation to have QuickBooks open the Undo Previous Reconciliation dialog box. The button label and the dialog box title don't match, but they both represent the same process.

Bottom: In the Undo Previous Reconciliation dialog box, click Continue. When the Undo Previous Reconcile Complete message box appears, click OK. QuickBooks returns to the Locate Discrepancies dialog box. Click Cancel if you want to modify transactions before attempting another reconciliation. Otherwise, click Restart Reconciliation to open the Begin Reconciliation dialog box for your next try.

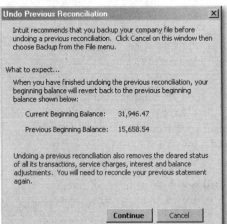

Tip: Although QuickBooks removes the cleared status on all the transactions including service charges and interest, it doesn't remove the service charge and interest transactions that it added. When you restart the reconciliation, in the Begin Reconciliation dialog box, don't re-enter the service charges or interest.

When Your Bank Makes a Mistake

Banks do make mistakes. Digits get transposed, or amounts are flat wrong. When this happens, you can't ignore the difference. In QuickBooks, add an adjustment transaction (page 353) to make up the difference, but be sure to tell your bank about the mistake. It's always a good idea to be polite in case the error turns out to be yours.

When you receive your *next* statement, check that the bank made an adjustment to correct its mistake. You can delete the adjustment or add a reversing journal entry to remove your adjustment and reconcile as you normally would.

Tip: For a reminder to check your next statement, create a To Do Note (page 69).

Managing Loans

Unless your business generates cash at an astonishingly fast rate, you'll probably have to borrow money to purchase big ticket items that you can't afford to do without, such as a deluxe cat-herder machine. The asset you purchase and the loan you assume are intimately linked—you couldn't obtain the equipment without the money you borrow.

But in QuickBooks, loans and the assets they help purchase aren't connected in any way. You create an asset account (page 36) to track the value of an asset that you buy. If you take out a loan to pay for that asset, you create a liability account to track the balance of what you owe on the loan. With each payment that you make on your loan, you pay off a little bit of the loan principal as well as a chunk of interest.

Note: On your company balance sheet, the value of your assets appears in the Assets section, and the balance owed on loans shows up in the Liabilities section. The difference between the asset value and your loan balance is your equity in the asset. Suppose your cat-herder machine is in primo condition and worth $70,000 on the open market. If you owe $50,000 on the loan, your company has $20,000 in equity for that machine.

Most loans *amortize* your payoff, which means that each payment represents a different amount of interest and principal. In the beginning of a loan, amortized loan payments are mostly interest and very little principal, which is great for tax deductions. By the end, the payments are almost entirely principal. Making loan payments in which the values change each month would be a nightmare if not for

QuickBooks Loan Manager, which is a separate program that comes with Quick-Books and can gather information from your company file. This program calculates your loan amortization schedule, posts the principal and interest for each payment to the appropriate accounts, and handles escrow payments and fees associated with your loans.

Tip: Loan Manager doesn't handle loans in which the payment covers only the accrued interest (called *interest-only loans*). For loans like these, you have to set up payments yourself (page 365) and allocate the payment to principal and interest using the values on your monthly loan statement.

Setting Up a Loan

Whether you use Loan Manager or not, you have to create accounts to keep track of your loan. You probably know already that you need a liability account for the amount of money you owe. But you also need accounts for the interest you pay on the loan and escrow payments (such as insurance or property tax) that you make:

- **Liability account.** Create a liability account (page 36) to track the money you've borrowed. For mortgages and other loans whose terms are longer than a year, use the Long-term Liability type. For short term loans, use the Other Current Liability type.

  When you create the liability account, add the account number but forego the opening balance. The best way to record money you borrow is with a journal entry (page 372), which credits the liability account for the loan and debits the bank account in which you deposited the money you borrowed. If you've just begun to use QuickBooks and have a loan that you've partially paid off, fill in the journal entry with what you owed on the loan statement that's dated just before your QuickBooks company start date.

Tip: For existing loans, be sure to enter any loan payments you've made since the statement date you used to specify the opening balance.

- **Loan interest account.** The interest that you pay on loans is an expense. Create an Expense account called something like Interest Paid.

Note: Although companies often assign interest paid to an Other Expense account type, Loan Manager doesn't show Other Expense account types in its account drop-down lists. When you use Loan Manager, create the account for interest paid as an Expense account type.

- **Escrow account.** If you make escrow payments, such as for property taxes and insurance, create an account to track the escrow you've paid. Because escrow represents money you've paid in advance, use a Current Asset account type.

- **Fees and finance charge expense account.** Chances are you'll pay some sort of fee or finance charge at some point before you pay off a loan. Set up an Expense account for these fees.

There's one last QuickBooks setup task to complete *before* you start Loan Manager. You have to create the lender in either your Vendor List or Other Names List (page 110).

WORKAROUND WORKSHOP

Where Are My Accounts and Vendors?

Loan Manager isn't a command within QuickBooks; it's a separate small program. When you start Loan Manager, it gleans information from your company file, such as the liability account you created for the loan and the vendor entry you set up for your lender.

If you forgot to create accounts or your lender in Quick-Books, you'll probably jump to your "Chart of Accounts" window or Vendor List and create them. The problem is you

still won't see those new elements in Loan Manager's drop-down lists.

You have to close Loan Manager (losing all the data you've already entered for a loan) and create those entries in QuickBooks. After you've created the vendor and all the accounts you need, choose Banking → Loan Manager to restart the Loan Manager program, which now includes your lender and loan accounts in the drop-down lists.

Adding a Loan to Loan Manager

Loan Manager makes it so easy to track and make payments on amortized loans, it's well worth the steps required to set it up. Before you begin, gather your loan documents like chicks to a mother hen, because Loan Manager wants to know every detail of your loan, as you'll soon see.

Basic setup

With your account and vendor entries complete (see the box above), follow these steps to describe your loan:

1. **Choose Banking → Loan Manager.**

   QuickBooks opens the Loan Manager dialog box.

2. **In the Loan Manager dialog box, click "Add a Loan."**

   QuickBooks opens the Add Loan dialog box, which contains several screens for all the details of your loan. After you fill in one screen, click Next to move to the next one.

3. **In the Account Name drop-down list, choose the liability account you created for the loan.**

   QuickBooks lists only accounts of Current Liability and Long-term Liability types.

---

4. In the Lender drop-down list, choose the vendor you created for the lender.

If you haven't set up the lender as a vendor in QuickBooks, you have to close Loan Manager. After you've created the vendor in QuickBooks, choose Banking → Loan Manager to restart the Loan Manager program, which now shows the lender in the Lender drop-down list.

5. In the Origination Date box, choose the date that matches the origination date on your loan documents.

Loan Manager uses the loan origination date to calculate the number of remaining payments, the interest you owe, and when you'll pay off the loan.

6. In the Original Amount box, type the total amount that you borrowed when you first took out the loan.

The Original Amount box is aptly named because it is *always* the amount that you originally borrowed. For new loans, the current balance on the loan and the Original Amount are the same. If you've paid off a portion of a loan, your current balance is lower.

7. In the Term boxes, specify the length of the loan, as shown in Figure 12-12. Click Next to advance to the screen for payment information.

The next section tells you how to deal with payment info.

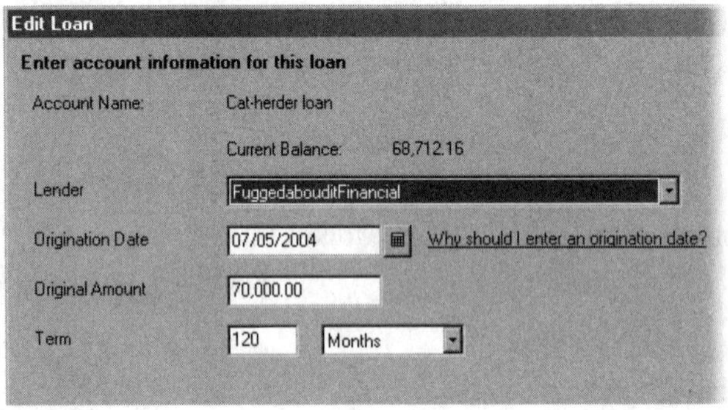

Figure 12-12:
Loan Manager automatically selects Months in the Term drop-down list. Specifying the number of months for a 30-year loan is a great refresher for your multiplication tables, but there's no excuse for confusing Loan Manager with an arithmetic error. In the Term drop-down list, choose the period (such as Years). Then, you can fill in the first Term box with the number of periods shown on your loan documents.

Payment information

When you specify a few details about your loan payments, Loan Manager can calculate a schedule of payments for you. To make sure you don't forget a loan payment (and incur the typically outrageous late charges), you can tell Loan Manager to create a QuickBooks reminder for your payments. Here's how:

1. In the "Due Date of Next Payment" box, choose the next payment date.

For a new loan, choose the date for the first payment you'll make. For an existing loan, choose the date for your next payment, which usually appears on your last loan statement.

2. **In the Payment Amount box, type the total payment for principal and interest.**

   If you don't know what your payment is, you can find it in your loan documents. Loan Manager automatically fills in the Next Payment Number box with the number 1. For loans that you've made payments on already, type the number for the next payment (this, too, should appear on your last loan statement).

3. **In the Payment Period drop-down list, choose the frequency of your payments.**

   Loans typically require monthly payments, even when their terms are set in years. Regardless of which period you chose in the Term drop-down list, in the Payment Period drop-down list, choose how often you must make loan payments.

4. **If your loan includes an escrow payment, first choose the Yes option.**

   Then specify the amount of escrow you pay each time and the account to which you want to post the escrow, as illustrated in Figure 12-13.

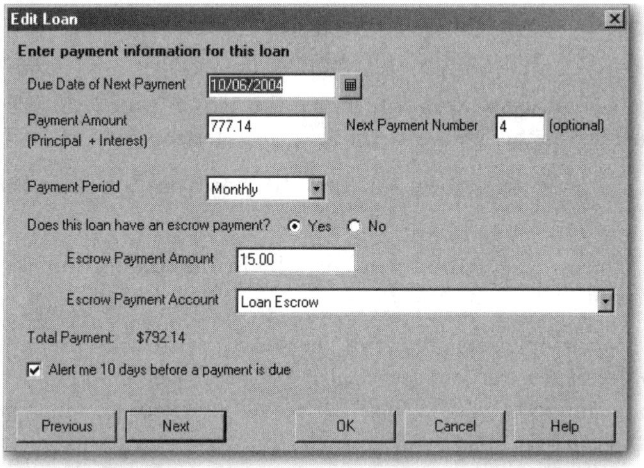

Figure 12-13:
Most mortgages include an escrow payment for property taxes and property insurance. Escrow accounts are asset accounts, because you're setting aside some money to pay expenses later. When you add an escrow payment, Loan Manager updates the value of the Total Payment to include principal, interest, and escrow.

5. **If you want a reminder 10 days before a loan payment is due, turn on the "Alert me 10 days before a payment is due" checkbox.**

   Loan Manager tells QuickBooks how often and when payments are due, so QuickBooks can create a loan payment reminder in the Reminders List (page 155).

6. **Click Next to advance to the screen for entering interest rate information.**

   The next section tells you how to deal with interest rate info.

Interest rate information

For Loan Manager to calculate your amortization schedule (the amount of principal and interest paid with each payment) you have to specify the interest rate. Here's how:

1. **In the Interest Rate box, type the interest rate for the loan.**

   Use the interest rate that appears on your loan documents. For example, although you probably make monthly payments, the loan document usually shows the interest rate as an annual rate.

2. **In the Compounding Period box, choose either Monthly or Exact Days, depending on how the lender calculates compounding interest.**

   If the lender calculates the interest on your loan once a month, choose Monthly. The other option, Exact Days, calculates interest using the annual interest rate divided over a fixed number of days in a year. In the past, many lenders simplified calculations by assuming that a year had 12 months of 30 days each, resulting in the Compute Period choice 365/360. Today, lenders often use the number of days in a year, which is the Compute Period 365/365.

3. **In the Payment Account drop-down list, choose the account from which you make your payments, whether you write checks or pay electronically.**

   In the Payment Account drop-down list, Loan Manager displays your bank accounts.

4. **In the Interest Expense Account drop-down list, choose the account you use to track the interest you pay.**

   Loan Manager displays only accounts of the Expense type. If you created the account as an Other Expense account type, close Loan Manager and modify the account type for the interest you pay. You'll have to re-enter your loan information in Loan Manager.

5. **Click Finish.**

   Loan Manager calculates the payment schedule for the loan and adds it to the list of loans in the Loan Manager dialog box, shown in Figure 12-14.

Modifying Loan Terms

Some loan characteristics change from time to time. For example, if you have an adjustable rate mortgage, the interest rate changes every so often. And your escrow payment usually increases as your property taxes and insurance go up. To make changes like these, in the Loan Manager dialog box (choose Banking → Loan Manager), select the loan and then click Edit Loan Details.

Loan Manager takes you through the same screens you saw when you first added the loan. If you change the interest rate, the program recalculates your payment schedule. For a change in escrow, the program updates your payment to include the new escrow amount.

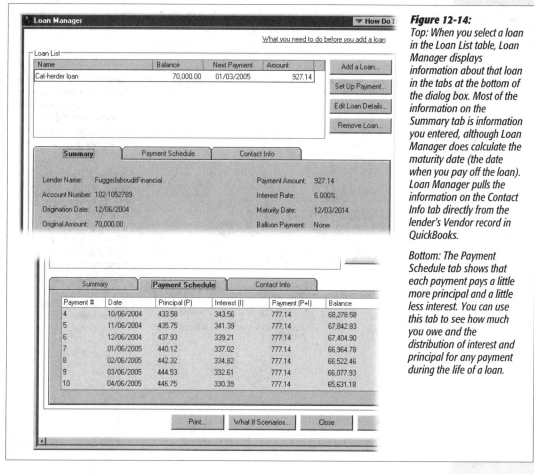

Figure 12-14:
Top: When you select a loan in the Loan List table, Loan Manager displays information about that loan in the tabs at the bottom of the dialog box. Most of the information on the Summary tab is information you entered, although Loan Manager does calculate the maturity date (the date when you pay off the loan). Loan Manager pulls the information on the Contact Info tab directly from the lender's Vendor record in QuickBooks.

Bottom: The Payment Schedule tab shows that each payment pays a little more principal and a little less interest. You can use this tab to see how much you owe and the distribution of interest and principal for any payment during the life of a loan.

Setting Up Payments

From Loan Manager, you can make a loan payment by writing a check or entering a bill in QuickBooks. Although Loan Manager can handle this task one payment at a time, it can't create recurring payments to send the payment that's due each month. When you see the QuickBooks reminder for your loan payment, you must run Loan Manager to generate the payment:

1. **In the Loan Manager dialog box, select the loan you want to pay and click Set Up Payment.**

   Loan Manager opens the Set Up Payment dialog box and fills in the information for the next payment, as you can see in Figure 12-15.

Tip: If you want to make an extra payment, in the "This payment is" drop-down list, choose "An extra payment." Because extra payments aren't a part of the loan payment schedule, Loan Manager changes the values in the Principal (P), Interest (I), Fees & Charges, and Escrow boxes to zero. If you want to prepay principal on your loan, type the amount that you want to prepay in the Principal (P) box. Or, if you want to pay an annual fee, fill in the Fees & Charges box.

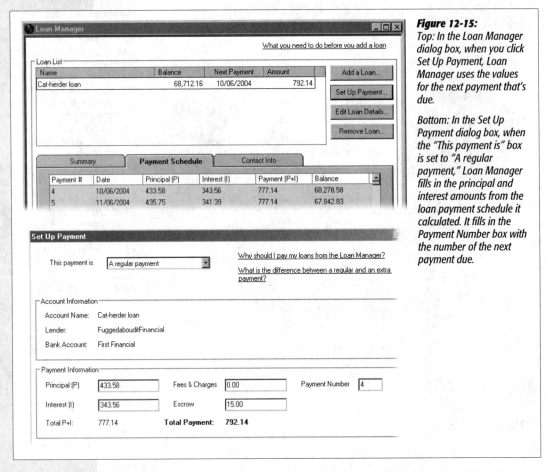

Figure 12-15:
Top: In the Loan Manager dialog box, when you click Set Up Payment, Loan Manager uses the values for the next payment that's due.

Bottom: In the Set Up Payment dialog box, when the "This payment is" box is set to "A regular payment," Loan Manager fills in the principal and interest amounts from the loan payment schedule it calculated. It fills in the Payment Number box with the number of the next payment due.

2. **In the Payment Method drop-down list, choose "Write a check" or "Enter a bill."**

   Loan Manager opens the QuickBooks Write Checks or Enter Bills dialog box, respectively, and fills in the boxes with the payment information. You can change the payment date or other values if you want.

Note: Because Loan Manager and QuickBooks are separate programs, you might notice a delay as one program communicates with the other.

3. **In the Write Checks or Enter Bills dialog box, click Save & Close.**

   When the Write Checks or Enter Bills dialog box closes and you're back in the Loan Manager dialog box, click Close.

If you want to print the payment schedule for your loan, click Print. Or, if you pay off a loan and want to remove it from Loan Manager, select the loan and click Remove Loan. Removing a loan from Loan Manager doesn't delete any loan transactions or loan accounts in QuickBooks.

What If Scenarios

Because economic conditions and interest rates change, loans aren't necessarily stable things. For example, if you have an adjustable rate loan, you might want to know what your new payment is. Or, you might want to find out whether it makes sense to refinance an existing loan when interest rates drop. The What-If Scenarios button is your dry-erase board for trying out loan changes before you make up your mind.

When you click What If Scenarios, Loan Manager opens the What If Scenarios dialog box. Take your pick from these five scenarios:

Note: The changes you make in the What If Scenarios dialog box don't change your existing loans. If you switch to a different scenario or close the window, Loan Manger doesn't save the information. If you want a record of different scenarios, click the Print button.

- **What if I change my payment amount?** Paying extra principal can shorten the length of your loan and reduce the total interest you pay. Choose this scenario and then, in the Payment Amount box on the right side of the dialog box, type the new amount you plan to pay each month. Loan Manager calculates your new maturity date and shows how much you'll pay overall and how much you'll pay in interest.

- **What if I change my interest rate?** If you have an adjustable rate loan, choose this scenario to preview the changes in payment, interest, and balloon payment for a different rate, higher or lower.

- **How much will I pay with a new loan?** You don't have to go through the third degree to see what a loan will cost. Choose this scenario to quickly enter the key information for a loan and evaluate the payment, total payments, total interest, and final balloon payment.

- **What if I refinance my loan?** When interest rates drop, companies and individuals alike consider refinancing their debt to save money on interest. With this scenario, type in a new term, payment, interest rate, and payment date to see whether it's worth refinancing, as shown in Figure 12-16.

• **Evaluate two new loans.** Type in the details for two loans to see which one is better.

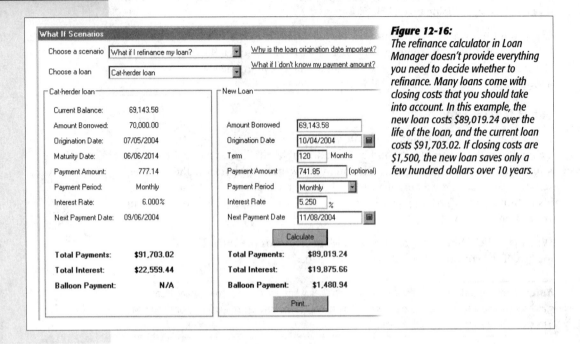

Figure 12-16:
The refinance calculator in Loan Manager doesn't provide everything you need to decide whether to refinance. Many loans come with closing costs that you should take into account. In this example, the new loan costs $89,019.24 over the life of the loan, and the current loan costs $91,703.02. If closing costs are $1,500, the new loan saves only a few hundred dollars over 10 years.

Tracking Petty Cash

Dashing out to buy an extension cord so you can present a pitch to a potential client? Chances are you'll get money from the petty cash drawer at your office. Petty cash is the familiar term for money spent on small purchases, typically less than $20.

Many companies keep a cash drawer at the office and dole out dollars for small company-related purchases that employees make. But for the small business owner with a bank card, obtaining petty cash is as easy as withdrawing some money from an ATM. Either way, petty cash is still company money. And that means you have to keep track of it and how it's spent.

Recording ATM Withdrawals and Deposits to Petty Cash

In QuickBooks, adding money to your petty cash account mirrors the real world transaction. You either write a check made out to Cash (or the trustworthy employee who's cashing the check), or you withdraw money from an ATM. To write a check for your petty cash account, you can simply open the Write Checks dialog box (choose Banking → Write Checks or, on the Home page, click Write Checks). Withdrawing cash from an ATM requires the Transfer Funds dialog box (choose Banking → Transfer Funds).

If creating transactions in the account register window (page 338) is OK with you, you can use the same steps whether you replenish your petty cash with a check or ATM withdrawal:

1. **In the "Chart of Accounts" window (press Ctrl+A to open), double-click your checking account to open the register window.**

   If the current date, which QuickBooks fills in automatically, isn't the day you add money to petty cash, choose the correct date.

2. **If you're withdrawing money from an ATM, clear the value in the Number cell.**

   If you're writing a check to get petty cash and QuickBooks fills in the Number cell with the correct check number, continue to the Payee cell.

3. **Whether you are writing a check or using an ATM, in the Payee cell, type a name such as Cash or Petty Cash.**

   If you made a check out to one of your employees, in the Payee cell drop-down list, choose the employee's name.

4. **In the Payment cell, type the amount that you're moving from the checking account to petty cash.**

   If you track classes in QuickBooks, this is one time to ignore the Class cell. You assign classes when you record purchases made with petty cash.

5. **In the Account cell, choose your petty cash account.**

   If you don't have a petty cash account in your Chart of Accounts, be sure to choose the Bank type when you create the account. When you do so, your petty cash account appears at the top of your balance sheet with your other savings and checking accounts.

6. **Click Record to save the transaction.**

   That's it.

Recording Purchases Made with Petty Cash

As long as company cash sits in the petty cash drawer or your wallet, the petty cash account in QuickBooks holds the cash. But when you spend some of the petty cash in your wallet or an employee brings in a sales receipt for purchases, you have to record what that petty cash purchased.

The petty cash account register is as good a place as any to record these purchases. In the "Chart of Accounts" window, double-click the petty cash account to open its register window. Then, in a blank transaction, follow these guidelines to record your petty cash expenditures:

- **Number cell.** Although petty cash expenditures don't use check numbers, QuickBooks automatically fills in the Number cell with the next check number anyway. The easiest thing to do is ignore the number and move on to the Payee or Payment cell.

- **Payee cell.** QuickBooks doesn't require a value in the Payee cell, and for many petty cash transactions, entering a Payee would just clog your lists of names. Leave the Payee cell blank. You can type the vendor name or details of the purchase in the Memo cell if you want a record of it.

- **Payment cell.** In the Payment cell, type the amount of the expenditure.

- **Account cell.** Choose an account to track the expense.

Tip: To distribute the petty cash spent to several accounts, click Splits. In the table that appears, you can specify the account, amount, customer or job, class, and memo for each split (page 307).

WORKAROUND WORKSHOP

Petty Cash Advances

Good management practices recommend against dishing out petty cash without a receipt. But suppose an employee asks for cash in advance to purchase a new lava lamp for the conference room? There's no receipt, but you really want the lava lamp to impress the CEO of a tie-dye company.

The solution in the real world is to write a paper IOU and place it in the petty cash drawer until the employee coughs up a receipt.

In QuickBooks, record the advance as if the purchase were already complete. For the lava lamp, create the transaction using entries like these:

- In the Amount cell, type the amount of money you advanced to the employee.

- In the Account cell, choose the account for the expenditure.

- In the Memo cell, include a note about the employee who received the advance, the IOU in the petty cash drawer, and what the advance is for.

When the employee comes back with a sales receipt, you can update the transaction's Memo cell to show that the IOU has been repaid. If the employee brings change back, create a deposit to replace that money in the petty cash account.

Making Journal Entries

Intuit claims that you don't need to know double-entry accounting (page 6) to use QuickBooks. Most of the time, that's true. When you write checks, receive payments, and perform several other tasks in QuickBooks, the program unobtrusively handles the double-entry accounting for you. But every once in a while, QuickBooks transactions can't help, and your only choice is moving money around directly between accounts.

In the accounting world, these direct manipulations are known as *journal entries*. For example, if you posted income to your only income account but have since decided that you need several income accounts to track the money you make, journal entries are the mechanism for transporting money from that original income account to the new ones.

The steps for creating a journal entry are deceptively easy, but assigning money to accounts in the correct way can be maddeningly difficult for weekend accountants. And unfortunately, QuickBooks doesn't have any magic looking glass that makes those assignments crystal clear. This chapter gets you started by showing you how to create journal entries and providing examples of journal entries you're likely to need.

Note: In the accounting world, you'll hear the term "journal entry," and see it abbreviated as JE. Although QuickBooks uses the term "general journal entry" and the corresponding abbreviation GJE, both terms and abbreviations refer to the same account register changes.

Balancing Debit and Credit Amounts

In double-entry accounting, both sides of any transaction must balance, as the transaction in Figure 13-1 illustrates. When you move money between accounts, you increase the balance in one account as you decrease the balance in the other—just as shaking some money out of your piggy bank decreases your savings balance and increases the money in your pocket. These changes in value are called *debits* and *credits*. If you commit anything about accounting to memory, it should be the definitions of debit and credit, because these are the key to successful journal entries and accurate financial reports.

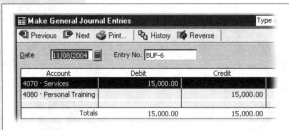

Figure 13-1:
For each transaction, the total in the Debit column must equal the total in the Credit column. To transfer money from one income account to another, you debit the original account (decrease the income) and credit the new account (increase its income).

Table 13-1 shows what debits and credits do for different types of accounts and can take some of the pain out of creating journal entries. For example, a loan payment is a debit to your loan account because it decreases your loan balance. A purchase of a machine is a debit to the equipment asset account because it increases the value of the equipment you retain. And (here's the real tongue-twister) a credit card charge is a credit to your credit card liability account because purchases on credit increase the amount you owe.

As you'll see in examples in this chapter, you can have more than one debit or credit entry in one journal entry. For example, when you depreciate equipment, you can include one debit for depreciation expense, but a separate credit for the depreciation on each piece of equipment.

Table 13-1. *How debits and credits change the values in accounts*

Account Type	Debit	Credit
Asset	Increases balance	Decreases balance
Liability	Decreases balance	Increases balance
Equity	Decreases balance	Increases balance
Income	Decreases balance	Increases balance
Expense	Increases balance	Decreases balance

Some Reasons to Use Journal Entries

Here are a few of the more common reasons that businesses use journal entries:

- **Reassigning accounts.** As you work with QuickBooks, you might find that the accounts you created originally don't track your business the way you want. For example, suppose you started with one income account for all the consulting services you offer. Now you have three income accounts: one for income from designing consumer surveys, a second for income for conducting surveys, and a third for the money you make working the statistics to deliver the right results. To move income from your original account to the correct new account, you debit the income from the original account and credit it to the new account, as described on page 374.

- **Correcting account assignments.** If you assigned an expense to the wrong expense account, you or your accountant can create a journal entry to reassign the expense to the correct account. If you've developed a reputation for mis-assigning income and expenses, your accountant might ask you to assign any questionable transactions to uncategorized income or expense. Then, when she gets the file at the end of the year, she can create journal entries to assign those transactions correctly. You can verify that the assignments and account balances are correct by running a trial balance (page 395).

Note: If you enter a transaction by mistake in QuickBooks, you can delete it. However, since most accountants prefer to keep records of *all* transactions, even erroneous ones, the common approach to correcting mistakes is to create a journal entry that moves money to the correct accounts.

- **Reassigning classes.** Journal entries can transfer income or expenses from one class to another. For example, nonprofits often use classes to assign income to programs. If you need to transfer money to a program, create a journal entry that has debit and credit entries for the same income account, but changes the class (see page 378).

- **Depreciating assets.** Each year that you own a depreciable asset, you decrease its value in the appropriate asset account in your Chart of Accounts (see Chapter 2). Because no cash changes hands, QuickBooks doesn't offer a command to handle depreciation as it does for transactions like bills, invoices, and checks. As you'll learn on page 379, a journal entry for depreciation debits the depreciation expense account (increases its value) and credits the asset account (decreases its value).

Tip: If you depreciate the same amount each year, memorize the first depreciation transaction you create (page 121). The following year, when it's time to enter depreciation, press Ctrl+T to open the Memorized Transaction List window. Select the depreciation transaction and then click Enter Transaction.

- **Recording transactions for a payroll service.** If you use a third-party payroll service like Paychex or ADP, the payroll company sends you a report. To get the numbers from the report into your company file where you need them, you can use journal entries. For example, you can move money to your payroll account, record paychecks, and record the additional expenses that employers incur.

- **Recording year-end transactions.** The end of the year is a popular time for journal entries, whether your accountant is fixing your more creative transactions or you're creating journal entries for noncash transactions before you prepare your taxes. For example, if you run a small business out of your home, you might want to show a portion of your utility bills as expenses for your home office. When you create a journal for this transaction, you debit the office utilities account and credit an equity account for your owner's contributions to the company.

WORKAROUND WORKSHOP

Creating Opening Balances with Journal Entries

QuickBooks has some arbitrary, but unyielding, rules about Accounts Payable (AP) and Accounts Receivable (AR) accounts in general journal entries. Each general journal entry can contain only one Accounts Payable or Accounts Receivable account, and that account can appear on only one line of the journal entry. And if you do add an Accounts Payable account, you must also choose a vendor in the Name field. For Accounts Receivable accounts, you must choose a customer name in the Name field.

These rules are a problem only when you want to use general journal entries to set the opening balances for customers or vendors. The hardship, therefore, is minute, because the preferred approach for building opening balances for vendors and customers is to enter bills and customer invoices. These transactions provide the detail you need to resolve disputes, determine account status, and track income and expenses.

You can get around QuickBooks' AP and AR limitations by setting up the opening balances in all your accounts with a journal entry based on your trial balance. Simply create the journal entry without the amounts for Accounts Payable and Accounts Receivable, as shown here. You must adjust the values in your equity account (like Retained Earnings) to reflect the omission of AP and AR. Now you can create your open customer invoices and unpaid vendor bills to build the values for Accounts Receivable and Accounts Payable. When your AP and AR account balances match the values on the trial balance, the equity account will match its trial balance value as well.

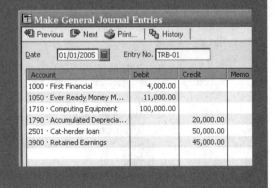

Creating General Journal Entries

In essence, every transaction you create in QuickBooks is a journal entry. When you write checks, the program balances the debits and credits behind the scenes.

To explicitly create QuickBooks general journal entries, you must first open the Make General Journal Entries dialog box using any of the following methods:

- Choose Company → Make General Journal Entries.

- If the "Chart of Accounts" window is open, right-click anywhere and then choose Make General Journal Entries.

- If the "Chart of Accounts" window is open, click Activities and then choose Make General Journal Entries.

Here are the basic steps for creating a general journal entry in QuickBooks:

1. **In the Make General Journal Entries dialog box, choose the date on which you want the general journal entry to occur.**

   Figure 13-2 shows you how it works.

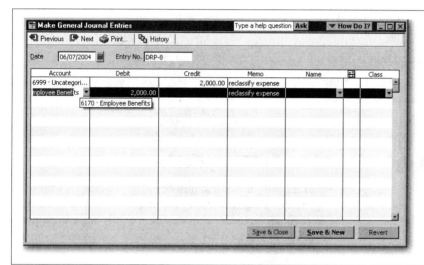

Figure 13-2:
If you're creating a general journal entry to reassign income or an expense to the correct account, you can use the date that you make the correction. However, when you or your accountant make end-of-year journal entries, for example, to add the current year's depreciation, it's common to use the last day of the fiscal year as the date.

2. **Although QuickBooks automatically assigns numbers to general journal entries, you can specify a different number. In the Entry No. box, type the entry number you want.**

   When you type a number, QuickBooks fills in the entry number for your next entry by incrementing the one you typed. For example, suppose your accountant adds several journal entries at the end of the year and uses the entry numbers ACCT-1, ACCT-2, ACCT-3, and so on. When you begin using the file again, you can type a number to restart your sequence, such as DRP-8. When you create your next journal entry, QuickBooks automatically fills in the Entry No. box with DRP-9.

You can also use words to indicate the type of journal entry you're creating. For example, you can label the journal entries that record payroll transactions for your outside payroll service with PAY.

Tip: If you don't want QuickBooks to number general journal entries automatically, you can turn off the automatic numbering preference in the Accounting preferences section (page 113).

---

3. **Fill in the first line of your general journal entry, which can be either a debit or a credit. For details about filling in each field in a general journal entry line, see the next section.**

   When you move to the next line, QuickBooks automatically enters the offsetting balance. For example, if the first line you enter is in the Debit column, QuickBooks helpfully enters the same amount in the Credit column in the second line.

4. **Fill in the second line of the general journal entry.**

   If your second line doesn't balance the debit and credit columns, continue adding additional lines until you've added debit and credit amounts that balance.

5. **When the debit and credit columns are the same, click Save & Close to save the general journal entry and close the Make General Journal Entries dialog box.**

   If you want to create another general journal entry, click Save & New.

Filling in General Journal Entry Fields

Each line of a general journal entry includes a number of fields, although for most general journal entries, the key fields are the Account field, either the Debit or Credit field, and the Memo field. But every field comes in handy at some point, so they're all worth knowing about. Here's what each field does and when you might fill them in:

- **Account.** Choose the account that you want to debit or credit. Every line of every general journal entry must have an assigned account.

- **Debit.** If you want to debit the account on the line, type the amount of the debit in this field.

- **Credit.** If you want to credit the account on the line, type the amount of the credit in this field.

- **Memo.** Entering a memo is a huge help when you go back to review your journal entries. For example, if you're reclassifying an uncategorized expense, type something like "Reclassify expense to correct account."

Note: In QuickBooks Premier and Enterprise editions, the Autofill preference (page 137) tells the program to fill each subsequent Memo field with the text from the first one.

- **Name.** If you're debiting or crediting an Accounts Receivable or Accounts Payable account, you must choose a name, as explained in the "Creating Opening Balances with Journal Entries" box on page 374. However, you might also fill in the Name field if you're creating a journal entry for billable expenses and want to assign the expenses to a customer.

- **Billable.** The column to the right of the Name column doesn't have a text heading, but the icon is meant to represent a flag for billable expenses. When you choose a name in the Name field, QuickBooks automatically adds the billable icon in the Billable field, as demonstrated in Figure 13-3. Leave this field alone when you create general journal entries to reassign some of your existing expenses to be billable to a customer.

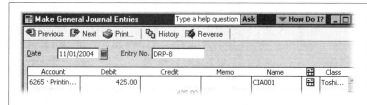

Figure 13-3:
If you don't want to make the value billable to the customer, in the Name field, click the billable flag to turn it off. QuickBooks indicates that the value isn't billable with a red X over the billable icon.

- **Class.** General journal entries are transactions just like checks and invoices, which means you should choose a class for each line to keep your class reports accurate. If you create a general journal entry to reassign income or expense to a different class, the Account on each line stays the same, but the class you choose is different.

Tip: You can use the Find feature to track down a journal entry. Choose Edit → Find. In the Find dialog box, select the Filter list and then choose Transaction Type. Next, in the transaction Type drop-down list, choose Journal. Click Find to display the journal entries you've created.

Checking General Journal Entries

If you stare off into space and start mumbling "Debit entries increase asset accounts" every time you create a general journal entry, it's wise to check that the general journal entry did what you wanted. Those savvy in the ways of accounting can visualize debits and offsetting credits in their heads, but for novices, thinking about the changes you expect in your profit and loss report or balance sheet is easier.

For example, if you plan to create a journal entry to reassign expenses in the Uncategorized Expenses account to their proper expense accounts homes, you'd expect to see the value in the Uncategorized Expenses account drop to zero while the values in the correct expense accounts increase. Figure 13-4 shows how you use a profit and loss report (see page 382) to check your general journal entries.

Tip: Some general journal entries affect both Balance Sheets and Profit & Loss reports. For example, as you'll see on page 379, a depreciation journal entry uses an asset account, which appears only in the Balance Sheet, and an expense account, which appears only in the Profit & Loss report. In situations like this, you'll have to review both reports to verify your numbers.

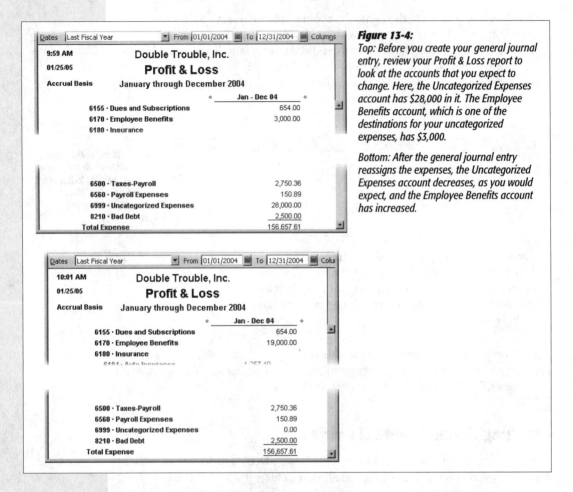

Figure 13-4:
Top: Before you create your general journal entry, review your Profit & Loss report to look at the accounts that you expect to change. Here, the Uncategorized Expenses account has $28,000 in it. The Employee Benefits account, which is one of the destinations for your uncategorized expenses, has $3,000.

Bottom: After the general journal entry reassigns the expenses, the Uncategorized Expenses account decreases, as you would expect, and the Employee Benefits account has increased.

Reclassifications and Corrections

As you work with your QuickBooks file, you might realize that you want to use different accounts. For example, as you expand the services you offer, you might switch from one top-level income account to several specific income accounts. Expense accounts are also prone to change—for example, when the Telephone account splits into separate accounts for landline service, wireless service, and Internet. For that matter, any type of account is a candidate for restructuring, as one building grows into a stable of commercial properties or you move from a single mortgage to a bevy of mortgages, notes, and loans.

Whether you want to shift funds between accounts because you decide to categorize your finances differently or you simply made a mistake, you're moving money between accounts of the same type. The benefit to this type of general journal entry is that you only have to think hard about one side of the transaction. As long as you pick the debit or credit correctly, QuickBooks handles the other side for you.

Debits and credits work differently for income and expense accounts, and Figure 13-5 shows you how to set them up for different types of adjustments.

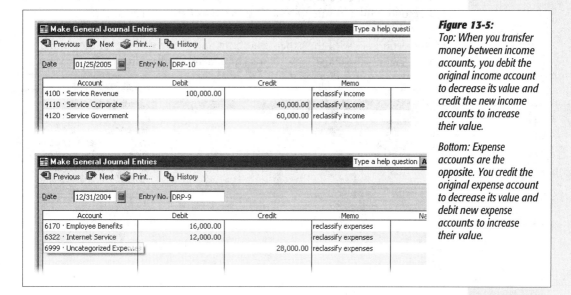

Figure 13-5:
Top: When you transfer money between income accounts, you debit the original income account to decrease its value and credit the new income accounts to increase their value.

Bottom: Expense accounts are the opposite. You credit the original expense account to decrease its value and debit new expense accounts to increase their value.

Accountants sometimes create what are known as *reversing journal entries*. These are general journal entries that move money in one direction on one date and then move the money back to where it came from on another date. Reversing journal entries are common at the end of the year, when you need your books configured one way to prepare your taxes and another way for your day-to-day bookkeeping.

Tip: It's easy enough to create two general journal entries, each using the same accounts, but with opposite assignments for debits and credits. In QuickBooks Premier Edition, the Make General Journal Entries dialog box includes a Reverse command, which automatically creates a reversing journal entry for you.

Depreciation

When you own an asset, such as the deluxe Cat-o-matic cat herder, the machine loses value as it ages and clogs with fur balls. *Depreciation* is an accounting concept, intimately tied to IRS rules, that reduces the value of the machine and lets your financial reports show a more accurate picture of the value of the assets you own.

But depreciation doesn't deal with hard cash, which is why you must create a general journal entry to enter depreciation. Unlike some other general journal entries with a wide choice of accounts, depreciation journal entries are easy to create, because the accounts you can choose are limited. The debit account is an expense account, usually called Depreciation Expense. (If you don't have a Depreciation Expense account, see page 36 to learn how to create it.) The offsetting account is another fixed asset account called Accumulated Depreciation.

For a depreciation general journal entry, you want to reduce the value of the fixed asset account and add value to the Depreciation Expense account. If you remember that debit entries increase the value of expense accounts, you can figure out that the debit goes with the expense account and the credit goes to the fixed asset account. Figure 13-6 shows how depreciation debits and credits work.

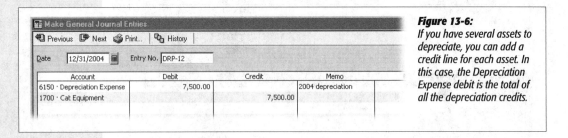

Figure 13-6:
If you have several assets to depreciate, you can add a credit line for each asset. In this case, the Depreciation Expense debit is the total of all the depreciation credits.

Working with Financial Statements

When you keep your company books day after day, all those invoices, checks, and other transactions blur together. But hidden within that maelstrom of figures is important information for you, your accountant, your investors—and the IRS. Consolidated and presented in the right ways, your books can tell you a lot about what your company does right, does wrong, could do better, and of course must pay to the Internal Revenue Service.

Over the years, the Financial Accounting Standards Board (FASB) has nurtured a standard of accounting known as GAAP (Generally Accepted Accounting Principles), which includes a triumvirate of financial statements that together paint a portrait of company performance: the income statement (also known as the Profit & Loss report), the balance sheet, and the statement of cash flows.

Generating financial statements in QuickBooks is easy—so easy, in fact, that you're likely to produce fodder for your paper shredder unless you understand what financial statements tell you, and you can spot suspect numbers. If you're new to business, get started by reading about what the three financial statements do. If you're already an expert, you can jump down to the section on generating these reports in QuickBooks (page 384).

Tip: These special financial reports are a must as you close out a year on your company books. You'll learn how financial statements fit into your year-end procedures in Chapter 15. If you're a business maven and know that there are plenty of other reports you need to manage your business, don't worry. All the reports that QuickBooks provides are described in Chapter 19, along with instructions for customizing reports to your demanding specifications.

The Profit & Loss Report

The Profit & Loss report is more like a video than a picture. It covers a period of time, usually a quarter or a year, and it shows whether your company is making money or hemorrhaging it.

Understanding the Profit & Loss Report

The money you make in sales sits at the top of the Profit & Loss report, gradually whittled away by your expenses until you're left with a profit or loss at the bottom. The Profit & Loss report in Figure 14-1 and the bullet points that follow explain the progression from sales to the net income your company earned after paying the bills.

- **Income.** The first category in a Profit & Loss report is income, which is simply the revenue your company generates by selling services and products to your customers. Regardless of how you earn revenue (selling services, products, or charging fees), the Profit & Loss report shows all the income accounts in your Chart of Accounts and how much you brought into each.

- **Cost of Goods Sold.** Unless you gather rocks from your yard and then sell them as authentic alien amulets, the products you sell carry some initial cost. For example, with products you purchase for resale, the cost is the original price you paid for them, the shipping costs you incurred to get them, and so on. In the Profit & Loss report, Cost of Goods Sold adds up the underlying costs associated with your sales.

Note: If you don't sell inventory items, you might not have a Cost of Goods Sold section. Most of the time, Cost of Goods Sold relates to the costs of buying materials and building the products you sell. But depending on the type of business, Cost of Goods Sold can include labor costs, product shipping, etc.

- **Gross Profit.** Gross profit is the profit you make after subtracting the Cost of Goods Sold. For example, if you sell equipment for $100,000 and you paid $60,000 to purchase that equipment, your gross profit is $40,000.

Tip: There is no question that sales are important. But the *percentage gross profit* you achieve is your first test of whether you're keeping up with your competitors. Compare the ratio of gross profit to sales to see if your company is in line with the industry. For example, in construction, gross profit between 40 and 60 percent is typical.

- **Expenses.** The next and longest section is for expenses—all the things you spend money on in the name of commerce, sometimes called *overhead*. For example, office rent, telephone service, and bank fees all fall into the overhead expense bucket. The name of the game is to keep these expenditures as low as possible without hindering your ability to make money.

• **Net Ordinary Income.** QuickBooks uses the term Net Ordinary Income to describe the money that's left over after you pay the bills. You've probably also run across this measure referred to as *net profit* or *net earnings*.

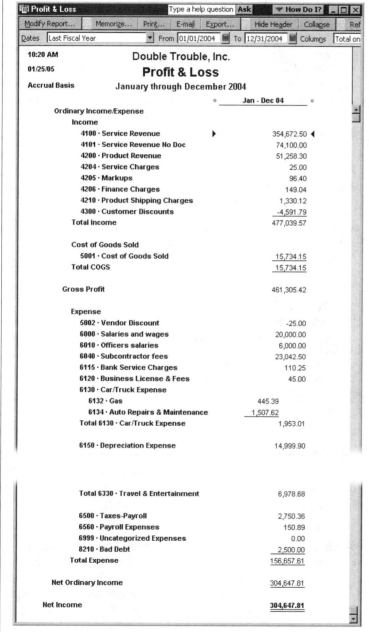

Figure 14-1:
If your company makes more money than it spends, your net income (also called net profit) is a positive number. Despite the report's name, QuickBooks doesn't label your result a loss when your company spends more than it makes; in the Profit & Loss Report, a loss shows up as a negative number for net income.

- **Other Income/Expense.** Income and expenses that don't relate to your primary business fall into the Other Income/Expenses category. The most common entrants are the interest income you earn from your savings at the bank or the interest you pay on your loans. In this category, income and expense are bundled together and offset each other. The result is called Net Other Income. For example, if you have only a smidgeon of cash in savings but a honking big mortgage, Net Other Income will be a negative number.

- **Net Income.** At long last, you reach the end of the report. Net Income is the money you have left after subtracting all the costs and expenses you incur. If Net Income is positive, your company made money. When Net Income is negative, your expenses were more than your income, and something's gotta give.

Generating a Profit & Loss Report

If you choose Reports → Company & Financial, QuickBooks gives you several built-in Profit & Loss reports to choose from. Choose Profit & Loss Standard to see a month-to-date report, which, if you've built your mom-and-pop shop into a merchandising monster, might be just the one you want.

But for many small companies, month-to-date numbers can be rather sparse. You can change the month-to-date report that QuickBooks produces into a year-to-date Profit & Loss report, as described in Figure 14-2.

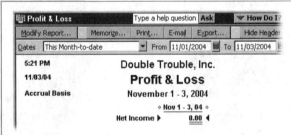

Figure 14-2:
If you see no numbers or very small numbers in your report, "This Month-to-date" in the Dates box could be the culprit. Particularly at the start of a month, you might not have any transactions to flesh out your report. If you choose "This Fiscal Year-to-date" in the Dates drop-down list, the dates in the From and To box change to the first of the year and today's date, respectively.

Other Profit & Loss Reports

Before you begin customizing reports, take a few minutes to see whether the built-in Profit & Loss reports fit the bill. Here's a guide to the other Profit & Loss reports on the Reports → Company & Financials menu and when you might use them:

- **Profit & Loss Detail.** Only the tiniest of companies—or the most persnickety of bookkeepers—uses this report regularly. The Profit & Loss Detail report is a year-to-date report that includes a separate line for every service and product you sold, every other charge that produced revenue, and every item on every bill you paid. It comes in handy when the numbers on your standard report seem a bit off and you want to find the culprit.

Tip: If you see numbers that are questionable in a Profit & Loss report, a closer inspection takes no more than a double-click of the number. QuickBooks displays a report with each transaction that contributed to the total (a Transaction Detail By Account report). When you spot the likely culprit in the detailed report, such as an invoice whose total looks too small, double-click the transaction to open the Create Invoices dialog box (or corresponding dialog box) to edit that transaction.

- **Profit & Loss YTD Comparison.** This report pits the Profit & Loss results for two periods side by side: the current month to date and the year to date. You might find a reason to run this report, but comparing a period to its predecessor from the previous year is usually more informative (see the next report), especially for seasonal businesses such as retail or landscaping.
- **Profit & Loss Prev Year Comparison.** If you own a gift shop, you know that sales are highest around the holidays. If you compare the last quarter of one year to the first quarter of the next, the Profit & Loss report would look pretty grim. Sales would be down and possibly exacerbated by returns from holiday purchases. To see whether your business is growing, compare your previous year to the current year with the report shown in Figure 14-3.

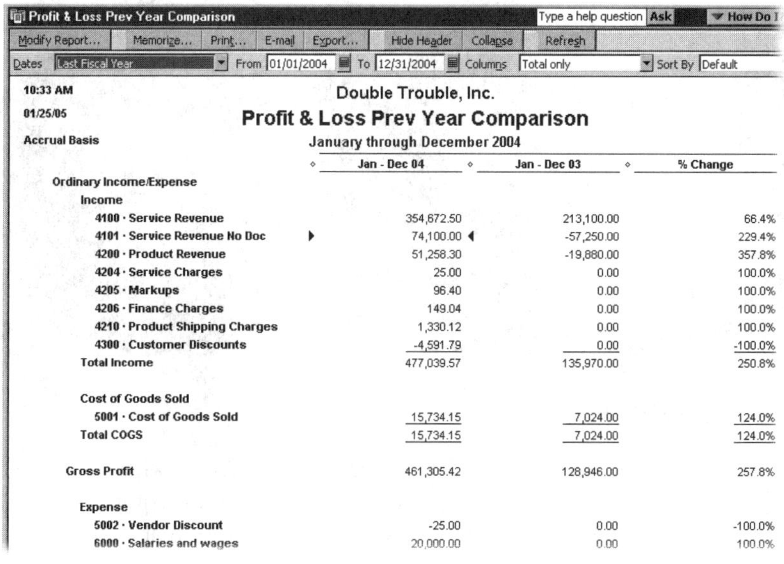

	Jan - Dec 04	Jan - Dec 03	% Change
Ordinary Income/Expense			
Income			
4100 · Service Revenue	354,672.50	213,100.00	66.4%
4101 · Service Revenue No Doc	74,100.00	-57,250.00	229.4%
4200 · Product Revenue	51,258.30	-19,880.00	357.8%
4204 · Service Charges	25.00	0.00	100.0%
4205 · Markups	96.40	0.00	100.0%
4206 · Finance Charges	149.04	0.00	100.0%
4210 · Product Shipping Charges	1,330.12	0.00	100.0%
4300 · Customer Discounts	-4,591.79	0.00	-100.0%
Total Income	477,039.57	135,970.00	250.8%
Cost of Goods Sold			
5001 · Cost of Goods Sold	15,734.15	7,024.00	124.0%
Total COGS	15,734.15	7,024.00	124.0%
Gross Profit	461,305.42	128,946.00	257.8%
Expense			
5002 · Vendor Discount	-25.00	0.00	-100.0%
6000 · Salaries and wages	20,000.00	0.00	100.0%

Figure 14-3: *The Profit & Loss Prev Year Comparison report sets the Dates box to "This Fiscal Year-to-date" and shows your results for the current year in the first column and those from the previous year in the second column. If you want to see where growth is strong or stagnant, include the columns that show the change in dollars or the change in percent (page 471).*

- **Profit & Loss by Job.** If you suspect that some of your customers and jobs are less profitable than others—and you want to learn from your mistakes—choose the Profit & Loss by Job report. In this report, each of your customers and jobs appears in its own column so you can compare how much you profit you made for each.

- **Profit & Loss by Class.** When you use classes to track performance for different business units or locations, use this report to produce a Profit & Loss report for each business entity. Each class has its own column. If you would rather generate a Profit & Loss report that shows only one class, modify the report to filter for that one class (see page 471). Unclassified is the label for last column in this report, which represents all the transactions that don't have a class assignment.

- **Profit & Loss Unclassified.** Before you pretty up and print your class-based Profit & Loss reports, display this one to see the numbers for transactions without class assignments. Depending on how you use classes, unclassified transactions might be perfectly acceptable. For example, if you track income by partner, overhead expenses aren't related to individual partners. You shouldn't see any non-zero values for income accounts, but expense accounts with non-zero values might appear.

WORKAROUND WORKSHOP

Making Year-to-Date Your Profit & Loss Standard

If you snort with displeasure every time QuickBooks displays a month-to-date Profit & Loss report, you *can* do something about it.

Memorizing reports is easy and saves you time and irritation. After you've memorized your ideal Profit & Loss report, you can choose it from one of the Reports submenus as easily choosing the program's built-in offerings. Here's how:

1. In the Profit & Loss report window, find the Dates drop-down list, and then choose the date range.

2. Make any other changes you want (see Chapter 19).

3. When you like the way the report looks, in the Profit & Loss window menu bar, click Memorize. QuickBooks opens the Memorize Report dialog box.

4. In the Memorize Report dialog box, type the name of the report. For example, for the year-to-date report, type something like "P&L Year-to-date."

5. To add the report to the Memorized Report list, click OK.

6. To view the report, choose Reports → Memorized Report → "P&L Year-to-date."

The Balance Sheet

A portrait analogy is more appropriate for the balance sheet, which shows how much you own (assets), how much you owe (liabilities), and the equity in the company. While a Profit & Loss report tells you whether you're making money, the balance sheet measures your company's financial strength.

Understanding the Balance Sheet

The funny thing about a balance sheet is that the total assets in the report always exactly balance the total of the liabilities and equity, as you can see in Figure 14-4. The key to a good-looking balance sheet is not having too much debt. How much is too much? If you closed up shop today and sold all your assets, would you have enough money to pay off your liabilities? If the answer is no, you'll have a hard time finding a bank to loan you more money. A balance sheet is strong when it shows a lot of assets but not many liabilities.

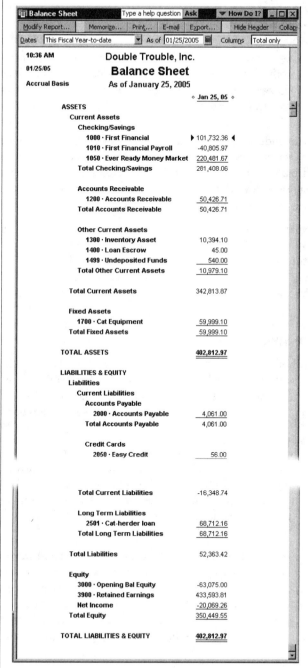

Figure 14-4:
This report earns its name because of math, not magic, and this is the formula that puts the balance into a balance sheet: Equity = Assets – Liabilities. As you buy more or borrow more, the value of your equity changes to make up the difference.

Here's what to look for in each section of a balance sheet:

- **Assets.** Assets are things of value that a company owns, such as equipment, land, product inventory, accounts receivable, cash, and even brand names. On a balance sheet, you want to see significantly more money in the asset section than in the liabilities section.

Tip: Even with assets, you can have too much of a good thing. Assets aren't corporate collectors' items. Companies should use assets to make money. Companies use a measure called return on assets (the ratio of net income to total assets) to see whether they're using assets effectively. Return on assets varies from industry to industry, but, typically, less than five percent is poor.

- **Liabilities.** Liabilities include accounts payable (bills you haven't yet paid), unpaid expenses, loans, mortgages, and even future expenses, such as pensions. Debt on its own isn't bad. It's *too much* debt that can drag a company down, particularly when business is slow. Debt payments are due every month whether your business produced revenue or not.

- **Equity.** Equity on a balance sheet is the corporate counterpart of the equity you have in your house. When you buy a house, your equity is the down payment you make. But both the increasing value of your house and the decreasing balance on your mortgage contribute to an increase in your equity. Equity in a company is the dollar value that remains after you subtract liabilities from assets.

Generating a Balance Sheet Report

A balance sheet is a snapshot of accounts on one date. The difference between the built-in balance sheet reports that QuickBooks offers is whether you see only account balances or all the transactions that make up those balances. Choose Reports → Company & Financial and you can choose any of the following reports on the menu:

- **Balance Sheet Standard.** This report includes every asset, liability, and asset account in your Chart of Accounts—unless the account has a zero balance. QuickBooks automatically sets the Dates box to "This Fiscal Year-to-date," so the report opens showing your balance sheet for the current date. If you want to see the balance sheet at the end of a quarter or end of the year, in the Dates box, choose This Fiscal Quarter or This Fiscal Year, respectively.

- **Balance Sheet Detail.** Printing the Balance Sheet Detail report is a good way to use up the last of your old printer paper, but it isn't that useful for managing your business. This report shows the transactions over a period in each of your asset, liability, and equity accounts. Should a number on your regular balance sheet report look odd, use this report to verify your transactions. Double-click the value for transactions to open the corresponding dialog box, such as Enter Bills.

- **Balance Sheet Summary.** If you want to see the key numbers in your balance sheet without scanning past the individual accounts in each section, this report shows subtotals for each category of a balance sheet, as shown in Figure 14-5.

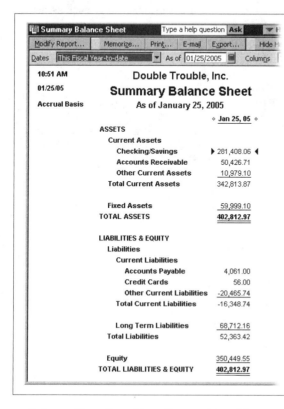

Figure 14-5:
For assets and liabilities, the summary report separates current assets from other assets. Current assets are those you can convert into quick cash to keep things going when business is slow. Similarly, liabilities can be either or current or long-term. Credit cards are current liabilities, since you must pay the bill each month. With long-term loans, the next twelve months of payments are current liabilities and the rest of the balance is long-term liability.

- **Balance Sheet Prev Year Comparison.** If you want to compare your financial strength from year to year, this report has four columns at your service: one each for the current and previous year, one for the dollar change, and the fourth for the percentage change.

Tip: When you review your Balance Sheet Prev Year Comparison report, you want to see decreasing liabilities. If liabilities have increased, then assets should have increased as well. You don't want to see more debt without more assets to show for the trouble. Equity is the value of your—and your shareholders'—ownership in the company, so it should increase each year.

The Statement of Cash Flows

Your balance sheet might look great—$10 million in assets and only $500,000 in liabilities. But if you don't have ready cash to pay your bills, you have a cash flow problem.

Understanding the Statement of Cash Flows

The concept of cash flow is easy to understand. In the words of every film-noir detective, follow the money. Cash flow is nothing more than the real money that flows in and out of your company—not the non-cash transactions, such as depreciation, that you see on a Profit & Loss report.

Figure 14-6 shows the three different sources of cash for companies.

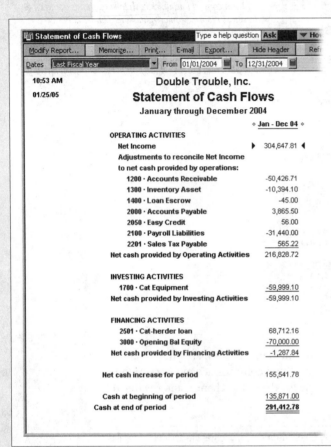

Figure 14-6:
Cash from operating activities is the most desirable. When a company's ongoing operations generates cash, the business can sustain itself without cash coming from other sources. Buying and selling buildings or making money in the stock market using company money are investing activities. Borrowing money or selling stock in your company brings cash in from outside sources. New companies often have no other source of cash.

Warning: When you sell an asset, which is an investing activity, it shows up as a gain or loss on the Profit & Loss report, which *temporarily* increases or reduces net income. Beware: the effect of investing activities on the Profit & Loss report can hide problems brewing in your operations, which is why you should examine the Statement of Cash Flows report. If your income derives mainly from investing and financing activities, instead of operating activities, you have a problem.

Generating a Statement of Cash Flows

To create a Statement of Cash Flows, QuickBooks deals the accounts that appear in your company's balance sheet into one of the three cash flow categories. And the program almost always gets those assignments right. Unless you're a financial expert or your accountant gives you explicit instructions about a change, you're better off leaving the QuickBooks account classifications alone.

Generating a Statement of Cash Flows is easy, because you have only one report to choose from. Simply choose Reports → Company & Financial → Statement of Cash Flows. QuickBooks creates the report (see Figure 14-6) with your cash flow for your fiscal year to date. To view the Statement of Cash Flows for a quarter or a year, in the Dates box, choose This Fiscal Quarter or This Fiscal Year.

Note: The Operating Activities section of the report includes the unfortunate label "Adjustments to reconcile Net Income to net cash provided by operations." QuickBooks calculates the net income at the top of the Statement of Cash Flows on an accrual basis (income appears as of the invoice date, not the day the customer pays). But the Statement of Cash Flows is by nature a cash-based report. So the program has to add and subtract transactions to get to net income on a cash basis.

POWER USERS' CLINIC

Expert Cash Flow Analysis

Thanks to today's accounting rules, cash isn't always connected to revenues and expenses. And a dollar in sales isn't necessarily a dollar of cash. Here's what financial analysts look for when they evaluate a company's health based on its statement of cash flows:

- If net income on the Profit & Loss report is close to the cash from operating activities, that means net income is mostly from business operations and the company can support itself.

- If cash from operations is growing at the same rate or faster than the growth of net income, that indicates that the company is maintaining or even improving its ability to sustain business.

- If cash is increasing, that means the company won't have to resort to financing to keep the business going.

- Negative cash flow is often the sign of a rapidly growing company—without financing, the company grows only as fast as it can generate cash from operations. If a company isn't growing quickly and still can't generate cash, something's wrong.

- If an increase in cash comes primarily from selling assets, the company future looks grim. Selling assets to raise cash sometimes mean the company can't borrow any more, because banks don't like what they see. Because assets often produce sales, selling assets means less cash generated in the future—and you can see where that leads.

The account assignments for the Statement of Cash Flows report are a collection of preferences you can find in the Preferences dialog box. If you want to view the account assignments or make change to them, here's how:

1. **Choose Edit → Preferences to open the Preferences dialog box.**

   In the icon bar, click Reports & Graphs, and then click the Company Preferences tab.

2. **Click Classify Cash.**

   QuickBooks opens the Classify Cash dialog box. As described in Figure 14-7, here's where you change your account categories.

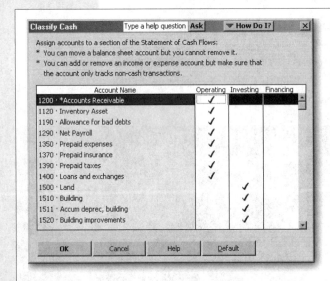

Figure 14-7:
To change the category to which an account belongs, click inside the cell in the column for the new category. If you made changes and fear you've mangled the settings beyond repair, click Default to reset the categories to the ones QuickBooks used initially.

3. **When the assignments are the way you want, click OK to close the dialog box.**

   That's it. You've reassigned the accounts.

Part Three:
Managing Your
Business

3

End-of-Year Tasks

As if your typical work day isn't hectic enough, the end of the year brings an assortment of additional bookkeeping and accounting tasks. As long as you've kept on top of your bookkeeping during the year, you can delegate most of the year-end tasks to QuickBooks with a few mouse clicks. (If you shrugged off your data entry during the year, even the mighty QuickBooks can't help.) This chapter describes how you employ QuickBooks for the most common tasks that companies perform at the end of the year.

Viewing the Trial Balance

The *Trial Balance* report is a holdover from the delightful days of paper-based accounting. The name refers to the report's original purpose: totaling the balances of every account in debit and credit columns to see whether pluses and minuses balanced. If they didn't, the bookkeeper had to track down the mistakes and *try* again.

QuickBooks doesn't make arithmetic mistakes, so you don't need a trial balance to make sure that debits and credits match. Nonetheless, the Trial Balance report is still handy. Accountants like to examine it for errant account assignments before diving into tax preparation or giving financial advice—and for good reason. The Trial Balance report is the only place in QuickBooks that you can see all your accounts *and* their balances in the same place, as illustrated in Figure 15-1.

Tip: If the account balances in your Trial Balance report look a little off, check the heading at the top left corner of the report. If you see the words "Accrual Basis" in the heading, but you use cash accounting for your business, you've found the culprit–likewise, if you see "Cash Basis" but use accrual accounting. To set things right, click Modify Report in the menu bar. In the Modify Report dialog box, choose the Accrual option or the Cash option, and then click OK.

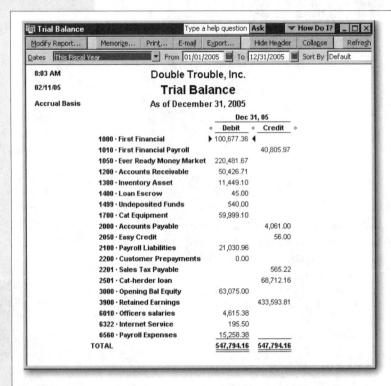

Figure 15-1:
To display the Trial balance report, choose Reports → "Accountant and Taxes" → Trial Balance. QuickBooks then generates a Trial Balance report for the previous month. If you want to see the trial balance for your entire fiscal year, in the Dates box, choose This Fiscal Year.

Generating Year-End Financial Reports

At the end of every year, tax preparation stimulates a frenzy of financial reporting as companies submit fiscal year Profit & Loss reports (page 382) and balance sheets (page 386) as part of their tax returns. But tax forms aren't the only reason for year-end reports. Before you hand over your company file to your accountant or prepare final reports for your tax return, run year-end reports for these reasons, too:

• Inspect year-end reports for funny numbers. They might mean that you posted a transaction to the wrong account or created a journal entry incorrectly.

• Analyze your annual results to spot problems with your operations or look for ways to improve.

After you complete your initial review of the year-end reports and make any corrections to transactions, your accountant (if you work with one) is next in line to
see your company file (page 399). If your accountant handles tax preparation, you
don't have to produce additional year-end reports. However, if you prepare your
company taxes, you'll generate another set of year-end reports *after* you've
inspected your results and corrected any mistakes.

The Year-End Profit & Loss Report

You'll need a Profit & Loss report for the entire fiscal year for your tax return.
Individuals receive W-2s to show how much money they made in a year. For *companies*, the Profit & Loss report shows the net income for the year. Whether you're
inspecting your report for accuracy or producing a report for taxes, here's how you
generate a Profit & Loss report for a fiscal year:

1. **Choose Reports → Company & Financial → Profit & Loss Standard.**

   QuickBooks opens the Profit & Loss window, which contains a report for the
   current month to date.

Tip: If you want to make a year-end Profit & Loss report as easy to access as the Profit & Loss Standard
report, memorize your year-end report as described on page 386.

---

2. **If the date on which you generate the report is within the fiscal year, in the
   Dates box, choose This Fiscal Year.**

   The program adjusts the dates as shown in Figure 15-2.

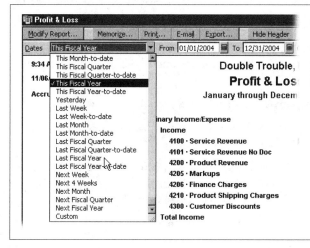

Figure 15-2:
*QuickBooks changes the date in the From box to
January 1 of the current year and the date in the To
box to December 31 of the current year. If you
generate the report after the end of the fiscal year, in
the Dates box, choose Last Fiscal Year.*

Even the most meticulous bookkeeper isn't likely to notice a few dollars missing from an account. But checking a report for glaring mistakes is worth the few minutes it takes. If you pay your taxes based on erroneous numbers and end up being audited, the ensuing tax penalties and interest are sure to cost more than the time you saved.

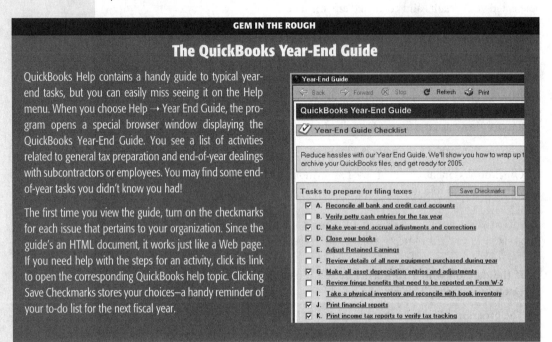

GEM IN THE ROUGH

The QuickBooks Year-End Guide

QuickBooks Help contains a handy guide to typical year-end tasks, but you can easily miss seeing it on the Help menu. When you choose Help → Year End Guide, the program opens a special browser window displaying the QuickBooks Year-End Guide. You see a list of activities related to general tax preparation and end-of-year dealings with subcontractors or employees. You may find some end-of-year tasks you didn't know you had!

The first time you view the guide, turn on the checkmarks for each issue that pertains to your organization. Since the guide's an HTML document, it works just like a Web page. If you need help with the steps for an activity, click its link to open the corresponding QuickBooks help topic. Clicking Save Checkmarks stores your choices—a handy reminder of your to-do list for the next fiscal year.

The Year-End Balance Sheet

A Balance Sheet report for the entire fiscal year also accompanies your tax return. Generating a Balance Sheet for a fiscal year is almost identical to generating a Profit & Loss report.

1. **Choose Reports → Company & Financial → Balance Sheet Standard.**

   QuickBooks opens the Balance Sheet window, which contains a report for the current year to date.

2. **If the date on which you create the report is within the fiscal year for the report, in the Dates box, choose This Fiscal Year. If you generate the Balance Sheet after the end of the fiscal year, choose Last Fiscal Year.**

   QuickBooks adjusts the dates, and you're good to go.

Note: Although a Statement of Cash Flows report (see page 389) isn't required for your corporate tax return, looking at cash flow can highlight financial problems before they snowball.

Generating Tax Reports

Whether your accountant has the honor of preparing your taxes or whether you keep that excitement for yourself, you can save accountant's fees and your own sanity by making sure your company file is ready for tax season. The key to a smooth transition from QuickBooks to tax preparation is linking each account in your Chart of Accounts to the correct tax line and tax form.

Check the tax readiness of your accounts by choosing Reports → Accountant & Taxes → Income Tax Preparation. QuickBooks displays a report showing every account, its type, and the tax line to which you assigned it (Figure 15-3).

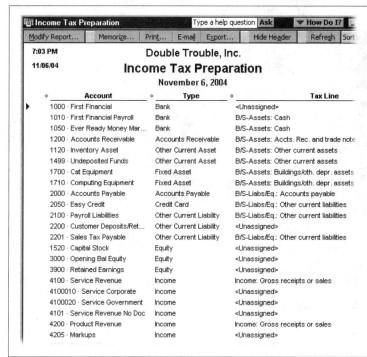

Figure 15-3:
If you see "Unassigned" in the Tax Line column, you'll have to assign a tax line to that account. To edit an account, press Ctrl+A to display the Chart of Accounts. Then select the account and press Ctrl+E to open the Edit Account dialog box. In the Tax Line entry drop-down list, choose the tax form for that account.

Sharing the Company File with Your Accountant

If you work with an accountant who uses QuickBooks, there are times when a tug of war over your company file is inevitable. You want to perform your day-to-day bookkeeping, but your accountant wants to review your books, correct mistakes you've made, enter journal entries to prepare your books for end-of-quarter or end-of-year reports, and so on. With a QuickBooks accountant's review copy, you and your accountant can stop squabbling, because you can each have your own copy of the company file.

Your accountant can work on the accountant's review copy in the comfort of his own office. You continue to work on your company file. When your accountant sends the updated accountant's review copy back to you, QuickBooks makes short work of merging your accountant's changes into the company file.

WORD TO THE WISE

Ways to Work with an Accountant

For most companies, QuickBooks is no substitute for an accountant. As financial professionals, accountants have the inside track on how best to monitor your business and keep you out of financial trouble. You can integrate your accountant's advice into your company file in several ways:

- **Working on-site.** An accountant can work on the company file right in your office with a login password from you. However, accountants are prone to doing things that require the company file to be in single-user mode, which might disrupt your day-to-day bookkeeping process.

- **The accountant's review copy.** For greatest ease and efficiency, create an accountant's review copy, as described below. Both you and your accountant can work on your own copies of the company file with only minor constraints.

- **A backup copy.** You can give your accountant *unrestricted* access to your company file by sending

her a backup copy of the file. When your accountant finishes evaluating your company file, you may have to make corrections or adjustments in your company file based on her recommendations. For example, your accountant can send you a document listing the journal entries you need to create to adjust your accounts. After you create those journal entries, your company file contains all of your transactions and the adjustments your accountant requested.

- **The paper method.** If your accountant prefers to work on paper (or doesn't use QuickBooks), you'll have to print the lists and reports that she requires. Then, when your accountant gives you a list of changes and journal entries, you make those changes in your company file.

In addition, QuickBooks Premier and Enterprise Editions include a remote access service, which lets your accountant access your QuickBooks company file over the Internet.

Creating an Accountant's Review Copy

Creating an accountant's review copy is a lot like creating a backup of your company file:

1. **Choose File → Accountant's Review → Create Accountant's Copy.**

   If several people work on the company file at the same time, you'll see a message that you must switch to single-user mode to create the accountant's review copy. Click OK to dismiss the message box. To switch to single-user mode, first make sure that everyone else logs out of the company file, and then choose File → Switch to Single-user Mode. Repeat step 1.

   QuickBooks displays a message that it must close all windows to create the accountant's review copy. Click OK. The program opens the Save Accountant's Copy To dialog box and automatically selects the folder in which you store your company files.

Tip: If you have a few dozen windows open and laid out just the way you want, there's no need to wail or gnash your teeth as QuickBooks undoes your window work. Before you create the accountant's copy, save the current window arrangement so the program can reopen all those windows for you (page 143).

Simply choose Edit → Preferences and, in the Preferences icon bar, click Desktop View. On the My Preferences tab, choose the "Save current desktop" option. If you would rather save the window layout that's active when you close the company file, choose the "Save when closing company" option instead.

2. **Choose the folder or media in which you want to save the copy.**

QuickBooks 2006 uses its new portable company file format (page 179) to create an accountant's review copy, so the resulting copy is small enough to email or save to a floppy disk or zip disk.

In the Save Accountant's Copy To dialog box, you can choose any drive or folder as the destination for your accountant's file, as illustrated in Figure 15-4. If you plan to email the accountant's review copy to your accountant or burn the file to a CD, the folder for your last backup file is as good a folder as any for your accountant's review copy.

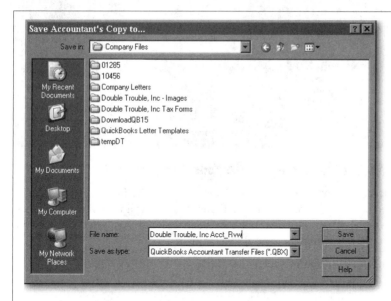

Figure 15-4:
QuickBooks automatically names the accountant's review copy using the company file name as the prefix and the extension .qbx (for QuickBooks Accountant Transfer File). As usual, you're free to edit the file name. To identify accountant's review copies more easily, you can append something like "Acct_ Rvw" to the end of the company name in the "File name" box.

3. **To create the accountant's review copy, click Save.**

To remind you that an accountant's review copy exists, in the QuickBooks program window title bar, you'll see the words Accountant's Copy Exists immediately after the company name.

Tip: If you use a password on your company file (and it's an excellent idea, no matter how tiny your company is), don't forget to tell your accountant the password for the administrator account.

FREQUENTLY ASKED QUESTION

Bookkeeping During Accountant's Review

Are there any limitations I should know about before I create an accountant's review copy?

QuickBooks locks parts of your company file when an accountant's review copy exists, so both you and your accountant must live with a few minor restrictions. Most of the taboo tasks can wait during the few weeks that your accountant has a copy of your file.

While you're sharing the company file, you can still create, edit, or delete transactions, so your bookkeeping duties are unaffected. You can also add entries to lists or edit the information in list entries. Here's what you *can't* do until you merge your accountant's changes:

- Delete an entry in a list.
- Rename or move an entry in a list.
- Change an account to a subaccount or vice versa.
- Rename an account.

Despite the file's name, your accountant can do more than review in the accountant's review copy. She can:

- View lists and transactions.
- Create journal entries.
- Adjust inventory values and quantities.
- Create reports and tax forms such as 941, 940, and W-2 forms.
- Print 1099 forms.
- Add, edit, and rename accounts.
- Add new items to the Item List and edit account and tax information for any item.

However, your accountant can't delete or make inactive any entries on your lists (because you might be using them), and she can't create any transactions other than journal entries (to prevent problems with automatic transaction numbering).

Merging Accountant Changes into Your Company File

When your accountant sends back your company file, the file extension changes from .qbx to .aif—which represents the file extension for an accountant's review copy import file. If you've imported data such as your customer records into QuickBooks, the following steps should be familiar:

1. **If your accountant sent you a CD or a disk, insert it into the appropriate drive on your computer. If your accountant sent the file as an email attachment, make sure to jot down the folder on your computer in which you saved the attachment.**

   If your company file isn't open, open it.

2. **Choose File → Accountant's Review → Import Accountant's Changes.**

   QuickBooks forces you to create a backup of your company file before you import your accountant's changes. Problems with data imports are always a possibility, so click OK to back up your file. After you complete the backup, the program automatically opens the Import Changes From Accountant's Copy dialog box.

3. **In the Import Changes From Accountant's Copy dialog box, navigate to the disk or folder that contains the accountant's file and double-click the file name.**

   QuickBooks imports your accountant's changes into your company file, but it won't tell you what those changes are. If your accountant didn't include a list of changes with the updated accountant's review copy, get on the phone and ask for one.

Tip: If your accountant has to correct some of your work, make a point of studying those corrections. Learning from your mistakes can translate into lower accountant's fees over the years.

Canceling an Accountant's Review Copy

From time to time, you might want to get rid of the accountant's review copy without importing any of the changes. For instance, you created an accountant's review copy by mistake or your accountant had so few changes that she told you the changes to make. Unlocking your company file so you can get back to performing any type of task requires nothing more than choosing File → Accountant's Review → Cancel Accountant's Changes. Click OK to confirm your action.

1099s

In QuickBooks, paying independent contractors is no different than paying other vendors. You enter bills from your independent contractors and then you pay those bills. No messy payroll transactions; no fuss with benefits or other regulatory requirements. But at the end of the year, you *do* have to generate 1099s for your independent workers.

If you set up QuickBooks to track 1099 payments (page 166) and your contractors as 1099 vendors (page 477), generating 1099s is a piece of cake. But before you push a stack of 1099 forms through your printer, it's a good idea to make sure your records are up-to-date and accurate.

Generating 1099 Reports

To review the amounts you've paid to 1099 vendors, choose Reports → Vendors & Payables, and then choose either of the following reports:

- **1099 Summary.** This report includes each vendor you've set up as a 1099 vendor and the total amount that you've paid the vendor. If any amount looks questionable, just double-click it to display the transactions for the vendor. Although the report lists only the vendors you set up as eligible for 1099 status, you can modify it to make sure you haven't left any 1099 vendors out, as demonstrated in Figure 15-5.

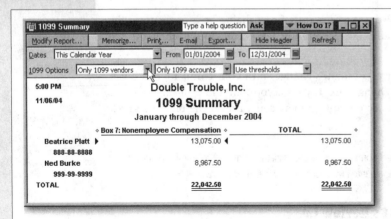

Figure 15-5:
The 1099 Summary report shows payments that you made to 1099 vendors through 1099 accounts. To make sure that you didn't forget to mark a vendor eligible for a 1099, in the 1099 Options drop-down list, choose All Vendors. To verify that you posted payments to the correct accounts, in the box that says, "Only 1099 accounts," in the drop-down list, choose "All allowed accounts."

Note: The federal government gives you the tiniest of breaks by setting thresholds for total payments to 1099 vendors. If you pay vendors less than the threshold, you don't have to generate 1099s for them. (For non-employee compensation, the threshold is currently $600.)

In the 1099 Summary report window, QuickBooks sets the last box for 1099 options to "Use thresholds." This choice filters the vendors in the report to those that exceed the government's threshold. If you want to see all of your 1099 vendors, regardless of what you paid them, in the third box, choose "Ignore thresholds."

• **1099 Detail.** If you pay your independent contractors on regular schedules, this report can pinpoint errors because it shows the transactions that produce the vendor's 1099 amount. If you see a gap in the payment schedule or two transactions in the same month, double-click a transaction amount to open the corresponding dialog box, such as Write Checks.

Printing 1099-MISC Forms

The steps to start printing 1099 forms are simple, but as with any printing task, fraught with nagging details:

1. **Load your printer with preprinted 1099-MISC forms.**

   1099-MISC and 1096 forms use special ink so government agencies can scan the forms. Intuit sells kits with preprinted 1099 forms. In your browser, navigate to *http://intuitmarket.intuit.com*. Then, under the 1099 Kits heading, click Learn More/Buy. You can also order 1099 forms directly from the IRS. Navigate to *www.irs.gov* and click the "Forms and Publications" link.

If you use a dot matrix printer, you might have to adjust the printer to handle the thickness of the multiple-copy forms.

Tip: If you use a printer that feeds individual sheets, don't bother placing a Copy 2 form after each Copy 1 form so that you can print multiple copies for each vendor. It's a lot easier to load the Copy 1 sheets and print a set of 1099 forms on those sheets and then load the Copy 2 forms and print a second set of 1099 forms. You'll send all the Copy 1 sheets to the 1099 vendors, while the Copy 2 sheets go to the government in one big batch.

---

2. **Choose Vendors → Print 1099s/1096.**

   QuickBooks opens the 1099 and 1096 Wizard, which makes it easy to verify your 1099 information before you begin printing.

3. **In the 1099 and 1096 Wizard, click Run Report to look at a Vendor 1099 Review report.**

   After QuickBooks runs the report, if you see vendors whose 1099 eligibility is incorrect, double-click their names to open the Edit Vendor dialog box and make changes.

4. **In step 2 of the 1099 and 1096 Wizard, click Map Accounts to review or modify your preferences for 1099 accounts.**

   QuickBooks opens the Preferences dialog box to the Tax:1099 section. On the Company Preferences tab, assign an account to each 1099 category that you issue 1099s for. For example, if you pay subcontractors for work, you can assign the account for subcontractors' fees to the Box7: Nonemployee Compensation 1099 category.

5. **In step 3 of the 1099 and 1096 Wizard, click Run Report to look at the 1099 Summary report.**

   This is your chance to make sure that you are printing 1099s for the right vendors and for the correct amounts.

6. **In step 4 of the 1099 and 1096 Wizard, click Print 1099s.**

   QuickBooks opens the "Printing 1099-MISC and 1096 Forms" dialog box with the date range set to the previous calendar year. If you're generating the forms during the calendar year, in the drop-down list for the top box, choose This Calendar Year.

7. **Click OK.**

   QuickBooks opens the "Select 1099s to Print" dialog box and automatically selects every vendor whose pay exceeds the government threshold. Besides columns for vendor name and total pay, the table in the dialog box includes the Valid ID and Valid Address columns. If you tend to create vendors on the fly without bothering to enter pesky details like their tax ID numbers or street address, scan these columns for the word No. If you see it in any cell, click Cancel and edit your vendors to add this essential information.

Tip: To add the tax ID or address to a vendor, on the Home page, click Vendors. In the Vendor Center on the Vendors tab, right-click a vendor and choose Edit Vendor. In the Edit Vendor dialog box, add the missing information (see page 110).

---

8. **When the Valid ID and Valid Address columns are awash with the word Yes, click Preview 1099 to see the final forms before they print.**

   In the Print Preview window, click Zoom In (if necessary) to verify the information. When you've reviewed the forms, click Close.

9. **Click Print 1099.**

   QuickBooks opens the Print 1099 window. If the preprinted forms are waiting in a printer other than the one that the program chose, in the "Printer name" box, choose the printer that holds your preprinted forms.

10. **Click Print.**

    Preprinted forms usually include Copy 1 for the vendor and Copy 2 for the government. But you'll also want a copy for your files. Instead of printing a third set of 1099s, run one of the printed sets through your copy machine or printer/scanner/copier.

Note: You can print 1099-MISC forms for up to 249 vendors. If you've got oodles more 1099 vendors—or even 250—the IRS requires you to file 1099 forms electronically. Bypass printing the forms in QuickBooks and use the government's hopefully easy-to-use system.

UP TO SPEED

Year-End Journal Entries

Journal entries run rampant at the end of the year. If your accountant makes journal entries for you or gives you instructions, you might be perfectly happy not knowing what these journal entries do. But if you go it alone, you need to know which journal entries to make.

For example, if you purchase fixed assets, you must create a general journal entry to handle depreciation. You might also create journal entries so you can produce accrual-based reports from your cash-based books.

If this book explained all the possible end-of-year journal entries, its mass might collapse it into a black hole. If you aren't an accounting expert, the cost of an accountant's services is piddling compared to the time it takes to research your journal entry needs. Chapter 13 explains how to create the most common journal entries.

Closing the Books for the Year

A few months after the end of a fiscal year, when tax returns rest fretfully under the gimlet-eyed scrutiny of the tax authorities, most companies close their books for the previous fiscal year. The purpose of closing the books is to lock the transactions for which you've already reported taxes or financial results, because the IRS and shareholders alike don't look kindly on changes to the reports they've received.

QuickBooks, on the other hand, doesn't care if you close the books in your company file. The closing task protects you from the consequences of changing the numbers in previous years (like altering the company file so that it no longer matches what you reported to the IRS). But you're free to keep your books open if you're not worried about editing older transactions by mistake. If you *do* close your books in QuickBooks, the program *still* gives you a way to edit transactions prior to the closing date. Unlike other bookkeeping programs in which closed means closed, in QuickBooks, people who know the closing date password can still change and delete closed transactions.

Note: Regardless of the fiscal year you use for your company, payroll and 1099 tasks run on a calendar year, because your employees and subcontractors pay taxes for a calendar year.

Closing the books in QuickBooks takes place in an unlikely location: the Preferences dialog box. Figure 15-6 shows you how.

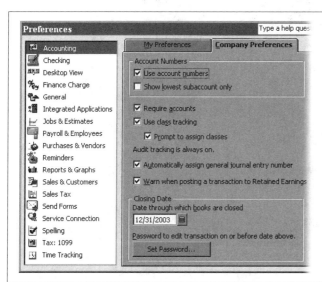

Figure 15-6:
Switch to single-user mode before you close your books. When everyone else has logged off, choose Edit → Preferences and, in the icon bar, click Accounting and then the Company Preferences tab. To close the books as of a specific date, in the "Date through which books are closed" box, type or select the last day of the previous fiscal year. Only a QuickBooks administrator can set the password for the closing date.

Once your books are closed for the year, most companies want to keep those transactions as they are unless there's an excellent reason to change them, such as an egregious error that you want to correct before you regenerate all of your end-of-year reports. If you want to allow only authorized people to make changes to the closed books, in the Edit Preferences dialog box, find the Accounting section, and then click Set Password. QuickBooks opens the Set Closing Date Password dialog box. In the Password box, type the password you want to assign (choose one that you can remember). Press Tab and, in the Confirm Password box, type the password a second time.

Tip: Don't cut and paste the password from the Password box to the Confirm Password box. These boxes display asterisks instead of the actual characters, which means you can't see typographical errors. If you set a password with a typo in it, you'll be unlikely to stumble on the correct password, and your closed books will remain shut as tight as a clam.

After you've set a password for the closing date, you'll have to enter that password whenever you want to modify transactions prior to the closing date. For example, if you try to edit a check that you wrote before the closing date, QuickBooks opens a message box with a Password box in it. Type the closing date password and click OK to complete your edit.

Tip: After you've completed all your QuickBooks year-end activities, create a backup of your company file (page 168). With all the data that contributed to your financial reports and tax forms in this backup, you're not going overboard by creating two copies of the backup: one to keep close by in your office and one stored safely off-site in case of emergency.

Managing Inventory

As you record inventory purchases and sales in QuickBooks, the program keeps track of your inventory behind the scenes, just as the point-of-service systems at the grocery stores do when a cashier scans the items you buy. The seemingly automatic tracking in QuickBooks isn't truly automatic. This chapter begins by reviewing the setup tasks you need to do to make the program work its magic.

Good inventory management comprises more than updating the number of items that QuickBooks thinks you have on hand. To keep the right number of items in stock, you need to know how many you have on hand, how many you've sold, and how many are on order. Making decisions like how much to charge or which vendor to use means evaluating your purchases and the prices you pay for your inventory. In this chapter, you'll learn how to make the most of the inventory reports that QuickBooks provides.

Another important yet trying aspect of inventory is keeping your records in QuickBooks in sync with what's sitting on the shelves in your warehouse. Inventory can go missing due to theft and damage of all kinds, so you might not have as many products in stock as you think you do. QuickBooks can't help all that much with the dusty business of rifling through boxes and counting products. But after the counting is complete, QuickBooks *can* help you adjust its records to match the reality in your warehouse. Adjusting inventory works for more than inventory counts. You can use this process to write off inventory that you *do* have in your warehouse but can't sell because it's dented, dirty, or too darned ugly.

The QuickBooks Inventory Process

Before you look at the tools that QuickBooks offers to manage your inventory, here's a quick review of how QuickBooks tracks inventory as you buy and sell products.

Setting Up Inventory Items

As you learned in Chapter 4, you set the stage for tracking when you create inventory items in QuickBooks. Items in your Item List contain purchase costs, sales prices, and accounts, all of which direct the right amount of money into the right income and expense accounts as you buy and sell inventory.

Here are the fields in an item record that QuickBooks uses to track your inventory:

- **Cost.** What you pay for one unit of the item.

- **Sales Price.** The price you typically charge for the item (for the same number of units represented in the Cost field).

- **Asset Account.** The asset account in which you want to store the value of the inventory you buy.

- **Income Account.** The account to which you want to post the income you receive when you sell this item.

- **COGS Account.** The account to which you want to post the item's cost when you sell it.

Note: As you sell inventory, QuickBooks deducts dollars from the inventory asset account and adds them to the cost of goods sold account. For a refresher on how inventory postings work, see the box on page 81.

TROUBLESHOOTING MOMENT

Working with Seasonal Items

The Item List is home to items for every service and product you sell, and it can grow lengthy, particularly when you sell different items at different times of the year.

For example, if you stock your store with lawn chairs in the spring, you don't want to scroll past dozens of outdoor items the other nine months of the year. Meanwhile, Quick-Books' reminders about reordering seasonal items quickly turn from helpful to irritating. For relief, you can make seasonal sellers inactive, which removes them temporarily from the Item List and silences the reminders.

To make an item inactive, in the Item List window (press Ctrl+I to open), right-click the item and choose Make Item Inactive from the shortcut menu.

When you want to reactivate the item, at the bottom of the Item List window, turn on the "Include inactive" checkbox. QuickBooks displays a column with an X as its heading and each inactive item sports an X in that column.

To reactivate the item, click the X next to its name. If the item includes subitems, in the Activate Group dialog box, click Yes to reactivate the item and all its subitems.

When you sell your time, you can always try to squeeze another work hour into your day. But when you run low on inventory, the only solution is to buy more. For products that you keep in stock, knowing how many copies you have on hand is essential. QuickBooks keeps a running total of how many units you've purchased and how many you've sold. The difference between these two numbers conveniently tells you how many should be in your warehouse. The running total of inventory on hand stays with the item in your Item List, as Figure 16-1 shows.

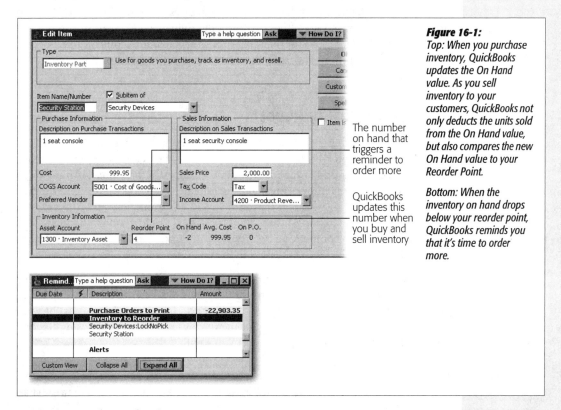

Figure 16-1:
Top: When you purchase inventory, QuickBooks updates the On Hand value. As you sell inventory to your customers, QuickBooks not only deducts the units sold from the On Hand value, but also compares the new On Hand value to your Reorder Point.

Bottom: When the inventory on hand drops below your reorder point, QuickBooks reminds you that it's time to order more.

The number on hand that triggers a reminder to order more

QuickBooks updates this number when you buy and sell inventory

Ordering and Purchasing Inventory

Unless you practice just-in-time inventory management, you need inventory in your warehouse to fill customer orders. Chapter 10 explains how to order inventory and then pay for the inventory you receive.

Companies typically create purchase orders for inventory products they buy (page 283). These business forms don't change anything in your QuickBooks company file (thus, they're called *non-posting transactions*). But they're useful for verifying that the shipments you receive match what you ordered—not unlike opening a pizza box before you leave the parlor to make sure you didn't get an anchovy and garlic pizza by mistake.

When you receive a shipment, you record it in QuickBooks, so you know that you have products to sell. The program increases the number of products on hand by the number in the shipment and adds the value of the shipment to the inventory asset account.

Selling Inventory

Finally, when you sell some of your inventory, the income makes all your bookkeeping seem worthwhile. When you create invoices, sales receipts, or other sales forms (see Chapter 8), QuickBooks deducts the units you sold from the item's On Hand value. The income from the sale posts to an income account, while the cost of the units you sold moves from the inventory asset account to a cost of goods sold account.

Running Inventory Reports

Checking the vital signs of your inventory is the best way to keep it healthy. When products are hot, you have to keep them in stock or you'll lose sales. And, if products grow cold, you don't want to get stuck holding the bag, box, or lime-green luggage. For all other temperatures, most companies keep tabs on inventory trends and compare them to what's going on in sales. For example, when the value of your inventory is increasing faster than sales, sales could be poor because your prices are too high, competition is encroaching on your market, or the Salvador Dali Chia Pets simply didn't take hold in the market.

Good inventory management means keeping enough items in stock to meet your sales, but not so many that your inventory grows obsolete before you can sell it. The inventory reports in QuickBooks aren't fancy, but they tell you most of what you need to know. You can run any of the inventory reports by choosing Reports → Inventory and then picking the report you want.

Tip: The QuickBooks inventory reports show only the active inventory items in your Item List. If you run inventory reports without reactivating all your inventory items (page 410), the inventory values in the reports won't be correct.

On the contrary, financial statements such as the Balance Sheet include your total inventory value for active and inactive inventory items alike.

Inventory Valuation: How Much Is Inventory Worth?

QuickBooks includes two reports that tell you how much your inventory is worth: the Inventory Valuation Summary and Inventory Valuation Detail.

Note: Prior to QuickBooks 2006, Inventory Valuation reports didn't let you change any of their columns. But now you can customize inventory reports (page 492) in the same ways as other types of reports.

The Inventory Valuation Summary report

The Inventory Valuation Summary report, shown in Figure 16-2, is a tidy over-view of the inventory you have on hand, what it's worth as an asset, and what it's worth when you sell it. The first column in these reports contains the names of the inventory items from your Item List. Subitems appear indented beneath their parent items. QuickBooks uses the current month-to-date for the date range for this report.

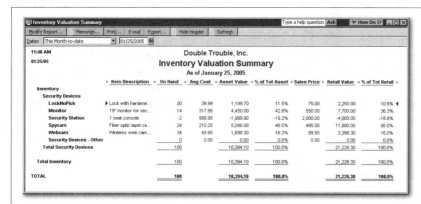

Figure 16-2:
Because the report is a snapshot of inventory value, Month-to-date, Quarter-to-date, and Year-to-date ranges all produce the same results. But if you want to see the inventory value as of a different date, in the To box, choose the date you want.

TROUBLESHOOTING MOMENT

When Inventory Loses Value

Inventory Valuation reports show the value of your inventory based on the average cost that you paid for your items. But that inventory value doesn't always tell the whole story.

If you have several cartons of (oh so passé) women's stirrup pants, the *true* value of that inventory is worthless. Although admitting that you made a mistake is painful, writing off that inventory as unsellable turns the inventory into a business expense, which reduces your net profit and, therefore, the taxes you pay.

In QuickBooks, you can write off obsolete inventory with an inventory adjustment (page 418). To remove the inventory from your QuickBooks item record, you change both the quantity on hand and the asset value to zero.

In the "Adjust Quantity/Value on Hand" dialog box (choose Vendors → Inventory Activities → Adjust Quantity/Value on Hand), choosing an expense account, such as Unsalable Inventory, as the Adjustment Account moves the value of the inventory from the inventory asset account into an expense account.

Here're the other columns in the report and why they are (or aren't) important to inventory health:

- **Item Description.** This is the description that you entered in the item record in the "Description on Purchase Transactions" box. A description doesn't help manage your inventory, but it does identify which inventory item you're looking at, particularly when you use part numbers or abbreviations for item names.

- **On Hand.** To calculate the On Hand value, QuickBooks subtracts the number of products that you sold from the number of products that you received. You can quickly check for items that are close to being out of stock. However, items sell at different rates, so the reorder point reminder is a better indication that something is perilously close to selling out.

Tip: When you add an item that is out of stock to an invoice, QuickBooks warns you but doesn't prevent you from selling products you don't have. When the On Hand value is negative, you know it's time to order more—and to ask for express shipping. Negative numbers can also remind you to receive inventory items (page 288) in QuickBooks.

- **Avg Cost.** Average cost is the only method of valuing inventory that QuickBooks can handle. QuickBooks uses the price you paid for every unit you've purchased to calculate the average cost of an inventory item. If you want to watch price trends so you can adjust your sales prices accordingly, review your most recent bills for inventory purchases.

- **Asset Value.** Asset Value is the average cost multiplied by the number on hand. Although changes in asset value over time are more telling, a snapshot of asset value can show trouble brewing. An excessive asset value for one item is one sign that inventory might be obsolete—the item hasn't sold, so you have too many on hand. If you know that the item *is* selling, streamlining your purchasing process can reduce the number you need to keep on hand.

- **% of Tot Asset.** This column shows the percentage of an item's asset value compared to the total asset value of all inventory items. Higher percentages might mean that a product is not selling well and you have too much in stock, but higher percentages can also mean a product is a significant part of your sales strategy. This measurement has meaning only in light of your business strategy and performance.

- **Sales Price.** This is the price you set for the item in the item record, which is meaningless if you regularly change the item's price or charge different prices to different customers. If you didn't set a sales price for an item, you'll see 0.00 in the report.

- **Retail Value.** Because the retail value is the sales price multiplied by the number on hand, this value is useful only if the value in the Sales Price column is the typical sales price for the item.

- **% of Tot Retail.** This is the percentage that the item's retail value represents of your total inventory retail value. Different products sell at different profit margins, which you can see when the retail percentage differs from the asset value percentage.

The Inventory Valuation Detail report

The Inventory Valuation Detail report lists every transaction that increases or decreases the number of items you have on hand. Although it can grow lengthy, this report can help you figure out where your inventory went (and perhaps jog your memory about inventory transactions that you forgot to add in QuickBooks). As in other reports, you can double-click a transaction to see its details.

Inventory Stock Status

As you might expect, Inventory Stock Status reports tell you where your inventory stands today and how that will change based on your outstanding purchase orders. The Inventory Stock Status by Item report is a great place to see which inventory items you need to reorder, as Figure 16-3 shows.

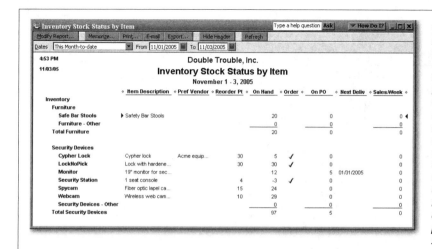

Figure 16-3:
For every active inventory item, the Inventory Stock Status by Item report shows you the reorder points (in the Reorder Pt column), the number you have on hand (On Hand), and how many are available to sell (Available). However, a checkmark in the Order column is the most obvious signal that you need to reorder. If you added an item to a purchase order, you can see whether that shipment is enough to restock your warehouse.

Tip: If you upgrade to QuickBooks Premier or Enterprise, the Inventory Stock Status reports also show how many items you've added to sales orders for future delivery.

The Inventory Stock Status by Vendor report shows the same information, but groups and subtotals items by vendor. If you seem to run low on products from a particular vendor, you might want to increase the reorder point for those products to fine-tune your lead time.

Viewing One Inventory Item

To see what's going on with one inventory item only, the Inventory Item Quick-Report is a fast yet thorough solution. In the Item List window, select the item you want to review and press Ctrl+Q. (You can generate the same report in the Item List window by clicking Reports and choosing QuickReport:<*item name*>.)

The Inventory Item QuickReport includes purchase and sales transactions for the item (Figure 16-4). In the On Hand As Of section, invoice transactions represent the sales you've made to customers, so the numbers are negative. Bills are your vendor purchases, which increase the number on hand. The On Purchase Order As Of section includes the number of products you've ordered but have not yet received. At the bottom of the report, the TOTAL As Of number tells you how many products you'll have in stock when all your purchase orders are filled.

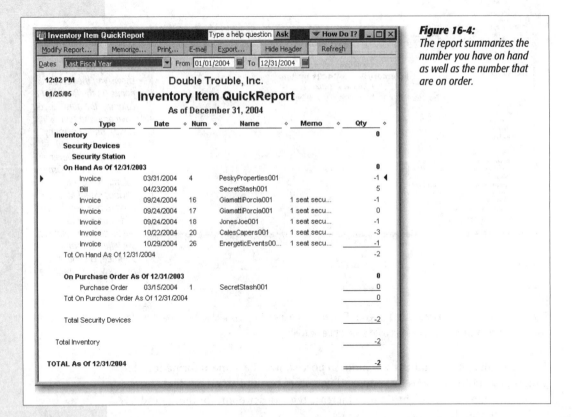

Figure 16-4:
The report summarizes the number you have on hand as well as the number that are on order.

Performing a Physical Inventory

Although QuickBooks can calculate how many products you have on hand based on your purchases and sales, it has no way of knowing what's happening back at your warehouse. Employees help themselves to products; fire consumes some of your inventory; or a burst pipe turns your India ink sketches into Rorschach tests.

Only a physical count of the items you keep in stock tells you how many units you *really* have to sell.

QuickBooks does the only thing it can to help you count your inventory—it provides the Physical Inventory Worksheet report, which lists each inventory item in your Item List and how many units should be on hand. To see it, choose Reports → Inventory → Physical Inventory Worksheet.

The Physical Count column has blank lines, so you can write in how many you find in storage. As you can see in Figure 16-5, the Physical Inventory Worksheet includes columns that have nothing to do with physically counting your inventory. If you want to nix those columns, you have to export the worksheet to Excel, as described in the figure.

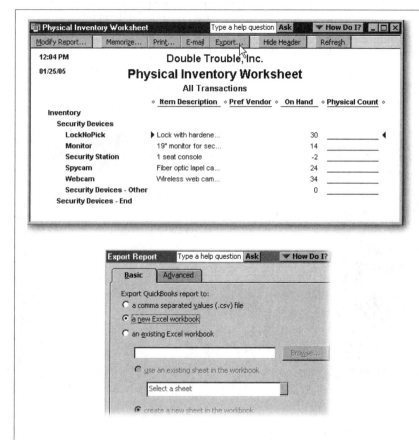

Figure 16-5:
Top: Your preferred vendor has nothing to do with counting inventory, yet the column appears on the Physical Inventory Worksheet. Unfortunately, you can't modify the columns that appear. Nor can you sort the inventory items, for instance to list them by the warehouse aisle in which they reside. To create a worksheet with only the columns you want and with inventory items listed in the order you want, in the icon bar, click Export.

Bottom: In the Export Report dialog box, choose "a new Excel workbook" or "an existing Excel workbook." When you click Export, QuickBooks opens the report in Excel. After you've made the changes you want, be sure to choose File → Save As to name the file and select the folder in which to save it.

Adjusting Inventory in QuickBooks

As you probably know, inventory can succumb to breakage, theft, and the damage caused by a paint ball fight in the warehouse. When these accidents occur, the first response is to report the loss to your insurance company. Adjusting the quantity of inventory in QuickBooks follows close behind. Similarly, if you have inventory that you can't sell, such as personal computers with 10 megabytes of disk space and 11-inch monitors, adjust the inventory in QuickBooks when you take the computers to the recycling center.

An inventory adjustment is also in order after almost every physical inventory count you perform, because the quantities for inventory in the real world rarely match the quantities in QuickBooks. *Shrinkage* is the polite name for the typical cause of these discrepancies. To be blunt, employees, repair people, and passersby attracted by an unlocked door may help themselves to a five-finger discount. And you not only take the hit to your bottom line, but you're stuck adjusting your QuickBooks records to account for the theft.

It's no surprise, then, that QuickBooks has a command for this multipurpose accounting task. Adjusting both the quantity of inventory and its value takes place in the aptly named "Adjust Quantity/Value on Hand" dialog box.

TROUBLESHOOTING MOMENT

Freezing Inventory While You Count

It's sheer madness to ship customer orders out and receive inventory shipments while you're trying to count the products you have on hand. QuickBooks doesn't offer a feature for freezing your inventory while you perform the physical count, but you can follow procedures to accomplish the same thing.

Because a physical inventory count disrupts business operations, most companies schedule it during slow periods and off hours. To keep the disruption to a minimum, print the Physical Inventory Worksheet just before you start the count. Then, until the count is complete, do the following to keep the inventory stable:

- **Sales.** In QuickBooks, create invoices for inventory sales as you would normally, but store these invoices in a special folder. When the count is complete, fill the orders and send the invoices.

- **Purchases.** If you receive inventory shipments during the count, don't unpack the boxes until you've completed the physical count. In QuickBooks, don't use any of the commands for receiving inventory (page 283).

Fiddling with inventory that you already own might not seem like a vendor-related task, but QuickBooks keeps all inventory commands in the same place—the Vendors menu. To open the "Adjust Quantity/Value on Hand" dialog box, choose Vendors → Inventory Activities → Adjust Quantity/Value on Hand. You can adjust the inventory item quantities and let QuickBooks calculate the dollar value, or you can control both quantity and value, as shown in Figure 16-6.

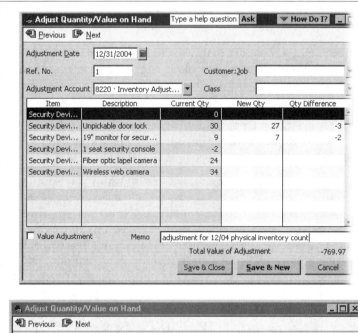

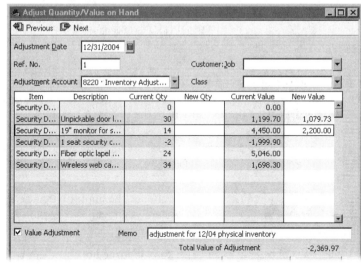

Figure 16-6:
Top: When QuickBooks opens the "Adjust Quantity/Value on Hand" dialog box, the Value Adjustment checkbox is turned off. All you have to enter are the quantities for your inventory items to match what's in your warehouse or to reflect inventory you're writing off. QuickBooks uses the average cost of each inventory item to calculate the dollar value that the new quantities represent.

Bottom: By turning on the Value Adjustment checkbox, you can enter actual values to mimic last in, first out or first in, first out costing (see page 421).

Adjusting Quantities

When you adjust inventory quantities, QuickBooks fills in or calculates some of the fields for you. Here are guidelines for filling in the remaining fields of the "Adjust Quantity/Value on Hand" dialog box when the Value Adjustment checkbox is turned off:

- **Adjustment Date.** QuickBooks fills in this box with the current date. If you like to keep your journal entries and other bookkeeping adjustments together at the end of a quarter or year, type the date on which you want to record the adjustment.

- **Ref. No.** QuickBooks doesn't require a reference number, but they come in handy when discussing your books with your accountant. QuickBooks increments the number in this box by one each time you adjust inventory.

- **Adjustment Account.** Choose an expense account to which you want to post the cost of the inventory adjustment. For example, if you adjust the quantity of an item to match the physical count, choose an account such as Inventory Adjustment. If you're writing off obsolete or damaged inventory, choose an expense account, such as Unsalable Inventory. Because you can assign only one account to each inventory adjustment, create one adjustment for physical count changes, and then click Save & New to start an adjustment for write-offs.

Tip: If the expense account that you want to use doesn't exist, choose *<Add New>*. In the New Account dialog box, fill in the boxes. When you click OK, QuickBooks fills in the Adjustment Account box with the account you just created.

- **Customer:Job.** If you want to send products to a customer or job without adding the items to an invoice, choose the customer or job in this drop-down list. QuickBooks assigns the cost of the adjustment to the customer or job.

Tip: A better way to give products to a customer or job is to add them to an invoice with a price of $0.00. Your generosity remains on the record lest your customer forgets.

- **Class.** If you use classes to track your sales, choose the appropriate one. For example, if one partner handles sales for the item you're adjusting, choose the class for that partner so the expense applies to that class.

- **New Qty.** When the Value Adjustment checkbox is turned off, you can type a number in either the New Qty or the Qty Difference cell, as you can see in the top image in Figure 16-6. If you're making an adjustment due to a physical count, in the New Qty cell, type the quantity from your physical count worksheet. On the other hand, if you know you lost four cartons of *Chivalry Today* magazine in a sprinkler head malfunction, it's easier to type the number you lost (such as *–400*) in the Qty Difference cell.

Tip: If you're ready to admit that the pet rock fad isn't coming back, you can write off your entire inventory by filling in the New Qty cell with *0*. In the Adjustment Account drop-down list, choose an expense account, such as Unsalable Inventory.

- **Memo.** To prevent questions from your accountant, in the Memo cell, type the reason for the adjustment, such as "2005 end-of-year physical count."

After you fill in all the boxes, click Save & Close or Save & New. If you decrease the quantity on hand, QuickBooks decreases the balance in your inventory asset account (using the average cost per item). To keep the double-entry bookkeeping principles intact, the decrease in the inventory asset account shows up as an increase in the expense account you chose.

Note: If the adjustment increases the quantity or value of your inventory, your inventory asset account balance increases and the balance in the expense account decreases.

Adjusting Quantities and Values

Calculating inventory value using the average cost for your items is convenient. But other methods for calculating inventory, such as first in, first out and last in, first out come in handy as well (see the box below). Because QuickBooks can handle only average cost for inventory, your sole workaround for achieving LIFO or FIFO costing is to adjust dollar values in the "Adjust Quantity/Value on Hand" dialog box.

UP TO SPEED

LIFO and FIFO Inventory Costing

First in, first out costing means that a company values its inventory as if the first products it receives are the first ones it sells. (Your grocery store always puts the milk closest to expiration at the front of the refrigerator, doesn't it?)

Last in, first out costing assumes that the last products in are the first ones sold. This method is like unpacking a moving van. The last valuables you packed in the truck are the first ones that come out.

The costing method that a business uses doesn't have to match the order in which it sells products. When you start your business, you can choose a costing method (but you have to stick with it). For example, when prices are on the rise (as they almost always are), last in, first out costing reduces your profit and taxes owed because you're selling the products that cost the most first. Unless you're sure which method you want to use, you're better off asking your accountant for advice on this matter.

Unfortunately, even with the Adjust Quantity/Value On Hand dialog box, you can't achieve true LIFO or FIFO costing in QuickBooks. The program still uses average cost to move money from your inventory asset account to your cost of goods sold account when you add products to an invoice or sales receipt.

When you turn on the Value Adjustment checkbox, QuickBooks displays the Current Value and New Value columns. To adjust the value of an item in inventory, in the New Value column, type the dollar value of the inventory. For example, to write off your entire inventory of pet rocks, in the New Value cell, type *0.00*.

Mimicking LIFO or FIFO costing takes some effort because you have to review the bills for all your purchases of the inventory item. Here's what you have to do to value your inventory using LIFO:

1. **Choose Reports → Purchases → Purchases by Item Detail.**

   QuickBooks generates a report that shows your purchase transactions grouped by inventory item.

2. **For the quantity of the item that you have on hand, add up the prices you paid for your earliest purchases, as illustrated in Figure 16-7.**

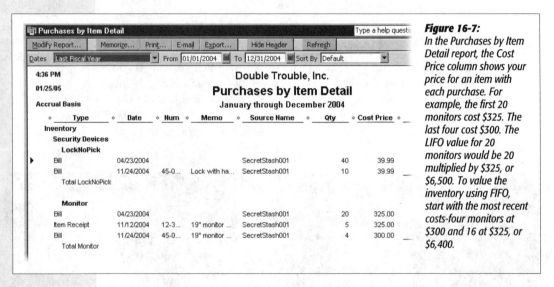

Figure 16-7:
In the Purchases by Item Detail report, the Cost Price column shows your price for an item with each purchase. For example, the first 20 monitors cost $325. The last four cost $300. The LIFO value for 20 monitors would be 20 multiplied by $325, or $6,500. To value the inventory using FIFO, start with the most recent costs-four monitors at $300 and 16 at $325, or $6,400.

3. **In the "Adjust Quantity/Value on Hand" dialog box in the New Value cell, type the amount you just calculated.**

   When you click Save & Close, QuickBooks decreases the balance in your inventory asset account using the value in the New Value cell instead of the average cost per item.

Tracking Time and Mileage

Services that you sell often boil down to time spent. Customers might pay for services, but they're really buying your knowledge of how to get something done and your experience doing it in the best or fastest possible way. That's why a carpenter who can barely hit the nail on the head charges $15 an hour, whereas a master who hammers faster and straighter than a nail gun charges $80 an hour.

If you charge by the hour, you know time is money, so you want to keep track of both with equal accuracy. But product-based companies track time, too. For example, companies that want to increase productivity often start by tracking the time that employees work and what they work on.

There are hordes of off-the-shelf and home-grown time tracking programs out there, and Intuit enters the fray with several ways to get time data into your company file. QuickBooks' time tracking isn't fancy. But for companies with simple time tracking needs, the advantage of this feature is that the time you record is ready to attach to an invoice (see Chapter 8) or payroll (see Chapter 11).

Mileage is another commodity that many businesses track—or should if they don't. Whether your business hinges on driving or merely requires the occasional jaunt, the IRS lets you deduct vehicle mileage, *but* it requires documentation of the miles you deduct. The QuickBooks mileage tracking feature helps you track the mileage of company vehicles, which you can use not only for tax deductions, but to charge customers for mileage.

Setting Up Time Tracking

For many businesses, *approximations* of time worked are fine. For example, employees who work on only one or two tasks each day can look back fondly on the past week and capture their hours in a weekly timesheet. But for people with deliciously high hourly rates, the QuickBooks Timer program captures every minute you work on an activity from the time you start to the time you finish—as long as you remember to start and stop the Timer at the right moments. The best thing about the Timer program is that you can record time without QuickBooks running. You can give all your employees and subcontractors a copy of the Timer program and they can send you time data to import into QuickBooks.

No matter which technique you use to capture time, the setup in QuickBooks is the same. You have to tell QuickBooks that you want to track time and then set up the people who must track their time (employees and outside contractors alike). You also need customers and items in QuickBooks, which you have already when you track time for billable work. To track nonbillable time, you need a few more entries in QuickBooks, which you'll learn about in the following sections.

Turning on Time Tracking

If you created your company file with the QuickBooks EasyStep Interview (page 20) *and* told QuickBooks that you want to track time, the preferences and features for time tracking should already be available. To see if time tracking is turned on, choose Edit → Preferences. In the Preferences dialog box icon bar, click Time Tracking and then click the Company Preferences tab, which appears in Figure 17-1.

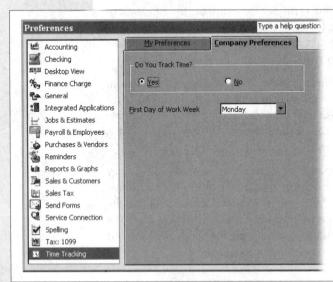

Figure 17-1:
Because time tracking preferences are on the Company Preferences tab, only a QuickBooks administrator can turn time tracking on and off. If you use this feature to generate hours for payroll, the QuickBooks work week should end on the same day of the week as your pay periods. For example, if you pay employees on Friday, start the QuickBooks workweek on Saturday so that it ends on Friday like your payroll.

If the Yes option isn't selected, click it. The only other time tracking preference is the first day of the work week. QuickBooks sets this preference to Monday to match the Monday through Friday workweek of so many businesses. For round-the-clock services, self-employed people, and workaholics, choose whichever day of the week feels most like the beginning of the week. For example, many companies on a seven-day week start the week on Sunday.

Setting Up the People Who Track Time

People can't track time with QuickBooks unless their names appear in one of your name lists (Employee List, Vendor List, or Other Name List). If a person whose time you want to track doesn't belong to a name list yet, here's how you decide which list to use:

- **Employee List.** Use this list *only* for the people you pay using QuickBooks' payroll features.

- **Vendor List.** Add subcontractors and outside consultants (people or companies that send you bills), whether or not their time is billable to customers.

- **Other Names List.** By process of elimination, anyone who isn't a vendor and isn't paid via QuickBooks payroll belongs on the Other Names List. For example, employees paid using a third-party payroll service or owners who take a draw instead of a paycheck qualify for this list.

POWER USERS' CLINIC

Building Paychecks from Time Worked

If you pay your employees by the hour *and* use QuickBooks payroll to generate employee payroll checks, time tracking can automate your payroll process a bit.

The people you pay via QuickBooks payroll must appear in your QuickBooks Employee List. But when you link your employees to their QuickBooks timesheets, the program takes care of calculating how much they've earned.

Here's how you link employees and timesheets to gain this small payroll improvement:

1. On the Home page, click Employees to open the Employee Center.

2. On the Employees tab, double-click the employee to pay.

3. When the Edit Employee dialog box opens, click the "Change tabs" drop-down menu and choose "Payroll and Compensation Info."

4. Turn on the "Use time data to create paychecks" checkbox.

5. Click OK to save the record.

Employees can still track time without this checkbox turned on, which is ideal if you *don't* need a connection between the hours worked and the employee's paycheck. For example, turn the check box *off* if you bill customers for employee time but pay those employees a straight salary.

Note: People who track time directly in QuickBooks (not with the Timer program) must have the program's permission to do so. When you set up QuickBooks users, you can set their permissions so they can enter time. Here's how: choose Company → Set Up Users (page 567). When the wizard opens, proceed to page 5, where you can edit time tracking permissions.

Setting Up Items and Customers for Time Tracking

The good news is that your setup for tracking billable time is already done. The Service items (page 92) and customer records (page 54) you create for invoicing also work for tracking billable time. You need additional items and customers only when you track *all* the hours that people work, both billable and nonbillable. For example, if you're trying to reduce your overhead costs, you might add items to track the time spent fixing software bugs, exchanging bad products, and holding meetings. The level of detail for nonbillable activities is up to you, as demonstrated in Figure 17-2.

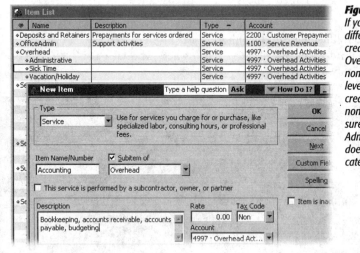

Figure 17-2:
If you want to capture time without differentiating nonbillable activities, create a single Service item called Overhead. For greater detail about nonbillable time, you can create a top-level item, such as Overhead, and then create subitems for each type of nonbillable work you want to track. Be sure to create one catch-all item, such as Administrative, to capture the time that doesn't fit in any other nonbillable category.

Here are hints for creating items to track time that you don't bill to a customer:

- **Type.** Use the Service item type (page 79) because that's the only item type that QuickBooks time tracking recognizes.

- **Rate.** In the New Item dialog box, the Rate box represents how much you charge your customers for the service. Because no money changes hands for nonbillable time, leave the Rate box blank.

- **Account.** You can't create an item without assigning it to an account. Go ahead and create an income account and call it something like Nonbillable Work or Overhead. If you number accounts, assign a number that places the account near the end of your Income type accounts. Because nonbillable time doesn't bring in any income, the account balance remains zero no matter how much nonbillable time you assign to it.

- **This service is performed by a subcontractor, owner, or partner.** Leave this checkbox blank for nonbillable items performed by owners and partners. However, if a subcontractor performs nonbillable work, create a separate item with this checkbox turned on. Then you can assign the subcontractor's costs to an expense account and use time tracking to make sure the subcontractor's bills are correct.

When you start entering time worked, you'll discover that QuickBooks requires a customer or job for time worked. To track nonbillable time, you must create a faux customer, such as Overhead or Administrative, solely to satisfy QuickBooks. Just like the income account for nonbillable work, this customer's balance remains zero.

Entering Time in Timesheets

In QuickBooks, you can enter and view time for a single activity or through a weekly timesheet. If you record time after the fact, the weekly timesheet is the fastest way to enter time. If you want to time work as you perform it, the Time/Enter Single Activity dialog box, explained in the section that begins on page 430, is the place to go.

UP TO SPEED

Copying Timesheets

People often work on the same tasks from week to week. Filling in row after row of customer, Service item, Payroll item, and Class when you filled in the same things the week before is bound to generate grumbling from employees who already have enough to do.

QuickBooks can reduce tedium by copying the entries from a person's last timesheet. Copying timesheets not only saves time for whoever enters time, but also helps prevent mistakes or omissions. Here's how you copy a timesheet:

1. In the Weekly Timesheet dialog box in the Name field, choose the person's name.

2. Click Copy Last Sheet. If the current timesheet is empty, the program fills in all the rows with the entries from the person's last timesheet.

3. If the timesheet already has values, QuickBooks asks whether you want to replace the entries or add entries to the timesheet. Click Yes to replace the entries with the ones from the previous week. Click No to append the entries from the previous week as additional rows in this week's timesheet.

Filling in Weekly Timesheets

The Weekly Timesheet is the fastest way to enter time for several activities or work that spans several days:

1. **Choose Employees → Enter Time → Use Weekly Timesheet.**

   QuickBooks opens the Weekly Timesheet dialog box.

Tip: You can also open the Weekly Timesheet dialog box from the Employee Center. To open it, click Employees on the Home page. Then, in the menu bar, choose Enter Time → Use Weekly Timesheet.

---

2. **In the Name drop-down list, choose the name of the person who performed the work.**

   Because time tracking is rarely limited to only the people with permission to run QuickBooks, you can enter time for yourself or anyone else. After you choose a name, the program displays the weekly timesheet for the current week and shows any time already entered for the week, as shown in Figure 17-3.

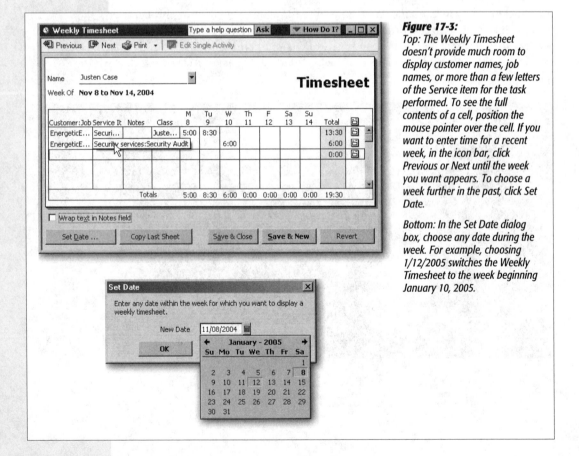

Figure 17-3:
Top: The Weekly Timesheet doesn't provide much room to display customer names, job names, or more than a few letters of the Service item for the task performed. To see the full contents of a cell, position the mouse pointer over the cell. If you want to enter time for a recent week, in the icon bar, click Previous or Next until the week you want appears. To choose a week further in the past, click Set Date.

Bottom: In the Set Date dialog box, choose any date during the week. For example, choosing 1/12/2005 switches the Weekly Timesheet to the week beginning January 10, 2005.

3. **To add an activity to the timesheet, in the first blank Customer:Job cell, choose the customer or job associated with the work performed.**

   If the work is billable, choose the customer or job that pays for it. If the time isn't billable, choose the customer you set up to track your overhead time (page 426). Depending on whether you keep your hands on the keyboard or the mouse, you can move to the Service Item cell by pressing Tab or clicking the Service Item cell.

4. **In the Service Item cell, choose the item that represents the work the person performed.**

   If you use QuickBooks payroll and pay employees by the hours they work, the Payroll Item column appears to the right of the Service Item column. In the Payroll Item column, you can choose the payroll-related item (page 318) that applies to the time worked. For example, for billable work, choose a payroll item, such as Salary or Employee Income. If the hours are for vacation or sick time, choose the payroll item you've created for that time.

5. **In the Notes cell, type additional information about the work.**

   For example, if someone receives comp time, but your company doesn't formally track it, you might use a Service Item such as Administrative and use the Notes cell to identify the comp time taken. If your customers require detail about the work performed, store that information in the Notes cell, which then appears on the invoices you create (see Chapter 8).

Tip: To see the entire contents of Notes cells, turn on the "Wrap text in Notes field" checkbox. Each row in the Timesheet table takes up more space, but you won't have to position the pointer over every cell to see what it contains.

---

6. **If you use classes to track income, in the Class column, choose one for the work.**

   For example, if you track income by partner, choose the class for the partner who handles the customer. If you use classes to track office branches, choose the class for the branch where the person works.

7. **To enter time for a day during the week, click the cell for that day or press Tab until you reach the right day.**

   You can enter time in several ways. If you know the number of hours, type the hours as a decimal or as hours and minutes. For example, for seven and a half hours, type either *7.5* or *7:30*. QuickBooks displays the hours in the timesheet based on the preference you set for time (page 150). If you know the starting and ending time, QuickBooks can calculate the hours for you. For example, if you type *9-5* in a cell, the program transforms it into eight hours.

As you enter time for each day of the week, the Total column on the right side of the table shows the total hours for each activity. The numbers in the Totals row *below* the table show the total hours for each day and for the entire week.

Tip: A row in a Weekly Timesheet represents one service item and one customer or job. If you perform the same type of work for two different customers, you must enter that time in two separate rows.

---

8. **If you aren't billing the customer for the work, in the billable column, click the billable icon, which strives to look like an invoice.**

   QuickBooks fills in the billable icon automatically. When you click the billable cell the first time, the program places a red X over the icon to indicate that the time isn't billable.

Tip: Adding billable time to customer invoices is easy and described in detail on page 204.

---

9. **To save the timesheet, click Save & Close or Save & New.**

   If you enter time for a number of people, click Save & New to save the current weekly timesheet and open a new blank one. Clicking Save & Close saves the timesheet and closes the Weekly Timesheet dialog box.

Entering Time for One Activity

Entering time in a Weekly Timesheet is quick, but the width of the columns makes it hard to see which customer and Service item you're tracking. If you prefer readability to speed, the Time/Enter Single Activity dialog box might be a better choice.

You have to fill in every field for every activity in the Time/Enter Single Activity dialog box. If you quickly grow tired of this form of time entry, in the dialog box's icon bar, click Timesheet to switch to the Weekly Timesheet dialog box. The Weekly Timesheet you see is for the person selected in the Time/Enter Single Activity dialog box and the week that contains the selected day.

Here's how you enter time one activity at a time:

1. **On the QuickBooks navigation bar, click Employee Center.**

   The program opens the Employee Center. (You can also open the Employee Center by clicking Employees on the Home page.)

2. **On the Employees tab, select the employee whose time you want to enter and then choose Enter Time → Time/Enter Single Activity.**

   QuickBooks opens the Time/Enter Single Activity dialog box with the Date field set to the current date, and the Name filled in with the selected employee. If you want to record time for another day, in the Date field, click the Calendar icon and choose the date on which the work took place.

3. **In the Name field, choose the name of the person who performed the work.**

The Name drop-down list includes vendors, employees, and names from the Other Names List. If you choose an employee who's not set up to send time data to payroll, QuickBooks asks whether you want to change the employee's setup. If you want to use the time entered to generate paycheck data, click Yes, which links the employee's time records to paycheck data.

4. **In the Customer:Job field, choose a customer.**

   If someone performs work for a billable customer or job, choose that customer or job whether or not you bill the time. To track overhead time, choose the customer you created for nonbillable work.

5. **If the hours are not billable to a customer, turn off the Billable checkbox.**

   The Billable checkbox isn't the next field in the dialog box, but choosing a customer is a reminder for whether the hours are billable. QuickBooks automatically turns on the Billable checkbox, so you have to worry about this checkbox only if the hours *aren't* billable.

6. **In the Service Item field, choose the item that represents the work performed.**

   Choose this item whether it's one you use to invoice customers or a nonbillable item you created to track overhead activities.

7. **In the Duration box, select the contents of the box and type the hours worked.**

   Type hours as a decimal or as hours and minutes. Or, if you know the starting and ending time, type the time range to have QuickBooks calculate the hours. For example, if you type *11-5* in a cell, the program fills in the box with 6.

   If you work in QuickBooks almost all the time, you can time a task that you're working on in the Time/Enter Single Activity dialog box, as shown in Figure 17-4.

Figure 17-4:
Unless you have a unique relationship with time, you can't run a stopwatch for work performed on a different day. To time your current activity, the Date field must contain today's date. To start the stopwatch, click Start. The colon in the Duration box starts blinking to show that it's timing your work. You won't see time until at least one minute has passed. If you want to pause the stopwatch to take a break or a phone call, click Pause. (Click Resume to start timing again.) When you finish the task, click Stop.

Tip: If you click Previous to display another activity and then click Start, the stopwatch feature starts adding additional time to what you've already recorded.

8. **If you track classes, in the Class field, choose the appropriate one. To add notes about the activity, type text in the Notes box.**

These notes appear in the Notes column in the Weekly Timesheet dialog box and, for billable work, appear on invoices you generate from time worked.

9. **To save the transaction, click Save & New or Save & Close.**

When you click Save & New, the saved activity represents time for only one day. To record time for the next day's work for the same worker, customer, and Service item, you have to create a new activity.

Setting Up the Standalone Timer

Copies of QuickBooks aren't cheap, so chances are that only the people who perform your bookkeeping have access to the QuickBooks software. Meanwhile, dozens of people might perform billable work and need a way to track the time they spend.

The Timer is a program that runs independently of QuickBooks. You can send this program to anyone whose time is important to you and track their time without spending more money on QuickBooks licenses. With the Timer, people can track their time as they work with a stopwatch mode or enter the time they work after they finish. They send the data captured by the Timer program to you to load into your QuickBooks company file for billing or payroll.

Here are the tasks you must perform to let other people use Timer and to load the time they send you into your company file.

Exporting Lists for Timer Users

Your QuickBooks company file contains all sorts of information that you need for tracking time:

- Your customers and jobs

- The people who perform work

- The items that represent the work they do

- The classes you use to track work in other ways

The Timer program needs all this information to function, so you have to send several lists from your company file to people who use the Timer. If you export these lists before you distribute the Timer software, you can include the export file along with the installation software.

Warning: If your lists change, you have to send updated export files to people who use Timer.

The Timer program reads files exported in the QuickBooks .iif format. After you've installed Timer (page 437) on the computer you use to run QuickBooks, Quick-Books includes a command to create the export file with all the information that Timer needs. Here's how you export lists for Timer:

1. **Choose File → Utilities → Export → Timer Lists.**

   QuickBooks opens the Export Lists for Timer dialog box, which initially includes a diagram of how data flows between QuickBooks and Timer, illustrated in Figure 17-5.

Figure 17-5:
Once you've seen this dialog box, you probably don't need to see it again. Before clicking OK to open the Export dialog box, turn on the "Don't display this message in the future" checkbox. The next time you export lists for Timer, QuickBooks immediately gets down to business creating the export file for you.

2. **Click OK to open the Export dialog box, and then choose the folder and the file name for the export file, as illustrated in Figure 17-6.**

   The Timer program is not sophisticated and doesn't recognize file name pre-fixes longer than eight characters. When you create the export file, your challenge is to identify the company and data that the file contains with an eight-character file name. And, because you send updated export files when your lists change, you need a version number, too. In the Export dialog box in the "File name" box, type up to eight characters for the file name prefix. (QuickBooks automatically assigns the .iif file extension for you.)

3. **Click Save.**

   You'll see a QuickBooks Information message box that tells you that your export was successful. When you click OK, the export file is ready to use with your own copy of Timer or to include with the software that you send to others.

Distributing Timer

You can distribute the Timer software to anyone using any digital method you want. Sending compressed files by email might be the easiest method for you, but a CD works for the greatest number of recipients. Distributing Timer on a CD is mostly about writing files from the QuickBooks CD onto a blank CD, so the steps vary depending on your operating system and computer setup.

Figure 17-6:
Store the export file in a folder with a memorable name. You can use a folder specifically for QuickBooks export files, called, say, Export Files. (But if you export lots of different kinds of files, you may want to keep time-related export files in their own folder.)

Note: The Timer installation files fit on three floppy disks. This is good to know for companies slow to adopt new technology.

Here's how you create a Timer CD if you run Windows XP:

1. **Insert the QuickBooks software CD into a CD drive.**

   If the QuickBooks Installation window appears automatically, click Quit.

2. **On your computer desktop, double-click My Computer.**

   The My Computer window opens, listing file folders, hard disks, and devices with removable storage connected to your computer.

3. **Double-click the CD drive that contains the QuickBooks software CD.**

   Another Windows Explorer window opens listing the folders and files on the QuickBooks CD.

4. **Right-click the QBTimer folder and then choose Copy. Then, in the Folders list, navigate to the folder in which you want to store the Timer program files. Right-click the folder and choose Paste from the shortcut menu.**

Tip: If your Windows Explorer window doesn't display folders in the left pane, choose View → Explorer Bar → Folders.

Because these files are for installation only, store them in a folder for downloads or other temporary files. After you've moved the installation files into a folder on your hard drive, you can install the software on your computer *and* create Timer CDs to distribute.

Tip: Although you can install the Timer directly from the QuickBooks software CD, installing Timer from the files on your hard drive has one advantage—you can document the steps you take to install the software on your computer and provide those instructions to the people who receive your Timer CDs.

5. **Use your CD recording software to write the files from the QBTimer folder to a blank CD.**

    Be sure to add the export file of lists to the CD as well so that your time trackers have all the files they need to use Timer. (And don't forget to label the CDs before you send them.)

Tip: You can send the Timer files via email, as long as you pay attention to a few potential problems:

  • Use file compression software, such as WinZip. You won't reduce the number of bytes you have to send because software files are concentrated, but at least you send only one file instead of several.

  • A compressed file is at least 3 megabytes, so you won't be able to email it to recipients whose ISPs limit the size of email attachments (often 1 megabyte or less).

  • Before you email a file this large, ask your recipients if it's OK. Make sure they have high-speed connections or don't mind the 30 minutes it could take to download the email.

Importing Workers' Time into QuickBooks

A few weeks after you distribute the Timer program (and the lists needed to run it), you'll begin receiving data files containing the time people tracked with Timer. Your mission: move that time data into your company file. Importing the time that people send you is easy, particularly when you keep time files in one folder on your computer. Here's how to import time as efficiently as possible:

1. **As you receive time files (by email, on a CD, or floppy disk), copy them into a folder specifically for time files.**

    Create a folder for exported time files where you store other company data. For example, if you have a folder for QuickBooks company files, create a subfolder for time-related files there.

2. **Choose File → Utilities → Import → Timer Activities.**

    Intuit engineers clearly consider the path that data takes between Timer and QuickBooks important because the "Import Activities from Timer" dialog box displays that diagram. Be sure to turn on the "Don't display this message in the future" checkbox before you click OK to begin importing a file.

3. **In the Import dialog box, navigate to the folder with your time files.**

The next time you import Timer activities, QuickBooks automatically opens the Import dialog box to the folder you chose the previous time. As long as you continue to store time files in the same folder, you perform this step for the first import only.

4. **Double-click the file name you want to import.**

After QuickBooks imports the data, it displays the QB Pro Timer Import Summary, which shows what was in the file. Click View Report to see the details for the imported time transactions. The report groups time transactions first by customer or job, and then by Service item. Each time record in the report includes the date, person's name, the date imported, and the number of hours.

Tip: Although QuickBooks has already loaded the time records into your company file, it's a good idea to review the Timer Import Summary report. If you spot an obvious typo, such as 26 work hours in one day, you can correct the activity in QuickBooks (page 444).

Also keep watch for list changes your employees might have made—even if by mistake. For example, if an employee created a new client or service item, QuickBooks imports those into the lists in your company file. If you find changes like these, be sure to reassign the time to the appropriate list entries and delete the ones imported from Timer.

---

5. **In the QB Pro Timer Import Summary dialog box, click Close.**

You're done.

After you import the time, it looks no different from time entered in QuickBooks using the Weekly Timesheet or Time/Enter Single Activity dialog boxes, as you can see in Figure 17-7.

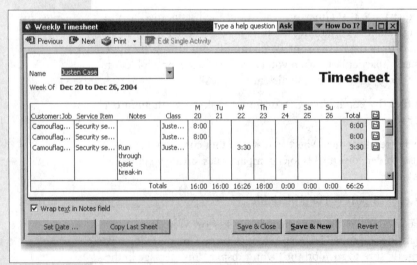

Figure 17-7:
You can edit the timesheet as if you had created it in QuickBooks yourself. For example, you can make an activity billable or not by clicking its billable cell (the one with the icon that looks like an invoice). Or, you can remove the notes that the person added. If you pay someone by the hours they work, discuss the changes you want to make before you actually change the hours reported.

Using Timer to Track Time

The previous section discussed the tasks that you must perform to distribute Timer and then import the time data you receive into QuickBooks. This section explains how people who track their own time use Timer and send the resulting time records to the person running QuickBooks.

Note: Even if your computer has QuickBooks installed replete with its built-in time tracking features, you might prefer to track time using Timer. This standalone program requires some setup, but tracking the time you spend with the Timer stopwatch and switching between different activities during the day is worth the effort.

Installing the Timer on a Computer

The Timer uses an installation wizard, so the steps to install the program should be familiar. Here are the installation steps (in case an employee isn't as experienced with a computer as you):

1. **As you should with any software installation, close any programs you've got running.**

   To ensure a smooth installation, it's also a good idea to stop any antivirus programs.

2. **In Windows Explorer, navigate to the CD or folder containing the installation files and then double-click the Setup.exe file.**

   The installation wizard opens the QuickBooks Pro Timer Installation window and displays a Welcome dialog box. Click Next to get to the good stuff.

3. **In the Destination folder for application screen, click Browse to select the folder in which you want to install the Timer software.**

   The installation wizard chooses a folder, such as *C:\Program Files\Intuit\Quick-Books\QuickBooks Pro Timer*, which is as good a place as any. However, if you want to keep the Timer software in a different folder, click Browse and choose a folder under Program Files, such as *C:\Program Files\QBTimer*.

   After you choose the folder you want, click OK.

4. **In the Destination folder for application screen, click Install.**

   You'll see a screen with a progress bar and a few inconsequential messages, but the installation takes less than a minute. When it's complete, the "Installation Wizard complete" screen appears.

5. **Click Finish.**

   The installation dialog box closes. QuickBooks Pro Timer joins the others on the Start → Program Files menu.

6. Before you remove the CD, copy the export file of QuickBooks lists from the CD to a folder on your computer.

The person who created the CD for you should have included an export file of QuickBooks lists. You must import the lists in the export file into the Timer program so that you can assign customers and items to the time you work.

Setting Up the Timer Program

The first time you run Timer, you have to set up the program before you can record any time:

1. On the Windows Start menu, navigate to the submenu that contains the Timer program, and choose QuickBooks Pro Timer.

The menu that holds Timer depends on the program folder you specified during installation. For example, if you added the program to your QuickBooks folder, choose Start → Programs → QuickBooks Pro → QuickBooks Pro Timer. (If you use QuickBooks Premier, choose Start → Programs → QuickBooks Premier → QuickBooks Pro Timer.

The Timer window opens, but so does the No Timer File Is Open dialog box. You must first create a file to hold the time that you track, as demonstrated in Figure 17-8.

2. In the New Timer File dialog box, click OK to create the Timer database.

Timer displays a message offering to show you how to import your lists into QuickBooks. If you've imported files before or if you prefer to read the instructions in this book (next step), click No. The Timer window now includes the name of the Timer file that you created in the title bar, though you still aren't ready to track time.

3. To import the QuickBooks lists from the export file you received with the Timer software, choose File → Import QuickBooks Lists.

The Import QuickBooks Lists dialog box opens, which includes a diagram showing how data flows between Timer and QuickBooks, turn on the "Don't show me this message again" checkbox, and then click Continue.

The Open File For Import dialog box opens.

4. In the Open File For Import dialog box, in the Folders box, find the folder in which you stored the QuickBooks lists export file (page 433).

For example, if you copied the export file to the same folder as the Timer software, the folder might be something like *C:\Program Files\QBTimer*.

Note: The Timer dialog boxes truncate folders, so the Program Files folder shows up as PROGRA~1.

---

5. **After you open the folder that contains the export file, double-click the export file name to import the lists into Timer.**

Click OK to dismiss the message box telling you that the import was successful. The Timer window doesn't look any different than it did before you imported the lists, but, if all went well, you can now track time.

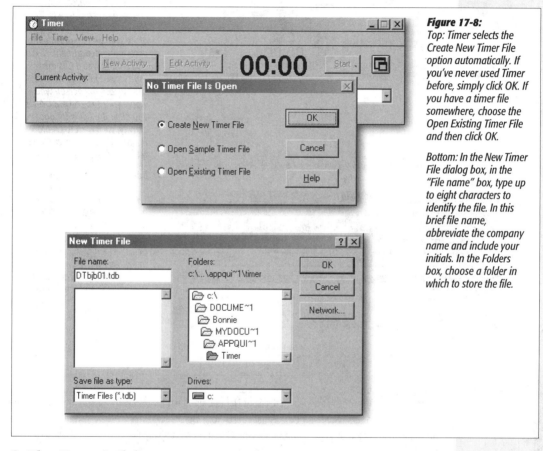

Figure 17-8:
Top: Timer selects the Create New Timer File option automatically. If you've never used Timer before, simply click OK. If you have a timer file somewhere, choose the Open Existing Timer File and then click OK.

Bottom: In the New Timer File dialog box, in the "File name" box, type up to eight characters to identify the file. In this brief file name, abbreviate the company name and include your initials. In the Folders box, choose a folder in which to store the file.

Setting Up an Activity

You track time on activities, so the next thing you do in Timer is set up one or more activities. Activities in Timer share most of the fields you find in the Time/Enter Single Activity dialog box (page 430), which should come as no surprise if you expect to import Timer records into QuickBooks. To create an activity, in the Timer window, click New Activity.

The New Activity dialog box opens with the Date box automatically set to the current date. If you intend to use Timer as a stopwatch, the Date box *must* contain the current date. However, if you're creating an activity for work you've already performed, choose the date that you performed the work.

Filling in the fields in the New Activity dialog box is mostly choosing from drop-down lists, as you can see in Figure 17-9.

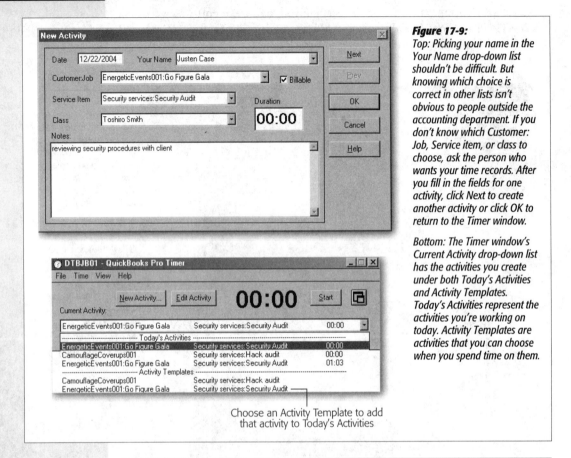

Figure 17-9:
Top: Picking your name in the Your Name drop-down list shouldn't be difficult. But knowing which choice is correct in other lists isn't obvious to people outside the accounting department. If you don't know which Customer: Job, Service item, or class to choose, ask the person who wants your time records. After you fill in the fields for one activity, click Next to create another activity or click OK to return to the Timer window.

Bottom: The Timer window's Current Activity drop-down list has the activities you create under both Today's Activities and Activity Templates. Today's Activities represent the activities you're working on today. Activity Templates are activities that you can choose when you spend time on them.

Choose an Activity Template to add that activity to Today's Activities

Note: If your name doesn't appear in the Your Name drop-down list, *you* can't add it to the Your Name list unless you're the person who exports name lists from QuickBooks. Tell the person who sent you the Timer program that your name is missing in the QuickBooks company file and (politely) ask for a new export file of QuickBooks lists with your name in it.

Entering Time

After you've set up at least one activity, you can time your work or type in hours that you've already worked. To record time either way, you must first select an activity. In the Timer window's Current Activity drop-down list, activities appear under two headings. Here's how you decide which activity to choose:

- **Activity Templates.** Every time you create a new activity (page 439), Timer adds it to the Activity Templates list. When you want to track time for that activity, click it under the Activity Templates heading. Timer adds the activity under the Today's Activities heading.

- **Today's Activities.** If you want to record time for an activity, choose the one that appears under this heading.

Stopwatch timing

In the Timer window, when you select an activity, you'll see one of three buttons, as Figure 17-10 demonstrates.

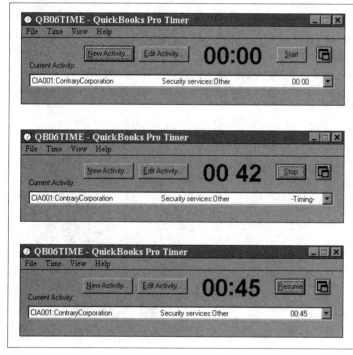

Figure 17-10:
Top: If you haven't recorded any time for the activity in the timer window, click Start.

Middle: When you click Start, the colon between the hours and minutes begins to blink and, in the Current Activity box, "-Timing-" appears at the end of the line. Because the elapsed time shows only hours and minutes, the initial 00:00 won't change until one minute has passed. The button changes to Stop, which you click when you want to pause timing or you've completed the activity.

Bottom: If you clicked Stop, you can restart timing by clicking Resume. If you choose an activity that has some recorded time, the Resume button appears instead of the Start button.

Tip: You can also pause timing on one activity by choosing a different activity in the Current Activity box. During a single workday, switching activities automatically pauses the current activity, and resumes timing to add more time to the next activity.

When you start the Timer the next day, your Today's Activities heading list is empty. The Current Activity box displays the text "Select an Activity Template from this list or click 'New Activity'." To work on an existing activity, choose its name under the Activity Templates heading. The Timer starts a new record with today's date for that activity and adds it under the Today's Activities heading. If you're starting an activity you've never worked on before, click New Activity.

Tip: If you like the stopwatch feature, but you want the Timer window smaller, click the button with the icon of two windows. The window shrinks to show only the elapsed time, the Edit button, the Start/Stop/Resume button, and the Window button—which reverts you to a full Timer window.

Typing in time

If you want to record time after the fact, in the Current Activity drop-down list, choose an activity and then click Edit Activity. In the Edit Activity dialog box, in the Duration box, type the hours and minutes you devoted to the work. You can type the time as hours and minutes or as a decimal. Click OK to finish up.

FREQUENTLY ASKED QUESTION

Customizing Timer

How can I make the Timer work the way I want?

Timer is relatively set in its ways, but you can improve its utility by setting a few preferences. The most helpful preference is Default Name, which lets you set the name that Timer automatically adds to the Your Name box.

- To set the Default Name preference, in the Timer window, choose File → Preferences → Default Name. In the dialog box that opens, choose your name and click OK.

- If you usually work on billable activities, turn on the "Time defaults to billable" checkbox. If you're a staff person who always works on overhead activities, turn off this checkbox.

- To keep your list of activities to a manageable number, you can set the number of days that Timer keeps activity templates (File → Preferences → Set

number of days to remember activities). For example, if you work on the same task for several weeks, you might set the number of days to 60. On the other hand, if you rarely work for the same customer from day to day, choose a low number, such as 5.

- Timer automatically turns on the Show Time When Minimized preference, which is a setting you're unlikely to change. When you minimize the Timer window, the button in the Windows taskbar includes the label Timer and the current elapsed time for the activity being timed.

For such a simple program, one-time messages are more annoying than they are helpful. But if you want to see those messages again, choose File → Preferences → Turn on All One Time Messages.

Creating an Export File of Your Time

If you're tracking time, the company you work for probably wants your time on a regular schedule. The most common reporting period is weekly, but you might have to send your time daily, every other week, or only when you've completed an activity.

Most of the time, you want to be sure that you're exporting the correct information, particularly when your paycheck depends on the time you've worked. In Timer, you can review, correct, and export your time all from the same dialog box. Here's how:

1. **In the Timer window, choose View → Time Activity Log.**

   The Timer opens the Time Activity Log dialog box, in which you can review and correct your time, as illustrated in Figure 17-11. To review the time you plan to export, in the Dates drop-down list, choose a date range, such as This Week. You can also choose From and To dates.

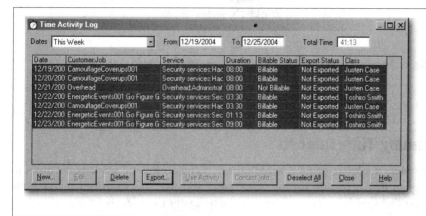

Figure 17-11:
In addition to listing all the activities for the selected date range, the Total Time box shows the total hours for all the activities displayed. If an activity is missing, click New and then add the activity and its time. To correct an activity, select it and then click Edit. To remove an activity that you added by mistake, select it and click Delete.

2. **To select all the activities shown in the dialog box, click Select All.**

   If you want to select some of the activities, select individual activities by holding down the Ctrl key as you click. To select contiguous activities, hold down the Shift key and click the first and last activities.

3. **Click Export.**

   If you see a window with more explanation, just click Continue. The Export Time Activities dialog box appears.

4. **In the Export Time Activities dialog box, choose the option for the time you want to export.**

   If you've already selected activities to export in the Time Activity Log dialog box, Timer automatically selects the "Selected activities" option. To export all activities through a specific date, choose the "All unexported time activities through" option, and then choose the date.

5. **Click OK to open the Create Export File dialog box. In the "File name" box, type the file prefix you want.**

   You can type a name longer than eight characters, but you'll receive an error message if you try to save the export file with that name. A good naming convention to identify the contents of the file is a combination of your initials and a version number, such as *bjb001*.

   Save the export file in a folder reserved for time and mileage export files.

6. **Click OK.**

When you see the message telling you that the export succeeded, click OK. Back in the Time Activity Log dialog box, the Export Status column displays the word Exported for all the activities that you included in the export file.

Tip: If you export activities during the day, Today's Activities are still available for the rest of the day. To keep your records straight, use Activity Templates to create new activities if you continue to work after the export.

---

7. **Send the export file to the person who imports data into QuickBooks.**

Time export files are usually quite small, which means email is the easiest way to send the file.

Running Time Reports

Customers don't like being charged for too many hours, and workers are quick to complain if they're paid for too few. Before you use time records, generate time reports that QuickBooks provides to make sure your time data is correct.

To generate a report, choose Reports → Jobs, Time & Mileage, and then choose the report you want. Here're the reports you can choose and what they're useful for:

- **Time by Job Summary.** Review the total hours worked on a job during a period. This report groups hours first by customer or job and then by Service item. Because of the high-level view in this report, it's perfect for spotting time charged to inappropriate Service items or hours that exceed job limits. If hours seem too high or low, you can drill down with the Time by Job Detail report to investigate.

- **Time by Job Detail.** If you want to verify that hours were correctly set as billable or nonbillable, use this report. It's grouped by job and Service item, but each time entry shows the date the hours were worked, who performed the work, and whether the work is billable. If hours are billable but not yet invoiced, the report shows the Billing status as Unbilled.

- **Time by Name.** This report shows the hours worked by person, with the hours worked for each customer or job. If a person reports too many or too few hours for a period, use the Weekly Timesheet dialog box to look for signs of inaccurate or missing time reports.

- **Time by Item.** This report groups hours by Service item and then by job. You can use this report to analyze where your billable and nonbillable time is spent, either to cut unproductive activities or to determine staffing needs.

Tracking Mileage

If you charge your customers for mileage, keeping track of the billable miles you drive helps you obtain all the reimbursements you're due. But *all* business-related mileage is tax-deductible, so tracking nonbillable business mileage is important, too. Customers and the IRS alike want records of the miles you drive, and Quick-Books can help you produce that documentation.

Note: The mileage tracking feature in QuickBooks tracks only the miles you drive using company vehicles, not other vehicle expenses, such as fuel or tolls.

Nor do you use QuickBooks mileage tracking to record miles driven by employees, vendors, or subcontractors. These miles go straight to an expense account. For example, if a vendor bills you for mileage, when you enter the bill in QuickBooks (page 276), you assign that charge to an expense account, such as Travel–Mileage. Likewise, when you write a check to reimburse an employee for mileage driven, you assign that employee reimbursement to the expense account for mileage.

Adding a Vehicle

To track mileage for a company vehicle, you must first add it to the QuickBooks Vehicle List. The Enter Vehicle Mileage dialog box presents all the mileage-related features you need, as you can see in Figure 17-12. To open this dialog box, choose Company → Enter Vehicle Mileage.

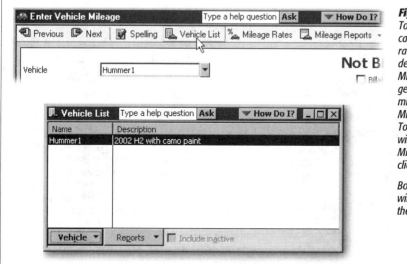

Figure 17-12:
Top: From this icon bar, you can set the standard mileage rate you use for tax deductions by clicking Mileage Rates (page 446). To generate reports of the mileage you've driven, click Mileage Reports (page 449). To open the Vehicle List window, in the Enter Vehicle Mileage dialog box icon bar, click Vehicle List.

Bottom: In the Vehicle List window, press Ctrl+N to open the New Vehicle dialog box.

Tip: The Vehicle List is also available on the Lists menu, but Intuit decided to hide it with customer and vendor lists. To open the Vehicle List window from the Lists menu, choose Lists → Customer & Vendor Profile Lists → Vehicle List.

In the New Vehicle dialog box, in the Vehicle box, type a name for the vehicle. To easily identify your company cars and trucks, include the type of vehicle and a way to differentiate it from others. For instance, if your company cars are all white Jeeps, the license plate number is a better method of identification than make and color. In the Description box, type additional information such as the year, make, model, the license plate number, the Vehicle Identification Number (VIN), etc.

Tip: To change vehicle information later, in the Vehicle List window, double-click the vehicle name, and then, in the Edit Vehicle dialog box, edit the name or description.

Setting the Mileage Rate

For tax purposes, you can deduct mileage expenses based on a standard mileage rate or by tracking the actual costs of operating and maintaining your vehicles. Using a standard mileage rate is convenient—simply multiply the miles you drove by the standard rate to calculate your vehicle deduction.

If you own an expensive car with expensive maintenance needs, actual costs might provide a larger deduction. But you have to keep track of what you spend on gas, tires, repairs, insurance, and so on, and deduct those costs on your tax return. As usual, the tax rules for deducting operating and maintenance costs are taxing. Before you choose this approach, ask your accountant or the IRS if you can deduct actual costs and whether it's the best approach.

Note: You can deduct either the standard rate amount or your actual costs, but not both.

QuickBooks stores multiple mileage rates along with their effective dates, because standard mileage rates usually change at the beginning of each calendar year. To set a mileage rate, in the Enter Vehicle Mileage icon bar, click Mileage Rates, which opens the Mileage Rates dialog box shown in Figure 17-13.

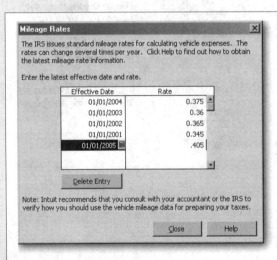

Figure 17-13:
QuickBooks displays the standard mileage rates with the most recent rate at the top and the other rates going backwards in time. This order ensures that the most recent rate appears at the top of the list, but adding a new rate can be confusing. If necessary, scroll down until you see a blank line in the rate table. In the Effective Date cell, choose the date that the new mileage rate becomes effective, such as 1/1/2005. In the Rate cell, type the rate in dollars (.405 per mile for 2005 as documented on the IRS Web site, www.irs.gov). Click Close.

Recording Mileage Driven

Here's how you fill in the Enter Vehicle Mileage dialog box to record billable and nonbillable miles you've driven:

1. **Open the Enter Vehicle Mileage dialog box (choose Company → Enter Vehicle Mileage).**

   In the Vehicle box, choose the vehicle that you drove.

2. **In the Trip Start Date box and the Trip End Date box, choose the days you started and completed the trip, respectively.**

   If you're recording mileage for one day of on-site work, choose the same day in both boxes. On the other hand, if you used a company car to drive to another city for several days, the Trip Start Date is the day you headed out of town and the Trip End Date is the day you returned.

3. **In the Odometer Start box and Odometer End box, type the vehicle mileage before you began driving and the mileage when you returned, as shown in Figure 17-14.**

   Actually, you can ignore the Odometer Start and Odometer End boxes. Instead, in the Total Miles box, type the mileage you drove. For example, if you know that a round-trip to your customer is 72 miles, in the Total Miles box, just type 72.

   The drawback to this approach is that your mileage record doesn't include the odometer readings that the IRS wants to see. But if every mile you drive is for business, you can prove your deduction by showing the IRS an odometer reading at the beginning of the year and one at the end of the year.

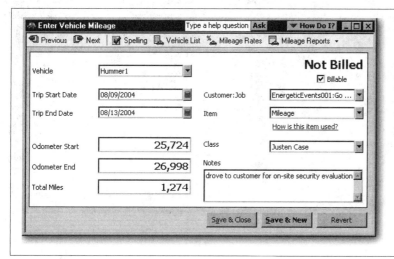

Figure 17-14:
You can type the mileage with or without commas. QuickBooks adds commas to numbers to make them easier to read and also fills in the Total Miles box with the difference between the Odometer End and Odometer Start values.

4. **If your mileage is billable to a customer or job, turn on the Billable checkbox. Then, in the Customer:Job box, choose the customer to whom you want to assign the mileage.**

   If the mileage is not billable to a customer, choose the customer you created to track time spent on administrative activities (page 426).

5. **If the mileage is billable, in the Item drop-down list, choose the item you created for mileage.**

   For guidance on creating an item for mileage, see the box below.

6. **If you track classes, in the Class box, choose the appropriate one.**

   For example, if you use classes to track branch performance, choose the class for the branch. However, if you track partner income with classes and the mileage is nonbillable, you don't need a class assignment.

7. **To further document the reason for the mileage, type text in the Notes box. Then, to save the mileage and close the dialog box, click Save & Close.**

   If you want to enter additional mileage for other customers and jobs, click Save & New.

FREQUENTLY ASKED QUESTION

Mileage Rates and Invoice Items

What if the IRS rate is different than the rate I charge customers for mileage?

The rates you enter in the Mileage Rates dialog box are the standard rates set by the IRS for tax purposes. The IRS doesn't care one whit what you charge your customers for miles.

For the reimbursable miles that you drive, you must create a Service or Other Charge type item in your Item List. (In the Enter Vehicle Mileage dialog box, the Item drop-down list includes only these two types of items.) When you create the item, you can assign the rate per mile or leave the rate at zero if you charge variable mileage rates.

For an Other Charge item, the "Amount or %" box is the place to enter the mileage rate, as shown in the figure. For a Service type item, use the Rate box. In the Account box, choose the income account you use for reimbursable mileage, whether it's specific to mileage or an overall reimbursable expense account.

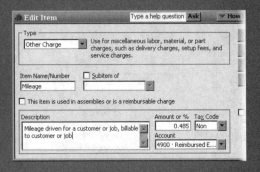

Generating Mileage Reports

QuickBooks includes four mileage reports that can help you prepare your taxes or discuss charges with your customers. The reports are simple, mainly because you don't track that much mileage information. To generate a report, in the Enter Vehicle Mileage dialog box icon bar, click the downward-pointing arrow to the right of the words Mileage Reports.

Tip: The reports are also available on the submenu you see when you choose Reports → Jobs, Time & Mileage.

Here are the reports you can choose and what they're useful for:

• **Mileage by Vehicle Summary.** This report shows the total miles and the associated expense (using the standard mileage rate) for each vehicle in your Vehicle List. You can change the date range to generate the data you need for your tax return, as shown in Figure 17-15.

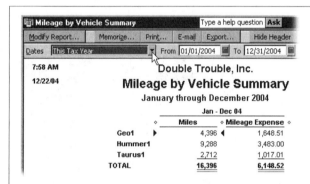

Figure 17-15:
If you like to spend New Year's Eve gathering your tax documentation, in the Date box, choose This Tax Year. If you wait until after January 1st, in the Dates box, choose Last Tax Year.

• **Mileage by Vehicle Detail.** This report shows each trip that contributed to a vehicle's mileage. For each trip made, the report includes the trip end date, total trip miles, mileage rate, and mileage expense. If you have questions about your deductions, double-click a trip entry to open the Enter Vehicle Mileage dialog box for that transaction.

• **Mileage by Job Summary.** This report shows the miles driven and the billable mileage for each customer or job.

• **Mileage by Job Detail.** If a customer has a question about mileage charged, this report is the quickest way to find the charges in question. The report groups mileage by customer or job, but lists each trip in its own line. The report shows the Trip Start Date, Trip End Date, miles driven, billing status, the mileage rate, and billable amount, so you can answer almost any mileage-related question a customer might have.

Budgeting and Planning

As you've no doubt noticed in business and in life, the activities that cost money almost always seem to outnumber those that bring money in. If you run your own business just as a hobby, maybe you don't need to plan ahead or use a budget. But most companies want to make money and most nonprofits want to do the most with the funds they have, so budgeting and planning are essential business activities.

Like any kind of plan, a budget is an estimate of what's going to happen. You'll never produce exactly the numbers you estimate in your budget. And, if you do, someone's playing games with your books. But comparing your actual performance to your budget can tell you that it's time to crack the whip on the sales team, rein in your spending, or both.

Budgeting in QuickBooks is both simple and simplistic. If you gather budget numbers from dozens of divisions and perform statistical analysis on the results to determine your final budget, plan on massaging your budget in some other program. But QuickBooks can handle basic budgets and even provide some very handy shortcuts for entering numbers quickly.

Beyond budgeting, QuickBooks includes a suite of decision tools primarily for beginners. These tools introduce some of the planning and analysis that organizations perform, but don't expect a thorough education on managing your business. You'll learn just enough to realize that you need to know more and, for that, you should turn to your accountant or take some business classes.

Types of Budgets

To most people, the word "budget" usually means a profit and loss budget—one that estimates what your income and expenses will be over a period of time. QuickBooks provides profit and loss budgets that are based on the income and expense accounts in your Chart of Accounts (see Chapter 2) and typically span the fiscal year for your company.

Balance sheet budgets aren't as common, but you can create them in QuickBooks as well. Balance sheets are snapshots of your assets and liabilities, and balance sheet budgets follow the same format by showing the ending balance for your asset, liability and other balance sheet accounts.

Note: Most companies plan outside of the budgeting process for major purchases and their accompanying loans. If a company needs an asset to operate, executives usually analyze costs, benefits, payback periods, internal rates of return, and so on before making purchase decisions. They evaluate cash flow to decide whether to borrow money or to use cash generated by operations. But after that, the additional income generated by the assets and the additional interest expense for the loans show up in the profit and loss budget.

QuickBooks profit and loss reports come in three flavors, each helpful in its own way:

- **Company profit and loss.** The most common type of budget includes all the income and expenses for your entire company. This is the budget that management struggles to meet or strives to exceed—whether that's to keep shareholders happy or to generate the cash needed to run the company. With a QuickBooks' Profit & Loss report (page 382), you can compare your actual results to your budget.

- **Customer or job budget.** A customer- or job-based profit and loss budget forecasts the income and expenses for a single customer or job. Projects that come with a lot of risk must offer the potential for lots of profit to be worthwhile. By generating a profit and loss budget for a customer or job, you can make sure that the profitability meets your needs.

- **Class budget.** If you use classes to track income and expenses—for instance, for different regions of the country—you can create profit and loss budgets for each class. Class budgets work particularly well when you track income and expenses for independent sections of your company: regions, business units, branches. If most of the company expenses are pooled and classes track only income and reimbursable expenses, you can still create class-based budgets. In those budgets, you ignore all the accounts that don't apply to your class-tracking scheme.

Ways to Build Budgets

If you've just started your business, you might have a business plan that includes estimates of your income and expenses. But you won't have any existing financial data to use as a basis for a budget. Either way, there's a method for building a QuickBooks budget. And, if you're willing to import and export data, QuickBooks offers two additional ways to build budgets. Here are your options and what each has to offer:

- **From scratch.** This is the most tedious method, but also your only option when you don't have budget numbers or existing data to use. Although you do have to type all the numbers, you only have to use this approach for your first budget.

- **From previous year's data.** If you have at least a year's worth of data in Quick-Books, you can build next year's budget using your previous year's actual income and expenses. No two years are the same, but it's much easier to use existing data as a starting point and edit only the values that change.

- **From previous year's budget.** If you created a budget for the previous year, you can use it as the basis for next year's budget. Although you might consider this a standard business task, copying budgets requires some exporting and importing games in QuickBooks (page 460).

- **From data in another program.** If you build budgets in another program or export QuickBooks budgets to work out what-if scenarios, you can import budget data into QuickBooks.

Creating Budgets in QuickBooks

If you want to build a budget directly in QuickBooks, the Set Up Budgets wizard is all you need. This wizard handles profit and loss budgets; balance sheet budgets; budgets for customers, jobs, and classes; and budgets built from scratch or from previous year's data.

These two setup steps are essential if you want your budgets to work properly:

- **Fiscal year.** QuickBooks uses the first month of your fiscal year as the first month in the budget. To check that you defined your fiscal year correctly, choose Company → Company Information. In the Company Information dialog box, head to the Report Information section, and make sure that the month in the First month in your Fiscal Year box matches the first month of your fiscal year.

- **Active accounts.** QuickBooks budgets cover only the accounts that are active in your Chart of Accounts. To activate any accounts that you want to budget, press Ctrl+A to open the "Chart of Accounts" window. Then turn on the "Include inactive" checkbox. For any inactive account that you want in your budget, click the X to the left of the account name to reactivate the account.

To start the budget wizard, choose Company → Planning & Budgeting → Set Up Budgets. Depending on whether you already have a budget in QuickBooks, the program displays two different windows, as shown in Figure 18-1.

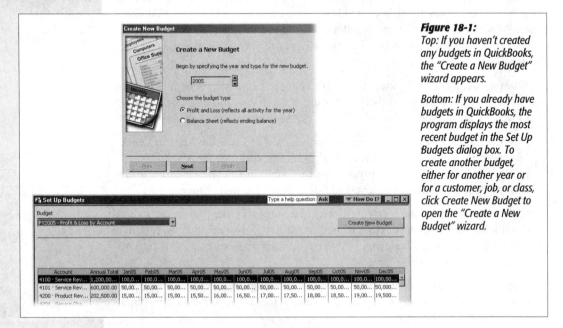

Figure 18-1:
Top: If you haven't created any budgets in QuickBooks, the "Create a New Budget" wizard appears.

Bottom: If you already have budgets in QuickBooks, the program displays the most recent budget in the Set Up Budgets dialog box. To create another budget, either for another year or for a customer, job, or class, click Create New Budget to open the "Create a New Budget" wizard.

Whether QuickBooks displays the Create New Budget dialog box automatically or you click Create New Budget, in the first "Create a New Budget" screen, you must specify the fiscal year for the budget and the type of budget. QuickBooks automatically fills in the next calendar year (perhaps assuming that you're done budgeting for the current year). The up and down arrows to the right of the year box increase or decrease the fiscal year. On this first screen, you also choose whether you want to create a profit and loss budget or a balance sheet budget.

Note: QuickBooks automatically selects Profit & Loss, so you rarely have to change the selected budget type option.

If you create a balance sheet budget, there's nothing to do but build the budget for your balance sheet accounts. In the "Create a New Budget" wizard, clicking Next displays a screen that tells you to click Finish. When you do so, a table containing your balance sheet accounts appears in the Set Up Budgets dialog box, and you can begin to type ending balances.

When you choose a profit and loss budget and click Next, the Additional Profit & Loss Budget Criteria screen appears, which contains three options, one for each flavor of profit and loss budget in QuickBooks:

- **No additional criteria.** Choose this option when you want to create a profit and loss budget for the entire company.

- **Customer:Job.** Choose this option to create a budget for a specific customer or job.

- **Class.** Choose this option to build a class-based budget.

After you choose the scope of the budget and click Next, the "Choose how you want to create a budget" screen includes two options: one for creating the budget by typing values, and a second for building the budget from your previous year's actual data. If you want to type in your budget numbers, choose "Create budget from scratch." If you have a year's worth of data and dislike tedious data entry, choose "Create budget from previous year's actual data," which transfers the monthly totals from the previous year for each income and expense account into the budget.

In the Set Up Budgets wizard, when you click Finish, QuickBooks displays a table with rows for each active account and columns for each month. If you opted to create a budget for a customer, job, or class, the Set Up Budgets dialog box includes either the Current Customer:Job drop-down list (containing all your active customer and jobs) or the Class drop-down list containing all your active classes. Before you begin entering values for a customer, job, or class budget, you must first choose the customer, job, or class.

Tip: If your screen resolution is less than 1024 × 768, the Set Up Budgets dialog box also includes the Show Next 6 Months button, because the screen can't display the entire year. QuickBooks initially displays January through June. Click Show Next 6 Months to display July through December, which also changes the button label to Show Previous 6 Months.

Filling in Budget Values

Regardless of which type of budget you create, filling in and editing values is the same. To add values to an account, in the Account column, click the name of the account. QuickBooks automatically selects the cell in the first month column in that row. If you're filling in the entire year's worth of numbers, type the value for the first month, press Tab to move to the next month, and continue until you've entered values in all 12 months, as shown in Figure 18-2.

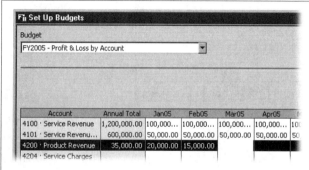

Figure 18-2:
As you add values to each month, the Annual Total column displays the total for all months.

Tip: If the account names are hopelessly truncated and you have screen real estate to spare, widen the
Set Up Budgets dialog box by dragging a corner. The Account column widens as well, showing more of
the account names.

Filling in a few budget cells is usually enough to convince you that data entry
shortcuts are in order. Because budgets are estimates, you don't need extraordinar-
ily detailed or precise values. QuickBooks provides two ways to enter values faster,
described next.

Copy Across the Columns

In the Set Up Budgets dialog box (choose Company → Planning & Budgeting → Set
Up Budgets), you can copy a number from one cell in a row to all the cells to the
right in the same row, as demonstrated in Figure 18-3.

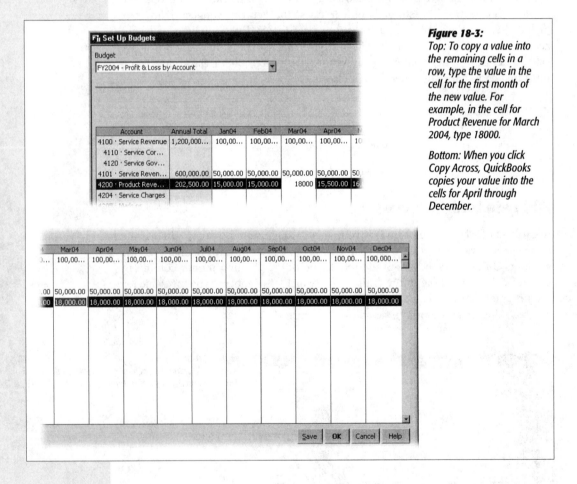

Figure 18-3:
*Top: To copy a value into
the remaining cells in a
row, type the value in the
cell for the first month of
the new value. For
example, in the cell for
Product Revenue for March
2004, type 18000.*

*Bottom: When you click
Copy Across, QuickBooks
copies your value into the
cells for April through
December.*

This shortcut is fabulous when a monthly expense remains the same throughout the year, such as office rent. But it still works if a price changes mid-year. For example, suppose the corporate concierge you've hired to run errands for your employees announces that his rates are going up in May. If your budget contains the old rate in every month, click the cell for May and type the new rate. Then, when you click Copy Across, the new rate appears from May through December.

Tip: If you mistakenly added values to cells that should be blank, Copy Across is the fastest way to empty a row. Clear the first month's cell by selecting the value and then pressing Backspace. Immediately click Copy Across to have QuickBooks clear all the following cells in the row.

UP TO SPEED

The Set Up Budgets Buttons

In the Set Up Budgets dialog box, several buttons help you manage the work you do on your budgets. Although you're probably familiar with their functions based on similar buttons in other dialog boxes, here's a review:

- **Clear.** Click this button to clear all the values for a budget—in every account and every month. This is the button to click if you want to start over.

- **Save.** When you've added or updated all the values in a budget, click Save to save your work on that budget. You can also click Save so you don't lose the

work you've done so far. Don't worry if you forget to click Save. If you click OK or choose another budget, QuickBooks asks you whether you want to record a budget.

- **OK.** Clicking this button records the values you've entered and closes the dialog box.

- **Cancel.** Clicking this button closes the dialog box without saving your work.

Adjust Row Amounts

In the Set Up Budgets dialog box (choose Company → Planning & Budgeting → Set Up Budgets), the Adjust Row Amounts button lets you increase or decrease monthly values by a dollar amount or a percentage, which has zillions of useful applications. Maybe you created a budget from previous year's data, but you want to increase this year's values by 10 percent. Or your company is growing quickly and you want to apply some heat to your sales force by increasing the income each month.

Changing all the cells in a row by a fixed dollar amount isn't as useful as you might think, because Copy Across basically does the same thing. But when you change budget amounts by percentages, QuickBooks takes care of the percentage calculations for you.

When you click Adjust Row Amounts, QuickBooks opens the Adjust Row Amounts dialog box and automatically selects "Currently selected month" in the "Start at" box, which starts adjustments in the cell that's already selected. If you choose "1st month," the program selects the first month of your fiscal year regardless of which cell is selected. Here's what the options do:

- **Increase each remaining monthly amount in this row by this dollar amount or percentage.** If the landlord tells you that rent is going up five percent, in the box for this option, type *5%*. QuickBooks increases the value in each cell by the percentage you specify.

  If you want to add a dollar amount to all the cells, type that dollar value. For example, to add $1,500 a month to the Rent cells, in the box for this option, type *1500*. Each subsequent cell in the Rent row increases by 1,500.

- **Decrease each remaining monthly amount in this row by this dollar amount or percentage.** When the budgeted amount decreases from month to month, which is as rare as hen's teeth, choose this option and type the dollar amount or percentage of the decrease.

You'll see the "Enable compounding" checkbox only when the "Start at" box is set to "Currently selected month." By turning on this checkbox, you tell QuickBooks to adjust each cell based on the value of the previous month's cell, as shown in Figure 18-4.

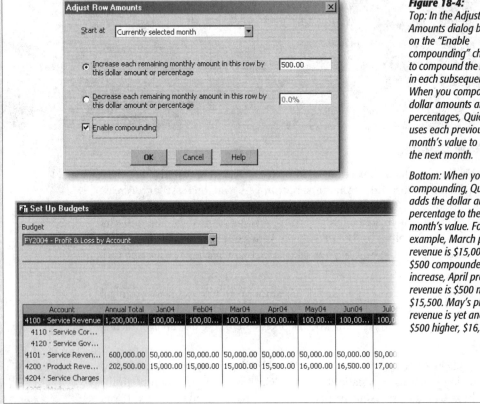

Figure 18-4:
Top: In the Adjust Row Amounts dialog box, turn on the "Enable compounding" checkbox to compound the increases in each subsequent month. When you compound dollar amounts and percentages, QuickBooks uses each previous month's value to calculate the next month.

Bottom: When you turn on compounding, QuickBooks adds the dollar amount or percentage to the previous month's value. For example, March product revenue is $15,000. With a $500 compounded increase, April product revenue is $500 more, or $15,500. May's product revenue is yet another $500 higher, $16,000.

Creating Additional Customer:Job or Class Budgets

In QuickBooks, there's no way to store several versions of a fiscal year budget that covers your entire operation. But you can create multiple budgets for the same fiscal year, as long as each budget applies to a different customer, job, or class.

After you create your first budget, the Set Up Budgets dialog box opens with the most recent fiscal year budget in the budget table. But if you've created at least one budget for a customer or job, the Budget drop-down list includes an entry like FY2005–Profit & Loss By Account and Customer:Job. And if you have at least one class budget, the Budget drop-down list has an entry such as FY2005–Profit & Loss By Account and Class.

Note: Class budgets work the way Customer:Job budgets do. In fact, if you replace every instance of "Customer:Job" in the following procedure with "Class," you'll have the instructions for creating Class budgets.

Here's how you create and save additional Customer:Job budgets:

1. **In the Budget drop-down list, choose the entry for customer and job budgets for the fiscal year you want to budget.**

   QuickBooks adds the Current Customer:Job box to the Set Up Budgets dialog box.

2. **In the Current Customer:Job drop-down list, choose the customer or job that you want to budget.**

   Any budgetary numbers that you've previously entered for the customer or job for the selected fiscal year appear in the budget table.

3. **In the budget table, type values for the Customer:Job budget.**

   Unlike a budget for your entire operation, customer or job budgets might include values for only a few accounts. For example, for a job that includes products, services, and reimbursable expenses, your budget might have values only for income accounts.

4. **After you've added the values for that Customer:Job budget, save the budget by clicking Save.**

   If you choose another customer or job without clicking Save, QuickBooks asks if you want to record the budget. In the Recording Budget message box, click Yes.

Copying Budgets and Creating What-if Budgets

If next year's budget is almost identical to this year's, copying your current budget and changing a few numbers should be quick and easy. But QuickBooks lacks a built-in mechanism for copying an existing budget to a new budget. Similarly, because QuickBooks only allows one budget of each type for the same fiscal year, you can't create what-if budgets to see which one is the best.

To do *any* kind of budget modifications beyond typing in values or using Copy Across and Adjust Row Amounts, you have to export your budgets to a spreadsheet program and make modifications or what-if copies there. Then, when you've got the budget you want, you can import the file back into QuickBooks to run Budget vs. Actual reports.

For example, you can export your QuickBooks budget into Excel and copy the budget into multiple worksheets. One worksheet could be a bare bones budget in case a client with shaky financials disappears. A second worksheet could represent your ideal budget if you snag that big new client. And a third worksheet could be your most likely results, somewhere in between the two extremes.

A command that copies a budget would be convenient—even Quicken, Intuit's software for personal finances, has one. But once you get the hang of exporting and importing budget files, you'll barely notice the extra steps.

Note: You can't export only the budget you want to copy or play with. When you export the Budget lists in QuickBooks, the export file contains entries for every budget for every fiscal year. If you created budgets for customers, jobs, and classes, you'll get entries for those, too. When you work on the budgets in a spreadsheet, you can ignore the entries for those other budgets—or you can delete those rows in the spreadsheet to prevent inadvertent changes to budgets you're happy with.

Here's how you export QuickBooks budgets and import your changes:

1. **Choose File → Utilities → Export → Lists to IIF Files.**

   QuickBooks opens an Export dialog box with checkboxes for each type of list you can export.

2. **In this first Export dialog box, turn on the Budgets checkbox and click OK.**

   QuickBooks opens a second Export dialog box, which looks like a Save As dialog box. However, the "Save as type" box is automatically filled in with IIF Files (*.IIF).

3. **In the second Export dialog box, navigate to the folder in which you want to save the export file and in the "File name" box, replace *.IIF with the name for your export file.**

To keep your files organized, save all your export files in the same folder, called something like QBExport_Files. Use a file name that identifies the contents of the file, such as QBBudgets.iif.

4. Click Save to export the budgets from QuickBooks.

When a QuickBooks Information box appears telling you that the export was successful, click OK to dismiss it.

5. In a spreadsheet program such as Excel, open the budget export file.

IIF files are tab-delimited text files (see Chapter 21). To open one in Excel, choose File → Open. In the Open dialog box, head to the "Files of type" box, and then choose All Files so you can see every file in your folders. Navigate to the folder that contains the IIF export file and double-click its file name. The Excel Text Import Wizard appears. You don't have to specify any special formats to tell Excel how to read the file; you can just click Finish to import the file into Excel.

6. While you're still in Excel, if you want to use an existing budget to create next year's budget, all you do is change the year in the STARTDATE column.

The Excel worksheet includes a column labeled STARTDATE, which contains the date that the fiscal year begins. Use the Excel Replace command (Edit → Replace or Ctrl+H) to change the year to the new budget (Figure 18-5).

To modify budget numbers, edit the budget values in the Excel worksheet.

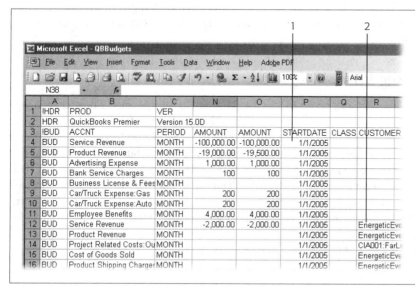

Figure 18-5:
1: The budget entries for 2005 budgets include "1/1/2005" in the STARTDATE column. To create a budget for 2006, change the contents of these cells to "1/1/2006."

2: Budget entries for customer, job, or class budgets include the customer and job name in the CUSTOMER column or the class name in the CLASS column. You can delete all the rows for budgets that you aren't changing before importing the file into QuickBooks.

Tip: If you create several what-if budgets in Excel, be sure to copy the data for only your final budget into a file for import into QuickBooks. Compare the keywords and column headings in the Budget list export file to those in the file you plan to import to make sure that the data imports the way you want. For example, a row that begins with !BUD contains the keywords that identify columns, such as ACCNT for your accounts and AMOUNT for your budget values. Rows for budget entries must begin with a cell containing the keyword BUD. For more information on importing and exporting data, see Chapter 21.

7. **Choose File → Save As and save the modified file with a new file name.**

   In the Save As dialog box, Excel chooses Text (tab delimited) as the file type, which is just what you want.

8. **To import the modified IIF file, back in QuickBooks, choose File → Utilities → Import → IIF Files.**

   QuickBooks opens the Import dialog box and automatically chooses IIF Files (*.IIF) in the "Files of type" box.

9. **Double-click the name of the IIF file that contains your edited budget.**

   When a QuickBooks Information box appears telling you that the import was successful, click OK to dismiss it.

10. **Choose Company → Planning and Budgeting → Set Up Budgets.**

    If you created a budget for a new fiscal year, in the Set Up Budgets dialog box, the Budget drop-down list now contains an entry for the budget for the new year. If you used a spreadsheet to edit an existing budget, in the Budget drop-down list, choose the entry for that budget to see your updated values in the budget table.

Running Budget Reports

A budget gives you a target to aim for. The Set Up Budgets dialog box lets you type values for income and expense accounts, but it doesn't show you whether your budget results in a net profit or loss. For that, you need a budget report. And to see how you're doing compared to your budget, you need a budget report that shows budget and actual numbers side by side. QuickBooks provides four types of budget reports, one to review budgets you've created and the other three to compare your performance to your plan. This section describes the types of budget reports, what they're useful for, and how to create and format them.

Tip: To learn about *all* the options for customizing any kind of report, see Chapter 19.

The Budget Overview Report

Because the Set Up Budgets dialog box shows your accounts and the values you enter for each month, you can't see whether your budget actually works. The Budget Overview Report shows budget numbers for each account and month, but it also subtotals values if you use top-level accounts and subaccounts in your Chart of Accounts, as shown in Figure 18-6.

Note: The Budget Overview Report includes accounts that have budget values and doesn't display accounts for which you didn't specify budget values.

To view the Budget Overview Report, choose Reports → Budgets → Budget Overview. In the Budget Report dialog box, you must first choose the budget you want to view and then the layout you want. When you click Finish, QuickBooks opens the Budget Overview Report window, shown in Figure 18-6.

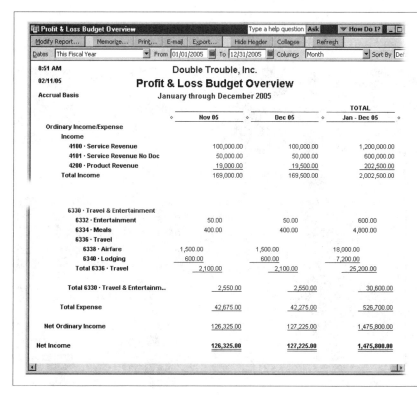

Figure 18-6:
Although you build budgets month by month, many businesses, particularly those with shareholders, focus on quarterly performance. To view your budget by quarter instead of by month, in the Columns drop-down list, choose Quarter. The Budget Overview Report helps you identify whether your budget balances income and expenses by showing the net income (income minus expenses) for each month and for the entire year.

Report layouts

If you create a report for a profit and loss budget for your entire company, the only layout option is Account by Month, which lists the accounts in the first column with each subsequent column showing one month of the fiscal year.

If you choose a Customer:Job budget, the Budget Overview Report includes these layout options:

- **Account By Month.** This layout lists accounts in the first column with months of the fiscal year in the subsequent columns. The values in the monthly columns represent the totals for *all* the Customer:Job budgets you've created.

- **Account By Customer:Job.** This layout lists accounts in the first column and includes additional columns for each customer or job you've budgeted. Each customer and job column shows its annual totals.

- **Customer:Job by Month.** This layout adds a row for each customer and additional rows for each job that customer has. The columns are for each month of the fiscal year. The value for a job and month represents the total budgeted value for all accounts.

Memorizing Budget Reports

When you generate budget reports, you must specify which budget you want to see and the layout of rows and columns. In addition, in the report window, you might click Modify Report to change the date range, the columns that appear, and so on. All in all, to get the budget report you really want might require a dozen or more small customizations.

Rather than reapply all these tweaks each time you generate the report, if you memorize the customized report, you can regenerate it with one click. Here's how:

1. In any report window, click Memorize. QuickBooks opens the Memorize Report dialog box.

2. In the Name box, type the name for the customized report, such as P&L Budget vs. Actual 2005.

3. If you want to save the report in a special group, turn on the Save in Memorized Report Group checkbox. In the drop-down list, choose the group. For example, for budget reports, you might store the report in the Company group. If you don't save the report to a special group, QuickBooks adds the memorized report to the Memorized Report submenu.

4. Click OK.

To run the report, choose Reports → Memorized Reports. If you didn't save the report to a memorized group, choose the report name on the Memorized Reports submenu. If you did save the report in a memorized group, on the Memorized Reports submenu, choose that group and then choose the report name.

Budget vs. Actual Report

The Budget vs. Actual report compares the budget you created to the actual income and expenses your business achieved. Run this report monthly for early warnings should your performance veer off track. For example, if your income is short of your target, the "% of Budget" column shows percentages less than 100 percent, as is painfully apparent in Figure 18-7. On the other hand, costs greater than 100 percent indicate that expenses are ballooning beyond your budget.

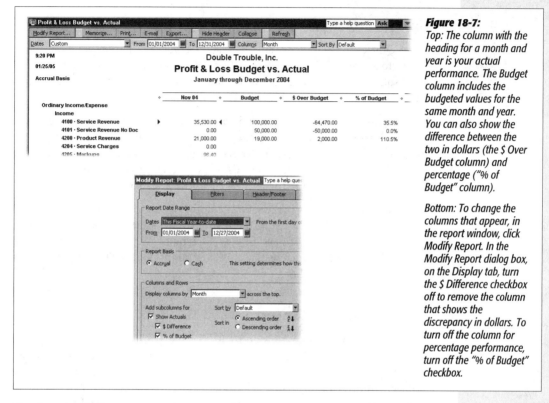

Figure 18-7:
Top: The column with the heading for a month and year is your actual performance. The Budget column includes the budgeted values for the same month and year. You can also show the difference between the two in dollars (the $ Over Budget column) and percentage ("% of Budget" column).

Bottom: To change the columns that appear, in the report window, click Modify Report. In the Modify Report dialog box, on the Display tab, turn the $ Difference checkbox off to remove the column that shows the discrepancy in dollars. To turn off the column for percentage performance, turn off the "% of Budget" checkbox.

To view the Budget vs. Actual Report, choose Reports → Budgets → Budget vs. Actual. You must choose the budget you want to view and the layout you want. When you click Finish, QuickBooks opens the Budget vs. Actual report window.

Tip: If the numbers in your report don't seem right, the culprit could be the wrong choice of Accrual or Cash reporting. Click Modify Report and click the Accrual or Cash option to match your reporting style.

Cash basis reporting records income when you deposit checks and records expenses when you pay for things. With Accrual accounting, you record income when you invoice a customer and record expenses when you receive bills. Page 159 tells you more about the difference.

Profit & Loss Budget Performance Report

The Profit & Loss Budget Performance Report also compares budgeted versus actual values, but initially shows the actual values for the current month to date with the budgeted values for the entire month in the Budget column. Two additional columns show the actual and budgeted values for the year to date.

Use this report to check your performance before the end of the month. Because the budget numbers represent the entire month, you shouldn't expect a perfect match between actual and budgeted values. However, if your income or expenses are way off the mark, you can take corrective action.

Budget vs. Actual Graph

To have QuickBooks automatically generate a graph comparing your budget to actual performance, choose Reports → Budgets → Budget vs. Actual Graph. This graph displays the differences between your budgeted and actual values in two ways:

- The upper bar graph shows the difference between your actual net income and budgeted net income for each month. When your actual net income exceeds the budgeted value, you've made more money than you planned. The bar is blue and appears above the horizontal axis. If the actual net income is less than the budget, the bar is red and drops below the horizontal axis.

- The lower bar graph sorts accounts, customers, or classes (depending on the report you chose) that are the furthest from your budgeted values (either above or below). For example, if you display a P&L by Accounts and Jobs graph, you can see the customers and jobs that exceeded your budget by the largest amount or that fell the furthest short.

Planning with QuickBooks Decision Tools

QuickBooks includes several decision tools, which explain choices managers must make. Some of these decision tools would be more aptly named training tools, because they mainly explain how typical businesses operate. For example, the "Employee, Contractor, or Temp?" decision tool discusses when it makes sense to use contractors or temporary workers and when to bite the bullet and hire employees. It also explains the pros and cons of each type of worker. To access the decision tools, choose Company → Planning and Budgeting → Decision Tools, and then on the submenu, choose the tool you want to use.

The tabs that appear vary, but each tab provides educational information that's helpful if you're inexperienced in an area of business management, as demonstrated in Figure 18-8.

Here're the decision tools that QuickBooks offers and what they cover:

- **Measure profitability.** This decision tool displays a graph of your net profit margin for the past four quarters. Net profit margin is the percentage of profit you earn for each dollar you make in sales. Downward trends in net profit margin are not a good sign. Read the information in the Measure profitability decision tool to find out how to stave off problems.

- **Analyze financial strength.** This decision tool shows your company's current ratio, which is the ratio of assets that can be quickly converted to cash divided by liabilities due in the next 12 months. For a margin of safety, companies typically keep at least twice as much money in short-term assets as they need to pay the short-term liabilities.

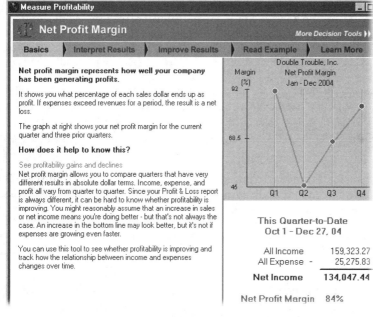

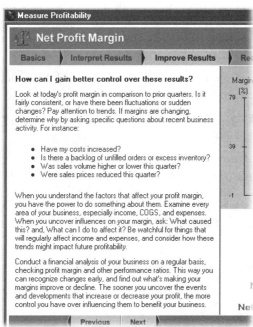

Figure 18-8:
Top: For the Measure Profitability decision tool, the Basics tab explains why net profit margin is important to your business. The Interpret Results tab tells you how to gauge your company's performance compared to typical businesses. If you absorb concepts better with examples, click the Read Example tab. The Learn More tab provides more detailed information and includes links to even more information.

Bottom: If your company is performing poorly in an area or if you want to do better than you are, the Improve Results tab explains steps you might take to improve performance in this area.

Note: This decision tool discusses the importance of the current ratio, but there's much more to financial strength than that. In addition, your current ratio doesn't show some of the problems you might have. For example, inventory is a current asset, but that inventory could be obsolete and worth almost nothing. Accounts receivable are a current asset, but might be uncollectible.

- **Compare Debt and Ownership.** This decision tool displays your company's debt-to-equity ratio for the last four quarters. Read the explanations in this tool to learn about the pros and cons of using other people's money to support your business.

- **Depreciate your assets.** Learn more about what depreciation is and the different ways you can depreciate your assets. The last tab in this decision tool includes a depreciation calculator. However, you must enter the information about the asset; QuickBooks can't gather the information from your Fixed Asset List.

- **Manage Your Receivables.** This educational tool explains why you should be careful when extending credit to your customers and how you can set up your business to urge your customers to pay on time.

- **Employee, contractor, or temp?** Learn about the different types of workers you can hire, when it makes sense to use each kind, and your responsibilities with each type.

- **Improve your cash flow.** Cash flow represents the cold hard cash that your company generates and is truly the fuel that feeds a growing enterprise. The QuickBooks decision tool doesn't deal with the underlying management challenges of cash flow, but instead focuses on QuickBooks features you can use to collect the money owed to your company, such as using online merchant services and accepting credit cards.

- **Track your taxes.** This decision tool explains how QuickBooks can simplify preparing your company records when tax season rolls around.

- **Prepare For Tax Filing.** This tool is one window with a few year-end tips and links to Help topics about taxes.

- **Periodic tasks.** This tool has tabs for tasks that you should perform weekly, monthly, quarterly, at the end of the year, and as needed. For example, weekly tasks include backing up your company file, paying bills, and printing invoices and other forms. Quarterly tasks include filing payroll forms and analyzing your financial performance. If business administrivia isn't your forte, open this tool regularly to see which tasks are due.

Tracking Your Business with Reports

QuickBooks comes with loads of built-in reports that show what's going on with your company finances. But a dozen report categories with several reports tucked in each category can make for a frustrating search, particularly if you're new to both QuickBooks *and* business. The first challenge is knowing what type of report tells you what you need to know. For example, an income statement or profitability report tells you how much income you earned, but a cash flow statement tells you how much cold cash your company generated.

The second challenge is finding the report you want in QuickBooks. After you decide you want to analyze the profitability of the items you sell, do you look for the corresponding QuickBooks report in the Sales category, Inventory category, or Jobs, Time & Mileage? (If you guessed Jobs, Time & Mileage, despite that category's project-oriented name, you're right.)

In QuickBooks 2006, the Report Center is a handy way to find the reports you want. Flipping through a book can be even faster, which is why this chapter describes some of the more popular built-in reports, what they're good for, and where you can find them.

A third challenge—for even the most knowledgeable QuickBooks aficionados—is that the built-in reports never seem to do exactly what you want. A date range is off, information that you don't want shows up, or the data is grouped in ways that don't make sense for your business. After using QuickBooks for a while, most businesses tweak the program's built-in reports. The second half of this chapter explains all the customization techniques you can apply to get what you want.

There's no point letting good customization go to waste, so you'll also learn how to memorize your customized reports, adding them to QuickBooks menus for fast access, and even how to exchange particularly handy customized reports between company files.

Finding the Right Reports

If you know what kind of report answers your burning business question, finding the right report can be as simple as dragging your mouse through the Reports menu to a likely category, and then, on the category submenu, clicking the name of the report you want. But when you need help figuring out what a report does for you and what one looks like, the Report Center could be your new best friend.

On the QuickBooks navigator bar, click Report Center. This window contains a clickable list of the same report categories as on the Reports menu. But unlike the menu, Report Center gives you all sorts of hints for finding the right report, shown in Figure 19-1.

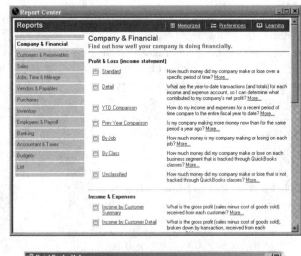

Figure 19-1:

Top: When you click a report category, under the category heading, QuickBooks summarizes what these reports do. The name of each report in that category appears as a link, which you can click to generate that report immediately. But before you do that, review the brief descriptions to find the right report.

Bottom: If you still don't know whether a report is what you want after reading its description, click More. QuickBooks opens the Help topic for the report, which often gives you hints about customization. If nothing but a visual example will do, find the report icon to the left of the report name. Position the mouse pointer over the icon to see an example of the report.

A Quick Guide to QuickBooks Reports

Some entries on the Reports menu are commands, but most entries are categories of reports. When you position the pointer over a category, a submenu with report names appears. Read the following sections to learn what each category of reports represents—a big help in finding the reports you want—and which reports are most likely to help. If you still don't find the report that you want, head to page 489 to bone up on customizing reports.

Company & Financial Reports

Knowing how your company is doing financially is a big part of business management. To give you some insight, QuickBooks' Company & Financial reports include several variations on the basic financial statements (Profit & Loss report or income statement, Balance Sheet, and Statement of Cash Flows). The Securities and Exchange Commission requires that publicly traded companies publish these three financial reports, which gives you a clue about how informative they are.

Because financial statements are a regular staple of the business owner's diet, Chapter 14 explains what each does and how to set them up. To generate a financial report, choose Reports → Company & Financial. Then choose one of the reports on the submenu. Chapter 15 gives you step-by-step instructions for producing Profit & Loss, Balance Sheet, and Statement of Cash Flows reports at the end of your fiscal year.

Profit & Loss reports

Profit & Loss reports start with income and then subtract expenses to show whether you made or lost money over a period of time. The Profit & Loss Standard report covers the current month to date, perfect for companies that manage month by month. If you want to see year-to-date performance, choose either the Profit & Loss YTD Comparison, which compares the month-to-date to the year-to-date, or the Profit & Loss Prev Year Comparison, which shows year-to-date values for this year and last year.

Tip: The Profit & Loss Detail report lists every transaction that contributes to income or expenses in every account, which is great if you're trying to find a transaction that got lost. Most of the time, this report includes too much information to be of much help, but you can filter the report (page 496) to focus it.

If you use classes to track income and expenses by office, division, or region, choose Profit & Loss by Class. And, for companies that primarily work on jobs, use Profit & Loss by Job to analyze your job winners and losers.

Tip: The Profit & Loss Unclassified report shows income and expenses that aren't assigned to any class, which is handy for two reasons. First, it shows your profit and loss for the part of your business not associated with classes. Second, if you track *everything* by class, this report should be empty. Double-click the values in this report to find transactions that are missing class assignments.

Income and expenses

If you're introducing enhanced services to keep your best customers or you're looking for customers that you *want* your competition to take, use the Income by Customer Summary report to see gross profit (sales minus cost of goods sold) for each of your customers. On the expense side, the Expenses by Vendor Summary report shows how much you spend with each vendor. Maybe it's time to negotiate volume discounts or set up electronic ordering to speed up deliveries.

Balance sheet

Balance sheets are a snapshot of assets, liabilities, and equity as of a specific day. The Balance Sheet Standard report shows balances for every asset, liability, and equity account, which is the report you typically generate for tax returns and shareholder reports. If you want to see an abbreviated balance sheet that shows only the totals for each type of account (such as current assets, fixed assets, current liabilities, long-term liabilities, and equity), choose Balance Sheet Summary.

Statement of Cash Flows

The Statement of Cash Flows report tells you how much cash you have—something that profit and loss reports can't do, thanks to non-cash accounting anomalies like depreciation. The Statement of Cash Flows reports your cash flow for the year to date based on the accounts you've tapped as cash flow accounts in Reports & Graphs Classify Cash preferences (page 160).

Are you wondering whether you have any invoices due that will cover a big credit card bill that's coming up? Are you hoping that income over the next few weeks is enough to meet payroll? Use the Cash Flow Forecast report to check for cash flow problems over the next four weeks, as demonstrated in Figure 19-2.

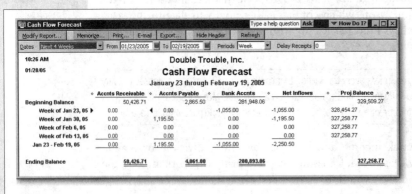

Figure 19-2:
If you want to review cash flow for a longer period, in the Dates drop-down list, choose Next 4 Weeks or Next Fiscal Quarter. Or type the exact dates you want in the From and To boxes. To change the length of each period in the report, in the Periods drop-down list, choose from Week, Two Weeks, Month, etc.

The Beginning Balance line shows the current balance for your Accounts Receivable, Accounts Payable, and bank accounts. QuickBooks sets up the report initially to show money flowing in and out over the next four weeks. To view additional weeks, in the From and To boxes, type the date range you want.

The Proj Balance column shows how much money you should have in your bank accounts at the end of each week. If that number starts flirting with zero, you're about to run out of cash. You'll have to speed up some customer payments (the Customers & Receivables reports in the next section can help with that), transfer cash from another account, or look into a short-term loan.

Customers & Receivables Reports

Customers & Receivables reports tell you how much your customers owe you and when the money's due. The longer you let customers go without paying, the less likely those customers are to pay you, so most companies review aging reports frequently. If an aging report shows that customers aren't paying on time, your next step is to run reports that tell you who's falling behind. When it's time to get on the phone, the Customer Phone List and Customer Contact List tell you who to call and the phone number to use.

Tip: If you want QuickBooks to prompt you to call tardy customers, you can set up reminders for overdue invoices (page 155).

Accounts Receivable Aging reports

When you have customers galore, the A/R Aging Summary report (page 248) is the fastest way to look for dangerously overdue accounts. The columns in this report start with amounts that aren't overdue, but each additional column means up to another 30 days late. For example, Current means the balance isn't due yet; 1–30 means the customer balance is between 1 and 30 days late. And so on.

You have two choices for reminding customers, which depend on whether you're an optimist or a pessimist:

- For the optimist who assumes that customers will pay, start with the >90 column (customer balances that are more than 90 days late). Call the customers with the oldest payments first and ask "Hey, did you forget about us?"

- The pessimist thinks that customers who *haven't* paid aren't *going to* pay. To the pessimist, payments older than 90 days are lost causes. So start working on the payments in the 1–30 column. By keeping after customers while your invoices are still fresh, you might prevent payments from reaching the >90 column.

Tip: If you really think old payments are hopeless, write them off (page 347).

The A/R Aging Detail report shows overdue invoices and statement charges grouped by lateness, but, if you're ready to call customers, the Collections report provides everything you need: each overdue payment, who to call, and phone numbers, as illustrated in Figure 19-3.

Customer balance reports

The Customer Balance Summary shows the total balance for every customer and job, whether or not the amounts are overdue. Although large balances aren't always a bad sign, you can double-click a row in this report to see all the transactions that make up a customer's balance.

Figure 19-3:
The report shows the company contact's name and phone number. Once you have someone on the phone and you need more detail about a late invoice, double-click the transaction to view its details in the Create Invoices or Enter Statement Charges dialog boxes.

Tip: Most Customers & Receivables reports focus on charges you've already invoiced. If you invoice customers for reimbursable expenses, be sure to regularly run the Unbilled Costs by Job report to look for job expenses that you've forgotten to invoice.

Customer lists

Most companies use other programs to keep track of customers and customer conversations. If you don't have a separate customer database, you can generate a Customer Phone List or the Customer Contact List in QuickBooks. Choose Report → Customers & Receivables and then choose the customer list you want. (These lists also appear when you choose Reports → List.)

The Item Price List might seem misplaced on the Customers & Receivables submenu; QuickBooks includes it for convenience in case a customer on the phone has a question about the items you sell. As you'd expect, the report also appears on the List submenu.

Sales Reports

Most companies analyze their sales to find ways to improve. Reviewing sales by customer, item, and sales rep tells you who's hot and what's not.

- The **Sales By Customer Summary** is a terse listing of customers and how much you've sold to each one. Choose Reports → Sales → Sales By Customer Summary to run it. The Sales By Item Summary shows how much you sell of each item in your Item List, starting with inventory items, then non-inventory parts, and finally service items. This report includes a column for average cost of goods sold (COGS) and gross margin, which apply only to inventory items you sell.

- The **Sales Graph** presents sales data in a cheery rainbow of colors, but you can quickly switch the graph to show the breakdown of sales by customer, item, and sales rep, as shown in Figure 19-4. Choose Reports → Sales → Sales Graph to generate it. The bar graph shows sales by month for the year to date. If you want to change the duration of the graph, click Dates and specify the date range you want. The pie chart shows sales distributed by category. In the window button bar, click By Item, By Customer, or By Rep to switch between distribution by item, customer, and sales rep, respectively.

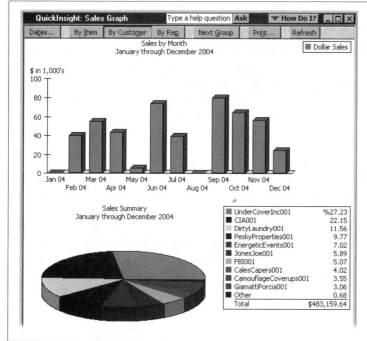

Figure 19-4:
This pie chart by customer shows that half of sales come from two large customers—which is a risk should either customer go out of business or find another vendor.

Jobs, Time & Mileage

QuickBooks puts reports for jobs, time, and mileage together, but the three are not necessarily related. Whether you want reports for jobs, the hours you charge, or the miles you drive, start by choosing Reports → Jobs, Time & Mileage, and then choose the report you want.

Job reports

If your business is based on jobs rather than ongoing work, job profitability is important. For example, if you consistently lose money when you build custom homes, but you make tons of money building banks, you might decide to target a different construction market. The Job Profitability Summary report shows your actual cost, actual revenue, and the difference between the two, which is your profit or loss on each job.

Profitability as a percentage makes it easy to gauge how well or badly you're doing, but QuickBooks doesn't include that measure in the report initially. Here's how to get that info: in the Job Profitability Summary window, click Modify Report. In the Modify Report dialog box, click the Display tab and then turn on the % Difference checkbox.

Note: The Profit & Loss By Job report appears on both the Jobs, Time & Mileage submenu and the Company & Financial submenu.

If you're in the retail business, you might think you can skip the Jobs, Time & Mileage report category. But one idiosyncrasy of QuickBooks classifications is that the Item Profitability report appears only on the Jobs, Time & Mileage submenu. This report shows how much you made or lost on each item in your Item List and can show the margin on your items if you modify the report to show the percentage of cost to revenue. The report begins with inventory items, but continues with non-inventory part items. It also lists your service items, other charges, and discounts—despite the costs on these items usually being zero.

Tip: Rare are customers who write you a blank check for a job, so most jobs require estimates of what the work will cost. When you've finished a job that you estimated, take some time to run the Job Estimates vs. Actuals Summary report to see how you did compared to your estimate. Do this a few times and the accuracy of your estimates should improve dramatically.

If you invoice jobs based on the progress you've made (page 219), run the Job Progress Invoices vs. Estimates report. This report compares your estimate to actual performance through your most recent progress invoice.

Time reports

If you charge customers for your time or request reimbursement for mileage, you'd better keep good records. For that matter, if you pay people by the hour, you can be sure that they'll raise a ruckus if you shortchange their paychecks. Time and mileage reports, covered in detail in Chapter 17, help you double-check invoices and payroll records.

QuickBooks includes time reports by job, by name, and by item. If you bill by the job, the Time by Job Summary report shows hours for each job, broken down by

Service items. Overly high or low hours—or Service items that don't belong on a job—are red flags for data entry errors.

When you want to verify that your workers properly set their time as billable, choose the Time by Job Detail report. Time is grouped by job and Service item, but each time entry shows when the hours were worked, who performed the work, and whether the work is billable. If hours are billable but not yet invoiced, the report shows the Billing status as Unbilled.

The Time by Name report shows the hours that each person works broken down by customer and job. QuickBooks sets the date range to This Fiscal Year-to-Date, but if you want to check timesheets for accuracy, you can change the date range to Last Week or Last Month.

Mileage reports

Mileage records come in handy when you prepare your taxes or if your customers question their mileage charges. You can generate mileage reports by choosing Reports → Jobs, Time & Mileage or in the Enter Vehicle Mileage dialog box (choose Company → Enter Vehicle Mileage) by clicking the Mileage Reports button.

For your tax backup, the Mileage by Vehicle Summary shows the total miles you drove each vehicle and the corresponding mileage expense (which QuickBooks calculates using the standard mileage rate in effect at the time). If you charge customers for mileage, run the Mileage by Job Summary report both for total miles driven and the billable mileage by customer and job. The Mileage by Job Detail report shows each trip separately with its start and end dates, miles driven, billing status, and mileage rate.

Vendors & Payables

After you've picked apart the income side of your business, it's time to look at your expenses. Vendors & Payables reports tell you how much you owe each vendor and when the bills are due. QuickBooks also includes special reports for 1099 tax forms and sales tax liabilities. Governments and tax agencies are quick to penalize you for not paying promptly, so these tax reports are particularly important. Choose Reports → Vendors & Payables and then choose the report you want to run.

A/P Aging and Vendor Balance reports

If your company is flush with cash and you pay bills as soon as they appear in the Pay Bills dialog box, your A/P Aging reports and Vendor Balance reports will contain mostly zeroes. In fact, because the Pay Bills dialog box lets you sort bills by due date, discount date, vendor, and amount, you might not find any reason to run these reports. For example, if you juggle payments to vendors to conserve cash, you can easily pay the oldest bills first by sorting bills by due date. But if you want an overview of how much you owe to each vendor and how much is overdue, use the A/P Aging Summary or Vendor Balance Detail reports.

1099 forms

If you hire independent contractors, the IRS wants to know how much you paid them. At the end of the year, you have to generate 1099 forms so the contractors can report their earnings. The 1099 Summary report shows which vendors need a 1099 form and the total you paid them. It's a good idea to review this report before printing the 1099-MISC forms, particularly since you print the forms on special paper (page 404).

Tip: If the total for an independent contractor looks wrong, double-click the row for that contractor to have QuickBooks automatically display the 1099 Detail report with every check you wrote to that person.

Sales tax reports

The Sales Tax Liability Report shows your taxable and nontaxable sales as well as the sales taxes you've collected for each tax agency. QuickBooks automatically sets the dates for the report to match the payment interval preference you chose (page 312). For example, if you set the payment interval to monthly to make sure you catch every required payment, in the Sales Tax Liability Report window, the program chooses Last Month from the Dates drop-down list.

Purchases

The reports in the Vendors & Payables category tell you how much you owe to your vendors, but the reports in the Purchases category focus on how much you've bought from each vendor you work with. When you run the Purchases By Vendor Summary report and see high dollar values, you might want to negotiate volume discounts or faster delivery times. These summary reports can also show when you rely too heavily on one vendor—a big risk should that vendor go out of business.

The Purchases by Item Summary report shows how many inventory items you've purchased and the total you paid. The Purchases by Item Detail report shows each purchase transaction with the quantity, cost, and vendor. If your supplies are dwindling, the Open Purchase Orders report shows when more items are due, as illustrated in Figure 19-5.

Figure 19-5:
For a report of open purchase orders, choose Reports → Purchases → Open Purchase Orders. The report shows only the date, vendor name, purchase order number, and delivery date. Double-click a purchase order to open the Create Purchase Orders dialog box, which shows the products on the order.

Inventory

After you review Purchases reports to see the inventory you've already bought, you can turn to Inventory reports (page 412) to find out how much inventory you have and whether you need to buy more. You don't want to run out of inventory, because that means lost sales, but neither do you want to tie up too much money in inventory—particularly products that grow obsolete quickly, such as clothing and high-tech gadgets. The Inventory Valuation Summary report provides a thorough overview of the inventory you have on hand. For each inventory item, you can see how many you have in stock, the average cost you paid, the asset value of your inventory, and the retail value if you sell it at your standard price (entered in the item record).

To see *all* the items you need to reorder, there's no better place than the Inventory Stock Status by Item report. Although the report shows quantity on hand and the number on purchase orders, a checkmark in the Order column means you should order more—that is, you have less than the number that's in the Reorder Point field for the item (page 96).

GEM IN THE ROUGH

Running Multiple Reports

Perhaps you perform the same tasks every month—calling customers with overdue invoices, checking inventory, and reviewing sales by item, for example—and you need reports to complete each task. If you run reports one at a time, you might sit for hours in front of the computer with nothing but the occasional click to break the monotony, while Quick-Books slowly transforms your data into report hard copies.

But you don't have to do it that way. Tucked away on the Reports menu is the Process Multiple Reports command, which runs all the reports you choose one after the other. Stock the printer with paper, make sure the toner cartridge isn't running low, and then use Process Multiple Reports to run dozens of reports while you do something else, or even better, head home (as long as the printer is located in a secure location).

Process Multiple Reports works only with memorized reports, because you have no opportunity to customize the reports it processes. So customize each report you run regularly to include the correct information and apply the formatting you want, and then memorize each one.

When you choose Reports → Process Multiple Reports, QuickBooks opens the Process Multiple Reports window. It

lists, but doesn't automatically select, all of your memorized reports. In the "Select Memorized Reports from" drop-down list, you can choose a memorized group of reports to have QuickBooks automatically select all the reports in that memorized group, as shown in the figure. To streamline Process Multiple Reports, create a memorized group (page 501) for each collection of reports you process, such as EndofMonth or EndofQuarter.

To include or remove a report, Ctrl+click the checkmark column. When all the reports you want to print have checkmarks, click Print. QuickBooks opens the Print Reports dialog box. All you have to do is choose the Printer name and the Number of Copies and click Print to start pushing reports through the printer.

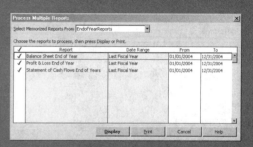

Employees and Payroll

If you use a third-party payroll service, you'll receive payroll reports from that service and you won't need payroll reports from QuickBooks. But if you use the QuickBooks payroll feature, payroll reports (see Chapter 11) let you review relevant data before cutting payroll checks. They also tell you what your payroll liabilities are and when you have to pay them to the appropriate government agencies.

The Payroll Summary report shows what you've paid on each payroll item, such as employee wages, taxes and other withholdings, and employer payroll taxes. QuickBooks generates the report for the current calendar quarter to date, but you can change the date range to see how much you've paid for a month, quarter, or entire year (in the Payroll Summary report window, choose a date range in the Dates drop-down list, or in the From and To boxes, type dates).

The Payroll Detail Review report shows how QuickBooks calculates tax amounts on paychecks. For example, the percentage for Social Security remains the same, but Social Security deductions stop when the employee reaches the maximum Social Security wage.

Because the penalties for submitting payroll liabilities to the government are meant to hurt, you won't want to skip the reports that show how much you owe in payroll taxes and when the payments are due. The Payroll Liability Balances report shows how much you owe for each type of payroll tax for the current quarter. The information you need to fill in on state tax forms appears on the Employee State Taxes Detail report.

Banking

Most of the time, you'll run the Reconciliation Discrepancy report from the Begin Reconciliation dialog box (page 350) only when you have discrepancies that you can't resolve. But the Banking submenu also includes the Reconciliation Discrepancy report and Previous Reconciliation report, which help you bring your QuickBooks company file back in line with your bank statements.

If a deposit shows up on your bank statement, but it doesn't appear in your QuickBooks bank account, you might have forgotten to receive or deposit the payment in QuickBooks. The Deposit Detail report shows payments you've received in QuickBooks and whether you deposited them in your bank account or the Undeposited Funds account. The Check Detail report and the Missing Checks report are both handy for finding checks that don't show up on your bank statement or checks with duplicate numbers in QuickBooks.

Accountant and Taxes

If you work with an accountant, you might never run a report from the Accountant & Taxes submenu unless your accountant asks you to. But if you go it alone keeping your books and preparing your tax returns, these reports (and reading Chapter 15) are key tasks at the end of each year.

If several people work on your company file, run the Audit Trail report frequently to watch for suspicious transactions—deleted invoices or modifications to transactions after they've been reconciled. People make mistakes, and the Audit Trail is also good for spotting inadvertent changes to transactions. QuickBooks initially includes transactions entered or modified today, but you can choose a different date range to review changes since your last review (in the Audit Trail report window, choose a date range in the Date Entered/Last Modified drop-down list, or in the From and To boxes, type dates). The Voided/Deleted Transactions report focuses on transactions that have been voided or deleted.

Whether you prepare your own taxes or let your accountant do the honors, a review of the Income Tax Preparation report can save you money on accountant's fees (and IRS penalties) as well as keep more of your hair attached to your scalp. This report lists the accounts in your Chart of Accounts and shows the tax line to which you assigned it. If an account isn't linked to the right tax line, or worse, not assigned to any tax line, the Income Tax Summary report, which lists each tax line on your tax return with the amount you must report, won't give you the correct values. See page 40 to learn how to connect an account to a tax line.

Budgets and Forecasts

Chapter 18 explains how to prepare budgets and how to use budget reports. Here's a refresher course:

The Set Up Budgets dialog box shows your budgeted amounts for each account, but it doesn't total the income and expenses for each month to show the net profit or loss. For that reason, the Budget Overview Report is an essential step to building a successful budget. After you create a budget, run the Budget Overview report to see whether you earned a profit for the year. Plus, if you see month after month of negative numbers for net income, you could hit a cash flow crunch.

To watch for problems in your company performance, run the Budget vs. Actual Report once a month. This report compares your budget to your actual income and expenses. If your income falls short of budget, you might have a problem with products, sales representatives, or your business plan. If expenses greatly exceed your budget, you might have to find ways to cut costs.

Tip: The key to comparing budget versus actual values is looking for reasons behind significant discrepancies between the budget and actual performance. Then, if the source of the difference is performance, address the problem. For example, it's OK if a large expense occurred earlier than planned but stayed within the budgeted amount. But you have a problem when office supply costs increase threefold because Pietro ordered pencils from Palermo.

List Reports

After you spend time building lists in QuickBooks—of your customers, vendors, items, to do notes, and so on—you might want to produce a report of those lists.

For example, you can create a price list of the things you sell, or a phone list for all of your customers. The List submenu contains entries to output several, but not all, of the lists you create, as you can see in Figure 19-6.

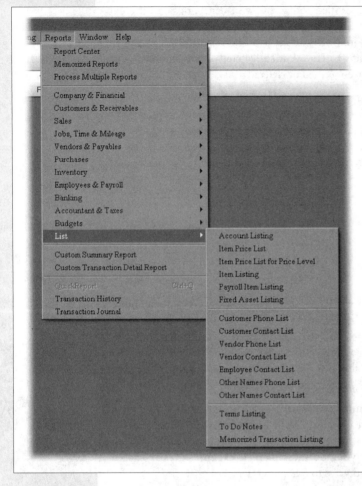

Figure 19-6:
When you choose Reports → List, you can choose reports for your accounts, items, item prices, payroll items, fixed assets, terms, to do notes, and memorized transactions. Other reports produce contact information lists for your customers, vendors, employees, and so on. (Although QuickBooks doesn't include a built-in Phone List report for employees, you can build your own by removing all columns except name and phone number from the Employee Contact List report.)

If you don't care about report formatting, you can print any list directly in Quick-Books. In the QuickBooks menu bar, choose Lists and pick the list you want to print. At the bottom of the list window, click the button whose label is the name of the list (for example, Terms for the Terms List) and then choose Print List on the shortcut menu. QuickBooks displays a message box recommending that you try list reports. But if you click OK, the Print Lists dialog box opens. Click Preview to see what the report looks like. If the report format works for you, click Print.

Custom Reports

If you make it all the way through the QuickBooks report categories without finding the report you want, don't give up hope just yet. The Reports menu includes two entries for building custom reports from scratch:

- **Custom Summary Report.** Choose this menu entry to build a report that displays subtotals by some kind of category. For instance, you could customize a summary report to create an income statement for all customers of a particular type. As soon as you choose Reports → Custom Summary Report, QuickBooks opens both the Custom Summary Report window and the Modify Report dialog box—because a custom report needs *some* kind of customization. You can set up the contents and appearance of the report any way you want, as shown in Figure 19-7.

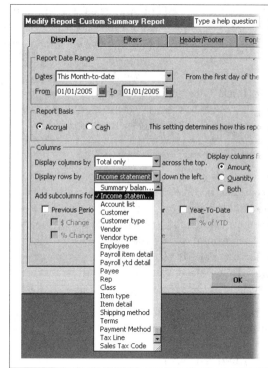

Figure 19-7:
In addition to date ranges, filters, and other customizations (page 489), you can control what QuickBooks displays in the rows and columns of a custom report. The entries in the "Display columns by" and "Display rows by" drop-down lists are the same, so you can set up a report to show your data across or down. A report that uses the same category for both columns and rows doesn't make any sense, so be sure to choose different entries for columns and rows. The Modify Report window for custom reports also includes checkboxes for comparing values to previous periods as well as showing dollar and percentage differences, like budget versus actual reports do.

- **Custom Transaction Detail Report.** This report lets you customize transaction reports to show exactly the fields you want to see. The Modify Report dialog box includes a list of fields that you can turn on and off, as well as checkboxes for specifying how you want to sort and total the results.

A Review of Report Preferences

Chapter 6 explains every preference you can set in QuickBooks, but a chapter devoted to reports wouldn't be complete without a brief review of report preferences.

Company-Wide Report Preferences

Some features on reports should remain consistent for every report that a company generates, such as whether you use cash or accrual accounting. A QuickBooks administrator can set company-wide report preferences to ensure that reports show financial information correctly and consistently. To set company preferences, choose Edit → Preferences. In the Edit Preferences dialog box, on the icon bar, click Reports & Graphs, and then click the Company Preferences tab.

Here are the company-wide preferences and what you can do with them:

- **Summary Reports Basis.** Select either the Accrual option or the Cash option to match the accounting method your company uses. When you upgrade QuickBooks, be sure to check that the installation didn't reset your Summary Reports Basis choice.

Note: When you choose the Cash option, your Profit & Loss reports show income only after you receive customer payments and show expenses only after you pay bills. With the Accrual option, income appears in Profit & Loss reports as soon as you record an invoice or other type of sale, and expenses show up as soon as you enter bills.

- **Aging Reports.** Whether you're checking on overdue invoices to see which customers to call or moving on to assess finance charges, calculating the age of invoices, statements, and bills shouldn't vary by customer or vendor. In the Aging Reports section, choose the option that best reflects your company's aging policy. If you choose the "Age from due date" option, age is the number of days that have passed since the due date. If you choose "Age from transaction date," QuickBooks calculates the age starting at the date of the transaction, which is the more punitive approach.

- **Reports—Show Accounts by.** QuickBooks automatically includes only account names in reports, which might not be very informative, particularly when you use abbreviated account names. In this section, choose an option to display account names only, account descriptions only, or both.

- **Statement of Cash Flows.** QuickBooks automatically associates accounts in your Chart of Accounts with the Operating, Investing, and Financing sections of the Statement of Cash Flows report. For example, accounts for fixed assets show up as investing, accounts for loans fall under financing, and accounts such as Accounts Receivable and Inventory appear as operating accounts. To ensure that your Statement of Cash Flows report (page 389) is correct, in the Statement of Cash Flows section, click Classify Cash to review the account assignments.

- **Format.** Anyone can format an individual report by selecting the information that appears in report headers and footers and by specifying the appearance of numbers and text. The QuickBooks administrator can set standard formats for all reports by clicking Format.

Individual Preferences

Here're the preferences people can set for the reports they generate:

- **Prompt me to modify report options before opening a report.** If you usually make small changes to every report you generate, turn on this checkbox so that QuickBooks automatically opens the Modify Report window every time you run a report. If the checkbox is turned off and you want to modify a report, in the report window, click Modify Report.

- **Reports and Graphs section.** This section would be better named Refreshing Reports and Graphs. If your QuickBooks data changes frequently, choose the "Prompt me to refresh" option, so you can decide whether you want to refresh your reports to show the most recent financial information. If a reminder about refreshing reports is too annoying, choose the "Don't refresh" option. However, if your reports must be accurate at all times, choose "Refresh automatically" and prepare yourself for interruptions as the program automatically updates your report.

Tip: If you don't choose "Refresh automatically," you can tell QuickBooks to refresh a report with current data in any report window by clicking Refresh.

- **Draw graphs in 2D.** If you want fast response more than fancy graphics, turn on this checkbox so that QuickBooks displays graphs in two, rather than three, dimensions.

- **Use patterns.** If you plan to print to a black and white printer, turn on this checkbox to substitute black and white patterns for colors on graphs.

Running Reports

QuickBooks tries to atone for any difficulties you might have finding the right reports by scattering commands to run reports in windows, menus, and centers throughout the program. Stick with the Report Center (page 470) if you want to learn about and choose from every built-in report that QuickBooks offers. When you're more familiar with what QuickBooks reports do, Figure 19-8 shows other ways to run reports.

Some reports take a long time to generate, because they pull data from every corner of the company file. And running your company file in multi-user mode exacerbates the problem. If you're hunkering down to a report-running session of epic proportions, here are some tips for speeding up your work:

- Wait until everyone else has logged out of the company file.

- If possible, log into QuickBooks from the computer that contains the company file. Otherwise, log into the fastest computer on your network.

- In QuickBooks, switch the file to single-user mode by choosing File → Switch to Single-user Mode.

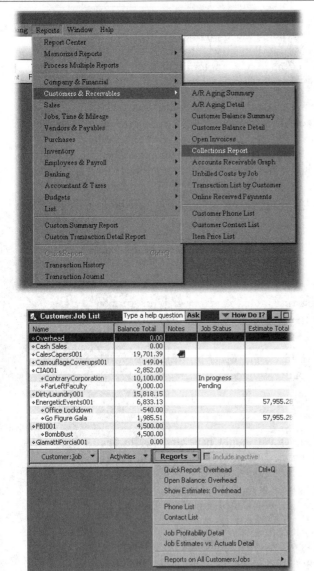

Figure 19-8:
Top: The Reports menu not only includes the built-in QuickBooks reports; it also launches the Report Center and contains the Process Multiple Reports command, described on page 479.

Bottom: At the bottom of every list window is a Reports button, which displays reports related to the list you're viewing.

Printing and Saving Reports

In QuickBooks, you can turn any report you create into either a hard copy or an electronic file. If you save a report as a file, you can use it to feed other programs or edit the report in ways that you can't do in QuickBooks.

Printing Reports

Printing a report doesn't take any imagination. In a report window, click Print. In the Print Reports dialog box that opens, QuickBooks offers most of the same printing options that you find in other programs, as you can see in Figure 19-9.

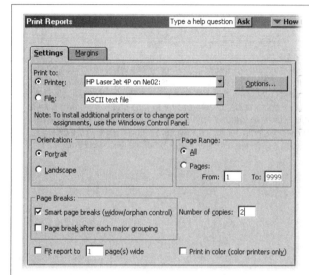

Figure 19-9:
Select the Printer option and then, in the Printer drop-down list, choose the printer to which you want to send the report. You can print reports in portrait or landscape orientation. You can also specify the pages you want to print, how many copies to print, where you want page breaks, and whether to print in color. If a report is a bit too wide to fit on one page, turn on the "Fit report to" checkbox, which lets you force the report onto one (or more) pages.

Saving Reports to Files

Intuit provides two places to transform reports into files. The Print dialog box contains an option to create ASCII text files, tab-delimited files, and comma-delimited files. But you can also create comma-delimited files and Excel workbooks by choosing Export in any report window. (The comma-delimited files that you create in both dialog boxes are identical, so you can generate them with whichever method you prefer.)

Here are the two ways you can create files for reports and the differences between them:

- **Print to file.** In a report window, click Print, which opens the Print Reports dialog box. Just below the Printer option are the File option and a drop-down list, which includes "ASCII text file," "Comma-delimited file," and "Tab-delimited file." After you choose the type of file and then click Print, QuickBooks opens the Create Disk File dialog box, in which you can specify the file name and where you want to save the file.

The ASCII text file format produces a text file that *looks* like the report, but it uses different fonts and uses space characters to position values in columns. This type of file isn't suitable for importing into spreadsheets or other programs, but you can use it to store an electronic version of your report. If you plan to import the information into another program, use a tab- or comma-delimited file, which use tab characters or commas, respectively, to separate each value. Many programs can read files in these formats.

- **Export to file.** In a report window, clicking Export opens the Export Report dialog box. In the Export Report dialog box, if you choose to export the report to a new workbook or a worksheet in an existing Excel workbook, click the Advanced tab to tell QuickBooks how you want to set up the Excel spreadsheet, as shown in Figure 19-10.

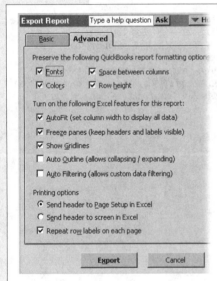

Figure 19-10:
The Advanced tab has three sections for setting up a report in Excel. The first section focuses on whether to transfer the fonts, colors, and spacing that you set up in your QuickBooks reports to the Excel workbook. The second section provides checkboxes for turning on Excel features such as AutoFit, which sets column widths wide enough to display all the data. The Printing options section can send the report header to the Excel header area (in Page setup) or to the top of the worksheet grid.

After you choose a file type and click OK, QuickBooks opens the Create Disk File dialog box, where you can type a file name and choose a location to save the file.

Tip: Creating a .pdf file of a report is a third way to save a report to a file. In a report window, click Print. In the Print Reports dialog box, choose the Printer option and then, in the Printer drop-down list, choose the Adobe PDF printer.

In the Print Reports dialog box, the Page Breaks section contains two checkboxes that control where page breaks occur in a report. If you want to add a page break after each major grouping (such as Income and Expenses in a Profit & Loss report), turn on the "Page break after each major grouping" checkbox. To stuff as much report onto the fewest pages, turn off the "Smart page breaks" (widow/orphan control) checkbox. When you do so, QuickBooks prints to the very last line of a page, even if it means that a single row of a section appears on one page with the rest of the section on another.

Fitting More Report onto Each Page

When a report is rife with columns, it's hard to fit everything onto a single page of paper. QuickBooks automatically prints the columns that don't fit on additional pages, but reports that span multiple pages cause paper rustling and lots of grumbling.

Try these approaches for keeping your report to one page across:

- Before you click Print, reduce the width of the report columns. In the report window, drag the diamond to

the right of a column heading to make the column narrower (or wider), as shown in Figure 19-14.

- In the Print Reports dialog box (in a report window, click Print), turn on the "Fit report to __ page(s) wide" checkbox and, in the number box, type *1*.

- In the Print Reports dialog box, choose the Landscape option for page orientation. When a report almost fits on an 8 1/2 × 11 sheet of paper, switching to landscape orientation should do the trick.

Customizing Reports

The report window is awash with ways to customize reports. Some customization techniques are available in several places:

- **Report window button bar.** Across the top of the report window, the button bar includes the Modify Report button, which opens the all-powerful customization tool—the Modify Report dialog box. The button bar includes other handy customization buttons such as Hide Header and Collapse, discussed in the box on page 492.

- **Report window tool bar.** Below the button bar is a customization toolbar, in which you can choose the date range, the columns to display, and which column to use for sorting the report contents.

- **Report window.** Hidden within the report itself are a few customization features. For example, by right-clicking text in a report, you can format its appearance. Dragging the small diamonds between columns changes the column width and, for detailed reports, you can drag columns to new locations.

Tip: To learn more about a report, including techniques for customizing it, in the report window title bar, click How Do I? and then choose "Learn more about this report" to have QuickBooks open the Help window and display the help topic for the report you've created.

Read on to learn about all the techniques available for making a report exactly what you want.

Date Ranges

Different reports call for different date ranges. Financial statements typically use fiscal periods, such as the last fiscal quarter or the current fiscal year. But most companies manage month by month, so sales reports often cover the current month or month-to-date. Payroll reports span whatever period you use for payroll, whether that's one week, two weeks, or a calendar month. And tax reports depend on the tax periods doled out by the tax agencies you answer to.

QuickBooks contains two dozen preset date ranges that work based on today's date. For example, if it's June 12, 2006, This Fiscal Year represents January 1 through December 31, 2006, but Today is simply 6/12/2006. And, if none of these date ranges do what you want, in the report window toolbar, you can set specific start and end dates in the From and To boxes.

The preset date ranges are numerous because they mix and match several types of date ranges.

- **Durations.** Some preset periods represent durations, such as Week, Month, Fiscal Quarter, Fiscal Year, Tax Quarter, and Tax Year. At the extremes, you can pick All to encompass every date in your company file, or Today, which includes only today.

- **This, Last, and Next.** For each duration, you can choose the current period, such as This Fiscal Quarter, the previous period (Last Fiscal Quarter), or the next period in the future (Next Fiscal Quarter).

- **Full and to-date.** You can also pick between a full period and the period up to today's date. For example, on June 12, "This Month" covers June 1 through June 30. "This Month-to-date" represents June 1 through June 12.

Tip: QuickBooks includes one additional choice, Next Four Weeks, which many businesses use when checking cash flow.

If the date range is the only thing you want to change, the report window toolbar is the best place. In the Dates drop-down list, choose the preset date range you want, or, in the From and To boxes, pick the starting date and ending date for the report, respectively. If you plan to change more than the date, click Modify Report instead. In the Modify Reports dialog box, the Report Date Range section includes the same date setting features as the report window toolbar—as well as several additional tabs and sections for every other type of customization.

Subtotals

Many of QuickBooks' built-in reports calculate subtotals. For instance, Profit & Loss summary reports include subtotals by income, cost of goods sold, expenses, and so on. Sales reports by customer subtotal the sales for all the jobs you do for a customer.

When you create a detailed report, such as Sales by Customer Detail, the report shows every transaction for that report, and you can subtotal the results in any way that makes sense for that type of report, as demonstrated in Figure 19-11.

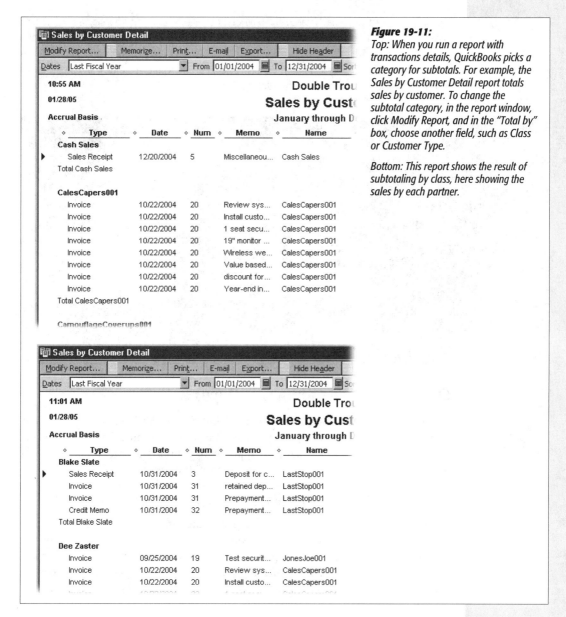

Figure 19-11:
Top: When you run a report with transactions details, QuickBooks picks a category for subtotals. For example, the Sales by Customer Detail report totals sales by customer. To change the subtotal category, in the report window, click Modify Report, and in the "Total by" box, choose another field, such as Class or Customer Type.

Bottom: This report shows the result of subtotaling by class, here showing the sales by each partner.

Depending on the report you pick, some choices in the "Total by" drop-down list are more appropriate than others. For example, you might decide to subtotal a sales report by Customer Type, Rep, or the Account list to see which types of customer provide the most business, which sales rep makes the most sales, or which income account pulls in the highest sales. Subtotaling a sales report by Workman's Comp Code doesn't make any sense—and QuickBooks isn't subtle about saying so: the report displays a zero balance and no rows of data.

Tip: When a selection in the "Total by" drop-down list empties your report, choosing a different field might not bring back your report contents. Close the report by clicking the report window Close button (the button with the X on the right side of the window title bar). In the Memorize Report box that Quick-Books displays, be sure to click No or you'll memorize an empty report. Then run the report anew by choosing it from the appropriate category within the Reports menu.

FREQUENTLY ASKED QUESTION

Viewing More Report on the Screen

How can I see more of a report on the screen?

If your computer monitor is a closer relative to your mobile phone than to your letterbox TV, you can use several techniques to stuff more of the report onto your screen:

- **Hide Header.** While you're working on a report, you don't need the report header to tell you which type of report you're using, your company's name, or the date range. In the report window button bar, click Hide Header to hide the report header and display more report content. The printed report that you

send to others still includes the header. To redisplay the hidden header, in the button bar, click Show Header.

- **Collapse.** You can get a high-level view of a report by hiding subaccounts, the individual jobs for your customers, and subclasses. In the report window button bar, click Collapse. QuickBooks totals the results for the subaccounts, jobs, or subclasses under the main account, customer, or class, respectively. Unlike the Hide Header button, Collapse affects the onscreen view *and* your printed report.

Customizing the Columns in Reports

Some reports start with only one column, but they don't have to stay that way. Depending on the type of report, you can change the columns that appear in several ways. Then, if you find that your appetite for columns is larger than your computer screen, you can remove, resize, and reorder the columns.

Adding and Removing Columns

As you manage your business, you'll generate the same reports for different date ranges. For example, during a year, you might create a Profit & Loss report a month at a time, for each fiscal quarter, and then for the entire year. If the report window toolbar includes a Columns drop-down list, choosing an entry there is the quickest way to change the categories that columns represent (see Figure 19-12).

Note: The Columns drop-down list appears whenever you create a summary-type report. You can make the same choices in the Modify Report dialog box using the "Display columns by" drop-down list.

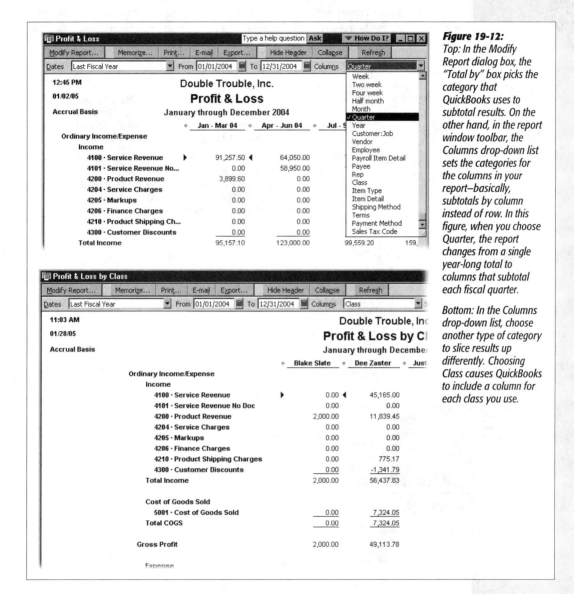

Figure 19-12:
Top: In the Modify Report dialog box, the "Total by" box picks the category that QuickBooks uses to subtotal results. On the other hand, in the report window toolbar, the Columns drop-down list sets the categories for the columns in your report—basically, subtotals by column instead of row. In this figure, when you choose Quarter, the report changes from a single year-long total to columns that subtotal each fiscal quarter.

Bottom: In the Columns drop-down list, choose another type of category to slice results up differently. Choosing Class causes QuickBooks to include a column for each class you use.

Reports that show transaction details, such as Profit & Loss Detail or Inventory Valuation Detail, use columns for data fields, such as Name or Memo. Because you can't categorize the columns in a detail report, you won't see the Columns drop-down list in the report window toolbar. To change the columns that appear in a detail report, in the report window, click Modify Report, and then choose the columns you want to add or remove, as demonstrated in Figure 19-13.

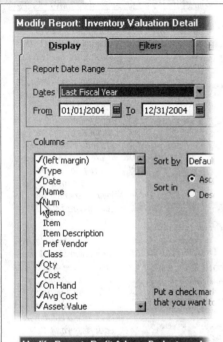

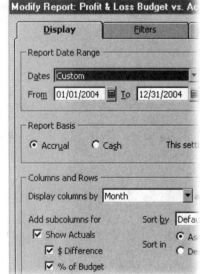

Figure 19-13:
Top: For a detail report, the Display tab in the Modify Report dialog box includes a list of fields you can choose to include as columns in the report. If a field is preceded by a checkmark, click the field to remove it from the report. If no checkmark appears, click the field to add it.

Bottom: When you create a report that makes comparisons, the Display tab on the Modify Report dialog box includes checkboxes for showing dollar and percentage comparisons. For example, if you want to focus on the percentage difference between budget and actual values, turn off the $ Difference checkbox.

The Modify Report dialog box provides different comparison checkboxes depending on the type of report. For example, when you click Modify Report for a Profit & Loss report, you'll find additional checkboxes to compare results to the previous period, previous year, or the year-to-date, *and* to show dollar and percentage comparisons.

The Profit & Loss Modify Report dialog box even includes checkboxes for "% of Column," "% of Row," "% of Income," and "% of Expense." For example, if you generate a Profit & Loss report by quarter and turn on the "% of Row" checkbox, the report shows each quarter's performance as a percentage of the full year's results.

Resizing and Moving Columns

Some columns seem to use more room than they need, while others truncate their contents. Figure 19-14 shows you how to resize columns or rearrange the order in which they appear.

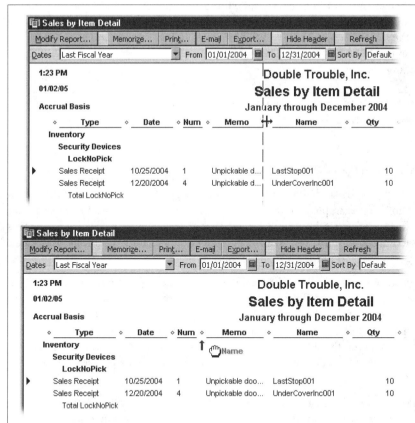

Figure 19-14:
Top: Any report you create that has more than one column also has a small diamond between each column heading. If you mouse over the diamond, it turns into a two-headed arrow. Drag to the right to make the column wider. Drag to the left to make the column narrower.

Bottom: In detail and list reports, when you position the mouse pointer over a column heading, it turns into a hand icon to indicate that you can move the column to another location. As you drag, the pointer shows both the hand icon and the name of the column. And, when you get close to the left side of a column, a red arrow appears to show where the program will move the column if you release the mouse button.

Sorting Reports

QuickBooks' built-in reports come sorted, but the order is rarely obvious. When you first generate a report, the Sort By box is set to Default, which means different things for different reports. For example, if you create a Sales by Customer Detail report, QuickBooks groups the transactions by customer, but it sorts the transactions for each customer from earliest to most recent. (Unlike Excel, QuickBooks sorts by only one field at a time.)

The fields you can use to sort depend on the report. For the Sales by Customer Summary report, you can sort by two columns only. The Sort By box includes Default and Total. Default sorts the report by customer name in alphabetical order. Total sorts the report by the total sales for each customer. On the other hand, the Sales By Customer Detail report includes several columns of information, and you can sort by any of them.

If a report is sortable, in the report window toolbar, you'll see the Sort By box. In the Sort By drop-down list, choose the column to use to sort the report. As soon as you change the Sort By box to something other than Default, the Ascending/Descending button appears to the right of the Sort By box. (It has the letters A and Z on the left and a blue arrow that points down when the sort order is descending and points up for ascending.) Click this button to toggle between sorting in ascending and descending order.

Note: The Modify Report dialog box also includes a Sort By drop-down list, but option buttons differentiate between Ascending and Descending order.

Filtering Reports

Reports that show individual transactions usually show more information than you want. For example, a Purchases by Item Detail report could run page after page, listing your weekly purchases of Turtle Chow. Filtering a report removes transactions that don't meet your criteria, so you can hone in on just the Turtle Chow purchases from Myrtle's Turtle Mart.

In QuickBooks, filters are unlike sorting in that you can apply as many as you want at the same time. Each filter adds one more test that a transaction must pass to appear in your report. For example, when you set the date range for a report, what you're really doing is adding a filter that restricts transactions to the ones that occurred between the starting and ending dates. Then, if you want to find the sales for only your corporate customers, you can add a filter based on the Customer Type field.

QuickBooks provides dozens of filters, from the most common, such as dates, items, and transaction types, to the less useful, such as Workmen's Comp Codes and FOB (that's Free on Board, discussed on page 200).

Built-in reports already contain some filters, but you can customize a built-in report by adding additional filters, editing the filters already there, or removing filters. In the report window, click Modify Report and then, in the Modify Report dialog box, click the Filters tab.

Depending on the field you choose as a filter, QuickBooks provides different criteria, one example of which is shown in Figure 19-15. For instance, if you filter by account, in the Account drop-down list, you can choose a category such as "All bank accounts," or you can choose "Selected accounts" and then click each one you want to include. Or you can click a single account.

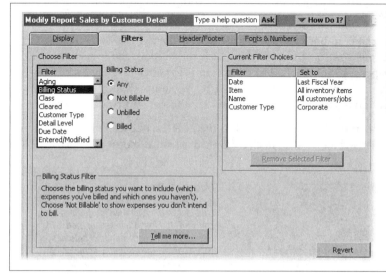

Figure 19-15:
When you choose a field in the Choose Filter list, the criteria for that field appear. If you're not sure what a field and its criteria settings do, click "Tell me more" to open the QuickBooks Help window to the topic about that filter.

After you set the criteria for a filter, QuickBooks adds the filter to the list of Current Filter Choices. To remove a filter, in the Current Filter Choices list select the filter and click Remove Selected Filter.

To edit a filter, in the Current Filter Choices box, select the filter you want to change. The Choose Filter section displays that filter's criteria. Make the changes you want.

Report Headers and Footers

You don't have free rein with what appears in report headers and footers, but you can choose from several fields common to all of them. For example, fields such as Company Name, Report Title, and Date Prepared are options for a header, and page number is one option for a footer. To change the header and footer contents for the report you're working on, in the Modify Report dialog box, click the Header/Footer tab.

Tip: To set standards for all report headers and footers, open Report preferences (page 484) and then set the fields you want.

QuickBooks pulls data from your company file to automatically fill in the header and footer text boxes. For example, if you use a built-in Sales by Customer Detail report, the program fills in the Report Title box with—you guessed it—Sales by Customer Detail. If you have a more eloquent title for the report, type it in the box.

The Show Footer Information section provides one field for typing whatever you want. The Extra Footer Line represents text that appears in the bottom left corner of the report page. This text isn't associated with any field in QuickBooks, so it's blank unless you type something.

The last checkbox in both the Show Header Information and Show Footer Information sections controls the pages on which the headers and footers appear. To conserve paper, turn off the "Print header on pages after first page" checkbox, so QuickBooks includes the header on the first page only. If you want to omit the page number on the first page, turn off the "Print footer on first page" checkbox.

The right side of the Header/Footer tab is the Page Layout section, which lets you position header and footer fields to a very limited extent, as shown in Figure 19-16.

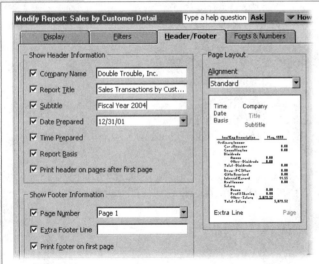

Figure 19-16:
If you want to realign the header and footer contents, in the Alignment drop-down list, choose Left, Right, Centered, or Standard. QuickBooks chooses Standard automatically, which centers the Company name and title; places the date, time, and report basis on the left; and positions the extra line and page number in the left and right corners of the footer.

Fonts and Numbers

The fonts you use or the way you display numbers doesn't change the underlying financial message, but an attractive and easy-to-read report can make a good impression. Just like the fields that appear in the header and footer, you can set QuickBooks' preferences to assign the same font and number formats for all your reports.

On the other hand, changing fonts directly in a report is quick, and has the added advantage of letting you see exactly what the report looks like with the new formatting, as Figure 19-17 illustrates.

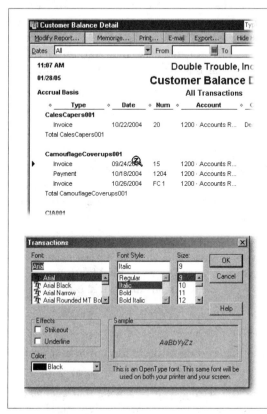

Figure 19-17:
Top: When the mouse pointer changes to the QuickZoom icon, to change text formatting, right-click the text you want to format, such as a transaction. When you change the format for text in a report, QuickBooks immediately displays it. If you don't like the format, right-click the text and try something else.

Bottom: The title of the dialog box tells you which report element you're formatting; otherwise, the dialog box is the same for every element. After you pick the font, style, size, color, and effects, click OK. QuickBooks opens a Changing Font box that asks if you want to change all related fonts. If you click No, it changes the font for only the report element you chose. If you click Yes, it changes related elements, often the entire report.

Tip: If you already have the Modify Report dialog box open, click the Fonts & Numbers tab. The Fonts section on the left side of the tab lists the different text elements of your report, such as Column Labels, Company Name, and Transactions. To change a font, select a text element and click Change Font, which opens the same dialog box you get when you right-click the element in the report.

The right side of the Fonts & Numbers tab has options for changing the appearance of numbers. Negative numbers are a curse in the financial world, so accountants use several methods to make them stand out. If you're not sure which style of negative number you like, choose an option and check the number in the Example area. In QuickBooks, you can choose among three ways to show negative numbers:

• **Normally.** This option shows negative numbers preceded by a minus sign.

• **In Parentheses.** This option places negative numbers within parentheses without a minus sign.

• **With a Trailing Minus.** This option places the minus sign after the number.

Note: If you use a color printer or display reports on your computer screen, make negative numbers even harder to ignore by turning on the In Bright Red checkbox.

To make big numbers easier to read, in the Show All Numbers section, turn on the "Divided by 1000" checkbox. This removes one trio of zeros from numbers, so that $350,000,000 shows up as $350,000 in a report. Turn on the Without Cents checkbox to show only whole dollars. And, if a report tends to contain mostly zero values, you can keep the report lean by turning on the "Except zero amounts" checkbox.

Memorizing Reports

If you take the time to customize a report to look just the way you want, it'd be silly to jump through those same hoops every time you run the report. By memorizing your modified reports, you can run them again and again with all your customizations just by choosing Reports → Memorized Reports, and then choosing the report name on the appropriate submenu.

When you memorize a report in QuickBooks, the program remembers the settings—things like date range and filter criteria—but not the data itself. For example, if you memorize a report whose date range is set to This Month, the report shows the results for June when you run the report in June, but shows results for December when you run the report in December.

Here's how you memorize a report that you've customized:

1. **Review the report to make sure that it contains the information and formatting you want.**

   If you notice later that you missed a setting, you can make that change and memorize the report again. If you use the same name for the memorized report, QuickBooks asks you to confirm that you want to replace the existing memorized report.

2. **In the report window, click Memorize.**

   QuickBooks opens the Memorize Report dialog box, which is small and to the point.

3. **In the Name box, type a name that indicates what the report does.**

   For example, P&L Budget vs. Actual 2004.

4. **If you want to save the report in a special group, turn on the Save in Memorized Report Group checkbox.**

   You can then choose the group, as demonstrated in Figure 19-18.

Note: If you don't memorize a report to a group, the report appears above the groups on the submenu, like the Secret Stash Orders report in Figure 19-18.

5. **Click OK to memorize the report.**

   Voilà. You're done.

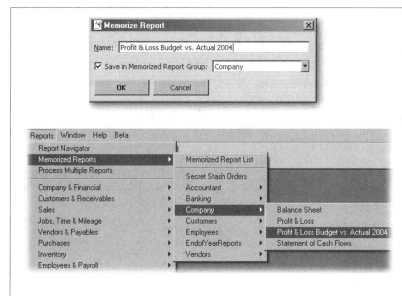

Figure 19-18:
Top: In the Memorized Report Group drop-down list, choose the group in which to memorize the report. For example, for financial statements, you might store the report in the Company group.

Bottom: When you add a memorized report to a group, you can run the report by choosing Reports → Memorized Reports. On the Memorized Reports submenu, choose the group and the report name. If you want to see all your memorized reports, choose Reports → Memorized Reports → Memorized Report List to open a window that lists groups and the reports within them.

TROUBLESHOOTING MOMENT

The Memorized Group Doesn't Exist

In the Memorize Report dialog box, search all you want, but you won't find a way to create a new memorized group. In fact, you must create a memorized group before you can add a memorized report to that group.

Unfortunately, QuickBooks doesn't make it easy to find the command for creating a memorized group. Here's the secret:

1. Choose Reports → Memorized Reports → Memorized Report List. QuickBooks opens the Memorized Report List window, which lists memorized groups and the reports they contain.

2. At the bottom of the window, click Memorized Report and then choose New Group.

3. In the New Memorized Report Group dialog box, find the Name box, and then type the group name. Click OK.

Now, when you memorize a report, the new group appears in the Save in Memorized Report Group drop-down list.

Tip: The Memorized Report List window also comes in handy if you want to edit or delete reports. In the window, select the report you want to work on and then click Memorized Report. Choose Edit to change the report name or the group in which it's memorized. Choose Delete to obliterate the memorized report.

Swapping Reports Between Company Files

Suppose you're one of several business owners who meet to share ideas. Some of your colleagues rave about the QuickBooks reports they've customized, and you'd like to use the reports they've created. If they're willing to share their ideas, you can swap reports by trading report template files.

Report templates contain the layout, filters, and formatting for memorized reports. Someone can export a memorized report as a report template, and someone else can import that file to save the report in a different company file. For example, if your accountant likes to see information in very specific ways, she can give clients a report template file so they can produce the reports she wants to see.

Most of the time, report templates play well between different QuickBooks Editions (Premier, Pro, and Enterprise) and from version to version (2005, 2006, and so on). However, here are a couple points to keep in mind:

- If you use QuickBooks Pro, you can only import templates that others create. You need QuickBooks Premier edition to export report templates.

- QuickBooks patches can affect the compatibility between versions. In that case, you might have to install the most recent QuickBooks update if you want to use someone else's report templates. (QuickBooks displays a warning if an update or version incompatibility exists with a report template you try to import.)

Exporting a Report

Whether you export one report or an entire group, QuickBooks stores the report settings in a single file with a .qbr file extension (for QuickBooks report). Because report templates are meant to move between QuickBooks company files, you don't have to specify any more than the reports you want to export and the file to which you want to export them:

1. **Choose Reports → Memorized Reports → Memorized Report List.**

   QuickBooks opens the Memorized Report List window.

2. **Select the single report or memorized group name that you want to export.**

   For example, if your customized reports are all memorized in the Special Reports memorized group, select Special Reports.

Note: In the Memorized Report List, you can select only a single report or a single group. Ctrl+clicking and Shift+clicking don't select several individual reports.

3. **Click Memorized Report, and then choose Export Template.**

   QuickBooks opens the "Specify Filename for Export" dialog box, which is nothing more than a Save As dialog box that automatically sets the file type to QuickBooks Report Files (*.QBR). The program also automatically applies the report or group name as the name in the "File name" box. If you want to use a different name, for instance to add the date you exported the reports, in the "File name" box, type the new name.

4. **Navigate to the folder in which you want to save the template.**

   For example, your folder for QuickBooks export files.

5. **Click Save.**

   QuickBooks saves the settings for the report or reports to the file. The next section tells you how to *import* a report template.

Importing Report Templates

Importing reports from a template file is even easier than exporting reports. In the Memorized Report List window (choose Reports → Memorized Reports → Memorized Report List), click Memorized Report, and then choose Import Template. QuickBooks opens the "Select File to Import" dialog box with the "Files of type" box set to QuickBooks Reports Files (*.QBR). All you have to do is navigate to the folder that contains the report template file and double-click the file name.

Note: If you try to import a report or group with the same name as a report or group already in your company file, QuickBooks displays a warning and recommends that you change the name of the report or group that you're importing. Click OK and remember to change that name.

Depending on whether you're importing one report or a group, QuickBooks opens a different dialog box:

- **Single report.** QuickBooks opens the Memorize Report dialog box. As you would if you were memorizing a custom report of your own design, in the Name box, type the name you want for the report, and if you wish, choose a Memorized Report Group.

- **Report group.** When you import a report group, the program opens the Import Memorized Reports Group With Name dialog box. QuickBooks fills in the Name box with the group name from the original company file, but you can type a different name. When you click OK, the program memorizes all the imported reports with their original names in the new group in your company file.

Note: QuickBooks won't export memorized reports with filters that reference an account, customer, or some other entry specific to your company file, because those report filters won't work in a company file that doesn't contain the account, customer, or entry that you use.

Part Four: QuickBooks Power

4

Online Banking Services

In the 20th century, you had to wait until your bank statement arrived (by snail mail) to find out what your account balances were and which transactions had cleared. But in the brave new world of online banking, you can view those balances and transactions any time and even download them into your company file.

By synchronizing your real bank accounts with the bank accounts in QuickBooks, you'll always know how much cash you have on hand. Before repaying your aunt the start-up money she loaned you, you can pop online and check your balance—and avoid an embarrassing family blowout instead of risking a bounced check.

Besides managing your cash flow, online banking services are much more convenient than the old methods. If you don't want to enter transactions into QuickBooks, you can download them from your bank (although you're better off keeping your account register up-to-date so you know how much money you have in the bank). Or you can transfer money between your money market account and the checking account when you find yourself awake at two in the morning.

If you use online billing, you can pay bills without having to write checks, lick stamps, or walk to the mail box. After you submit payment transactions online, the billing service either transfers funds from your bank account to the vendors or generates and mails paper checks. Online billing also lets you set up recurring bills so you can go about your business without worrying about missing a payment.

All this convenience requires some setup. QuickBooks needs to know how to connect to your bank, and your bank needs to know that you want to use online services. This chapter explains how to apply for and set up online services. With your accounts enabled and your online services activated, you'll learn how to download transactions from your bank and make online payments. If you enter transactions in QuickBooks, you'll learn about matching them with the ones you download—and correcting any discrepancies.

Note: QuickBooks Merchant Services and Billing Solutions transmit deposits and payments electronically. To learn more about these services, choose Help → Add QuickBooks Services to open a browser to a QuickBooks Web page with more information and online applications.

Setting Up Your Internet Connection

QuickBooks uses an Internet connection for more than online banking, so chances are you've already told the program how you get online. If QuickBooks is still isolated on your computer, start by choosing Help → Internet Connection Setup. QuickBooks opens the Internet Connection Setup wizard. The first screen has three options, which encompass the three possibilities for the state of your Internet access, as shown in Figure 20-1.

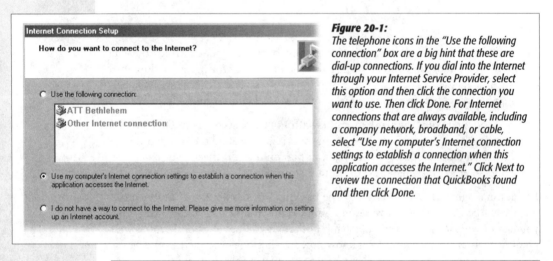

Figure 20-1:
The telephone icons in the "Use the following connection" box are a big hint that these are dial-up connections. If you dial into the Internet through your Internet Service Provider, select this option and then click the connection you want to use. Then click Done. For Internet connections that are always available, including a company network, broadband, or cable, select "Use my computer's Internet connection settings to establish a connection when this application accesses the Internet." Click Next to review the connection that QuickBooks found and then click Done.

Note: QuickBooks connects to the Internet to update your version of QuickBooks, access additional information on the Intuit Web site, and run any of QuickBooks Add-On Services (page 542).

If you don't have Internet access, don't bother choosing the third option. The additional information it promises doesn't give you anything concrete. Instead, click Cancel. Do your own homework to find an Internet Service Provider and obtain Internet service. When you have a connection, return to this wizard, and choose the appropriate option.

Setting Up Your Accounts for Online Services

Connecting your bank accounts with your accounts in QuickBooks is a lot like running a dating service. You have to prepare each participant for the relationship and then get them together.

The services you can subscribe to and the price you pay depends on your financial institution, but the services fall into one of these three categories:

- **Online account access.** This service is often free. Your bank won't admit it, but letting you check your account balance and transaction status online is cheaper than letting you chat on the phone with customer service representatives.

- **Online bill paying.** This service usually comes with a fee, which is often a good deal when you consider the price of stamps and printed checks.

- **Online credit card access.** You can download credit card transactions as you do checking transactions, as long as you set up your credit card in QuickBooks as a liability account and enter individual credit card charges. Setting up a credit card as a vendor and entering only the monthly bill payment won't work.

TROUBLESHOOTING MOMENT

When Connections Don't Appear

The dial-up connections you've configured for your computer *outside of* QuickBooks should appear in the "Use the following connection" box. If your dial-up connection isn't listed, click Cancel to close the Internet Connection Setup wizard.

Use your dial-up connection to access the Internet as if you were planning to check email. While the connection is running, reopen the Internet Connection Setup wizard, which should now list your connection. Choose the connection and click Done.

If QuickBooks doesn't recognize your dial-up connection no matter what you do, don't panic. Choose the "Use my computer's Internet connection settings" option. Before you perform any task in QuickBooks that requires Internet access, be sure to dial into the Internet outside of the program.

Applying for Online Services

The first step in linking QuickBooks to your bank accounts is to apply for online banking services with your financial institution. If you use more than one bank, you must apply separately to each one. If you've already started the application ball rolling, you can skip this section. If you haven't, QuickBooks helps you apply for the services your bank offers.

Choose Banking → Online Banking → Available Financial Institutions. Peruse the Financial Institution Directory to find your bank and apply for its online services, as demonstrated in Figure 20-2.

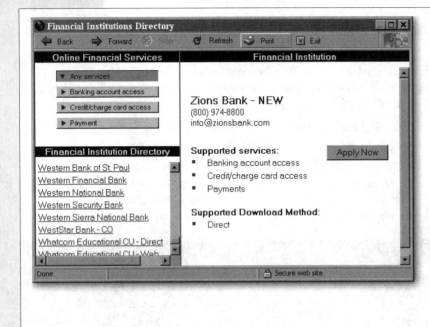

Figure 20-2:
In the Online Financial Services section, you can click one of the four buttons to limit the list to institutions that offer that service. QuickBooks automatically selects "Any services" so that every financial institution that it works with appears. Scroll through the directory to find your financial institution. When you click the link for your bank, you'll see its phone number and email address, the online banking services it offers, how to connect, and any special sign-up offers the bank might offer, such as a 30-day trial. An Apply Now button appears if the bank offers an online application.

Note: Choosing Banking → Online Banking → Setup Account for Online Access starts the Online Banking Setup Interview wizard on the Apply Now tab. However, after clicking through several screens of options, you'll find yourself in the same place that the command Online List of Available Financial Institutions takes you to directly.

When your financial institution sends you confirmation information and a PIN (personal identification number) or password, check that the information that you received, such as the account number, is correct. Now you're ready to set up your account for online services.

Activating Online Services for Your QuickBooks Account

The confirmation letter from your bank that your online services are ready to go is in your hand. You have your customer ID and your password or PIN. Now all you have to do is set your corresponding account in QuickBooks to use these online services. The Online Banking Setup Interview wizard walks you through the steps:

1. **Choose Banking → Online Banking → Setup Account for Online Access.**

   QuickBooks launches the Online Banking Setup Interview wizard and automatically selects the Apply Now tab. But you've already completed your application, so you can click the Enable Accounts tab and then click Next. You should now see the "Add a financial institution" screen.

2. **Click Add Financial Institution.**

   QuickBooks opens a Web browser window, which lists all the financial institutions it works with. Unlike an online service application process, you can enable accounts for several institutions at the same time.

3. **In the list of financial institutions, turn on the checkbox for each institution from which you've received your online service confirmation and then click Done.**

   When a message box appears saying that the next step is to connect to the Internet to download identification information, click OK. You'll see several progress windows as QuickBooks goes out to the financial institution Web sites and gathers information you need to enable your accounts. When the program finishes collecting information, the Web browser window closes and the Online Banking Setup Interview wizard is visible once more. However, the wizard has switched to the "Select a financial institution" screen.

4. **In the "I would like to enter information for my accounts at" drop-down list, choose one of your financial institutions and click Next.**

   The next screen asks whether you've received your confirmation letter from your financial institution.

5. **Assuming that you didn't start this procedure unless you did receive that critical piece, select the Yes option and click Next.**

   The next screen that appears is the beginning of several steps of entering information about your financial institution.

   If you don't have your customer ID and password, don't bother selecting No. Click Leave. (Selecting the No option and then clicking Next tells you something you already know—that you need your confirmation letter and PIN. And you still have to click Leave to close the wizard.)

6. **On the financial institution information screen, use the information from your confirmation letter to fill in the boxes, as shown in Figure 20-3.**

   After you've filled in the routing number and Customer ID, click Next to advance to the Select a QuickBooks Account screen. QuickBooks automatically selects the "Use my existing QuickBooks account" option.

7. **In the "Use my existing QuickBooks account" drop-down list, choose the bank account in your Chart of Accounts that corresponds to the bank account you're enabling for online services and then click Next.**

   The next screen you see is the "Enter additional information about your <*name of bank*> account" screen. (You'll see the name of your bank instead of <*name of bank*>.) This screen lets you specify information about the account you're enabling.

Figure 20-3:
The Routing Number is an identification number for your bank. Besides the confirmation letter you received, your printed checks show the routing number in the lower left corner. The Customer ID is the ID that the bank assigned to you for online services. This number might be your Federal Employer Identification Number, your social security number (for sole proprietors), or another number altogether. The Customer ID should be on the confirmation letter.

Note: When you open a new account at a bank and immediately apply for online services, you can create the account in QuickBooks and enable it at the same time on this screen. Select the "Create a new QuickBooks account" option.

8. **In the Account Type drop-down list, choose the type of account, such as checking, savings, and so on.**

   In the Account Number box, type the account number assigned by the bank.

9. **Turn on the checkboxes for the services you plan to use and then click Next.**

   For bank accounts, you can turn on the online account access checkbox and the online payment checkboxes. If you enable a credit card account, you'll see only the checkbox for online credit card services.

10. **On the final screen, review the information you've entered. If the information is correct, answer "Do you wish to enable additional accounts?" by selecting Yes. Then click Next.**

    The link between your bank account and the one in QuickBooks is now active. The program takes you to the "Select a financial institution" screen. If you have other accounts to turn on, return to step 3 to set up the accounts at the next institution.

11. **If you have no other accounts to enable, click Leave.**

That's it. You're ready to bank electronically.

Exchanging Data with Your Financial Institution

Your financial institution takes the lead in controlling how QuickBooks can communicate with it. There're two ways your bank can set up this pipeline:

- **Direct connection** uses a secure Internet connection that links directly to your bank's computers. With this type of connection and a financial institution that offers the services, you can download your bank statements and transactions, transfer funds between accounts, pay bills online, and email your bank.

- **WebConnect** uses a secure connection to your bank's Web site to download your statement information. With WebConnect, you must then import the downloaded information into QuickBooks.

Note: Regardless of the method you use, the online balance usually isn't the true picture of your cash balance, because it doesn't show all transactions, such as checks you've written that the bank hasn't received.

Connecting to your financial institution begins in the Online Banking Center, regardless of which type of connection you use (choose Banking → Online Banking → Online Banking Center). Going online is quite simple, as Figure 20-4 shows.

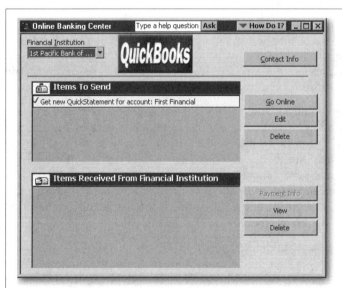

Figure 20-4:
If you have online services with more than one bank (say, your checking account with one bank and a credit card with another), in the Financial Institution drop-down list, select one to connect to. In the Items To Send box, QuickBooks automatically selects all requests. For example, if you want to download transactions, you must send a request for a QuickStatement. If you don't want to send an item, uncheck it. Click Go Online to send the checked requests and connect to the bank's Web site. After you send your requests, the Items Received From Financial Institution box shows the balances for your online accounts and any messages that your bank sent you.

Downloading Statements with WebConnect

When you click Go Online in the Online Banking Center, QuickBooks opens a browser window and displays your bank's Web site; use your customer ID and PIN or password to log in. The easiest approach to acquiring your data is to download it. Select an account and then click Download to QuickBooks to load the recent transactions into your company file.

Note: Depending on your financial institution, you don't have to go through QuickBooks to access your bank's Web site. Use your browser to log into the site directly. Look for the Download to QuickBooks button or another button that creates a file of your transactions that you can import into your company file.

UP TO SPEED

Using Intuit Online Banking Services

If your bank is behind the times and doesn't offer an online bill payment service or online credit card access, Intuit is happy to earn more of your business. The company offers an add-on Bill Pay Service and a QuickBooks MasterCard.

To find these services, choose Help → Add QuickBooks Services. In the bottom-right corner of the browser window that opens, click QuickBooks Bill Pay Service or QuickBooks Business MasterCard.

This Web page contains links to other services, such as Merchant Services (page 543), which make it so that you can accept credit card payments from your customers or Intuit Payroll Services (page 544) to help you with paying your employees.

Exchanging Data via a Direct Connection

Going online when your financial institution uses a direct connection is pretty much the same as going through WebConnect. The difference with a direct connection is that you set up your fund transfers, requests for downloads, online bill payments, and emails *before* you connect. Here's what you do to send requests and receive replies with a direct connection:

Choose Banking → Online Banking → Online Banking Center to open the Online Banking Center window. If you use more than one online-enabled bank, in the Financial Institution drop-down list, choose the one you want to reach. In the "Items to Send" box, QuickBooks automatically selects them all. For example, QuickBooks considers your fund transfers, online bill payments, requests for QuickStatements (statements of cleared transactions that the bank sends in a format that QuickBooks can read), and emails as items to send. If you don't want to send an item, click it to remove the checkmark. Click Go Online.

In the Access dialog box that appears, type your PIN or password and then click OK. QuickBooks transfers your online requests to your bank and brings back any items that your bank sent to you, which you then see in the Items Received From Financial Institution box. For example, a QuickStatement that you requested or a message from the bank might appear in this box.

Tip: If you want to change your password or PIN, which is a good idea for preventing unauthorized access to your accounts, in the Access dialog box, click Change PIN.

Working with Online Items

In the Online Banking Center window (choose Banking → Online Banking → Online Banking Center), you can make changes to items to send before you go online. Once you're connected, it's too late. After you receive items from your bank, you can view them or delete them. Here's how you use the buttons in the Online Banking Center window:

- **Edit.** Before you go online, you can edit any items other than a request for a QuickStatement. Select the item and click Edit. Make the changes you want and click OK.

Note: QuickBooks adds a request for a QuickStatement to the Items to Send list every time you open the Online Banking Center window. A QuickStatement is simply a list of the transactions that cleared in your account since the last time you retrieved information formatted in a way that QuickBooks can import.

- **Delete.** If you set up a fund transfer between accounts that you no longer need or want to remove another type of item, in the Items To Send list, select the item and then click Delete.

  You'll find that your bank is fond of sending you messages about new services or holidays. There's no reason to clutter the Items Received From Financial Institution with these messages. In the Items Received From Financial Institution box, you can also select an item and then click Delete.

- **View.** In the Items Received From Financial Institution box, select an item and click View to see it. When you want to match the transactions in a QuickStatement to your QuickBooks bank account transactions, select the QuickStatement and then click View.

Creating Online Items for Direct Connections

Banks that work with direct connections can do more than those that use Web-Connect. Depending on which services your bank offers, you can do some or all of these tasks online:

- Transfer funds between accounts

- Receive transactions that cleared in your account

- Pay bills

- Exchange messages with your bank

Sending a Message to Your Bank

If you have an email address for your bank, you can send messages from outside QuickBooks (that is, from your regular old email program). But when you use online banking services, your bank sends you messages that you receive in the Online Banking Center. By sending messages back through the Online Banking Center, you can see all the messages that you've exchanged (until you decide to delete them).

Choose Banking → Online Banking → Create Online Banking Message. QuickBooks opens the Online Banking Message dialog box. If you're addicted to email communication, the fields shown in Figure 20-5 should be very familiar.

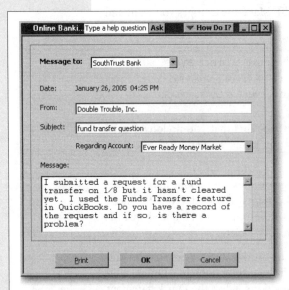

Figure 20-5:
In the "Message to" drop-down list, choose the bank you want to send a message to. QuickBooks automatically timestamps the message with the current date and time and adds your company name to the From box. In the Subject box, type a short but informative subject. If you have more than one account enabled for online services, in the Regarding Account drop-down list, choose the account. In the Message box, type your message or question. If you want to save a copy of the communication, click Print before you click OK to send it.

Transferring Funds Between Accounts

When you have two accounts at the same financial institution and they're both enabled for online banking services, you can set up online funds transfers in QuickBooks.

Choose Banking → Transfer Funds as you would for a non-electronic transfer (page 347). However, in the Transfer Funds dialog box, in addition to filling in the fields, be sure to turn on the Online Funds Transfer checkbox. When you save the transaction, QuickBooks adds the transfer as an item to send to your bank.

Note: Online fund transfers using QuickBooks work only with two online-enabled accounts at the same bank. You can't transfer funds electronically using QuickBooks if the accounts are at different financial institutions. Neither can you transfer funds electronically using QuickBooks if one of the accounts at your bank is enabled for online services but the other isn't.

Viewing and Matching Downloaded Transactions

Every time you connect to your financial institution (in the Online Banking Center dialog box, click Go Online), QuickBooks requests a QuickStatement of all the transactions that cleared since the last time you went online. After you connect, in the Items Received From Financial Institution box, you'll see a QuickStatement entry. To view the transactions in this QuickStatement and pull them into your company file bank account, select the entry and click View.

QuickBooks opens the Match Transactions dialog box and tries to match the QuickStatement transactions to the ones you already entered in QuickBooks, as you can see in Figure 20-6.

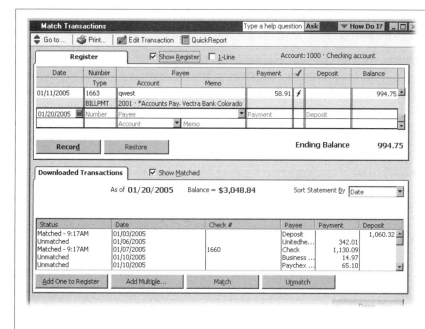

Figure 20-6:
Initially, all the transactions show up as unmatched. If you don't enter transactions in QuickBooks, this status shouldn't surprise you. But if you dutifully enter all your transactions before you download, dozens of unmatched transactions might make you nervous. You must first turn on the Show Register checkbox for QuickBooks to compare the downloaded transactions to the ones in your account register. If the program finds a match, you'll see the word Matched next to a QuickStatement transaction. Otherwise, the transaction is labeled Unmatched.

Note: The first time you download transactions for an online account, QuickBooks looks at transactions marked as cleared in your account register. For all subsequent downloads, the program tries to match only transactions that haven't previously cleared.

If QuickBooks matches every transaction, your work is done. In the account register in the Cleared column, you'll see a lightning bolt for every matched transaction. If you're not so lucky, read the next section.

Note: When you reconcile an account, the mark in the Cleared column changes from the lightning bolt to a checkmark for transactions that have cleared.

Matching the Transactions QuickBooks Couldn't Match

Unsuccessful attempts to match transactions can occur for several reasons, but the source of the problem is *almost* always a mistake in your account register. Here are the different problems you might see and the steps to take to correct them.

Unmatched checks

For downloaded transactions that include check numbers, QuickBooks looks first for a matching check number and, if it finds one, only then does it check the amount. The program considers check transactions matched only if both the check number and amount match. This means there are three reasons that QuickBooks can't match a check:

- **The check number in your register is wrong.** For example, if you wrote several checks at the same time, you might have entered them in QuickBooks in a different order than the paper checks you wrote out. Open the register window (in the "Chart of Accounts" window, double-click the name of the bank account). Find the check transaction and edit the check number.

Note: QuickBooks might warn you about duplicate check numbers. Go ahead and use the check number. After you've edited all the check number transactions, you should be back to unique check numbers.

- **The amounts on the checks don't match for some reason.** If the amounts disagree, first look at the account register to see if you typed the amount correctly. In the account register, correct the amount of the check.

Tip: If you're sure that the check amount is correct, change the check amount anyway. Your bank won't go back and edit that transaction. Contact your bank and work out the discrepancy. If the bank was at fault, it will issue a separate transaction to correct the error, and you can then download the corrected version.

- **You never entered the check in QuickBooks in the first place.** When there's no sign of a check transaction in QuickBooks for the one you downloaded, you forgot to enter the transaction. For checks that are payments for bills, you should use the Pay Bills dialog box to enter the transaction (page 292) so that your bills in QuickBooks show up as paid. For checks that aren't linked to bills or refunds, use the technique shown in Figure 20-7.

Unmatched deposits

If transactions from the bank don't include check numbers, QuickBooks scans transactions without check numbers in your account register for matching amounts.

If the program doesn't find a match, you have two options, which depend on the type of transaction downloaded.

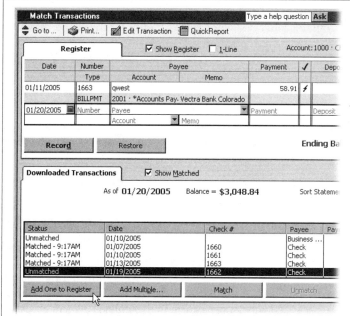

Figure 20-7:
In the QuickStatement, select the check that you didn't enter in QuickBooks and then click "Add One to Register." In the Account box, choose the account to which you want to post the expense and click Record. This technique works for deposits that aren't linked to customer payments and bank charges.

Deposits for payments can go missing in your company file in a couple of ways. For example, if you receive a cash payment from a customer, you might forget to record it in the Enter Sales Receipt dialog box (page 268). Or, when you use the Receive Payment dialog box to record check or credit card payments you receive, you might place the payment in your Undeposited Funds account and forget to make the deposit to your bank account using the Make Deposits dialog box (page 271). When a deposit transaction doesn't have a match in your company file, first make sure that you've recorded all your customer payments in QuickBooks and moved deposits from the Undeposited Funds account into your bank account.

If you have a deposit that doesn't link to a customer payment, such as an insurance refund check you received, you don't have to enter the transaction manually. In the QuickStatement, select the deposit, and then click "Add One to Register." In the Account box, choose the account to post the deposit to and then click Record.

Note: For transactions without check numbers, QuickBooks matches a downloaded transaction with the oldest transaction of a matching amount. For example, suppose you withdrew $200 from your checking account twice last month. When you download a $200 withdrawal transaction, QuickBooks matches it to the oldest matching transaction in your register.

Bank charges

Even with online banking, you don't know what your bank charges are until you download them. For charges including monthly service fees, bounced check charges, and so on, in the QuickStatement, select the transaction and click "Add One to Register." In the Account box, choose the account for the charge and click Record.

Paying Bills Online

Whether you use the bill paying service that your financial institution offers or whether you subscribe to QuickBooks Bill Pay service, you don't have to use any special dialog boxes to make electronic payments. Here's how you turn the three ways you make payments into electronic transactions:

- **Pay Bills.** In the Pay Bills dialog box (page 292), in the Payment Method drop-down list, choose Online Bank Pmt.

- **Write Checks.** In the Write Check dialog box (page 305), turn on the Online Payment checkbox.

- **Account register window.** If you "write" checks by entering a transaction in your checking account register window (page 306), you can turn a transaction into an online payment by right-clicking it and then choosing Edit Check. When the Write Checks dialog box opens, turn on the Online Payment checkbox and save the transaction.

When you set up a payment as an online transaction, QuickBooks adds the payments to your list of items to send. When you open the Online Banking Center window, you'll see these online bill payments in the "Items to Send" box.

When you click Go Online, QuickBooks sends these electronic payments along with any of your other requests. Once the bill payment service receives your online payment information, it transfers money from your account to the vendor's account—providing the vendor accepts electronic payments. Otherwise, the bill payment service generates a paper check and mails it to the vendor.

Note: When you enabled accounts for online services, you told QuickBooks which account acts as your bill payment service.

Sharing QuickBooks Data with Other Programs

Most businesses use lots of programs besides QuickBooks to keep things running smoothly. Data from QuickBooks could be very useful in many of those programs for doing things like studying your company's financial ratios, calculating employee bonuses based on hours worked and services sold, or sending special sales letters to customers on their birthdays. Likewise, other programs might contain data that you could use in QuickBooks. For example, if you use an estimating program that has all the products and services you sell in its database, there's no reason to re-enter those in QuickBooks.

QuickBooks doesn't share its most intimate details with just any program. It reserves its data for a few select programs—or the ones you tell it to play with nicely—and then it gets really chummy. For example, in QuickBooks, you can set up letters to send to some of your customers—and the program automatically opens Microsoft Word with your customer data merged into form letters and envelopes. If you use Outlook or Act! as your contact management tool, keeping records up to date is easy. By synchronizing your QuickBooks company file and your contact database, you enter changes in one place and the programs automatically copy data from one file to the other.

All programs that can read a QuickBooks company file, be they Word, Act!, Outlook, or others, have to ask permission to grab QuickBooks data. The QuickBooks administrator (or other QuickBooks users that the administrator anoints) can say whether another program can have access and how much. For software that can't read a company file directly but that *can* provide valuable assistance processing your financial data, such as an Excel spreadsheet that calculates financial ratios that

QuickBooks doesn't, you can revert to exporting and importing data between programs (page 534).

This chapter doesn't just describe how to integrate QuickBooks at whatever level of trust you prefer. It also tells you about add-on services that Intuit provides and how to find third-party programs that work with QuickBooks.

Mail Merge to a Word Document

Business communications are the perfect marriage of QuickBooks data and word processing. You can generate your letters and envelopes in no time by pulling customer contact and other data from QuickBooks into Microsoft Word mail merge documents. QuickBooks includes dozens of ready-to-mail letters as Word documents that cover the most common business communications, from customer thank-you notes to the less friendly denials of request for credit. In addition to popular form letters to customers, vendors, and employees, QuickBooks offers generic "Other Names" documents containing the basic mail merge fields, leaving the creative content up to you. If nothing less than Pulitzer Prize quality will do for your business letters, you can modify the built-in letters and envelopes in Word or write your own.

The best place to start when you want to prepare letters in QuickBooks is Company → Prepare Letters with Envelopes, which displays a submenu with the following entries:

- **Collection letters.** These are letters that include the invoices or statements that are overdue, and they remind the customer to pay up. QuickBooks automatically pulls the overdue balance and overdue invoices from your company file.

- **Customer letters.** Other customer letters pull only the customer contact and address information from QuickBooks to address the letter and envelope. The rest of the letter is boilerplate for situations such as thanking customers for their business, apologizing for a mistake, or sending a contract.

Note: In previous versions of QuickBooks, you could also access customer letters by choosing Customers → Customer Letters with Envelopes. QuickBooks 2006 has removed this redundant menu command and restricted letter production to Company → Prepare Letters with Envelopes.

- **Vendor letters.** This small category includes credit requests, disputed charges, payments on your account, and two blank templates for sending or faxing a vendor.

- **Employee letters.** Employee letters cover birthdays, sick time, vacation, and general communications.

- **Letters to Other Names.** Because the Other Names list attempts to cover a hodge-podge of different recipients, QuickBooks doesn't even try to guess what letters you need. The only template is a blank letter with basic mail merge fields.

- **Customize Letter Templates.** QuickBooks covers all the bases with customizable letters. You can create a brand new template, convert a Word document that you've already created into a letter template, edit an existing letter template, or organize the templates you already have, as described in the box below.

POWER USERS' CLINIC

Customizing Letter Templates

To create, edit, or otherwise manage your letter templates, choose Company → Prepare Letters with Envelopes → Customize Letter Templates. In the Letters and Envelopes wizard, choose one of these options:

- **Create a New Letter Template From Scratch.** You can specify the type of letter you want to create and the name of the template. QuickBooks sends a blank letter template to Word along with the toolbar shown in the figure. In addition to authoring the content of the letter, you can add fields from QuickBooks to automatically fill in your company and customer or other recipient information.

- **Convert an Existing Microsoft Word Document to a Letter Template.** You can specify an existing Word document as the foundation for a new template. Then, once you specify the type of letter, you can add more text or QuickBooks fields to the document as if you were creating a new template from scratch.

- **View or Edit Existing Letter Template.** You can open and edit any existing template.

- **Organize Existing Letter Templates.** When you choose this option, you can navigate through each category of letter template, choose a template, and then delete, duplicate, or rename it. If the template is in the wrong category, you can move it to another category.

QuickBooks stores the Word documents for letter templates in subfolders within your QuickBooks software folder. For example, if you install QuickBooks in the folder *C:\Program Files\QuickBooks*, your letter templates are in *C:\Program Files\QuickBooks\QuickBooks Letter Templates*. There's a subfolder for each category of template (Collections Letters, Customer Letters, and so on).

Creating Letters and Envelopes in QuickBooks

Though preparing any kind of letter with the QuickBooks letter wizard takes no more than a few clicks, the collection letter wizard has some extra smarts. For most letters, you can tell QuickBooks whether you want to include active and inactive names and then select the names you want to receive letters. The collection letter wizard can also filter the customer list by how late payments are.

Here are the steps for creating letters and envelopes using a collection letter as an example:

1. **Choose Company → Prepare Letters with Envelopes → Collection Letters.**

   QuickBooks opens the Letters and Envelopes wizard and shows the recipient options that apply to collection letters, as illustrated in Figure 21-1.

   (For non-collection letters, you still choose active or inactive customers and whether to send letters to each customer or to each job, but your only options are whether the names are active, inactive, or both.)

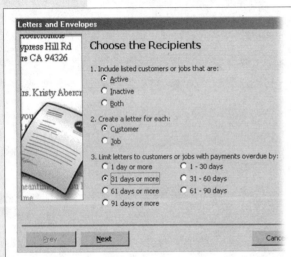

Figure 21-1:
On the "Choose the Recipients" page, choose an option to include all customers and jobs or only active or inactive ones. If each job has a different contact person, choose the Job option to create a separate letter for each job. For collection letters only, you must also specify how late the payment must be before you send a letter.

2. **After you choose the filters you want to apply for your letter recipients, click Next.**

   For collection letters, QuickBooks displays a message if any customers have unapplied credits or payments. Rather than dealing with the embarrassment of sending a collection letter to a customer whose payments are up-to-date, you're better off canceling the wizard and applying credits and payments before preparing collection letters.

   The next screen you see is "Review and Edit Recipients." QuickBooks automatically selects all the names that passed your filters.

3. **If you've already talked to some customers about their payments and want to remove them from the list, click the checkmark in front of their names.**

   If the list of names is long, you can click Mark All or Unmark All to select every name or clear every name, respectively. If you want only a few names, it's faster to click Unmark All and then click each name you want.

   (For letters to vendors, employees, and other names, the first screen you see combines the options for filtering names and the list of selected names.)

4. **When you've selected the customers you want to send letters to, click Next.**

QuickBooks moves you to the "Choose a Letter Template" screen.

5. **Select the collection letter template that you want to send, and click Next when you're done.**

QuickBooks includes three types of collection letters. The formal collection letter is a straightforward request for payment. The friendly collection letter assumes the customer simply forgot. The harsh collection letter includes the threat of turning the account over to a collection agency. The friendly and formal collection letters can't do any harm, but if you're considering sending harsh letters, you might want to create your own template for that communication. Click Next.

6. **On the "Enter a Name and Title" screen, in the Name box, type the name that you want to include in the letter signature block. In the Title box, type the signer's title.**

When you click Next this time, QuickBooks sends the information to Microsoft Word, as demonstrated in Figure 21-2. Depending on how many letters you're sending, you might have to wait a few minutes before Word launches with your letters. You print the letters from within Word.

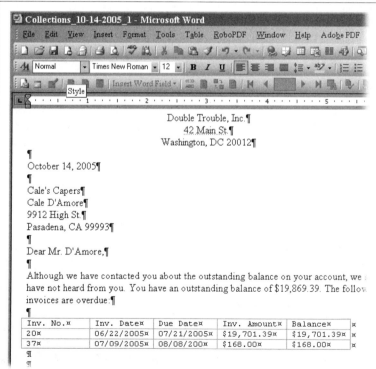

Figure 21-2:
All the letters you create are in one Microsoft Word document, with each letter starting on a new page. You can edit the letters in the Word document to make small changes, but you must make the changes in each letter individually. (Editing the Word document doesn't alter the templates in QuickBooks.) Word names the file automatically with the type of letter and the date. To print the letters, in Word, choose File → Print.

7. Back in QuickBooks, the Print Letters and Envelopes screen appears. Click Next if you want to print the envelopes that go with the letters you just printed in Word.

If you don't want to print envelopes, click Cancel.

8. If you choose to print envelopes, QuickBooks opens the Envelope Options dialog box. In the Envelope Size drop-down list, choose the envelope you use.

If your envelopes already include your return address, turn off the "Print return address" box. Turn on the Delivery Point Barcode if you're mailing letters in the US and want the post office bar code printed on the envelopes. When you click OK, you'll see a preview of the envelopes in Word.

9. Click Finish.

Make sure you've got envelopes in your printer because the print job runs right away.

Synchronizing Contacts

If you keep information about contacts in Microsoft Outlook or Act! (3.0.8, 4.0.2, or 2000), you can synchronize those records with your QuickBooks contact data. In addition to saving time by not duplicating data entry, synchronizing your contact information helps reduce errors. As long as you enter an update correctly in the one program, you're sure to get the correct information in your other contact database. Regardless of which program you update contact information in, you can transfer any changes to the other database.

Using QuickBooks Contact Sync for Outlook

You can synchronize Microsoft Outlook 98 and 2000 directly with QuickBooks. However, if you use QuickBooks 2005 or 2006 (and Outlook 2000, 2002, or 2003), there's an easier way to synchronize—QuickBooks Contact Sync for Outlook. Here's how to download this tool and put it to work:

1. To download QuickBooks Contact Sync for Outlook, navigate to *http://quickbooks.com/contact_sync*. Click Download Now.

You can save the installation file or run it immediately to install the software.

Installing is easy. First, be sure to close Outlook. Then, in the installation wizard, choose a destination folder, and then keep clicking Next until you see the Finish button. Click it to complete the installation.

2. After you install QuickBooks Contact Sync for Outlook, launch Outlook.

The Contact Sync Setup Assistant appears, offering to help you import your contacts form QuickBooks into Outlook. After you click Get Started, a "Connecting to QuickBooks" message box appears while Outlook and QuickBooks introduce themselves to each other.

Eventually, the QuickBooks Contact Sync Setup Assistant dialog box opens and selects the company file that's open in QuickBooks.

Tip: If you want to import contacts from a different company file, click Cancel and, in QuickBooks, open the company file with the contacts to import.

---

3. **Click Next to begin the setup in earnest.**

   The Choosing Contact Types screen appears. To synchronize all contacts, turn on the Customers, Include Jobs, and Vendors checkboxes. For each checkbox you turn on, the Setup Assistant creates a subfolder within the Outlook Contacts folder.

4. **Click Next to map QuickBooks customer fields to Outlook fields, as illustrated in Figure 21-3.**

   The Mapping Customer Fields screen displays the QuickBooks fields for contacts and its initial assumptions about how the fields in the two programs correspond to each other.

   If you turned on the checkboxes to import vendors and jobs, you'll repeat this step to map their fields to the corresponding Outlook fields.

5. **When the Import button appears, click it to bring your QuickBooks contact data into Outlook.**

   When the import is done, the Setup Complete screen appears, showing you how many customers and vendors it found and added to Outlook.

6. **Click Close.**

   The QuickBooks Contact Sync Setup Assistant dialog box closes.

From now on, you can update contact information with just one click. In Outlook, in the Contact Sync toolbar, click Synchronize. Contact Sync analyzes the changes in the two programs and updates both as necessary.

Setting Up Contacts in Act!

QuickBooks needs some help choosing the contacts in Act! that you want to synchronize and determining which type they are. Once you've synchronized the two databases, you can't move a contact to a different category, so before you try to transfer data, open Act! and identify each contact as a type of QuickBooks name (Customer, Vendor, Employee, or Other Name). The categories in the programs don't match up exactly. You must add each contact to one of the following categories (if you don't want to synchronize a name, choose QB Ignore):

- QB Customer
- QB Vendor

- QB Other

- QB Ignore

Here's how to assign an Act! contact to a QuickBooks category: edit the contact. In the User 5 field, type the appropriate QuickBooks category. If the User 5 field already contains a category, type a comma and then type the QuickBooks category.

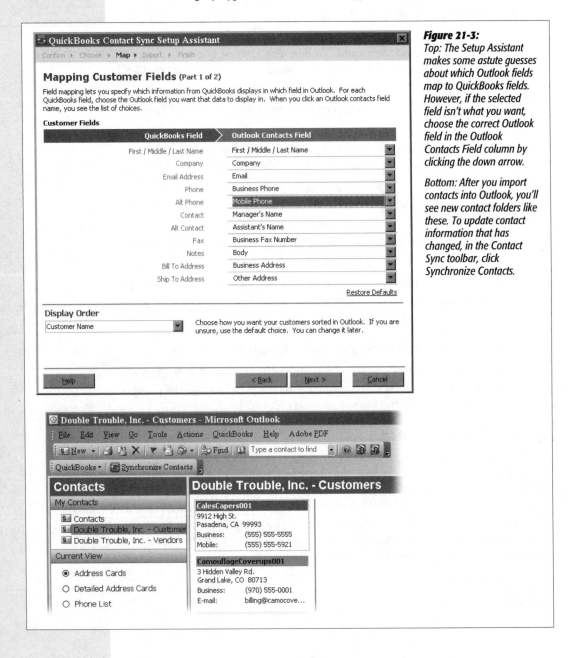

Figure 21-3:
Top: The Setup Assistant makes some astute guesses about which Outlook fields map to QuickBooks fields. However, if the selected field isn't what you want, choose the correct Outlook field in the Outlook Contacts Field column by clicking the down arrow.

Bottom: After you import contacts into Outlook, you'll see new contact folders like these. To update contact information that has changed, in the Contact Sync toolbar, click Synchronize Contacts.

Synchronizing Data with Act!

After you categorize your contacts in Act!, the synchronization process is usually straightforward. QuickBooks recommends that you back up both your contact database and your QuickBooks company file before you synchronize—which is advice you should follow, particularly if you have hundreds of contacts that you don't want to recreate.

Warning: If you jumped the gun and already opened the Synchronize Contacts window, be sure to click Cancel and then back up your company file and your contact database.

Here are the basic steps to synchronize your data:

1. **If you work on your company file in multiuser mode, first switch to single-user mode (choose File → Switch to Single-user Mode). Then choose File → Utilities → Synchronize Contacts.**

   QuickBooks opens the Synchronize Contacts wizard. The first screen shows your current synchronization settings, such as type, file and folder, the QuickBooks lists you synchronize, and filters you use. Click Continue.

Tip: After you've run the synchronization wizard at least once, in the Synchronize Contacts screen, you can click Sync Now to use the current settings, or click Setup to change the settings.

---

2. **In the "Select your contact manager" screen, choose Act! and then click Next. Then, on the "Select a type of synchronization" screen, choose whether you want to transfer data in one or two directions.**

   If you're prone to making contact changes in whichever program you happen to be in, choose "Two way." The Synchronization sends changes in Act! over to QuickBooks and any changes in QuickBooks back. On the other hand, many people find it easier to keep track of changes if they always make them in the same database. In this situation, choose the "One way" option. If you make changes in QuickBooks, then choose "QuickBooks to Act! only." For changes made in Outlook or Act!, choose "Act! to QuickBooks only." Click Next.

3. **On the next screen, choose the Act! database that you want to synchronize with.**

   For Act!, click Browse and navigate to the folder that holds your Act! database and double-click the database name.

Note: If you synchronize in both directions, the next screen includes checkboxes for turning on the QuickBooks lists you want to synchronize (Customers, Vendors, and Other Names). If you synchronize in one direction, you can specify names to exclude, like those marked as Private in Outlook.

---

4. **In the "Select how you want conflicts to be resolved" screen, choose the option you prefer for handling synchronization problems.**

You have to tell QuickBooks what to do in case it and your contact database both contain changes to the same record. For example, a customer moved and the Zip code in QuickBooks includes the new Zip+4 code, but Act! contains only the old five digit Zip code. To keep the synchronization running, choose "QuickBooks wins," "Act! wins," or "Ignore both." If you want to specify which change is correct, choose the "Interrupt synchronization and let me decide each case" option.

5. **Click Sync Now.**

   The programs start transferring changes.

6. **In the Confirm Changes screen, review the changes that QuickBooks plans to make. If you see problems, click Cancel. If the changes are OK, click Accept.**

   The synchronization charges ahead.

Finding Third-Party Integrated Applications

Because QuickBooks is so popular with small businesses, plenty of companies besides Intuit develop applications to fill the niches that QuickBooks doesn't handle itself—or doesn't handle very well.

The QuickBooks Solutions Marketplace

The QuickBooks Solutions Marketplace Web site is one place to look for third-party programs. Point your Web browser to *http://marketplace.intuit.com* to reach the QuickBooks Solutions Marketplace, shown in Figure 21-4.

Third-party programs come in handy even if you already use one of QuickBooks' industry-specific editions. For example, the Solutions Marketplace has programs in the Construction area that produce estimates more easily than QuickBooks' Construction Edition and that generate documents that conform to industry association standards—while still sharing data with your QuickBooks company file.

Intuit lists third-party programs in two ways: by industry and by business function. For example, if you're looking for contact management software, you don't have to navigate every industry link looking for programs. Under the Find Software Solution By Business Function heading, click Contact Management.

Other Ways to Find Third-Party Programs

The QuickBooks Solutions Marketplace doesn't show you *every* third-party program that integrates with QuickBooks. The Marketplace Web page would scroll forever. If you use Google (*www.google.com*) to search for some basic terms, say "QuickBooks third-party applications," you'll get over 100,000 results. Of course, if you focus your search (add "medical office," for example) you can narrow the results (to about 20,000 in this case). And, if you use all 10 keywords that you can enter in a Google search to describe the QuickBooks add-ons you seek, you might get a few dozen links worth investigating.

If you're familiar with Web sites like Download.com (*www.download.com*), try using "QuickBooks" as a keyword for a search. Download.com has several dozen programs that work with QuickBooks, some of which aren't industry-based at all but are still incredibly valuable. For example, one of the most frequently downloaded programs helps you recover forgotten QuickBooks passwords.

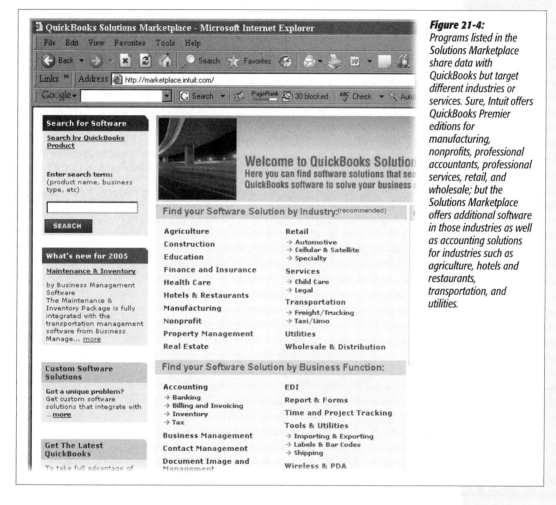

Figure 21-4:
Programs listed in the Solutions Marketplace share data with QuickBooks but target different industries or services. Sure, Intuit offers QuickBooks Premier editions for manufacturing, nonprofits, professional accountants, professional services, retail, and wholesale; but the Solutions Marketplace offers additional software in those industries as well as accounting solutions for industries such as agriculture, hotels and restaurants, transportation, and utilities.

Setting Up an Integrated Application

Integrated applications don't read data from exported text files; they actually access your company file for information. To protect your data from programs that *shouldn't* read your company file, you have to tell QuickBooks which programs you *do* want digging into your financial data.

Letting programs access your data is something you set up with preferences. Choose Edit → Preferences, click the Integrated Applications icon, and then click the Company Preferences tab. Here, you can turn on the "Don't allow any applications to access this company file" checkbox to keep all programs out. But you're reading this section, which means you probably want at least one program to access your QuickBooks data.

Tip: Initially, only the QuickBooks administrator can give programs access rights, but the administrator can also set up other users with that same power (page 568).

As long as the "Don't allow any applications to access this company file" checkbox is turned off, when a program tries to access your company file, QuickBooks displays an Application Certificate dialog box, in which you can specify whether to let the program look at your data, as shown in Figure 21-5.

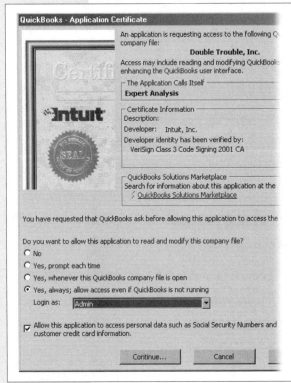

Figure 21-5:
If you are the QuickBooks administrator or another user with the permission to dole out file access, choose an option to set the program's access to the company file. Obviously, choosing No keeps the program out. But you have several options when you want to let the program in.

Here are the three options you can choose to allow access to your company file:

- **Yes, prompt each time.** When you're letting another program access your data, this is the safest option. The program can only get in when someone with the rights to approve access says so—a small assurance that the wrong person can't run the program after breaking in after hours. But if someone who can approve access isn't available to say yes, the integrated application (or the person who's running it) is out of luck.

- **Yes, whenever this QuickBooks company file is open.** This option is a bit more trusting. As long as someone is working on the company file, the integrated application can access the file without asking permission.

- **Yes, always; allow access even if QuickBooks is not running.** By far, this is the most lenient of answers. The program can help itself to your financial data even if no one with a QuickBooks login is working on the file. This option is exactly what you need if the integrated application is a resource hog that you run at night.

  When you choose this option, you can specify the QuickBooks user for the login. Rather than use the login for one of your employees, you can create a QuickBooks user (page 566) specifically for an integrated application, which lets you control the type of data the application can access without affecting someone else's login.

After a program has accessed your company file, you can change its access rights in the Edit Preferences dialog box, as illustrated in Figure 21-6.

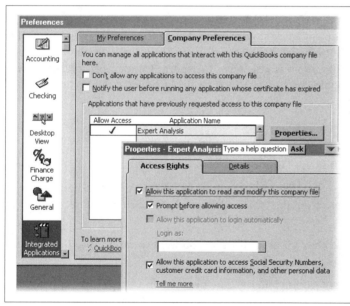

Figure 21-6:
On the Company Preferences tab, select the application and then click Properties. In the Properties dialog box, you can turn checkboxes on and off to remove access or change the level of access the program has. The Details tab shows the program name, the company that developed it, the version, and its certificate.

Warning: Sometimes, third-party programs alter QuickBooks features, like your Chart of Accounts. So before you try to integrate a new program, back up your QuickBooks file. After you integrate a program, check your QuickBooks file for unauthorized changes, like new accounts that you don't want to use. If the program made changes you don't like, you can restore your backup or modify your lists manually in QuickBooks (see Chapters 3, 4, 5, or 6, depending on the list).

Exporting QuickBooks Data

Programs that don't integrate with QuickBooks can still do things that Quick-Books can't. For example, you can export a report to Excel and take advantage of a wider range of formatting options and calculations. To get data out of your Quick-Books company file and into another program, you have two choices:

- **Export file.** You can create a delimited text file that contains various types of data from your QuickBooks file. For example, you can generate export files for QuickBooks lists, such as your Item List or Sales Tax Code List. For the named records in QuickBooks, such as your Customer:Job and Vendor Lists, you can produce export files that contain only address information.

- **Report file.** Create any report in QuickBooks and you can then export it to a file that you can use in another program. Compared to exporting an entire list, a report gives you more control over the exported information. If you want to export data from several lists or from transactions, exporting reports is your *only* choice.

Exporting Lists and Addresses

When you export lists to QuickBooks delimited text files, or .iif files, the export file contains all the fields associated with those QuickBooks lists. Creating export files is easy, and your only choice is which lists to export. If you export several lists, the .iif file that QuickBooks creates contains every field for every list you chose.

Exporting lists

Exporting one or more lists to a delimited file takes only a few quick steps:

1. **Choose File → Utilities → Export → Lists to IIF Files.**

   The program opens an Export dialog box, which contains checkboxes for each list in QuickBooks from the "Chart of Accounts to Customer" List to Sales Tax Code List.

2. **Turn on the checkbox for every list that you want to export into the same file and then click OK.**

   If you want to export lists into separate files, you must repeat all of these steps for each .iif file you want to create. For example, if you want to export your Customer List and your Item List to two different files, repeat steps 1–4 twice through.

3. **In the second Export dialog box, which is basically a Save As dialog box, navigate to the folder in which you want to save the export file and, in the "File name" box, type the name of the file.**

   Your export files are easier to find if you create a folder specifically for them. For example, you could create a subfolder called Export IIF Files within the folder that holds your company files.

4. Click Save to create the file.

Now, you're ready to import the file into Microsoft Excel or another program, as described later in this chapter.

Exporting addresses

With QuickBooks features to generate mail merge letters, export contact list reports, synchronize your company file with some versions of Outlook or Act!, there isn't much reason to use the tab-delimited address files that QuickBooks produces. However, if you need a text file of names and addresses, here's what you do:

1. **Choose File → Utilities → Export → Addresses to Text File.**

   If an Export Addresses message box appears and suggests that you try Write Letters, turn on the "Do not display this message in the future" checkbox and then click OK to close the message box.

2. **In the Select Names for Export Addresses dialog box, choose the category of names you want to export. Then click OK.**

   To select all names, in the drop-down list, choose "All names." You can also choose categories of names, like "All vendors," or individual names.

3. **In the Save Address Data File dialog box, select a folder in which to save the exported file, type a file name in the "File name" box, and then click Save.**

   QuickBooks automatically assigns a .txt extension to the file. You can now import it into any program that likes tab-delimited addresses.

Tip: Exporting QuickBooks data can help you learn the format you need to *import* data into your company file. For instance, once you've entered a sales tax code or two (using the laborious process described on page 86), you can export them and then, in the export file, create the rest of your codes using the same format. Then import that file back into QuickBooks.

Exporting Reports

If you remember all the way back to Chapter 19, you know that you can customize reports to contain just the information you want, presented just the way you want. When you want to export only *some* of your QuickBooks data or export it in a specific way, your best bet is customizing a report to contain that data in the way you want and then exporting the report.

You can export a report to a comma-delimited file if that's what another program needs. If another program is as fussy about data as QuickBooks is, making those changes in Excel is easier than trying to do the same in a text editing tool such as Windows Notepad.

Start by running the report you want to export as you normally would just to view or print it (page 485). In the report window button bar, click Export. The Export

---

Report dialog box lets you choose the file and options for the export, as shown in Figure 21-7, top.

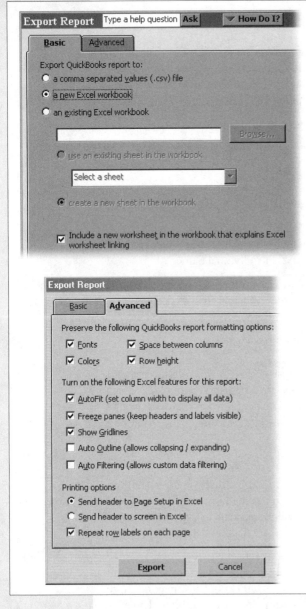

Figure 21-7:
Top: In the Basic tab, choose "a new Excel workbook," if you want QuickBooks to create a brand new Excel file for the report. To export the report to an existing file, choose "an existing Excel workbook." This option is ideal if you're planning to calculate ratios and want your most recent financial statements in the same workbook as statements for previous periods. If you export to an existing file, you can also choose options to create a new worksheet for the report or add the report to a sheet already in the workbook.

Bottom: On the Advanced tab, you can set the formatting you want to transfer from QuickBooks to Excel, Excel features you want the workbook to turn on, and where you want the report header information stored. Unless you have special requirements for your workbook, you won't go wrong keeping the choices that QuickBooks makes.

Tip: If you want a worksheet with tips for working with the resulting Excel worksheet, be sure to leave on the "Include a new worksheet in the workbook that explains Excel worksheet linking" checkbox.

After you've selected the export file and options, click Export. QuickBooks launches Excel and copies the data in the report to the Excel workbook you specified, placing the data in the report columns into columns in a worksheet, as shown in Figure 21-8, bottom.

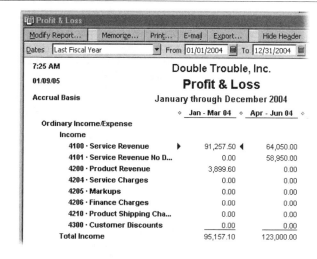

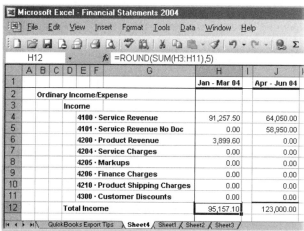

Figure 21-8:

Top: A report in QuickBooks has a header, columns, and rows. When you export a report to Excel, the data in report columns and rows transfer into columns and rows in the worksheet.

Bottom: You can choose whether the report header transfers to the worksheet header or appears in the worksheet itself. Exporting a report to a workbook isn't a mindless transfer of values. The subtotals in the workbook actually use the Excel SUM function to add up the workbook cells that make up the subtotal. If you requested a worksheet of tips, click the QuickBooks Export Tips tab and read about how to customize, update, and manage the exported reports.

Importing Data from Other Programs

Importing data from other programs comes in handy mostly for generating lists in QuickBooks. The biggest requirement for importing data is that the files be either Excel workbooks (.xls file) or delimited text files, which separate each piece of information with commas or tabs.

Importing an Excel Spreadsheet

If you're familiar with importing Excel spreadsheets into other programs, import-ing them into QuickBooks is a snap. You set up a *mapping*, which is geek-speak for simply matching up Excel columns with the corresponding QuickBooks fields. QuickBooks can't figure out on its own where the data belongs, so you have to tell it. Here's how the whole process works:

1. **Choose File → Utilities → Import → Excel Files.**

   QuickBooks opens the "Import a file" dialog box. The Set Up Import tab includes options for selecting an Excel file and setting up the import mapping. The Preferences tab lets you tell QuickBooks how to handle errors and dupli-cate records. (QuickBooks sets the Duplicate Handling option to "Prompt me and let me decide," so you're in complete control.)

2. **Click Browse and select the Excel file that you want to import.**

   QuickBooks fills in the "Choose a sheet in this Excel workbook" drop-down menu with the worksheets from the workbook you selected. Choose the work-sheet to import from the drop-down menu.

   QuickBooks automatically turns on the "This data file has header rows" checkbox, which is the perfect choice when the first row of the Excel workbook contains text labels for the columns.

3. **In the "Choose a mapping" drop-down menu, choose <Add New>. Then, in the "Mapping name" box, type a name for the set of correspondences between fields and columns you're about to choose.**

   QuickBooks lets you give the mapping a name, so you can use it again the next time you import the same type of spreadsheet. You can just choose the map-ping from this drop-down menu instead of setting it up all over again (see Figure 21-9, top).

4. **For each QuickBooks field listed in the left column, in the "Import data" col-umn, choose the corresponding Excel header or column name (Figure 21-9, bottom).**

   If you don't see the fields you want, try changing the Import type, which changes the list of fields in the QuickBooks column.

5. **After you've mapped all the columns you want to import to QuickBooks fields, click Save.**

   QuickBooks closes the Mappings dialog box.

6. **In the "Import a file" dialog box, click Import.**

   Importing isn't reversible, so take QuickBooks up on its offer of backing up your company file before continuing.

After the import is complete, QuickBooks shows you a message saying whether the import was successful and how many records had errors.

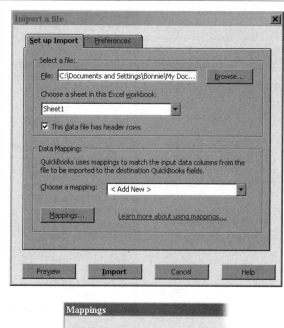

Figure 21-9:
Top: Once you've set up a mapping, you can reuse existing mappings by clicking Mappings and selecting the mapping you want. Leave the box set to <Add New>, as shown here, if you're importing this type of file for the first time.

Bottom: The correct column is easy to pick when the workbook contains column headers in the first row. Otherwise, picking is a lot like a Chinese menu with names like Column A and Column B.

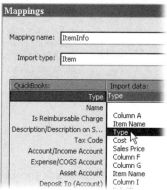

Importing a Delimited File

For delimited files, QuickBooks needs to know the *kind* of data you're importing—and it learns that from special *keywords* for row and column headers. Keywords are strings of characters in a delimited file that identify QuickBooks records and fields. Before you import data from another program into a QuickBooks list, you need to know the correct keywords for the import file. The easiest way to see the keywords for a list is to export that list from QuickBooks and examine the keywords at the beginning of the rows and at the tops of the columns.

Deciphering keywords requires a smattering of computerese. For example, when you see the column heading Billing Address, you know instantly what kind of information you're looking at. But the only way QuickBooks recognizes the first line of a billing address is from the keyword BADDR1. Figure 21-10 explains all.

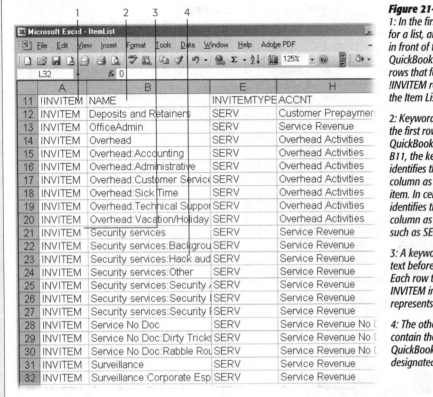

Figure 21-10:
1: In the first cell in the first row for a list, an exclamation point in front of the keyword tells QuickBooks that the data in the rows that follow are for that list. !INVITEM represents data for the Item List.

2: Keywords in the other cells of the first row for a list specify the QuickBooks field names. In cell B11, the keyword NAME identifies the values in that column as the name of each item. In cell E11, INVITEMTYPE identifies the values in that column as the type of item, such as SERV for Service.

3: A keyword for a row is the text before the first comma. Each row that begins with INVITEM in the first cell represents another item record.

4: The other cells in a row contain the values that QuickBooks imports into the designated fields.

Here's how you create the export file to get the keywords:

1. **Choose File → Utilities → Export.**

   QuickBooks opens the Export dialog box, which contains checkboxes for each type of list.

2. **Turn on the Item List checkbox (and checkboxes for any other lists you want to export) and then click OK.**

   QuickBooks opens a second Export dialog box where you can choose the folder and the file name for the export file. The program automatically sets the "Save as type" box to IIF Files (*.IIF)—the QuickBooks' file extension for export files.

3. **After you specify the folder and file name, click Save.**

   QuickBooks displays a message box telling you that the data was exported successfully. Click OK to dismiss the message.

4. **In Excel, open the export file.**

Choose File → Open to display the Open dialog box. In the "Files of type" drop-down list, choose All Files, so you can see the .iif export files. Navigate to the folder that holds your exported list and double-click the file name.

Although the Text Import Wizard has options for telling Excel how to read the file, you won't need them. Just click Finish to display the exported file in Excel.

Shipping out of QuickBooks

Making regular runs to the FedEx or UPS office gets old quickly. But sitting quietly within QuickBooks is a free service that could change the way you ship your packages. Shipping Manager is already built into QuickBooks, so you can sign up for shipping services and start sending out your packages right away.

You can print FedEx and UPS shipping labels, schedule pick-ups, and track package progress right in QuickBooks. The Shipping Manager fills in shipping labels with customer addresses from your QuickBooks invoices, sales receipts, or customer records. All you pay are the FedEx or UPS charges on your shipment.

Using Shipping Manager isn't just about convenience. By setting up a FedEx account through Shipping Manager, you get discounts of up to 16 percent on FedEx Express and 12 percent on FedEx Ground service. (Discounts don't apply if you use QuickBooks Online or QuickBooks for the Mac.)

In case you haven't noticed Shipping Manager, here's where it's been hiding in QuickBooks:

- If you're creating an invoice for products you plan to ship, in the Create Invoices dialog box (press Ctrl+I), on the toolbar, click Ship. In the QuickBooks Shipping Manager dialog box, choose which shipping service to use and then follow the instructions to set up a shipment. On the Create Invoices toolbar, click

the downward-pointing arrow to display a drop-down menu with commands for shipping packages or choosing shipping options to schedule a pick-up or track a package that's already on its way, as shown in the figure.

- The Sales Receipt dialog box toolbar also includes a Ship icon.

- Choose File → Shipping and then choose Ship FedEx Package or Ship UPS Package.

- To set up Shipping Manager and an account with FedEx, UPS, or both, you'll need your QuickBooks Registration Number (for QuickBooks 2004 and earlier) or QuickBooks License and Product Number (QuickBooks 2005 and 2006). If you don't memorize these crucial numbers, choose Help → About QuickBooks to open a window that displays them.

- The first time you launch Shipping Manager, the program steps you through setup and creating an account with either FedEx or UPS.

Now that you've created an .iif file with the correct keywords, here's how you import an .iif file into QuickBooks:

1. **Choose File → Utilities → Import → IIF Files.**

    QuickBooks opens the Import dialog box with the file type set to IIF Files (*.IIF).

2. **Navigate to the folder that contains the file you want to import and double-click the file name.**

QuickBooks displays a message box that tells you that it imported the data successfully. If you didn't set up the keywords correctly or QuickBooks ran into other problems with the data in your IIF file, it tells you that it didn't import the data successfully.

QuickBooks Add-on Services

Not every company runs payroll or accepts credit cards for payment. If yours does, you might like the idea of business services that perform those functions using your QuickBooks data. Intuit offers several business services you can subscribe to—for additional fees. The price might be worthwhile when you take into account the cost of your employees' time or—far more valuable—your being able to relax on the weekend instead of catching up on company paperwork.

QuickBooks Business Services require an Internet connection. To scour Intuit business services using your regular Web browser, navigate to *http://quickbooks. intuit.com* and then click links to find out more, as illustrated in Figure 21-11.

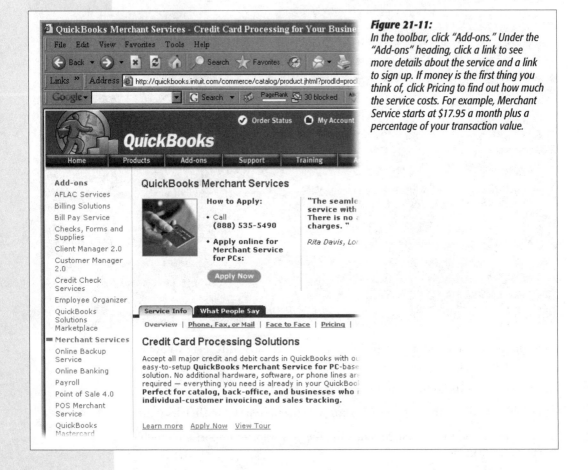

Figure 21-11:
In the toolbar, click "Add-ons." Under the "Add-ons" heading, click a link to see more details about the service and a link to sign up. If money is the first thing you think of, click Pricing to find out how much the service costs. For example, Merchant Service starts at $17.95 a month plus a percentage of your transaction value.

Here are some of the more popular business services that Intuit offers, what they do, and why you might consider using them.

Merchant Services

QuickBooks Merchant Services provides two very important features with one service. First, you get a merchant account, which is a bank account that handles credit card payments from your customers. The merchant account you get through QuickBooks accepts all major credit cards, which might mean more business for you, and it charges discounted rates you might not get from your bank. Then, with a QuickBooks Merchant Account in place, you can download your credit card payment transactions directly into your company file.

Here's more detail on Merchant Services:

* **Accept credit card payments.** When a customer pays with a credit card, in the Receive Payment dialog box, you enter information about the payment as usual: the customer name in the Received From box, the amount, and the type of credit card in the Pmt. Method box. The only difference is that you also turn on the "Process *<credit card name>* payment when saving" checkbox (see Figure 21-12).

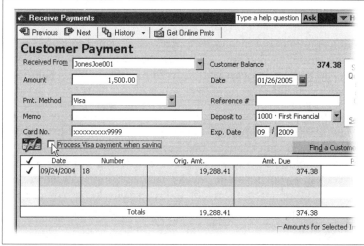

Figure 21-12:
When you save the transaction, QuickBooks not only records the payment in your company file; it transmits the payment to your merchant account and authorizes it. The Enter Sales Receipts dialog box also includes a "Process credit card payment when saving" checkbox for handling merchant account credit card payments.

If customers hand you their credit cards in your store, you can buy a card reader from Intuit that sends credit card data to QuickBooks. Even better, the rate you pay for swiped card transactions is lower than transactions you enter directly in QuickBooks.

* **See transaction status.** The QuickBooks Merchant Service collects credit card payments and deposits them to your bank account in batches. The Funding Status tool tells you which payments have been deposited.

* **Download and reconcile fees.** Merchant accounts charge fees for their services, and the QuickBooks Merchant Account is no exception. In QuickBooks, you can download processing fees and service fees to keep your records up-to-date.

Tip: With QuickBooks Virtual Terminal Plus, you don't have to be in your office to process credit card payments. Suppose you attend a trade show and you have a computer and Internet connection. You can accept credit card payments at the show and download them into QuickBooks when you get home using Virtual Terminal Plus.

In addition to one-time credit card charges, you can set up recurring credit card charges, such as the monthly membership fee for the More or Less Body Building and All You Can Eat Buffet exercise studio.

If you decide that you want to accept credit cards using QuickBooks Merchant Services, click the friendly yellow Apply Now button on the Web page or find the toll-free phone number to sign up.

Intuit Payroll Services

Intuit offers several options for payroll services that not only simplify payroll processing but also automatically update your company file with payroll transactions. If you need more convincing, Intuit also assumes the liability for fees and penalties incurred for late or incorrect payments. Chapter 11 explains the services they offer and how to set them up to run payroll.

QuickBooks Billing Solutions

QuickBooks Billing Solutions is a medley of services, all designed to help you get payments from your customers more quickly and easily. If $14.95 a month plus tax sounds reasonable, on the QuickBooks Add-ons Web page, click Billing Solutions. Here's what the services include:

- **Let QuickBooks mail your invoices.** In the Create Invoices dialog box, if you choose the Mail Invoice command, one of the options in the Send Invoice dialog box is "Mail through QuickBooks." Invoices mailed through this feature of QuickBooks Billing Solutions go to a centralized mail center, which prints customized invoices using your logo and invoice template, stuffs envelopes, and mails the invoices with remittance tear-offs and return envelopes. You can also find out whether customers have viewed invoices you email to them.

- **Get reminders about overdue payments.** QuickBooks reminds you when payments are overdue if you set up Reminders properly (page 155). With Billing Solutions, the service not only reminds you about overdue payments, it also lets you email payment reminders to your customers.

- **Let customers help themselves.** With Billing Solutions, customers can set up a password-protected Web page for paying their invoices, viewing past billing, and submitting customer service questions.

- **Receive online payments.** If you combine Billing Solutions and Merchant Services, your customers can pay via credit card. You can also download the online payments into QuickBooks.

Customizing QuickBooks

QuickBooks 2006 comes with a new Home page that provides instant access to all the accounting tasks you perform. Between new Center panels for vendors, customers, and employees and your old friend, the icon bar, you can take your pick of helpful shortcuts to the features you use the most. But your business isn't like anyone else's. If you run a strictly cash sales business, you couldn't care less about customer lists and invoices, but making deposits is a daily event.

You don't have to accept QuickBooks' take on convenience. The Home page and the icon bar come with a set of popular shortcuts, but you can add, remove, rearrange, and otherwise edit which program features appear. This chapter covers all your options.

QuickBooks helps you get up and running with built-in business form templates. They'll do if you have to blast out some invoices. When you finally find a few spare minutes, use them to customize your own templates. You can show the information you want, format the forms, and lay them out to work with your letterhead. Create as many versions as you want. For example, you can create one invoice template to print to your letterhead and another that includes your logo and company name and address for creating electronic invoices that you email. This chapter starts with the most efficient way to create forms—using built-in templates as a foundation for your own forms. But you'll also learn how to start from scratch.

Customizing the Home Page

The QuickBooks Home page is a chameleon that changes to fit your business's workflow. The program performs its magic by incorporating your answers from the EasyStep Interview with your Company Preferences settings (Figure 22-1). For example, if you don't have inventory, the tasks for buying, receiving, and paying for inventory are nowhere to be seen on your Home page. And if you don't have employees, the entire employee panel disappears.

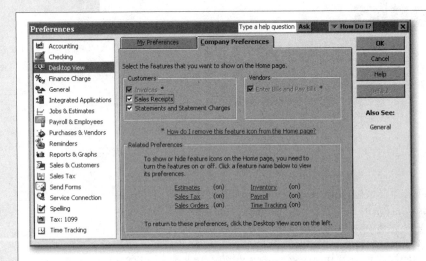

Figure 22-1:
*The Preferences →
Desktop View →
Company Preferences
tab is where you
customize your Home
page. To turn some of
the basic tasks on or off,
turn their checkboxes on
or off. For example, if
you don't send
statements to customers,
turn off the "Statements
and Statement Charges"
checkbox. To show or
hide feature icons (like
Payroll), simply turn the
features on or off in the
bottom panel.*

If you've recently hired your first employees, say, or decided that you'll no longer provide customers with estimates, you can modify the Home page to include the tasks you now need (Payroll) or remove tasks (Estimates) that no longer apply. To tweak your Home page, on the right side of the Home page in the Customize section, click "Customize Home page and set preferences" (if the Home page isn't visible, click Home on the navigation bar).

Customizing the Icon Bar

In QuickBooks 2006, the first icons you'll see are Home (page 144), Customer Center (page 55), Vendor Center (page 110), Employee Center (page 322), and Report Center (page 470). These new interfaces are phenomenally helpful, and Intuit apparently agrees, since it's made these icons impossible to hide. To the right of these, the icon bar includes several icons that take you to the program's most popular features. If you opt to use QuickBooks' Home and Centers, the icon bar is still good for quick access to your favorite memorized reports or other windows you open often.

Tip: You might run out of room if you add more than a few icons to the icon bar. To keep all your icons visible, point to the vertical bar on the left edge and drag down, positioning the bar on its own row below QuickBooks' Home and Center icons.

Unless you're a keyboard shortcut fanatic, clicking Accnt on the icon bar is the fastest and most consistently available way to open your Chart of Accounts. Sure, the Home page has a link to Chart of Accounts, but you can click the Accnt icon no matter what window is in front of you. Invoices, bills, checks, and other features are equally easy to get to. If Intuit's assumptions about which features are useful don't jibe with what you do every day, you can replace the icons with others for the features you *do* use. What's more, you can change the appearance of the icon bar in several ways, as described in the following sections.

The icon bar must be visible before you can customize it. If you choose View when the icon bar isn't visible, the Customize Icon Bar entry is dimmed. To display it, choose View → Icon Bar.

Adding and Removing Icons

The icon bar that QuickBooks puts together is a good guess of what most companies use regularly. If you know which icons you want and don't want, you can make those changes in one marathon session, as Figure 22-2 demonstrates. To make several changes at once, first open the Customize Icon Bar dialog box by choosing View → Customize Icon Bar.

The Add Icon Bar Item dialog box doesn't list every QuickBooks window, but that doesn't have to stop you from adding a window to the icon bar. Once you realize that you open the same window again and again, you can add an icon for that window to the icon bar without going anywhere *near* the Customize Icon Bar dialog box. Here's how:

1. **Open the window for the feature or report you want to add to the icon bar.**

   You can add a window for a standard QuickBooks feature, such as Make Deposits. Even handier, you can add an icon for a memorized report that you've created. (To add an icon for a memorized report, you must first run the report so it appears in a report window.)

2. **Choose View → Add *<window name>* to Icon Bar; *<window name>* is the name of the window you just opened.**

   If the wrong window name appears, be sure to activate the window you want before continuing. When you choose View → Add *<window name>* to Icon Bar, QuickBooks opens the Add Window to Icon Bar dialog box.

3. Because you've already selected the window, all you have to do is click the icon you want to use and, in the Label and Description boxes, type the text you want for the icon label and description.

   In the icon bar, the text in the Description box appears as a Tool Tip when you position the mouse over the icon.

4. Click OK to add the window to the icon bar.

   That's it.

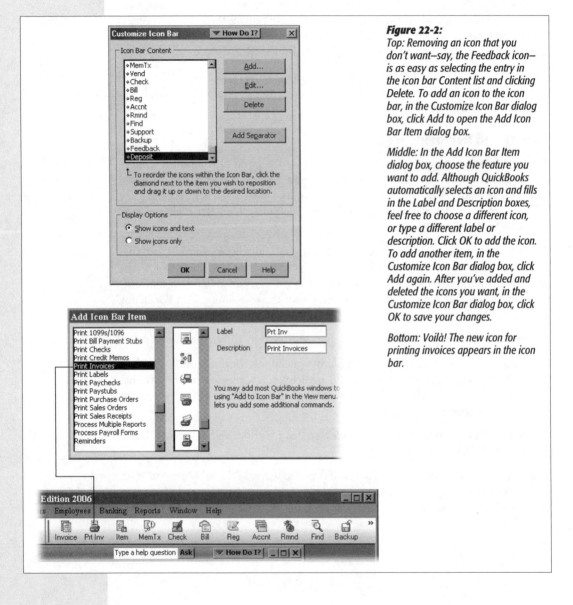

Figure 22-2:

Top: Removing an icon that you don't want—say, the Feedback icon—is as easy as selecting the entry in the icon bar Content list and clicking Delete. To add an icon to the icon bar, in the Customize Icon Bar dialog box, click Add to open the Add Icon Bar Item dialog box.

Middle: In the Add Icon Bar Item dialog box, choose the feature you want to add. Although QuickBooks automatically selects an icon and fills in the Label and Description boxes, feel free to choose a different icon, or type a different label or description. Click OK to add the icon. To add another item, in the Customize Icon Bar dialog box, click Add again. After you've added and deleted the icons you want, in the Customize Icon Bar dialog box, click OK to save your changes.

Bottom: Voilà! The new icon for printing invoices appears in the icon bar.

Changing Icon Appearance

To change an icon or its associated text, choose View → Customize Icon Bar. Select the entry whose icon you want to alter and then click Edit. QuickBooks opens the Edit Icon Bar Item dialog box, which lets you change three features of each icon:

- **Icon.** To change the icon that the program displays in the icon bar, in the icon list, select the graphic you want.

   (You can't demonstrate your creativity by designing your own icons. But Quick-Books doesn't care whether you choose an icon that fits the feature you're adding. For instance, a faucet with a drip of water might be good for Writing Checks, but you could choose the icon that looks like a smiling hippo if you prefer.)

- **Label.** If you don't like the label that QuickBooks provides or want to shorten the label to condense the icon bar, in the Label box, type your own.

- **Description.** To change the text that appears as a Tool Tip for the icon, in the Description box, type your own.

Tip: If screen real estate is at a premium, you can shrink the height of the icon bar by removing icon labels. In the Customize Icon Bar dialog box, select the "Show icons only" option. Without icon labels to identify what the icons represent, you can see a hint by hovering the pointer over one to display its Tool Tip description.

Changing the Order of Icons

If you want to group related icons, you can change the order of the icons in the icon bar and add separators to make the groups stand out. Open the Customize Icon Bar dialog box to make these changes. Figure 22-3 illustrates the process of rearranging icons.

Figure 22-3:
The Icon Bar Content list starts with the leftmost icon on the icon bar and continues to the rightmost. To move an icon, drag the diamond to the left of the icon name to the new position. Dragging the two-headed arrow up and down in the list moves the icon to the left and right in the icon bar, respectively. To add a separator between groups of icons, select the last icon in the group and then click Add Separator. To save the changes, click OK. QuickBooks immediately displays the changes you make to the icon bar.

Note: In QuickBooks 2005 and earlier, the Shortcut List was an aptly named shortcut to the windows that you opened all the time. In QuickBooks 2006, the Shortcut List is no more. Instead, you can use the Home page to access common accounting tasks and add icons to the icon bar for shortcuts to your favorite report windows.

Customizing Forms

Like it or not, everything you do says *something* about your business—even the business forms you use. For a small company or someone with devastatingly bad taste, the built-in QuickBooks invoices and other forms work just fine. But if you want business forms that convey your sense of style and attention to detail, customized forms are the way to go.

In QuickBooks, form customization comes in two levels:

- **Customizing what's already there.** When you have a form to work with, you can quickly format text and numbers as well as change whether or not fields appear in the form. For example, you can turn off the company name and address to create an invoice that prints on your company letterhead. The Customize dialog box, which opens when you edit any template, contains everything you need for these types of changes.

- **Laying out and designing a form.** With the Layout Designer, you can design a form from scratch, adding fields, laying them out where you want, and formatting them as you please. For example, you can resize and reposition fields to emphasize the balance due. The Layout Designer works just as well for redesigning existing templates or enhancing the aesthetics of a built-in template.

Note: To change the format and layout of a built-in template, you must first duplicate it and make the changes on the customized copy (page 561).

Editing an Existing Form

The easiest way to build your own forms is to start with a template that QuickBooks provides or use another customized template that you've put together. Whether you plan to make minor adjustments or major revisions, you won't have to start from scratch. Here're the steps for editing an existing template:

1. **Choose Lists → Templates.**

   QuickBooks opens the Templates window, which displays built-in templates and any that you've created. If you're looking for a specific type of form to start with, the Type column displays the type of form, such as Invoice or Credit Memo.

   Select the template you want to modify.

2. In the button bar at the bottom of the window, click Templates and then choose Edit Template from the shortcut menu (or simply press Ctrl+E).

QuickBooks opens the Customize *<template type>* dialog box. For example, if you edit an invoice, the title of the dialog box is Customize Invoice.

Tip: If you're in the midst of creating a transaction and realize you need to modify the template, the Customize dialog box is reachable without interfering with the transaction in progress: in the transaction dialog box (Create Invoices, for instance), make sure that the template you want to use (and modify) appears in the Template box. Then, click the Customize button, which lurks just above the name of your template, begging you to make some changes. In the Customize Template dialog box, click Edit to open the Customize *<template type>* dialog box.

---

3. Make the changes you want by following the instructions for customizing and laying out forms (page 552).

When the form looks the way you want, in the Customize *<template type>* dialog box, click OK.

Creating a New Template

For radically different forms, it just might be easier to start from scratch. If you're prepared to add all of the fields, position them, and format the text and numbers, follow these steps:

1. Choose Lists → Templates to open the Templates window.

QuickBooks opens the Templates window.

2. Press Ctrl+N or click Templates, and then choose New.

QuickBooks opens the Select Template Type dialog box.

3. Select the option for the type of form you want to create.

Each type of business form has its own collection of typical fields, which QuickBooks adds to the tabs in the Customize *<template type>* dialog box. For example, when you select Purchase Order, you can include the Expected field for the date you expect to receive the order. You can choose Invoice, Credit Memo, Sales Receipt, Purchase Order, Statement, or Estimate as your basic template types. When you click OK, the program opens the Customize *<template type>* dialog box with the typical fields for that type turned on.

Tip: If you use QuickBooks Premier or Enterprise, you can also customize Sales Order forms.

---

4. In the Template Name box, type the name for the template.

Type a name that tells you something about the template: the type of form, whether it focuses on services or products, and any other hints to help you choose the template you want. For example, if you create an invoice template that you email to customers, name it something like Service Invoice Email.

5. **Choose the fields to include in the form.**

Click through each tab in the Customize *<template type>* dialog box, turning the checkboxes for fields on or off. When you create a new template, QuickBooks still makes some assumptions and positions the fields you turned on. If you want to redesign the layout, click Layout Designer.

6. **When the new template is complete, click OK.**

The Customize *<template type>* dialog box closes.

Now when you click the downward arrow in the Templates box in a dialog box, like Create Invoices, your template appears in the list. Choose it to use it for your business form.

Customizing Form Content

The Customize *<template type>* dialog box has tabs mainly for choosing the fields you want to display in the form, as demonstrated in Figure 22-4. The Format tab and the Printer tab are the exceptions, with options for formatting the printed forms.

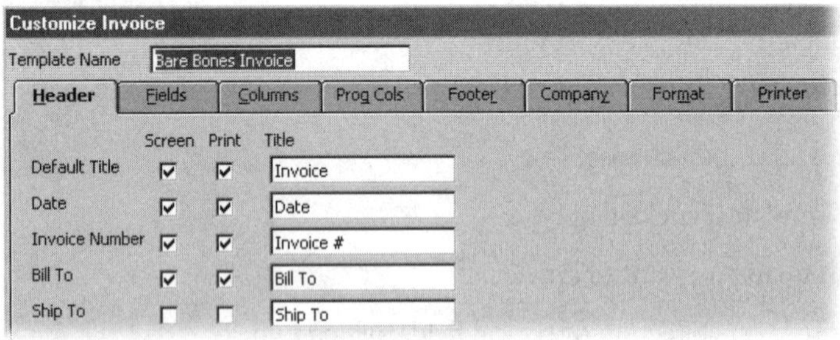

Figure 22-4:
To include a field onscreen, turn on its Screen checkbox. To print a field, turn on its Print checkbox. The Title boxes contain the field label. QuickBooks fills them in with either the field name or a label that identifies the type of form, such as Invoice for the Default Title field. You can edit the labels in Title boxes.

The tabs are the same for every type of form unless you create an invoice and have the Progress Invoicing preference turned on (page 151). Then QuickBooks adds the Prog Cols tab so you can pick the columns you want to add for progress billing. Each tab relates to a different area of the form, as Figure 22-5 illustrates.

Setting up the fields on the tabs is straightforward, but a few of them have extra features that make a complete tab review worthwhile:

- **Header.** These fields appear at the top of the form. The only field that isn't turned on automatically is the Ship To field, because you need that only if you're shipping products.

- **Fields.** As you look at a form, the fields on the Fields tab appear horizontally above the table area—for example, fields like Terms and P.O. Number appear just above the table area of line items in an invoice.

Tip: You can choose whether to display fields on the screen and on the printed form. Some of the checkboxes are dimmed if a choice doesn't make sense. For example, the checkbox for displaying the Project/Job on the screen is dimmed, because the Create Invoices dialog box (and other dialog boxes) include the Customer:Job field, which tells you the same thing.

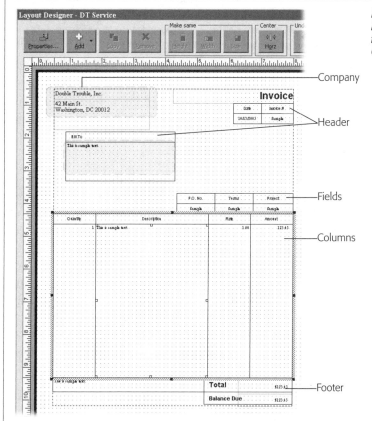

Figure 22-5:
Each form contains five areas for fields: Company, Header, Fields, Columns, and Footer.

- **Columns.** These fields determine the columns in the table area of a form, such as the item description, quantity, rate, and amount for each line item in an invoice.

- **Footer.** The Balance Due field shows up as a checkbox for the Footer of a form, but most companies omit that field on invoices. Typically, each invoice shows the amount for just that invoice. Statements, mailed separately, show the customer's account status, including invoices, payments, overdue balances, and credits.

The Long text box lets you add a substantial block of text on a form. If you want to include a legal disclaimer or other lengthy notes, add this field to the form and type the text in the box. Long text appears only on the printed form, not on the screen.

- **Company.** QuickBooks automatically turns on the Print Company Name and Print Company Address checkboxes, which is perfect if you print to plain paper. But if you have letterhead with your company name and address preprinted, be sure to turn these checkboxes off. You can also turn on checkboxes to print the company phone number, fax number, email address, and Web site address.

- **Format.** The Format tab lists different components of a form, such as Labels (for the field labels), Data (for the values in fields), and Title (for the title of the form). To change the font for any of these components, in the Change Font For list, select the component name and then click Change. The dialog box that opens contains all the usual font formatting options, just like the dialog boxes you see when you format a report (page 498).

  The Format tab includes a few additional formatting options. QuickBooks automatically turns on the "Print page numbers on forms with more than 2 pages" checkbox, in which the checkbox label sums up its function rather well. Remember the status stamps that QuickBooks adds to forms, such as PAID, which appears as a watermark on an invoice when you've received the payment? If you want to *print* these status stamps, turn on the Print Status Stamp checkbox. If you bill to fractions of an hour, turn on the Print Trailing Zeros checkbox, which adds zeros and a decimal point, so that whole number and decimal quantities all line up.

- **Printer.** You can set up printer settings for different types of forms by choosing File → Printer Setup, picking the form, and then choosing the settings you want. But if you have a special form that doesn't follow the other templates in that category, you can specify a different orientation, number of copies, and paper size for just that form. In the Customize *<template type>* dialog box, on the Printer tab, select the "Use specified printer settings below for this *<form>*" option.

Laying out Forms

When you want a form to look just so, the Layout Designer is the tool to use. Once you master the art of selecting objects (labels, fields, and images) on a form and dragging sides or whole objects, you'll be amazed at how quickly you can design a form. And the Layout Designer goes beyond dragging and dropping objects. Work the other Layout Designer commands into your repertoire to finish your form even faster—or spend the time you save making your form even better.

Laying out a form is a combination of zeroing in on areas to position objects and then viewing the entire form to see whether it's readable and reasonably attractive. As you work, you can zoom in and out any time you want. In the Layout Designer toolbar, click Zoom In or Zoom Out.

Tip: As with any kind of design, laying out forms can be fraught with choices that don't work out. If you make changes that you don't want, click Undo to reverse up to the last 50 actions. If you change your mind, click Redo to put back the action you just undid. For the keyboardist, press Ctrl+Z to undo actions.

Selecting Form Objects

Laying out a form means moving, resizing, and formatting the objects on the form. *Before* you can do any changing, you must first select the objects you want to modify. QuickBooks displays a shaded border around selected objects, as illustrated at bottom in Figure 22-6.

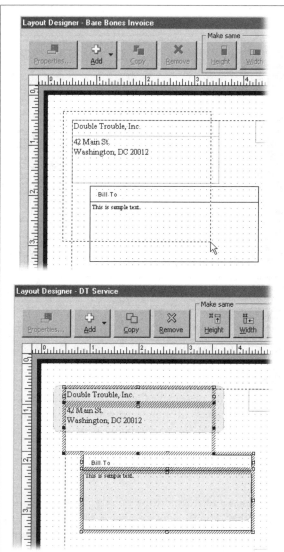

Figure 22-6:

Top: QuickBooks displays a dashed rectangle as you drag the mouse. To select an object, be sure that the center of the object lies within the dashed rectangle.

Bottom: Selected objects have a shaded border. You can grab the object handles to move and resize the object.

Choose any of the following methods for selecting objects:

- **One object.** Click the object. For example, to select the company name, click the company name text. To select one of the columns in a form table, click anywhere within the column.

- **Multiple objects.** Shift+click each object that you want to select.

- **Objects within an area.** Drag the mouse from one corner of the area to the opposite corner, as shown at top in Figure 22-6.

UP TO SPEED

Adding a Logo to a Template

To create a professional-looking form even on plain paper, on the Company tab, turn on the "Use logo" checkbox. QuickBooks immediately opens the Select Image dialog box, in which you can navigate to the folder that holds your logo image file. The program sets the "Files of type" box to All Image Files, so you'll see any kind of graphic file in a folder. Double-click the file name to select the logo.

QuickBooks wants to keep the logo file close to your company file. If you choose a file stored in a folder for your corporate graphics, QuickBooks copies the logo file and tucks it into a subfolder within the folder that holds your company file.

For instance, if your company file is named Allyoucaneat.qbf and resides in a folder *C:\QBCompanyFiles,* QuickBooks creates a folder for you: *C:\QBCompanyFiles\Allyoucaneat - Images,* and places the copy of the logo file there. If you decide to edit your original logo file, be sure to copy the edited file into the QuickBooks image folder.

On the template, your logo appears initially in the top left corner of the form. If you want to reposition it, do so within the Layout Designer (page 554).

After you add a logo to a template, it sometimes disappears. Rather than panic, simply repeat the steps in this sidebar to relink the logo to the template. If the logo still doesn't appear, exiting and restarting QuickBooks usually solves the problem.

Moving and Resizing Objects

You don't have to stick with the size and placement QuickBooks gives fields. For instance, if your company name and address fit in a narrow space, you can resize the boxes for those fields, which might give you room to add your company telephone number and email address.

Moving objects

You can move one or more objects at a time. Select the objects you want to move (by clicking or Shift+clicking). When you've selected all the objects, click anywhere within one of the selected objects' boundaries and drag it to a new position. To center the selected objects horizontally in the form, select the objects and then click Horz.

If you want to fine-tune the position of objects, select the objects and then press an arrow key to move them one pixel in that direction. If you have one or two objects to position precisely and you don't have to move them a great distance, using the arrow keys saves you the trouble of turning grid snapping on and off (page 560).

Resizing objects

Each selected object has six handles you can drag to change the height, width, or both. To resize an object, select it and then drag one of the handles until the object is the size you want. When you resize a logo, QuickBooks maintains the original height-to-width ratio, so that your resizing doesn't distort the logo by stretching it more one direction than the other.

You can resize the columns in a table, but the columns are inextricably linked to each other. If you widen one column, you narrow the next. To resize a column and its neighbor to one side, in the Layout Designer window, click within the table. Position the pointer on the border of the column and drag to move the border.

Tip: Dragging the edge of a column that also happens to be the edge of the table changes both the width of the table and the width of the column.

Dragging object handles is easy, but you can resize only one object at a time. In addition, forms look better when you keep related fields in the same size boxes. The Layout Designer tool bar includes a few buttons to change objects to match the size of another object on the form. In the Layout Designer window, Shift+click each object you want to resize, but be sure to choose the correctly sized object *last*. Then, you can use these commands to match the object dimensions:

- **Height.** This button changes the height of the selected objects to the height of the last object you selected.

- **Width.** This button changes the width of the selected objects to the width of the last object you selected.

- **Size.** This button changes the height and width of the selected objects to the height and width of the last object you selected.

After QuickBooks resizes the objects, they might not line up with their neighbors any more. Just select the objects that are out of position and drag them back into place.

Adding, Removing, and Copying Objects

When you use the Customize dialog box to tweak a form, you can include only the fields that QuickBooks displays on the Customize tabs. But in the Layout Designer, you can add just about any company or customer field you want by using the buttons available for adding, removing, and copying objects.

The Add button lets you add text boxes, data fields, and images to a form, as Figure 22-7 demonstrates.

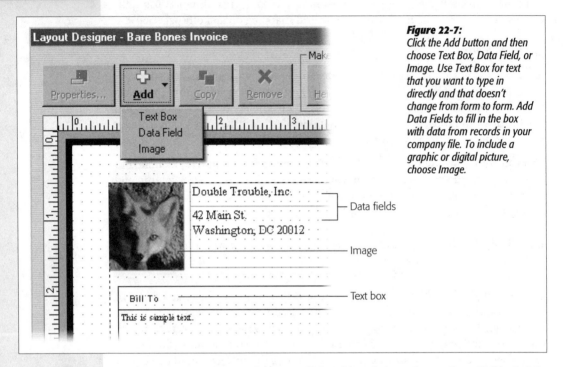

Figure 22-7:
Click the Add button and then choose Text Box, Data Field, or Image. Use Text Box for text that you want to type in directly and that doesn't change from form to form. Add Data Fields to fill in the box with data from records in your company file. To include a graphic or digital picture, choose Image.

In the Layout Designer, when you click Add and then choose Data Field, Quick-Books opens the Add Data Field dialog box. Click a field name in the list and then click OK. The program adds both a text box with the field name as a label and a Data Field box in the middle of the form. Drag the boxes to where you want them.

In the Layout Designer, if you click Add and then choose Image, QuickBooks opens the Select Image dialog box. Find the image file you want, and double-click it to add it to the form. QuickBooks displays a message telling you that it is copy-ing the file to the image folder for your company file.

To remove an object already on the form, select that object and then click Remove. Unlike the Add command, Remove deletes only the boxes you choose, not the pairs of labels and data fields.

Copying an object is easy—select the object and click Copy. The program copies the selected boxes and places the copies slightly offset from the originals. Copying is useful when you want to add several labels of the same size. You can add the first text box and get it to the size you want. Then copy that text box for all your labels. After the text boxes are in position, you can edit the text for each label.

Formatting Forms

For text boxes and data fields, you can add some formatting to spice up the form. In addition to all the typical font formats for text, you can add or remove borders around boxes and choose background colors to emphasize information. To make changes like these, in the Layout Designer window, select the object that you want to format and then click Properties. Figure 22-8 shows what you can do to Data Fields and Text Boxes.

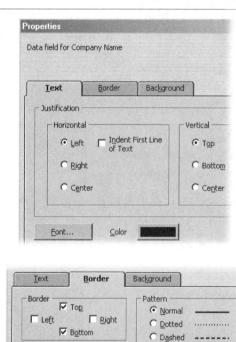

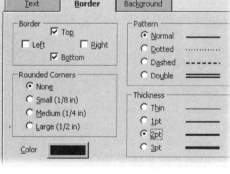

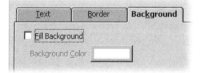

Figure 22-8:
Top: The Properties dialog box tells you whether you've selected a Text Box or Data Field, and tells you which Data Field you've chosen. On the Text tab, you can set the horizontal and vertical position of the text within the box. For example, Data Fields usually position text beginning at the top left corner of the box. However, the Text Box for the form title is right-justified to make the type of form stand out. You can also choose the font and color for the text.

Middle: Click the Border tab to add or remove borders around the box. You can add a border to one or all of the box sides, and you can choose from four line patterns and four thicknesses. You can round the corners of boxes to make them a bit more stylish.

Bottom: For background colors, all you have to do is turn on the Fill Background checkbox and then choose the color you want. If you don't use a color printer, you can still choose shades of gray to make fields stand out.

Note: Unless you print forms on a color printer, don't bother choosing colors for text, borders, and backgrounds.

POWER USERS' CLINIC

Changing the Layout Designer Grid

In the Layout Designer, points appear in a regular grid to help you line up boxes, text, and images on your forms. The human eye picks up even the tiniest offsets in alignment, and the result of these small mistakes is a sloppy form that simply looks unprofessional.

To help you line up objects, QuickBooks snaps the objects on a form to the grid. The wider the grid, the easier it is to see that you've snapped to the right grid point, but the less flexibility you have in positioning objects.

QuickBooks sets the grid to the smallest spacing, which is 1/16 inch, but you can change the grid to spacing up to 3/8 inch. On the other hand, to position elements precisely, such as your logo, you can turn snapping off entirely.

Here's how you manage the Layout Designer grid:

1. To change the grid or turn off grid snapping, at the bottom of the Layout Designer window, click Grid. QuickBooks opens the "Grid and Snap Settings" dialog box.

2. If you want to change the spacing between grid points, in the Grid spacing drop-down list, choose the spacing you want.

3. To kill grid snapping, turn off the "Snap to grid" checkbox. You can turn off grid snapping while you position one or two objects, and then turn it back on to align text and boxes.

4. Click OK.

If you don't want to see the grid, in the "Grid and Snap Settings" dialog box, turn off the "Show grid" checkbox.

Other Handy Layout Tools

A few Layout Designer features remain. Although they aren't related to each other, they're all worth knowing about.

- **Show envelope window.** If you print forms that you stuff into Intuit's envelopes with windows, turn on this checkbox. QuickBooks then displays transparent blue boxes at the window locations for Intuit's standard window envelopes. If you move the Company and Bill To Address fields so they appear within the shaded areas, you'll be able to mail the envelope without printing separate mailing labels. (You can't move the shaded areas, so this feature won't help if you use another brand of envelopes with windows in different positions.)

- **Margins.** The light dashed rectangle around the edge of the Layout Designer window shows the current margin settings. To set margins for the form, at the bottom of the Layout Designer window, click Margins. You can make margins as wide as you want, but you can only make them as narrow as the margin settings for your printer.

Note: Many printers can't print closer than one quarter of an inch to the edges of the paper. If you're determined to squash as much information as possible onto a form and set margins too narrow for your printer, QuickBooks warns you that the margin won't work based on the printer you designated for that type of form in Printer setup (page 235).

Managing Templates

Like many of the list windows in QuickBooks, the Templates window includes commands for managing the list entries (in this case, templates) you create. In the Templates window button bar, click Templates and then choose a command on the shortcut menu. Besides some of the obvious tasks, such as New, Edit, and Delete, there are some other helpful things you can do with your templates.

Tip: You can delete only templates that you create. If you try to delete a built-in QuickBooks template, the program tells you that you're out of luck.

Duplicate

If you want to create a new template based on one that already exists, the Duplicate command works like a charm. If you plan to edit an existing template, duplicate it first in case your edits go awry.

In the Templates List window, head to the Name column, and then select the template you want to edit or duplicate. Click Templates and then choose Duplicate. The Select Template Type dialog box appears. As it turns out, you can choose any type of template for the duplicate, regardless of what the original template type is. In the Select Template Type dialog box, when you click OK, QuickBooks adds the duplicated template to the list with the name *DUP:<original template name>*.

Warning: If you duplicate a template to create a new one, be sure to edit the duplicate's name to identify what the form does. If you duplicate a template as a backup in case you mangle the original, first check that the duplicate is what you want. The *DUP:* that QuickBooks adds to the beginning of the template name tells you that it's a backup. After you've modified the original template and you're completely confident that the edited template is correct, you can delete the duplicate.

Make active/inactive

If you want to keep a template, such as an original that you've duplicated, but you don't want it to appear in the Template list, you can make it inactive, just as you do some customers, vendors, and invoice items. To make a template inactive, in the Templates List window, select the template, click Templates, and then choose Make Template Inactive. You can reactivate it by first turning on the "Include inactive" checkbox to display all templates. Then click the X to the left of the template name.

Export

If you want to trade form templates between company files, you can export templates from one company file and import them in another. To create a form export file, in the Templates List window, select the template you want to export. Click Templates and then choose Export. In the "Specify Filename for Export" dialog box, navigate to the folder in which you want to save the file, and, in the "File name" box, type the name of the file. QuickBooks automatically sets the "Save as type" box to Template Files (*.DES).

Templates Without the Tedium

Say you find the QuickBooks built-in templates boring, but you don't have the time or design know-how to put together templates of your own. You can download spiffier templates from the QuickBooks Web site. For example, contractors can choose invoice templates with a drill or tape measure as a background.

In the Templates List window, click Templates and then choose Download Templates. The program launches a Web browser opened to the QuickBooks Template Gallery. You can search for report or form templates and specify the type of report or form and even a specific industry, as shown in the figure.

Click the name of a template to view a larger sample. When you find a template you like, click Download, which saves a template export file (with a .des file extension) onto your computer. In QuickBooks in the Templates List window, click

Templates and choose Import on the shortcut menu. Select the file you downloaded and then click Import. (The process for importing a template export file is the same as importing a report export file [page 503].)

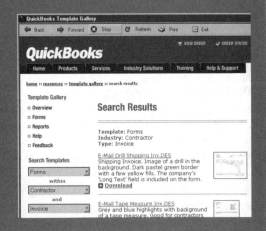

Keeping Your QuickBooks Data Secure

Your QuickBooks records are indispensable. They help you invoice your customers and prepare your taxes, prevent you from overdrawing your checking account, and provide the information you need to plan for the future. A company file does so much—and yet, many companies don't take the time to keep their financial data safe and secure.

Losing data to a hard disk crash is a shock to your system (both hardware-wise and emotionally), and rebuilding your records is inconvenient, time-consuming—and, if you hire Intuit to do it, costly. But having someone embezzle the money from your accounts could send years of hard work down the drain. Protecting your QuickBooks data takes so little time that there's no excuse for not doing it.

If you're the untrusting type or simply have no one else willing to do your bookkeeping, you can skip the discussion of creating users and setting up user permissions. The administrator login is all you need to work on your company file—and QuickBooks creates *that* automatically. Although you might not let other people access your financial data, that doesn't mean that someone won't try to access it *without* your permission. Good security measures, such as firewalls, up-to-date antivirus software, and passwords that strangers can't guess go a long way to prevent unauthorized fiddling with your finances.

When you have other people work on your company file, security is a bit trickier. Each person who accesses your financial data is a potential problem, whether intentional or inadvertent. By setting up users in QuickBooks and specifying which areas of the program they can access, you can delegate work to others without worrying about security quite so much. With the audit trail on your company file (page 572), every transaction that's modified or deleted is there for you to review.

Setting Up the Administrator

In QuickBooks, the administrator is all-powerful. Only that person can create new users, assign permissions and passwords to other users, and set QuickBooks company preferences. If you use the EasyStep Interview to create your company file, the wizard won't let you finish until you specify the user name and optional password for the QuickBooks administrator (page 21). If you skip the EasyStep Interview, you can create, open, and close a company file without any sign of a login screen. But behind the scenes, QuickBooks logs you in as the administrator user because no password is set. As soon as you try to set up additional users, QuickBooks first asks you to specify the administrator's user name and password—the process for which is described next.

Tip: One of the first things you should do in QuickBooks is set a password for the QuickBooks administrator. If you don't, anyone who opens your company file has full access to every feature of QuickBooks and every byte of your QuickBooks data.

WORD TO THE WISE

Password Guidelines

Because the QuickBooks administrator can do anything in a company file, choosing a trustworthy person for that role is only your first step against financial misfortune. Your efforts are in vain unless you secure the administrator's access with a good password. In fact, assigning passwords to all QuickBooks users is an important security measure.

Ideally, a password is almost impossible to guess, but easy for the rightful owner to remember. It's easy to meet the first criterion by using random combinations of uppercase and lowercase letters, numbers, and punctuation, which then of course make the password very hard to remember. And unfortunately, if people have trouble recalling their passwords, they'll write them down somewhere, shooting holes in your security.

Here are some tips for creating passwords in QuickBooks that are both secure and yet easy to remember:

• Don't use family birthdays, names, phone numbers, addresses, or Social Security numbers.

• Make your passwords at least six characters long, and combine upper- and lowercase letters, numbers, and punctuation. (QuickBooks passwords are case-sensitive and can include up to 16 characters.)

• To make guessing more difficult, replace letters with numbers or punctuation that look similar. For example, replace the letter "l" with the number 1 or an exclamation point (!). Or replace the letter "s" with the number 5, or the letter "e" with the number 3.

To make remembering easier, use names, birthdays, phone numbers, or addresses of people not obviously connected to you. For example, if no one suspects that Kevin Spacey is your favorite actor, Kev!n5pacey72659 would be a good password (but not anymore).

Assigning the Administrator User Name and Password

If you haven't set up the QuickBooks administrator, choosing Company → Set Up Users opens the Set up QuickBooks Administrator dialog box. Before you can set up other users, you must set up the Administrator, as demonstrated in Figure 23-1.

Don't copy and paste the password from the Administrator's Password box into the Confirm Password box. If you copy a typographical error from one box to the other, you won't know what the Administrator password is, and you won't be able to open your company file. In an emergency, Intuit can remove the Administrator's password from your file. However, password removal takes about five days and isn't free, so you're better off making sure you know the administrator's name and password—and keeping a record of them in a safe place. (You can also obtain a program from Download.com that retrieves forgotten passwords, as described on page 531.)

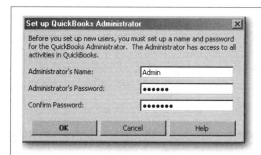

Figure 23-1:
QuickBooks automatically fills in the Administrator's Name with the user name "Admin." Using the name Admin makes it easy for more than one person to share administrator duties. (If one person acts as the QuickBooks administrator, give the current password to the new administrator. Let her reset the administrator user name and password.)

Changing the QuickBooks Administrator

Only the current administrator can change the user name and password for the administrator login, which makes it hard to keep the password a secret. Here's how to change the administrator's password without spreading the new password around:

1. **Choose File → Open Company/Login.**

   In the Open a Company dialog box, double-click the company file you want to open.

2. **In the QuickBooks Login dialog box, in the User Name and Password boxes, type the user name and password for the QuickBooks administrator and then click OK.**

   QuickBooks opens the company file with permission to do anything you want—including resetting the administrator login.

3. **Choose Company → Set Up Users.**

   QuickBooks opens the User List dialog box. Because you've logged in as the administrator, it includes the words "(logged on)" after the administrator's user name. The program automatically selects the first name in the list. If the first name *isn't* the administrator, click the administrator user name.

4. **Click Edit User.**

   QuickBooks opens the "Change user password and access" dialog box.

5. If you want to change the user name for the administrator, in the User Name box, type the new name.

Remembering the administrator password is challenging enough without having to remember a regularly changing user name, too. As long as you assign a password to the administrator login, leaving the User Name as "Admin" is safe enough.

6. In the Password and Confirm Password boxes, type the new password for the administrator. Click Next, and then click Finish.

For advice on picking a good password, see the box on page 564.

Warning: When you add or change the administrator password, remember that passwords are case-sensitive. If you have trouble logging in with a new password, first check your Num lock and Caps lock keys. If all else fails and you have a recent backup of your company file (page 168), you can restore the backup and log in with the old password. You can then reset the administrator password, but you'll also have to re-enter transactions since you made the backup.

FREQUENTLY ASKED QUESTION

How QuickBooks Serves Up Files

How does QuickBooks let different people use a file at the same time without getting confused?

In QuickBooks 2006, you access the data in your company files through a database server. Unlike previous versions, when someone performs a task in QuickBooks, their copy of the program asks the database server to send information

or to make changes. The database server makes the changes, retrieves information, and sends it back to the user—and at the same time makes sure that the changes don't conflict with changes someone else wants to make.

But you don't need to know any of this—just concentrate on your business and let multiuser mode take care of the file sharing.

Creating QuickBooks Users

Setting up users in QuickBooks has the same advantages as setting up users in the Windows operating system or on your network—you can restrict people's access to only the financial data they need to see, and you can keep track of what they're doing. By setting up user logins for the people who work on your company file, you can:

- **Keep sensitive data confidential.** User names, passwords, and permissions (page 570) help protect both your and your customers' sensitive data from prying eyes.

- **Prevent financial hanky-panky.** By limiting each employee's access to only job-relevant data and checking the audit trail for changes or deletions (page 572), you can prevent embezzlement—or catch the culprit early. These measures protect your data from unintentional corruption by new or careless employees as well.

• **Let several people work in QuickBooks at the same time.** You need to set up multiple users in QuickBooks in order to use multiuser mode (see the box below). QuickBooks has no way of knowing if several people share the same user name. If you want to protect your data or identify who's doing what in your financial records, each person who accesses your company file needs a unique user name and password.

UP TO SPEED

Sharing Your Company File

You might set up several users for a company file, but that still doesn't let more than one person work on the file at the same time. If you want your company file bustling with financial activity, you must first purchase a copy of Quick-Books (Pro, Premier, or Enterprise) for each computer on which you want to run QuickBooks and also switch the company file to multiuser mode.

To turn on multiuser access, choose File → Switch to Multi-user Mode. When multiuser mode is on, the title bar of the QuickBooks window includes the text (multiuser)(<*user name*>) to indicate that several people can work on the file simultaneously and the user name for the current session.

For example, if you're the QuickBooks administrator but you also perform bookkeeping tasks, it's a good idea to log in as the administrator only to perform the tasks that only the administrator can do. For your bookkeeping duties, log in with your other user name, ClarkKent perhaps, particularly if you want the audit trail to record who makes transaction changes.

After you begin using your company file in multiuser mode, you soon discover that some tasks in QuickBooks require single-user mode: backing up and condensing your company file, exporting or importing data, some changes to lists, and some types of setup. If multiuser mode is turned on and you try to perform a single-user mode task, Quick-Books tells you that you need to switch modes.

Single-user mode runs faster than multiuser mode. If you have monumental reports to generate and a tight deadline, switch to single-user mode to get the job done more quickly.

To switch a company file to single-user mode, first ask others to exit QuickBooks. (If you need single-user access for more than a few minutes, appease your coworkers by scheduling your work when others aren't in the office.) After everyone has logged off, choose File → Switch to Single-user Mode.

Adding New Users

Only the QuickBooks administrator can create additional users. After you log in as the administrator, here's how you create other users:

1. **Choose Company → Set Up Users.**

   QuickBooks opens the User List dialog box.

2. **Click Add User.**

   QuickBooks opens the "Set up user password and access" dialog box.

3. **In the User Name box, type the name that the person types in to access the company file. And in the Password box, type a password for the person.**

   In the Confirm Password box, retype the password.

Note: The people who use other user names can't change their own passwords, which means the administrator truly can do anything—including log in as someone else.

4. **Click Next to begin setting permissions, which are described in detail in the next section.**

   When you click Next to begin specifying the areas of QuickBooks that the person can access, the program selects the "Selected areas of QuickBooks" option automatically. Selecting the "All areas of QuickBooks" option instead requires only a few more clicks to complete the user setup, as shown in Figure 23-2, but gives this login access to all your financial data.

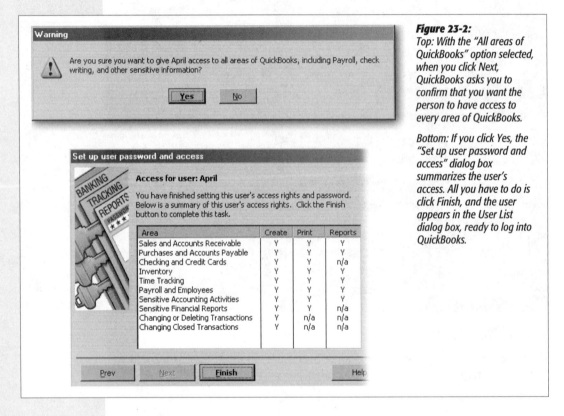

Figure 23-2:
Top: With the "All areas of QuickBooks" option selected, when you click Next, QuickBooks asks you to confirm that you want the person to have access to every area of QuickBooks.

Bottom: If you click Yes, the "Set up user password and access" dialog box summarizes the user's access. All you have to do is click Finish, and the user appears in the User List dialog box, ready to log into QuickBooks.

Restricting Access to Features and Data

When several people work on your company file, it's safer to limit what each person can do. For example, Trusty Ted has earned his nickname, so you could set his login up with access to every QuickBooks feature, including sensitive financial reports and accounting activities. Myra Meddler can't keep a secret, but there's no one faster for data entry, so you want to make sure that she gets no further than checking, credit cards, and paying bills.

If a person chooses a command and doesn't have permission for that feature, QuickBooks displays a warning message that identifies the permission needed to perform the action. In case the lack of permission was a mistake or an oversight, the warning message also suggests asking the QuickBooks administrator to grant that permission.

UP TO SPEED

Common Sense Security Measures

Your QuickBooks company file isn't the only place that you keep sensitive information. Be sure to set up your computers so that your QuickBooks data *and* all your other proprietary information are secure:

- **Back up your data regularly.** Back up your company file and other data and store the backups in a safe place. Check that your backups save the files you want and that your backups restore without any problems.

- **Update your operating system with security updates.** If you run a Windows operating system, review the articles about the latest security updates at *www.microsoft.com/security*.

- **Use antivirus software and keep it up-to-date.** These days, you need antivirus and anti-spyware software. Because the rogues who write viruses, worms, Trojans, and spyware don't look like they're going to stop any time soon, be sure to update your antivirus and anti-spyware programs regularly.

- **Install a firewall.** An Internet connection without a firewall is an invitation to nosy nerds and criminals alike. A firewall restricts access from the Internet to only people or computers you specify.

- **Plan for problems.** Cross-train your employees so that more than one person knows how to do each procedure in your company, including working with QuickBooks. Store the QuickBooks administrator's password in the company safety deposit box or give it to a company officer for safekeeping.

What the Access Areas Represent

The "Set up user password and access" dialog box groups QuickBooks features into nine areas, but there's some overlap. The names of these areas provide hints about what the permissions allow, but each area actually covers a lot of ground:

- **Sales and accounts receivable.** This area includes creating sales transactions with any kind of sales form (invoices, sales receipts, statements, and so on) and with any additional features (receiving payments, reimbursable expenses, finance charges, and so on). With sales and accounts receivable permissions, you can modify sales-related lists, such as the Customer:Job, Customer Type, and Ship Via lists, and customize sales forms. Full access includes printing and creating sales-related reports.

Tip: In QuickBooks, you can create an invoice, print it, and then *not* save it. Someone intent on embezzling could send out invoices, which don't appear in your company file, intercept the checks that the customer sends, and then cash them. This loophole in QuickBooks' invoicing is a good reason to limit people's access to sales and accounts receivable features. You can also export (page 534) a list of invoices to Excel each month to look for missing invoice numbers.

- **Purchases and accounts payable.** These permissions include all aspects of bills and vendors: entering and paying bills, working with purchase orders, entering reimbursable expenses and credit card charges, and paying sales tax. You can also modify purchase lists, such as the Vendor and Vendor Type lists, and customize purchase forms. Full access includes printing 1099s and reports about vendors or purchases.

- **Checking and credit cards.** Permissions in this area let users write checks (expense checks and refund checks, but not payroll checks), enter credit card charges, and make deposits.

- **Inventory.** People with these permissions can maintain the inventory items on the Item List, receive products into inventory, adjust inventory, work with purchase orders, and generate inventory reports.

- **Time tracking.** Time tracking permissions include the ability to enter time transactions in the weekly and single activity timesheets, import and export Timer data, and generate time reports.

- **Payroll.** Payroll permissions include writing and printing paychecks, setting up and paying payroll liabilities, using the selected payroll service, maintaining the Employee and Payroll Items lists, and generating payroll forms and reports.

- **Sensitive accounting activities.** Sensitive accounting activities don't belong to any one area of QuickBooks. Reserve these permissions for people who are not only trustworthy, but who understand how your accounting system works. With these permissions, someone can maintain your Chart of Accounts, make general journal entries, transfer funds, reconcile accounts, access accounts through online banking, work in balance sheet account registers, and create budgets. Other permissions include condensing data (which removes details of past transactions), using Accountant's Review, and generating the payroll report.

- **Sensitive financial reports.** These permissions let someone print every report in QuickBooks, including your most sensitive financial information, such as Profit & Loss, Balance Sheet, Cash Flows, and audit trail reports.

- **Change or delete transactions.** As an extra precaution, you can give people permission to create transactions in an area, but not let them change or delete the transactions that they've created. For example, for trainees just learning the ropes, you might remove their permission to edit transactions, so they must ask someone more experienced to make changes. An additional option lets people change transactions prior to the closing date. (Ideally, give this permission only to those who really know what they're doing—like your accountant.)

Setting Access Rights

In the "Set up user password and access" dialog box, if you go with the "Selected areas of QuickBooks" option, clicking Next begins the journey of specifying access to areas of QuickBooks. For each area of QuickBooks, you can give someone no access at all, full access to the area, or the right to perform some tasks in the area, as shown in Figure 23-3.

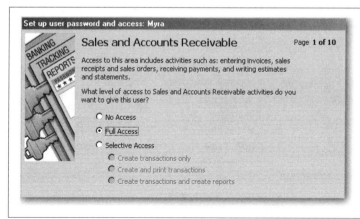

Figure 23-3:
QuickBooks automatically chooses the No Access option. To give a user any access to an area, you must choose either Full Access or Selective Access. In the upper right corner of the dialog box, QuickBooks shows which access page you're on. Each area of QuickBooks appears on its own page (nine pages of permissions and one summary page). To set up permissions, you must step through each page.

Here's a guide to what each level of access lets people do:

- **No Access.** People can't open any windows or dialog boxes for that area of QuickBooks, meaning they can't perform any actions in that area.

- **Full Access.** The person can perform every task in that area of QuickBooks.

- **Selective Access.** The person can perform some tasks in the area of QuickBooks. When you choose this option, you must also select the option that specifies what the person can do. Selective Access separates tasks into creating transactions, creating and printing transactions, or creating transactions and generating associated reports.

The final page in the "Set up user password and access" dialog box is a summary of the access rights that you chose for the user, as shown in Figure 23-4.

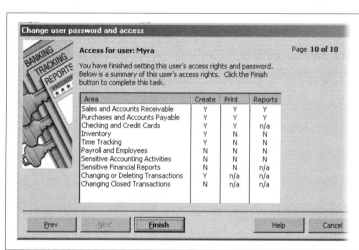

Figure 23-4:
The Summary screen separates access into the same categories as the Selective Access level: Create, Print, and Reports. In most cases, giving someone full access means that "Y" appears in all three columns. No access usually displays "N" in all three columns. When a permission isn't applicable to an area, QuickBooks displays "n/a." For example, there aren't any reports associated with the right to change or delete transactions.

Audit Trails

In QuickBooks 2006, the audit trail feature is always turned on, keeping track of changes to transactions, who makes them, and when. You check this permanent record—the Audit Trail report—to watch for unseemly activity. See Figure 23-5 for an example.

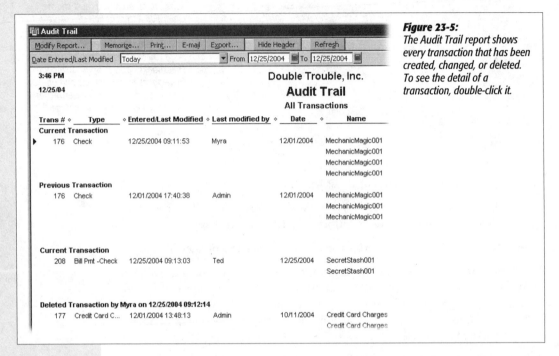

Figure 23-5:
The Audit Trail report shows every transaction that has been created, changed, or deleted. To see the detail of a transaction, double-click it.

You must be the QuickBooks administrator or have permission to generate sensitive financial reports to generate the Audit Trail report. If you pass muster, choose Reports → Accountant & Taxes → Audit Trail.

Tip: The Clean Up Company Data wizard (page 182) removes all the audit trail information up to the clean-up date that you specify. So if you're watching transaction activity, print an Audit Trail report *first*, and, as always, back up your company file regularly.

Part Five: Appendixes

5

Installing QuickBooks

QuickBooks doesn't have a lot of options in its installation procedure. You either install from scratch or upgrade a previous version. When you upgrade from a previous version, you can choose to run both versions on your computer at the same time. For business owners, this option isn't as helpful as you might expect, because once you open a company file in a new version of QuickBooks, it won't run in the earlier version. But upgrading and maintaining the previous version is an essential option for bookkeepers and accountants who work with company files from many clients.

Several people can access a company file at the same time. For business owners, this multiuser access adds a small burden to the installation because everyone must run the same version (QuickBooks 2006, for example). In addition, where you store your company file affects performance.

Although the QuickBooks Startup Guide that comes with your software CD is surprisingly thorough in its coverage of installation, the information for installing every edition from QuickBooks Pro to Enterprise could be overwhelming. This chapter distills what you need to know to install QuickBooks Pro or Premier.

Tip: You don't have to pay list price for QuickBooks ($199.95 for a single license of QuickBooks Pro; $399.95 for a single license of QuickBooks Premier). Your local office supply store, Amazon.com, and any number of other retail outlets usually offer the program at a discount. In addition, accountants can resell QuickBooks to clients, so it's worth asking yours about purchase and upgrade pricing.

Before You Install

Intuit recommends at least a 1 GHz processor and 256 MB of RAM (512 MB of RAM for more than one concurrent user)—but for most people, doubling the recommended amounts probably brings you closer to number-crunching speeds you'll find acceptable. You also need at least 850 MB of free disk space to install the program.

If you're planning to use the integration features that QuickBooks offers, the versions of your other programs matter, too. For example, writing letters and exporting reports requires Microsoft Word and Excel 2000 or later. To synchronize contacts requires at least Outlook 98 or Symantec ACT! version 3.08.

If you have several QuickBooks users, don't update the company file to the new software version until you've upgraded everyone's copy of QuickBooks. Otherwise, your colleagues won't be able to work in the company file until they have the newest version of software.

POWER USERS' CLINIC

Installing Multiple QuickBooks Versions

If you work with clients running different versions or editions of QuickBooks, don't panic. QuickBooks versions and editions run on the same computer *mostly* without squabbling with each other.

For example, you can run QuickBooks Pro 2005, QuickBooks Pro 2006, and QuickBooks Premier Edition 2006 all on the same machine. If you access each company file with only one version or edition of the program, you'll be fine. However, in two situations, QuickBooks updates company files, which means you won't be able to use the files in the previous version or edition:

- Opening a company file in a new version updates the file to work with the new version, which prevents earlier versions from opening the file. For example, once you open your company file with QuickBooks 2006, your accountant who's running QuickBooks 2005 won't be able to access your data.

- Opening a company file in QuickBooks Enterprise Edition optimizes the file for faster performance. Once you open a company file in this edition, the file is off-limits to QuickBooks Pro, and Premier.

Installing QuickBooks

If you have a single-user license for QuickBooks, installing or upgrading the program is incredibly simple. Even on a network with a multiuser license, installing QuickBooks is mostly common sense. Here are the steps for installing QuickBooks:

1. **Log in as Administrator or as a user with administrator rights.**

   Windows NT, Windows 2000, and Windows XP require administrator rights to install QuickBooks.

2. **Shut down any programs you have running, including your virus protection programs (a good idea for any installation). Then put the QuickBooks CD in your CD drive.**

   Most of the time, the installation procedure starts on its own, and the Quick-Books Installation window appears on your screen.

Tip: If the installation window doesn't appear, try using the Windows installation feature. Choose Start → Settings → Control Panel, and then double-click Add or Remove Programs. In the large dialog box that opens, click "CD or Floppy," select the QuickBooks CD, and then follow the onscreen instructions.

---

3. **In the QuickBooks Install Shield Wizard window, click Next.**

   Your CD drive begins whirring and a window appears with the heading "Welcome to the InstallShield Wizard for QuickBooks Financial Software."

4. **Click Next a second time. When the Remove Installation Files screen appears, choose whether to remove the installation files from your hard drive.**

   If you are short on disk space or don't plan to run setup again, select the first option, which removes the installation files. Selecting the second option keeps the installation files on your hard drive, which will save time if you someday need to change your installation.

   When you click Next, the wizard begins extracting the files from the installation package. No matter how fast your computer is, you have time to reheat your coffee before the "Welcome to QuickBooks Installation Wizard" window appears and you can begin the installation in earnest.

5. **In the QuickBooks Installation window, click Next.**

   The QuickBooks 2006 Software License Agreement screen appears.

6. **After you read the software agreement carefully, select the Accept option and click Next.**

   You can select the Accept option without reading the agreement, but the safer approach is to first make sure that the agreement doesn't demand something you're not willing to provide.

7. **Fill in the License Number and Product Number boxes with your QuickBooks license number and product number. Then click Next.**

   The license number and product number are hard to miss on the bright yellow sticker on your QuickBooks CD sleeve.

   As you complete typing the digits in one box, QuickBooks automatically jumps to the next box. If you're confident on the keyboard, you can keep your eyes on the yellow sticker and type all the digits for the license number without a break. To move to the Product Number boxes, press Tab.

8. **The Select Installation Folder screen appears, but you do more than select a folder if you're upgrading from a previous version, as Figure A-1 indicates.**

After you specify the installation folder (and the type of install for an upgrade), click Next.

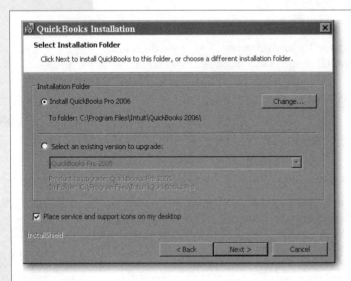

Figure A-1:
If you are running a previous version of QuickBooks, this is where you tell the program whether you want to install QuickBooks 2006 in a separate folder or upgrade your previous version. Unless you like your desktop ablaze with shortcuts, turn off the "Place service and support icons on my desktop" checkbox. You can reach the same services from the Help menu with commands for contacting QuickBooks technical support (page 585) and finding third-party integrated applications (page 530).

When no previous version of QuickBooks is present, the installation wizard automatically selects the Install QuickBooks *<edition>* 2006 option. (In the option label, *<edition>* represents the edition of QuickBooks that you're installing, such as Pro, Premier, or Enterprise.) Choose a different folder for the software by clicking Change. When you click Next, the installation wizard takes you to the screen described in step 10 on page 579.

When a previous version of QuickBooks is already present on the computer, the installation wizard automatically selects the "Select an existing version to upgrade" option and displays the most recent version in the box. You'll see the path in which the previous version is stored; the wizard upgrades to that same folder.

If you want to run two versions of the same computer, select the "Install QuickBooks *<edition>* 2006" option. On a PC, the wizard automatically selects *C:\ Program Files\Intuit\QuickBooks 2006* as the installation folder. To choose a different folder, click Change and navigate to the folder you want.

Tip: If you keep numerous versions of QuickBooks on your computer, you can choose the version you want to upgrade. However, if you've been running each version separately to support clients on numerous versions, continue separate installations by selecting the "Install QuickBooks *<edition>* 2006" option. To remove a truly ancient version of QuickBooks, uninstall it.

---

9. If you're running other versions of QuickBooks, the Copy QuickBooks Settings screen appears. Choose settings to tell the wizard about any customizations that you want to keep.

The wizard gives you a chance to copy any customizations you've made to previous versions of QuickBooks to your new version. In the "Select the version of QuickBooks from which you want to copy the settings" drop-down list, choose your previous version.

The wizard automatically turns on the "Copy User Preferences and Printer Settings" checkbox, which is how you want it to stay, unless your business model has changed significantly. Turning on this checkbox brings over all the preferences you've set (see Chapter 6) and the settings you've chosen for every printer you use to print QuickBooks documents. The wizard turns off the Copy QuickBooks Letters checkbox. If you have customized letters, be sure to turn this checkbox on.

10. Click Next to display the "Multi-user Access" screen. Then, choose the option for whether other users will access QuickBooks company files.

If more than one person works on your company files, select Yes. If you're the only QuickBooks user for the moment, select No/Not Sure/Will Decide Later. The wizard customizes the installation based on your answer. (You can change the multiuser setting later, as described on page 567.)

11. Click Next to finally reach the "Ready to install QuickBooks" screen.

The Installation Summary box shows how the installation will proceed, as shown in Figure A-2.

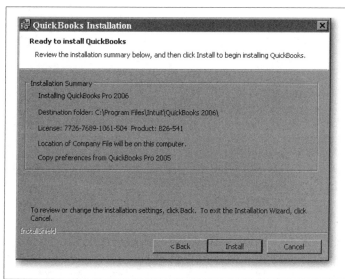

Figure A-2:
If the settings are correct, click Install. If you want to change, say, the folder you're installing to or the preference settings you're copying, click Back.

12. **Click Install to install QuickBooks 2006.**

When you click Install, the CD starts whirring again and your hard drive makes busy sounds. The wizard shows the installation task it's performing and progress bars indicate how far it's gotten. When the marketing information about new features appears in the dialog box, you know that the installation might take some time and you can get some coffee or return phone calls. The process continues for a few minutes after the progress bars reach the right side of the window. But eventually, the QuickBooks Installation Complete screen appears.

13. **Click Finish.**

To launch QuickBooks, double-click the desktop shortcut or choose Start → Programs → QuickBooks → QuickBooks <edition> 2006, where <edition> is the edition of QuickBooks that you've installed, such as Pro, Premier, or Enterprise. If you're upgrading your version of QuickBooks, the program displays a dialog box that asks if you want to convert your company file (page 28). In the text box, type Yes and click OK. If the program displays a message about Automatic Update, click OK to install updates made since the CD came out.

Tip: When Intuit releases software *patches* for QuickBooks (small, free upgrades to the program), the Automatic Update option downloads and installs those patches for you. But many people prefer to do these updates themselves, so they don't get taken by surprise when the software changes. To learn about QuickBooks Automatic Update or to turn this feature off, in QuickBooks, choose Help → Update Quick-Books.

At long last, the Welcome to QuickBooks <edition> 2006 window appears. Click "Open an existing company file" if you've upgraded from a previous version or your accountant built your company file for you. If you're restoring from a backup, click "Restore a backup file." To create a brand new company file, click "Create a new company file."

Registering QuickBooks

The Register QuickBooks dialog box doesn't appear until the first time you open a company file with the new version of the program. If you're new to QuickBooks and create a brand new company file, the EasyStep Interview walks you through the entire process without a whisper about registration. But when you open the file you've just created, you'll see the Register QuickBooks dialog box. And although you've purchased QuickBooks, the program runs only 15 times unless you register your copy.

Registration provides other valuable features besides running the program that you've purchased. You receive 30 days of free callback support from the day you first register and you receive updates that Intuit releases for the program.

Make sure that you're connected to the Internet and then click Begin Registration. The registration tool connects to the Intuit registration database via the Internet. The next step depends on whether you've already registered this copy of QuickBooks:

- **If you've registered the copy of the software before,** the QuickBooks Online Registration tool asks you to confirm the last four digits of your telephone number and your postal code. For example, if you installed QuickBooks on a computer whose hard drive has since gone to heaven, you don't have to re-enter every registration field for the program when you install it on a new hard drive.

- **If you've never registered this copy of the program,** you must answer a few questions about your company, which Intuit uses later to display messages about other products and services that they'd like to sell to you. For example, if you use a payroll service other than QuickBooks, you're sure to see an advertisement for payroll services. Click Next. The program opens a Web browser for registration. You must provide your contact information and company information.

In both cases, when you click Next, you see a message thanking you for registering your software. To complete registration, click Next. Sure enough, links to other Intuit products and services appear in the Web browser. Click Finish Registration to close the browser window so you can finally do some accounting.

Tip: When you open a company file, the first thing you see is the QuickBooks Learning Center window. This window includes tabs that take you to tutorials about different areas of the program. The What's New tab tells you about new features and enhancements in this version. But when you're ready to use QuickBooks and don't want further interruptions, turn off the "Show this window at startup" checkbox and then click Begin Using QuickBooks.

Setting Up QuickBooks on a Network

To let several people work on the same company file from different computers, the computers running QuickBooks must be networked together. Making this arrangement work requires a few extra—but simple—setup steps. Each user in a multiuser environment must:

- Run the same version of QuickBooks (QuickBooks 2006, for example).

- Have permission to read, write, create, and delete within the folder in which the company file resides. A network administrator typically sets up each user for these permissions. If you're responsible for getting users set up, but you never wanted network administrator as your job title, choose Start → Help and Support and then, in the Search box, type *Share folder* to find the instructions for sharing a folder using your operating system.

Tip: You can also simplify access to the company file folder by mapping a drive to that folder. In the Windows Help and Support window, search for "Assign drive."

• Have a valid License Number and Product Number. You need a separate QuickBooks license for each computer on which you install the program.

QuickBooks Pro and Premier can handle up to five people accessing a company file at the same time. Intuit is happy to sell you more than five licenses for QuickBooks to install on other people's computers, but only five of the licensed users can work on the company file simultaneously. QuickBooks Enterprise comes with 5-, 10-, or 15-user license packs and expands the number of simultaneous users to 15.

Storing Company Files

Where you store your company file can determine whether the people who work on the file see blisteringly fast response or nod off waiting for commands to complete. The location of your company file depends on the type of network you use:

• **Peer-to-peer networks** don't use dedicated file servers, so you can store your company file on any computer on the network. However, for the best performance, store the company file on the computer on the network with the most memory, the fastest processor, and the most available disk space. In a peer-to-peer network, computers that run QuickBooks must use either a Windows 2000 or Windows XP operating system.

• On a **client-server network,** the company file typically resides on a file server, a dedicated computer for sharing files. Every computer on the network that has QuickBooks installed can access the company file, but one of the computers must host multiuser access. Intuit recommends installing QuickBooks and the company file on the server, which must run either the Windows 2000 Server or Windows Server 2003 operating system.

In some cases, however, you *can't* install QuickBooks on the computer that holds the company file (if you use a Novell file server, for instance). You must log into the computer that you want to use as the *host* and open the company file in multiuser mode (page 567). When the program asks if you want this computer to host multiuser access, click Yes. This computer then plays traffic cop for several people working on the company file at the same time.

Tip: When you perform resource-gobbling tasks, such as running massive reports or reconciling accounts, performance is paramount. On a peer-to-peer network, log into QuickBooks on the computer that holds the company file to perform these tough tasks. On a client-server network, use the fastest computer on the network.

Finding Help

Between questions about how to do something in QuickBooks and about how to handle something in accounting, you probably need help more often than not. Finding answers isn't always easy, however.

Although online help is renowned for telling you what you already know, QuickBooks 2006's Help system is worth a look. As you'll learn in this appendix, you can access Help topics in several ways depending on how you like searching for information. But if the QuickBooks help you find isn't so helpful, you'll also learn about other resources that might do better.

QuickBooks Help

For the most flexibility finding the help you want, choose Help → QuickBooks Help (or press F1). On the left side of the QuickBooks Help window are three tabs, each of which provides a different way to find the information you want. The pros and cons of each are demonstrated in Figure B-1.

Tip: As you navigate from one help topic to another, on the QuickBooks Help icon bar, click Back to display previous help topics or click Print to print the current one.

Choosing Help → Access Support Resources provides the same Help content you find in the Help window, but with a different look and feel. The QuickBooks Support Resources window (Figure B-2) focuses on searching for answers to questions. For example, you can search the Knowledgebase for detailed instructions, by clicking "Search the Support Knowledgebase." If you want to post a message on the QuickBooks message boards to see if someone has an answer to your dilemma, click "Go to the QuickBooks Online Community." To find an expert in your area who provides QuickBooks support and other services, under Certified QuickBooks ProAdvisor, click Learn More.

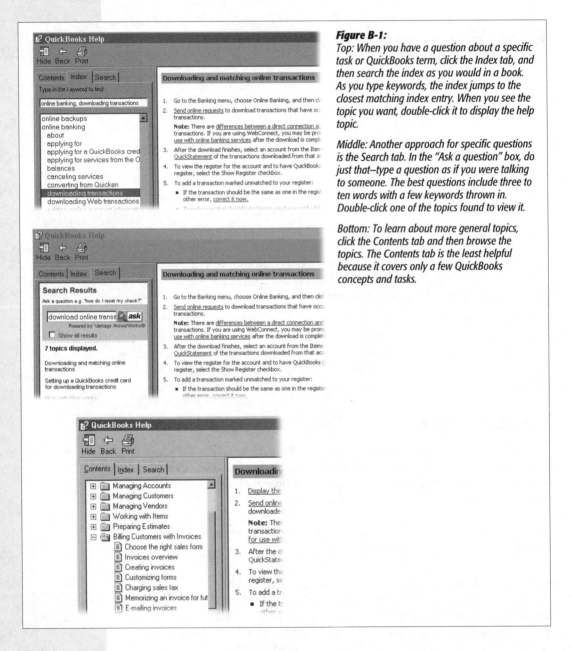

Figure B-1:

Top: When you have a question about a specific task or QuickBooks term, click the Index tab, and then search the index as you would in a book. As you type keywords, the index jumps to the closest matching index entry. When you see the topic you want, double-click it to display the help topic.

Middle: Another approach for specific questions is the Search tab. In the "Ask a question" box, do just that—type a question as if you were talking to someone. The best questions include three to ten words with a few keywords thrown in. Double-click one of the topics found to view it.

Bottom: To learn about more general topics, click the Contents tab and then browse the topics. The Contents tab is the least helpful because it covers only a few QuickBooks concepts and tasks.

If you're really stuck and want an answer from Intuit, you can choose from four Contact Us links in the QuickBooks Support Resources window:

- For the first 30 days after you register your software, click Contact Us under **QuickBooks 30-Day Included Support.** You receive free support with no waiting on hold during this brief but enjoyable honeymoon.

- For help with installation, errors, and so on, click Contact Us under **Installation, Upgrade, and Error Message Assistance.** You receive free support for problems regarding installing or upgrading QuickBooks, as well as error messages you receive or behavior that you suspect is a bug.

- If the idea of an ongoing support package appeals, click Contact Us under **Support Plans.** You pay an initial charge and monthly fees to receive unlimited, round the clock technical support.

- To buy just one support phone call, click Contact Us under **One-Time Support.** At $49.95 per call, this is the option for rare but desperate situations. If you suspect that you'll want to call support several times, a support plan is more cost-effective.

Figure B-2:
Both free and for-a-fee options appear in the QuickBooks Support Resources window. You can also purchase training delivered by CD-ROM, online, or in person: under the QuickBooks Training heading, click Learn More.

Help As You Work

You're working away and you have no idea what an option or button does. Choosing Help → QuickBooks Help, typing in keywords, and clicking entries seems like too much trouble, so you cross your fingers and hope for the best. But there's no reason to ignore options or bypass buttons with unknown consequences. Most QuickBooks windows and dialog boxes have help features built right in (Figure B-3). For instance, in the "Chart of Accounts" window, the How Do I? list includes "Add new accounts and subaccounts." You can also type a question in the Ask box, and then click Ask. If the search finds a help topic that sounds interesting, click the link to view it.

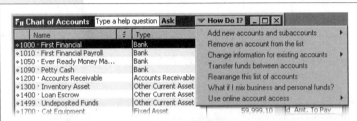

Figure B-3:
For help with the current window or dialog box, click the How Do I? button and choose one of the tasks.

WORKAROUND WORKSHOP

Hiding the %$^&*# Help Window

Besides telling you what you already know, the QuickBooks Help window has another annoying quirk. It won't get out of the way when you click a different QuickBooks window. Clicking another window or dialog box makes that window or dialog box active, but the QuickBooks Help window obstinately sits on top, blocking your view (and your ability to turn on checkboxes or otherwise complete your task).

If you want to read the Help instructions *and* perform the steps of a task at the same time, a large computer screen is the ideal solution. If you aren't so fortunate, here're some other options:

- **Hide.** In the QuickBooks Help window icon bar, click Hide, which reduces the width of the window by hiding the pane with the Contents, Index, and Search tabs. All you see is the pane with the text for

the help topic. When you want to find another topic, in the icon bar, click Show to display the Contents, Index, and Search tabs again.

- **Minimize.** In the top-right corner of the QuickBooks Help window, click the Minimize button, which hides the window (and the instructions). When you're ready to read about the next step, in the Start menu bar, click the QuickBooks Help button to display the window.

- **Resize panes and windows.** Make the Help window smaller by dragging the border between the search pane and the Help topic pane. Drag the right side of the Help window to make it narrower. QuickBooks wraps the contents in both panes to fit the new slimmer profile.

In some dialog boxes, you'll see a Help button, which takes you to a Help topic specifically about the features in the dialog box. Some of these topics do help, but others don't. For example, in the Edit Customer dialog box, when you click Help, the QuickBooks Help window opens the "About the New, Edit Customer window" topic. This topic has some useful information, such as the fact that customer records require only a customer name. Within that topic, if you click the "Address Info tab" link, you can view information about each of the fields. Unfortunately, some of the entries aren't worth either the time it took a tech writer to type it or your time to read it. For example, click Company Name and the "help" you get is nothing more than "If applicable, fill in the customer's company name." The topic says nothing about typing a brief but meaningful code for the customer in the Customer Name text box and using the Company Name text box for the organization's full name.

Other Help Resources

For answers that don't cost money, try a QuickBooks message board. Intuit has one (see below), but independent message boards abound. Quickbooksusers.com (*http://quickbooksusers.com*) is one of the best. This Web site has forums for different editions of QuickBooks, including one each for QuickBooks overall, QuickBooks Pro, Premier Non-profit, and Premier Manufacturing and Wholesale. People post some gnarly problems on these message boards, but each question gets at least one reply. In some cases, you might receive several different solutions for the same problem.

Tip: If you're looking for an add-on program or having problems with one, check out the QuickBooks 3rd Party Software Forum on Quickbooksusers.com. When you really get going with QuickBooks, you can even prowl the QuickBooks Jobs forum.

The Quickbooksusers.com message boards are free. This site supports itself by selling data recovery services and tech support. Yes, it also has advertising. Then again, a data recovery service might be just what you're looking for.

If you're tired of figuring things out on your own, you can find plenty of accountants and bookkeepers who are QuickBooks experts. Intuit has a certification program for accounting professionals, and the Certified QuickBooks ProAdvisor Search helps you find the ones in your area. ProAdvisors have passed tests to prove their QuickBooks expertise. Finding a ProAdvisor is free, but the ProAdvisor's services aren't. When you find ProAdvisors near you, ask about their fees before hiring them.

To find an advisor, choose Help → Access Support Resources. Under the Certified QuickBooks ProAdvisor heading, click the Learn More link. QuickBooks opens the Certified QuickBooks ProAdvisor Search window. Besides your location, you can specify the QuickBooks version and other products you use, the services you're looking for, the industry the advisor needs familiarity with, and professional designation (such as Certified Public Accountant).

UP TO SPEED

QuickBooks Tutorials

If you're new to QuickBooks and prefer to see steps instead of reading about them, choose Help → QuickBooks Learning Center. The QuickBooks Learning Center includes elementary tutorials for typical tasks in QuickBooks. Each tutorial is only a few minutes long, so don't expect in-depth training.

The Learning Center starts with a "Welcome to QuickBooks" section, which is an overview of what QuickBooks does. If you've already purchased QuickBooks, presumably you don't need this tutorial to tell you that you made the right decision. Here're the other sections of the Learning Center:

- **Understanding the Basics.** This section includes tutorials about QuickBooks accounts, items, and reports—three concepts you can't do without.

- **Customer & Sales.** This section is the most fertile of the Learning Center sections. You can start with an overview of the new QuickBooks 2006 Customer Center or learn how to bill customers using invoices, sales receipts, and statements, as well as additional tasks, such as putting together estimates.

- **Vendors & Expenses.** Learn how to enter and pay bills, or track and pay sales tax.

- **Inventory.** If you sell inventory, view these tutorials to learn the basics of setting up inventory, purchase and sell your inventory, and run reports about inventory.

- **What's New.** If you've used previous versions of QuickBooks, but you want to find out what's new in this version, click the What's New tab. This section has one multimedia tutorial in addition to links that explain the new features.

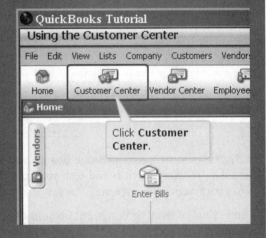

Keyboard Shortcuts

You can start almost every task you perform in QuickBooks with a click on something—a menu command, a button in a toolbar or icon bar, or a link in one of the Centers (new in QuickBooks 2006). But the seconds you spend mousing and clicking add up over time, especially when you have to move overlapping windows out of the way to find the place to click.

If you use QuickBooks every day, it pays to learn the keyboard shortcuts that take you where you want to go in a fraction of a second, regardless of which windows are open. Here are some of the QuickBooks keyboard shortcuts.

Tip: Each section in this appendix starts with shortcuts that you're most likely to commit to memory.

Task Shortcuts

These keyboard shortcuts open the windows and dialog boxes for the bookkeeping tasks that you perform the most.

Task	Keyboard Shortcut
Open the QuickBooks Help window to the topic for the current window or dialog box.	F1
Open the "Chart of Accounts" window.	Ctrl+A
Open the Customer Center window to the Customers & Jobs tab.	Ctrl+J
When a list window is active, open the dialog box for creating a new element in that list.	Ctrl+N

Task	Keyboard Shortcut
Open the Memorized Transaction List.	Ctrl+T
Open the Create Invoices dialog box to a new invoice.	Ctrl+I
Open the Write Checks dialog box to a new check.	Ctrl+W
Print the current transaction or report.	Ctrl+P
When an account is selected in the "Chart of Accounts" window, open the register window for that account.	Ctrl+R

Transaction Shortcuts

Whether you're creating, editing, saving, or deleting transactions, these keyboard shortcuts make your work move faster.

Task	Keyboard Shortcut
For a transaction selected in a register window, open the corresponding dialog box with that transaction displayed.	Ctrl+E
Record the current transaction (when the OK, Next, Previous, Save & New, or Save & Close button is highlighted).	Enter
Record the current transaction (anytime).	Ctrl+Enter
Memorize a transaction or report.	Ctrl+M
Close the active window or dialog box and clear any data entered or changed in the current transaction.	Esc
Copy the selected transaction in a register window.	Ctrl+O
Paste a copied transaction in the register window.	Ctrl+V
Find a transaction.	Ctrl+F
When a transaction is selected in a report or an item is selected in a list, generate a QuickReport for that transaction or item.	Ctrl+Q
For a transaction that spans two accounts with registers, such as a payment, which moves money from Accounts Receivable to a bank account, open the register window for the other account.	Ctrl+G
For an Accounts Receivable transaction, such as a payment, or an Accounts Payable transaction, such as a bill, show the history of the transaction.	Ctrl+H
For a transaction selected in a report, show the history of the transaction.	Ctrl+Y
Delete the current transaction or item.	Ctrl+D

Although some of the following keyboard shortcuts are old friends, they all help you edit portions of a transaction more quickly.

Task	Keyboard Shortcut
Recall a name and fill in the field (QuickFill).	Type the first few letters of the name and press Tab.
Undo the edits in the current field.	Ctrl+Z
Increment an invoice, check, or other transaction number by one.	+ (Plus key)
Decrease an invoice, check, or other transaction number by one.	– (Minus key)
Delete a line in a transaction table, such as an item in an invoice.	Ctrl+Del
Insert a line in a transaction table, such as an item in an invoice.	Ctrl+Ins
Cut the selected characters.	Ctrl+X
Copy the selected characters.	Ctrl+C
Paste cut or copied characters.	Ctrl+V
Open the list window for the list associated with the current field.	Ctrl+L
Delete the character to the right of the insertion point.	Del
Delete the character to the left of the insertion point.	Backspace

Date Shortcuts

When you choose the date for a transaction, keyboard shortcuts are often faster than selecting from the calendar or even typing the date. When a date field is active, press the following keys to change the date.

Task	Keyboard Shortcut
Move to the next day.	+ (Plus key)
Move to the previous day.	– (Minus key)
Change the date back to today.	T
Choose the first day of the week.	W
Choose the last day of the week.	K
Choose the first day of the month.	M
Choose the last day of the month.	H
Choose the first day of the year.	Y
Choose the last day of the year.	R
Display the Date calendar.	Alt+Down arrow

Tip: For M, W, and other shortcuts that move to the beginning or end of a financial period, pressing the key repeatedly advances the date incrementally. For example, if pressing M once goes to March 1, pressing M twice more goes to January 1.

Window Shortcuts

These shortcuts apply to QuickBooks windows and dialog boxes.

Task	Keyboard Shortcut
Move to the line below in a table (such as in the Create Invoices dialog box) or in a report.	Down arrow
Move to the line above in a table or in a report.	Up arrow
Move to the next field.	Tab
Move to the previous field.	Shift+Tab
Move to the beginning of the current field.	Home
Move to the end of the current field.	End
Move to the next word in the field.	Ctrl+Right arrow
Move to the previous word in the field.	Ctrl+Left arrow
Choose the first item in a list or the transaction dated the previous month in a register window.	Ctrl+Page Up
Choose the last item in a list or the transaction dated the next month in a register window.	Ctrl+Page Down
Move to the next column to the right in a report.	Right arrow
Move to the next column to the left in a report.	Left arrow
Move down one screen in a scrolling window.	Page Down
Move up one screen in a scrolling window.	Page Up

Miscellaneous Shortcuts

Here are a few shortcuts with specialized uses.

Task	Keyboard Shortcut
Launch QuickBooks without opening a company file.	On the Start menu or in the QuickLaunch bar, Ctrl+double-click the QuickBooks icon.
Open a company file without displaying any desktop windows.	In the Open Company window, press Alt while the company file is opening.
Display information about QuickBooks, such as the number of entries in lists.	F2

Index

Colophon

Marlowe Shaeffer was the production editor for *QuickBooks 2006: The Missing Manual*. Marlowe Shaeffer and Reba Libby proofread the book. Sanders Kleinfeld and Claire Cloutier provided quality control. Johnna Dinse wrote the index. Loranah Dimant provided production assistance.

The cover of this book is based on a series design by David Freedman. Karen Montgomery produced the cover layout with Adobe InDesign CS using Adobe's Minion and Gill Sans fonts.

David Futato designed the interior layout, based on a series design by Phil Simpson. This book was converted by Keith Fahlgren to FrameMaker 5.5.6. The text font is Adobe Minion; the heading font is Adobe Formata Condensed; and the code font is LucasFont's TheSans Mono Condensed. The illustrations that appear in the book were produced by Robert Romano, Jessamyn Read, and Lesley Borash using Macromedia FreeHand MX and Adobe Photoshop CS.

Better than e-books

Buy *QuickBooks 2006: The Missing Manual* and access the digital edition FREE on Safari for 45 days.

Go to www.oreilly.com/go/safarienabled
and type in coupon code BTEZ-PPED-4KPA-CDDX-E9IZ

Search
thousands of
top tech books

Download
whole chapters

Cut and Paste
code examples

Find
answers fast

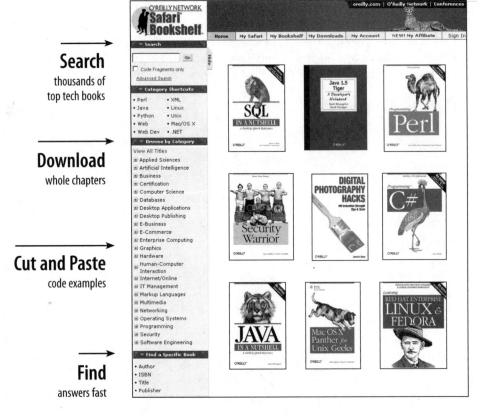

Search Safari! The premier electronic reference library for programmers and IT professionals.